MODERN FAITH AND THOUGHT

MODERN FAITH AND THOUGHT

by HELMUT THIELICKE

Translated by Geoffrey W. Bromiley

GRAND RAPIDS, MICHIGAN
WILLIAM B. EERDMANS PUBLISHING COMPANY

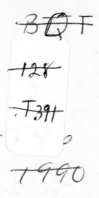
Copyright © 1990 by Wm. B. Eerdmans Publishing Co.
255 Jefferson Ave. S.E., Grand Rapids, Mich. 49503

Printed in the United States of America

Originally published as *Glauben und Denken in der Neuzeit*, © 1983 by
J.C.B. Mohr (Paul Siebeck), Tübingen.

Library of Congress Cataloging-in-Publication Data

Thielicke, Helmut, 1908-
    [Glauben und Denken in der Neuzeit. English]
    Modern faith and thought / by Helmut Thielicke; translated by
Geoffrey W. Bromiley.
      p.   cm.
    Translation of: Glauben und Denken in der Neuzeit.
    Includes indexes.
    ISBN 0-8028-3685-2 (hard)
    1. Theology, Doctrinal—History.   2. Religion—Philosophy—History.
I. Title.
BT21.2.T4613   1990
230'.09'03—dc20   90-45870
                                              CIP

To the Memory of My Friend
Hans P. Schmidt
Professor of Theology
at the University of Frankfurt
1926-1980

One age bears the guilt of others but can seldom undo it except by fresh guilt.

Friedrich D. E. Schleiermacher

As the blood and sweat of past generations water the cultural field on which our modern life blossoms or decays, so the mistakes of seeking and striving spirits are the steps on which we move ahead.

Martin Kähler

CONTENTS

Contents ix

PREFACE

This book is based on lectures delivered over many years—with revisions—in the universities of Tübingen and Hamburg in a three-year cycle. They involved four-hour classes stretching over two semesters. I have now worked over all the material again, partly reshaped it, and extensively added to it. The important chapter on Goethe became so large that it threatened to make the book too big (and expensive), and so, not without some difficulty, I have left it out and published it as a smaller supplementary work (*Goethe und das Christentum* [Munich: Piper, 1982]).

The lectures were constantly augmented by discussions, and what I learned in thrust and counterthrust, in question and suggestion, has found its way into the presentation and had an impact. The desire of young students to know what they could actually do with the material, what it meant for them and their lives, has, I hope, helped to make the work more relevant. The isolation of the study is, of course, unavoidable in a book of this kind. But the other pole of vital dialogue should go hand in hand with it.

As regards goal and method, enough is said in Chapter 1. I might simply say here that I am not dealing with the epochs of Protestant theological history as a historian but from the standpoint of specific issues, especially the question of the interrelationship of faith and thought. This problem is not picked out at random as a special theme. It seems to me to be the leading problem in the theology of the last centuries right up to our own time. Perhaps it will also be didactically fruitful for young students—whom I naturally have in mind, and not just older and more informed readers—to be presented in this way with a thematic center around which they can group the material and which can give the material its contours.

A second goal is linked with this purpose. I want especially to show how the problems discussed today arose. I might put it this way: I want to present the great systematic sketches of the past century in the light of our modern problems.

There is no doubt that the study acquires in consequence a subjective accent. The historical movements and their representatives do not stand at a suitable distance. The stance of the observer decides the difference in perspective between what is closer and more distant. Whether this is a loss or a gain, or both, the reader must say. I for my part simply want it to be known that the situation is clear to me and that I adopt it deliberately.

For one thing the definition of "our modern problems" is definitely subjective. Here at least they are essentially the problems with which the author has wrestled for decades in his theological work and with which he has dealt in his systematic writings. Many may miss questions that are important to them, although I believe that the thematic axis of the ensuing deliberations—especially the polarity of doubt and rejection related to the field of faith and learning—is one of the fundamentals that occupy everyone who is concerned about the questions of theology and the philosophy of religion. The criterion by which I have chosen theological thinkers is the question how and how far they have significance for this thematic axis.

The result is that I have had to do a great deal of omitting. Great figures who would have been significant in other areas have been partly passed over and partly treated only in cross-references, of which I make abundant use. (The fact that Karl Barth could not do much more in his important *Protestant Theology in the Nineteenth Century* is a comfort to me.) Nevertheless, the work carries generous references to other theological themes and figures, and especially to the theological and philosophical work of our own century. This is unavoidable if past figures are not to belong only to the past but are to be regarded as partners in the current debate. Tension thus arises between the sense of temporal distinction and the concern to see them as contemporaries. This tension has a dramatic side. Theological history thus takes on for me the air of a drama, with fear and catharsis and all the rest.

I dedicate the book to my late friend Hans P. Schmidt, who unfortunately had a fatal accident with his youngest son at Christmas 1980. He leaves a sad gap in the ranks of younger theologians. His writings, which have been and will be so impressive for many, display his penetrating intellect and his ability to discern modern theological problems, but they do not adequately present his human vitality and spontaneity, his joy and suffering in the faith, his Swabian humor, and his gift of friendship. These things are all treasured up in the hearts of his students and friends. I myself have lost in him a most loyal companion, although his independent bent never allowed him to be a theological disciple.

He was only sixteen when after a lecture he came to me for the first of many times, so that I could share in his development and help to guide him a little. Later, after coming home from a difficult time as a prisoner of war, he studied with me at Tübingen and then became my assistant at Hamburg. I helped him through his doctorate. When at a certain stage in his growth he tended toward an abstraction which seemed to me to be suspect, I sent him for a time to the sturdy and popular evangelist Wilhelm Busch in Essen for training in a city mission, where he learned to speak to the simplest of people who had hardly been touched at all by Christianity. He withstood this test and learned to function in this very different area. That faith produces great originality—God's handiwork, as it were—we can see very plainly in Hans Schmidt. With sorrow and gratitude I think of all that I owe to his friendship.

I might conclude with a personal note. In the preface to volume III of *The Evangelical Faith* I wrote that my academic work was complete with the conclusion of my systematic endeavors. That I have been enabled to add this historical supplement, that I could work on it afresh while still looking back with pleasure on my favorite lectures, I count as a special gift of grace.

ABBREVIATIONS

CD	K. Barth, *Church Dogmatics*, I-IV (1936ff.)
Clemen	O. Clemen, ed., *Luthers Werke in Auswahl* (1912ff.)
DAS	Deutsches Allgemeines Sonntagsblatt
EA	Erlangen Edition of Luther's Works
EF	H. Thielicke, *The Evangelical Faith*, I-III (1974ff.)
EK	Evangelische Kommentare
ET	English translation
EvTh	*Evangelische Theologie*
Hampe	J. C. Hampe, ed., *Die Autorität der Freiheit. Gegenwart des Konzils und Zukunft der Kirche im ökumenischen Disput*, I-III (1967)
Heppe	H. Heppe, *Reformed Dogmatics*
HK	Herder-Korrespondenz
HWP	Historisches Wörterbuch der Philosophie
KuD	*Kerygma und Dogma*
LBK	*Die Bekenntnisschriften der evangelisch-lutherischen Kirche* (1935)
LC	Luther's Large Catechism
LMH	*Lutherische Monatshefte*
LThK	*Lexikon für Theologie und Kirche*
LW	Luther's Works
NR	*Die Neue Rundschau*
NT	New Testament
NZSTh	*Neue Zeitschrift für systematische Theologie*
OT	Old Testament
PhB	Philosophische Bibliothek
RE	*Realenzykopädie für protestantische Theologie und Kirche*, 3rd ed.
RGG	*Religion in Geschichte und Gegenwart*
Salnar	Salnar's *Harmonia confessionum fidei*, ed. A. Ebrard (1887)

SW	Sämtliche Werke
Tappert	T. G. Tappert, ed., *The Book of Concord: The Confessions of the Evangelical Lutheran Church* (1959)
TDNT	*Theological Dictionary of the New Testament,* I-X (1964ff.)
ThBl	*Theologische Blätter*
ThE	H. Thielicke, *Theologische Ethik,* I-III (1951ff. [ET *Theological Ethics,* altered and abridged, 1966ff.])
ThL	*Theologische Literaturzeitung*
ThR	*Theologische Rundschau*
ThSt	Theologische Studien
TRE	*Theologisches Realenzyklopädie*
WA	Weimar Edition of Luther's Works
WW	Werkausgabe
ZAW	*Zeitschrift für alttestamentliche Wissenschaft*
ZSTh	*Zeitschrift für systematische Theologie*
ZThK	*Zeitschrift für Theologie und Kirche*
ZZ	*Zwischen den Zeiten*

PART I

HISTORICAL PROLEGOMENA

CHAPTER 1

Goal and Method

I. GOAL

A. DIALOGICAL PURPOSE

In such an extensive complex of facts and problems as that which is found in the history of theology and philosophy during the past centuries, it is as well to consider the goal of our study and the method we propose to use in reaching it.

I do not approach this field with a predominantly historical interest. My presentation will be that of a systematic theologian who regards past thinkers as partners in a dialogue and who wants to discuss the question of theological truth with them. I shall not ignore the dates and settings of those whose portraits I give. On the contrary, it is for me almost a matter of pride to make the great figures as vivid and immediate as possible, to present them in the stimulating polarity of their evident humanity on the one side and the truth that grips them and encircles their thinking on the other. How else can a system of thought, and especially the story of the search for truth, be described except as we let each author make an impact on us and put the question of the background of his thinking?

The theological work which we ourselves undertake is also a human work which is done with great passion, to which the whole of our existence is committed, whose consuming flame often burns up completely all that might be called "private." Yet often theology is pursued according to an indolent law of traditions and amounts to little more than a commentary on inherited theses.

Most theologians are very busy people, and those who study the biographies of theologians will often be struck by the many academic

3

hours they put in and the extent of their published writings. Often they were fencers who found edification in polished aphorisms while alienating, provoking, and shocking their contemporaries. Lessing and Kierkegaard were of this type.

Some simply wanted to be builders presenting the Christian faith in an intellectually orderly way. Others wanted to tear down and destroy so as to rebuild on the leveled site (e.g., D. F. Strauss). Others again were fishers and missionaries whose hearts were afflicted by the plight of the secular world. Yet others were apologetic anglers who could throw out the hooks of their sagacity and sought to catch as many fish on their line as possible in the sea of the world.

In short, theology is always a very human work and is done by living people, some of whom have a true appearance of sanctity but others only a false appearance. It is pursued by people who develop their greatest enthusiasm on the rostrum or in the pulpit, who are missionaries or scholars, and often both, who stand in the service of their Lord or their ambition, and often both.

Because this is so, because theology is a very human work, Luther's statement is apposite that the person does—and characterizes—the work. The proclaimer does not merely speak the message but also confesses the self in all its concern or lack of it. The spirit of the age intermingles with the scholar, wittingly or unwittingly and often unwillingly. Those who come after scent it better.

I thus come to what seems to me to be the first principle of writing theological history. The personal relationship of the theological task means that we cannot write theological history merely as a history of theological thoughts and ideas. We have to consider the way in which specific people of a specific time adopted the kerygma and how they met the temptation posed by the spirit of their time, no matter whether it came to expression in an Enlightenment worship of reason, a historical materialism with its exclusive sociopolitical concern, or the romantic cult of feeling in various forms.

Theological reflection arises when the message—the primary event—finds forms and figures of thought in which the people of a particular time reflect. The message comes first. It cannot be fused into the forms and figures. It is always in tension and competition with them. But if it prevails, if it leads on to faith, the paradoxical state arises that we have to state and express it in our time-bound categories if we are not to relapse into dumbness and silence. The tension between the eternal that is present and the time-bound means of appropriation is always noticeable. Concepts begin to flicker when they have to express something that does not conform to their previous ideological content but transcends it. When John's Prologue speaks about the incarnation of the Logos, it uses Stoic or Gnostic terms. But it only "uses" them. For the term *Logos,* to express the mystery of the incarnation, has to shed its previous meaning as a symbol for the cosmic principle and fill itself with a content that is basically alien to it.

Thus language reaches its limit and the vessels of words are shattered by their contents. A sign of this is that paradox is unavoidable. Paul, Luther, and later Kierkegaard all take refuge in paradox, and Karl Barth could refer to the "impossible possibility" of speaking God's Word in our human words.

Often the tension between the onrushing kerygma and our means of reflection and reception is relaxed by integrating the message into the means and thus giving them a position of rule instead of instrumentality. In this case we assimilate the message to the world and let it say and state only what we know already. We accord it at most the task of giving what we know a higher sacral significance. This may be done in sublime processes of thought. But it may also take a crude, popular form, in which case it is all too obvious. We need only think of certain conformist theologies in ideological dictatorships. Thus the "German Christians" of the Third Reich took their philosophical norms from the Nazis. What they advanced as the supposed Christian message was adapted and integrated. The tension of the message with the spirit of the time—and hence its point—was eliminated.

Here it is paradigmatically clear how theology always involves a debate between the kerygma and the self-understanding of an age, or, in popular terms, between eternity and time. For this reason the lives of those who do theology can never be ignored. They play a part. They have a major role. They are the battlefield between eternity and time. In them the decision is taken who or what rules and who or what serves as an instrument. A few considerations will show this.

If we define theology as thought-out faith, its form as reflection, then the history of theology has to do with the history of faith, or, more precisely, of believers, or, more precisely still, of people who confess their faith and themselves by the thinking form of their faith. But this is not all. An important factor is part of the history of faith and reflection upon it: its polar structure.

B. POLAR STRUCTURE OF THEOLOGICAL THINKING

Faith believes *against* as well as *in.* In the history of theology and the underlying faith we thus have a history of specific attacks against which people believe and mobilize theological arguments.

For Luther the point against which he mobilized his theology was the attack of legal righteousness. Against this he brought his polemical confession of justification by faith alone.

For theologians of the Enlightenment—Reimarus and Semler—the point lay in the hardened anachronism of orthodoxy and its dogmatic metaphysics, which could no longer be adopted credulously and uncritically by those who wanted to be honestly enlightened and to maintain their identity as people permeated by a rational faith.

For Schleiermacher the point lay in the field of the historical and scientific criticism of a biblically based faith. History challenged the supranatural picture of history in the Bible and threatened to dissolve it in historical relativism. Science criticized biblical cosmology and replaced its reference to transcendence (in its demonstrable pre-Copernican form) by self-resting finitude interwoven by natural law. This truly radical criticism could no longer be met by apologetic evasions, by a "Yes, but in detail. . . ." It posed the need for a great strategic retreat to a calm plateau of inwardness, feeling, and experience which scientific criticism could not reach. In Kantian terms, an a priori of religious statement had to be attained equal to that of theoretical judgments. Schleiermacher attempted this in the Introduction to *The Christian Faith*, as we shall see. His theology is a great effort to provide a prophylactic against what he suspected would be a time of scientific credulity. A mere confession of religious truth would be defenseless and sterile against this so long as it did not find a *rocher de bronze*, i.e., a new foundation of faith which scientific criticism would gnaw at in vain.

Finally, for the biblical theologian Martin Kähler—to note his paradigmatic significance too—the source of the attack lay in the historical leveling down of Christianity and the problem of the relationship between revelation and history. Should critical historical research determine in which Christ we may confidently believe? Should faith in Christ be limited to what the critical subtraction of history left of him? Here too, as in Schleiermacher but with a different theological thrust, anticriticism cannot be content with petty squabbling about historical details. There must be an attack in principle on the attempt of historical criticism to make a scientifically reconstructed "Jesus of history" the only basis of faith. The concept of history which underlay this enterprise must be destroyed. Kähler did this, as we shall see, in his formative work *The So-called Historical Jesus and the Historic, Biblical Christ*.[1]

One might go on and describe the history of theology not only as the history of faith and its form of reflection but also as that of the

---

1. Originally published as *Der sogennante historische Jesus und der geschichtliche, biblische Christus* (1892); the partial ET is based on the 2nd German ed. (1896).

attacks on this faith. Theology always arises under assault or not at all. Luther's well-known statement that temptation makes a theologian shows that the challenge over against which we believe also evokes theological arguments with whose helps faith seeks clarification. (Authors like Albert Camus and Gottfried Benn, who move on to their own insights by way of nothingness, have perceived the same problem at least in formal analogy.) Dostoyevski can say of himself that his "hosanna is achieved through the great purgatory of doubt."[2]

It is typical of confessional writings that their structure reflects this origin in attack. They combine their "we confess" with a "we reject," their faith *in* with faith *against*. We should not be misled by the fact that the negative statement follows the positive statement, for the historical genesis takes the opposite course. The attack of a heretical position provokes faith to clarify itself in reflection, and a confessional statement results.

That theological statements arise by way of attack explains why there are no timeless theological statements and no perennial theology. Theology arises out of a challenge (Toynbee) and is thus always related to its historical time and place. Its statements can have lasting validity only as they are transposed into other times and places. They thus need hermeneutical mediation. This obviously applies to preaching too, as may be seen simply from the fact that even the sermons of great theologians, e.g., Luther or Schleiermacher, cannot be repeated today. The preacher is committed to his own age and contemporaries.

This is why theology by its very nature points not only to a superior, eternal basis derived from revelation but also to specific constellations of the spirit of the age within and against which it makes its statements. To this extent it has a polar structure. Three aspects of these constellations may be noted.

C. SIGNIFICANCE OF THE SPIRIT OF THE TIME AND TIME-BOUND EXPRESSIONS

First, the attack is that of the specific time with which the message finds itself confronted. Today, as indicated, we have to think of natural science and the universal sense of the idea of a self-related cosmology closed to anything outside. Modern historicism has a similar effect with its relativizing tendency. Finally, we have to think of the philosophical influence

2. For Luther see WA, 11, 70, 13; 20, 461, 23. Cf. also my article "Temptation" in *Encyclopedia of the Lutheran Church*, III (1965), 2327ff.

of sociology and psychology, both of which in their own ways tend to reduce all intellectual and spiritual phenomena to immanent factors and to understand them psycho- or sociogenetically.

These various approaches give rise to the problem of how far the old Christian doctrines can be stated in relation to these new constellations and explanations without alert contemporaries seeing in them either an unreasonable sacrifice of the intellect or the flight into a double concept of truth. The stir caused by Bultmann's demythologizing and J. A. T. Robinson's *Honest to God* can be explained only by the fact that they raised the basic question whether Christianity can still be espoused within the modern understanding of the world. Must not its dogmas at least be modified? Must we not take seriously only the existential self-understanding which is contained in that kerygma that is now encased in time-bound mythical and supernatural forms? Do we not have to pry out this self-understanding?

This question is elemental because it has to do with the credibility of Christian proclamation and theology. The latter can be credible only if I can so receive it that it does not plunge me into conflict with a rationally based understanding of existence and the world such as I hold in ordinary life (e.g., as an artisan or scholar). My "I" must not be divided. Credibility cannot be maintained if I must engage in intellectual repression in order to believe.

An obvious example is the problem of explaining the resurrection of Christ as the basis of my faith. To do so with a good conscience I must ask how far I view the resurrection as a historical event. If I call it this, I must then ask at once in what sense I am speaking of history here. Do I mean it in the same sense as when I speak about Christ's crucifixion or the birth of Napoleon, i.e., when we plainly have to do with objective and objectifiable events in time and space? If I have reservations here—as I must, for the resurrection transcends the historical continuum and the Gospels do not narrate it in the same way as the crucifixion—then I am compelled to say what concept of history I am using and how my theological concept of history relates to that which I normally lay claim when I have the usual facts of world history in view.[3]

The new and changed constellations of the understanding of the world and history compel me, then, to face their challenge to faith. They do so, at least, if I am not just to reproduce the traditional deposit naively and self-confidently, if I want to be credible and to accept the challenge in solidarity with my contemporaries, if I take up myself the task of

3. On this problem see *EF,* II, 423ff.; also R. R. Niebuhr, *Resurrection and Historical Reason* (New York, 1957).

meeting it. Theologians to a high degree have the task of representatively carrying the intellectual and spiritual conflict on behalf of their contemporaries. Here, if we are not afraid of an overloaded term, is the *apologetic* task of theology. We best fulfil this task historically. All the theological thinkers that we shall study confront us with the question of what the conflict was for them and how they faced and overcame it.

Second, the constellations of the spirit of the time contain changing questions for proclamation and theology. Luther's question of how to find a gracious God is not—or not at least directly—our question. We hardly ever hear it in a cafe, at a table, or in a railroad car. The problem is not the gracious God but God's existence. This problem itself is seldom stated openly. It is put in cipher. It is hidden under the question of lost meaning, in complaints about its loss, in the suffering of meaninglessness.[4]

If I do theology outside such questions, I give answer to questions that are not asked and ignore those that trouble my contemporaries. I then take up a reactionary attitude and do theology anachronistically within the framework of an older age whose theology answered the questions of that age. Hence there is no contact between theology and (time-bound) existence, and inevitably I produce indifference. The second task resulting from the confrontation between theology and current questions I call (alongside the first apologetic task) the task of *actualization*.

Third, the constellations of the spirit of the age set us before a final problem arising out of the changing conceptual instruments. These are usually forged by the humanities (earlier philosophy, today mostly psychology and sociology). Every age with its questions and challenges forces a stock of concepts upon us which usually pass into theological reflection, and which have to do so if theology takes seriously its hermeneutical task, its actualizing function, its proximity to its time. Thus modern theology, especially from the Enlightenment, can express itself only along with philosophy and its conceptual schemata. D. F. Strauss can be understood only in the light of Hegel, A. Ritschl and W. Herrmann only in the light of Kant, and Bultmann only in the light of Heidegger. The relations are not always so evident, but they always exist, even in Barth's theology.[5] Indeed, the problem is present in the

4. This is why the younger generation is influenced by the Sisyphus idea of Albert Camus or the idea of our chance existence in the molecular biology of Jacques Monod, *Chance and Necessity* (New York, 1972).

5. As regards Barth, cf. F. Gogarten, *Gericht oder Skepsis* (1937), which shows how existential philosophies and identity speculations affect him. Modern theolo-

NT itself, where Gnosticism and Hellenistic Logos speculations offer schemata of thought.

The same question arises in Roman Catholic theology, especially as the Aristotelian bases of Thomism forge such a close link between theology and philosophical concepts. In contrast, the normative Jesuit theologians of Lyon-Fourvière in their series *Sources chrétiennes* and *Théologie* championed the thesis that the close link between theological thought and the Scholastic-Aristotelian synthesis leads to anachronism and deprives of relevance. Thus the Jesuit H. Boillard in his *Bekehrung und Gnade beim hl. Thomas von Aquin* (1944) concludes that Thomas's doctrine of grace, through its relation to the Aristotelian schema of form and matter (*eidos* and *hyle*) is now outdated, and therefore, not being relevant, is necessarily false. The demand of the French Jesuit school, especially Henri du Lubac and Jean Daniélou, is that modern theology should take its questions and forms of expression from the situation in its own age and that existentialism (and then other things) should replace Aristotle. They thus allow the influence of Kierkegaard and Rudolf Otto free rein in their theology. This demand took form, e.g., in Lubac's work on the eucharist and the church in the Middle Ages (*Corpus mysticum,* 2nd ed. 1949), in which he tried to show that using the Aristotelian terms "substance" and "accident" to depict Christ's presence in the sacrament entails unbearable restriction, at least when this schema claims permanent validity. Similarly, Daniélou tried to bridge the gulf between the church and the modern world by arguing that every living theology must be in touch with the questions and vocabulary of the age. Thus subjectivity, which is stressed both in existentialism and Marxism, must be given its due in theological thinking as well.

This program exerted such a fascination through its modernity that Pius XII felt compelled to criticize this new French theology in his encyclical *Humani generis* (1950). His main argument was that any attempt to replace the "perennial philosophy" of Scholasticism by modern philosophical trends leads to dogmatic relativism. In Scholastic philosophy we do not have a short-lived philosophical system that may be changed at will. It is a manifestation of how divine revelation comes to the aid of human thought. Ecumenical councils used these philosophical schemata and thus set on them the seal of definitiveness. This papal intervention shows how basic and at times dramatic is the struggle

---

gians of hope (on the Protestant side J. Moltmann) use Ernst Bloch's principle of hope, and theologians of social ethics go back to the Frankfurt school (especially J. Habermas).

for actualization in theology and for the relationship among theology, philosophy, and the humanities.

These deliberations enable us to define our task more precisely. Within the schemata of expression we have to find the material goal of what each thinker is saying. In this way we have to make the temporal setting clear and find a contemporary partner in debate. Hence we cannot be content merely to state what Lessing, Schleiermacher, Ritschl, Barth, and others said (with quotations), or what is objectively there. (This would be rather dull and tedious.) The question must be: What were they trying to say with the schemata at their disposal? What was the intention behind their statements?

Theoretically it is easy to formulate the task. But carrying it out involves many difficulties. These are not just technical. They relate to a basic problem of understanding. For time-bound modes of expression do not merely "serve," so that distinction can easily be made between the statement itself and the conceptual instrument. There is instead a kind of revolt of the conceptual means. These can cause their ideological contents, which they have in contemporary philosophy, to penetrate the material sphere of theological statements and overwhelm these statements. Many examples might be given, and we shall have to mention them continually in the critical questions that we address to thinkers of the past.

At this point I might adduce two examples by way of preliminary illustration. First, before the Johannine Prologue could formulate the statement that the Word was made flesh, Greek philosophy, especially Stoicism, had played with the logos concept and given it cosmological significance as world reason or the subjective *ratio* that is analogous to the cosmic logos. When the Prologue adopts the term to describe the mystery of the incarnation, John strips it of its ideological content and uses it as an empty shell, a mere synonym for the Word of God. He thus avoids defining the phenomenon of Christ by the Stoic concept and in this way integrating Christ into the sphere of Greek thought. The reverse happens. What Logos means in John's Gospel is defined by Christ, i.e., by what follows in the ensuing chapters. In second-century Apologists like Justin Martyr, however, we find the very opposite. To make Christianity understandable to those stamped by the Greek tradition, to bring it closer to them, an attempt was made to show that the Greek philosophers were in a sense precursors of Christ. What they said about the logos contained serious particles of truth and indications of what Christ would reveal in fulness and perfection as the manifestation of the world logos. The apologetic aim was that those influenced by Greek thought should not find in Christ something absolutely new and hence scandalous and offensive (1 Cor. 1:23), but a confirmation of their own thinking and a transcending and completing of their own fragmentary knowledge. This missionary view presupposed the need to accommodate the Christian message to Greek thought and hence to define Christ by the Greek *logos,* in contradistinction from John's Gospel. Clearly, many essentials of the gospel, e.g., the folly of the cross (1 Cor. 1:18; 2:6ff.) or miracles, fell by the wayside with this procedure. The logos concept loses its servant role as a conceptual instrument and takes on a normative and governing role. Christ is subsumed under the concept and becomes a mere illustration. We thus have here a classical example of the revolt of the conceptual means. In such cases it is impossible to extract the mere form of the term and cast off the material intention. The form becomes the content. This is the hermeneutical difficulty we constantly encounter.

A second example may be seen in the way in which Bultmann adopts the philosophical terminology of Heidegger. Here I may be brief (for a fuller discussion see *EF,* I, 55ff.). Bultmann's view of biblical interpretation, which takes over Heidegger's concept of existence, can regard biblical statements as binding only as they are relevant to me and unconditionally apply to me (Tillich). Hence Bultmann has to try to detach time-bound (mythical or Gnostic) statements from the kerygmatic core. The question is: How far is this possible when one's own conceptual means and criteria—taken over in this instance from Heidegger—acquire normative significance and become hermeneutical principles which may at times be alien to the text? The decisive criterion whether a passage is existentially meaningful will see to it that what does not seem to be meaningful will not be received, and hence there will necessarily be excisions such as we see in Bultmann's attitude to miracles or to the resurrection. The criterion of what is mythical (the presence of a divine element) seems indeed to demand that the incarnation itself has to be viewed as at least dubious. Bultmann's theology is thus an experiment which illustrates particularly well the problem in separating the form of a statement from its intention.

From what has been said it should be clear that we cannot write a history of theology as an abstract history of ideas. If we simply consider how the rigid principle of authority in orthodoxy unleashed the desire for adulthood and liberation, i.e., the Enlightenment, or how the newly dominant concept of reason engendered the critical idealism of Kant and the metaphysical idealism of Fichte, Hegel, and Schelling, and then provoked the opposition of the left-wing Hegelians and Kierkegaard; if we are interested only in this evolution of ideas, then we miss the decisive problem, not perceiving the distinction between matter and form, because we do not see the concrete people who are tied to the historical situations, the people who approach the Christian message with their time-bound schemes of thought and try to understand it in interrelationship with these schemes. Our purpose, then, is to find these concrete people with their concrete historical locations and to enter into self-critical dialogue with them concerning our own historical determination.

Along these lines I want to achieve understanding not as a historian but with a systematic purpose. This means negatively that my primary aim is not to see how things are "in themselves." I do not seek to give a complete picture of the people concerned or of the intellectual, cultural, and political trends in which they are set. My concern is to consult them on certain theological and philosophical problems, or, better, to traverse with them some essential spheres of inquiry that are posed both for them and for us.

Selection is thus necessary from the very outset. From the rich historical data I will take figures that represent dominant modern themes which cause us to "stamp and glow" (Lessing). Such figures, we hope, will serve as partners in a dialogue which will help us to master the themes by criticism and countercriticism.

In this attempt to make headway with modern problems by dialogue with the past, the period beginning with the Enlightenment is especially attractive because it covers the whole field of basic theological questions. Some new problems make their first appearance in this period, e.g., the tension between faith and history. They emerge with dramatic force from daring revolutionary discoveries. They also have the freshness of first experience. They have not yet been "domesticated" by skeptical familiarity as among us. (*We* know only too well that hard and perhaps insoluble problems are posed by the relation between faith and history or faith and science, so that we have almost come to terms with them, except for young students who come across them for the first time.) It is thus attractive to look at these basic problems on their first appearance.

D. PROGRAM

In a preliminary schematic survey I want to set out the most important problems that arise when we have this goal in view and that will occupy us later. The first is that of the relation between revelation and reason. The urgency of this question increases as the focus shifts after Descartes to the emancipated I and its subjectivity, and in and after the Enlightenment the basis of the worth of this I is found in the fact that it is the bearer of reason. The awareness thus develops that we are capable of adult autonomy and are under obligation to seek it. This necessarily entails tension with the authoritarian and heteronomous claims of every kind of revelation or dogma that seek to deprive us of adulthood. The main representative in whom to study this basic tension is Lessing. With his program of emancipation Lessing initiates debates that continue to this day with variations, especially in Bonhoeffer, Gogarten, and their successors.

The second problem is that of the relation between God's commands and the human conscience. Here is a first variation on the basic tension. The relation between authority and autonomy finds thematic expression in the relation between command and conscience. If the autonomous moral I is discovered and systematically established by Kant, the question runs, can one retreat into the religious sphere and be bound by the mandates of an external court, a non-*autos*, i.e., God? Are not divine commands in principle a *heteros nomos*? Is not theonomy heteronomy? Is it not to be rejected at least in ethics? Or is there some solution to this conflict? Can God's commands commend themselves as "moral" before the normative court of conscience and thus be accepted as a legitimate norm even by our autonomy? On the other hand, is it in keeping with the dignity of divine mandates to have to legitimize themselves before the forum of the moral I and to have to recognize this forum as a final authority? We shall deal with this problem as we analyze Kant's concept of autonomy and the theological deductions Kant draws from it. We shall then see how the nineteenth-century theology that Kant influenced followed up this philosophical approach and handled the tension between autonomy and theonomy. This will bring us into dialogue with Albrecht Ritschl and especially Wilhelm Herrmann.

Since this is a permanent problem irrespective of its Kantian origin, we must look at some modern instances of it. In the famous debate between Karl Barth and Emil Brunner it comes to expression in the quarrel about the so-called point of contact which the law and the gospel find in our structure of consciousness, especially reason and conscience. Brunner thinks that these in some sense prepare the way, but Barth radically rejects any point of contact on the ground that merely to consider a basis for the understanding and acceptance of the kerygma robs the Word of God of the freedom and power of its creative work and thus yields to the ancient temptation to change theology into anthropology.[6] This controversy (to which we shall return in chap. 15

6. See Brunner's "Nature and Grace" and Barth's "No!" in *Natural Theology* (London, 1946).

below) may not be too attractive in its modalities but it points us to the core of the debate between autonomy and theonomy, to the question of the analogy of being which is relevant in the debate with Roman Catholic theology, i.e., to the question how far there is agreement between our nature (our natural structure of consciousness) and revelation ("supernature").

As we draw out the lines we constantly leave the historical situation and come into the present. We are more interested in the problems than in the thinkers in whom we first see them appearing. These serve as models for material discussions.

The third problem is that of the general relation between theology and philosophy. In this problem the relation between revelation and reason is given its broadest basis. We shall pursue it in Hegel and his school and follow it up in the reactions of the left-wing Hegelians and Kierkegaard.

The fourth problem is that of the significance of the modern historico-critical study of scripture for faith based on the Bible. Here questions already considered from the previous standpoints take on actuality. A special issue is that of the hermeneutical conditions grounded in subjectivity. Is a critical study of the biblical text really so presuppositionless and neutral as many supposed—especially at the beginning (Reimarus, D. F. Strauss)—when they called faith a presupposition that has to be tied down to the facts by the human understanding and then critically overcome? To this context belongs the problem of distinguishing between the (nonbinding) world picture of the Bible and the kerygma itself, i.e., the problem of "demythologizing," as our generation calls it. Long before Bultmann similar problems arose with Semler in the age of the Enlightenment.

The fifth problem is that of the general relation between revelation and history which was discussed by such classical thinkers as J. C. K. von Hofmann, J. T. Beck, and later Martin Kähler, and which is still an issue today.

The sixth urgent question is that of the relation between the gospel and the world's religions. Schleiermacher dealt with the concept of religion but did not go into historical details. The so-called history of religions school—we shall take Troeltsch as its sole representative—confronted the empirical forms of the world's religions and was thus plunged into the debate about absolute and relative truth. The question, to put it briefly in its original form, is whether Christianity is simply one of the many phenomena of religious history. If it is, then missionary impulses must give place to a dialogical exchange between the religions. On the other hand, may it be that the gospel has transcendent origins which finally set it in contrast with the world of religions even though it is embedded in forms of expression that belong to the religious background and typology?

Seventh, secularism brings some tendencies in Enlightenment thought to a head when it does not merely advance a religion purified by reason but gives reason a dominant role in which it "unmasks" religion as ideology or projection. Karl Marx, Ludwig Feuerbach, and Friedrich Nietzsche are paradigms of this criticism of religion and ideology.

According to this survey I am looking for normative representatives of each basic question (especially those who helped to initiate the discussion). I shall analyze these representatives and relate them to their precursors or successors.

II. METHOD

I have said that we shall be guided by primarily systematic rather than historical interests, but this principle needs qualification. Even a "purely" historical concern to understand texts of philosophical or theological provenance cannot achieve the "in itself" of the past. It enters into a partnership of common inquiry with the past and summons it to engage in a present, here-and-now dialogue. The thinking of the past can be taken seriously only when there is this interweaving of historical and systematic interest.

This leads us to the problem of understanding. Since in this book we have to expound and understand texts of this type, since it is also our task to engage in "polemics," i.e., to accept, to reject, and to evaluate, it is essential that at the very outset we should clarify our hermeneutical principles. Two considerations demand this in any work on the systems of the last two centuries.

First, hermeneutical discussions have strongly shaped this period, so that we do not have here mere preliminary skirmishing but the very substance of the thinking of the time. A decisive question, as we shall see, is how far dogmas that are based on the Bible and handed down by tradition can be understood and above all appropriated by an altered consciousness.

Second, hermeneutical discussions are essential in an analysis of the last centuries because in our temporal proximity we are shaped by certain preunderstandings and prejudices, and above all by conscious or unconscious evaluation. Have not the romantic subjectivism of a

Schleiermacher, the Kantianism of a Ritschl, and the liberalism of a Harnack been long since overcome and outdated? Are they not to be regarded as of mere historical or antiquarian interest? This is simply a rhetorical question for many people in our generation.

No wonder that study of the past is often noninvolved and tedious, that it produces new strains in the sickness of nonhistoricity. The shelves of modern theologians will usually include many heretical books, and the readiness to hand them around is one of the most highly developed spontaneities in the discipline, and that not merely among critical younger theologians.

The question, then, is how we are to understand someone like Schleiermacher. What standards are to be used in his theological appraisal? If in a naively orthodox way we use only confessional writings in a gloatingly superior obscurantism, we shall, of course, find it easy. But how foolish and disrespectful that would be!

To what principles are we to subject the process of understanding and evaluating theological statements? This is our chief question, and with it we come upon a problem that stands, as we have said, at the center of almost all the newer theologies. What did the Enlightenment or Lessing do but propose a new hermeneutical program? This program is as follows. We cannot let ourselves be governed in our secular and religious commonplaces by certain Christian traditions. We are too responsible for what we regard as truth to be simply a point of transition on the assembly line of tradition. We have to measure the rank and value of these traditions, including holy scripture, by the truth-criteria of reason and conscience. Did not Schleiermacher, too, propose a hermeneutical program (not just explicitly but implicitly in every statement of *The Christian Faith*) when he tried to harmonize revelation and self-consciousness and thus to avoid dichotomy between the general and the religious self-consciousness? Did not the Ritschlian school do the same when it used moral and religious criteria to differentiate the obligatory content of revelation from the time-bound vessel of its expression? And Martin Kähler in his controversy with historical substraction, and Karl Barth with his pneumatic exegesis, and . . . ?

Even radical progressives, in an age of sociology run wild, practice hermeneutics in their own way. They consult the texts from the standpoint of the impulses of renewal and change and revolution that they contain. Under the control of this criterion the question can arise whether a more important guiding function in Protestantism is to be ascribed to Martin Luther or Thomas Münzer.[7]

7. Cf. Dieter Forte, *Martin Luther und Thomas Münzer* (1971).

During the whole period we thus encounter the hermeneutical problem in different forms. Here I shall simply look at three main types, to which I might add, as a fourth, my own principle of interpretation. I have chosen these types because modern historians and philosophers, and to some extent theologians, approximate to one or the other of them.[8]

A. PRAGMATICALLY DETERMINED HERMENEUTICS

This first type finds classical expression in Nietzsche's early work *Vom Nutzen und Nachteil der Historie für das Leben* (1873/74). From three standpoints Nietzsche shows the creative significance of history for the discovery of identity.

History has this significance first when I view it as monumental history. I focus in this case on its great figures and moments, on the march of humanity across the centuries. Humanity may be seen here in terms of its extreme possibilities. These are *my* possibilities, for I am the race.

History then has existential significance when I pursue anti-quarian history. Nietzsche means by this the concentration on local history, the history of one's own locality. In this I find my extended self. I understand the walls of the town, the tower, the constitution, and the festivals as a pictorial diary of my own youth, and find myself in them.

Finally, history leads to self-discovery when I engage in critical history. To do this we must have the strength to break and dissolve our own past so as to live. We do this by judging it, investigating it, and finally condemning it. It is hard to put the knife to our roots and trample on our pieties. But even with this critical distance, as Alexis de Tocqueville saw, I need history in order to mature by its "for and against" and to become myself.

Nietzsche is not interested in an objective or disinterested

8. For the modern history of hermeneutics the three-volume work of Joachim Wach, *Das Verstehen* (1926), is still significant. Among the many new works I might mention R. Bultmann, "The Problem of Hermeneutics," in *New Testament and Mythology and Other Basic Writings* ed. S. M. Ogden (Philadelphia, 1984), pp. 69-93; G. Ebeling, *Wort und Glaube*, II (1969), 99ff.; idem, "Hermeneutik," *RGG*, 3rd ed., III, 242ff. (bibliography); idem, *Dogmatik des christlichen Glaubens*, I (1979); H.-G. Gadamer, *Truth and Method* (New York, 1982). A. Schopenhauer ("Zur Wissenschaftslehre," in *Die Welt als Wille und Vorstellung*, III, 133) points out that hermeneutics is a late science and can arise only after acts of understanding have actually taken place. There is a clear analogy here to Kleist's essay "Über den Weltlauf."

understanding of history and the texts that it has handed down. He is not concerned about the "in itself" of what has happened. If we make this our goal and build up a gigantic mass of historical data, then, Nietzsche thinks, we shall become cripples, academic invalids, whose mind and limbs will be crushed beneath the weight, so that we lose our own identity.

For Nietzsche the problem of historical knowledge and understanding is not an epistemological matter (for in that respect we can achieve only approximate certainties) but an existential matter. I throw my own existence into the scales, I involve and risk myself, when I seek historical understanding. Two possibilities open up.

(1) I might do history in such a way that I give myself to it, that I commit myself to the past (in an ascetic desire for objectivity). If I do this, I emigrate from the present to the past and totally immerse myself in it. But I then let myself be flooded, absorbed, and consumed by alien materials. I become a petty academician who is taken over by these materials and loses the ability to live his own life, to exist historically. In this way, Nietzsche thinks, people eternally lose their subjectivity or suffer from overblown objectivity.

Those who pursue history in this way are not independent enough to stand over against it, to interrogate it, to evaluate and appraise it. To take a theological example, they can no longer understand or take seriously a figure like Schleiermacher. He cannot be for them a partner in debate to whom they listen, whom they address, whom they criticize, or over against whom they come with better theses. Instead, with overblown objectivity they become lost in Schleiermacher, or at any rate become no more than Schleiermacher experts. Only an empty husk remains of their own theological ego.

This is the "accursed immanence" of understanding of which Peter Schneider complained during the student revolt of 1968 in his article in *Zeit* (26, 1968, p. 24). Speaking of absorption in *The Prince of Homburg*, he argued that in this accursed immanence we enter into his despair without asking *why* he despaired. We prepared for death with him, we were reconciled with him. When reading Schiller we became great and lofty as he is, when reading Thomas Mann we became sick and ironical as he is. We did not read or think or feel as ourselves. This cry echoes Nietzsche's ironical description of absorption in an alien immanence, of the surrender of one's own identity in thinking, feeling, and willing.

(2) The second possibility is that I might risk my own existence, maintaining myself over against history, not letting what I have to understand gain monumental mastery over me. I may be grateful to

history for giving me some examples of life and work but for the rest I
will reject it, taking up an attitude of measurement and evaluation,
keeping my distance, remaining myself.

This is obviously a more considered position, for in it I take a
historical figure more seriously. I do this by entering into dialogue about
right and wrong, truth and falsehood. I contract with it a partnership
of Yes or No. I am not just a camera to which it is all one whether the
person at whom it is pointed is Albert Schweitzer or Adolf Hitler.

Yet we can argue that this is a more considered position only if
we distinguish more precisely. An existential relationship alone is not
enough. For there are many variations of this. In connection with
Nietzsche I will mention only two.

First, I may feel solidarity with a historical figure in relation to
norms that govern us both. Thus, if I am theologically a Luther scholar,
the normative authority of holy scripture stands over both Luther and
myself. I speak with Luther on the basis of this authority. I ask both him
and myself whether we do justice to this authority in our teaching and
preaching. If I do not do this, if I interpret Luther only intellectually, if
I see him only as the initiator of what takes shape as Lutheranism, I am
at best only a morphologist.[9] At root a Buddhist, Muslim, or atheist
might offer the same kind of presentation. It does not relate to my own
existence. If, however, I come under sharp mutual questioning with
Luther, I adopt an attitude of "affection" and make him a contemporary
in dialogue. Thanksgiving and criticism will govern my attitude. It is no
wonder that terms from Kierkegaard suggest themselves to describe this
attitude, e.g., the infinite passion of inwardness, or the involvement of
subjectivity.[10]

The second form of an existential historical approach is when
I debate with my historical partner in dialogue, as Nietzsche demands
and does, i.e., when I do not accept a common norm for the simple
reason that there are no final norms. Nietzsche himself polemically
rejects authoritative norms such as the good, the true, and the beautiful.
He believes that norms of this kind have been invented only to rob
people of their autonomy, to domesticate them, and in this way to
promote a decadent slave-morality. But if there are no norms that
embrace the historical subject and me, I myself become the point of

9. I have in mind Werner Elert's great work *The Structure of Lutheranism*
(1962), originally published as *Morphologie des Luthertums* (1931/32).
10. For an extreme example of this attitude cf. Christoph Schrempf, "Mein
erstes Bekenntnis zu Kierkegaard—und zu mir" (1884; *Gesammelte Werke*, XII [1935],
1).

reference for everything. There is nothing over me to which I, too, am referred. Hence the existential reference to the historical subject is either that it is useful to me or harmful. I myself am necessarily the criterion of history. Nobody and nothing can criticize me. I am not interested in the "truth" but only in the question of what impulses history contains for my own self-development, or, in modern terms, what motifs it has to offer for action and programs of world change. In this way I myself become the center of perspective on the historical landscape. It hardly needs to be pointed out that in this way I forfeit a true understanding of the past, or lose interest in such an understanding. The pragmatist is interested only in himself.

Marxist-Leninist writings (even the reports of the Moscow Academy) bring out the final consequences of this pragmatism. In the last resort natural and historical science—even astronomy—does not have the (sole) significance of bringing truth to light. Its task is to confirm our own doctrines or philosophical axioms. A scientific statement can take on an ideological point or achieve propaganda effects. It can be part of an objectifying trend. The polemical debate with Einstein offers an example. A philosophical affinity to belief in creation is feared in Einstein's thesis of the finitude of the universe. The thesis of the infinite possibilities of material progress is opposed to it. This is mediated by the idea of the limitless nature of incalculable creative impulses.[11] I also recall the teaching of the botanist T. D. Lysenko, who has since fallen out of favor, concerning the philosophically postulated inheritance of acquired characteristics, which then had to be confirmed scientifically.[12]

It is important that we should illustrate this type of existential historical interpretation by Nietzsche so as to be immune against the prejudgment that the existential reference as such is an unequivocally positive factor in hermeneutics. This is not so. The existential reference is in itself only an empty form and ambivalent as such. Otherwise such radically different thinkers as Marx, Kierkegaard, Nietzsche, and Bultmann—to mention only a few—could not take it as their starting point. We have to say precisely what the existential reference is in each case, whether it involves acceptance and solidarity under final norms or mere pragmatism. Along these lines we need critical alertness in testing the program of existential interpretation in Bultmann.

At any rate, we now note how easily the concept of the existential can become a mere slogan, and how an existential reference can lead to

11. See G. A. Wetter, *Der dialektische Materialismus* (1952), pp. 358ff., 319, 616.

12. Cf. *ThE*, II, 2, §§ 235ff.; ET II, 39-40.

darkness and misunderstanding instead of to understanding and the clarification of truth.

B. HISTORICO-PSYCHOLOGICALLY DETERMINED HERMENEUTICS

In modern theology this type is seen with particular clarity in Troeltsch and "liberal" theology. But the principle was classically formulated by Schleiermacher in his later lectures on hermeneutics.[13] More recent proponents have been W. Dilthey, E. Spranger, and to some extent H.-G. Gadamer.[14] In what follows I shall deal in essence only with Schleiermacher and Dilthey. We need to grasp their view of understanding if we are to comprehend the modern hermeneutical debate and especially Bultmann's principles of interpretation. These are governed by the controversy with the historico-psychological mode of understanding. Here is the break between past and present which we propose to illustrate as impressively as we can.

Schleiermacher in particular distinguishes between a divinatory and a comparative method of understanding. The two methods are related and together form the complete act of understanding. We shall briefly analyze both.

1. The Divinatory Method

According to Schleiermacher's famous definition, the divinatory act consists of changing oneself into the other, of seeing the other from within. In modern terms, it means adopting the self-understanding of the other and judging him by his own criteria. Only thus, thinks Schleiermacher, can we achieve a direct, intuitive, or congenial view of the other's individuality. Along similar lines Goethe thinks that the genius of the poet in shaping alien characters is determined by the ability to have been these characters.

But how can one change oneself into others? In putting and answering this question the historian J. G. Droysen,[15] and after him Dilthey, expanded Schleiermacher's idea of the divinatory and gave it

---

13. Schleiermacher, *Sämtliche Werke*, 1, vol. 7 (1838).

14. W. Dilthey, "Die Entstehung der Hermeneutik" (1900), in *Gesammelte Schriften*, V (1957), 317ff.; idem, "Das Verstehen anderer Personen und ihrer Lebensäusserungen," in *Gesammelte Schriften*, VII, 204ff.; E. Spranger, *Lebensformen*, 7th ed. (1930), pp. 410ff.; H.-G. Gadamer, *Truth and Method* (New York, 1982).

15. Droysen, *Grundriss der Historik*, 3rd ed. (1882; repr. 1925), § 9.

a broader anthropological setting. Over against others and their forms and expressions, we feel essential similarity and antithesis, each being self-enclosed, and each opening itself to the other in its expressions. In a simple formula, this means that we are all spirit of the same spirit and flesh of the same flesh. We are in human solidarity and can understand one another analogically. Negatively, we are not related intellectually because we deal with the same themes, e.g., the meaning of life, or God. We are not just common points of reference in respect of such themes, so that we know what the issues are. We are related and understand one another because we are analogous as human beings. Only for this deeper anthropological reason do we ask the same questions.[16] Thus according to Droysen the act of understanding is a direct intuition, the immersing of soul in soul, not unlike conception. This is possible, thinks Dilthey, only because individual differences are not finally based on qualitative personal differences but merely on quantitative differences in intellectual processes. This is why the expositor can achieve the reconstruction of the life of another.[17] The basic anthropological condition for this possibility is that there can never be anything in the individual self-expression of another that is not present in the life of those who lay hold upon it.[18]

We can understand, then, only things that have points of contact or a bridgehead in ourselves. Theologically, in connection with a problem that runs through the whole period, this means that if God's revelation is absolutely transcendent it is inaccessible to us. It discloses itself only because it uses our speech and addresses our reality as we know it already in our natural humanity (conscience, guilt, suffering, longing for peace, etc.) even prior to revelation.[19]

The possibility of understanding rests on the affinity (analogy) between the subject of understanding and the object. This is the presupposition of what Schleiermacher calls the divinatory act, the immersion in another. On the basis of this hermeneutical principle he finds something akin in revelation, and not the wholly other, like Kierkegaard. Thus in *The Christian Faith* he tries to harmonize the human self-consciousness with the dogmas, and he regards as a valid theological statement only that which coordinates with given intellectual data and

16. Cf. K. Jaspers, *Allgemeine Psychopathologie*, 4th ed. (1946), pp. 250ff., for the distinction between understanding (as an interpersonal act) and expounding.

17. Dilthey, *Gesammelte Schriften*, V, 329-30.

18. Ibid., p. 334. The view of Troeltsch is quite different; see chap. 15 below.

19. In Paul this problem occurs in connection with tongues (1 Cor. 12; 14). Paul demands that the individual experience of transcendence be put in ordinary speech by an interpreter. Cf. *EF*, III, 73ff.

may be integrated into them. Believing because absurd *(Credo quia absurdum)* is thus impossible. More appropriate to the understanding of revelation is Goethe's saying that the eye could not see the sun were it not itself sunny.[20]

This hermeneutical theme raises an urgent problem in the 18th and 19th centuries, and one that is still with us. One might formulate it thus. Do we not find it too easy since Barth to speak about God as the Wholly Other with no bridgehead in our natural I? Not as though Barth did not have good grounds to oppose, especially in his *Romans,* certain synthesizings of cultural Protestantism. Yet once one makes a thesis out of this antithesis, Bloch's ironical comment is not unjustified when he refers to Barth's secret cabinet and mighty fortress of transcendence.[21] Does not the hermeneutical question drop away altogether within this framework? The later Barth of the *Church Dogmatics,* of course, made some corrections by modifying his radical rejection of the principle of analogy.[22]

What stands behind Schleiermacher's divinatory principle theologically is a refusal to reduce theology to a positivistic *Deus dixit.* This would make the content of revelation into an alien court. Instead, everything depends on the possibility of appropriation. This is a valid goal, and our only question is whether the proposed hermeneutical means are also valid. What is the crux of appropriation? Does it lie in the anthropological presuppositions, i.e., the presence of an analogy between subject and object? Or does it lie in the testimony of the Holy Spirit? Or again, do we really have to choose between appropriation *by* and appropriation *to?* This is the question that we shall have to keep in view, and it will be constantly with us in our proposed dialogue.[23]

2. The Comparative Method

In this form of understanding what is to be understood is first posited as something general, and then the individual or specific aspect is worked out by comparison. Figuratively, one might depict the comparative act as looking at a thing through a microscope, first more broadly, then in detail.

A few examples will illustrate this. Schleiermacher's *Christian Faith* seeks to present the nexus of Christian teaching. The larger view

---

20. Cf. Tillich's principle of correlation, *Systematic Theology,* I (1959), 59ff.
21. E. Bloch, *Atheism and Christianity* (New York, 1972), pp. 42ff.
22. See the Epilogue below.
23. Cf. *EF,* I, chaps. 7–11, and vol. III.

displays the master concept, i.e., religion, under which Christianity is to be subsumed. Monotheism is also a more general concept and thus comes under the broader view. The more detailed view brings to light the differences compared to other religions or monotheisms. To argue on Schleiermacher's own level, the larger view acquaints me with the universal feeling of dependence, while the more detailed view leads to a distinction between relative dependence on finite entities and the feeling of absolute dependence. The first form of dependence is relative and broken because I can still counter it with some freedom, however small. The feeling of absolute dependence shows me that this freedom is not my own but has been received, and that I am thus dependent on its reception. Absolute dependence refers to an entity that transcends all finite objects. I thus call the object of this dependence "God." Further steps in detailed knowledge show me how the Christian religion works out the concept of God and in comparison with other constructions helps me to establish its specifically Christian character.

Eduard Spranger offers a good example of the process of comparison. To understand Socrates, I first (1) subsume him under the general concept of a philosopher, then (2) place him in some field of philosophy, e.g., dialectics, ethics, or pedagogics, then (3) note that he does not fit in any of these fields but is a unique person full of contradictions. Thus the picture of a new totality arises which stands on its own feet and cannot be subsumed. The uncontrolled total impression of Socrates is finally (4) refined, tested, and augmented by comparison, and at last all these acts of understanding produce a new and valid portrait of Socrates.

This technique of comparative understanding is at first very illuminating. We all use it every day. I make a new acquaintance. In no way arbitrarily, I classify him according to current criteria, e.g., as a solid citizen, playboy, or snob. I regard him as normal or eccentric, noble or petty, vital and full-blooded or a shrunken intellectual. In relation to women I may say that someone is my "type." (But before I marry my type, I look more closely, following the course of comparison recommended by Schleiermacher, and more specifically testing her way of thinking, feeling, reacting, and cooking!)

This everyday form of comparative understanding often enough runs into a crisis even in daily life. Some people cannot be subsumed but themselves serve as normative models. Mothers are an example. They cannot be related to a prior principle of motherliness. They themselves become in our consciousness the image of what motherliness means for us.

Something of the same applies to love at first sight. The very spontaneity is in this case a sign that I do not have to perform an act of comparison in order to establish a degree of loveability. From the first encounter I relate to that encounter all that I experience in the sphere of eros. The encounter becomes a normative thing which cannot be measured or subsumed. If someone then begins to compare—as old and resigned husbands are supposed to do in their hunger for life—and sets the freshness of a young girl in competition with the maturity of a life partner, if there is thus a relapse into comparison, marital understanding does not *begin* here (as it ought to according to Schleiermacher) but ceases. Comparison is a sign of alienation, of drifting apart.

This sad example of marriage shows how oversimplified, if clear, is the common picture. I will thus go on at once to a theological evaluation. The hermeneutical principles of Schleiermacher and, as we may say without exaggeration, of modern liberal humanism, run into a twofold crisis which is particularly evident in the theological sphere.

First crisis. Comparison presupposes a common measure under which to set the individual specimen. An example is religion, under which I set Christianity or the Reformation. But supposing the gospel rules out subsuming, being itself the measure of religion, its judgment and fulfilment, instead of having to validate itself as a suitable actualization before the forum of a general concept of religion? Might we not have here a suspicious parallel to the older married man? If I begin to compare the gospel to parallels in religious history, and if I do this, not out of an obviously justifiable academic interest, but because I am not sure of the moral and religious superiority of the gospel, i.e., whether it is really the supreme and absolute form of religion, might not this preliminary comparative skirmish be an indication that in relation to the gospel I have become uncertain, tired, and resigned, that I no longer understand its true features? In terms of intellectual history, might not this be the sign of a later time which has fallen victim to the resignation of relativisim?

Rudolf Kittel offers an instructive example in his essay "Die Zukunft der alttestamentlichen Wissenschaft."[24] The expositor of any religion, he says, must assign it its place within the religions. If we try to do this for OT religion, it is soon clear that it stands at the head of all ancient religions. When we realize with what purity and loftiness it expresses the idea of God, i.e., the idea of a universal God who dispenses salvation to all and who is also moral will and the holy director of history; when we consider how there grows out of this the ideal of the personality that has real worth only as it is moral and holy; when, finally, we come under the influence of its powerful moral and social universalism, we

24. *ZAW* (1921) 96ff.

can only be astonished at Harnack's thesis that the OT is not the equal of the NT. When we become aware of those things, OT religion is not just the blossoming of all ancient religion but comes so close to the very idea of religion itself that we ourselves have to accept its truth-content and maintain its abiding worth.

Here we find all the signs noted. We have normative entities such as religion, morality, personality, etc. The OT is not an unquestioningly accepted rock whose evidence immediately convinces us. We approach it apologetically because we are uncertain even though emphasis conceals our secret resignation. The OT is criticized by Harnack in a system of coordinates, i.e., that of morality and religion. It does not stand comparison with other religious documents, especially the NT. It has thus to be defended within the system. The OT can no longer be the measure of itself. No place is left for holy scripture to be its own interpreter. It has to be validated within the moral and religious criteria of an enlightened humanism. This type of comparison follows the same pattern as that adopted by the second-century Apologists when they tried to commend the Christian message to the Greeks by arguing that it not only does justice to the schema of Greek thought and may be integrated into it, but that it is supreme within this system. In the light of these and other alien laws, can one recognize any longer what is really proper to the OT itself?[25]

Second crisis. As we have seen, the divinatory principle means immersing oneself in others. Our analogical psychological structure makes this possible. It is assumed that we understand others when we grasp their psyche. Along these lines the Ritschlian Wilhelm Herrmann constructs an inner life of Jesus and thus reaches the level of an analogy on which we may meet and understand him.[26]

A test question, however, is whether we really have to do with the psyche of Isaiah if we want to understand him. Is this psyche crucial in the act of understanding? Who is Isaiah when he speaks to us as a prophet? He is the one to whom a message (kerygma) is entrusted and who is used and in some sense consumed by this message. He himself, his personality, is not at issue. At most it is at issue only insofar as we are concerned about his personal credibility, i.e., whether we can be certain that he obeys God rather than men, whether his kerygma is for him a

---

25. Among these alien laws one might list christological criteria that are projected into the OT, esp. by W. Vischer, *Das Christuszeugnis des AT,* 2 vols. (1934-1942); vol. I translated as *The Witness of the OT to Christ* (1949); and even more radically by H. Hellbardt, *Abrahams Lüge,* Theologische Existenz heute, 42. Cf. *ThE,* I, §§ 573ff.; ET I, 100ff.; *EF,* III, 145, 189.

26. Cf. W. Herrmann, *Communion with God* (1906), pp. 33ff., 57ff.

reality to which he bears witness with his life. Apart from that, the real issue is not the man himself but his message, which applies to us no less than to him.

If we still ask who Isaiah is personally, we are led into byways if we give a psychological answer and think that this is relevant, e.g., that he has a very stormy temperament, that he is sanguine, that he has great faith (or credulity), that he is obsessed with submission, that he has a striking eloquence, and that he has a considerable metaphysical gift for perceiving the lines of theological history. Isaiah might well have had these qualities. But he would have been the first to say that they do not matter in themselves but only as God impresses them into service. His true being is that he is claimed by God. External things, not inner qualities, shape him. All that he might be apart from being claimed by God can be understood only in the light of this claim. It is raw material which has neither shape nor form until it receives shape when he is taken into God's service.[27]

If this is true, what is finally needed is not the divinatory act of immersion into Isaiah but a dialogue with him about his message. To understand him, I must not grub around in the raw material of his psychological qualities. I must question him about the kerygmatic theme by which he is governed and by which I must be governed too, which applies to both of us equally, and in face of which we are in solidarity. This brings us to a third type of understanding.

C. EXISTENTIAL INTERPRETATION

In view of all that has been said, Bultmann is undoubtedly right on one point, i.e., when he argues that "understanding or interpretation is always oriented to a certain way of asking questions or to a certain objective."[28] I understand Isaiah when I look into the matter by which he is determined. I do not understand him when I merely examine the psychological presuppositions or use him simply as a source of the history of Israel's religion and culture. I may do this, and sometimes I

27. For a fascinating example of this kind of approach cf. Günter Jacob, *Dar Gewissensbegriff Luthers* (1929). Jacob shows that conscience is not an ontic construct or theme for Luther. It is never neutral but is always shaped by whoever claims it. Since it changes according to whoever claims it, *before* faith God is our accuser and conscience our defender, but *in* faith conscience is our accuser and God our defender. Cf. *ThE*, I, §§ 1596, 1674ff.; ET I, 298ff.

28. Bultmann, "The Problem of Hermeneutics," in *New Testament and Mythology and Other Basic Writings* (Philadelphia, 1984), p. 72.

have to do it. But when I use him in this way as a historian, i.e., as a source by means of which to achieve certain ends of my own in cultural or social history, I can hardly claim either to understand Isaiah or to be wanting to do so. I am like the person in charge of costumes in a theater, who fits out the actors for Schiller's *Kabale und Liebe,* and tries to give an accurate picture of Frederick the Great or his father, getting the uniforms right and dressing the women in rococo style. Why should not an expert of this kind use historical material about Frederick as a source for this honorable task? But in distinction, perhaps, from many historians, who have a blind spot in this regard, this expert will hardly claim that getting the uniforms right results in a divinatory relationship with Frederick and discloses his inner nature. Real understanding comes only as we raise the question of purpose. The intended goal is the essential core of the alien individual, i.e., that which determines the core.

There is no doubt at least that this applies to kerygmatic texts whose author knows that he is taken into service. If the theme of Paul, e.g., guilt and justification, is not important to me, I do not claim to have the key to his existence and therefore I do not understand him even though I am a qualified expert in NT Greek. Paul *exists* by this theme. His existence *has* a theme.

We have thus to do justice to Bultmann on the historico-psychological front, and yet the positive side of his hermeneutical theses is still suspect. He says that understanding is oriented to an intention, that interpretation "is never presuppositionless; more exactly, it is always guided by a preunderstanding of the subject matter about which it questions the text. Only on the basis of such a preunderstanding is a way of asking questions and an interpretation at all possible.[29]

What does it mean to have a preunderstanding? First, it refers to what I already know about the kerygmatic theme. I bring a preunderstanding to Paul's teaching on sin when, at least in the moral sense, I know something about good and evil, about my conscience which accuses me, about my alienation. At least in his earlier works Bultmann thinks that the totality of what we bring naturally by way of preunderstanding is representatively stated and analyzed by Heidegger. Only because I have this preunderstanding can Paul's themes find an echo in me and come into my field of vision. This preunderstanding, which philosophy expresses when it talks about human guilt, alienation, and inauthenticity, is then corrected by encounter with the kerygma itself and made into authentic understanding.

Second, although the first concept of preunderstanding is

29. Ibid., pp. 72-73.

generally known and often mentioned, the term has another content which figures less frequently in discussion. This second concept is more obscure and has perhaps more serious consequences. It relates to a specific mode of self-evaluation. We regard ourselves as lost, or as fallen from our true destiny. Even in our natural state, thinks Bultmann, we know about this lostness or disorder. Philosophy as well as theology speaks about it. Heidegger's philosophy calls us back from it to our true selves.[30] We also know our finitude. We know that we are doomed to die. We know finally that we are the victims of anxiety who are not at home in the world. Preunderstanding is thus a kind of native self-understanding. It implies self-evaluation.

The decisive question is this: What role does this preunderstanding play when it encounters revelation or the kerygma? One might describe this role very simply by saying that there takes place a transvaluation of the previous self-understanding. It is set in another frame of reference.

By nature we have to see ourselves as subject to finitude and judgment. We cannot revise our past. But in Christ's death and resurrection a new future opens up for us. We are now ordered to *zoe*, to life. We thus attain to a new self-understanding.

We recognize that our natural self-understanding is only very *conditionally* ready for transvaluation. It asks what impulses there are for this in the kerygma. We are interested only in this. What does not touch our given self-understanding, what cannot be interpreted anthropologically, is irrelevant to us. It is not pertinent.

Certain conditions must thus be met in advance if an NT statement or story is to qualify as kerygma. "Understanding reports of events as the act of God presupposes a preunderstanding of what in general can be called God's act."[31]

Such an act cannot have the same objectivity as the fact of a battle or the biography of a statesman. Thus the historical character of the kerygma, the facticity of the crucifixion and resurrection, is relatively irrelevant and unimportant. It necessarily belongs to the sphere of an invalid objectification of God, i.e., of miracle and myth. The facticity of these saving events is not needed for a transformation of our self-understanding. Such a transformation might be brought about by any doctrine of salvation, or by Plato. An imaginary poetic figure like Faust, or figures from Dante's *Divine Comedy*, might take on transforming significance for my self-understanding.

30. Bultmann, "New Testament and Mythology," in ibid., p. 25.
31. Bultmann, "The Problem of Hermeneutics," in ibid., p. 87.

Bultmann, of course, makes a more precise distinction. He does not abandon historicity altogether. But the autonomous and normative force of the concept of preunderstanding allows him only a very slender history which hardly goes beyond the historical character of a figure like Plato. Thus Christ's resurrection is not a historical fact in the external world but a visionary reflection in the minds of the disciples evoked by their encounter with him who walked on earth.

While it is only a visionary dream, however, this dream is not just an inner process. It carries within it its basis as a present reality. The disciples' vision was imaginary only insofar as they projected its object on the spatial, sensory world. The object of their vision was not imaginary.[32] The historical element is reduced to an X which unleashes the visionary effect and works in it as a present reality.

In other words, the preunderstanding is not content to be simply a temporal "pre-" which I bring to the kerygma. It has the force of a material postulate and works as a controlling criterion that decides what is legitimate in the kerygma. I ask the kerygma: What have you to say about my problems? This question has the force of a prejudgment. The preunderstanding works like a sieve through which the kerygmatic contents are filtered. Only that gets through which, as truth that is relevant to me, can become the content of my preunderstanding.

At root, then, it is not history that takes place according to Bultmann. What comes about is consciousness. The preunderstanding takes on the rank of a criterion or norm which works secretly and nonobjectively.

Bultmann, then, is not interested in whether we have fact or myth in such NT data as those of Christmas, Easter, and Pentecost. The idea-content of a historical event and that of a myth might both work on the understanding of my existence equally. I thus lose nothing as a Christian if everything in which God is viewed objectively is brought under the rubric of myth. The story itself is not eliminated. When it is interpreted, when its idea-content is extracted, it may be just as fruitful existentially.

At this point we have some decisive objections to raise against Bultmann's hermeneutical principles. The principle of preunderstanding is alien to the Bible. It operates as a criterion that is imported from outside. If I insist on it, I can no longer regard anything as possible. The historical facticity of the events of salvation is not open to

32. Cf. my "The Restatement of New Testament Mythology," in R. Bultmann, et al., *Kerygma and Myth*, ed. H. W. Bartsch (New York, 1961), pp. 138ff., esp. p. 152.

discussion because it cannot be used existentially or enter into my self-understanding.

We see here the limit of Bultmann's thesis that we must seek the intention of a text. He assumes that this intention is an existential theme, a theme of my self-understanding. He does not reckon seriously with the possibility that the biblical text is questioning me, or, better, that it is piercing the phalanx of my own questions and teaching me to ask the right questions. He does not reckon seriously with the possibility that as regards the kerygma more takes place in heaven than in my nous, which forms my self-understanding. He seems to be blind to the apparent axis of the NT message, namely, that more important than my dying and rising with Christ is the fact that quite apart from my acceptance or rejection Christ himself died and rose again, and that the resultant facticity has ontic primacy over my dying and rising with him.

Bultmann is not without presuppositions. His preunderstanding prejudices what he regards as legitimate kerygma. This prejudice may be seen in the question how far a text can be interpreted existentially, i.e., how far it can become the content of possible self-understanding.

We have here an essential problem that I can only indicate in this context. In fact I cannot escape this questioning of the text for two reasons.

First, no Christian proclamation, especially preaching, can avoid exegeting a text ad hominem and clarifying its setting. This means, however, that in proclamation I am addressing the self-consciousness of the hearers, their hopes and fears, their false security and despair, all that makes up their lives.

Second, if I do not ask how a text relates to my prior self-understanding, I renounce every hermeneutical criterion and run the risk of falling into a rigid doctrine of verbal inspiration, a doctrine that compels me to accept everything as God's Word or kerygma simply because it is there. When I come to the eschatological jungle of the last book of the Bible, how can I survive without the critical principles of hermeneutics? The eschatological fantasies of many sects show where ignorance of such principles leads.

In fact, then, we need some points of understanding by which to orient ourselves. As regards the OT, Luther's question how far it "promotes Christ" plays the part of such a point of orientation.[33]

Our question to Bultmann is simply this: How far has he taken these principles from the text, and how far has he imported them by

33. Cf. *EF*, III, 112ff., 140ff., 144ff.

way of the concept of preunderstanding and the modern worldview? I myself suspect the very idea of a hermeneutical "principle." A principle suggests a fixed, static, axiomatic, and permanent standpoint. Over against kerygmatic texts, however, I must be ready to let my prior reservations and assumptions and prejudices be revised and transcended.

This problem is constantly illustrated in the dialogues of Jesus. People bring specific questions to Jesus, e.g., that of eternal life, or that of the division of an inheritance. These questions show that they have presuppositions about Jesus, that they see something specific in him, e.g., a teacher of wisdom, a judge, a revolutionary, or a Messiah of some kind.

It is typical, however, that questions put against such a horizon of expectation cannot be answered simply. Jesus reacts to them with counterquestions. This is an indication that he will not let himself be known on the level of human judgment. He will let himself be known only when people are ready to allow their previous views to be revised as they listen, to experience a total surprise which throws all their hermeneutical presuppositions to the winds. The existential expositor, it seems to me, questions the texts in relation to his existential concerns but does not let himself be turned around and with equal strictness question his own principles in the light of the text (i.e., question the self-evident validity of the modern, immanentist picture of the world).

Only when I let myself be questioned in this way do I take the historical object seriously. If I do not let myself be questioned, I am in danger of taking seriously only myself and my presuppositions of thought, and therefore of projecting my own spirit into the object of interpretation.

In this sense I am concerned as presuppositionlessly and self-forgetfully as possible to look at the present figures under discussion. For I want to take them seriously. I want to understand them in terms of the theme which they espouse. We cannot be completely without presuppositions. We cannot jump over our own shadows. But with critical vigilance we can take our presuppositions into account, see in them a blind spot (and hence a necessity, not a hermeneutical virtue), and thus keep them under control.

We have now passed through the vestibule of our subject with all the questions of principle and method that it poses. We move on to the material itself.

CHAPTER 2

The Scope of Theological Thinking from the Enlightenment: Doubt

In the confusing variety of philosophical and theological thinking during the last centuries, we would do well to seek a red thread or common scope that will guide and facilitate our orientation. Naturally, it would be less didactically than materially appropriate to seek this thread in the material itself and not to present it in advance. But for many readers to whom the material may be new, some advance information might be didactically helpful.

In fact, I think I can discern a guiding theme which governs the period and gives unity to the multiplicity. Apart from a few outstanding mavericks such as Kierkegaard, Johann Tobias Beck, and the Blumhardts, the thinkers of the era are like a choir with different voices. Some of them are atonal, but they still make up a choir.

If I were to reduce the common theme to a short formula I would say that the 18th and 19th centuries, along with the preparatory and succeeding systems, are centuries of doubt. These are different forms of doubt from those found in the history of the early and medieval church. In general, and in much simplified form, I would see four main types of theological doubt, two of which play an essential role in the epoch. There is doubt of God's mercy, doubt of his justice, epistemological doubt, and pragmatic doubt.

I. DOUBT OF GOD'S MERCY

As regards the first form of doubt, Luther might serve as a representative. This doubt arises in face of the judicial law. It is doubt of God's mercy, which one hesitates to trust, and hence there is despair. If I move in the schema of law and try to fulfil God's demands by way of merit and achievement, can I really count on God's mercy? Being justified by works means, in modern terms, being able to achieve self-fulfilment (which Marxism thinks is possible, since we are dependent on social structures, and a change of structures can produce new people). But can I in any way make myself a *kaine ktisis* (a new creature) and thus earn acceptance with God? I find that I cannot press beyond myself, that I am stuck with my alienated being, that I cannot silence the accusation of the law. I remain imprisoned in the vicious circle of "I ought but I cannot." I see myself confronted by God's wrath and not his mercy. Luther's struggles in the cloister are a lasting illustration of this form of doubt. The only possible human consequence of doubt of God's mercy is shown to be either despair on the one side or security on the other.

From a historical perspective, I venture the thesis that we have here the final specifically medieval doubt. This doubt obviously does not arise out of the concrete, empirical form of life. It does not arise out of observation of the course of the world and the unfathomable hiddenness of human destiny. It is related in every way to the transcendent sphere of revelation. It arises within the dialectic of law and gospel and hence on the autochthonous ground of the sacral rather than through secular observation of the course of things. Doubt of God's mercy implies that one questions neither God's existence nor the self-disclosure of this God.

II. DOUBT OF GOD'S JUSTICE

The second form of doubt is more modern. To be sure, it occurs in Job, Ps. 73, and many other parts of the OT, and it is at least as old as the first form. Yet only in the modern age does it become a main theme and an initiator of theological destruction. As distinct from doubt of God's mercy, questioning of his justice implies a loss of confidence in any meaningful government of the world. The final result, then, is doubt of God's very existence. A God that cannot rule the world is a contradiction in terms. If chance is lord, if lightning strikes haphazardly, the world can no longer be understood as creation. A supposed Creator is thus viewed as mere wishful thinking.

This escalation of doubt occurs not only on Judeo-Christian soil but may be seen already in later Greek antiquity. In the *Heracles* of Euripides the hero destroys his own children in madness that Hera has brought upon him. Looking at their corpses in a lucid moment, he asks where his madness comes from if it does not come from a god, and if the god is really a god if it does come from a god. Here we see clearly the transition from doubt of meaning, of the just ordering of things by divine action, to doubt of the divine quality and therefore of the existence of God. For Euripides the gods are no longer beyond question. He has reached the stage of doubt and theological resignation. This swarm of doubts arises from observation of reality as it gives, in a phrase of Jean Paul,[1] the impression of cold, eternal necessity and meaningless chance.

The contradiction between what God is according to his own declaration—namely, a righteous God, merciful, and of great kindness—and the experience of senseless reality in which the wicked are often rewarded and the good punished, this collision between revelation and concrete reality, between faith and experience, raises always the problem of theodicy. We know it in our own time in the rhetorical, resigned question: "Why does God allow that?" This question implies the alternative that only one thing is possible. Either there is a just God who directs the world meaningfully, as faith believes, or there is the opposite, as observation seems to show. Nonsense quickly gains the upper hand against faith in God.

The Lisbon earthquake of 1755, in which 30,000 to 60,000 people died, was also an earthquake in the shaky religious world. Leibniz had shortly before promulgated the optimistic view that ours is the best of all possible worlds, that it is an organism which is meaningfully guided and divinely governed. Voltaire in his poem on the *Désastre de Lisbonne* fully exploited the crisis in meaning, the shattering of belief in divine justice. Goethe in his *Dichtung und Wahrheit*, however, was able to look beyond the destructive impression that led to a crisis of faith.[2] The Nazi concentration camp at Auschwitz has taken on similar significance for our time to that of the Lisbon earthquake in the 18th century. Not just a few voices are raised to say that after Auschwitz we can no longer sing: "Praise to the Almighty who over all things so wondrously reigneth. . . ."

As regards this form of doubt, we should note that it always arises out of the observation and interpretation of reality. Modern empiricism, which makes possible the age of science and technology, focuses on objectifiable reality.[3] Even though we find observation very early, and in sacrally controlled ages, it is plain that to the extent that

1. In his "Sermon of the Dead Christ"; cf. *EF,* I, 236ff.
2. For guidance on the result of the crisis cf. W. Lütgert, *Die Erschütterung des Optimismus durch das Erdbeben in Lissabon* (1901).
3. The text adduced from Jean Paul, J. P. Jacobsen's *Niels Lyhne,* and the so-called death-of-God theology all display clearly this origin of doubt.

this world is systematically investigated, and humanity begins to be empirically oriented at the Renaissance, this form of doubt necessarily becomes dominant. Secularism makes the discovered structural laws of this world the criterion of all reality, and hence, of course, the criterion of the reality of God.

But there is more. Doubt not only increases *quantitatively* but becomes *qualitatively* more radical. The Psalmist and Job quarrel with God about his government of the world. They find it unjust until they get through to God with a Nevertheless, not an understanding or conjectural Therefore. As an obvious and unchallenged partner in the dispute, even though he is called to order, God is for them an undisputed reality. His hiddenness, his being as *Deus absconditus*, is seen as part of his nature. The unknowability of his tracks, the concealment of his being under its opposite, is simply a sign of his majesty and his higher thoughts. Ps. 77:19 is typical: "Thy way was through the sea, thy path through the great waters; yet thy footprints were unseen." Note that this complaint that God's tracks may not be seen, that he cannot be known from the evidence of just and meaningful operations, is stated in the form of a prayer. Hence it does not merely count on the existence of this hidden God; it cherishes the certainty that he will hear the complaint. (The analogy to the dereliction of Jesus on the cross suggests itself.) So uncontested is the reality of God, so constant is the trust that he is and always will be "my" God.

Martin Buber radicalizes the question of how life with God is possible in the period after Auschwitz. The hidden and sinister nature of things has become too terrible. There might still be "faith" in the God who has permitted such things, but can we still speak to him? Can we call upon him? Dare the survivor of Auschwitz, the Job of the gas chambers, thank the Lord for his goodness and grace?

How about Job himself? He does not just complain—he complains to God. God has set aside his right. The Judge of the whole world is not acting justly. Job also receives a response from God. What God says, however, does not answer or even deal with his complaint. The response is simply the manifestation of God. His remoteness becomes proximity. Job's eye sees him. He recognizes him. But nothing is explained or settled. The injustice has not become justice. The horror is no less. The only thing is that Job hears God's Word. The mystery is still a riddle but it has become our own.[4]

In Ps. 77 the hiddenness of God is not the occasion for a complaint against him. It comes within a song of praise, a doxology. This

4. Buber, *Die vierte Rede über das Judentum* (1952).

means that the greatness of God which transcends our thoughts is what is denoted when we do not know him, and transitory things are *not* simply a perceptible likeness.

In this context God does not show himself in reality. On the contrary, reality is simply a source of doubt (even though we can think of exceptions such as the liberation from Egypt or the passage through the Red Sea). In the OT certainty about God arises out of his Word, which is accompanied by signs, and in which he reveals himself directly and not by inference from reality. The demand that we should consider the end of the wicked (Ps. 73:17) is an anticipation of eschatological thoughts which contain the promise that only with the end of this age will the hour come when we see clearly what we now see only in a mirror (1 Cor. 13:12) and in such distortion that we can hold fast to it only in a venture of faith.

As it traverses this doubt, faith achieves self-clarification. It is not just faith *in* but always, to the end of the aeon, faith *against*—the faith of a Nevertheless. If here there is doubt within faith in God, a radical mutation takes place in the history of modern doubt. The existence of God now begins to be doubted. The prayer in which doubt has previously been expressed breaks off and becomes itself an object of doubt.

Why is this so? God is identified with a self-evident notion of justice. We do not learn from himself who he is and how his righteousness is to be understood. Our own standards become the criterion of the concept of God. But when God is integrated into our own table of values, he becomes questionable. At the end of the history of doubt, belief in fate replaces faith in God.

The philosophical explanation of this new belief lies in the sense of tragedy. The persons of the gods are swallowed up by *moira*, by the lifeless ineluctability of things. The heart of the eternal yields to *ananke*. Classical authors begin to write tragedies again. The acceptance of the tragic seems to me to testify more forcefully to their break from Christianity than many confusing quotations from their directly religious utterances.[5]

Doubt of God's justice and finally of his existence as this results from the experience of meaninglessness reaches its final stage in the modern period. It leads to the acceptance of meaninglessness and the recognition of the creativity of the nothingness with which we are confronted. Here we have more than the sad statement that reality does not harmonize with the theses of tradition or the postulates of reason. In

5. Cf. H. Thielicke, *Schuld und Schicksal. Über das Tragische* (1936).

a dialectical leap meaninglessness itself is seen to be full of meaning. The absurdity expressed by Camus in the figure of Sisyphus is viewed as a productive liberation. Faced with an empty universe in which there are no laws or norms and nothing by which to orient myself, I have to make myself the author of law and am thus ready for a radical autonomy.[6]

III. EPISTEMOLOGICAL DOUBT

The third form of doubt brings us to the typical problem of the 18th and 19th centuries and preparatory movements of thought. It relates not to doubt of God's mercy or justice but to the dubious nature of religious knowledge as a whole.

The questions that trigger this change in the structure of doubt are these: What valid grounds are there for the self-evident truths of our time, and especially for the Christian tradition from which they derive? By what right do we believe, e.g., in a transcendent God who has made himself known through the birth, death, and resurrection of his Son? Are the *historical* accounts of this so secure that we may base on them such an extravagant report as that of the resurrection of the body of Christ, which runs contrary to all historical analogies? Or are there some *logical* arguments which credibly support this unusual event? Is there valid knowledge of the facts of salvation by any recognized means of attaining certainty, whether historical or logical? (These are questions which, among others, were posed by Reimarus and Semler.) Only when there are such means of attaining binding certainty can we be Christians without forfeiting our intellectual integrity.

In all circumstances, then, one thing is impossible. (In this negation there erupt the volcanic passions of the spirit which set in motion, like the shuddering of a ship, the thinking of G. E Lessing, that most honest of all the figures of the Enlightenment.) What is impossible is that we should indolently accept tradition and believe on authority. When he was twenty years of age, in 1749, Lessing in a letter to his father said that Christianity is not something that we can take on trust from our parents. Two years later his poem *Religion* put the religious subject, not religion, at the center with all the attendant problems.[7] The Muslim

---

6. The microbiologist J. Monod, a friend of Camus, tries to support this thought scientifically in his work *Chance and Necessity* (1972). I am also reminded of Nietzsche; cf. *EF,* I, 249ff.

7. See O. Mann, *Lessing* (1949), p. 47.

Saladin in *Nathan der Weise* speaks to the same effect when he says that
we cannot stay where an accident of birth has set us, or we can do so
only because we see and choose what is best (III, 5). And Nathan himself
asks whether we can put truth in our heads like money in a bag. We are
not passengers on the ship of tradition who have to accept things
passively. We are responsible helmsmen.

The skeptical view expressed in many different ways is this. We
cannot inherit truths and put them in a bag. Under certain conditions,
however, we may still accept the old truths. (There is here no purely
revolutionary impulse, no seeking of novelty or change for its own sake.)
But we can accept these truths only because we see and choose them as
the best, only because we find them to be true. We have to attain to them
and not just accept them on authority. If we do not—especially in the
case of religious truths—we are not really the subject of our belief in a
truth; we simply believe the belief of others. In a sharp expression aimed
against this epigonal degeneration, Alexander Schweizer (b. 1888) once
uttered the bitter statement that our fathers confessed their faith but
theologians today are often merely seeking to believe the confessions of
the fathers.[8] Our main task must be to set forth a truly credible faith for
contemporary Christianity. Every serious theological program must aim
at this. We may surely say that, in intention at least, a credible faith is
the concern of a thinker like Bultmann when he tries to separate the
kerygma that claims our faith from the time-bound setting which we no
longer find credible.

The question of the credibility of faith which honest seekers of
the Enlightenment try to establish and orthodox fanatics dismiss with
blasphemous self-certainty does not have to carry with it a whiff of
"rationalism." Credibility is not the same as rational demonstrability.
Credibility may also be the issue when I try to show that religion is truth
in a unique sense with no historical or logical postulate. Thus Schleiermacher deals with the credibility of faith when he locates it in contemplation and feeling and tries to make it clear to his contemporaries that
emotional subjectivity already harbors religious truth, so that this truth
does not meet us as an authority from outside. And does not Tillich have
something of the same in view when he thinks religious truth is appropriated with certainty when it applies unconditionally to us?

We see at any rate that epistemological doubt has its own worth.
I beg the reader to note that it involves wanting to *know*, not just wanting
to *believe*. This is why the Enlightenment presents such a confusing

8. Cf. F. Kattenbusch, *Die deutsche evangelische Theologie seit Schleiermacher*
(1926), p. 57.

picture. There is a will or readiness to believe. Most, if not all, the thinkers of the Enlightenment agree on this. But they want to believe for themselves. They do not want to believe the belief of others, which is no true faith at all. Belief is not the only issue. Equally important is respect for the religious subject, which wants to remain autonomous and not to be infiltrated by alien matter. The human self is inviolate only so long as it can be identified with its belief, only so long as the belief is *its own.*

There is thus resistance to the threatening schizophrenia of the modern consciousness and its slippery slope, i.e., the inclination to be an unthinking believer at one level of the consciousness and a pagan intellectual at the other. A struggle takes place for the wholeness and unbrokenness of humanity and hence for humanity itself. The religious motif of credibility and the human motif of totality are inseparable.

Walter Freytag, the Hamburg missiologist, tells of an extreme example of the division which might serve as an illustration. A young Chinese astronomer was educated in the West. When he returned home, he took part in noisy demonstrations by night which were designed to drive off the moon. He did not do this because he was hypocritically accommodating himself to a custom that he had transcended inwardly but because he was divided into two dimensions of consciousness.

At this juncture theologians are under assault. They cannot evade the assault. They face up to it. Their questions are still with us today. To treat them only historically, or with theological assurance to think that we are above them, is a mistake. We are in the dialogue with them which is the concern of this book. We have not advanced beyond them. We cannot look back on them victoriously. We are still contemporary with them.

IV. PRAGMATIC DOUBT

Pragmatic doubt is the final form of doubt developed in the 19th century. This kind of doubt is much too resigned to want to recognize final truths (i.e., truths that have to do with the basis, goal, and meaning of life, and that thus bear a religious signature). It is much too resigned to regard them as a possible object of knowledge. Those who are resigned in this way quickly appreciate the irony in Pilate's question: "What is truth?" In what was previously regarded as truth in the sphere of theology and philosophy, they find ideologies, i.e., unreal reflections of real being that lie beyond truth and falsehood. The championing of such dubious reflections is usually bound up with vested interests. To use the Marxist example, the deceitful support of supposed truth has as its real concern the pacification of the exploited. They are either given the consolation of a world to come or they are appeased by the alleged higher thoughts of providence.[9]

This approach leads to the following conclusions. First, whereas truth (presuming there is such a thing) has to be regarded as absolute and once-for-all, ideologies are always relative. The question whether a religion or philosophy is true is inappropriate on the soil of ideological thinking. The question assumes that truth is a supratemporal norm, but here it is only a function of other more real and actual things.

Second, whereas truth (if there is such a thing) is timeless and constant, even though it is developed in time-bound forms of expression, ideology is by nature time-bound and variable. It develops as social and economic realities change or the biological structure of those who produce it differs.

Third, this leads to the specific form of doubt that can arise only within this system of thought. Doubt can no longer relate to the question whether what is said in an ideology is true. The question of truth itself is misguided and dubious at this level. Doubt can relate only to the question whether a given ideology—or a religious statement interpreted as such—is adequate for the social situation and the state of consciousness determined thereby, above all whether it is *still* adequate, whether it may perhaps reflect a situation that is long since outdated. In clear if popular terms the common reproach that is made against Christianity from this angle is not that it states what is not true, or tells lies, but, ironically, that it is behind the times, that it has not grasped the spirit of the age. The worst offense is to be out of date, not to be immoral or untrue. This prepares the way for the charge that Christianity is *reactionary*.

Nietzsche's diagnosis of the age in *The Gay Science* is to be understood in this framework. "The ice that still supports people today has become very thin; the wind that brings the thaw is blowing; we ourselves who are homeless constitute a force that breaks open ice and other all too thin 'realities.'"[10] The ice here is the Christian culture of the West whose values, good and bad, are outmoded. (I might observe

9. On the concept of ideology cf. *ThE*, II/2, §§ 133ff., 154ff.; ET II, 22ff., 33ff. The most succinct definition may be found in the Communist Manifesto of 1847/1848. It does not occur only in the materialistic view of history, however, but also in biological materialism, in which the *logos* is the superstructure of *bios*, i.e., of basic reality. Cf. the Königsberg philosopher Hans Heyse, *Idee und Existenz* (1935).

10. Nietzsche, *The Gay Science* (New York, 1974), p. 338.

that we never regard our own diagnosis as ideology or relativize it as the mere superstructure of a true reality. We grant it the old-fashioned rank of a norm of truth.)

For the theologians and, in part, the philosophers of the 18th and 19th centuries, there arises in face of the forms of doubt that they represent (if they are intellectually fruitful) the question of how they can overcome doubt. A common conviction in this regard is that when doubt springs up we cannot evade it but have to go through with it if the religious subject and its humanity are not to be destroyed. This is what happens when Christian dogmas are viewed as necessary propositions that must be hurled against doubt. We cannot just quote the Bible, then, as if nothing had happened. We cannot simply take over the tradition of the Reformation and mark off a "nature reserve" of pure doctrine. This would only lead to theological unreality, for it would mean overlooking the historical nature of theology and treating its statements as timeless mathematical truths. It would also entail the loss of the most vital spirits of the age and those most ready to think.

One might formulate as follows the new theological point which is still with us. Theology can be pursued only in dialogical encounter with the generation in which it is set. It has always a twofold orientation: first, to the Word of revelation which it repeats, and then, in correlation, to those with and for whom it thinks. The humanity of theology lies in this twofold orientation. A perennial theology is reserved for the angels.

V. THE QUESTION OF APPROPRIATION

On the positive side, doubt involves the problem of appropriation. This gives us a second slogan by which to define the theological subject matter of the time. As theology and its theme cease to be self-evident certainties, one has either to cut loose from them or to find a way to make theological statements *accessible* as credible and intelligible statements.

Connected with this is the fact that from the time of Schleiermacher (to the present) two areas of theological teaching have come more and more into the foreground. The first is the area of theological principles, i.e., religious philosophy and what is academically called dogmatics.[11] The issue here is the controversy between faith and con-

---

11. Scholasticism deals with the relation between revelation and reason on the basis of the principle of analogy (see *ThE*, I, Index *"Analogia entis"*; *EF*, I, Index "Analogy of Being"). It can thus establish theological principles. But this is hardly

sciousness, or revelation and reason, which is triggered by the problem of doubt and appropriation. The possibility of intellectual honesty on the part of believers is thus involved.

The second area is that of homiletics. If I simply need to recite the biblical text as an unquestioned authority, and to paraphrase it homiletically, the homiletical problem is latent. It becomes virulent only when I have to ask about *targeted* proclamation. When I face this question, it is obvious to me that merely declaimed truth may not be relevant because my hearers, having different presuppositions of thought, do not see how it applies to them, and because the philosophical or time-bound setting of the textual statements conceals their point from them.

An anecdote might help to make this clear. Under the Third Reich, an assembly in the Berlin Sports Palace mocked the suffering figure of the Crucified and sought to replace it with a heroic Christ. A man who felt impelled to confess cried out in protest: "*Christ* is the Messiah." But he aroused only passing attention in his immediate vicinity. Another then cried out: "Christ is our Leader in time and eternity; those who reject him are seducers." He was saying just the same as the first person but formulated his statement in terms of the leader-cult of Nazism. Thus the first person was not understood and people did not see the relevance of what he was saying. But things began to happen when the second person cried out. He was inviting martyrdom because his confession was understood.

The question of the personal application and actualization of the message arises only when the ego has become problematic, when its self-evident relation to the message has been lost, when there is a greater awareness of one's own subjectivity.[12] The question then necessarily arises: Who is the one to whom I am speaking, and what preunderstandings, prejudgments, or doubts will the message encounter?

The homiletical problem arises in a radical sense, then, only when my hearers are not a blank page on which I can simply write the kerygma but are already written upon religiously and philosophically by the spirit of the age. I then have the task of removing these debit items or expunging these prejudices so as to make room for my own writing.

---

possible in the Protestant dogmatics of the 17th and 18th centuries even in the chapter on reason. The great breakthrough in this regard comes with the Introduction to Schleiermacher's *Christian Faith*. Cf. G. Ebeling, *The Study of Theology* (1978), pp. 136ff.; idem, *Dogmatik des christlichen Glaubens*, I (1979), 13ff.; H. G. Pöhlmann, *Abriss der Dogmatik*, 2nd ed. (1975), pp. 13ff.

12. In *EF,* vol. I, I have described as "Cartesian theology" the theological orientation based on the emancipated modern self.

Here one must put the critical counterquestion whether things are not quite different in the encounter of the gospel with the natural human being, whether the existing writing is not removed, not by preliminary apologetic work but by the act of proclamation itself, whether what takes place is not so much preparation *for* the truth as liberation—from prejudgments too—*by* the truth. Naturally, the prejudgments see to it that on a first hearing things are not properly understood, and a theology focused on the human ego has to be deeply unsettled. We have only to think of the confusion caused by a moral misunderstanding of the term *sin* and the resultant implausibility of the correlative terms *redemption* and *justification*.

This regard for the inner situation of the hearers and their ego is the chief thing that caused the 19th century to develop a doctrine of preaching. Even where this task is not a specific theme, always between the lines of the different theologies one may discern the question how the message is to be addressed to its "cultured despisers." The title of Schleiermacher's work characterizes the problem. The cultured are the most burdened with prejudgments and their subjectivity has to be freed from all kinds of religious misunderstandings.

Our sketch of the main problems will have shown us already what questions are posed for our own dogmatic and homiletical thinking. Have we not forgotten many of the questions to our hurt? Many sermons today might just as well have been preached in 1800. This does not imply that their contents are timeless but that they are bypassing their hearers and are thus boring. Secular hearers who come on occasion, or perhaps at Christmas, ask with astonishment what the preachers are really talking about. A conventional church member might say that "it is all perfectly correct, but I do not come into it; hence it does not grip me." This is why the most vital spirits of the age are seldom in the pews, and the pews are filled only with those, e.g., old people and children, in whose lives the question of the credibility of belief and the broken relation between the ego and the message does not for the most part arise.

What we have to consider is how theologians have tried to deal with doubt and appropriation since the Enlightenment. This is the theme of the present book. The theme both determines and limits the choice of material. It might serve to indicate the main lines of treatment, which are often blurred, if I briefly characterize the two main types that will meet us in the encounter with doubt and the task of appropriation.

The first type of appropriation is when a synthesis is sought between revelation and doubting reason. To put it briefly and crudely, such a synthesis involves the thesis that the Christian revelation is the direct and deepest answer to all the doubts and questions of reason. The original type of this thesis may be found in the second-century Apologists, to whom we have already referred. The doctrine of the analogy of being, of which Protestant theology makes abundant use in the present age, forms the theological background of the intended synthesis.

In synthetic presentations the problem of the point of contact has great importance. Revelation has a bridgehead in our subjectivity. Grace finds in nature something that comes to meet it and on which it can build.[13]

A statement by F. A. G. Tholuck in his famous work *Guido und Julius*[14] might help us better here than a theoretical discussion. That within us which God intends when we feel that we are drawn by the related spirit that moves toward us from the Christian revelation, he says, is filled by sacrificial love for the related one. The longer we try to penetrate and master and understand it, the more we do so, and this understanding is simply an appropriation of the beloved object, an entry into it. What takes place here is no different from what takes place in any act of vital understanding. In the case of the Pietist Tholuck the synthesis that makes divinatory understanding possible is based, not on the analogy of reason and revelation, but on that of emotional religious subjectivity and revelation.

The second principle of appropriation that has been exploited is that of diastasis. This is not yet the form of diastasis that is theologically formulated by Kierkegaard and later by Barth, and that finds in God a Wholly Other. The analogy between the religious subject and that which triggers the religious impulse (the universum or dogmatic truths) is maintained. The element of diastasis, e.g., in Schleiermacher, lies elsewhere. In view is the total difference between the subjective dimensions of theoretical and moral thinking on the one side and religious appropriation on the other. In the latter we have "contemplation" and "feeling," i.e., specific forms of reception, or, in the later Schleiermacher, a unique "self-consciousness." The act of religious appropriation, then, differs from

---

13. The classical model here is the Scholastic doctrine of the *analogia entis* (cf. E. Przywara, *Religionsphilosophie katholischer Theologie* [1927], pp. 22ff.). The Thomistic doctrine that grace builds on the presuppositions of nature (cf. F. Diekamp, *Katholische Dogmatik*, II, 9th ed. [1939], 48ff.) needs to be supplemented, as modern Roman Catholic theology stresses, by the statement of the Lateran Council of 1215 that we can postulate similarity between Creator and creature only if a greater dissimilarity is included. On the analogy of being see Vatican I, chap. 4: *De fide et ratione*, Denzinger, 3015ff.; G. Söhngen, *Die Einheit in der Theologie* (1952), p. 235; *ThE*, I, Index. The debate between Barth and Brunner in *Natural Theology* (Brunner's "Nature and Grace" and Barth's "No!") is also important for this whole theme.

14. Tholuck, *Guido und Julius* (1823), p. 159.

all other mental acts. Later, along the same lines, reference is made to a special religious a priori.[15] The last great proponent of this kind is Karl Heim. In his view of dimensions he relates religious experience to the nonobjective subject and strictly differentiates it, as a primal and inexplicable fact, from the objective thinking of empirical experience.[16]

VI. SURVEY OF THEMES FOR DISCUSSION

If we are right to pick on doubt and appropriation as the main themes in modern theology, we may establish a typology of theological and religio-philosophical conceptions on this basis. This typology will strengthen the method envisioned at the outset. I shall not try to expound the great systems in their historical sequence. I shall try instead to present some features of the type of thinking in the areas of doubt and appropriation as they occur throughout the period. In this way we shall find clear, objectively defined partners in the dialogue that we plan. Indeed, we shall see at different levels that the theological and philosophical thinkers are themselves already engaged in dialogue as this is triggered by differences within the same type. We have seen already that the polar processes of doubt and appropriation arise out of the modern emancipation of subjectivity, i.e., the increasing self-awareness of the ego. It is as well, then, to relate the typology to the broad concept of subjectivity with its many nuances. But in so doing we shall have to practice the great art of omission.[17]

A systematic typology will run somewhat as follows: (1) Epistemologically determined subjectivity (Descartes, Lessing, Kant). At issue here are the conditions of experience, including religious experience, inherent in subjectivity.

(2) Religiously enflamed subjectivity (Schleiermacher). The basis of religion is sought in feeling or self-consciousness. What we find in the word-form of the Bible or dogma can be appropriated only if it is integrated into established subjective conditions.

15. Cf. E. Troeltsch, *Gesammelte Schriften*, II (1913), 754ff.; A. Nygren, *Die Gültigkeit der religiösen Erfahrung* (1922); *EF,* I, 308.
16. Karl Heim, *Leitfaden der Dogmatik*, I, 3rd ed. (1923), 754ff.; idem, *Glaube und Denken*, 4th ed. (1938), pp. 102ff., 184ff.; idem, *Glaubensgewissheit*, 4th ed. (1949), pp. 140ff.
17. This survey does not mean that I shall deal with everything mentioned in what follows. Many things will be discussed in other contexts or referred to only in passing.

(3) Awakened Christian subjectivity (Tholuck, von Hofmann). The primary subject of theological reflection is not the word-form of Christian truth but the Christian (and the Christian's subjective inwardness) in whom this word is at work and takes form. Schleiermacher's view of religion is expanded here in the sense that the theme is not religious subjectivity as such but religious subjectivity as it is governed by the Christian message.

(4) Personal ethical subjectivity (Kant, Ritschl, Herrmann). In Kant the morally autonomous I is autarchous and needs no transcendent guidance or direction. Such guidance and direction simply cause conflicts in theologians who follow this course. Conscience is the subjective locus of religion. God is not an entity that heteronomizes conscience. Theological Kantians, then, try to harmonize the Christian concept of God with autonomous conscience. Their influential and widespread school has essentially propagated the moralizing of Christianity that we still see today.

(5) Idealistic subjectivity (Hegel and the left-wing Hegelians). The absolute spirit thinks itself by means of the finite spirit which is in a sense its instrument (Hegel). Or, as the left-wing Hegelians of all kinds would say, the finite spirit with its subjectivity, conditioned for its part by material things, is the only reality, the absolute spirit being merely its superstructure and projection. This movement stands Hegel's view on its head.

(6) Historical subjectivity (Troeltsch, Kähler). The dominant question here, to which various answers are given, arises out of the fact that subjectivity stands at some distance in time from the biblical event of salvation. What is the significance of this difference between things that are related in time? Does it lead to the slippery slope of relativism inasmuch as every historical phenomenon is conditioned and none can represent the absolute? If so, the historical Jesus is subject to this relativizing (Troeltsch). How can history possibly be understood in such a way that the relativizing distance, especially in relation to Jesus, is overcome? This is Kähler's question. It leads to a distinction between history in the sense that implies distance *(Historie)* and history as that which takes me up into itself *(Geschichte)*.

(7) Existential subjectivity, first in its theological form (Kierkegaard, Bultmann), which has to do with the varied relation between existence (rather than one part of subjectivity such as feeling or reason) and the Word of revelation, then in its areligious or atheistic form (Nietzsche and some modern existentialists), in which existence wins from itself its understanding of itself.

(8) Additional wrestling with subjectivity (Barth, Brunner, Tillich).

PART II

PREPARATORY CONCEPTIONS: DESCARTES AND THE ENLIGHTENMENT

CHAPTER 3

Descartes: The Breakthrough to the Human Subject

It is not that "I think, therefore I am," but conversely, or in Hebrew, "he is, therefore I think," and with this inversion of so simple a principle the whole system perhaps takes on a different vocabulary and direction.

J. G. Hamann to Jacobi, 6.2.1785

Bibliography. Primary Works: *Méditations; Discours de la méthode;* ET *Discourse on Method and Meditations* (New York, repr. 1960); *Principia philosophiae;* ET *Principles of Philosophy* (repr. 1984).
Secondary Works: K. Barth, *CD,* III/1, 350ff.; E. Cassirer, *Descartes. Lehre, Persönlichkeit, Wirkung* (1939); W. Dilthey, *Gesammelte Schriften,* II, 6th ed., Index; Kuno Fischer, *Geschichte der neueren Philosophie,* I-II, 4th ed. (1897); K. Jaspers, *Descartes und die Philosophie,* 2nd ed. (1948); G. Krüger, "Die Herkunft des philosophischen Bewusstseins," *Logos* 22 (1933) 225ff.; R. Lauth, *Die Frage nach dem Sinn des Lebens* (1953); L. Richter, *Dialoge mit deutschen Denkern* (1949).

I. THE PLACE OF DESCARTES IN THE HISTORY OF PHILOSOPHY AND THEOLOGY

Descartes opens the list of thinkers who make doubt and its conquest their theme and who struggle for the appropriation of legitimate knowledge. He is a thinker who starts at the very beginning, questioning

51

all that is traditionally regarded as self-evidently valid and initiating the process of gaining certainty.

The focal statement of his *Meditations,* "Cogito, ergo sum," stands on the threshold of modern thought. One might call it the initial thesis of secularization. The new note as compared with the Middle Ages is immediately apparent when we realize that this general thesis with a verb in the first person begins: "I" think, so that the subject and subjectivity are emphasized. Three things are significant in the statement.

First, neither the thinking subject nor the act of thought is of primary importance in the Middle Ages and antiquity. The almost exclusive concern is with being, the "is," and only then with thought. The ontic aspect takes precedence over the noetic aspect.

This is clear in the way in which Anselm speaks about the truth of knowledge and the truth of action (which also exists).[1] If what I will and do is to be right, it depends on whether I have in view the values posited in the objective order of being. Yet rightness does not appertain only to what is deliberately willed. It may apply also to unconscious things and processes. A thing can be true when it is what it ought to be. Fire does what is right and true when it burns and warms. It ought to do this. It is meant to do so by its very nature. In so doing, it fulfils the role that is allotted to it in the order of being. Human thought and action are true when they, too, take the form that they are assigned in the order of being. This is posited with the order of values that the Creator has given to being. But since our thought and action do not usually coincide with the intended value, but only approximate to it, we have to assess the amount of truth. There is not only truth and untruth; there is also more or less truth. It may seem strange to us, but there are degrees of truth. These depend on how close our thought and action are to the *telos* that the Creator has set in being. The final goal of creation is perfect truth. The degree of approximation to the final goal determines the degree of truth. We are significant only as a form of this created being, and in our thought and action we are thus subject to the same norms of truth as other forms of being such as plants, animals, and stones.

I have put in this short excursus on Anselm so as to give an impression of how things have changed since Descartes. In Anselm's world the Cartesian I could not possibly stand over against the world as an independent norm. The I plays a role in Anselm only as one being among others. It is subject to the same demands as others. It must fit in with the organism of the creaturely cosmos and achieve its truth in this way. It must not fall out of the order or stand over against it.

1. Cf. the discussion of truth in the preface to *De incarnatione Verbi,* Patrologia Latina, 158, 259ff.

In Descartes, interest shifts from objective being to the subject that stands over against this being, that does not integrate itself to it, that no longer wants to have a secure place in it. This landslide of thought—it is no less—is obviously possible only because uncertainty develops concerning objective being, God, and the world. For this reason the first task is to investigate the conditions in the liberated subject under which knowledge is possible. Epistemological theory, like hermeneutics, is a sign of skepticism and a loss of certainty.[2] The slogan "I think" replaces being, and the act of thought replaces the content of thought. Thinking about thinking now becomes the theme. We are no longer at home in the structure of the world. There are shifts and cracks in the timbers. We have gone outside and are alone.

Second, concentration on the "I" and the "I think" tells us more. In the Middle Ages, as in Aquinas or Luther, self-knowledge means knowledge of the relationship to God. The nature of the self cannot be abstracted from the fact that it is created by God, that it has guiltily broken free from him, and that it is visited and redeemed by him. We are those who have a history with God. This is the point of our existence. The point is not to be found—primarily—in ontic qualities, e.g., the possession of reason or the upright stance. If the history with God constitutes our being, this being can only be defined *relationally*. It is a being under judgment and grace. Our worth is also relational. Ours is an alien dignity.

We can thus know who we are only as we know who and what God is. But we learn about God only as he reveals himself in Jesus Christ. We can know ourselves, therefore, only as we relate ourselves to this self-revelation. We find *our* humanity in the humanity of Jesus Christ. We see in him the original of humanity. We perceive our goal in a living person. We cannot say of ourselves who we are, for we cannot say of ourselves who God is. In this sense anthropology is always for Christians a part of theology.

Epigrammatically, one might say that we learn our nature through revelation. We are ourselves an object of faith. To try to know our nature by listing ontic qualities is thus pointless. As Norbert Wiener says bluntly and ironically, it leads us only to the definition of ourselves as "featherless bipeds," puts us in the same category as plucked hens, kangaroos, and jerboas, and does not seize on anything specific to us.[3] In contrast, Augustine's *Confesssions* is the classical expression of a Christian anthropology. This biography is in fact a history of divine leading. The underlying relationship finds formal expression in the fact that it is conceived of as a prayer.

2. Cf. the brilliant essay by H. von Kleist on the course of the world.
3. N. Wiener, *Mensch und Menschmaschine* (1952), p. 14.

In Descartes, the initiator of the new era, we find the very opposite. His thesis is: I can know myself only as I reflect upon myself as an isolated I. Only when I have established *that* I am, *who* I am, and *how* my noetic apparatus works, can I take the further step of asking how I can know what is outside me, e.g., the world or God.

To describe the new tendency in a succinct formula, I might say that whereas Luther's thought is governed by the thesis that I must know who God is to know who I am, Descartes says that I must know that and who *I* am to know who and what *God* is. I must be clear about the conditions (posited in the I) under which a valid theological statement is possible.

When we put it thus, we note how this approach still exerts an influence today. I simply recall what I said in the introductory chapter about the existential interpretation of the Bible. This uses an existential analysis (related to the Cartesian analysis of the I) to establish the conditions under which an event may rank as a work of God.

In Descartes, then, certainty about the self precedes certainty about God. His first statement is not "God says" or "God is," but "I think, therefore I am." This statement, as we have seen, has axiomatic rank. Everything else, every theological statement, is deduced from it. If the subject of knowledge—the I of the *cogito*—is not known precisely, if its ability to know is not made plain, I am a hopeless victim of uncertain metaphysical assertions, of every supposed revelation, and of all kinds of superstition. I have no way of distinguishing the true from the false. Modern critical theologians (modern and critical are more or less synonymous) are very anxious at this point. They are afraid that careless repetition of the conventional will mean a surrender of the subjectivity of the I and an attack on the dignity of humanity. It is because Descartes wants to avoid this slippery slope that he begins with the impregnable axiomatic basis of all knowledge, the *cogito*.

Third, this leads on to the phenomenon of doubt—a theme we want to keep in view. If I am uncertain about objective being, if the existence of God and the world around me is doubtful, there is no point in making no more than small tactical maneuvers designed to wrest a supposed certain fact or two from the prevailing uncertainty. Thus I might argue that the desk at which I am sitting is unquestionably there, as is also the person I love, etc. For Descartes rearguard actions of this kind are a fatal patchwork, an apologetic maneuvering which cannot reestablish what has become doubtful; I must do something much more radical.

Instead of tactical actions I must engage in a strategic retreat. I must be ready to give up everything that has become uncertain, i.e., everything outside the certainty of the I, the *sum*. I must not try to show that this or that is certain. I must accept the movement of skeptical destruction in which I am engaged. I must carry it through to its bitter or happy end. I must affirm the process willingly and welcome the necessary result of my thinking.

In other words, I see that I am now given the task of doubting, and of doing so deliberately and radically. I must even question that which has previously seemed to be certain and guaranteed.

Only when I do this can I surely expect to reach the deeper level of that which cannot be doubted or destroyed, if there is such a thing. I must make of the necessity of having to doubt the virtue of being under obligation to doubt. The doubt that comes upon me at the first stage thus takes on the rank of deliberate doubt that serves a methodological purpose. It becomes a program. Only when I reach in this way the basic script of being, immediate self-certainty, do I have a tenable ontic foundation. Only then can I try to move out afresh from this inmost line of knowledge and conquer new territories for knowledge.

Although Luther never made doubt or temptation a means of theological knowledge, he resembles Descartes in some ways. He, too, suggests that only through trial can we reach certainty of faith, for all false supports drop away in affliction, temptation, and doubt, and I then retreat to the center of the divine promise that God will be "my" God.[4] The saying of Isaiah that temptation teaches us to pay heed to God's word (Isa. 28:19) is a constant refrain in Luther. So long as people enjoy peace and security they despise and neglect the Word. Trials alone make them certain of the truth of the Word, so that the power and truth of the Word lie in temptation alone (WA, 25, 189, 15). In this sense the greatest temptation is the absence of temptation (6, 223, 31ff.; LW, 44, 47). In temptation and tribulation we repeat Christ's passion and therefore share his consolations (5, 158, 18).

There is here no dialectical mechanism that can be used as a method. What we have is the promise of God's presence in temptation or trial. This decisively marks off Luther's teaching on doubt from the use of doubt by Descartes. The theocentric focus of Luther's view derives from the fact that God has to shatter the security that we find in philosophical systems and to reduce us to nothing with the help of temptation, so that at this lowest point he might begin his work in us. Thus in the exposition of the seven penitential psalms Luther says that it is God's nature to make something out of nothing, so that he can make

4. Cf. P. Althaus, "Gottes Gottheit als Sinn der Rechtfertigungslehre Luthers" (1931), in *Theologische Aufsätze*, II (1935), 1-30.

nothing of us if we are not nothing; in contrast, we make one thing out of another, a futile and unnecessary work (1, 183, 39–184, 3).

Descartes had indeed a grand strategic plan in view. But in detail his plan is not as important as a fact which is basic and revolutionary in the history of theology, namely, that doubt is here given a new and creative function.

In the Middle Ages doubt is a necessity and not a virtue. In the form of temptation it causes anxiety and disquiet and is finally a sign of sin. Even Luther, as indicated, never makes it a program for faith, although God—not we—can give it a role in salvation history. In the Middle Ages doubt is something that we catch, like an infection or virus. We cannot deliberately initiate it as a kind of healing fever.

When doubt is present, of course, as in Luther's case, we should not treat it "alleopathically" by using an antidote to suppress it. Instead we should treat it "homeopathically," treating like with like, i.e., carrying it through on its own level, not for methodological or strategic reasons but for theological reasons. If I fight doubt with my will and try to suppress it, this is a kind of autonomous cooperation and therefore a righteousness of works. This happens when I make it a method on the way to certainty, as Descartes does.

Like Luther, and unlike Descartes, I ought to treat doubt as follows. I may accept it calmly because I know that it can shatter only penultimate certainties and that when I let these go I come upon a solid and impregnable layer which—for Luther at least—cannot be shattered. This layer is the certainty about God which is reached in the first commandment, namely, that he is my God and is always in relationship with me. On this basis I ask again about the lost certainties, e.g., the cross of Christ and his atoning death, which might for a moment have become doubtful to me. On the solid rock of the first commandment it is clear that God wanted to go this way which I cannot establish rationally.[5] Luther never doubts intentionally; doubt is always something he accepts. The contested certainty of the penultimate is always upheld and encircled by the certainty of the ultimate to which I flee and to which I may cling as to the horns of the altar.

In the Cartesian strategy doubt is assigned a *creative* role. It is no longer a mere necessity. It is a virtue worth striving for. It is a means of knowledge. Faith does not lead to knowledge. The fear of the Lord is not the beginning of wisdom (Prov. 1:7; Job 28:28). The opposite is true. Doubt is the first step to knowledge. It is thus the beginning of wisdom. Only when it is set aside can the fear of the Lord begin. Only

5. Ibid.

thus is this fear protected against the verdict that it is uncontrollable superstition.

Thus doubt is a sign of human adulthood. Self-awareness responsibly controls the I. It is not at the mercy of what others say or of supposed plausibilities. We moderns are free, and on our own methodological initiative we create our own certainties. We break the taboo of what are collectively regarded as self-evident truths.

In the Middle Ages doubt was sin because it questioned God. For Descartes and the modern age, doubt, by unmasking and investigating conventional plausibilities, is now a virtue, for within the questioning, as a final reality that cannot be questioned, it finds the I and its *cogito* (or some other final reality). The sin for Descartes would be a naive adoption of Anselm's certainty of being (the formal similarity between their proofs of God, about which we shall speak, should not cause us to overlook the fundamental differences).

There thus arises a kind of infatuation with doubt, a metaphysical narcissism. At any rate, Cartesian doubt is an opening chord that calls for quiet, and the concert of the modern age begins. In our own century various forms of existentialism are the modern rage. Camus, after all his questioning, comes face to face with nothing. Heidegger speaks about our liberation. Sartre distances himself from fixation on the *essentia* that has controlled us from the time of Aristotle, or on what others expect of us.

All these things express an extraordinary shift in the human spirit and the history of theology. Descartes represents this shift. This is why we may pay special attention to him. I will sum up the shift in three brief theses. First, epistemological interest moves away from objective being to subjectivity and the epistemological conditions that it involves. Second, certainty of the self takes precedence over the certainty of God. Third, doubt undergoes a change of structure.

I am not saying too much if I venture the opinion that from the time of this shift there is always a pinch of Cartesian salt, if not a whole container, in modern theology.[6] Those who understand Descartes understand the point of the great theological and philosophical systems of the modern age, in both their affirmation and their contradiction.[7] For the focal point lies in doubt and the struggle for certainty. We are thus brought back to the theme that lies at the heart of our Introduction.

6. Cf. my characterization of a whole type of modern theology as Cartesian in *EF,* I.

7. When I say "contradiction" I have Barth, but not Barth alone, in mind.

II. THE PERSONALITY OF DESCARTES

Descartes lived from 1596 to 1650.[8] His manner of life is in keeping with his philosophizing. It is so symbolic that I will try to sketch his portrait, limiting myself to what is theologically relevant, and thus leaving out many dimensions of his thought, e.g., the mathematical dimensions. Philosophers do not always practice what they preach (neither do theologians!). Here, however, idea and life, *bios* and *logos*, are very closely akin.

The main source of what follows is the *Discourse* of Descartes, in which he tells us many things about his development as a philosopher. This autobiographical interest is in keeping with the trend of the *cogito*. Autobiography is a modern phenomenon. Augustine's *Confessions* are autobiographical, but one should not forget that they are viewed as a prayer, so that we do not have, in the strict sense, an autobiographical depiction of Augustine's own entelechy, notwithstanding the sublime psychological analyses. We have the description of a history with God and a dialogue with God about this history and Augustine's nature. In Descartes, however, the I as such stands at the center, and we thus have the author's monologue with himself. Kuno Fischer calls the *Meditations* a monological drama.

Descartes's whole life was, in fact, monological. It has been said of his philosophy that it was born in his study and not on the outside in *dialegesthai*. It is the product of a mind that focuses on itself and is completely introverted. Problems do not arise for Descartes as he inquires into the meaning of the world and history, or seeks the idea of justice in the pain of pressures.[9] They arise parthogenetically from the act of thought itself.[10]

By no means arbitrarily we see him as a thinker who is wrapped up in himself. As he says in the First Meditation (6), he is sitting there at the fireplace in his winter coat with paper in his hand. Who can make him doubt that he is in fact sitting there and that the hand and his whole body

8. For a brief survey of the life and work of Descartes, and the many dimensions of his thought and research as a philosopher, an opponent of Scholasticism, a mathematician, a physicist, an anatomist, and a physiologist, see Rainer Specht, *Descartes* (1966).

9. In this regard I think of a contrasting figure like Hesiod, the father of natural law, who is led to the idea of justice and eternal law by bad experiences of the perversion of law (*ThE*, I, §§ 1910-12; ET I, 396-97).

10. This does not have to mean that Descartes is not influenced by the history of philosophy and especially the study of Stoicism. In the *Discourse* (1) he can even say that the motif of doubt is suggested by a consideration of the way in which scholars defend different opinions on the same subject even though there can be only one true opinion. Cf. Dilthey, *Gesammelte Schriften*, II, 295.

are his? If he did, he would be like a mad person whose brain is so weakened by black moods and hostile vapors that he obstinately maintains that he is a king when he is really a beggar, or that he has an earthen head, or that he is a pumpkin or is made of glass, when he is in fact mad.

Thus Descartes thinks about himself in order to establish his identity. He is no pumpkin but a man in a comfortable robe. He is himself. His philosophizing starts here. He begins by identifying the subject of *cogito*. This philosophy is independent of encounters. It involves no communication. It is solipsistic. It begins with the introspection that Goethe rejects for those who want to know themselves, commending activity and encounters instead as the true means to achieve self- certainty.[11]

It is not as though Descartes was always a stay-at-home or always shut himself off in splendid isolation. He was one of the most widely traveled people of his day. Before writing his works he spent some profitable years of wandering that took him from Rome to Stockholm, from Holland to Transylvania. He saw the emperor crowned in Frankfurt and the doge married in Venice. He was at the jubilee year in Rome, enjoyed Paris, and was the guest at several courts.

Yet one can still say that these travels did not lead to encounters which influenced him. It seems as if he hardly felt himself to be touched by the enigmas, defects, and wonders of the world. He remained remarkably self-contained. The world did not present him with any obscure fate. As he once said, it was for him a book in which he wanted to "read." In the light of modern phenomena, we might better say, and more precisely, that it was an illustrated journal or a show on television. The media bring it about that the array of murders and ceremonies and sensations and everyday things can touch us only as spectators without causing any disturbance in our own lives. With very few exceptions we quickly accept what we see. A book by Wilhelm Raabe or a song by Matthias Claudius, in which very little happens, can make a deeper impact on us. The colorful plethora of sensations (especially in the gutter press) hardly makes a dent.

In fact, this kind of distant experience is very close to the way that Descartes experiences the world. He himself points out that he is in the world as *spectateur* or *voyeur* rather than *acteur*. He sees it passing in front of him (rather like a film). He has not the slightest urge to work on it, to wrestle with it, or to change it. His quietistic role as a spectator brought down upon him the considerable scorn of his family, which had a great zest for life.

11. Cf. *ThE*, II/1, §§ 1387ff.

Strictly, then, Descartes is outside the world, not in it. Distance marks the spectator. His maxim that to lie low is to live well shows how much he feels isolated from the world. He is a definitely *worldless* man. This is one of the points in his life from which one may draw a straight line to the solipsism and worldliness of many modern existentialisms.

Sometimes he expresses this sense of distance very vividly (as in the *Regulae*). He looks out from the window, sees people passing, and notes their hats and coats. He wanders through the markets of Amsterdam and sees people as trees. They are not personal Thous. They fill up space. They are not different in principle from things. They are extensions of things. The fact that they have souls is never a theme in his experience or philosophy. Neither love nor hate has a home in it. Descartes lives alone.

His role as a spectator comes to constant expression in his letters even when he is full of admiration for his partner, e.g., Balzac. When he commends to him a place to stay in Amsterdam, the reasons are that he can be passive there and will be at a safe distance. In a letter dated May 5, 1631, he says that every day he walks among the confusion of a large population with as much freedom and peace as in quiet streets, and he sees people as trees in the woods or the animals that feed there. Seeing peasants at work in the fields, he reflects that their work serves to make the site of his dwelling beautiful and to see to it that he lacks nothing. Even the ships that he sees at anchor in the port evoke only the thought that they richly provide goods from the Indies. The army protects his undisturbed security. For the rest, one might say that in great part his letters are more monological than dialogical.

As concerns his role as a spectator, it is significant that he lives when painting reaches its peak in Holland. He is thus in an atmosphere of observation and depiction. More precisely, light and shadow are more important than objects. The half-light interposes itself between him and reality.

In fact, I think that Dutch painting leads us directly to the heart of his philosophizing. The *Discourse* confirms this. Painters, he says, cannot on a flat surface present all the different aspects of a three-dimensional body. They thus select the most important and put these in the light. They then let us see the others only insofar as they can be seen when one looks at the lighter side. This is how he himself proceeds as a philosopher.

In interpreting this most essential feature of his self-understanding one might note simply that the spectator cannot see every aspect of a thing at once. To present reality we must choose the side that faces us and that we know best. We can only suggest the rest, and we may have to let it fade into semidarkness, as in Rembrandt's paintings.

Perhaps what I have in mind is that the point of comparison between painting and the philosophy of Descartes is the principle of perspective. The need for perspective entails a distinction between foreground and background, between what is clear and what is unclear. This distinction arises because perspective is entailed by the standpoint of the spectator. To make a pointed application to Descartes, it is linked to the relation to the I.[12]

Applied to philosophy this means that when we reflect on being we can present directly only that which faces us. But ultimately this is our own existence. This alone is certain. This is the foreground that is plainly and evidently before us. All else lies in semidarkness and uncertainty. I do not control the outside world so directly or plainly. I have it only by inference, i.e., in relation to my own existence. This is why Descartes writes as he does about perspective.

From the standpoint of painting Descartes is at the opposite pole from Caspar David Friedrich. Friedrich in his landscapes presents a world *with no people*. His landscapes are transhuman: a lonely ship coming home, a rugged polar world (although this contains confessional self-depiction). By contrast, in Descartes we have *worldless* people. The philosophical problems of the modern age constantly oscillate between these poles. Awakened to doubt, we have lost God. Hence our relation to the world has become problematic. The bond has snapped. Loss of the vertical brings a crisis in the horizontal. Problems like this arise: Is being simply a phenomenon of the human consciousness? The high idealism of Fichte offers a solution along these lines. Or is consciousness simply a phenomenon of matter, a function of the surrounding world, a reflection (ideology) of social and economic conditions? The various forms of materialism, especially that of Marx, take this view.

In the history of theology the crisis in the relationship with God means uncertainty in ethics as well as dogmatics. This comes out in the question that runs like a red thread through the history of modern ethics (Ritschl being perhaps the first to wrestle with it): How far can we be subject to God's law? Are we not enclosed and integrated into a worldly nexus, e.g., that of economic processes which threaten to determine us autonomously?

In this sense David Friedrich Strauss can say of the ethics of war that war is like lightning or electricity and is thus a meteorological, not

---

12. This link occurs for the first time (in distinction from Egyptian painting) when Apollodorus of Athens and Agatarchos of Samos discover perspective; cf. *ThE*, III, §§ 3258-61.

a moral, problem. It is meaningless, then, to say that God's laws forbid it or to try to bring it into a system of good and evil. It is amoral, fate.

The theological question, then, is whether we are the exponents of determinative cosmic laws or whether we confront this world in the name of God's commands. How does God's law relate to the autonomy of structures and processes? In all these unavoidable questions the uncertainty in the relation between I and the world finds expression. This uncertainty itself arises because according to the biblical view we have moved out of unbroken fellowship with God and his world into a zone of mere encounter with the self. Once in train, this process is irreversible, for the new situation imposes new responsibilities that we cannot escape.

For the rest, this process is not just a modern affair that Descartes helps to initiate. Fundamentally, the fall is the beginning of the process, and the Cartesian questioning of the I-world relation simply offers an elucidation of the fall. Naturally, the modern crisis in the I-world relation expresses a different nuance from that implied by the doubt of Descartes. For methodological reasons, as we shall see, Descartes reckoned with the nonexistence of the world. Today the crisis is that of a sense of alienation from the world—the feeling that Jacques Monod describes as a gypsy existence on the margin of a universe that has accidentally arisen and been hurled into being.

If we trace the lines from Descartes both backward and forward, we shall see what a crucial and representative role he has in respect of the modern shift in the history of philosophy and theology.

III. THE TEACHING OF DESCARTES

A. HIS PROOF OF THE EGO

After this initial biographical sketch we can turn to those parts of his teaching that are of particular theological relevance.

His methodological doubt, as I have said, begins with a radical questioning of the existence of the outside world. We have already shown why he questions it. By the device of consistent doubt he wants to see whether he will finally arrive at something that cannot be questioned. This will then have the strategic significance of an inner line of defense from which fresh advances can be made to recapture the lost world.

Now we can easily follow him in thinking that everything we

experience and regard as real rests on mere imagination and is simply a dream. When we dream, do we not think that what is happening is real? To use Goethe's theory of color as an example, and to extend even further the questioning of reality, are colors really red, blue, and yellow outside of us and independently of our eyes?

Even if we can in fact enter into this thought that reality is a mere dream, the critical question obtrudes at once: Can this dream-hypothesis be carried through finally and radically? The mathematical statement that $2 + 2 = 4$ can be "proved" to be true and is thus not subject to the verdict that it might be merely dreamed by me. Or is it?

Descartes himself raises this objection and accepts the impregnable truth of the proposition. But he does not think it has any bearing on the question of reality. His thinking on the matter is startling.

He concedes that the relations in mathematic equations and geometric figures are in harmony. But might it not be possible, he asks, that there are no extended spatial constructs to which they apply? In itself the truth of $2 + 2 = 4$ is only a mathematical game abstracted from reality. It can contain a concrete, ontological statement only when I add being and say, e.g., that 2 eggs and 2 eggs make 4 eggs. But the existence of these eggs is still in doubt. The sum does nothing to establish it. Only the relations are unequivocal. The truth and existence of the things that are set in relation remain doubtful. There is thus uncertainty about their facticity (First Meditation).

To this extent our relation to history as a realm of fact is also uncertain. Only that which applies (as in geometric proportions), not that which is, has final certainty.

This form of doubt is still with us, although not with the same methodological radicalness. Is it not echoed in Lessing's well-known saying that the temporally accidental truths of history cannot establish the eternally necessary truths of reason? Lessing reverses the question of Descartes. He questions whether we can move on from being, from what is reported to exist or to have happened, to unconditional truth. If a miracle is said to have really happened, can we deduce divine omnipotence from it, or, better, a dogma of divine omnipotence? Just as this inference is doubtful, so is its opposite, i.e., inference from an eternal truth to being. In both cases—this is the point of comparison—being, or the factual side, is uncertain, be it as a premise, as among Lessing's orthodox opponents, or as a conclusion, as in the inference of being from the relations in which it is set.

I venture to go further in my questions and insights. May we not see the same Cartesian doubt today in the kerygmatic theology of the Bultmann school? Here the factual or historical element— being—

is uncertain. This uncertainty extends to the kerygmatically superimposed and theologically interpreted events in Israel's history and also to the accounts of the years 1-30, which have been affected by later community theology. The crisis in the concept of the "historical Jesus" arises out of this uncertainty. But does not a valid relation replace the dubious facts? What is the real rock of certainty in this theology? My reply would be that it is the relation between the kerygma and faith. And do we not find the same relation in the "liberal theology" from which Bultmann's position arises by thesis and counterthesis? In Adolf von Harnack what counts is not the existence of Jesus or the mighty acts of God, which belong to the sphere of facticity, but the validity of the teaching of the Nazarene, which is as little dependent on anything factual as is the validity of the Pythagorean theorem on the existence of its author. What is valid is the message of trust in God, humility, the forgiveness of sins, neighborly love, and the infinite worth of the human soul.[13] The Father alone and not the Son is the theme of the gospel as Jesus proclaimed it.[14] To look at the Son brings us into the zone of historical facticity. With the Father, however, we are in the sphere of an eternal relation which the title of a collection of sermons from this milieu pregnantly describes: "God and the soul," "The soul and its God."[15]

After this look to the future, which helps us to understand what the doubt of Descartes initiates, we return to Descartes himself. For anyone in the Christian tradition—as Descartes was—the question at once arises whether theological arguments might be used with success to remove this doubt about the existence of the outside world. Is not faith in the Creator of heaven and earth a guarantee that heaven and earth exist? But this line of thinking does not help us in the view of Descartes. A preliminary appeal to the Creator God is philosophically invalid. For who is to guarantee the truth of the dogma, or, even more sharply, God's own existence, the existence of *this* God?

The doubting question cannot stop at God. Although, in part at least, Descartes has an ontological proof like that of Anselm, he does not regard its theological presuppositions as simply given, and especially not the spiritual order of being, which was conceived by God as basis of its meaning, and which thus points to God as the supreme being. Because Descartes no longer accepts this background of the understanding of being, at least as self-evident, his doubt can rise to a bold

13. Harnack, *What Is Christianity?* (New York, 1957), 4, 2 (pp. 63ff.); 5, 3 (pp. 68ff.).
14. Ibid., 8, 1 (pp. 132ff.).
15. Rittelmeyer (1906).

and even mad extreme. We cannot rule out the possibility that instead of a supremely good God a *demon* has constructed this sham world as a deceptive setting for me, and that he takes a cynical and even "sadistic" joy in deceiving me in this way (Second Meditation, 7). This is the utmost limit to which the passion of doubt can lead.

Descartes is here caught in a circle which in spite of every doubt points him to a final and abiding certainty of being and of God and shows that his radical methodological doubt is simply a bold experiment and no more. Dilthey has drawn attention to this circle.[16] The existence of the deity, whose truth is supposed to guarantee the validity of the means of knowledge, can itself be deduced only by way of the law of causality and the concept of substance. The evidence for these is given intuitively, but the validity of what is evident is proved only by the truth of God, whose proof presupposes this objective validity. These common notions, however, are not related only to the proof of God. Descartes could not fail to see that the *cogito sum* presupposes the validity of simple concepts. Such concepts are already contained in all knowledge as its condition. It seems to follow, then, that fundamentally there is a closer relation to Anselm than the experiment in doubt might immediately suggest.

Even if the contents of my thinking and experience imply an evil and deceitful fate, it is still true that I exist as one who thinks and doubts. Doubt itself carries a final and evident reference to facticity. It is a *fact* that I doubt, that *I* doubt, that the process of doubt and its subject exist: *dubito ergo sum*. (The statement *ergo sum* is not an inference but a self-evident truth, so that it is more appropriate to say *cogito [dubito] sum*.) The existence of the I as a final substratum of reality is incontestable.

Again I would like to pause to point out how, when being is uncertain and forgotten, doubt is still used as a methodological means to secure an ontic basis (even though the method is handled differently and does not end with the Cartesian I).

I might take as a first example Paul Tillich's book *The Courage to Be*.[17] I have doubts about meaning, Tillich argues, and am thus under the threat of nihilism. But I discover—this is the point of the book—that I doubt in the name of something that is given me in the very act of doubt. I doubt in the name of norms, e.g., that of meaning. I find that reality does not correspond to what I presuppose to be meaning. But there can be no pure nihilism with no reference at all to meaning. For I always have meaning behind me. I come from it. I would not have

16. Dilthey, *Gesammelte Schriften*, II, 6th ed. (1960), 350.
17. Tillich, *The Courage to Be* (New Haven, 1952).

seen, however, that it is always there as a norm if I had not doubted but had naively counted on it as self-evident. Thus those who are threatened by nihilism have a great chance to find an elementary basis of meaning.

Existential doubt is similar. Doubt here means that I accept nothing as given or self-evident; I accept no tradition; I accept nothing that merely seems to be plausible. Precisely in questioning these things, however, I achieve my own existence. I resist the dissolution of my existence in anonymity and find it as an existing I. The sense is not the same as Descartes's "I doubt and therefore I am." It is the fuller one: "I doubt and therefore I come to existence, I find my true being, I achieve existence." I no longer travel as a mere passenger on the ship of self-evident truths. I myself ask whether I am on the right course. I go to the bridge and assume responsibility. The nuances differ, but in both cases there is an analogy to Descartes's questioning. The issue is doubt which leads to something evidently ontic.

If we now return to the Cartesian *cogito sum*, our point is as follows. The I that as an existing subject lies behind the act of thought is brought to light only by an inward view of thought itself. Negatively, this means that the certainty of the I does not come from encounter with the outside world whose existence is doubted. Descartes's experiment with certainty differs emphatically from what we learn elsewhere about the rise of self-consciousness and self-certainty.[18] Thus we are taught that a child experiences itself in encounter with the outside world. It learns to know and understand itself as it experiments with the world around it. It leans too far forward and falls on its nose. It thus finds out that it is not pure spirit, that it has a body that is subject to the laws of gravity. It is good and is rewarded; it is naughty and is punished. By these reactions of the outside world, represented in such cases by its parents, it achieves experience of itself as a moral person, as an I. (This

18. Cf. E. Husserl, *Logische Untersuchungen*, esp. vol. II (1901), who teaches that self-consciousness arises through contact with the outside world and *direct* access to it. His "phenomenology" takes the opposite view to that of Descartes, who achieves certainty of the outside world only *indirectly* by way of deductive operations. Husserl's direct subject-object relation, which is posited in the consciousness, is described by him as intentionality. Nevertheless, in his *Ideen zu einer reinen Phänomenologie* (1913), he advances theories which recall Descartes's experiment. He engages in a "reduction to pure consciousness." This is still intentionally oriented and is thus a consciousness of the world and things. But it leaves aside their existence and brackets it experimentally. There is thus something of a break here with his original view in which he stresses the direct presence of the world to the subject. Later, in the twenties, his interest in the world in which we are implicated revives, so that this question occupies him: What achievements of the consciousness bring it about that we mostly move about in the world naively and unreflectingly as though it were all self-evident?

is still true even though later it may come to this experience more through its emancipation from these reactions.)

Gerardus van der Leeuw makes this point when he says that play is the original expression in which we discover ourselves.[19] We find ourselves in the resistance we meet, i.e., on the borders, as it were, of play, on what happens in it. A child reaches for the bars of its cot and also for its big toe, and it gradually finds out what belongs to the outside world and what belongs to itself. Similarly, we adults experience ourselves in life as things come upon us and as we react to them. We learn to know ourselves as, like Alpine climbers, we reach the limit of our capabilities or test our convictions at critical moments.[20] As the author finely puts it, we do not only play but are played with. Our last emotion is the terror of death. Our play is disrupted. It has an end as soon as it begins. It has hardly begun before it ends. Human life is projected backward. It is life for death. In its finitude, in its encounter with that which limits it, and finally with death, we experience ourselves.[21]

We thus maintain that Descartes does not experience the I in encounter; rather, the I experiences itself as the subject of an act of thinking that is not related to the outside world but takes place as the only reality in an unreal world of appearance. The act of thinking does not think something; it thinks; it is a pure act. This act is the only assured reality.[22]

19. *Der Mensch und die Religion* (Basel, 1941), p. 35.

20. In this light we can appreciate the problems in modern self-exploration groups and their narcissistic orientation to the ego.

21. The question of self-knowledge, not by introspection or concentration on the ego but by encounters, is an important theme in Goethe's anthropology; cf. *ThE*, II/1, §§ 1387-92.

22. The many contemporary objections to this thesis of Descartes deal only in part with the *cogito*. (In this case the main interest is in the structure of the subject and the question of the material substratum and mode of the act of thinking.) The inferences, especially the proof of God, are the most important target of criticism. A notable objection to the Cartesian *cogito*, and therefore to the central point of the *Meditations*, has been raised in our own time by philosophical structuralism, which has its home in France. One of its main champions, Michel Foucault, reverses the starting point of Descartes's concern for self-certainty. Thinking does not impart to its subject, the thinking I, any certainty as to its existence. In thinking the I is not alone. It is with something else. It is in the sphere of suprapersonal structures. It thinks within these. Unnoticed, they direct its viewpoint by means of the language at its disposal. The subject of thinking does not recognize this other that is with it, and hence it does not control it. The I underlying the *cogito* is never alone as Descartes thought. It is thus mistaken as to its identity if it wants to be certain of its existence without suspecting that it is not alone but with that other. Hence this subject of knowledge has necessarily to be given up (*Von der Subversion des Wissens*, ed. W. Seitter

We may suspect that the Cartesian I as the subject of *cogito* has no personal traits but is an artificial abstraction. The I that has no counterpart, that exists in relation to neither God, a Thou, nor an It, loses its human quality. It becomes the docetic ghost of a *res cogitans* which is beyond love and hate, good and evil, and which reminds us of the shadowy and solipsistic I that much later Max Stirner (= Caspar Schmidt) presents as the final reality in his work *Der Einzige und sein Eigentum* (1845).

"What am I?" asks Descartes in the Second Meditation (14). He replies, "A thinking being." And what is that? "It is a being which doubts, which understands, which conceives, which affirms, which denies, which wills, which rejects, which imagines also, and which perceives." Thus the I does not have the starry heaven above it. No beloved awakens passions in it. It is moved by no work of art. It does not feel secure in the peace of God. It does have feelings of security, eruptions of enthusiasm, and emotions. But these are not movements that flow between the I and what is outside it. They are waves above the depths of the I, and they sink back at once into the I. They are ghostly actions in a vacuum.

We are reminded of the scene when Descartes was looking at people at the Amsterdam market, and they were like trees— extended things. We see here, perhaps, how an intellectual feature of the new age is taking on its first contours. It means the treating of people as objects. They are relevant only in terms of their functions. In this regard it is not decisive whether the function consists of an act of thinking (as in Descartes) or technical manipulation. A first vision of the world of computers swims into our ken at this point.

B. HIS PROOF OF GOD AND THE WORLD

The ballad of solipsism has a happy ending in Descartes. He finally rediscovers the world even if it is a very anonymous, abstract, unspiritual, and depersonalized world. How does he achieve certainty that in spite of the impression of illusion there is an outside world, there are realities beyond the inner sphere of the I?

He reaches this certainty by means of the proof of God. If I

[1974], pp. 83ff.). Particular stress on the importance of speech as a structure that carries and frames the individual act of thinking is laid by the founder of structuralism (though he did not use the term), Ferdinand de Saussure, in his famous *Cours de linguistique générale* (published posthumously, 1916; ET *Course in General Linguistics* [New York, 1966]).

advanced earlier the negative thesis that to lose God is to lose the world because it is to erase the bracket that binds things together, the corresponding positive thesis is that to regain the world, or outside reality, we need to be sure of the divine bracket around it. Once we see that there is a God, that everything depends on him, and that he is no deceiver, and once we have deduced from this that everything that I see plainly and clearly is necessarily true, nothing can make us doubt; we have true and certain knowledge (Fifth Meditation, 17).

With this statement Descartes arrives at the theological basis of all ontology. There can be no direct relating of thought and being, of I and the world, of I and Thou. It is a hopeless philosophical endeavor to try to deduce one side of this relation from the other. We can infer neither the existence of the world from the I nor the existence of the I from the world. We cannot do this although it has often been attempted in intellectual history subsequent to Descartes, e.g., by idealism when it derives the manifold phenomena of the world from the structure of the I, or by materialism when it derives the knowing I from the material structure of being. As Descartes saw, the subject-object relation demands a third thing. It is possible only when, in the modern vocabulary of Jaspers, we know an underlying something which cannot be grasped objectively. That which constitutes the relation, Descartes calls "God." Stoicism had already pointed to the same thing with its concept of the cosmic logos. Only because there is this logos that governs the cosmos can we gain an understanding of being with our noetic logos, i.e., reason, and control it as subjects.

We thus see that although Descartes's proof of God may seem strange to us, and although his God may seem to be just as much a ghost as the I that thinks him, Descartes is led by his premises to the truly basic question in all philosophy, namely, the question whether the concept of God (no matter what it may be) does not have to be the inherent principle of all philosophical certainty.[23]

But how can Descartes reach a valid idea of God from the autarchy of his closed world of the I? He seeks it with the help of the realistic ontological system of thought of Scholasticism in a way similar to that taken by Anselm in his proof of God. Even though I must greatly

23. Kant answered this question in the affirmative when he stated in *The Critique of Pure Reason* that reason must form the idea of God, because the idea belongs to the terms of reason's thinking. With this, it would present "the idea of something at hand, upon which all empirical reality grounds its highest and necessary oneness" (Appendix to the Transcendental Dialectic; Weischedel ed., WW, IV, 586-87; see also pp. 557-58).

compress his train of thought, and can hardly give any impression of the sublime circumspection and the multiplicity of controls at each detailed step, we may at least take note of the main points.

The initial thesis is that I find the idea of God in myself (cf. the Third Meditation). This does tell us whether any reality corresponds to the idea. I find other ideas in myself to which no outside realities correspond. I may have the idea of a triangle. Poets have the idea of sirens and other legendary figures. As C. G. Jung might add, we have a subconscious archetype of humanity. Nevertheless, the "realistic" structure of thought demands that there be some relation between that which produces and that which is produced. We naturally perceive that there must be at least as much reality in an efficient cause as in the effect that it produces. For where can the effect get its reality if not from the cause (Third Meditation, 19)? But I myself cannot be the cause of the idea of God, for as a cause I have not enough reality to produce the idea of an eternal and almighty God. If the reality of my ideas is so great that I know for certain that neither formally nor materially does it lie in me, and that consequently I cannot be the cause of the idea, then it necessarily follows that I am not alone in the world but there exists another cause which is the cause of this idea (Third Meditation, 22). I am thus driven to the conclusion that God and not my consciousness produces this idea. We thus arrive at the definition that by the term *God* we mean the infinite, independent substance, full of supreme insight and power, by which I myself am created, and all else that exists, if it does indeed exist (Third Meditation, 27).

Parenthesis on the Difference between Descartes and Anselm

As is well known, Anselm's proof of God begins with a prayer. This contains the decisive key to an understanding of the proof. It refutes the idea that Anselm intends to give a "proof." It comes at the beginning of chapter 2 of the *Proslogion* and is essentially a request that the God who gives faith will also give understanding, the knowledge that God is, as we believe, and that he is what we believe him to be, namely, the one than whom no greater can be thought.

The "proof" of God is connected with the prayer and falls within the realistic system of thought of Scholasticism. In brief it is as follows. If in our believing consciousness we have the idea of a being than which no greater can be thought, this being must also exist, for if it did not, it would not be the greatest.

It is not my purpose to criticize this proof (which would be easy enough after Kant, and hence banal). I will simply interpret it with Descartes in view.[24]

Anselm thinks within a secure knowledge of God. This prior certainty is the basis of his reflections in the *Proslogion*, not their product. What is certain in faith does not have to be proved. What might look like a proof, therefore, serves a different purpose. In a proof we move on from lesser certainty to greater or even to absolute certainty. In geometry I can achieve some certainty by repeated measurement, but the geometrical proof makes empirical probability into certainty. It makes the transition from even a high degree of probability to assured or demonstrated knowledge. In Anselm, however, the process is different. Anselm does not begin with a moderate, conditional, or deficient certainty about God which the proof of God will turn into absolute certainty. He already has absolute certainty before he embarks on the proof. The introductory prayer shows this. In it he confesses the certainty which is already present in faith.

Why, then, bother about the "proof"? The aim is undoubtedly not to achieve certainty but to transform certainty from the level of faith to that of the intellect. Unreflecting faith is given the form of intellectual and argued knowledge. Faith wants to impart its certainty to reason so that reason, too, may join in adoring prayer. Thus faith seeks understanding, it seeks reason, it seeks to bring reason to its side. In contrast to Descartes, certainty of God precedes certainty of self. Anselm does not know exactly who or what he is, how his subjective conviction relates to the intellectual dimension of the I, how the blurred and at first contradictory elements of the I synchronize. It is not too much to say, perhaps, that in modern terms Anselm does not see himself as a subject that is adequate to its theme, at least as an estranged intellect. His intellect limps behind his faith. It lies in the half-light of uncertainty. He thus needs to move on from believing certainty to rational clarity, and in this way to synchronize his believing I and his intellectual I. It is for this consensus that he prays.

Descartes, however, reverses certainty of God and certainty of reason or the self. (The formal similarity on the basis of scholastic-realistic ontology should not mislead us.) His doubt is modern. He asks in radical fashion whether God might not be an illusion, or, as Feuerbach would later put it, a projection. Might not that which we call the outside world be a dream?

Anselm, in contrast, lives and thinks on the soil of an unshaken

24. For a more extensive theological interpretation of Anselm see K. Barth, *Anselm: Fides quaerens intellectum* (Cleveland, 1960).

certainty about God and about equally evident and incontestable being. Since God is the final end of being, being displays a final order. Its elements may be known as our reason establishes their place within the order, i.e., in relation to the final end. This relation is their *rectitudo*.

Things are true, and their *veritas* and *rectitudo* are clear to us, when they fully represent their nature, i.e., when they are what they are meant to be according to their destiny and final end. An event is true inasmuch as it corresponds to its purpose. Fire—I have already mentioned this example—is true and right when it warms, as it is meant to do.[25] Because the truth of a thing is oriented to its ontological and teleological reference, there are degrees of truth, not just truth and untruth. Closeness to the final end is the norm. Hence quartz is more true than a pebble, and a crystal more true than quartz.[26] Thus I myself, as one who knows, am "true" (and know the truth) when I am integrated into the order of being which has its final end in God, and when I think in terms of this final end.

Anselm, then, would probably accuse Descartes of untruth because he emancipates himself from the order of being as a thinking being, as the subject of the *cogito sum*. Renouncing certainty of God in favor of self-certainty, he necessarily (from Anselm's standpoint) plunges into worldlessness and a total loss of being. The attempt to move on from the worldless I to a new certainty of being by way of a speculatively achieved certainty of God cannot but seem abstruse and incomprehensible to Anselm, who takes the opposite path.

Thus, although both men work within an ontological system of thought, it is apparent that they are radically apart. The gap is between one who still finds unbroken certainty of being in God and one who on the threshold of the new age is freed to call all things in question. The fact that doubt is a methodological experiment for Descartes, not a personal or confessional matter, should not mislead us as to the distinction, for the experiment shows that he is ready to question everything. It could never have entered Anselm's head to engage in such an experiment.

We pause for a moment. The God whom Descartes finds in his solipsistic consciousness has no personal features. He is simply an infinite "thing." He knows neither love nor wrath. Impersonal, he is beyond either judgment or grace. Personal traits arise only in the encounter of I and Thou. But this God does not encounter us. He is simply an abstract point that I construct beyond my sphere of empirical

25. See R. Allers, *Anselm von Canterbury* (1936), p. 97.
26. On Anselm's ontology cf. *EF,* I, 276ff.

vision with the help of various geometrical loci. Personality can never be made present by a conclusion.

If, for example, I want to find out deductively what eros is, and what love for a friend or spouse entails if it is to correspond to the idea of eros, I have put myself outside the sphere of personal encounter in which we humans breathe. The conclusion does not lead me to personal realities but at best to things or values. It follows, then, that God is for Descartes a thing or substance.

There is some analogy here to Spinoza, in whose system God is substance, *natura naturans*. Spinoza may speak of an intellectual love of God but this is a very impersonal love (and thus a contradiction in terms), formally very like Nietzsche's love of fate. I myself cannot love as a personal God the God who does not love me personally. The Apology for the Confession of Augsburg takes the directly opposite position when on the basis of God's turning to us it calls him a lovable object whom I may love in return.[27] The formal term *object* is a deliberate exaggeration and almost stylistic irony.

Things are much the same in Enlightenment deism as in Descartes. God is not so much a thing now as a principle of order. He is the epitome of cosmic teleology and the basis of solid optimism. Here again Descartes is a pioneer. Looking at his system we find pointers to whole stretches of philosophical and theological history. There is an increasing depersonalizing of God, whether as substance or idea.

C. THE DOUBTING AND THE BELIEVING DESCARTES

We have still to consider the copestone of Descartes's system and to ask how he moves on from the demonstrated (or apparently demonstrated) reality of God to that of the outside world.

"God is no deceiver" is his guiding thesis. We may feel at once that we should ask how he knows this, since honesty and deception are personal qualities. In keeping with his approach, however, he depersonalizes them, arguing that deception means imperfection. But God is perfect by definition as the supreme being (Fourth Meditation, 3). It is thus evident that he is no deceiver, and the existence of things follows.

Since God is no deceiver, it is plain that he does not send the ideas that I have of houses, people, sun, moon, and stars, either directly from himself or by the mediation of any creature. God has given us no capacity to know but a great inclination to believe that the ideas come

27. Cf. the Apology, III, 8, *LBK*, 185-86, ET Tappert, pp. 125ff.

from bodily things. I do not see, then, how we can know that he is not a deceiver if they come from anything but bodily things. Hence bodily things exist (Sixth Meditation, 21).

If the certainty of being is linked to the fact that God exists and that he is not a deceiver, it turns out that Descartes does not despair *radically* but only in a methodological experiment, so that his despair has only conditional existential rank. In other words, he plainly despairs only within a certainty that is always present latently and very indirectly and that is not totally set aside in spite of all the emancipation. The decisive indication of this is the focal position that he gives to the ontological proof of God. Everything depends on this proof. But the proof rests on the secret assumption that concepts come from being, and that being is teleologically structured and oriented to a *summum ens,* a supreme being. This organism of being—what the Stoics would call its orientation to the logos— naturally imparts itself to the concepts that derive from it. In the form of being as it is thus understood, there is naturally a meaningful correspondence between thought and being. For the rectitude of the order of being manifests itself in the fact that thought has a meaningful function corresponding to the order. As fire is true when it warms, so thought is true, i.e., in harmony with being, when it represents the same logos as governs being, and thus affirms this logos.

The ontic law that the greater cannot be contained in the smaller (e.g., an elephant in the stomach of a mouse) applies also to thought, to the thought that is analogous to being and reflects it. The inference is then valid that an idea of the infinite that occurs in me as a finite being cannot have grown up in the microconstruct of my intellect. It thus relates to a real existence outside me.

Using this mode of reflection and giving the proof of God a key role in the overcoming of doubt, Descartes shows that he is thinking in the name and within the frame of a certainty of being that is not *totally* shattered. With the help of a metaphysical inference I thus reach the conclusion that truly and existentially Descartes is not in fact the (total) doubter he makes himself out to be. He is hardly in danger of perishing of doubt, for he is not really at the front but is playing at sand castles. He is on maneuvers, not in battle. He is acting "as if." Yet even to arrive at the idea of such an experiment is an indication that his certainty of being is no longer self-evident, and that his experiment has—to put it cautiously—an existential element. When we begin to question, we are on shaky ground. For Anselm, as noted, the experiment would have been absurd. But Descartes stands on the threshold of the modern era and therefore of a skepticism for which the plausibilities of earlier tradition no longer hold water.

IV. SUMMARY AND PROSPECT: DESCARTES AS THE INITIATOR OF COMING MOVEMENTS

In Descartes religious understanding is based on thought and not on a real encounter with God. This thought doubts everything except itself (and its ontological structure). Hence Descartes initiates movements which come to full fruition only in the 18th and 19th centuries and which still have an incisive and pregnant impact upon the history of theology today.

(1) He prepares the way for the philosophical concept of the postulate which comes to fulfilment in Kant's transcendentalism.

In Kant, too, God is not the content of an encounter. The possibility of such an encounter as it might take place in the form of God's revealing action is not, of course, denied.[28] Yet the theme of Kant's concern in the philosophy of religion centers on the noetic problem of revelation, i.e., the philosophical establishment of a fact that he might accept as a Christian. For Kant a matter is valid as a philosophical statement when it derives from the conditions of thought itself. The question, then, is whether God is contained in the conditions of thought. Does thought, when it analyzes itself, come upon God? When we formulate the question thus, the relation to the approach of Descartes is plain.

According to Kant, one cannot at first say that thought—at least that of pure reason—does lead us necessarily to God.[29] For God is not objectifiable in our experience. He is not in the sphere of what Kant calls transcendental apperception. But the idea of God occurs much more emphatically, as we shall see, in the conditions of practical reason. Here he is a postulate of the *summum bonum* in which the concretely incompatible concepts of duty and happiness achieve metaphysical

28. Cf. the fact that along with the religion of reason Kant can speak of revelation and divine inspiration in Christianity (*Critique of Practical Reason*, Great Books 44, p. 351; *Religion within the Limits of Reason Alone* [1960], pp. 102ff., 133). This is true even though his accent is on the religion of reason and revelation seems to be relevant for him only insofar as its confirms rational postulates of God and of norms. Kant is very reserved toward that which transcends these postulates in revelation, so that he can say that only as a last resort can we feel forced to presuppose a divinely inspired faith, preferring instead to formulate maxims that accord with the faith of pure reason (*Religion within the Limits*, p. 129).

29. The idea of God arises only weakly even in the epistemological self-criticism of reason which investigates the conditions of knowledge (cf. chap. 10 below on Kant). Purely theoretical reason does lead us to the idea of something on which all empirical reality bases its supreme and necessary unity (*Critique of Pure Reason*, IV, Great Books 44, pp. 171-72), but this idea, called "God," is not an object of knowledge but remains in the twilight of an "as if" postulate.

unity. Since we cannot avoid postulating this suprapolar point of indifference, this transcendental catalyst, it is morally necessary to assume the existence of God.[30] Hence the idea of God resides in the conditions of thought itself when it is a matter of practical reason.

To the degree that the human I sees itself as a *res cogitans*—as is conditionally the case in Kant, at least in the sphere of pure reason—God enters a zone of total indirectness. He is not a power that meets us, nor an experienced reality. He is contained nonobjectively in the conditions of thought. He is no more than the point of intersection of two lines of thought. As we have seen, Heine can thus speak of the death of God in Kant.[31]

(2) Descartes's idea that thinking doubts everything except itself also finds an important result in Kant's ethics, not merely in his epistemological theory in which the thinking subject focuses on itself (even if in relation to the outside world), but especially in the *Critique of Practical Reason.* For this in its own way doubts everything by way of normative claims from outside and suspects them of heteronomy. It doubts everything except itself, so that in pointed dependence on Descartes one might say that an unconditional "You ought" sounds forth in me, therefore I am, or, more precisely, I am a moral subject.

(3) Finally, Descartes inaugurates the ideal productivity of a reason that is elevated to the rank of a myth, as in Hegel when he deduces reality from reason, from the reason which as the cosmic spirit comes to self-awareness in the finite spirit.

When one considers that the views of Kant and Hegel gave nineteenth-century theology its normative shape, it is plain with what volcanic force the revolutionary thinking of Descartes affected the traditions of the Christian West and what impulses of modern, secular thought were programmatically triggered by it for the first time. It is thus a sound theological principle to conduct our debate with secularism under the auspices of the Cartesian approach. The struggle for such concepts as the point of contact, preunderstanding, and appropriation must always be waged in such a way as to echo the Cartesian program. The thought of Descartes is indeed the salt that can be tasted in all the dishes which the table of nineteenth- and twentieth-century theology provides.

In conclusion, we may state that materially the doubt of Descartes has the appearance of a methodological trick. Three points are important if we are to understand this.

First, this doubt arises parthogenetically, as we have seen, from

30. *Critique of Practical Reason,* p. 345.
31. See *EF,* I, 268ff.

the act of thought itself as the thinker experiences the self as a subject and as the only thing that has certain being. It is thus a methodological trick because real, existential doubt takes the very opposite course. It does not arise from the fact that the thinker is the only true subject, the only thing that has unquestionable being when all else is doubtful. It ultimately arises from the very opposite experience that the thinker simply is or might be no more than the object of external influences, and that the I- or subject-quality is set in question. This doubt is the result of the question: Am I just the object of a blind force of *tyche*?[32] Much of the meaninglessness of life might suggest this. But in this case doubt of God is, in the last resort, unavoidable. Another form of the same question leads to the same conclusion: Am I simply the effect in a causal nexus which determines me and thus robs me of freedom and personality. Am I just the product of economic and social forces around me, or of certain glandular functions, and hence of material factors? If so, I have every reason to doubt the personal character of both God and myself.

In Descartes these questions are still below the horizon. In the ghetto of the inner I, he thinks outside the zone of real encounters in which the basic doubters that affect existence arise. His doubt is a heuristic construction which leads to the goal, with the help of consistent but purely experimental doubt, of finding a final layer of being that cannot be shaken.

Second, as we have seen in investigating Descartes's ontological structure of thought, we must also say that from the very first the premise "God" has been secretly smuggled in, i.e., that the nonexistence of God is an impossible thought for him because God is the normative basis of his structure of thought. What is controversial for him is not the existence of God but his conceivability, and this only because in Descartes the ontological thinking of the Middle Ages comes up against and begins to wrestle with, the empirical thinking of the modern era. Descartes's solution is that the structure of Scholastic thinking takes on new force, and he thus advances the thesis that God is a necessity of thought.

Yet now that the empirical pole of his thinking has momentarily made this necessity an open question, as it never could be for Anselm, the question of necessity soon becomes the problem of possibility. In this form the question runs through the whole of the 19th century and finds a good final discussion (on the Protestant side) in the theology of Karl Heim. Here it appears as the question: How can we think of the absolute within relativity? Can it be thought of in this realm? Is it a possibility of thought?

The first issue is whether God is a necessity of thought, but then

32. I recall again Monod's *Chance and Necessity* and the role of Sisyphus in Camus.

the issue is his existence or nonexistence. What is at first an experiment of thought (triggered by the first step into the area of modern thought) takes on greater seriousness in the sequel. It becomes the probing question whether faith in God is "still" possible.

Third, a final question that arises especially in respect of a figure like Spinoza or later idealist philosophy, both of which stand on the shoulders of Descartes, is this. Is the divine X that Descartes believes to be a necessity of thought, is this omnipotent being and *natura naturans* really the Father of Jesus Christ? Can a point be fixed here, with the help of the aforementioned geometrical loci, at which the Father of Jesus Christ may be localized *when* he declares himself historically? Is there an advent expectation of theoretical reason, or, better, can we construct an advent line of thought on which the point Christmas may be placed as the event of the incarnation? Do we really have here, in religious philosophy, the prolegomenon to a possible theology?

We have to say that we do not, and historically and concretely we see from the impersonal substance of Spinoza, the impersonal first cause of deism, and the world spirit of Hegel that it is not really so, that in place of the Father of Jesus Christ we have an imaginary construct which can never be equated with the God of the Christian tradition as Descartes desired and intended. Jesus Christ obviously bursts open all these preunderstandings and postulates *when* he declares himself. The Holy Spirit does not creep into the waiting skins (the *old* skins, Matt. 9:17) of the human spirit and its postulating acts of thought.

The theology of the 19th century, which is idealistically determined, may be regarded as an attempt to capture the Spirit in this way, to change him from the Pneuma into the human nous. It is also a history of the impossibility of doing this. We shall have more to say about this later.

In spite of all these efforts, in spite of his repeated imprisonment in systems, the Holy Spirit constantly raises up new theology to break the systems like earthen vessels. The fact that he does so "almost" amounts to a proof of God. No less astonishing than the resurrection of Jesus Christ from the tomb is his resurrection from the bondage of systems. It is amazing that he does not die when systems perish but ever and again rises above them and upholds his rank as *Kyrios*.

We see, then, the unheard-of way in which Descartes's thought is full of implications foreshadowing all the basic and essential problems of modern theology. This is why I have had to treat him more fully than many later figures. Perhaps we speak so readily of "modern" theology — as though it were the last word — just because so little attention is paid to Descartes, as though he were "only" a philosopher!

CHAPTER 4

Reimarus and Deism

I. GENERAL PROBLEMS OF THE ENLIGHTENMENT: RATIONALISTIC AND EMPIRICIST VARIATIONS

In the attempt to give a picture of Enlightenment thought, I will limit myself to a sketch of the basic features, and in this I will stress the decisive points with thetic brevity.

First, we have to realize that the Enlightenment has two basically different forms which have had a similar impact on theology, philosophy, and ethics, and which still have. I refer first to the rationalistic Enlightenment in Germany, which we will study in Reimarus, Semler, and Lessing, and second to the empiricist Enlightenment in Britain, which is represented by Hume. The one thinker who inherits but also seeks to transcend both is Kant, about whom we shall have to speak later.

I will characterize these two forms in a few strokes, showing that they are not historically accidental, but logically necessary variations. We see how the Enlightenment splits into these antithetical forms when we realize what is the oldest and as it were the "permanent" problem of philosophy. We have referred to it already in Descartes—I mean the relation between thought and being, the I and the world, the subject-object relation.

One may relate the I and the world by using the I as the point of orientation, as is supremely the case in Descartes. One uses the I here— the thinking or sensory I—as the incontestable basis of all external observation. What is outside is then a phenomenon for the I. The German Enlightenment takes this line when it defines the rational I as the subject of all our knowledge of nature and history. I add at once that what the I perceives is not a mass of discontinuous and amorphous impressions but may be understood in its basic structure, i.e., relative to the laws of nature

79

that obtain in it. In the objective sphere of our knowledge, this principle holds, there is nothing that is not also contained in its living comprehension. (We recall Dilthey's formulation in elucidation of the principle of analogy in divinatory understanding.)[1] We can thus grasp the outside world only because it obeys the same law as our reason, being just as rational as our reason. The noetic and the ontic reason are analogous.[2] Our understanding functions as a kind of causal law. It ties together premise and consequence, cause and effect. The outside world (to think again of the laws of nature) obeys the same law. The structure of being is spirit of our spirit. This is why we can understand it.

Negatively, this means that if we encounter something incomprehensible or, in principle, irrational, that withstands acceptance by our reason, e.g., a miracle outside the bounds of natural law, the alarming suspicion is kindled that this inconceivable thing has no real basis, that it is not true, that it is evil. Thus the Enlightenment agrees with the dictum of C. Morgenstern that nothing can be which ought not to be. The irrational ought not to be, for it is unthinkable. This principle of analogy reaches a climax in Hegel, for whom all being is rational, because it is an emanation of the world spirit thinking itself in our finite spirit.

Theoretically, however, the opposite course is also possible, namely, that of viewing the subject-object relation from the standpoint of observation of the outside world and regarding the I only as an exponent or even as a product of this world (as later in various forms of materialism). The father of positivism and empiricism, the great David Hume (1711-1776), took this path. Kant's transcendentalism, and especially his doctrine of the a priori, was formed essentially in opposition to Hume, or, better, was antithetically stimulated by him. In summing up the decisive theses of Hume, I will differentiate him from German rationalism.

(1) For Hume the rationalistic path of the German Enlightenment is itself only a disguised metaphysics. It presupposes what is for him an unprovable thesis, namely, that there is agreement between the structural law of thought, the subject of knowledge, and the structural law of being. Only on the basis of this presumed preestablished harmony can one be a rationalist. But this presupposition is for Hume a metaphysical hypothesis and not a scientifically objectifiable principle. At best one can presuppose only an analogy. One can believe in this, but not prove it. Hence one should not act as though pursuing an unpreju-

1. Cf. above, chap. 1, § II.B.
2. In the Greek world the term *logos* means both *nous* and *ousia;* cf. H. Kleinknecht, *TDNT,* IV, 77ff.

diced and rationally sober science. The German Enlightenment may work with the coolness of objectivity, but for British empiricism it is full of religious and metaphysical assumptions.

(2) As Hume rejects all metaphysical postulating of laws, he is forced to restrict very considerably the radius of human knowledge. The knowing I can do no more than receive impressions of the outside world. It cannot claim to track the laws that determine the course of the realities underlying these impressions. What we can establish as the content of our consciousness consists only of impressions and then of ideas, i.e., concepts which are gradually formed by the accumulation and repetition of impressions, and which preserve the impressions.

(3) Ideas are not already there for experience, as in Plato; they are the product of experience. They do not rest on recollection; they arise from observation. The same applies to the laws of nature. Only on the basis of statistical experience are we sure that the sun will rise each morning. We cannot appeal to an inferred physical law. Experience is not based on the fact that I know the laws of phenomena (e.g., their causality). It rests on the law of averages.

There thus arises the positivist standpoint, not only in natural science, in which I can be sure of facts and processes by repeated experiments, but also in law. Here there is no prior law of justice, only what we would now call the normativity of facts. Law rests on social decisions that harden into conventions.

The same applies to conscience in ethics. According to Herbert Spencer (1820-1903), who follows this line later, conscience has no normative function. It simply records what is done, what proves itself. It sums up the finding of experience that the good is what has shown itself to be the most useful and worthwhile, e.g., that we cannot get away with lying, but things always come to light. Here positivism joins hands with utilitarianism. This eudaemonistic utilitarianism is the exact opposite of what Kant advances as a moral principle. It forms the background of the conviction: "My country—right or wrong" (along with the misuse of this principle, as in the Third Reich).[3]

(4) The content of the consciousness, insofar as it consists of impressions and ideas, forms a copy of the outside world, a kind of photograph. Here, then, we have a reversal of the Cartesian approach in which the worldless I is isolated as the subject of the act of thought.

A critical consideration suggests itself at this point. At root this kind of Enlightenment positivism runs into the same problem as German rationalism. Hume, too, can establish a relation between the I and the

3. On Spencer, cf. *ThE*, I, §§ 1465-83.

outside world only by an unstated and very indirect metaphysical postulate. German rationalism postulated a preestablished harmony between the ontic and the noetic logos. Hume postulates the laying of the one on the other and hence something that embraces them. If the outside world triggers impressions in the I, and if the I can function as an antenna or receiver, there obviously has to be some basic connection between them. This presupposed connection can no more be objectified than the analogy between noetic and ontic reason in German rationalism.

I will try to illustrate the problem of this connection with an example. If I want to record impressions on a film, it will not do simply to hold up any kind of film and expose it to impressions. No contact will be made. I will be acting just as foolishly as the person who tried to trap sunlight in a sack. Sunlight and sack do not work together. The necessary analogy is not present. (The basic philosophical problem of the subject-object relation is thus involved.) To get a copy I have to use the right kind of film, one which is receptive to light and can thus serve as a suitable vessel for what is to be received. The thin strip that is receptive to light serves this purpose.

In this sense Descartes remains the great sign and summons on the margin of every epistemological theory, for he shows that the I and the outside world cannot be strictly related, and he tries to present their relationship with the help of an embracing factor, a proof of God, i.e., the intervention of a metaphysical act. What the English and German Enlightenment does secretly takes place openly and programmatically in Descartes. The Cartesian solution to the problem may indeed be problematic as regards the ontological proof. More important, however, is the fact that no one before Kant saw the problem of the relation between the I and the world or the subject and the object as Descartes did.

(5) The results of Hume's positivism for the philosophy of religion I will sketch only briefly. It can form neither the speculative nor the experiential basis for the recognition of a religion of revelation: the former because speculation would mean confirming the legitimacy of the supposed revelation with the help of a rational proof (i.e., an a priori legalism which does not exist), the latter because experience, which alone remains and which is a mental copy of the outside world, can never validate the religion of revelation, but can only contribute a veto of every kind of supposed religious experience, since in the normal encounter between the I and the world there are no signs of a transcendental reality such as are usually seen in miracle or other exceptions to the usual course of things. Even though Hume cannot argue that the extraordinary lies outside natural law, which, strictly, does not exist for him, he

can point out that it lies outside all experience. Morgenstern's saying that what ought not to be, cannot be, is as it were turned by him into the dictum that what has never been, and has never been experienced, cannot be. One might perhaps say that for him there is no law of causality by which to rule out the extraordinary. (Such a law amounts to no more than the statistical regularity of what is constantly observed.) But there is for him a law like that in the saying of Rabbi Akiba, namely, that everything has already been and hence all true perceptions will be like those that have gone before. Hume engages in the same type of positivistic criticism of religion as became popular in the 19th century, anticipating the common view of the half-educated in our own time.

Equally typical is his positive solution. Religion is a historical force, a palpable reality, and hence a de facto subject of experience. It exists. Even Hume can see the cultus, hear preachers and chorales, and smell incense. Or he can hear others speak about these things. But these experienced impressions of the senses, being the content of experience, rest only on experience. This means that we cannot trace them back to metaphysical causes but only to empirical realities on the horizon of possible experience. As the realities that produce religion Hume recognizes certain basic human emotions which may be verified psychologically, especially fear and hope, a concern for life, and the need of security. In face of destiny, the menacing power of fate, and other destructive forces, religion arises as the belief in higher powers which supplement or complete our own resources and thus make us a match for the pressure of the natural world.[4] Religion is an illusion which is to be explained psychologically or psycho-empirically. It seeks to make life bearable and is thus a kind of dulling opium.

This view dispenses entirely with the question of truth. Religion is not taken seriously as a normative statement. In modern terms, it is seen as a device of the unconscious which is to be understood psychoanalytically. Even with no special development one may thus see the line which leads to the view of religion found in Marx and Freud. We also perceive that the way is powerfully prepared for the modern concept of ideology.[5]

After this general sketch of the intellectual history of the Enlightenment and its theological relevance, we may now turn to that aspect of Enlightenment thinking which forms the direct introduction to German theology in the 19th century.

4. Cf. A. Ritschl, *Die christliche Lehre von der Rechtfertigung und Versöhnung*, III, 2nd ed. (1883), 186; Hume himself would not put it this way.
5. Cf. *ThE*, II/2, §§ 133ff., 108ff., 294ff., 196ff., 765ff.; ET II, 26-27, 33ff., 53ff.

II. THE DEISTIC THEOLOGY OF REIMARUS

Cf. especially the *Fragments* in editions of Lessing. Also A. Schweitzer, *The Quest of the Historical Jesus* (New York, repr. 1968). Apart from histories, dissertations, and occasional references, Reimarus is virtually ignored in theology (even by Barth). See D. F. Strauss, *H. S. Reimarus und seine Schutzschrift* (1862); idem, *Der alte und der neue Glaube* (1872); E. Hirsch, *Geschichte der neueren evangelischen Theologie*, IV (1954), 144ff.

A. PERSONALITY AND WORKS

Reimarus was born near Stettin in 1694. He spent most of his life as a professor of Oriental languages in Hamburg. His esotericism is typical of his whole life and work. He was held in high regard by Christians, attended church, and was on the best of terms with the clergy. Secretly, however, he radically rejected churchly Christianity. His posthumous *Fragments,* made known and extolled by Lessing,[6] are a Christian detective story which tries to show that all the biblical miracles are a fraud and the supposed revelations are an invention. Reimarus does not stop at saying that the disciples are behind the times and belong to a mythical age but act in good faith. For him they are crafty deceivers and conjurers whose actions often break the rules of honesty and indeed of natural and civil law.

With this damaging posthumous account, which burst like a bomb, he saw to it that shocked Christians would henceforth view the Enlightenment as the "ancient foe." He himself seemed to fit the role of a hypocrite,[7] and the charge of hypocrisy would stick to him in the further history of theology. In church history a person usually lives in the light of any great shock that he may cause his contemporaries. Such a shock is fertile soil for fixed ideas (cf. Darwin and this theory of evolution). The fixed idea regarding Reimarus is that he was a hypocrite. Perhaps this is why he is so seldom treated seriously in theology.

One may concede that Lessing emerged as his defender, if not on the altar at least on the rostrum, and that with the publication of the *Fragments* he became his foremost propagandist. And Lessing is reckoned as one of the most honest and incorruptible persons of the modern

6. The proper title is *Apologie oder Schutzschrift der vernünftigen Verehrer Gottes. Fragmente eines Ungenannten.*

7. One may compare Prince Bülow, whose *Denkwürdigkeiten* (memorable occurrences) Wilhelm II described as *Denkunwürdigkeiten* (unworthy, disreputable).

era (and hence as far removed from hypocrisy as possible). How do we explain this?[8]

If we examine more closely the view of Reimarus as a hypocrite, we come upon the esotericism of the Enlightenment which Reimarus represented. What do we mean by this?

In some eras of theological history the problem of knowledge, even in religion, comes to the fore. It did so in the Enlightenment.[9] But as a result faith might seem to be merely preliminary to knowledge.[10] It is a first and primitive thing in the developing process of knowledge. Since it is incapable of abstract statements, it uses the symbolical language of myth. Its failure to achieve exact knowledge may also be seen in the fact that it is mere conjecture. Epistemologically it is a preparatory sensing rather than knowing, a mere viewing of this or that as true, an "it seems to me." The statement that faith is personal trust transcending objectifiable knowledge is impossible on this view, particularly because the impersonal concept of God in deism blocks the path to *fiducia* (trust).

At the stage of faith, then, I simply hold uncritical conjectures. I jump too quickly past the exact investigation of the innate causes of an event and accept instead such metaphysical causes as God or miracle. I once saw a propaganda sheet in the Soviet Union which graphically expressed this. It showed two pictures of the same family during a thunderstorm. On the one they were praying that they might not be hit by lightning. The other prominently displayed a lightning conductor and showed the family peacefully at table enjoying a meal. They had found out what causes thunderstorms and how to avoid their dangers instead of attributing them to God or his wrath. Knowledge had now gone beyond the primitive stage of faith.

True knowledge has to do with the immanent causal nexus or with empirical statistics (in Hume's sense). Faith cannot handle these. It thus finds a supernatural origin for whatever seems inconceivable to it. It belongs to the unenlightened mythical stage of human history. Development seems to lead from myth to logos.[11]

These terms have been differently understood at different

8. J. S. Semler (1725-1791), whom we shall discuss later, expressly disapproved of Lessing's editing the work. He did not accept Lessing's explanation that he was imply bringing to light the poison in the dark and giving theologians the chance to defend Christian truth the more solidly. He responded with a very satirical anecdote (see H. von Campenhausen, *Theologenspiess und -spass* [1973], pp. 116ff.).

9. With some reservations this is also true of some modern overemphasizing of the hermeneutical and epistemological question, e.g., in the school of Bultmann.

10. We cannot make this objection to the Bultmann school!

11. Cf. W. Nestle, *Vom Mythos zum Logos*, 2nd ed. (1942).

times. Myth is not always a preliminary stage of logos. There can also be new myth after the logos stage. This is because the mythical is a form of statement which covers what logos can no longer say, i.e., the depth of being.[12] Plato is an outstanding example. Although the Enlightenment is behind him and he no longer believes in the Homeric gods, he presents philosophy against the background of the myth of Apollo[13] and invents mythical pictures like the images in the cave. Similarly, in our own century we see remythologizing as well as demythologizing, especially in poetry. We need only refer to R. M. Rilke, Ernst Jünger, Gerhard Nebel, James Joyce, T. S. Eliot, Eugene O'Neill, etc.[14]

As the act of knowledge takes center stage, the question of *who* knows as well as *what* is known becomes an urgent one. This "who" has a history and the act itself also has a history. The who stands either on a primitive mythical level or an enlightened rational level. Or else he is moving between the two.

It has often been said that the Enlightenment has no feeling for history. This is only partly true. It is true inasmuch as the Enlightenment seeks the timeless, nonhistorical truths of reason. Thus Lessing opposes such truths to the contingent truths of history. But it is not true when we consider that the act of knowledge itself has a historical quality. The historical dimension has now been put in the sphere of the subject rather than the object, as may be seen in Reimarus, Semler, and Lessing. The Enlightenment thus focuses on a side of historicity that is important in modern hermeneutics. I mean that of the understanding.[15] We have developed the idea of the Enlightenment in this regard only to the extent that we can no longer see the history of the understanding as an evolution in the way that Reimarus and Lessing did, for whom it would end with an eternal age of reason and hence an all-sufficient and direct understanding. We today have to be content with the fact of the history. The Enlightenment idea of progress now seems naive to us, in direct antithesis to their self-understanding.

At any rate, on the Enlightenment view of history each stage of

---

12. Cf. M. Schroeter's introduction to J. J. Bachofen, *Der Mythus von Orient und Okzident* (1926), p. XC. Cf. also symbolism, *EF,* I, 74-75.

13. See G. Krüger, *Einsicht und Leidenschaft. Das Wesen des platonischen Denkens* (1939), p. 31.

14. Cf. *EF,* I, 76-77.

15. That the understanding is bound to a historical place and its conditions change has been increasingly recognized since Dilthey's hermeneutical discussions (*Die Entstehung der Hermeneutik,* in *Gesammelte Schriften,* V, 317ff.), and it plays a role in all hermeneutical writings today; cf. G. Ebeling, *Word and Faith* (1963), pp. 17ff.; idem, *Wort und Glaube,* III, 488ff.; idem, *RGG,* 3rd ed., III, 244-45. Symptomatic is the fact that hermeneutics itself has a history.

humanity has its own way of knowing. Reason, too, has a history which leads it out of prerational half-light into its own light.

But this raises a pedagogical problem: May I assume such knowledge in everybody?[16] This is clearly impossible. Lessing, stating a common Enlightenment opinion, issues an express warning against ascribing too much developed knowledge to those at a naive, prerational stage. The cleverer ones who have reached the last page of the primer must consider the weaker students who have not yet reached what they are now beginning to see.[17] For, we might add, these backward contemporaries will regard you as disturbers of the substance of religion if you blab out what you have learned too hastily and foolishly. You will thus destroy it in their eyes inasmuch as they are not yet ready for your insights. They do not have the ability to differentiate which would enable them to see that you are only developing and not erasing what they believe and what can at first be grasped only in faith, that you are demythologizing and spiritualizing it without destroying its identity. The weak do not have such categories and thus they can see in you only people who cut the ground from under their feet.

The weaker brethren can also be a theme in Paul when he speaks about the use of Christian freedom. He warns the mature who are aware of the nothingness of idols against eating idol meats with sovereign freedom when the weak and uncertain are present. For many do not have the same awareness (1 Cor. 8:7), believe they are eating the meat offered to real gods, and thus stain their consciences. Premature encounter with higher knowledge can be destructive. Such knowledge must be concealed, must remain esoteric. Luther, too, can put the problem when in the preface to his *Romans* he calls the doctrine of predestination "strong wine" that is not for babes, i.e., for beginners in the faith. Some truths are related to specific stages; each doctrine has its time or age.[18] Paul, Luther, and Lessing are at one in their sense of the historical character of knowledge.

But this raises the problem of the esoteric which Reimarus puts so vividly as he walks among his contemporaries under the guise of conventional churchmanship while his true face carries the features of a mature scholar who has long since defected. This forces us to seek the boundary between guilty honesty and guilty (pedagogic) caution. But

16. Cf. the hermeneutical problem of a work with many layers of meaning suitable to various stages of development and degrees of understanding. Thus Origen refers to three senses: the somatic or literal, the intellectual or moral, and the spiritual or mystical and allegorical.

17. Lessing, *Education of the Human Race*, § 68.

18. Munich ed., VI, 106; LW, 35, 378.

this question takes a deeper form. Can I hide the core of my faith, or my understanding of the faith, from those who trust me?

Although the Enlightenment initiates the conflict acutely, with Reimarus as its particularly radical spokesman, the problem reaches beyond that period. The plight of much modern preaching is that it recognizes the hermeneutical difficulties that have been raised by historico-critical research but dares not bring them to the pulpit because the congregations do not seem to be ready for them. (On this basis poor work may undoubtedly be done; it may be an excuse for didactic laziness, incompetence, unbelief, or cowardice, just as it may also denote a profound and serious problem.) At any rate, the struggle for a correct understanding of hermeneutical questions, for the kerygma in the text, is put in the ghetto of the study or of expert theological discussion until the magazines come and proclaim from the rooftops in distorted form that which is still under the arcane discipline of unfinished debate.

The problem of Reimarus, which comes so close to home, cannot be dismissed briefly. If in the style of the lectures of J. T. Beck (1804-1878) I may make a few observations, they are as follows.

First, theology has a vicarious function vis-à-vis the community. This means that there is a class or order of theologians who face the problems and difficulties of the search for truth. The struggles and emergencies that this search causes, and that may grow larger, are the unavoidable sufferings incurred in this vicarious work. But they are also the greatness and power of theology. For with the risks of the epistemological process our horizons expand. Thus it is a fatal mistake to see in historico-critical research only a burden or pressure for faith, as though it merely reduced it. This research has been able to set aside many misunderstandings of the faith. It has brought out the full richness of biblical statements by showing how many witnesses there are, by displaying the historicity of truth, and by enabling us to hear the polyphony of the kerygmatic choir. If the hermeneutical question becomes acute, it shows us the difference between the spiritual center and the periphery, between the form of statement and its substance. The opportunities of spiritual knowledge thus achieve a richness that is denied to a fundamentalist view which puts every biblical text on the same level of homogeneous revelation. Incalculable gain accompanies the threatened loss if we dare to seize it in a venture of faith. Theological knowledge is thus a front and not a mere succession of stages.

Second, the vicarious function of theology also means that we are dealing with the same truth, not a higher or different truth, as the devout old person in the pew. The only point is that here the truth is dearly bought, although perhaps also deepened, through the need for intellectual honesty.

Only from this standpoint do we come upon the basic hypocrisy of Reimarus. He had the illusion of a higher and different truth. Or, more sharply, he did not attack the half-truth, or mythically concealed truth, of his Christian contemporaries in the name of a fulness of truth; in the name of ostensible truth he attacked the open falsehood of the biblical authors, a refined falsehood which they carried out with criminal means.

Esoterically tarnished with this fatal knowledge in his heart, he lived in the church; this was his own falsehood. We cannot excuse it simply by pointing to the fear of tradition as a compelling force. Lessing finally dared to publish his views in his lifetime, even if, as one must concede, with tactical assurances that exaggerated the accidental nature of their discovery and the expected distancing from his own person.

To live theologically in untruth as Reimarus did leads at once to untruth in theological statement. This is the judgment which like a sword of Damocles hangs over the head of every theological utterance.

Reimarus himself was hardly aware of the gap in his total theological conception. On the one hand, he argued that Jesus and his disciples, as regards the kerygmatic core, championed the purest moral and religious teaching. On the other, he maintained that they pursued their noble work only with the basest of motives and even criminal means. Clearly, one can hardly have it both ways. It is important, however, to stress this obviously unnoticed conflict between the two theses, for it expresses the relation between life and theology. The disorder and contradiction in the life of Reimarus projects itself into his theological statements. Jesus and his apostles are presented as deceivers in the same sense as those who secretly know the truth but like Reimarus conceal it with mendacious mythology.

A general theological secret comes to light here, and we are dealing with the theological theme when we refer to Reimarus. Valid theological statements are possible only when theologians claim the redemption about which they speak, only when their lives are oriented to "being in the truth" in the Johannine sense. Every secret bondage or disorder in life affects theological statements. Redemption gives epistemological freedom. It enables us to see that theology needs forgiveness and can hardly claim the title of sacred study.

We thus come across some of the problems which arise when Lessing publishes the *Fragments*. Of other works we may refer only to a work which appeared in 1754, when Reimarus was sixty years old, *Vornehmste Wahrheiten der natürlichen Religion*. This work expounds deism. It is not aimed at orthodoxy but at a cheap materialistic atheism, i.e., at the other front. It mistakenly won the applause of many of the Christian contemporaries of Reimarus and did nothing to clear up the misunderstanding that we have noted.

B. REIMARUS AS A REPRESENTATIVE OF DEISM

The total nexus into which Reimarus fits his deistic view of God is mechanistic. The world is a machine that the divine mechanic has set going in favor of its highest creatures, human beings.[19]

Three factors come into play: God, the world, and humanity— the mechanic, the instrument, and those who use it. This is more than a mere comparison. It expresses strictly the basic relations that obtain in the universe. Surveying these relations more closely, we ask: (1) Why and to what end does God make the machine? (2) How does it work? (3) What does the comparison imply for the view of God in the Christian tradition? (We deal essentially with this third question in discussing the other two.)

(1) Why and to what end does the divine mechanic set the machine going?

To achieve first a standard by which to evaluate the deistic answer, we recall that this question of the why of creation often occurs in the specifically Christian tradition. Sketching the Christian answer, of which there are many varied forms, one might say that God created the world and humanity so as to have fellowship with a Thou made in his image, and to glorify himself in his works.[20] At the fall humanity sabotaged this divine plan by breaking off fellowship and trying to substitute equality with God for the divine likeness. The Thou-partner of God is also the risk that can destroy God's plan.

This crude sketch shows that we can speak about the basis, goal, and meaning of creation only as those who have broken free from it and who by the ongoing covenant grace of God are destined for visitation and alienation. This can mean only that we cannot speak speculatively and a priori about the basis and goal of creation; we can do so only as we achieve the certainty that God gives when he declares himself to be the Creator in his Word and reveals himself in the event of salvation, keeping to his plan in spite of our unfaithfulness and turning to us in grace. But

19. When eighteen years old, Nietzsche expressed a similar view in some verses which compare the cosmos to a rolling wheel (WW, ed. H. J. Mette, II, 1934, 68).
20. See *ThE*, I (Index "Creation, Doctrine of").

the gracious will of God which is the normative content of the historical telos can only be revealed to us and *told* us. In negative terms, it cannot be the content of a mere postulate of reason. Here is the decisive boundary beyond which the deism of Reimarus begins to think.

Offering the model of the machine, Reimarus constructs a world whose ends may be known a priori. We can see its goal; we do not have to learn it from a contingent communication. Reimarus counts on certain self-evident axioms from which he deduces the laws and telos of the cosmos. Deducing, not listening, is the main thing in deistic thought. Herein lies the magic of the rationalistic view. In virtue of its logical structure, the cosmos makes deductions possible.

The chief axiom in this deductive procedure is that God exists and that he is perfect. The idea of a perfect being is a necessity of thought. Further statements follow from this, especially those concerning the basis and goal of creation.

It seems important to me that we can fix here the very point where the deistic view of creation contrasts with Christian theology. I will clarify this point with the help of various antitheses.

Christian theology, especially in its Reformation form, says that to know creation we must know the Creator. Only when I know a person can I know that person's intentions, in this case, the telos of creation. God's self-revelation, the revelation of his person in his Word, is the condition.

Deism says that to know creation, the functions of the world machine, I must first be clear about the concept of perfection. This concept already implies a statement about the telos. Perfection is possible only where there is meaning or telos and this telos is achieved by the shortest route.

Reformation theology says that if I must first know the Creator, I am referred to his self-demonstration. In Kantian terms, I know him only a posteriori as he declares himself by his Word and Spirit.

Deism says that the idea of perfection is present self-evidently, so that I can make a priori statements about the goal of creation.

How does the idea of perfection arise and how do we discover its implications? The idea is won with the help of the same techniques of thought as we find, with little hope of disentanglement,[21] in Scholastic ontology, Lessing, and Spinoza. The most pregnant example is in Lessing's *Christianity of Reason*, whose arguments are found in much the same form in Reimarus.[22]

§ 1. From all eternity the one most perfect being can only be

---

21. Cf. Erich Schmidt, *Lessing*, II, 3rd ed. (1909), 463ff.
22. Cf. the Witkowski ed., 6, 308ff.

occupied with the contemplation of what is most perfect. Subject and object are here united in the absolute knowledge which corresponds to the concept of a most perfect subject.

§ 2. Imagining, willing, and creating are one in God. All that he thinks of, he creates. If God were to contemplate what is perfect without willing it, he would lack ethical perfection. If he were to will it without creating it, his ontological perfection would be in question.

§ 4. God can think in only two ways, either by thinking all his perfections at once and as the epitome of them, or by dividing and separating them, and putting them at a distance from himself. In the first case this leads to the creation of a being that lacks none of his own perfections. Scripture calls this being the Son of God (§§ 5-6). In the second case, the result is the creation of the world.

§ 13. God thought of his perfections in divided form, creating beings which each had some of his perfections, for with God every thought is a creation.

The goal of creation, of the world machine which is here set in motion, is thus the self-actualization of God's perfection. But this goal is especially related to humanity. It demands anthropological formulation. Belonging to this perfect creation, we humans must achieve this perfection. Happiness, eudaimonia, is the goal of this perfection.

Kant's definition might help us to grasp what this eudaimonia means, for it plainly echoes the deistic understanding. Happiness as the state of a rational creature in the world rests on the agreement of nature with its total goal.[23] No less than a creature's own identity lies in this agreement. The aim is perfection, and humans are links in the process which leads from the divine idea of perfection to its actualization. Finally reaching agreement with the goal, they attain happiness. The resultant imperative that derives from our very nature is that we should act in a way that accords with our individual perfections.[24]

We thus see the answer to our first question of why and for what end God set up the machine. The answer is: For the sake of eudaimonia.

The second question is: How does the machine function?

Its course is so regulated that the teleology of its functioning is obvious and enables us to see the perfection of its maker. Theologically speaking, we can trace the footsteps of the Creator in world events, in nature and history. Natural theology is possible; the cosmic process is a source of revelation. Philosophically speaking, we find a posteriori, i.e., by an empirical diagnosis of the perfection of the cosmic process, a

23. See *Critique of Practical Reason,* p. 345.
24. See Lessing, *Education of the Human Race,* § 26.

confirmation of that which we already affirm in a speculative way a priori by reflection on the idea of perfection. Both speculatively and empirically, a well-considered and well-rounded teleology results.

Although Voltaire in his *Philosophe ignorant* (1767) accepts the sensualism of Locke, he can say deistically that for him the most convincing theology is that which is deduced from the order and purposiveness of the world. "Shall I tell you the truth, dear child?" he has nature say to the philosopher. "People have given me a name that does not fit. They call me nature, and I am art." God, the eternal mathematician, is the artist behind the world as a work of art. Voltaire adds a moral argument in favor of teleology. A God is needed to reward and punish, to represent the moral order. If there were no God, we should have to invent one.[25]

Only when we grasp this basic idea of a consistent teleological view can we understand the many vital expressions of deistic piety, especially in sermons. Starting at this point deism feels impelled in two directions which it follows with true passion.

First, it must constantly demonstrate the perfection of the cosmic process. Obsession with this matter lies behind both scientific research and religious meditation (in strange contrast to the concern of Monod today to prove the accidental nature of life, especially human life).

Second, deism feels impelled toward the alien moralism that runs through its sermons. It has to demand that we live according to nature. This means integrating ourselves into the ends of the divine order, and it is thus regarded as worship. We are exhorted to avoid excess (e.g., in dancing), or to sleep with the bedroom window open so as to let in the fresh air. Similar precepts are legion. We find such things not merely in books of hygiene but also in sermons. (Rather maliciously, I have to ask whether our modern sociological preaching is not doing in its own way precisely what the preaching of the Enlightenment does with its borrowing from hygiene, agriculture, and other secular sources of knowledge, except that today we do it with considerably less humor.) Conversely, books of hygiene often take the form of theological ethics.

Before giving way to my desire to share some examples with the reader, I might say that in spite of the oddness in detail we have to be impressed by the fact that here for the last time in modern history the world is seen as a whole. Science, history, and theology are seen to be united and complementary, and they all emerge as elements in a comprehensive teleology. Furthermore, we here encounter once again

25. Cf. his article on "Nature," in *Dictionnaire philosophique. Questions sur l'encyclopédie* (1774-1775).

the leading ethical theme of the Enlightenment, namely, a concept of humanity which stakes all on maintaining a unified picture and avoiding division into separate sectors of the I, especially when it comes to faith and knowledge. This worthy background motif must be kept in mind when we survey the odd phenomena in the foreground.

I will now give a few examples of the way in which the search for traces of God in the world comes to expression. I will also add some theological comments. Reimarus is insistent that we can find God in the purposive organization of animal organisms,[26] e.g., in the folds in the skin of the rhinoceros.[27] In general the skin of the rhinoceros is thick and hard, but at its joints it is folded, soft, and pliable, i.e., at the very points where pliability is needed for movement. What points us to the Creator is the fact that the animal does not achieve this elasticity by its movements—if it did, the phenomenon would have no theological significance—it has the elasticity from birth. We may thus infer a wise providence and the existence of God. Numerous examples of this kind, e.g., the hare which doubles back and thus outwits the dog by native instinct rather than reason, are assembled by Reimarus with a view to making the same point, namely, that these inborn instincts and powers must have an infinite understanding as their first cause.

Yet the details which give signs of teleology and hence of the existence of God are also responsible for the crisis in the theological concept. For they give rise to individual difficulties. (This is perhaps why Hegel avoids being specific when he sketches the self-development of the world spirit. He seems to fear that he will come across exceptions that cannot be subsumed if he studies the details.)[28] When we look at the deistic search for the ways of God and his providence, we are aware of ambivalent emotions. On the one hand, we find the joy of discovery, but hard by we also find a kind of apologetic nervousness. What are we to do if in some detail we come across meaninglessness, if in some little matter we find complete absurdity, so that we cannot fit it into the teleological concept? Anxiety is palpable in this respect. One example of meaninglessness will wreck the whole system. Only an ironical thinker like Voltaire does not feel the anxiety. Instead he takes pleasure in rooting out such intractable details, in detecting absurdities, in mocking

26. He devoted a special work to the theme, *Allgemeine Betrachtungen über die Triebe der Tiere* (1760). In chap. 11 he tries to show that animal instincts are significant for a knowledge of the Creator. Apart from this theological interest, he is a pioneer of animal psychology.

27. Ibid., pp. 261ff.

28. Cf. *EF,* I, 259ff.

the Leibnizian idea of the best of all possible worlds and the whole deistic concept of cosmic harmony (although sometimes we catch other notes).[29]

As an example of the passionate apologetic desire to find providential purposiveness even in the smallest things, I know of no more vivid or typical example than the great work of Gottfried Ohnefurcht Richter, *Ichthyotheologie* . . . (Leipzig, 1754), which runs to no less than 912 pages, with no index.[30]

The general lauding of fish as tasty food is relatively simple. It readily supports the deistic thesis that all created things serve final ends and aim at our eudaimonia. The main line of argument is thus easy enough. In detail, however, the author has a hard struggle against threatening meaninglessness. It is for him a serious problem that many people are drowned and devoured by divinely created fishes. So as not to let this obscure the purposiveness of creation and the justice—or even the existence—of God, in this and similar cases he finds relief in the fact that such people must have done something false or wicked to deserve such a death. This thought redresses the balance. Even the sad recollection that many people choke on fish bones or eat rotten fish makes no difference. After careful research Richter finds comfort in the conclusion that either they did not test the fish or they ate too quickly.

After endless discussions of apparent rifts in the harmony of God's direction of the world, Richter turns to a particularly delicate and apparently insoluble problem. Typically it is the most farfetched. For the deists the most threatening questions arise on the extreme limits. In this case, there are deep-sea fish which we never see, which have nothing to

29. Cf. his *Candide* (1759) with its absurd Dr. Pangloss, who has to allow that Columbus brought his sexual ailment but finds something positive in the fact that he also brought chocolate and cochineal. In discussions of negative features original sin and our wolfish nature are sometimes cited as possible causes of dubious or destructive elements. But Pangloss weakens the concept by integrating evil into the best of all possible worlds. Voltaire finds the culmination of meaninglessness in the Lisbon earthquake, which shatters the Enlightenment idea of cosmic harmony. Faced with its horrors, the corpses and destruction, Candide, the previously loyal pupil of Pangloss, is forced to ask: "If this is the best of all possible worlds, what would the others be like?"

30. Richter was one of the so-called physio-theologians who tried to prove divine providence by means of natural phenomena. Among them are Friedrich Christian Brockes with his famous poem *Irdisches Vergnügen in Gott* (1735), and Friedrich Christian Lesser with his *Lithotheologie* (1735) and *Testaceotheologie* (1744), in which he tries to use rocks and shellfish as proofs of God. W. Philip, *Das Zeitalter der Aufklärung* (1963), has collected extracts from these works. Behind them, as their philosophical basis, stands Christian Wolff's celebrated *Vernünftige Gedanken von Gott, der Welt und der Seele des Menschen, auch allen Dingen überhaupt* (1733).

do with us, and which in consequence can never contribute to our eudaimonia. Meaning is thus menaced from the depths of the ocean. But a theologian of the Wolffian school, Johann Gustav Reinbeck, shows how these demons of the deep can be fitted meaningfully into the cosmic order. The Creator's purpose was that these creatures should set the water in movement and hence keep it from becoming dirty.[31] A stroke of the fin, and harmony is preserved.

Examples might be multiplied, but I will be content simply to refer to a few of the most striking (and amusing). First, some verses from the Hamburg senator B. H. Brockes, whose *Irdisches Vergnügen in Gott* came out in 9 volumes between 1721 and 1748.[32]

One of its recitatives speaks of the fivefold utility of mountains in producing milk, butter, cheese, skins, and whey. Utility is what serves human eudaimonia. Grass presents a difficulty, for it does not seem to be of any use to us, but the solution comes in a fine song, for God enables us to live on grass by means of cows. Thus in his song on the misuse of nature Brockes finds confirmation of the thesis that God and nature never do anything in vain.

A second example is less easy to grasp today. I refer to the Swabian priest Michael von Jung and his work *Melpomene oder Grablieder* (1839).[33] This Roman Catholic pastor had the idea that instead of preaching funeral sermons he should compose these songs and sing them at the grave to a lute accompaniment, using popular tunes, and bringing in great crowds.[34] His collection deals especially with unexpected deaths (e.g., by accident or suicide), for which the style is very well suited, and which offer opportunity to trace God's purposive action even in the terrors and discords of life, and thus to beat down the lurking temptation to doubt. Typical titles refer to a hunter who was shot, the death of a prominent teacher, a man who froze to death while drunk, and a woman prisoner who was decapitated. When Jung has laboriously found the meaning in his rough verses, he adds moral admonitions to keep to the goals of creation as God has established them and thus to integrate ourselves into the ontic order. Thus when speaking of a young

31. Richter, *Ichthyotheologie*, p. 444.
32. A fine facsimile edition came out in 1965. The work ran through several editions and was even made into an oratorio.
33. I have edited these songs with an explanatory essay, Herder-Bücherei, no. 599.
34. These tuneful melodies are included in the above edition. With an audience of beadles and attendants, who were much impressed, although not the original hearers, my students rendered them with great historical accuracy when in my course I came to lecture on the Enlightenment.

man who danced himself to death, he says that the wise dance but only slowly, rationally, and infrequently.

To conclude this brief survey of examples of the Enlightenment adjustment to God and nature, with its fine moral, I might adduce the verdict which August Tholuck (1799-1877) passed on a popular preacher at Halle who embraced Enlightenment theology: "To his credit, he preaches the usual strict morality, and at times he even makes some use of Christianity."[35]

Apart from the crises of cosmic teleology which arise in matters of detail and on the borders, the Enlightenment has to mobilize its apologetic resources of thought against two fundamental threats. The one is that of evil, the other that of death. Here the problem of theodicy is particularly acute.

III. THE BASIC PROBLEM OF THEODICY

A. EVIL

We have seen already that there is a foreground solution to this problem. The harmony of the moral world order is preserved if evil can be seen as punishment for incurred guilt. But this equation can be asserted only with limitations. In Job the absolute failure to discern any such equation is a problem. The Lisbon earthquake seems to be a drastic refutation of it. For the Enlightenment it shattered the harmony of their cosmic order. It destroyed both good and bad alike. Making no distinction, it obviously made of evil an inexplicable enigma. Evil resisted the attempt to find any meaningful explanation for it.

How does deism try to overcome this problem apologetically? How can it prevent the shattering of the basis of its teleological vision, its reduction to absurdity? The deists, Reimarus among them, solve the problem in principle in the same way as Leibniz in his *Theodicy*. This is the only solution, the classical one, that the doctrine of a closed system of ends can find.

To see teleology as a whole, instead of signs of it in the skin of a rhinoceros or the doubling back of the hare, insight is needed into the totality of the system. To achieve this one must come close to the world spirit of Laplace (1748-1827) and find a cosmic formula in past and present situations which makes a comprehensive glance possible. But

35. See L. Witte, *Das Leben Tholucks,* I (1884), 375.

being limited, we can never see the system as a whole. Hence the ends of innumerable small things are hidden from us. They seem to be meaningless, to lack any purpose. But they do so only because our field of vision is limited. As Reimarus says, only an infinite understanding can assess the perfection or imperfection of the whole world, both as a whole and in detail, according to space and time. Since we do not have this insight, it is a mistake to say that anything is useless, imperfect, or evil, for we do not know what good purpose it might serve,[36] i.e., we do not see ends, even though they are surprisingly clear in places—but only in places.

Pain, doubt, and anxiety are the result of a lack of insight into the totality of the system. If we know the system as a whole, we should hear the symphony of creation.

The comparison leads to two essential statements. Musical people are edified when they hear a symphony because, as Kant says in his *Kritik der Urteilskraft,* they see the immanent teleology of the work. For it is an essential feature of a work of art that it should be a system whose totality in space, or, in the case of music, in time, can be perceived.[37] A dog howls when it hears a Bach fugue because it cannot understand the whole and hears only an amorphous collection of highly unmotivated sounds which cause it discomfort. We ourselves are in the same position as the dog when we hear the shrill dissonances and formless impressions of noise that random disasters produce in the symphony of life. We do not perceive how or in what context these noises fit in with the whole.

Hence it is not an ontic deficiency in being that brings the perfection into question; it is a noetic lack in the observer. Frederick the Great agrees with this view when some years before his death he comes upon the statement that we must not blame God's wisdom but confess our own lack of insight.[38] Deism thinks we can see the harmony of creation only in the light of the eschaton, for only in this light can we see world events as a whole, as a system. We have here what is in fact a *secularized eschatology.*

This is the one point in the deistic view at which I find indicated that which Christianity calls faith, not in the sense of purely precognitive conjecture, but in the sense of trust *(fiducia).* Deism here surrenders its claim to base everything on evidence and understanding. Reimarus

36. Reimarus, *Die vornehmsten Wahrheiten,* p. 580.
37. Along these lines Gottfried Benn calls a work of art a kind of protective wall against the threat of the formless, the chaotic, or even nothingness. On Kant's theory cf. *ThE,* III, §§ 3123ff.
38. WW, XIV, 18-20.

demands of us that on the basis of a purely partial insight into teleology we should trust that the whole that we cannot see is meaningfully directed to divine ends. He is confident that the few scattered harmonies which reach our ears amid the unintelligible sounds of the universe are a guarantee that even the macro-chaos of meaninglessness will prove to be a cosmos on a higher view.[39] Thus a breath of eschatological faith wafts over this cold religion of reason.

We might say, then, that we agree with deism at the point where it is inconsistent when measured by its own axioms. I am reminded of an earlier remark that theology betrays its deepest secrets in moments of inconsistency. Reimarus shows here that with one finger he is still touching the hem of a lofty robe and that his world would collapse if he did not secretly do this. Who is to say whether this incidental contact is not more essential, even for Reimarus, than the whole structure of thought which is built upon him in the history of philosophy?

B. DEATH

A final and more serious obstacle still threatens the deistic view of meaning or faith in meaning. The question is as follows.

Supposing a person dies through a totally meaningless and nonteleological mischance? Supposing Job, for example, had died before he was restored? For such a person all that is said about the symphony of life as a whole could have no meaning. For life would be broken off at a specific point. This disaster in detail would call in question the symphony as a whole.

To explain the difficulty that death presents to the Enlightenment I should like to set it against the background of our own day. For I think this will show that at this point the Enlightenment has some premodern features typical of medieval Christianity.

For modern atheists or nihilists with their characteristic modern views, death is not the serious problem it was for Reimarus. This is related to the decline of a sense of personality. When personality is integrated into the collective, its organs are socialized,[40] and there is no spirit to surrender or soul to breathe out. The person is dissolved in suprapersonal entities and hence transcended. Could not Reimarus have accepted a similar solution? Am I not just one note in the symphony

39. Reimarus, *Die vornehmsten Wahrheiten*, pp. 614ff.
40. Cf. K. Marx, "On the Jewish Question," in *Early Writings* (New York, 1975), pp. 221, 234; also my *Living with Death* (Grand Rapids, 1983).

of all life? When I die, do I not merge into the whole, so that death, as a transition into the transpersonal, presents no problem? Why cannot the Enlightenment accept this—apparently obvious—idea?

It cannot do so because it thinks wholly in terms of the individual. The whole world machine is meant to serve our eudaimonia. Hence in solving the problem of death there can be no bypassing of the individual. This would be to rob world teleology of its telos and therefore of its point. Humans and their eudaimonia are the final goal. The idea of a suprapersonal society into which I merge, serving it with my sacrificial death, is thus totally unacceptable to the Enlightenment.

This individualism, this idea that individuals are ends in themselves, might seem to be an artificial abstraction and hence a mark of sickness. Yet one should consider that, even if in distorted form, the Christian tradition is at work here with its view that we are made in God's image and thus have an indelible character. The force with which we assert our worth echoes the ancient Christian doxology which praises the Creator and his gracious resolve to make us in his own likeness. Deism undoubtedly foreshadows depersonalizing, as we may see in the concept of the *res cogitans* in Descartes, yet the process has not yet gone so far that the transpersonal offers a solution to the problem of death, whether in terms of merging into an idea or into a collective to which individuals sacrifice themselves.

For Reimarus, who speaks here for the Enlightenment as a whole, only one solution can maintain the link between perishing individuality and the total symphony. This is belief in a future life. He has to flee to a hereafter beyond the boundary of death to answer the pressing question of theodicy. Since contrary events (like the fate of Job or the sufferings of the righteous) come not infrequently in this life, God's wisdom, love, and righteousness to us could not be saved if there were no life, in which these discords can be resolved and, in a final act of the play, suffering innocence is crowned and blustering wickedness punished.[41]

Thus the doctrine of individual immortality is given a new basis. If from the middle of the last century atheistic, socio-revolutionary movements have threatened to take away from Christianity this comfort of the hereafter, giving as their reason the fact that it prevents the exploited from deploying all their resources to change living conditions in this world, their objection has been less against Christian eschatology than against this kind of continuation of the symphony of life beyond the stage of our temporality.

41. Reimarus, *Die vornehmsten Wahrheiten*, p. 665.

The problem of immortality is the point where the Enlightenment fails in its attempt to solve the riddle of the world and humanity with the help of the understanding alone, and to set faith on one side. We have seen why the attempt fails. From no finite standpoint can we see the totality of being or hear the whole symphony of life. The postulate of immortality is the valve which relieves the pressure of the mounting and insoluble problem. The resulting position midway between understanding and faith is clearly unavoidable if individuality is regarded as a basic fact of humanity that cannot be abandoned. In such a case the only possibilities are either to solve the pressing problems of life and theodicy within the stretch of time between birth and death or to prolong the existence of individuality beyond death. Facing these alternatives, Reimarus is involved in a model problem which has more than contemporary relevance and reaches into areas in which the history of philosophy and theology has ever and again had to face up to similar questions.

To mention only one example, tragedy often struggles with the question of how basic conflicts can be solved in a finite lifetime. It is perhaps because Christianity thinks that our existence is more than finite that there can be no Christian tragedy in the strict sense. The tragic hero, e.g., the Oedipus of Sophocles, has only a limited time to deal with the problem of guilt and destiny (patricide and incest). He cannot take refuge in a life after death. He finds the solution in a patient acceptance of his fate. The basic orders of being have to be challenged and violated if it is to be evident that they avenge themselves and hence cannot be broken. Oedipus has the role of the one who, half-guilty and half-innocent, provokes them. He is a sacrifice to their vengeance and thus helps to publish their sacred taboo. His final acceptance of his fate is thus the tragic solution, within the stretch of being between birth and death, to a conflict which defies any speculative solution.

We cannot leave the teaching of Reimarus and deism without finally pointing out that even in the solution of immortality a factor that is critical for teleology cannot be avoided, namely, how harmony is to be restored if there is a balancing out of things in the hereafter. What is needed is the punishment of blustering wickedness, and this entails the necessary positing of hell. Hell is a spatial symbol for the fact that the idea of harmony is not total, that the resolution of dissonance does not occur at one point. To relieve this problem and to avoid this remaining discord the idea of universal reconciliation and theories of reincarnation seem to be designed.

We do indeed find such thoughts in the Enlightenment. Sometimes there is reference to the kindly and loving course of reason which no hell or accompanying furies serve. Reimarus himself does not reflect further on hell or the eternity of its penalties. The issue is a marginal one. As soon as he lights on it, he glances away. Perhaps with his focus on experience and concreteness he thinks such matters belong too much to the sphere of speculation and their outline is too hazy to call for discussion. Divine judgment and wrath are an offense to the optimistic cheerfulness of his thinking. It is better to ignore them. If we speak about them, they might prove to be a dangerous explosive that would wreck this beautiful and cheerful ship with its awnings. Some primitive elements in the Christian kerygma might begin to have an impact again— elements which are to be feared because they reopen questions that are suppressed.

Nonetheless, deism cannot totally ignore what is suppressed because of the difficulty of the issue. It has to go further. It has to attack actively that which remains deep within it as an undiscarded remnant of the Christian tradition. Yet it cannot do this in the zone of eschatology; the air in this zone is too thin for Enlightenment tastes. It will proceed in the sphere of history. This brings us to the final question that calls for discussion in Reimarus.

IV. IMPLICATIONS FOR THE ATTITUDE TO CONVENTIONAL CHRISTIANITY

Reimarus draws the implications in his *Apologie*. This is less an apology, a defense of deism against conventional belief, than a vehement attack on the Christian position. In it Reimarus uses the same strategy as we constantly find in deism. He uses the double bookkeeping of both a priori and a posteriori arguments.

At the outset we find his a priori thesis that the natural religion of deism, which is speculatively deduced from the perfection of God, is the only true religion validated by reason. What is advanced speculatively is confirmed empirically. The world proves to be a logical and purposive nexus. As a result—again an a priori conclusion—any religion (including Christianity) which rests on supernatural or transcendent interventions has to be false. This is the a priori presupposition with which Reimarus attacks orthodoxy from the very first.

The second thesis, an a posteriori one, is as follows. The detailed historical data on which the Christian religion bases its transcendent origin are untenable. The Christian religion as such is thus untrue. Here is also an a posteriori confirmation of the a priori assertion that deism alone is true religion. The results are the same if the calculation is correct.

Reimarus thus enters into historical criticism and becomes a pioneer of the historico-critical method in biblical research. When we study this start of a new theological discipline, we see that in the eyes of the community and the silent majority it calls for condemnation and plays the role of a bogeyman.

This has led to many conflicts, and especially the split between the theology of the schools and that of the church, and a refusal to deal with questions of biblical criticism before the forum of the community. The result has been that the discipline has lived in a ghetto. The way has led to an esotericism similar to that found in the Enlightenment, and in an extreme form in Reimarus. It is unfitting that we should snobbishly ignore the reserve of the community. To understand it, we need to remember that biblical criticism emerged in the form of a mortal attack, not merely on the mythical clothing of biblical truth, or on the excesses of popular piety, but more radically on the Christian message itself. The resultant shock has prevented people from seeing that in the meantime criticism has undergone a radical reappraisal. Today, in all its many forms, it works with a definite *theological* intention. Reimarus had the tendentious aim of confirming a rationalistic and speculative pre-supposition. The later goal has been that of working back behind the interpretative theology of the community and legendary stylizations and establishing what really happened or what was really said. But apart from a few exceptions this is not a destructive process. The many witnesses who have been disentangled within the basic unity of witness, and the many individual notes that have been discovered in the polyph-ony of the whole Bible, have helped us to appreciate its wealth and kerygmatic fulness. Only when we contrast what Reimarus intended with what is now done theologically in biblical criticism do we discern the change of thrust that has taken place in this field.

As we see from our survey of the strategy, the historico-critical theses of Reimarus are not the results of research. They are there before the research begins, or, at any rate, the point is there. They are theses with a purpose. They have simply to be strengthened empirically. The initial a priori argumentation has already established what alone can be true historically because it is true speculatively. Once this is clear, we may look at the critical work of Reimarus, not with shock, but with a good deal of humor.

Along these lines, we might summarize the famous theses as follows: (1) The saving facts on which the Christian religion rests are demonstrably untenable. (2) The people and supposed eyewitnesses to whom we owe the accounts of the "revelations" are not serious and act deceitfully. (3) The doctrines that come with a claim to revelation, e.g., justification and substitution, are not only philosophically contradictory but fall down because the historical facts with which they are linked (the resurrection, ascension, etc.) are untrue. (4) The supposedly verbally inspired scriptures are demonstrably of human and even obscurantist origin.

These theses lead on to the destructive criticism which reminds us at many points of a criminal investigation. Reimarus is not even afraid of defaming the figure of Jesus. On the contrary, the questioning and unmasking strike a nerve in this respect. The attack on Jesus Christ himself involves a strange mixture of respect and scorn. It seems as if Reimarus is at odds with himself here, so that only with a great effort can he free himself from the shackles of a deep-seated restraint.

Contradictory and irreconcilable features combine in his strained portrait of Jesus. On the one side, not without some warmth, and even an obvious inward sympathy, he extols him as the champion of the purest moral and religious teaching, i.e., rational teaching. Thus he recognizes that Jesus accords only a lesser rank to the ceremonial law as compared with moral duties and conversion, and he refers to the fine Sermon on the Mount.

On the other side, however, Jesus no less than the apostles uses the basest means to enforce his requirements and especially to give himself validity. He is a teacher of virtue but also a strategist of the kingdom of God. He thinks he can impose his ethical laws, not by mere appeals, but only by placing them under this messianic rule and enforcing them by leadership that is backed by secular power. The noble end of virtue can be achieved only by force and cunning. (The Jesus of Reimarus is more like the Grand Inquisitor of Dostoyevski than his partner in dialogue from Nazareth.) He thus has to usurp the throne of David. To do so he engages in propaganda designed to promote his messianic hopes. He has to stir up the masses against the Romans with a view to producing a great revolt out of their hope of redemption. He has to make sure that when the revolt comes he will be chosen as the leader. He thus engages in a clever campaign. He stages the spectacle of his baptism, at which his cousin John, a real swindler, assists. The scenario demands that they act as if they did not know each other. The voice from heaven (how is *this* managed?) is thus all the more impressive when it proclaims Jesus as the divinely planned messianic ruler. The people fall for this, especially as cunningly contrived miracles seem to validate the messianic mission. With calculated tactics Jesus waits for the right moment—not too soon—to accede to the people's desire to proclaim him king. Even what Wrede will later call the "messianic secret"[42]—i.e., the command not to make the miracles known—is only a refined trick. It is meant to stimulate the spread of rumor, and it obviously achieves this result.

I can break off here, for this sample is enough to fill out the picture of the grotesque way in which Reimarus does his unmasking. (And we recall that in Hamburg he was pretending to be a devout churchman, naively participating in the swindle which he alone had seen through!)

We can imagine how violently he handled the resurrection stories. Here he takes malicious pleasure in the fact that he is up to all the tricks. He examines the witnesses separately, notes how they entangle themselves in contradictions, and thus unmasks the charade.

Reimarus applies his critical methods of detection to the OT first. Here there are fewer kerygmatic texts than in the Gospels. Nevertheless, when he unmasks a miracle like that of the Red Sea as a hoax (Exod. 14:19ff.),[43] the attack does lose any of its destructive impact, especially when it is directed against orthodox Lutheranism. For if even one peripheral passage is shown clearly to be untrue, it cannot have been inspired by the Holy Spirit. This makes it plain that Reimarus is dealing a mortal wound at a vital point, namely, the orthodox doctrine of inspiration. We see this from two angles.

First, this doctrine is totally refuted if at only one point the historical, geographical, or scientific impossibility of the narrative is demonstrated, especially when an explanation can be furnished which shows how the error arose (e.g., a tendentious purpose, a confusion of sources, or distortion in the course of the tradition). The attack in this regard comes in matters of detail on the extreme periphery (as in the case of deep-sea fish for the deists). There is thus a certain resemblance between the critical elements in secular teleology on the one side and confessional orthodoxy on the other.

Second, the doctrine of inspiration is vitally affected because it is shown to be unable to appreciate the historicity of revelation. This historicity involves the concursus of divine and human factors: divine direction and inspiration on the one side, disobedient and fallible

---

42. W. Wrede, *Das Messiasgeheimnis in den Evangelien* (1901); ET *The Messianic Secret* (Cambridge, 1971).

43. Here Reimarus calculates that if the army numbers 600,000, with 4 members to each family, the total number of the people must have been over two and a half million. At ten abreast its march would have spread over 190 miles, and crossing the Red Sea would have taken, not the three hours available, but ten days. Consequently the story is demonstrably false.

people on the other. The theological fault of the doctrine—if one may put it thus—is that for all its frenzied and dogmatically sanctioned acceptance of the biblical histories, it denied the historicity of revelation and disembodied the word of scripture. At the very point of a supposedly supreme orthodoxy it fell into the heresy of a docetic view of the Bible.

When we see this, then against the background of orthodoxy the picture of Reimarus perhaps takes on a different aspect, and we have to take a fresh look at the problems posed by historical theology. I might put the relevant question as follows.

Reimarus was fighting against the nonhistorical docetic element in the orthodox doctrine of scripture. The Christianity with which he had to do was totally docetic in this regard. In his own setting he was thus attacking Christianity itself.[44] But who was to blame, if we may talk of blame? Orthodox Christianity, which surrendered to nonhistoricity, which thus sublimely denied the incarnation of the Word, which fell victim to legalism, and which thus substituted a dubious codification for the incarnation—or that remarkable preacher of repentance Reimarus, who threw out the (kerygmatic) baby with the (docetic) bathwater? Could Reimarus have differentiated the two? Was it a personal hardening that prevented him from doing so, or was he blinded by the spiritual world around him? Who is responsible if Reimarus tears off the veil at *one* point, seeing some of the sharp contours through the rent, but failing to see the context? The grotesque distortions that we find in Reimarus might be explained along these lines. To present truths out of context— that is the creative art of caricature.

If I may speak personally for a moment, I take pleasure in not snobbishly depicting a figure like Reimarus as completely outdated and superseded, in not regarding him as belonging merely to the Enlightenment and then passing on, but in taking him much more seriously. Precisely at this extreme our program must prove itself. We have to enter into dialogue with thinkers of the past and hence respect them as partners in discussion.

If with this end in view we talk about our common theme with Reimarus, relating him to our own purpose, we shall have to say this to him. From what angle and with what criteria do you attack a nonhistorical biblical docetism? Do you not mount your criticism from the standpoint of a very definite and highly secular view of historicity, namely, that everything must take place "naturally," that it must keep

44. Similarly, Nietzsche's attack on Christianity can hardly be understood except against the background of the liberal, moralistic Christianity of his day.

to the laws of causality, analogy, and immanence (as Troeltsch would later put it), if it is to be regarded as possible and consequently as true? (Pardon us, Reimarus, if clever people have made all this clear to us, and we are thus better instructed, whereas for you such matters were still in the womb of the future!) As we now see, did you not, Reimarus, attack that nonhistorical orthodoxy with weapons that could be turned not merely against a docetic falsification of the kerygma but against the kerygma itself, so that you found yourself in the painful position of not being able to require something so revolutionary from your contemporaries, and were thus forced into the role of a hypocrite? The rationalistic presuppositions of your criticism can never—not even later—be harmonized with historically understood revelation. Would it not have been better for you to attack docetism in the name of the kerygma itself? You would then have had to find your norm in the fact that God chose concrete people, patriarchs, prophets, and apostles, who understood him, in their own categories, in their own pictures of the world, and, as I would see it, in their own mythically determined mentality. (It would then have been clear to you, as it has become clear in the course of time and our own faulty experience, that these people, with their contemporaries, constantly ran the danger of setting their historical presuppositions and their own self-assertive desires above the divine Word, thus valuing the earthen vessel more than its contents.) We are not just being pharisaical if in the light of subsequent history we ask you whether you could not have fought docetism better from the standpoint that the Bible documents God's visitations, his wrestling with disobedient and fallible people, that this document thus bears the servant form of the historical, and that there is only *one* in whom the Word became totally and undividedly and inviolably flesh.

But this you could not do, Reimarus, because your premises did not allow you to think of God as a person but only as the idea of perfection. You thus found in orthodoxy only a divine person that seemed to be no more than an idea: the idea of a subject of inspiration, a mover of goose-quills, which mechanically wrote down what he dictated. Nor do you find persons in the patriarchs, prophets, and apostles; for you they are no more than the automatically functioning scribes of an inspiring Spirit. They are thus no more than machines with no flesh and blood (computers, as we would say nowadays, into which data are fed). What is left then, Reimarus, but another idea, your idea of divine perfection, to play off against the ideas of docetism? What else do you have?

Yet who of us may dare judge here if we take our hermeneutical program seriously, neither holding our historical distance and not taking the great theologians seriously, nor unhistorically measuring them by our own theological insights?

When we ask questions such as these we find that we are not given the role of judges but that with Reimarus we ourselves stand under judgment, the last judgment. We can only talk with one another—and we have to argue with one another—like patients waiting for the same doctor.

This does not mean that we are relativists who have abandoned all absolute norms in theology. We might seem to be advocating something like relativism but only because we know the absolute of the last judgment. This judgment is not at our disposal as a norm because only one person sits on the judgment seat and this person knows the heart, whereas we know only theological arguments.

Thus this Reimarus who seems to be so shallow, this Enlightenment figure who is so laughed at and outdated, brings us up against the final mysteries of theology. Who is really to blame, the deist Reimarus or the orthodox docetists? This is the decisive question. The guilt of orthodoxy called down upon it the judgment of deism. But was this real judgment and no new guilt? The history of theology is the history of thoughts that need forgiveness. So long as theology is aware of its plight and need, it remains healthy, for it stands under justification. Theology does not merely teach justification; it lives by it. Hence it should be pursued only by those who know the remission of sins. Because there are always such people, theology never ceases. I can name no other reason why the history of dogma with its confusion has not ended in absurdity and sunk into a miserable grave above which the community sings its songs of praise without theology.[45] For this reason alone theology lives on until the last day.

From this standpoint I would bid you hear and understand the saying of Schleiermacher which I chose as a motto for this book and with which I will close this chapter. It occurs in a letter to F. H. Jacobi and shows how much Schleiermacher was aware of the mystery of theology: "One age bears the guilt of others but can seldom undo it except by fresh guilt."[46]

45. As is well-known, D. F. Strauss called the history of dogma *(Dogmengeschichte)* the judgment of dogma *(Dogmengericht)*.

46. Cf. *Schleiermachers Leben (Briefsammlung)* (1858), II, 343. For modern views of rationalism cf. the debate between H. Albert and G. Ebeling: Ebeling, *Kritischer Rationalismus? Zu H. Alberts Traktat über kritische Vernunft* (1973); Albert, *Theologische Holzwege. G. Ebeling und der rechte Gebrauch der Vernunft* (1973). Cf. also the important work by S. Scharrer, *Theologische Kritik der Vernunft* (1977), and the comprehensive account by H. Hempelmann, *Kritischer Rationalismus und Theologie als Wissenschaft* (1980).

CHAPTER 5

G. E. Lessing: The Question of the Unconditioned in History

Bibliography. For primary and secondary sources readers should consult W. Drews, *Gotthold Ephraim Lessing in Selbstzeugnissen und Bilddokumenten* (1962). Cf. also my *Offenbarung, Vernunft and Existenz. Studien zur Religionsphilosophie Lessings,* 5th ed. (1967). I am using the edition by Georg Witkowski (cited as Witkowski). For translations of some of Lessing's works cf. H. Chadwick, ed., *Lessing's Theological Writings* (1957).

I. BIOGRAPHY

In this area one may consult the work by Drews, the brief sketch by C. Bertheau in *RE,* 3rd ed., 11, 406ff., and the article by O. Mann in *RGG,* 3rd ed. Lessing died at the age of 52 in 1781.

The debate between rationalism and orthodoxy which runs through Lessing's theological writings, especially his dispute with the Hamburg pastor Goeze, can hardly be understood apart from his family background. His father, Johann Gottfried Lessing, was a worthy Lutheran minister who published pietistic songs as well as learned works. Particularly well known is one of these songs in which he sings about the feeding of the multitude, and which refers to the false reckoning of the disciples as compared to that of Jesus, who can add and multiply even when there are only noughts. The scholarly tradition of the family continued in the son, who even at school read the authors of antiquity on his own initiative. His student years in Leipzig, Wittenberg, and Berlin led him away from his first field, that of theology, into philosophy, philology, science, and medicine. We see here the broad range of cultural interests that encounter us particularly in his critical works. He spent many years in Berlin, which made a great impact, but he never had any true calling, not even in the theater at Hamburg or the library at Wolfenbüttel. He rejected an invitation to a professorship of rhetoric at Königsberg. Hence he never really settled anywhere and worked as an independent author. In his personal life he was always harassed by poverty, and his wife died only fifteen months after they were married. He died lonely and embittered and almost blind on a difficult journey to Brunswick. Yet for his great plays especially, and also for his critical writings on drama and religion, he is one of the few classicists who is more influential today than many who had classical rank in their own time (e.g., Herder, Klopstock, and Wieland), but who hardly count on the modern cultural scene.

II. LESSING'S WRESTLING WITH THE RELATION BETWEEN REVELATION AND HISTORY

A. LESSING THE SOCRATIC-DIALECTICAL THINKER

Although Lessing's thought is marked by crystal clarity and precision, in his critical, polemical statements about theology we seem to enter an impenetrable labyrinth in which even he himself has trouble finding his way. When I say "he himself," I have his personal existence in view, his own articles of faith as compared to his many antitheses. Even when one studies him for decades, he still seems to be mysteriously aloof and yet exercises all the fascination of an inexplicable nearness.

The difficulty in getting a hold on him may be traced not least to the man himself. Kierkegaard in his *Concluding Unscientific Postscript* gives us the clue when in his affectionate explanation of Lessing he says: What result did he reach? "O wonderful Lessing! He reached none at all, not even the trace of a result." Why not? Because he is not a systematician who expresses truths in fixed form; he is an existential thinker to whom the truth comes, for whom it is an event, who has a lively history with the truth. In this respect he is like his beloved Socrates, whose entelechy was directed by the fact that he did not just teach truths but triggered them, releasing an encounter with the truth by maieutic arts.

Socrates and Lessing make what Kierkegaard calls an appeal. They do not import ready-made truths but engage in the production or reproduction of truth and help people to achieve maturity. They give rise to what one might call "existence."

This maieutic thought takes on a polar structure. It posits tension with those to whom it imparts itself. Since there are many combinations of this tension, the act of thought is unending. This is why no one can say what Socrates, Plato, Luther, or Lessing taught as such. No one can pour their teaching into set molds. Each generation and individual must make a new encounter and at root can only have a unique dialogical history with them. This dialogue never ceases during the lifetime of the student.

Lessing, however, is especially in dialogue with himself. To understand him, then, we must enter into this dialogue and share it. What form does it take?

His I as it is tied to the historical tradition of Christianity speaks with his other I which understands itself as a rational being and can recognize only universally valid truth, or what Kant would call synthetic judgments a priori. Thus the epic poet in him talks with the dramatist, or as he once put it, the pagan in his head with the Lutheran Christian in his heart. Because these tensions cannot be resolved in quick syntheses, but the polar members remain strictly apart, Lessing's thought acts as a kind of acid. Much of it serves a divisive purpose inasmuch as he is the foe of all compromise or synthesis. I will give a few examples.

(1) He rejects the mixture of positive and natural religion in the rational Christianity of Reimarus and wants both lights to shine on separately.

(2) He distinguishes between letter and spirit, between the religion of Christ and the Christian religion. What he means is that we should not project church dogma back into the religion of Christ. We should not try to validate normative ideas by their historical genesis and thus create a false form of security—false because it heteronomizes an authority and at the same time invents it. Those of us familiar with modern debates about the problem of the historical Jesus and the early Christian kerygma are astonished to see how far they are foreshadowed in Lessing.

(3) He also differentiates between the accidental truths of history and the necessary truths of reason, between typifying poetry and individualizing history.

(4) Finally, he distinguishes between the individual genres of literature, drama and epic, tragedy and comedy.

Only within these distinctions can one understand Lessing the dramatist. Even if only on the margin, this is relevant to our theme. Lessing is a dramatist for two reasons.

First, he is a dialectician through and through. He is a man in debate. This may be seen in the dialogical style of his writings. He works with exclamation marks and question marks. He uses scorn and adjuration. He is always addressing someone. In contrast to Descartes, he does not work out his philosophy in the study or by the hearth. He does not give birth to it in quiet moments. It does not spring out of his brain as Pallas Athene does from Zeus. He always has a partner in discussion. Truth is not for him a timeless mathematical proposition but something that actualizes itself, that takes place, that needs to be provoked by antithesis if it is to emerge.

This means that truth is historical. It comes with debate. *The Education of the Human Race* shows this. Here truth eventually achieves freedom by a process of crystallization. It arises through what Toynbee calls "challenges." These bring it out of the darkness of mythical concealment and into the light of reason. Because truth is an event that encounters us, drama is the best form in which to express it. Even in his theological works Lessing is wholly the dramatist.

In these works, too, he can express himself only in *dialegesthai*. Indeed, some parts of his anti-Goeze writings take the form of dialogue: he and I. The constant hermeneutical question of whether he speaks *gymnastikos* or *dogmatikos* finds an answer in this dialogical form of statement. Dialogue poses the question whether individual statements receive their emphasis from the matter or the opponent. Each train of thought in Lessing is a complex picture in which partner and matter are entangled and both come together to form a complete figure.

The second reason why Lessing turns to drama is his desire for synthesis. For all the passion of division and distinction, this desire is also present.

The dialectician divides and isolates the members. The dramatist brings them together and gives them life. If Hebbel's description of the dramatic process is right when he says that drama is a profounder reconstruction of life, one might say that in Lessing the comparative "profounder" denotes the universal validity of the reconstruction. For Lessing, however, universal validity means purified from the play and contingency of history. Drama depicts a typical process, a prototype of events. It presses beyond the accidental truth of history. It seeks out the rational truth of life and the historical process. Here, then, we note a final common background to his theological and aesthetic ideas. This is why I have mentioned these matters.

B. LESSING'S THEME: HUMAN NATURE AND THE THREAT TO IT

We have in fact been led to the basic theme of his existence as a thinker. This theme might be formulated as follows. How can I, as a rational being, accept myself as a historical being, without being disloyal to my existence?

What I here call existence is defined in Lessing by the fact that I am a bearer of the logos. In contrast, history is the heteronomous and irrational outside which threatens the logos structure of my nature.

I must develop this basic theme for a moment so as not to give the impression that in the expression *rational being* we simply have a remote phenomenon of the Enlightenment which does not affect us directly, even though along the lines of Wilhelm Röpke we might say with some basic right that we are living in a new phase of the Enlightenment, an Enlightenment of the second degree.

If we are to engage in a true *dialegesthai* with Lessing, we have to realize that Lessing is concerned about the definition of human nature. I have a nature, or what Goethe would call a daimon or entelechy. This nature of mine, the core of my being, is threatened from outside (as Goethe says in his *Orphische Urworte*). It is threatened by moira, eros, and other things. All these are trying to turn aside the chariot of my destiny (as Goethe puts it in his *Egmont*) and to distort my nature.

Goethe believes in the indestructibility of the entelechy. He is certain that although it may be disturbed it will keep its original direction like the needle of a compass. But Lessing is a skeptic. He sees the risk that he might be untrue to his nature and therefore lose it. We shall see how this loss may come about. But first it is important to see how Lessing puts the question of the destiny of human nature.

His definition of this nature as a rational nature is secondary. In this regard he is simply claiming the conceptual framework of his day. To enter into relevant *dialegesthai* with him, we are right to bring our own framework, putting for Lessing's rational nature what we have been taught by our own anthropology and philosophy to understand by human nature. What we should probably say is character, existence, essence, being, personality, or, in the Christian sense, the "spiritual man."

This being or nature of mine is threatened. This is the decisive point. The threats may vary according to the way I understand my nature. If in Kant's sense I view it as the moral person, the threats are heteronomy, the dictatorship of the senses, bondage to an alien will, and eudaemonism. If in the sense of Heidegger or Sartre I view it as existence, the threat is that of generalization, fixation on others, or the authority of an alien *essentia*. If in Lessing's sense I view it as a rational nature—rationality being more than intellectuality, although I cannot show that here—then the threat is that of history, the sphere of the contingent, the sway of something alien.

The fact that I stand in a living history and tradition means that certain values and norms posit themselves as self-evident. To take examples from a different area than that found in Lessing, one might say that I perhaps live under a monarchy and think that there is no other social order than the feudal system. Or perhaps I live in the Communist bloc and think that dialectical materialism is the self-evident axiom of every scientific view of the world.

These are not my own convictions. I myself did not invent them. They are not the superstructure of my own existence. Something else is thinking through me. Alien values and impulses have found a beach-head on the terrain of my I. Yet even though I am constantly directed from outside, I think that I am moving under my own steam in the direction that I myself have chosen.

This is why history with its imported values is a heteronomous entity which threatens to overwhelm my own nature. I have to wrestle with it. I have to mark myself off from it in order to be myself. It is for me a provocation, a maieutic challenge, which forces me either to find myself or to lose myself wholly in it. (In his early *Vom Nutzen und Nachteil der Historie* Nietzsche classically describes this wrestling with history.)

C. HISTORY AS THREAT

For Lessing this problem of an external history which robs us of the self is of existential urgency. It leads him to question what he has received as the Christian tradition. It is easy to see why.

The Christian message has the structure of an account. The Bible is a book of history which tells us about events, about divine messages ("Thus saith the Lord"), about human deeds, about miracles of healing, about the forgiveness of sins and the raising of the dead.

How far is it permissible for me to receive from historical materials of this kind statements and impulses which are decisive for my existence? This is the question for Lessing, or, rather, this is his life's problem.

First, if as a rational being I am conversant with the maximal degree of certainty, i.e., that of logical judgments, can I be content with the dubious certainty of a purely historical account? Can I base my existence on records of the supposed resurrection of a Son of God which are not subject to any final control?

When it is a matter of the ultimate basis of my existence, my destiny, I have to act absolutely. But does not this need to act absolutely stand in contradiction with the very relative certainty that is all that historical accounts of what is alleged to have happened can give me?

The certainty that can be reached in this field is limited by three decisive elements and seems to run contrary to the unconditional certainty that I need in matters of belief. (a) Historical certainty is limited because it does not come from my own rational entelechy but is imported as the statements of others who tell me about the miracles. (b) As distinct from mathematical propositions or rational truths, historical certainty means approximation and can have at best only the rank of probability. (c) Finally (and in this regard Ernst Troeltsch pressed Lessing's questioning to its extreme limit), if something is to be historically verifiable and therefore to be certain to me, it must satisfy the criteria of analogy, causality, and immanence: of analogy inasmuch as there is nothing unique in history which might not in principle occur elsewhere; of causality inasmuch as we cannot conceive of any event without a cause; and of immanence inasmuch as our consciousness is unable to find a place for events which are radically outside the objectifiable nexus of occurrence. In this light, however, what is presented to me as the historical basis of Christian truth escapes all possible verifiability. The resurrection of Christ, the axis of Christian dogma, is without analogy. It is unique. It belongs to no causal nexus. It cannot be fitted into the immanent nexus of events.

Lessing draws attention to his startling difficulty, which brings everything into question, in his famous thesis that accidental truths of history cannot be the basis for necessary truths of reason. We need to see how radical his question is.

Here, then, is the first and epistemological part of Lessing's question concerning the relation between the human self and history. But the question has also a second part.

Even if belief might arise out of historical records, can it become my own conviction? Will it not be merely the repeating of what others have believed before me? (As we have seen, Alexander Schweizer in the last century stated that whereas our fathers confessed their faith, theologians are often devoting all their efforts to believing their fathers' faith. They do not fulfil their own existence with their faith. They are creeping into the existence of others. They are then pretending that they are making a confession, an original confession.) This is the second and existential part of the question.

The two parts of the threat that the encounter with history poses merge into one another and achieve their greatest force when Christianity is the history that encounters us. I might illustrate the twofold threat from the work *Über den Beweis des Geistes und der Kraft* (1777; ET *On the Proof of the Spirit and of Power*, in *Lessing's Theological Writings*, pp. 51-56). Miracles are one thing when we have the chance to see and test them for ourselves and quite another when we only know historically that others saw and tested them. Is not this incontestable? What is the objection to it? If I had lived in Christ's day, I would have seen the prophecies fulfilled in his own person. If I had seen him work miracles, I would have had no reason to doubt that they were real miracles. I would have had such confidence in this remarkable man that I would willingly have subjected my own understanding to his, trusting him in all the things in which undoubted experiences did not happen to him. But accounts of fulfilled prophecies are not themselves fulfilled prophecies, nor are accounts of miracles themselves miracles. Fulfilled prophecies and miracles that I see have a direct effect; accounts of them work only through a medium that robs them of their force.

We see from this that Lessing's distinction between the accidental truth of history and the necessary truth of reason has a more radical meaning and seriousness than we customarily think when we talk about the Enlightenment and the dominion of an insipid rationalism. To be sure, we cannot as Christians accept his saying about the timeless truth of reason. As a thesis his saying is an impossible description of what Christian faith has always meant.

But how about the saying as an antithesis to the accidental truth of history? More precisely, Lessing's question to us is this: Does not Christianity in fact degenerate, is it not affected in substance, when it is made to depend on the letter of historical narratives (for then it no longer lives by trust in the truth, but becomes historical belief, a feverish acceptance of historical facts, which can be maintained only by a constant sacrifice of the intellect and the conscience)?

D. THE MISTAKE OF ORTHODOXY: FALSE ASSURANCES

At this point Lessing hits indeed on the wound of orthodoxy as it meets him in the very respectable form of Goeze, the leading minister of Hamburg. A theology that is tied to historical belief unavoidably degenerates because it has to focus all its forces on saving the historical letter without regard for the loss incurred, namely, the loss of intellectual integrity. It has to become feverishly apologetic.

Recent theological history offers an illustration and confirms what Lessing foresaw. We need only think of the apologetics of the positive theology of the turn of the century, which thinks that the faith stands or falls with whether or not the four Evangelists wrote the Gospels ascribed to them and attempts with truly deluded energy to prove that the disciple John wrote the Fourth Gospel. One need only think of theology's fear of "legend" and of the resultant efforts to save the faith by historical constructions and forced historicizing.

We note the same apologetic feverishness in the relationship between orthodoxy and natural science, e.g., in the attempt to make the scientific theory of descent less threatening by using dilettante biological arguments to establish gaps in the continuity of evolution from animals to humans and rejoicing at every such gap as though it saved the biblical story of creation.

If the promise of faith is true, Lessing reminds theology that hell will not prevail against either him or the community of faith, and if the hell of historical and scientific temptation cannot prevail, then it is undoubtedly unbelief to try to gain the victory over this hell, i.e., to try to establish the historical foundations of the faith with force, feverishly, and in a way that is intellectually dishonest.

Fundamentally, Lessing accuses Goeze of inauthenticity and unbelief along these lines. He does not simply play off reason against faith but a faith that is responsible to reason against unbelief. This is, it seems to me, an astounding situation. Lessing is protecting faith and not reason. He is fighting the pastor of St. Katherine's on the ground of his own presuppositions. Goeze should not merely take note of this; he should be ashamed. To be inconsistent with one's own presuppositions is scandalous. Those who have the promise of their divine teacher that the gates of hell will not prevail against his church should be ashamed. They should simply believe that that can happen only if they themselves prevail against the gates of hell. Lessing sees unbelief when hell, in this case the historical assault, becomes a counterfront for human enterprises and tactical evasions. A rescue operation is then mounted for an impotent God. On another occasion Lessing asks when people will stop suspending all eternity on a spider's thread, i.e., on such evasions. When will they stop basing the unconditionality of faith on what is conditioned? I know of no place where Lessing is closer to the issues which have been with us since the time of Troeltsch, Kähler, Barth, and Bultmann.

The certainty of faith is not menaced by historical criticism but by the search for false assurances. You fools, Lessing tells Goeze and those like him, who try to ban the stormy wind from nature because here it drives a ship on to a sandbank and there it smashes it on a cliff. You hypocrites, we know you. You are not concerned about the unfortunate ships but about your little garden, about your own little comfort and pleasure. That bad wind. Here it has taken the roof off your summer house and there it has badly shaken your full branches. There it has overturned your costly orangery in seven earthen pots. What do you care what good the same wind does in nature in other places? Could it not do it without damaging your own little garden? Why did it not blow on past your fences?

The storm wind of historical criticism, the offensive of honesty against the accidental truths of history, has also its good side, thinks

Lessing. It is creative. It brings healing to those who dare put themselves in the storm. It may mean destruction for the great armada of orthodoxy, i.e., the concrete form of clerically and historically self-assured Christianity. But those who blame the wind and seek its lee side only show thereby that they pander to a secret pragmatic desire to protect and preserve their faith like a nature reserve. This private concern of a handy and practical Christianity, however, is not the foundation of truth on which alone faith can be built. On this slime, even though it might contain some grains of gold, our neighbors boldly and defiantly place the whole building of their faith.

What gives me final certainty has to be my own personal, subjective possession. It has to be "appropriated" by me. It has to be *my* truth. What is assured and told me from outside, and thus stays within the confines of the contingent, can never be the basis of my certainty, faith, or eternal destiny.

E. LESSING'S CONCEPT OF SUBJECTIVITY

With the question of appropriation we come up against the problem of subjectivity. Modern theology and philosophy, especially in the 19th century, have had two different views of this. If we understand these views, I believe we have in our hands the red thread which will guide us through the labyrinth of this epoch in intellectual history. Lessing's prophetic power in posing problems may be seen clearly in the fact that both views of subjectivity may already be discerned in him.

The first view arises out of the question: Who am I? And how, then, must the truth that I can appropriate look? The answer in Lessing is this: I am a rational being and can base myself neither on authorities nor on irrational contingencies. The opposite of authority is the autonomous understanding and individual insight. The opposite of the contingent is the necessary.

The second view of subjectivity is quite different. It results from the question: What is truth? And how, then, must I act in such a way as to be able to appropriate it? The parable of the ring in Nathan helps us to answer this question.

Exact study can give no objective certainty as to which is the genuine ring. By nature the truth in question is not the content of exact findings but an event that overtakes us. The authentic ring cannot be known materially. A jeweler cannot diagnose it through his magnifying glass or by means of a chemical reaction. The true ring can do something in my life. It can make me agreeable to God and others.

This ability cannot be diagnosed objectively. It may be known only as I am exposed to its effects and cooperate with it, only as I act in a certain way and become something. Objective uncertainty about the genuine ring releases the subjective passion of assurance and provokes action.

The answer to the question of truth in the second form of subjectivity is thus as follows: what is at issue is existential, not objective, truth. I myself have to be involved. I have to relate to it with passionate inwardness if I am to appropriate it.

The result of the first view is that Christianity is assimilated to the religious and moral subject. In theological history we have here the line that leads to Schleiermacher and Ritschl and beyond, with many variations. At work is the ontological and epistemological discovery of the subject as it may be seen in different ways in Descartes and Kant. Lessing is the mediator between the philosophical forms of this understanding and its theological application in which Christianity is assimilated to the sphere of human understanding.

The result of the second view is worked out by Kierkegaard. Christian truth, he argues, is of a very specific quality. It does not consist of dogmatic propositions that I can understand or that I have to regard as true. It consists of a person who says of himself: "I am the truth," and that I have to trust. There is an infinitely qualitative difference between a proposition and a person. This may be seen in the fact that they claim our subjectivity in very different ways.

A proposition claims universal validity. This means that subjectivity is interchangeable for it. It transcends love, hate, and passion. It does not demand action or cooperation from me. In the strict sense objectivity means no inwardness. In a person, however, the truth is quite different. Everything depends here on my attitude of love and trust or of hate.

Subjectivity, then, entails inwardness. When I know next to nothing objectively about a person I love (Kierkegaard uses this example in *Training in Christianity*), when I note in a person that I love and trust that he or she does incomprehensible or even dubious things and my objective mind can find no way to resolve the contradiction, then my attitude to that person, my inwardness, reaches its highest level of passion. To the degree that God is not objectively available, whether by a historical revelation or in such a way that I can grasp and see him plainly in the phenomena of providence, the intensity of my faith increases to a supreme level and claims my subjectivity totally. The truth lies, not in the object, but in the relation to it. It does not matter whether something "is" objectively true. What matters is whether I "act" truly toward it, i.e., in a way that is appropriate. What matters is where I "am" in the truth. In Christian terms, this relation is faith.

It is not difficult to see a connection between this form of subjectivity, i.e., the position of Kierkegaard, and the position of Lessing vis-à-vis the truth. The understanding of truth in the parable of the rings manifests the same passion of inwardness and the same objective uncertainty as the truth of faith in Kierkegaard. In both cases the truth is not a valid something that one may state but a process, something that sets itself going in me. The strongest emphasis, then, is not on the fact of the fixable truth that results but on the way that I must go and the commitment that I must make. Thus Lessing says in *Duplik* that our worth does not consist of the truth that we possess or think we possess but of the sincere effort that we make to get at the truth. For it is by the search and not by possession that we develop the powers in which all our maturing perfection consists. Possession make us quiet and slothful and proud. I can place objective knowledge in the archives of my consciousness. I can let it alone, for it carries itself. I do not need to carry it, to be responsible for it, or to accept and confess it.

F. LESSING AS A PRECURSOR OF KIERKEGAARD

Jaspers used the positions of Galileo and Bruno to illustrate these different forms of truth and the different ways of relating to them.

Galileo represented an objective truth. If he denies it and thus evades commitment, this does not harm it, for it does not depend on any subjectivity that identifies itself with it. He can thus recant and still say ironically (at least according to the story): "Yet it still moves." He can do this because he knows that in virtue of the evidence his astronomical truth will establish itself without him, without the advocacy of a confessing subjectivity.

Bruno's panentheistic (philosophical) truth, however, is not objective. It is present in a specific attitude to the world, an existence. Its fate is bound up with this. If the existence denies it, it suffers a mortal wound. It needs the witness who is related to it and represents it. Hence Bruno cannot recant.

Here, then, the truth is set in a committed subjectivity. In another place Lessing says that if God had all truth in his right hand and a constant urge to seek the truth in his left, with the proviso of constant error, and if God told him to choose, then he would humbly ask for what is in the left hand, with the acknowledgment that pure truth is for God alone. We are not to take this saying in a Faustian sense, as is often done. Nor does it wave a white flag of surrender as regards final, unconditional truth. It is simply an indication of the path to take in the search for truth and of the structure of the truth itself. This structure is not an objective system. It is a relationship that defines my connection with the truth.

In an astonishing way this saying may be put word for word into the vocabulary of Kierkegaard. The urge to seek the truth becomes the passion of inwardness. Constant error describes what Kierkegaard means by objective uncertainty. Finally, the assertion that possession of the truth makes us slothful and proud is the exact opposite of what Kierkegaard in the *Concluding Unscientific Postscript* describes as the development of the existential thinker. Objective thinking lays all the emphasis on the result, but subjective thinking stresses the development and ignores the result, partly because this is proper to thinkers as they go their way, and partly because, as they exist, they are constantly developing, as are all those who are not misled into becoming objective and losing their humanity in speculation.

When we look at him in terms of this aspect of his thinking and questioning, do we not see here another Lessing who at least at some points has left the Enlightenment behind him, and who can no longer be understood in deistic categories, but who has to be interpreted in the light of Kierkegaard?

This leads us to our last question, namely, whether his style in the theological works is to be understood in the light of this position. Both Lessing himself and his contemporaries noted and in part deplored the fact that he spoke *gymnastikos* and not *dogmatikos,* that his thinking had no point on which one could fix. I said at the outset that the *dialegesthai* of Lessing's mode of communication may be seen in this. Yet obviously it is not just a methodological problem of communication. The *gymnastikos* is not just a tactical device, and it is more than an expression of the dramatic element in Lessing. His style deems to be determined by his concept of truth. *Gymnazein* means to exercise, to practice. The truth to which one relates, in which one "is," which one does not just "know," has to be practiced. It cannot be stated as a mere result.

Ultimately, then, Lessing is not a preacher or teacher, and certainly not a speculative philosopher. He is a trainer. His concern is the intellectual training in which the truth will emerge, in which it will be shown to be truth. In many respects he is a new Socrates. He has schoolmasterly moments. He can be superficially rationalistic. He is sometimes led astray by the fascinating wealth of his ideas and words. But if he is these things too, he is more than these things. He is a man whose existence everywhere transcends his formulas. He is the prophet and initiator of coming developments. As a prophet, he often does not know what he is saying. He has to be understood in the light of fulfilments that are often greater than himself.

All the things that the ensuing epochs in theology have been thinking about right up to our own time are variations on a theme that Lessing's intellectual ear picked up and that he then spoke about.

We can think further only if we have this theme in our ears. And how can we do so unless we grant a place in our hearts to this most eloquent of all thinkers, and perhaps greet head pastor Goeze with a friendly nod as well.

III. LESSING'S WRESTLING WITH THE RELATION BETWEEN REVELATION AND REASON

A. CONFUSING CONTRADICTIONS

The issue here is not Lessing's character but what he means by Christian truth in his theological works. Was he of the Enlightenment like Reimarus, and hence an esoteric like Reimarus? As we have seen, Reimarus kept to himself his inner liberation, his emigration from the *corpus christianum,* because he thought his contemporaries were not yet ready for what he knew. What was Lessing's real view of Christianity? What lies behind his statement that he is a pagan in his head and a Lutheran Christian in his heart? How can we reconcile the two? Is there any synthesis or must they remain apart?

The core of the problem, it seems to me, is that for Lessing the unconditioned or absolute cannot occur in history because history is an accumulation of the accidental and irrational. Unconditional truth can occur only within the bounds of reason. At its center, however, Christianity is a historical revelation. It consists of an account of events. This source of truth comes under the verdict of the accidental. Hence it offers no access, or at least no direct access, to the unconditioned. Renunciation of historically mediated truth seems to lie behind the statement that the accidental truths of history cannot be the proof of the necessary truths of reason,[1] and that there is here a broad and ugly ditch which he cannot cross no matter how often or how strenuously he tries. If any can help him to do so, he asks and even adjures them to do so; they will deserve a divine reward from him.[2]

Lessing obviously wants to unite history and reason. He wants to maintain his identity as a rational being without giving up the Christian tradition which rests on history. But how can he do this? When

1. Witkowski, 7, 22.
2. Ibid., p. 84.

we look for evidence of the polarity in his writings, we soon feel very helpless, because we are confronted by a list of contradictory statements. We have seen this already in discussing the dialectical and Socratic element in Lessing.

Thus in the anti-Goeze works he expressly keeps his distance from the rational faith of Reimarus and points out that he has never written or publicly said anything that would expose him to the suspicion of being a secret enemy of the Christian religion.[3] Yet there are also statements (eagerly seized on by Goeze), such as we find in the apocryphal discussion with Jacobi, in which he takes a pantheistic line, will hear nothing of transcendental interventions, and wants everything "natural."

Equally confusing is the secondary literature, in which commentators usually say that one of the two standpoints is Lessing's real view, mostly that which brings him close to Reimarus and the Enlightenment. Yet often interpretation oscillates between the two positions. This is explained by the fact, already noted, that his style is *gymnastikos* and not *dogmatikos,* and that he does not express himself in theses. He is a Socratic thinker who holds back his opinion and by provoking others as the devil's advocate starts up trains of thought which finally lead them to his own position.

Another interpretation of the contradictions refers to Lessing's dramatic development which leads him now to one position and now to another. It thus depicts him as a passionate seeker. But this will not do. For one thing, this supposed development would be like the erratic movement of a fever and would have him contradicting himself only a short time after he has made a statement. The two positions may also be found in the same work, and even in his most systematic work, *The Education of the Human Race.* In this work §§ 4 and 77 are hard to reconcile. I will come back to this later.

B. HISTORICAL AND RATIONAL CONCEPTS OF TRUTH AND THEIR LIMITATIONS

I shall try to make headway in this question by advancing the heuristic thesis that revelation and reason have a kind of complementary significance in Lessing. Neither of the two courts—transcendental revelation and immanent reason—can of itself mediate final certainty. The one needs to confirm the other. This is my provisional thesis.

The fact that revelation, which comes in the mode of historicity,

3. Ibid., p. 269.

cannot alone grant final certainty results for Lessing, as for Reimarus, from an epistemological consideration of the degree of certainty that historical insight can afford. I recall once again the central saying in his *Über den Beweis des Geistes und der Kraft*,[4] namely, that miracles that I can see and test with my own eyes are one thing; miracles of which I know only historically that others have seen and tested them are another.

Revelation cannot convey final certainty because it is never imparted to me as the content of actual experience. It is mediated by historical agents. As regards its historical certainty, it is thus subject to only limited control.

The indirectness puts the certainty of the content of revelation on the level of mere probability or approximation. Only with probability can we establish the credibility of the witnesses on which revelation rests.[5]

But how then, as Kähler once asked, can I see any unconditional certainty of faith, or any basis of life in a form of certainty that is conditional in principle? Indeed, in his *Nachlass* Lessing says that the more a religion claims the authority of revelation, and thus tries to establish itself historically, the more suspect it seems to him.[6]

For two reasons, then, the truth of revelation is inferior to the truth of reason. First, it is historically mediated and hence has only a degree of probability. Then the probable fact of revelation, which can be accepted in some way only on authority, is itself accidental or contingent, and hence cannot be convincing a priori. This is why the accidental truths of history fall behind in rational certainty. This is why there is the broad and ugly ditch which Lessing tries in vain to cross.

All this does not mean that Lessing fundamentally disqualifies the truth of history as compared to the truth of reason. He often says that the proofs of the two truths are quite different. If the accidental truths of history cannot be the proof of the truths of reason, the opposite is also true, that the truths of reason are not so convincing or comprehensive that we may present them as truths of revelation and rely on them alone. Revelation contains many truths which are out of the reach of reason and thus force it into a kind of captivity.

If, then, certain truths of reason are self-evident, this is not so when rational speculation reaches after metaphysical truths which are beyond its grasp and which, if they come upon reason from outside as truths of revelation, force it into that captivity. That captivity means the

4. Ibid., pp. 79ff.; ET pp. 51ff.
5. Ibid., 6, 417.
6. Ibid., p. 417.

renunciation of proof, at least in some areas. It means renunciation of the claim to do more than advance postulates in some areas. The lack of evidence, or, positively, the fact that some insights are mere postulates, denotes subjectively a lack of certainty.

C. THE COMPLEMENTARY RELATIONSHIP OF THE TWO CONCEPTS

The truths of reason and revelation, if isolated from one another and considered alone, share in principle the same uncertainty.

As regards reason, its autonomous speculations about immortality can never escape uncertainty or the character of mere postulates. Reason alone cannot find in the inequalities of this life a strict proof for the immortality of the soul or a life hereafter.[7] That inequality, as reason perceives it, can lead at most, as Kant's doctrine of the supreme good explicitly and pregnantly shows, only to the postulate of immortality. Only an analogous content of revelation can give this rational postulate the character of certainty. But on its own this content too remains uncertain. Only when the proclamation of Christ meets the postulate of immortality does the doctrine become trustworthy.[8]

For certainty or trustworthiness, then, a correlation of reason and revelation is needed. Once God is known and this correlation is set up, we can no longer be "untrue" to God by refusing certainty about him or resisting his claim.[9] But if the correlation cannot be set up, the corresponding truths still have only the uncertainty of postulates. This is shown by the doctrine of eternal recurrence at the end of *The Education of the Human Race*. This idea lacks any support in revelation and hence remains in doubt.[10]

We thus conclude that in Lessing revelation and reason are made for one another and form an indissoluble whole. This may be deduced already from the metaphysical axiom of the *Education*, which tells us that the whole history of reason and revelation can be written only with the help of a reason which has been educated and has made progress by means of revelation. The correlation of reason and revelation is not just the theme of the system but its presupposition. It is ultimately the metaphysical background which alone gives certainty to truths that go back to this final correlation.

7. Lessing, *Education of the Human Race*, § 28.
8. Ibid., § 58.
9. Ibid., § 40.
10. Ibid., § 94.

In the context of the problem of certainty, we might finally formulate the correlation as follows. In order to be certain, revelation needs the witness of reason in the form of the possibility and fact of perception. In certain religious and metaphysical fields, reason needs the confirmation of revelation. Final certainties come only in the second part of the history, when truths of revelation are perceived, i.e., when reason illumines revelation and the correlation is achieved. In the first part revelation guided reason, and now reason suddenly lit up revelation.[11]

D. REASON REPRESENTATIVE OF THE TOTAL PERSON AND NOT JUST THE RATIONAL SECTOR

In this illumination of revelation by reason (i.e., by its witness), we have to consider that reason represents the whole person, so that what is at issue is not just the rational side of the content of revelation but the consent of the whole person to it. Thus Lessing can find testimony to the truth of revelation, and therewith subjective certainty, in the fact that we experience it to be true, that we feel blessed in it.[12]

In a remarkable way we see here an important factor in intellectual history. In Lessing the Enlightenment does not merely represent isolated rationality but human existence as a whole, even though the quality of being rational is its main feature.

Reason does not cover all of human existence. There is a surplus element which is at work in achieving certainty of truth. This surplus element is what Lessing calls experience and a feeling of blessedness. He thus anticipates what Schleiermacher later means by religious self-consciousness, namely, the feeling of absolute dependence (again a "feeling"), and what Troeltsch later still calls experience.

For Lessing, too, there are forms of religious certainty which have an—existential—breadth relative to which reason is only a single province, albeit the province in which the capital of humanity is situated. The certainty that the witness of reason, i.e., the consent of the whole person, brings can thus take on unconditional forms and finally be independent of the reliability of historical testimony. It can regard the correlation with history as absolute in virtue of subjective certainty, and hence as no longer in need of any controls. When a paralytic experiences the beneficial shocks of an electric spark, what does it matter whether Nollet or Franklin or neither of them is right?[13]

11. Ibid., § 36.
12. Witkowski, 7, 54.
13. Ibid., p. 54.

This despising of historical counterarguments is due to the thesis that a historical basis may be false, as a mathematical conclusion may be incorrect, and it makes no difference so long as the resultant truth is right.[14] Euclid's geometrical theorem, Lessing thinks, need not be tied to the authority of its author; it is indeed totally independent of this authority. It is thus unnecessary and nonsensical to equate a dispute about the historical basis of a truth with a dispute about the truth itself. The certainty of an evident truth is not affected thereby.[15] This form of direct certainty, which is content with the evidence of the truth without making it dependent on its apocryphal or historical character,[16] points us away to suprahistorical thinking.

Certainty of this kind is also proof against rational objections—a further sign that the witness of reason embraces not merely rational speculation but the consent of the whole person. Even if we could not meet all the objections that reason is so busy in bringing against the Bible, Lessing still thinks that religion would continue unaffected and undisturbed in the hearts of those Christians who have achieved an inner feeling of its essential truths.[17] The witness of feeling has here become the substance of the consent that marks the summit of religious certainty in the correlation of the person and revelation. For Lessing, then, it is no longer vulnerable to rational criticism. Here is a solid rock of truth which can no longer be questioned.

These two forms in which certainty finds a place which is impregnable against historical and rational arguments are the most impressive indication that the truths of reason and revelation are related and complementary.

E. THE ABIDING TRANSCENDENCE OF REVELATION AND ITS RATIONAL CONTENT

The problem of subjective certainty, which is solved by the idea of complementarity, gives rise to the further problem, that of defining the concept of truth that corresponds to this certainty.

At first it seems that this question is easily answered. For since the universally valid truth of reason is the goal of history, it seems that the concept of truth extends to the rational core of the content of revelation as this is determined by its goal.

14. Ibid., p. 85.
15. Cf. *Über den Beweis*, in Witkowski, 7; ET pp. 51ff.
16. Ibid., p. 85.
17. Ibid., p. 185.

It seems all the easier to define this core inasmuch as the truth of revelation, which will later become free-floating rational ideas, must be oriented even now, i.e., in history as it actually takes place, to those superior free-floating ideas. Religion is not true because the Evangelists and apostles taught it; they taught it because it is true. Even what God teaches is not true because he wills to teach it; he teaches it because it is true.[18] As the history of dogma knows, we are reminded here of the debate between the Thomists and Scotists. Lessing belongs on the side of Thomas. At any rate, the rational core emerges plainly. For Lessing characterizes the content of revelation very clearly as the function of a rational idea of truth which can be detached from its historically conditioned and therefore broken form.

The indifference to all historical conditions which is achieved along with final certainty is reflected here in the objectivity of the concept of truth. Thus the problem of this concept seems to be solved. The problem arises only because an objective and timeless entity—the age of the gospel of pure reason which lies beyond history—has entered the brokenness of historical processes. The Lord of history arranged this, Lessing thinks, so that this eternal truth might accommodate itself to history-bound beings, fit in with their epistemological status, and thus stimulate their own active development.

Hence we do not have here the dualism of heterogeneous elements, i.e., of two irreconcilable concepts of truth. In virtue of the rational content of dogma we have instead a continuum between the aeon of the time-bound truth of reason and that of the immediate truth of reason. Even the truth which is implicated in history and which shimmers in the vacillation of its outward forms is transparent to the true point which will manifest itself in history's eschaton. A continuum of truth running across every age is thus unmistakable.

Yet in Lessing this definition of the concept of truth is dubious for the following reasons.

(1) So long as history continues, even in its more advanced stages, the rational core of revelation, the content of timelessly objective truth, is not available with basic universality. If it were, the age of reason could be achieved at once by a simple act of abstraction, and revelation in the full sense would lose its force. Lessing instead speaks cautiously about a great distance which still separates him from the rationality of truth. Factually available truth at every stage of ongoing history is made up of two things, neither of which can be detached from the other by pointing to some overarching rationality.

18. Ibid., p. 214.

The first of these two things is revelation insofar as this is "understood" by religious subjects and perceived by their reason, insofar as they "know" it or reach a felt agreement with it. It is truth of revelation newly changed into truth of reason.

The second thing is the truth of revelation insofar as it goes ahead of reason and transcends it, insofar as it is still "believed" and not yet "known."

For Lessing, then, revelation stands at any point where history has not yet reached its telos, partly beneath and partly above the "water level" of reason. The objectivity of the concept of truth is thus called in question again by the subjectivity of the observer. For since this is entangled in historicity, like the truth that is offered in dogma, the rational core of dogma, whose knowledge alone provides a timelessly objective and continuous concept of truth, cannot really be perceived in terms of this subjectivity.

The place of the observer in history manifests once again the momentous significance of the observer in Lessing's thought. The profound coherence of his system may also be seen here. The very fact of the historical situation which makes the concept of objectively timeless and continuous truth impossible forms at the same time the systematic reason for the division of Lessing's thought into exoteric and esoteric components. The same phenomenon may be seen in both. Both times the act and content of thought are codetermined by the historical subjectivity of the observer, and they are thus inconstant. There can be no thought of any timelessly objective and therefore absolute content in the sphere of history, neither by the establishment of what dogma finally has in view nor by the establishment of the esoteric in an exoteric shell.

(2) The following consideration also makes the setting up of an objective concept of truth very doubtful. For Lessing, as we have seen, revelation as a historical fact, as a truth of history, is always burdened with the character of being "accidental" and singular in contrast to the "necessary" and universal truths of reason. The question of the universal validity of truth is thus made all the more difficult. There is the difficulty already caused by subjectivity, namely, that of seeing the universal in the singular, that which is esoterically future in what which is exoterically present. But there is the even greater difficulty that many singular and accidental truths of history occur together and can all claim to carry universally valid and objective truth. This problem becomes acute when many historical revelations compete with one another and raise a claim to primacy. Formulated with philosophical strictness and sharpness, this is the ultimate problem in the parable of the rings in *Nathan*. I must be content simply to refer to it here.

F. THE DEPENDENCE OF TRUTH ON THE STANDPOINT OF THE OBSERVER

The problem of objective truth in Lessing is thus plain. Within history, in the existential situation, one can talk about objective truth, not bound to time, only insofar as revelation is rational or has become significant in religious feeling. In such cases it is perceived. In such cases, too, the telos posited in revelation is shown not to be reached only at the end of historical evolution. To that extent the age of reason has already dawned, at least in places.

Thus from Lessing's historical standpoint the objective truth-content of the dogma of satisfaction may be seen in isolation from any time-bound factors (although limited in this case by the probing with which the objectivity is met). In the case of other dogmas their release from bondage to time is awaited. The objectivity of their validity has not yet come to light.

Theoretically (i.e., apart from the existential situation), the objective truth of all the contents of revelation is potentially perceptible because the place of their historical relativization is known. We say "potentially" because provisionally only the fact of the objective truth-content can be postulated; the manner is totally unknown. We are not yet a match for the NT. We do not yet perceive all its objective and timelessly valid content. It may thus reflect, Lessing suggests, many truths which we admire as revelations until reason learns to unite them with other truths,[19] i.e., until their objective validity is plain and may be detached from the authority of the form of proclamation as a geometrical theorem is from the authority of Euclid.[20]

Objective, absolute truth exists, then, for those who are capable of theoretical contemplation, for advanced individuals, but only as expectation and question: as expectation inasmuch as the fact may definitely be postulated and may thus be awaited with progress in time; as question inasmuch as the manner in still unknown, for so far reason cannot derive the content of revelation from other truths and unite the two.

In sum, then, the existence of objective truth has the same certainty as that of the age of reason. As yet, however, neither has achieved more than a broken and provisional form.

The relation between the "accidental truth of history" and the "necessary truth of reason," which Lessing investigates in the work aimed at Schumann of Hanover,[21] and which he depicts in his *Education*, is thus connected very radically with his systematic approach.

19. *Education*, § 51.
20. Ibid., § 72.
21. *Über den Beweis* (1777), in Witkowski, 7; ET pp. 51ff.

G. SOLUTION TO THE CONTRADICTIONS: TWO CONCEPTS OF REASON

We have seen that truth has two dimensions for Lessing. There is truth which is timelessly and unconditionally valid. There is also truth which is under the pressure of history, which is found first, in accordance with the various stages of human maturity, in mythical ciphers or figurative language, but which gradually frees itself from its historical carrier and in the eschaton comes out plainly, no longer concealed.

This view of things sheds light on the contradiction which we noted between §§ 4 and 77 of the *Education*. In § 4, as we recall, education (i.e., the transcendental direction of the race, or revelation) gives us nothing that we might not have on our own; it simply gives it more quickly and easily. It anticipates, but does not exceed, our own potential development. In § 77, however, we are told that revelation tells us things about divine and human nature which human reason could never find out for itself. There are in it elements which radically and permanently transcend the sphere of reason. It discloses truths that escape the grasp of reason.

How can we resolve this contradiction? Is there a solution? In dealing with this question, one thing seems to be decisive to me. Reason is understood differently in the two passages. In § 4 it is a universal, transcendental capacity that corresponds to the subject-side of time-free objective truth. It is used in much the same way as Kant uses it when he refers to the critique of reason, i.e., of transcendental, not empirical reason.

Now we have seen that in Lessing the goal of the history of revelation is objective, timeless truth which can be detached from its historical connection with myth. With the same right one might also describe as the goal of history our liberation for the purely transcendental form of reason purified from empirically historical dross. This means that for Lessing the final aim of the historical process is to free the religious content from bondage to historical relations and to set it in the subject and the subject's autonomy. To this extent that which revelation intends and contains is nothing that exceeds reason or that reason cannot reach on its own. Like empirically distorted reason, or reason graded according to historical levels, revelation is simply a popular paraphrase for the Platonic idea of reason.

As regards the timelessly valid outcome of history, reason (the "pupil") is not in any sense below revelation but alongside it and above it. This is why the two are equated in principle in § 4. The equation is justifiable if the transcendental (Platonic) concept of reason underlies it.

On Lessing's own terms the postulate is thus reasonable that left to itself reason would reach the same goal as that to which it is in fact led by its education by revelation. For the goal is finally reason itself in its transcendental immediacy, i.e., as the correlate of the objective truth which is the outcome of history as this is directed to its goal.

But this can only be a postulate, for in the *Education* there is no such thing as a reason that is left to its own devices, i.e., the Platonic idea of reason exists only eschatologically and not in the present. Since reason within history is only historical and not absolute reason or reason as such, the possibility that it will reach the goal when left to itself does not in fact come into consideration. In the form in which it might be left to its own devices it is not reason as such but empirical reason, reason broken by history.

This explains § 77. Whereas § 4 deals purely theoretically with the possibility of an autonomous self-development of reason as such, which does not exist, § 77 deals with the factual or historical impossibility of any such self-development. The inability of reason to arrive on its own at better and more precise concepts of divine and human nature and our human relations with God, or to avoid the aberrations of millions of years of self-development, is connected with the empirically historical form of reason. In practice both individuals and the race have only a quantitatively limited degree of reason and not a form commensurate with the transcendental concept.

It is thus clear that the divergent statements on whether reason can reach the telos of history on its own find their explanation in the dualism of the concepts of reason in Lessing's view of things. If transcendental reason is at issue, then all the goals intended by revelation may be reached in principle by reason alone, since reason, or the objective truth known by it, is the goal of all the ways of revelation. If, however, the historical shadow of the Platonic original of reason is at issue, the limit of all empirical self-development is plain. And since for Lessing reason is primarily a historical concept, since he thinks in terms of the concrete givenness of reason and not its nonhistorical prototype, the deus ex machina of revelation is for him unavoidable if the duality of the two concepts is not to destroy the unity of the meaningful structure of things. Here again, at the very core of his view of the world, we see the enigmatic character of Lessing's thought.

Perhaps the saving act of revelation is itself only a postulate like the deus ex machina which tragedy called in as a postulate or a metaphysical cry for help. Perhaps this very act is no more than the mythical reconciliation of the hopeless duality of being such as the "holy Spinoza" sought elsewhere and tried to find by positing reality in God and the empirical in the timeless rest of substance.

But even if the *Education* is no more than a postulate or cry for help, or a leap with which the aging fighter attempts for the last time to jump across the broad and ugly ditch, the revelation which relaxes the tension makes sense only if it is regarded as transcendent, for the severity of the dualism is revealed by the fact that we happily organized children of nature cannot resolve it and therefore need help from outside.

If, then, we merely have a request or call for revelation, it is still a request or call for a transcendent revelation. Interpret it as we will, we are here at the core of Lessing's thought. If we think we can avoid the problem of transcendence by the methodological devices of exoteric and esoteric thinking, we have not yet looked deeply enough nor penetrated beyond the forecourts of the discussion.

Lessing's "true insight," which his many expositors seek, was a "question," and at root it was very much an "unclarified question." We can discuss only the direction of the question and the provisional answer which Lessing, the seeker, wrung out of himself. The radical openness of the question itself must be respected.

If for a moment we may try to clarify the dark background of thinking which outwardly seems to be crystal clear, it seems to me that Lessing's view of history has three emphases.

First, in Enlightenment fashion Lessing devalues the irrationality of historical life, regarding it as no more than the temporal depiction of timeless ideas. Second, he affirms the irrationality of history when it is viewed as a self-posited image of immanence. But he does not do this in a pure sense, which brings us to the third point: He gives irrational historical life a new teleological reference in terms of the transcendent and assured direction of human reason, which, left to itself, is only empirical reason, and hence *ir-ratio*.

Thus the problem of transcendence, around which all Lessing's metaphysical thinking circles, finds expression in a respect for actual history which resists its rationalistic degradation. We see here that the Enlightenment reaches its limit in the *Education* and will go on at once to pass it.

Even if Lessing reaches this limit only in the posture of a questioner, I do not think we should deny the respect with which he raises the question in this final form, whether or not the question is sincerely meant as such. For we are led on from it to the personal encounter which at the deepest level awaits objective analysis when the subject is religion or a worldview. And here, more strongly than on the first stages of the way, historical analysis realizes that in spite of its desire for exactitude it finally involves pondering and venturing. This is the great surprise when we come to the precise Enlightenment thinker, the fencer of the spirit, the master of cabalism.

IV. CRITICAL SURVEY OF LESSING'S INFLUENCE

Much of what Lessing and his inquiries mean for the history of theology right up to our own day will have emerged already from my attempted interpretation. In conclusion, however, I should like to focus on two important points. The first is the problem of appropriation; the second, the question of the tenability of an idea of truth detached from history.

A. THE PROBLEM OF APPROPRIATION

All Lessing's religiophilosophical inquiries rest on a single premise which becomes dominant with Descartes's *cogito sum* and achieves its first great development in the Enlightenment.

I refer to the discovery of the I as the central point from which to view the world. This is not just a question of perspective. Nor is the issue merely the transcendental ego of Kant which is correlative to all possible experience of the world and objects. The issue is also that of the I in its normative function. What can be meant by this?

In the Enlightenment the I finds itself in its human rank, its possible adulthood. If we respect this rank, we can no longer misuse this I, the bearer of the practical logos in Kant's sense, as the mere means to an end. We cannot make it the object of claims from outside (even though these are the claims of God's commands or some other authorities). Knowing its adulthood, the I has discovered its autonomy, its role as *autos*. In virtue of this autonomy, it faces the question whether it can or should appropriate certain claims or reject them as heteronomous and degrading. Awakened to self-consciousness, the I can no longer let anything have authority over it if it is not to renounce itself and bury its pound of humanity.

Kant alludes to this new situation in his famous essay of 1784, "What Is Enlightenment?"[22] "Enlightenment is man's release from his self-incurred tutelage. The definitions are important. Tutelage is man's inability to make use of his understanding without direction from another. Self-incurred is this tutelage when its cause lies not in lack of reason but in lack of resolution and courage to use it without direction from another. . . . Have courage to use your own reason."[23]

For Kant, then, the problem of immaturity is not a deficiency of intellect or a cognitive weakness or a low intelligence quotient. If it were

22. See "Was ist Aufklärung?" in *Werk-Ausgabe,* ed. W. Weischedel, 11, 53ff.; ET "What Is Enlightenment?" in *The Critique of Practical Reason and Other Writings in Moral Philosophy,* tr. and ed. L. W. Beck (Chicago, 1949), pp. 286-92.
    23. "What Is Enlightenment?," p. 286.

this he surely would not attribute guilt. No, the immature in his sense are those who suppress their power of thought because they are not ready for the venture of being responsible subjects who think for themselves. As Sartre might put it, they will not condemn themselves to freedom.

Thus the main impulse behind the Enlightenment is not the promoting of better knowledge or the raising of intellectual standards. The motive force is ethical. The Enlightenment appeals to the will to be ready for selfhood, for the venture of adulthood. It appeals to the dignity of humanity which cannot permit the suppression of individual responsibility or the rending of the unity of self-consciousness. This unity is in fact shattered if as merchants or scientists we calculate rationally in one dimension of the ego but think uncritically in another (the religious dimension), accepting what we are told, and not allowing our rational nature to function, but negating it.

Kant's point is not that prior to the Enlightenment people knew only what was false or as Christian believers fell into the trap of superstition. They might have reached the truth as Christians. Christian dogma might be true. But how did they handle the truth? They simply used the understanding of others, e.g., the prophets, apostles, or fathers.

Lessing, too, can say that in this way they came into contact with the truth. For the holy scriptures contain the truth even if in cipher and accommodated form.

But those who accept the truth on authority and find it based on a supposed *Deus dixit*, not appropriating it or finding their own truth of reason in such texts, have an alien and depraved relation to the truth even though they possess it objectively.

The point, then, is that the issue is not the truth itself but *how* we find it. The issue is our *relation* to the truth (cf. § I of this chapter and the comparison of Lessing and Kierkegaard).

Truth wants to be a power of conviction. If I am not convinced but only persuaded or led or forced, I have—paradoxically—an untruthful relation to the truth. There is such a thing, and Kierkegaard with his idea of the existential thinker was the great accuser of this untruthful relation to the truth.

The decisive point is made in John's Gospel when it says that only those who *are* of the truth hear the voice of Jesus (which is the voice of the truth, 18:37). What is meant is that only those who follow Jesus, who let the truth be a force in their whole being, come to Jesus and enter into a hermeneutical relation of analogy which enables them to understand the truth, so that it becomes their *own* truth, their *appropriated* truth.

Part of the ethos of those who achieve adulthood or autonomy is that they use their own understanding and thus resist all outside direction, all leading by the hand, all heteronomy.

Neither in Kant nor Lessing does this have to mean the rejection outright of all authority or all authoritative claims; God's voice on Sinai with the Ten Commandments is not discredited in advance. Here again the question is how I receive it. In this respect the rule is that all such claims must pass the censor of our own understanding and receive the stamp of their aptness to be appropriated by us.

But why any authority at all? one might ask. Why not a transition to full and free autonomy? We have seen Lessing's caution at this point. Two things especially hold him back. First, we are not yet at the end of time but as advanced individuals we are still mastering the primer of revelation. Second, it is conceivable that insights might be hidden which reason can never discover on its own.

Luther, who in his own way also protested against authority and knew something of the adulthood of Christians, probably found a more profound answer which hits closer to home today, because we are like children who have burned their fingers and have experienced the bankruptcy of the rationality which is so often demanded. Luther saw to what extent reason is directed by fear and hope. He saw that it often simply produces arguments to show that fear is unfounded and hope well-founded. This insight stands behind his often misunderstood saying that reason is a "harlot." His point is simply that reason offers the body of its arguments to its inferiors (the forces of fear and hope). One cannot trust a variable reason of this kind (Lessing's concrete, historical reason) without being led astray. In a modified sense Luther might thus have adopted Kant's view that reason must be brought to understanding.

The basic ethical problem of the Enlightenment, as we have seen it also and especially in Lessing, is thus plain. It is the problem of the appropriation of the truth, and therefore of the relation to it. If I do not appropriate things that I regard as true, I divide my consciousness and destroy its unity. Lessing alludes to this when he says that he is a pagan in his head and a Lutheran Christian in his heart.

The point of Lessing's theology, and also of Schleiermacher's, is the counteracting of this division. Schleiermacher is concerned about the effect of orthodoxy on the more highly educated. Those who are schooled in natural science, who are won over by the self-enclosed economy of natural forces, have to suppress all this, and hence make a split, if they want to believe in miracles in the orthodox sense. If they refuse to do this, they necessarily become irreligious, despisers of religion. Schleiermacher's passionate concern is to reconcile religion with the critical modern consciousness. He tries to do this by interpreting religion as an independent content of the consciousness side by side with contents from the academic world.

But here a further problem arises, for the adult understanding immediately wants to be the criterion or censor. It at once becomes normative. This transition can take place in such a way that I say: All that I can honestly appropriate must be rational, for I am a rational being. Logically, everything nonrational must be excluded. Ultimately, all that is left is the flat rationalism of moral teaching that I can produce for myself. Precisely because I can produce it for myself, I finally do not need the rational side of the biblical message anymore. I need not import what I can produce for myself. There is thus a definitive parting from everything that has previously claimed to be revelation. Is not this parting from positive religion intimated already in *Nathan the Wise*?

This transition from criterion to norm continues up to our own day, e.g., in Bultmann's existential interpretation of the Bible, as I have pointed out already. We see here the same principle even if the normative court is no longer reason in Lessing's sense but existence in the modern sense. There can be truth for me in the biblical texts, Bultmann thinks, only if its significance is apparent to me. This is an existential significance. Only that is significant for me which claims me at the basis of my existence, which has reference, e.g., to my anxiety, my suffering from finitude, my mortality, my burdening with the question of meaning, my false trust in this world. Only thus is the kerygma relevant. Only thus does it qualify as kerygma. The criterion of relevance is my inner (existential) situation.

We see at once how this criterion at once takes on normative rank. Whatever cannot be interpreted existentially, e.g., the cultural precepts or miracle stories of the OT, is definitively denied kerygmatic rank.

We can see this in the Enlightenment inquiries that are found in Lessing. These trigger real problems even if in a dubious way. We cannot escape the questions. At issue is the appropriation of Christian materials in a changing consciousness, in a consciousness which is becoming increasingly critical.

We now turn to the second problem which arises as we consider the influence of Lessing.

B. THE QUESTION OF THE TENABILITY OF AN IDEA OF TRUTH DETACHED FROM HISTORY

By this "idea of truth" I mean the result of a constantly seen process of abstraction, i.e., of the attempt to establish certain Christian "principles" with no dogmatic or historical connection, e.g., such principles as love or hope (cf. Ernst Bloch). In this process one obviously trusts in the self-evident nature of these principles.

Because they are self-evident, no appeal to a basis in salvation history is needed any longer. The Johannine statement that God so loved the world that he gave his only begotten Son (3:16) is superfluous. It bases love on the Christ event. But the principle of love, like Nathan's direction to be agreeable to God and others, is obvious without any such appeal. It needs no historical basis.

This development seems to be illuminating, but I should like to bring an objection which arises out of historical study of the liberation. When Christian principles are distilled out in this way, they are no longer present *as such* but usually have an ideological framework into which they are integrated.

Marxism is a sufficient example. The humanitarian ideas of the young Marx are undoubtedly a secularizing of the Christian concept of love and humanity, but these are at once integrated into the system of historical materialism.

Thus the so-called Christian principles are not merely detached from their historical origin; they are also set in another system of coordinates. They are never "naked," as it were, but in some way they are at once ideologically clothed.

We can see this process close up in the sixties and seventies. I am thinking of the social and political passions of young Christians, of their championing of oppressed racial, social, and religious minorities, of their passionate protest against unjust structures. A Christian motive of love undoubtedly served as the starting point. But as things developed this faded more and more into the background and evaporated into a general humanitarian impulse. Here again—we need only think of the student groups of the last decade—the humanitarian principle was filled out at once ideologically. The Christian motive was put in a Marxist setting. Student societies became political clubs. In his own time, when the age of ideology had hardly dawned, Lessing could not see that an age of pure reason would never come but that even in the future the truth of reason would find clothing, not now mythical clothing, as in the first stages of the education of the human race, but ideological clothing of various kinds.

A further observation seems to me to be essential in this context. When Christianity is freed from dogma and supposedly reduced to basic ideas, at first it is usually greeted with joy by contemporaries. The Christian "idea" of love suits heart and mind and reason. It is a welcome guest. It is recognized and hailed as a kindred spirit. It now enters without the baggage of dogma. Christianity now seems to conform to the age. It deserves to be called "modern."

But this readiness to find a conformist and dogma-free Christianity acceptable is fleeting. People soon see that what is being said by it is known already. Pleasure in this self-confirmation does not last long.

The question quickly arises: Why should we be told in this alien dogmatic form something that we can derive more naturally and easily from the depths of our own consciousness?

This, then, is the end of a development which may be seen today and which in theology does not just take up the questions of its day and relate its message to them (which is valid) but dissolves its message in these questions and reduces itself to the mere representative of ideas that conform to the day. In doing this it not only exposes itself to secularization but integrates itself into this and in so doing loses itself. This is the decisive question which we children of the 20th century, who have burned our fingers, have to put to Lessing, the child of the still naive 18th century.

In this light many problems of secularization take on a new look. Once the real motor is turned off—the saving event reported in the NT—the wheels of a Christian culture that it has set in motion may continue to roll for a time. But the movement will gradually slow down. Finally, human activism, especially in the form of ideological urges, will see to it that the wheels keep on turning, unless we go back to the power of the event which initially started the movement.

Lessing had perhaps some inkling of this final consequence and did not shrink from it. How else can we explain the fact that as a more able individual stamping and glowing on the last page of the primer,[24] he not only took care not to let his weaker fellow-students notice what he was beginning to see; he also refused to dismiss altogether what he had experienced as revelation or to believe it to be compromised as mere projection in Feuerbach's sense. He continues the inner dialogue between his natural and his spiritual self, between the Christian who is tied to history and the advocate of a gospel of reason.

He thus remains in contradictory tension between the historical basis of revelation and an emancipating truth of reason. In all the heat of controversy (to which I have already drawn attention) he can thus greet his main theological adversary, chief pastor Goeze, respectfully from afar, even though the greeting is essentially a challenge.

Lessing's answers, his various evasions when pressed, may seem dubious to us today and time-bound in many respects. But his questions will always be with us.

We can never grow out of these questions. We can only grow into them. They are above all the question whether we realize what faith means, and whether we dare to appropriate what it means.

24. Lessing, *Education*, § 68.

CHAPTER 6

J. S. Semler: The Question of the Conditioning of Revelation by History

Bibliography. Primary Works: "Einführung" to the 3 volumes of S. J. Baumgarten, *Evangelische Glaubenslehre*, vol. I (1759, quoted as Baumgarten); *Abhandlung von freier Untersuchung des Kanon*, 4 vols. (1771-75, quoted as *Kanon*); *Versuch einer freieren theologischen Lehrart* (1777, quoted as *Lehrart*); *Über historische, gesellschaftliche und moralische Religion der Christen* (1786, quoted as *Religion*); *Lebensbeschreibung*, 2 parts (1781-82, quoted as *Leben*); *Beantwortung der Fragmente eines Ungenannten* (1779, quoted as *Fragmente*); *Letztes Glaubensbekenntnis über natürliche und christliche Religion*, ed. C. G. Schütz (1792, quoted as *Glaubensbekenntnis*).

Secondary Works: K. Aner, *Die Theologie der Lessingzeit* (1929); E. Hirsch, *Geschichte der neueren evangelischen Theologie*, IV (1952), chap. 37; G. Hornig, *Die Anfänge der historisch-kritischen Theologie* (1961); H.-J. Kraus, *Geschichte der historisch-kritischen Erforschung des AT* (1956), pp. 93-102; W. G. Kümmel, *The New Testament: The History of the Investigation of Its Problems* (Nashville, 1972), pp. 62-69; C. Mirbt, "Semler," *RE*, 3rd ed., 18, 203-9; A. Schweitzer, *The Quest of the Historical Jesus* (1952), pp. 15ff.; L. Zscharnack, *Lessing und Semler* (1905).

I. BIOGRAPHY

Semler was born in 1725 and died in 1791, and was thus a contemporary of Lessing. From early youth he gave himself to academic study and had an unusual memory. His father, once a Dutch preacher and later archdeacon in Saalfeld, had a lively theological interest and was at odds with the pietism of the day. But for pragmatic reasons he forced himself and his son to participate in the movement. The impulsive and non-academic thrust of pietism as the young Semler encountered it in Saalfeld, especially in devotional meetings, produced a strong aversion which would be with him all his life and which simply stimulated his intellectual interest. He tells us about it in his autobiography. He went to Halle in 1743, and liberation came when he met his great teacher S. J. Baumgarten, whose follower he became and whose dogmatics he later edited with an introduction by himself which set forth his own position. He could not always remain a pupil, however, although he continued to honor Baumgarten so long as he lived, being called to Halle through his influence in 1752, and working alongside him as a colleague. Later he moved increasingly away from the theological traditions that Baumgarten had espoused. In particular he engaged in the historical, nondogmatic canon criticism which became his main work. But he accomplished his breakthrough, not with revolutionary élan, but with timidity and hesitation, spending many anxious hours over the conflict between his own initial studies and so much theological literature.[1] His theological interests embraced almost every discipline in the faculty. Even though the emphasis lay on OT and NT research, he also read church history, dogmatics, and ethics. A list of his works, drawn up by J. G. Eichhorn shortly after his death,[2] carries 173 independent publications.

II. SEMLER'S BREAKTHROUGH TO NEW HERMENEUTICAL QUESTIONS: THE CRITERIA OF UNDERSTANDING

All the essential questions that are found in Lessing occur in Semler as well. They develop here out of difficult historical investigations of the biblical text, and their systematic consequences are unfolded. We thus have a conjunction of a historical approach, the controlling or resultant hermeneutical questions, and powerful systematic reflection which raises the problems to the level of discussions of principle, especially regarding the question of biblical revelation and the needed criteria of understanding. All this tempts us somewhat boldly to call Semler the Bultmann of the 18th century. In fact, the decisive questions and theses of the one

---

1. *Leben*, II, 314.
2. Eichhorn, *Allgemeine Bibliothek der biblischen Literatur,* V (1793), 184ff.

may also be found in the other. The analogy is astonishing, and it is surprising that no one so far seems to have noticed it, not even Bultmann himself.[3] The expression *systematic reflection* should not be taken to imply that Semler formally espoused a system. He was hardly in a position to do so. Only occasionally in his main work can he follow progressive trains of thought; most of the work is polemical. His style is not marked by systematic clarity; it is often obscure and requires repeated reading.[4] Yet he has systematic significance inasmuch as he draws basic inferences from his historical studies and uses these as materials for a doctrine of the historical conditioning of revelation—a doctrine which represents a radical breakthrough as compared with orthodoxy, pietism, or the Enlightenment religion of reason. Semler is thus the father of modern biblical criticism if not of hermeneutics in general.

For Semler a historical understanding of the canon is the basic condition of all understanding. For the orthodoxy of the time this is a revolutionary thesis. This starting point makes it plain that he rejects a verbal inspiration which sees the Bible as falling direct from heaven. In place of this, and without completely ruling out inspiration, he sets up the antithesis that God as the author of revelation works in the horizontal dimension of historical development. But in this case the canon can no longer be regarded as a homogeneous whole whose parts are all equally inspired and which therefore offers a dogmatic system with no contradictions. The canon must be seen as the product of a process in which many historical factors are at work. Its views and expressions are temporal and historical. It includes mythical and social and many other matters which form the husk around the true kernel of revelation.

There thus arises at once the task of distinguishing husk and kernel so as not mistakenly to make what is secondary into articles of faith. What is really binding, the kernel, must be discovered. But making the differentiation cannot be left to the instinct or taste of Bible students. More valid hermeneutical criteria are needed which all can use.

These criteria can be found only on one condition, namely, that the biblical authors envisaged and presupposed rational readers and hearers of holy scripture. This is incontestable. For otherwise we could have no possibility of distinguishing a true divine revelation from a

3. Nor is it perceived in the book by C. Hartlich and W. Sachs, *Der Ursprung des Mythosbegriffs in der modernen Bibelwissenschaft* (1952), though this work deals with Semler. So far as I can see, Semler is not mentioned in the basic work of W. Schmithals, *An Introduction to the Theology of Rudolf Bultmann* (Minneapolis, 1968).

4. E. Hirsch complains that his was the worst German that any German of intellectual rank ever wrote (*Geschichte*, p. 50).

purely alleged one. We would be groping blindly and helplessly between what is authentic and what is inauthentic. We would accept as genuine coinage everything that is set forth in the name of a *Deus dixit*. Not only that, but if the biblical revelation did not presuppose reason, and hence the use of rational criteria by its recipients, we would not be able to enter into a moral relation with it and therefore to confess it with mature responsibility. Many other peoples as well as Christians could also claim a true and authentic divine revelation and we would have no arguments against such claims. We would then be in danger of causing our Bible to be confused with some other book. The essential condition that revelation banks on rational readers also presupposes, however, that God's self-revelation in holy scripture can never contradict what we can discover by the use of reason and our natural intellectual powers.[5]

When Semler regards rational beings with their criteria as the subjects of the biblical revelation, we may see here a rationalistic Enlightenment element and hence a historically conditioned factor. This is true. Yet far more vital is the fact that another motif is present here which even within a rationalistic mode of thought points far beyond a narrow rationalism to an ethical humanism. For if revelation were bound up with the demand that we should dispense with the other bases of human knowledge, from the use of the senses to more general cognition, this would mean no less than that we would cease to be the true subjects of our own ideas.[6]

Here, then, is the real nerve of the argument. For here is an ethical appeal to our view of humanity. We have to be people who can appropriate the truth of texts as responsible subjects. The reader or hearer must be an *autonomos*. For this reason, we have to seek criteria that will enable us to make a responsible judgment about the truth enclosed in the texts and separate it from the time-bound and therefore merely relative mode of statement. The only alternative is to accept every biblical saying piecemeal as the Word of God and thus to degrade ourselves into mere objects of a canonical claim, i.e., to surrender the dignity of being subjects as rational beings. This would carry with it even greater damage, for it would split us into a rational part, which has to be violently cut out, and another part which irrationally and uncritically lets itself be forced into slavish obedience and mere functioning.

We have seen already, not least in Lessing, how fervently the Enlightenment championed at this point the inviolability of humanity. But we then have to be ready to relativize the rational-Enlightenment

5. Baumgarten, pp. 39-40.
6. Ibid., pp. 36-37.

character of the criterion of reason. This is only the time-bound cipher for a much deeper problem which affects all subsequent ages, namely, that of differentiating the Bible and the Word of God, the eternal and the time-bound, the content and the form, or, if one will, the kerygma and its mythical garb.

This attempted differentiation is still the task even if other criteria are used instead of the *ratio* of the Enlightenment, e.g., the concept of existence, as in Bultmann. The decisive thing for Semler, and it will remain decisive in the future, is that the connection between Christianity and humanity should not be broken and that there should be no break with existence and consciousness in the achieving of faith. As special revelation, the Bible seeks to make Christians, not people. But Christians are still people, and they can now be so more fully. They are not prevented from being philosophers, jurists, scholars, or artists any more than they cease to eat and drink, to have bodily needs, and to have rights and obligations over against the others with whom they are associated.[7]

Semler lays much stress on the fact—a first sign of distinction from Reimarus—that his focus on humanity and the criteria of reason cannot mean the subjecting of scripture to reason. We do not make physics God's overlord when, in order to live, we follow the laws of the body and do not expect daily exceptions from God because he sustains us. Similarly, we lay claim to reason in physics, astronomy, history, geography, and psychology without doing violence to God. We are not subjecting God to reason; we are recognizing the task of distinguishing from the things that we know those things which we cannot perceive or know only by revelation.[8]

We have expounded Semler's theological interest and also his human interest in hermeneutical criteria. These criteria are demanded theologically by the fact that we must distinguish the Bible and God's Word for the sake of the dignity of the Word. They are necessary on the human level so as to protect the dignity of the human subject from being destroyed. We may add that this subjective dignity is regarded as a pledge from God.

7. Ibid., pp. 52-53. Semler goes on to explain that Christians cannot possibly be content with the Bible alone. Their humanity demands that they consult natural law and secular wisdom. It is irrational and fantastic pietistically to regard schools as useless institutions, as human inventions and baubles.

8. Baumgarten, p. 48.

II. SURVEY OF SEMLER'S INFLUENCE

With this question of criteria of exposition and the resultant distinction between what is binding and what is not binding in the text, Semler becomes the father of modern hermeneutics. But his influence depends on a further insight into the process of understanding.

According to Semler, not merely subjective norms like the criterion of reason are essential in hermeneutics, in the act of understanding, but also conditions laid down by the object, i.e., the text. Hermeneutics has first to consider what is meant. What is the theme? The approach to understanding depends on a prior understanding of what is there. It makes a great difference whether we are dealing with the understanding of a religious kerygma, a historical account of Napoleon, or a scientific fact. The theme at issue determines the choice of hermeneutical categories. We have to understand this basic hermeneutical fact if we are to assess the true significance of Semler. When we consider the historical situation in which he broke through to this insight, his achievement is most impressive.

Two things may cause us to lose sight of the hermeneutical problem, and both these things were present in the intellectual milieu in which Semler grew up and lived.

The first is when the subject, as a rational being, is absolutized. In this case I hear in a kerygmatic text only that which I may make my own, only that which confirms me, only that which I know already and which objectifies rational certainties. What does not do this is rejected as unacceptable. To make the distinction, no hermeneutical principles are required. The self-confirmation of reason and the shock of what is against reason are both spontaneous. They are immediately evident in virtue of the self-certainty of absolutized reason.

How self-evident and automatic this rationalistic encounter with the text may be we can see in Reimarus. Here everything is clear from the very first. As if centrifugally, what is rational is separated from superstition. Nowhere is there any attempt at a deeper understanding. Nowhere is the question asked how the meaning is to be differentiated from the medium. The naive and banal result of the interpretation of the text by Reimarus shows that to absolutize the rational subject nips hermeneutical reflection in the bud, if it ever reaches that point.

The objection to absolutizing of the subject need not be brought only against rationalism. It applies to many types of pietists (not all, but certainly those that aroused such a strong aversion in the young Semler). In this case pious subjectivity hears in the texts only that which strengthens itself. It does not hear by way of the times things that are alien to it.

It ignores the times. It does not ask what the biblical author meant in his own time. It does not ask about the recipients who helped to determine the form of his proclamation.

The second thing which obscures the hermeneutical problem is present when the object, i.e., the text that has to be expounded, is absolutized. The orthodox doctrine of inspiration is the classical instance of this. Here every text is accepted piecemeal as God's Word. No longer, or not yet, can there be any hermeneutical discussion leading to the question: What is the text saying to me, and where does it not speak? What did it say to its first recipients? What process is necessary to see which items out of the mass of what is time-bound apply to the present?

The hermeneutical question arises only when the subject and object, the one who seeks to understand and that which is to be understood, are neither of them absolutized but are brought into relation and seen in tension. This happens when we start out from the point that the two situations are different and yet are bound together by a third factor. By way of example, we might cite the two creation stories in Genesis. Modern readers feel at some distance from these. They are strange inasmuch as they combine a kerygmatic statement with an ancient view of things. The earth is solid ground between the lower and upper waters (Gen. 1:6). The post-Copernican world differs radically from this cosmological medium. Even today some semi-educated persons still appeal triumphantly to the outmoded thinking of the stories, appealing to science, which has refuted it all. This shows how urgent is the task of distinguishing between the point of the message and the time-bound nature of the medium in these accounts. Apart from this task we are forced—to put it brutally—*either* to believe the ancient cosmology along with the kerygma, swallowing it even though we know better, *or* to reject the whole message in the name of our advanced cosmological knowledge.

In neither case is appropriation possible. In the former case it is impossible for us to be the true subject of our beliefs. We hold them as the objects of some other authority. To accept them we have to renounce our autonomy and thereby block the possibility of appropriation. In the second case appropriation is impossible because we set aside the whole story ostensibly in the name of science.

The fact of the differing situations of biblical proclamation on the one side and its recipients on the other poses the task of hermeneutics. Hermeneutics has first to take this difference seriously and for this reason it has to investigate the past situation: Who is speaking here and to whom? What medium is available? In the sense mentioned it must then distinguish between the point of the statement and the means of expression. The leading question in this case is as follows: What applies directly to me within the historical framework? What is relevant to me?

This question presupposes that as a modern reader I myself become the subject of my inquiry. It implies that I am clear as to who the "I" is to whom the message is relevant.

The hermeneutical question thus involves not merely the past situation but also *my* situation, *my* view of humanity. In this respect Semler reminds us of the historical framework in which he thinks. This is naturally the rationalistic and ethical framework of the Enlightenment.

To understand him aright, then, we have to distinguish between the message and the medium in him too. It would be a mistake to equate these and hence to dismiss him as merely a man of the Enlightenment. We need to handle him as we do the Bible and to see that in the time-bound medium he offers a hermeneutic that transcends his time and raises questions that are directly relevant to us today. Like the biblical authors whom he interprets, he accommodates himself to his contemporaries. But to interpret him today, we must try to accommodate him to us.

The hermeneutical problem points us in three directions. It investigates the situation of the biblical authors. It investigates that of the interpreter (whether Semler, Luther, Aquinas, or other past expositors). It then investigates our own situation as we try to understand the Bible and its expositors, the sources of revelation and the fathers who interpret it.

We thus arrive at a question which we shall now discuss, and before which Semler himself places us.

IV. ACCOMMODATION TO THE RECIPIENTS OF PROCLAMATION

In talking about the time-bound character of the biblical authors, we must be on guard against a relativism which controls the biblical statements through their horizontal setting and which sees them evaporating in this horizontal element. A kerygmatic content of unconditional rank is in no way affected by our understanding of the medium as time-bound and the resultant distinction of kernel and husk. For Semler the works are time-bound because the authors have to accommodate themselves to the notions of their contemporaries. Goethe, in obvious agreement, points out that it has been held for a long time that God is guided by human modes of thoughts and powers of understanding, that those who were inspired by the Spirit did not lose their character or individuality, and that Amos the herdsman did not speak in the same way as Isaiah, who was supposedly a prince.[9]

To be clear about the point, which is, of course, hermeneutically decisive, one has thus to consider whom the authors are addressing. As Semler sees it, one can understand the OT only if one remembers that it was written for Jews. In Matthew one must bear in mind that it was written for Jews outside Palestine, in John that it was directed to Christians of Greek culture. People at different religious stages and of different ideas were in view. Paul broke away most fully from the Jewish spirit which is elsewhere so much pandered to. He could thus make Christianity into a world religion. The stories of Esther and Samson are crass examples of Judaizing in the OT, which also uses mythical notions.[10]

The distinction between the binding content and the relativizing vessel comes to a climax when Semler applies it just as rigorously to the situation of modern hearers and readers. Quite early he came to see the difference between religion and theology.[11] We have to distinguish between public and private religion. By the former Semler means the complex of all church dogmatics as laid down in the confessional writings and reflected in contemporary theology. This complex, too, compels us to differentiate message and medium. Individuals cannot take it over as a whole. They may be stimulated by it in their private religion but they must choose in free responsibility what seems to them to be obligatory, what can become God's Word for them.

Nowhere is the kerygma present, naked and direct—not in the Bible, in church statements, or in private religious convictions. It is always clothed. It wears different garments according to current taste in thought and vocabulary. No kerygmatic or dogmatic statement as it stands can be binding on all Christians in every age and place. What is true is always an X which is concealed behind the local and temporal accommodation of every statement, including my own in my private religion. The moment I inquire into this X and state it for myself, I put it in my own system of coordinates, which is right only for me.

Thus there is something fleeting in all religious statements. No one can avoid this. No one can make them static, permanent, or lastingly valid. There can never be any such thing as a perennial theology.

The result of these deliberations might be formulated as follows. Not the biblical texts alone are historical but also our relation to them. We can never evade this historical reference. This is why there can never

---

9. *Dichtung und Wahrheit*, Part 2, Book 7.
10. *Kanon*, II, 182ff.
11. Cf. *Leben*, I, 96ff.

be an objective and universally valid dogmatic norm. This is why we must investigate the temporal and local accommodation of every religious utterance. What we find and state in such investigations is also valid only for a moment, for in its very appropriation it falls victim to fresh accommodation. Thus it cannot be a Christian principle that all Christians must derive their religion from all the books of the OT and the NT and be led to their convictions in some way by them.[12]

This raises, however, the question of the hermeneutical criteria which must guide our investigation of the binding kerygmatic X. The answers to this question are scattered through Semler's works and constantly recur in similar forms. I will simply choose a few sentences by way of clarification.

When, following Luther, Semler can make the demand—the first hermeneutical criterion—that we must examine whether and where the Spirit of Christ is to be seen in a biblical text, it may be asked, of course, what he means by the Spirit of Christ. We see that he does not have in view christological data such as the sacrificial analogies or high-priestly ideas of Hebrews, nor such titles as Son of God, nor what Christ says about the kingdom of God. Semler thinks all such things are borrowed from Judaism, to which the Evangelists and apostles were laboring to make the new religion understandable. The Spirit of Christ as Semler understands it—and we can see here the accommodation of this Spirit to the age of the Enlightenment—can only be something that is useful for present-day Christians and that they can see plainly to be a moral norm. But this norm can consist only of something that promotes moral betterment. Semler can go so far here as to say that the essence of Christianity consists of a new covenant, i.e., of new and better principles in the worship of God. But he would have this understood only as a general framework which in view of the great number of those who become Christians, and their many differences, can comprehend a great variety of possible ideas and judgments.

If we look more closely, it is clear that Semler does not just use his hermeneutical criteria to distinguish between content and time-bound form, between the eternal and the temporal; he also presumes to judge what the content *can be.* Hence his criteria are more than helps in interpretation. They are normative courts which tells us what we may regard as inspired and therefore as kerygma. This holiest of all scripture can only be that wherein Enlightenment morality finds confirmation. Here people of God speak to people today. They express their own religious experiences but in so doing they affect us too. What

12. *Leben,* II, 139.

they say as the mediators of scriptural revelation is approved by God but it is still their own. They speak as rational writers.[13] For this reason they touch on something that is human in us, for the Bible, as revelation, makes Christians, not humans, and Christians are still humans in every possible relationship, and may still be philosophers, etc., just as they do not stop eating and drinking.[14] For all the differences of time and place, what we have here are people speaking to people. Thus we today understand these authors of yesterday when they get down to the ultimate normative content which unites us across all time. By this content Semler, being bound to his own time, has in mind that which promotes moral betterment.

If our own reason meets a fellow-reason in the Bible (rational authors), and our morality is struck by something that promotes our moral betterment, it is easy to see why Semler is so sure that the scriptural revelation cannot contradict what human reason perceives. This does not mean the subjection of scripture to reason. It simply means that the scriptural revelation is in full agreement with what we, as rationally thinking persons, can always see and know in the sphere of morality, natural theology, and psychology. If in this way revelation and reason form a continuum within which there can be no contradictions, revelation still adds something extra that is beyond reason's sphere of competence. On this account it cannot be subject to reason. We must not reckon among the things known by reason that which we do not see or know but can learn about only from revelation.[15]

This plea for the primacy of revelation over reason makes it plain that Semler does not want to be regarded as a deist in the sense of Reimarus and his *Fragments*, notwithstanding his Enlightenment view of virtue and his hermeneutical criteria, which are of the same provenance. He expressly emphasizes that he does not want to be identified with the natural theology of Reimarus. At the end of the fifties he points out that his concern is with Christian salvation and that this is not possible without Christian knowledge. Although moral betterment is included in this goal of Christian salvation, this does not mean that there can be no moral betterment without Christian betterment.[16] Some weight is attached to autonomous (natural) morality which can be present even without Christian motivation. (Semler does not want to discredit morally either the author of the *Fragments* or his deistic col-

---

13. Baumgarten, pp. 40-41.
14. Ibid., pp. 52-53.
15. Ibid., p. 49.
16. *Lehrart*, p. 260.

leagues.) The Christian faith is for Semler a motor which is of significance for the ethical level.

Yet we have to say that for Semler faith and morality are not
qualitatively different but belong to the same plane. He finds only a
quantitative distinction, a "more" and "higher," between natural morality and sanctification by faith. We often get the impression that only with
difficulty does Semler find elements in the Bible which at least occasionally, here and there, and not very often, transcend and surpass the
system of natural religion. Most of the Bible, he says in the Introduction
to Baumgarten, simply repeats natural religion. Only a smaller part, the
few sentences in which holy scripture differs from natural religion, tell
us about what is specifically Christian, namely, the possibilities of supreme union with God and agreement with all his purposes for us.[17]

V. SPECIAL IMPLICATIONS FOR THE QUESTION OF THE CANON

Our deliberations show that Semler cannot have been inclined to accord
any normative canonical significance to the biblical canon. This canon
is simply a complex and heterogeneous starting point where we must
find something binding with the help of hermeneutical operations. We
may sum up as follows (with some references) the reasons why the canon
cannot be for us a direct revelation, a direct Word of God.

First, the hermeneutical rule of what applies unconditionally to
us (Tillich), and can thus be religiously binding, prevents us from
adopting the canonical texts as a whole. This rule, as we have seen, is that
of moral betterment. But, Semler states, we are not improved morally by
all the twenty-four books of the OT, and hence we cannot be convinced
of their divinity.[18] Why are we not improved by these writings apart from
some exceptions? Because the OT canon largely consists of primitive
Jewish prejudices which are opposed to Christianity, and only a small
part contains for the Jews divine and inspired writings in which useful
and serviceable truths may also be found for Christians.[19] For this reason
there is a difference between holy scripture and the Word of God.[20]

Second, the temporal and local accommodation means that

17. Baumgarten, pp. 51ff.
18. *Kanon*, III, 26.
19. Ibid. In the canon we also find, e.g., Ruth, Esther, Canticles, etc., but
not all the books called holy belong to the Word of God which makes people of all
ages wise until salvation.
20. *Kanon*, I, 75; cf. also pp. 25-26.

even apart from extreme forms of Judaizing the literary form of the biblical statements, namely, the address to contemporaries in their changing settings, implies that not all the biblical statements are meant for us today.

Third, those who first seek edification in scripture, and relate its utterances directly to this end, impose themselves on scripture and no longer truly listen to it. Expositors, says Semler, must not import their own thoughts into scripture; they must make scripture their own and find confirmation from its contents. The idea of accommodation is still present when in the same context he adds that the same degree of edification is not available to all (otherwise accommodation to different positions would not be necessary), just as the same knowledge is not possible. It is thus a mistake to think that holy scripture always effects edification first and must be used directly for this purpose. True historical knowledge must be achieved first, and only then that which is to salvation.[21] Edification, if it is not to serve arbitrary worship and not to involve importing our own ideas into the text, must be subject to the prior exertions of a hermeneutical concern for the text. Only then does the text offer to our free, private, Christian religion, which always rests on our own distinctive insights,[22] something special. We cannot find this special thing, which is particularly for us, if we have not first settled on the special thing which is contained in the text itself.

Fourth, the biblical canon cannot be a Word of God that has fallen from heaven, partly because the Holy Spirit himself has chosen the way of time-bound accommodation, but partly also because an all too human element has helped to relativize the canon as bishops and other clerics have manipulated the text, i.e., canonized things that correspond to their own interests and doctrines, and rejected things that do not suit them. Thus in the 4th century the bishops made the canon a means of rule. This brotherhood of bishops served a purely external end which did not enhance the Christian religion in such a way as to serve all Christians and their private religion. What was achieved was the domination of the ecclesiastical leaders over Christians who had thus far been externally free.[23]

In Semler's final confession of faith harsh formulations of this kind rise to a crescendo. The clergy forced themselves on the people, not as teachers, but as rulers who order and command. Doctrines simply come from religious parties and serve an external purpose. We have to

21. *Kanon;* cf. Kümmel, *New Testament,* p. 66.
22. *Glaubensbekenntnis,* p. 36.
23. Ibid., pp. 34ff.

ask, then, where the true Christian religion is to be found. We can find it only in the minds of all true Christians of all parties.[24]

If we finally list the very heterogeneous elements assembled in the Bible and church history, three antitheses may be found in Semler.

(1) True and authentic religion has to be disentangled from the texts of the Bible with their various costumes. In contrast to this is the external order of religion which is partly conditioned by the aim to accommodate, partly by a (pragmatically oriented) social contract.[25]

(2) We then have moral religion, whose proponents regard older historical statements (including miracle stories and the hope of sharing in Christ's earthly kingdom) as simply husks and symbols in which moral Christians find universal truths which they constantly use to their inner benefit. In contrast, naive people accept all the texts that are held to be sacred, take them at face value, and make them the content of their faith.

These two classes, namely, those who worship the symbol and the truly enlightened who can distinguish sign and thing signified, are both present in every age.[26] They correspond to the different stages of development in Lessing's *Education of the Human Race.* Sometimes considerable conflict arises between them, leading to painful struggles. On the one hand are those who take the forms of expression, the figures and myths, to be the inspired Word of God. On the other are advanced individuals who are already stamping and glowing at the last lines of the primer.

(3) We then have a final tension between the truth of revelation itself and the work of the mediators of the scriptural revelation who, even if with God's approval, write something of their own.[27]

Semler's hermeneutics is thus an intellectual and theological breakthrough inasmuch as he does not deistically and superficially regard the Bible as compromised by immanent contradictions or by the tension between biblical revelation and the religion of reason, but interprets it historically and in so doing regards it as meaningful and finds the true tasks of understanding. Semler thus takes up the human thrust of the Enlightenment but turns it in a different way to the Bible. Consistent deism, as in Reimarus, thought that human dignity and maturity could be guaranteed only by the liberation of reason from the scriptural revelation. Semler, however, makes no such distinction. He

24. Ibid., pp. 48ff., 61-62.
25. Ibid., pp. 64ff.
26. *Religion* (1786), pp. 142ff.
27. Baumgarten, pp. 39ff.

leads mature Christians to a discovery of their inner moral religion *in* the biblical texts, and to its extraction from these texts. In this process of exposition they maintain their adulthood because they are no longer subject to the control of the scriptural revelation but meet it as subjects who investigate it with existential criteria and can thus differentiate the eternal from the time-bound, that which was valid then and that which is valid for Christians today.

VI. CONCLUSIONS

It would be a mistake to describe Semler's position as one of religio-historical relativism such as we find in Lessing's parable of the ring in *Nathan*. In *Nathan* the view of religion is close to Feuerbach's theory of projection. The reality of the ring, as a symbol of the reality of the event of revelation, is in doubt. But even if it is only imaginary, it can still release the activity which makes us agreeable to God and others. This activity is the true reality. Hence revelation and religion are derivative. They are a kind of superstructure or a mere projection.

For Semler, however, there is a real, objective kerygma. But this kerygma is a transcendental X, a "thing in itself," which is available to us only in brokenness and transposition into our own modes of reception. (Not by accident we tend to speak here in terms of Kant's doctrine of categories.) Of course, there is objective truth, Semler can say with reference to the objective reality of the kerygma, which is not generated by our own reason or consciousness. No, it is historically real in the event of revelation, and as such it affects our consciousness. But whether we are close to the objective truth or far from it, Semler continues, "there is always something different, which has to be different because it is a moral judgment."[28] In this quotation, which I owe to F. A. G. Tholuck, Semler's position finds pregnant expression in two ways.

First, the understanding subject plays a part and cannot be excluded in any kerygmatic statement. We see here, in some sense, the presence of the Cartesian I. But it plays a part without being in any way creative. Hence religion itself is not relative, only the way of expressing and understanding it.

Second, no objective statement can be made about the extent of the breaks and transpositions that come with the subject. If it could

28. Tholuck, *Vorbereitung auf die königl. grossbritische Aufgabe von der Gottheit Christi* (1787), p. 59.

be, then the breaks and transpositions could be subtracted and we should have the kerygmatic content in pure form and could formulate it as a perennial theology outside time and history. This is impossible, however, because I myself, when trying to differentiate husk and kernel, am a victim of the husk of my own age, and cannot free myself from it. I cannot jump out of my own standpoint and join those who see the kerygma from other standpoints. At least, I can do it only in the name of Semler's moral judgment, not in the name of any objective insight. In modern terms, I can do it only in the form of a daring existential judgment which alone can make such a union possible.

Obviously, Semler, who renounces all objective judgments, is hard to pin down objectively as regards his own theological position. He was a riddle to his contemporaries. Orthodox, Pietists, and Deists all claimed him and then rejected him, finding in him a flexibility bordering on a complete lack of distinctives. It has now become clear that many elements in his apparent vacillation may be explained by his theology, and especially by his idea of accommodation. Lessing had to suffer the same accusations from his contemporaries.

Yet there are also incompatible features in Semler as a person. He lived in the rational brightness of his age. He left the dark lanes and corners of the Middle Ages. He settled in a city with its modern streets. Yet he had a yearning for the mystical and obscure. In this respect, too, he belonged to his age. The Enlightenment had mystical components. As it investigated the historical, psychological, and epistemological conditions of the subject, it came upon the mysteries of the nonobjective I. Introspection became an art, as in the psychological novels of Mme. Guyon, the mystical as well as rational pedagogics of Pestalozzi, and the mystical popular philosophy of the Roman Catholic theologian Fénelon. The same union of rationalism and mysticism may be seen especially in the Rosicrucians, who had an influence on Freemasonry. At every end and corner the rationally controlled life stands above and leaps across the framework in which it is meant to be set.[29]

But not life alone stands above and transcends rationality; so does Semler's own Christianity. I have already pointed out that in the theologians at issue we should note this additional element which in their systems usually seems to be an inconsistent factor that they have not mastered and that resists the system. Thus in Descartes we have seen a resistant belief in the divine goodness and in Reimarus a confidence that the partial impression made by God's creation cannot deceive us if we are open to the symphony of the whole.

29. Cf. in this regard what Spengler calls "secondary religiosity."

In conclusion, then, we should at least mention how Semler at the end of his life found words that are obviously above the level of his arguments and therefore above the problems that necessarily arise on this level. When we hear them we might ask who is the real Semler, and who finally are we ourselves, the authentic we.

Are we thinkers prior to the last judgment, and therefore fallible thinkers? Or are we living beings, living in the light of Good Friday and Easter, reflecting in the broken mirror of this light, and taking comfort in the fact that the mirror is broken and that the immediacy of vision will replace it? Who are we truly?

The famous Halle pietist Tholuck (the teacher of Martin Kähler), who admired and perhaps even loved Semler, quotes such a word which does not belong to his work as a thinker.[30] In it Semler says that he often sighs at the extreme grace of God which helps him into the invisible kingdom of eternal light which Jesus, the Christ of God, so trustworthily reveals and which the Holy Spirit has inaugurated in all true Christians. His heart is open to all such emotions. No one can know what he feels when he thinks about God's mercy and the weight of his own unworthiness. Quoting Luther's dictum that prayer, meditation, and temptation make a theologian, he can also admonish his students to try to practice morning devotions for the sake of their office and standing, and in a short time they will feel an inner power which is peculiar to our Christian knowledge of God; they may then let those high-flying spirits go their way which mock at our religion and accept the standard only of their own self-made religion.[31]

Again we have to ask: Who was the real Johann Salomo Semler?

---

30. Cf. *RE*, 2nd ed., XIV, 116.

31. Semler, *Nähere Anleitung zu nützlichem Fleiss in der Gottesgelehrsamkeit* (1757), § 41.

PART III

THE GREAT SYSTEMS OF THE 18TH AND 19TH CENTURIES AND THEIR INFLUENCE

CHAPTER 7

F. D. E. Schleiermacher: The Correlation of Religion, Christianity, and Consciousness

Bibliography. Primary Works: Three main works have been used: *Über die Religion* (ET *Speeches on Religion*, cited as *Speeches*); *Der christliche Glaube* (ET *The Christian Faith*); and *Sendschreiben an Lücke*, ed. H. Mulert (1908, cited as Lücke). Also cf. the *Monologen* (ET *Soliloquies*); *Weihnachtsfeier* (ET *Christmas Eve*); *Dialektik; Grundriss der philosophischen Ethik* (cited as *Ethik*);[1] *Die christliche Sitte* (cited as *Sitte*); *Kurze Darstellung des theologischen Studiums* (ET *Brief Outline on the Study of Theology*, cited as *Outline*); *Predigten*. For a selection of texts cf. the *Schleiermacher-Auswahl* in the Siebenstern ed., with an epilogue by K. Barth (1968). For letters cf. *Aus Schleiermachers Leben in Briefen*, 4 vols., ed. L. Jonas and W. Dilthey (1858ff., cited as *Briefe*); also a selection by H. Mulert (1923).

Secondary Works: W. Dilthey, *Leben Schleiermachers* (1870, 2nd ed. rev. H. Mulert, 1922; cited as Dilthey); K. Barth, *Protestant Theology in the Nineteenth Century* (Valley Forge, repr. 1976), pp. 425-73; E. Brunner, *Die Mystik und das Wort* (1924); O. Kirn, *RE*, 3rd ed., 17, 587-617; R. Hermann, *RGG*, 3rd ed., V, 1422-35; E. H. U. Quapp, *Christus im Leben Schleiermachers* (1972); G. Ebeling, *Wort und Glaube*, III (1975), 60-136; G. Wehrung, *Die Dialektik Schleiermachers* (1920); W. Trillhaas, *Schleiermachers Predigt und das homiletische Problem* (1933); H. J. Rothert, "Die Dialektik F. Schleiermachers," *ZThK* 2 (1970) 183-214; F. Mildenberger, *Geschichte der deutschen evangelischen Theologie im 19. und 20. Jahrhundert* (1981).

1. Cf. A. Schweizer, *Entwurf des Systems der Sittenlehre* (1835).

Dilthey's is a sympathetic account of Schleiermacher and a brilliant depiction of the era. In view of his opposition to Schleiermacher, Barth achieves an astonishing insight into his personality and work, in sharp contrast to the young Brunner. The works on the dialectic and the preaching reflect the tension in Schleiermacher and the debate regarding his true position. Mildenberger offers a comprehensive view of theological development from Schleiermacher's day to the present.

I. PERSONALITY AND INTELLECTUAL PHYSIOGNOMY

A. SCHLEIERMACHER'S PLACE IN INTELLECTUAL AND THEOLOGICAL HISTORY

If with some astonishment we must admit how far the figures discussed hitherto prefigured or at least foreshadowed later theological developments, especially the fixing of the relation between history and revelation and the unfolding hermeneutical problem, face to face with Schleiermacher we have to confess that the whole tree of the 19th and 20th centuries is present in seed-form in him so far as the link between theological and intellectual history is concerned. Either respectfully or ironically, he has rightly been called the church father of the 19th century. This is true to the degree that all later theologians have had to be either for or against him, and often both. With the enormous breadth of his subject matter he embraces the whole Western tradition. His calling as a Christian theologian is the axis of his life, but he is also a philosopher who pursues questions of universal interest. Not least of all he is a translator of Plato. No wonder that he was one of the leading charter members of the University of Berlin. He dominated the faculties.[2] The two streams of Western culture, the Greek and the Christian, flowed together in him.

Yet the event of his thinking—it was truly an event!—is overshadowed by the dark suspicion that the Western tradition with its polarity of Christian divinity and Greek humanity can no longer be fused into a synthesis, not even by Schleiermacher's heaven-storming

---

2. In this respect we are reminded of A. von Harnack, who not only wrote his monumental *History of Dogma* but also wrote a history of the Prussian Academy (1900), was Director General of the Prussian State Libraries, and helped to found the Kaiser-Wilhelm Society for the Promotion of the Sciences (1911); cf. the biography by his daughter Agnes von Zahn-Harnack (2nd ed., 1951).

systematics. In this mediating spirit we see the impossibility of viewing the divine and human aspects in analogy, no matter how much he longed and strove to accomplish this.[3] The pain of this helplessness reminds us of F. Hölderlin's poem *Der Einzige*, in which he vainly attempts to bring Christ and Olympus together in his thoughts.[4]

Nevertheless, it is a mistake, constantly made by dialectical theologians, to accuse Schleiermacher of being a synthesizer and analogist who tried to harmonize the facts of revelation with the modern consciousness and in so doing fatefully secularized Christian dogma and assimilated it to the spirit of the day. This is unquestionably a crude and misleading caricature which expresses only one side of his concern. He himself realized that the age of such analogies is past and that everything claiming to be transcendent revelation is an alien body or erratic block on the modern landscape. Thus an essential effort of the mature Schleiermacher is to show that the Christian revelation is indeed this alien, historical thing, not a mere product of our own consciousness. He is also asking how far we can regard and acknowledge it as such without damage to our intellectual integrity.

We thus see in Schleiermacher the tragedy of the modern spirit whose home—the Christian faith—has become a foreign land that it must struggle to reach again. I think the secret of Schleiermacher's whole theological enterprise is to be found in this comparison. The diastatic element in his thinking comes to expression in it. He is compelled to view the sphere of Christian revelation as something alien and by no means self-evident, so that to a large degree the Christian tradition of the West is no longer intelligible. Yet the synthetic element in his thinking also comes to expression here. It consists of the attempt to convince his age that only a relinking, a *religio*, with this alien and by no means self-evident world can grant us fulness of life and thus bring us back home.

One may readily conjecture that a thinker who lives in the polarity of doubt and appropriation will see and anticipate all the essential individual questions of modern theological thought. In what follows I will first try to sketch these problems. We will constantly come across them as we discuss the vital works.

(1) At the center of Schleiermacher's theological principles the thesis of the autonomy of religion runs through every variation. Religion, including its intellectual form as theology, is not a resident alien in the territories of, e.g., philosophy or morality. It is independent. This

3. This striving may be seen in almost all his work from the *Speeches* to the *Dialektik*.

4. See *EF,* III, 343-44.

is the basis of later efforts to establish its independence, to postulate a separate religious a priori.[5]

(2) Schleiermacher constantly discusses the problem of understanding. (We shall shortly be looking at his ideas of the divinatory and the comparative in the act of understanding.) For him the hermeneutical problem arises out of the question: How do I meet the authoritative claim of a traditional religion? More precisely: How do I meet this claim in such a way that I am not subject to a distorting heteronomy but achieve my own religious self, or, as we would say today, my identity? An answer to this question is possible only if I can show that this entity that meets me from outside, from history, has a bridgehead in my consciousness, and that I am not, therefore, subject to any authority. Everything depends, then, on an analysis of the consciousness and a discovery in it of categories which meet this entity. The Introduction to *The Christian Faith* takes up this task. It leads on to the third problem.

(3) How do I make the Christian faith my own?—the question familiar to us from the time of Lessing. Can I believe the prophets simply because of their prophetic authority or canonical status? If I agree to this, the threat of heteronomy at once arises again. But if I begin by asserting that the truth of the prophets (like any religious truth) encounters certain contents of my consciousness, then I do not just play the role of a "consumer" regarding it, but can see in its proclamation only a spur or appeal, so that it helps me to develop something of my own that is already present in my consciousness. Motifs are thus touched on which will be taken up later by Kierkegaard and existential philosophy (especially Karl Jaspers).

(4) Schleiermacher is also the first great modern apologist in two respects. First, he tries to settle religion on its own impregnable and sheltered territory.[6] (The prefigured idea of the religious a priori has drawn our attention to this.) His specific apologetic goal is that of meeting prophylactically the threat posed to the Christian religion by a total historicism and a self-resting immanence introduced by the natural sciences. He expresses this motif, and offers his vision of such coming threats, especially in his *Sendschreiben an Lücke*.

His anthropological starting point is also a kind of apologetic motif. Since he understands us as a unity in all our intellectual departments, he has to view as a unity, too, the system of sciences which we

---

5. Cf. E. Troeltsch, *Zur Frage des religiösen Apriori* (1909), idem, *Gesammelte Schriften*, II, 754ff.; R. Otto, *The Idea of the Holy* (New York, 1958), chaps. 13, 16; A. Nygren, *Die Gültigkeit der religiösen Erfahrung* (1922).
6. Dogmas should free us from entanglements with science (Lücke, II, 40).

bring forth as intelligible beings. Religion may be unique in the sense that one cannot derive it from metaphysics or morality, but the moment we begin to reflect about religion theologically we come up against the system of sciences and have to relate our theology to it. How carefully Schleiermacher does this and avoids integrating Christian theology into that system we shall see. But if he were simply to ignore the relation he would necessarily be betrayed into a dubious axiom such as that of twofold truth, and into a rending of our unity.

(5) Schleiermacher begins in a modern way with the subjective consciousness. With his understanding of subjectivity he overcomes the Enlightenment view, for he no longer conceives of human subjectivity as mere rationality. In the *Speeches* he characterizes it instead as contemplation or feeling, and in *The Christian Faith* as self-consciousness, which embraces a multiple rational, moral, aesthetic, and religious complex. We shall have to analyze in greater detail this central concept.

The dynamic element in Schleiermacher's view of subjectivity— this much we may say already—is that objective (or, better, transsubjective) historical facts correspond to it. For him the Christian religion is by no means an expression or projection of subjectivity. Jesus Christ is its central content—and *he* is an entity that transcends the subjective I and comes to it from history. How Schleiermacher combines the subjectivity of the religious self-consciousness with the transsubjective entity of Christ is the great problem in interpreting his theology. The resultant hermeneutical question is given its edge by Christology. It runs as follows: Can the consciousness really be combined with something that transcends it? Or does the attempt at combination lead to a conjuring trick in which *either* Christ is accommodated to the preunderstanding of the consciousness and thus dehistoricized, *or* the religious starting point in the self-consciousness has to be abandoned?

(6) Schleiermacher tries for the first time, to my knowledge, to deal with a problem that is still unsolved, namely, what we mean by Christian theology. He is the first modern theologian who, at least in principle, wants to relate theology to the available concept of science with a view to maintaining the unity of the consciousness. What I here call "relating" later becomes a firm "linking" such as we find in contemporary philosophy. Thus Schleiermacher's independence of theology is for the most part quickly surrendered. We need only recall how under the domination of Hegel's philosophy Christian theology becomes no more than a specific form of philosophical thought.[7] The theology of

---

7. Cf. A. E. Biedermann's view of theology, *Christliche Dogmatik* (Zurich, 1869), § 2. Remarkable in Biedermann (as in Semler) is the contrast between his

Ritschl and W. Herrmann is essentially controlled by Kant. Similar affinities between theology and philosophy may be seen today.[8] All this goes to show that theology was not just led astray by Schleiermacher, as the dialectical theology thought. Often enough, and to its own hurt, it failed to follow Schleiermacher.

Schleiermacher definitely refuses the idea that theology is a science like any other[9] or that it may arrogantly seek to be called such. He follows Schelling in thinking that a science is present in the full sense only when it is developed out of the idea of the absolute. Theology is definitely not deduced in any such way. It is not a speculative metaphysics that traces back all its theses to a superior principle. Schleiermacher is thus proof against Hegel.[10] His position is that the object of theology is not an idea. It finds this object and is thus based on historical data. It rests on the fact that there is a Christian fellowship, the church, that this church is historically present, and that it reflects on itself and the basis of its existence.[11] In this reflection it comes across two facts from which it derives, namely, primitive Christianity and Christ. It also finds that Christian states of feeling correspond subjectively to these objective data. This religious structure of the subject makes it possible to categorize that which comes from outside and to meet it with divinatory understanding.

The church is marked by historical objectivity and also by the religious makeup of its members. Both factors are in play. They form the dramatic knot of Schleiermacher's thinking, especially the correspondence between the transsubjective (or historical) data and the receptivity of the subject, but also the relation between the religious individual and the community.

We shall not now go into the way these factors work together. More essential in this first and general survey is that Schleiermacher bases theology on the existence of the Christian fellowship and regards it as this fellowship's self-reflection. If he does refer to theological "science" in this connection, he means only that theology is a positive science, i.e., an academic undertaking which is based on positive data.

---

highly abstract and impersonal theology and his childlike piety. As C. J. Riggenbach pointed out, his heart kept breaking through his system.

8. Cf. the influence of Heidegger's *Being and Time* on Bultmann or of Hegel on Pannenberg.

9. Specifically in *Outline*. In what follows I rely on the essay by S. Scholz.

10. The two could not stand one another. Hegel rejects Schleiermacher's supposed irrationalism as fawning sentimentality (WW, XX, 4th ed. [1968], 19, 27); cf. Rothert, *ZThK* 2 (1970) 200.

11. *Outline*, § 43; idem, *Christian Faith*, § 6, Postscript.

Being tied to the historical entity of the Christian community, it cannot be pursued in the vacuum of mere abstractions.

In the second *Sendschreiben an Lücke* Schleiermacher passionately defends himself against the accusation that the Introduction to *The Christian Faith* builds on philosophical principles which according to the judgment of interpreters who do not understand that the work will lead to pantheistic conclusions.[12] That *The Christian Faith* has a speculative tendency seems to him to be the worst and crudest misunderstanding.[13] What might seem to support it in the Introduction are only initial philosophical formulas, empty spaces which will later receive their content from the reference back to positive foundations.[14] To avoid such misunderstandings he considered the idea of putting the true Christian materials first and letting the introductory discussions follow.[15]

As concerns the nonspeculative or positive basis of theology, a further distinction must be made. Theology is not just related to the church. It can be done only in the individual confessions and denominations, for we have the Christian community only in positive forms.

In thus relating theology to the church Schleiermacher goes so far as to add to the positive historical and communicative connection a pragmatic orientation. The aim of theology is to supply leadership to the church.[16] He does not mean, of course, that theology simply gives direction to church bodies. I can well believe that he shrank back from the idea that he would find guardians of the theological grail among church leaders. What he means is rather that a coherent church leadership or church government is not possible if academic knowledge and practice are ignored.[17] The necessary significance of theology for church government rests on the fact that theology, as already noted, refers back to the original and exemplary form of Christianity (Christ and primitive Christianity), to the "idea" of Christianity, as it were,[18] and thus has the task of seeing to it that the "true essence" of the Christian life is transferred from the past by way of the present to the future, that this true essence represents itself more purely in every future moment.[19]

If theology has, then, a certain instrumental point relative to church government, this is not because the institution claims it, in

12. Lücke, II, 32.
13. Ibid., p. 34.
14. Ibid., p. 32.
15. Ibid., pp. 33-34.
16. *Outline*, §§ 5, 81, 84.
17. Ibid., § 5.
18. Ibid., § 27.
19. Ibid., § 84; cf. § 81.

modern terms as an ideological support, but because theology, in a kind of self-consecration, places itself at the disposal of church government and forces it to do its proper work. For the rest, theology is kept from being a mere means to an end by being seen in connection with other activities of the human spirit, for the pious communities in which it is pursued can be shown to be necessary for the development of this spirit.[20]

By thus defining theology as a positive science and relating it to the church, Schleiermacher sovereignly cuts the bond which tied theology to speculative metaphysics and by which it threatened and threatens to become a purely academic discipline foreign to the community at large. Yet his concern also connects religion and theology with the other activities of the human spirit, wards off the danger of the ghetto, and offers protection against the possibility that theology will become no more than the ideology of the ecclesiastical institution.

Unmistakably, theology is thus seen to be encircled by very different influences and temptations. On the one hand, concern to avoid the ghetto, the possible otherworldliness and cultural isolation of theology, might expose it to the inducement to establish itself as a province in a general philosophy of culture. On the other hand, the concern not to be a mere squatter on some other intellectual territory might increase the need for liberation and lead it to create a monopoly on the scale of psychological experience.

At any rate, Schleiermacher's program demands that he steer a careful course between many forms of Scylla on the one hand and many forms of Charybdis on the other. The knot of a dramatic development of thought is in any case tied. Traditional tedium is certainly not to be feared. Paul and Plato, primitive and modern Christianity, all have a part in this play of forces, and one may expect that a multidimensional, multifaceted theologian like Schleiermacher will be beset by the hatred and favor of parties, that one interpreter will seek to explain him in terms of some components of his system and another of others, and that the presentation of his character will vary accordingly in history. The influence of such a man will be equally rich and full of tension. Where kings tread, carriers follow.

B. BIOGRAPHY

Dilthey is certainly right when he introduces his biography of Schleiermacher with the observation that Kant's philosophy can be understood

---

20. Ibid., §§ 21-22.

apart from the life of its author,[21] but in the case of Schleiermacher a look into his biography is an essential aid to interpretation. We must bear this in mind in the following sketch, regretting only that it has to be so short.[22]

Schleiermacher was born on November 21, 1768, as the son of a Silesian military chaplain. Already at school (cf. the musical gifts of the boy Mozart) much of the intellectual entelechy might be seen which is found in developed form in his mature works. His mother wrote that he was the smallest boy in the school but first in all his classes.[23] Very early, then, he received a call to supradimensional primacy, although he suffered from a secret sense of inferiority. The reason for this feeling of inadequacy is typical of both the boy and the man. Before he completed his tenth year he was tormented by the fact that he did not understand coherently and systematically the sum of what he had learned at school. Already as a child he had some inkling that an accumulation of detailed information does not mean intellectual possession, but that such possession comes only with understanding. For the child Schleiermacher understanding means grasping things in context and appropriating them by systematic penetration. Quite literally, then, we have here a foreshadowing of his later hermeneutical theory. This theory will simply put into theses what the child dimly spied in advance. He found it strange, and it gave him a lonely feeling, that he did not find the same unease in his small fellow-students. In his naivete he thought that unlike himself they had grasped the bond which inwardly holds the world together. He lived in constant anxiety lest his teachers would find out how deficient was his eye for interconnections.

The same thought occurs again later when he was studying at Halle and with the same unrestricted desire for mastery worked through Semler, Wolff, Kant, and Jacobi, while still devoting time to mathematics and modern languages. This superabundance of new and varied materials perhaps drove him to the confession that he did not think he could work out a system which would enable him decisively to answer all the questions that he might be asked in the context of all the rest of his knowledge. He had always thought that testing and investigating and hearing every witness and party was the only way finally to achieve

21. While the observation may be accepted in general, nevertheless some knowledge of Kant's life gives color and relief to many of his works, esp. *The Critique of Practical Reason;* cf. Dilthey, *Immanuel Kant. Sein Leben in Darstellungen von Zeitgenossen* (Berlin, 1912).

22. For this reason I shall be using Dilthey's work even where I do not give the actual references.

23. Dilthey, p. 11.

accessible certainty, and especially to establish the border between that on which one must take a position and that which may be left undecided with no prejudice to one's peace or happiness.[24]

This saying of the young theological student shows not only how important a system is for understanding but also what systematic principles are at work in Schleiermacher's thinking. If I understand correctly what Schleiermacher is saying here, he is distinguishing between two thematic spheres, namely, that which may be systematized and that which may not, i.e., that which is outside the understanding and its order, that which might be called the zone of the irrational. Such a distinction could never be made by a speculative philosopher like Hegel. For Hegel all things can be subsumed under first principles, e.g., the self-unfolding of spirit. There is no irrationality here. All forms of being are spiritual and rational inasmuch as they may all be deduced from a single principle. Distinction between what may be systematized and what may not (i.e., the irrational) is possible only when one proceeds inductively and not deductively, i.e., when one is exposed to the fulness of the world of experience, including that of religion; when one faces positive facts, and tests, investigates, and listens patiently. Only then does one stumble across the fact that life is richer than our systems and that the totality cannot be forced without a break into a systematic order but sticks out in every corner and at every end. For Schleiermacher, as we shall see, the sermons are the place where what sticks out finds expression and where many theological statements are ventured which are hard to integrate into the systematic web of his theological teaching.

It is impressive to note how Schleiermacher's spiritual entelechy gradually develops and yet remains extremely true to itself. The whole may already be seen in germ in his young spirit. In what follows I will be content to pass on biographical data in which one may see the form which comes to vital development in his great writings.

Particularly significant in this regard is the fact that Schleiermacher grew up under the influence of Herrnhut. We may recall how pregnantly the Herrnhut brotherhood affected the leading spirits of the century even if only by their decisive impact on Lessing, Schleiermacher, and indirectly even Goethe (chiefly by stimulating them, and especially by releasing their own originality).

The lively piety of Herrnhut pietism at first engulfed the young Schleiermacher. In a certain sense it remained with him his whole life long. Even in his riper years he could call himself "a Herrnhuter of a higher order." What we find subjective in pietism is a permanent

24. *Briefe*, I, 82-83.

element in his thinking even if under another sign. As the Christianity of Herrnhut cannot simply be dismissed as subjectivism, as it displays a vital contact with the *extra me* of the biblical revelation, so in Schleiermacher the correlation between the subjective and the transsubjective is never severed.

As an example of the youthful piety of Schleiermacher I will mention only his saying as a sixteen-year-old to his sister Charlotte that for just over two years now he had been a boy in the community and had experienced a great deal in that time, both bad on his side and grace on that of the Savior. When he considered what was required of a brother, he could only tremble were he to attempt it in his own strength, and he asked to be remembered the more assiduously before the Savior.[25]

Toward the end of his time at Herrnhut he had a decisive religious crisis which is also typical inasmuch as its essential marks affect all his later life. The main source for this is in his letters to his father, and in both human and theological terms these are certainly among the most shattering that we find in German letters. The break in his unconscious conformity with the pietist tradition, whose air he breathes, is prepared for in this alert and open spirit when he notes that the teachers at Herrnhut do not allow anything of the exegetical and dogmatic controversies of the time to penetrate their well-guarded seminary with its defenses against all attacks. This creates in him and many of his fellow-students, as he mentions in a letter of 1786, the suspicion that many of the objections of the moderns must be very acceptable and hard to refute, since they are afraid to present them to us. The doubts that now arise about what had previously been regarded as self-evident come upon the young scholar and student from two directions.

First, he has doubts about the orthodox pietistic doctrine of the atonement, and implicitly about dogmatic supranaturalism in general. "I cannot believe," he wrote to his father, "that the eternal true God called himself the son of man, or that his death was a substitutionary atonement, for he himself never expressly said this, and I cannot believe it was necessary; God made us for striving, not for perfection. He cannot want to punish us eternally because we are not perfect." Schleiermacher's pain in writing this letter prevented him from giving a full account of his soul's history, but he asked his father to regard these doubts as deep-rooted and not just passing thoughts; they had been with him for almost a year and caused him long and earnest reflection. He begged his father not to try to refute them, since he did not think he could convince him. He knew how much this news would shock his father and therefore he wrote

25. Dilthey, p. 21, and cf. pp. 31ff. for the brief quotations that follow.

with a trembling hand and with tears. In a second letter he tells how the brethren torment and threaten him now that they see him as a renegade. They say that his father will drop him and that he can no longer stay in the community. He admits that his blood boiled when he heard how lacking in love they judged his father to be.

His father's answer depresses and shakes him, for it contains none of the expected arguments but expresses the pain of the father at the prodigal who has left for the far country. His father asks who has bewitched him that he does not obey the truth. Jesus Christ was set before his eyes and has been crucified by him (cf. Gal. 3:1). He accuses him of disturbing the rest of his sainted mother and seeking the glory of the world. He thinks his pride of heart is strong, but not his objections, which even a child could overcome. With sorrow he finally has to renounce him because Schleiermacher no longer worships the God of his father or bows before his altar with him. He begs him, if possible, to come back: "If it is possible . . . hear the request of your beseeching father: Return, my son, return."

In an age whose pedagogic wisdom teaches that fathers should let go of their children, and that it is neither a service to young souls nor in keeping with the Christian faith to cultivate an unbroken, untested faith in them, this reaction is hard to understand. It shows under what unusual inner and outer pressures new religious directions had to be sought in the age of the Enlightenment and after. The painful struggle that we saw in Lessing is constantly repeated. To put the knife to the roots, which Nietzsche regards as a task of "critical history," unavoidably causes deep wounds.

We are moved to find a similar conflict between Adolf von Harnack and his orthodox Lutheran father Theodosius. In this case it came at a riper age. Rumor soon had it in Harnack's hometown of Dorpat that the young Adolf was "liberal," and his *Unterricht in der christlichen Religion,* as he remarked in a much later letter,[26] seemed to be subtracting from the dominant teaching of the age. He wrote to his honored Dorpat teacher Moritz von Engelhardt about his struggle with the dogmatic tradition of positive theology and his breaking with it. It is typical that in his case, as in that of the young Schleiermacher, skepticism begins in the sphere of Christology, involving the doctrines of the Trinity and the two natures.[27] It gave him great sorrow that he

---

26. To a close relative, Marie von Oettingen; cf. Agnes von Zahn-Harnack, *Adolf von Harnack,* 2nd ed. (1951), p. 73. The references that follow are from this biography.

27. Ibid., pp. 65, 72.

had to give up ideas he had known and loved from childhood. He expresses the pain of parting in the letter to Marie von Oettingen, stating that the question of the person of Jesus is one that he would have left willingly if it would have left him, but every point or position that he has to abandon fills him with deep remorse as though he had committed a crime, and yet, as his head tells him, he is only breaking with old ideas and traditions.[28] The pain of his father Theodosius is just as emotional and nonargumentative as that of Schleiermacher's father. He thinks that if he had been more faithful his son would hold a more positive position. He asks him by all that is dear not to let his vanity be enticed by modern theology and its negative criticism, for which it makes no odds whether it tears one page out of the Bible or rejects the whole. He begs him to follow the consciousness of the church and not that of the world, since the choice is only between the two.[29]

In the case of the young Schleiermacher the theological problem of his life begins very early when doubts arise about Christology and he questions the traditional view of the atonement. This was still the critical point in *The Christian Faith*, where the subjective starting point— the feeling of absolute dependence (earlier, contemplation and a feeling for the universe)—struck hardest at the historical facticity of a person. What he could not deal with from his first encounter with the problem was the twofold argument that the doctrine of the atonement was not rational and that it had no support in the teaching of Jesus himself. Yet the doctrine is given out as dogmatic truth. It is a truth that one cannot understand even though it moves on a rational level (as in Anselm). It is contrary to the known historical facts, and it cannot be assimilated except at the cost of intellectual honesty.

The theological crisis of the young Schleiermacher also arises from his observation that the pietism of Herrnhut lives on an island and is closed to the breadth of the spirit. As he found as a student, it is opposed to every attempt to understand the world or to let itself be understood by it. It has no relevance to secular things. Neither natural science nor culture in the wider sense is related to its religious inquiries; faith lives apart and in isolation.

The program imposed daily worship and sealed off the students from the world. An odd censorship forbade the reading of Kant and even Lavater. The great poets were not available even in expurgated editions when a worldly sense was suspected. A widespread and very painful spying system controlled everything.

28. Ibid., p. 75.
29. Ibid.

If the link with learning, art, and culture is snapped, life threatens to become a meaningless desert in which only the lonely and restricted oasis of religion gives evidence of a breath of life. This Christianity of the conventicle reduces to a minimum that which human life was meant to be by creation.

The emptying of secular life of all meaning has a result to which Ernst Troeltsch and Max Weber draw attention in their analyses of the sociology of religion.[30] The one thin thread that still binds worldly life to religion is the task of subduing the earth and honoring God by activity in the world—not idle contemplation. If this task is combined with a view of things which excludes all ideal content, all joy in learning, art, and culture, the outcome is that hard work, a mercantile spirit, and even avarice associate themselves with a stern Christianity.[31] When this final reality becomes normative, and the penultimate reality ceases to control or permeate it, uncontrolled activism and secularization follow. The close interrelationship of intensity of religious life and a naked desire for gain is not simple hypocrisy, even though it may seem to be so from outside. It corresponds to a theological conception which gives religion and the practice of piety a monopoly and hence does not see the present order, or hardly does so, from the standpoint of eternity, but leaves it to itself.

These remarks about the Herrnhut of the time, with its exemplary significance, must here suffice. We had to make them in order to show how Schleiermacher's spirit came to oppose this form of life and how this form of life was the spur which contributed to his essential lines of thinking. The cleavage in personality which this kind of piety involved was, in fact, totally opposed to his need for a unitary view, for the interdependence of all secular and religious truths that he was already seeking as a child.

It would certainly be a mistake to link the opposition of the young Schleiermacher to Herrnhut *solely* with a certain desire for culture which found the ideal goods of humanity withheld and rebelled against this despoiling. This may well have played a part in so richly orchestrated a spirit as that of Schleiermacher. But undoubtedly the true and sustaining impulse behind his opposition is his rejection of the severing of faith from systematic contact with all the other phenomena of life and the consequent disparaging and denaturalizing of faith as well as culture: of faith to the extent that it becomes no more than

30. E. Troeltsch, *The Social Teaching of the Christian Churches* (New York, 1931), pp. 807ff.; M. Weber, *The Protestant Ethic and the Spirit of Capitalism* (New York, 1958), pp. 155ff.; idem, *Gesammelte Aufsätze zur Religionssoziologie*, I, 4th ed. (1956), 192ff.; ET *Essays in Sociology* (New York [1946]).

31. Dilthey, p. 24.

religious habit, is reduced to a restricted sector of humanity, and even in its form as theological reflection forfeits all correlation with the questions of the age and the surrounding world; and of culture because its spiritual salt is taken out of it, so that as an expression of a world left to itself it becomes in part the sphere of a developing and undirected desire for gain and in part the epitome of temptation and of all that is seductive in the field of faith. Finally, humanity itself inevitably degenerates because it is brought under the gravitational pull of a completely inauthentic polarity and hence ceases to be the point of unity relating all life's functions.

Thus the period at Herrnhut is for Schleiermacher a creative stimulation which kindles his own thinking and causes it to shine for the first time. As in Goethe's *Orphische Urworte* his "daimon" finds the occasion here to let itself be affected by something that threatens it, to oppose the threat, and thereby to find its way to its own identity.

After discussing this vital and formative inner history, I need refer only briefly to other points in his biography. (For details cf. *RE* or the letters.) At Halle he studies Semler, Wolff, Kant, and Jacobi, and also mathematics and modern philology. He is then a tutor in the house of Graf Dohna-Schlobitten; he gives a lively account of this period in his letters. He then becomes the preacher at the Berlin Charité in 1796. Here he enters the Romantic Circle, becomes a close friend of Friedrich Schlegel, and is active in the Berlin salons, especially that of Henriette Herz. At this period his translation of Plato, which he planned with Schlegel, is begun; he continues it even after the crisis in their friendship. After an interlude as court preacher in Stolpe (1802-1804), he is called as professor and university preacher to Halle (1804-1806), where he lectures on dogmatics, ethics, and the New Testament in an unbelievably full program. The dissolving of the university by Napoleon brings him again, and this time finally, to Berlin as his center of action (1807). In close association with W. von Humboldt he prepares the ground, both by writing and organizing, for the founding of the University of Berlin, and from 1809/1810 he combines his pastorate at Trinity Church with a professorship at the university, and from 1811 with a fellowship in the Academy of Sciences. As a professor he lectures on most subjects, apart from the OT, and also on various systematic and historical materials in philosophy. At the academy he also gives many lectures that testify to his universal cultural range. He also participates actively in church politics, championing the Union, but at the same time opposing the royal establishment of the liturgy, partly on principle, because he favors congregational independence over against state absolutism, partly on matters of detail, because he has to combat liturgical decisions which he finds intolerable in view of his Reformed background. If we think finally of his sociable life-style, his work as a preacher, his time-consuming devotion to relations with his students, and his rich literary output, we are left with the impression of almost incalculable achievement. In this respect, too, we are reminded of Harnack.

More important than the survey of biographical details is the need to show how the spirit of the young Schleiermacher manifests itself and to give some hint of the developed humanity of the mature Schleiermacher.

Schleiermacher was a very sociable person. For self-expression he needed to be triggered by a Thou. Dialogue was his intellectual métier. (This is not perhaps the final reason why Plato's dialogues attracted him.) One of his finest works—*Christmas Eve*—uses the form of dialogue.

The Berlin of his day, with its cultured gatherings, which had not yet become superficial cocktail parties, offered his nature rich opportunities for development. He was a dominant figure in the salons of the Berlin Romanticism hosted by highly cultured ladies. Here he had the chance to engage in abundant conversation. His almost daily visits to such places of dialogue were not based on any desire to discharge burdensome social duties. In sharp contrast to our own days, the expenditure of time was worth it, because the time spent was rich, relaxing, and creatively stimulating.

One of the leading salons was that of Henriette Herz, which attracted all who had any name or rank in Berlin, and was frequented by the Humboldts. Herz herself was well educated, spoke eight languages, and later learned Turkish and Sanskrit. Yet these great ladies of Romanticism were not professional scholars. We cannot imagine Humboldt or Schleiermacher addressing them or even thinking of them as such. Their intellectual structure was different from that presupposed in university scholars. Thus Schleiermacher speaks characteristically of the "passive learning"[32] of Henriette Herz. What he means is that her learning is simply an instrument of her charisma. This charisma is the gift of stimulating masculine spirits and triggering all their possibilities. We do not have here the feminist ideal of doing the same as men do, of an equality of nature and rank between the masculine and the feminine intelligence. A polar division of roles was seen between the sexes, whose creativity so exalted the rank of the feminine that the feminist desire for equality could not even be considered.[33]

32. Dilthey, p. 236.
33. Naturally, this solution to the ranking of the sexes among the intellectual elite of a salon cannot be regarded as a norm for the universal regulation of the

A tragic shadow was thrown over Schleiermacher's life by his friendship with, and love for, another woman, Eleonore Grunow, the childless wife of a Berlin minister who was unhappy in her marriage. Schleiermacher recounts the happiness and unhappiness that this love brought him, and its final end, in moving letters to his sister Charlotte.

Friedrich Schlegel, with whom he lived for a time and had a stimulating friendship, was the one who above all brought him into the Romantic Circle. It is through his influence that in many phases of his life we find a certain playful approach to literature which helped Schleiermacher to develop his literary style. His *Vertraute Briefe über Schlegels Lucinde* (1801)[34] belongs to this category. It is a serious and almost shocking commentary on what was then regarded as a pornographic book by his friend. (Let us imagine Karl Barth or even Paul Tillich writing on Vladimir Nabokov's *Lolita*!) To this period, too, belongs his *Idee zu einem Katechismus der Vernunft für edle Frauen*,[35] which makes its serious points in playful form and with a delight in startling epigrams.

Thus in expounding the first commandment Schleiermacher says that women may be friends but without playing at love or indulging in coquetry or adoration. As regards the second he tells them not to make an ideal either of an angel in heaven or of a hero from a poem or novel; they should love men as they are, for nature is a stern deity that visits the madness of girls to the third and fourth generation of their emotions. In relation to the tenth he tells them not to desire the culture, art, wisdom, or honor of men.

That Schleiermacher was a significant preacher may be seen from his published works. Perhaps one might say—as examples will show—that his Christianity finds its most direct expression in the pulpit. Here he breaks through a certain restriction imposed by his theological system, expresses himself more freely, and develops many christological and eschatological ideas that are hardly covered in *The Christian Faith* but play a role in his personal piety. In their printed form the sermons are wide-ranging discussions that still give evidence of heartfelt warmth and feeling. Their wealth of thought and compactness of statement keep the rapt attention of hearers and presuppose a high level of reflection. He was an academic preacher. His homiletical principle is marked by the fact that he presents no ready-made dogmatic theses and directs no

---

relation between the sexes. This would be an unjust use of the model of the salon. In a general survey of the problem many sociological aspects call for consideration.

34. *Kleinen Schriften und Predigten*, ed. H. Gerdes, I (1970), 83ff.
35. *Athenaeum* 1 (1798) 109.

proclamation at the community but brings his hearers with him into his train of thought. He strives to convince, and believes that the best way to do this is to show what line of thinking has led him to accept the truth that he proclaims. Hence he does not confirm the traditional community in its own presuppositions, but in the pulpit, too, has in mind cultured despisers of the faith or seekers. He thus avoids the confessing confrontation which would not help them and takes them up into his thinking process, to which they can give themselves willingly and with awakened interest, whether they finally agree with his confession or not. He does not spare them this confession. It is dominated by the figure of Christ. Perhaps this is why OT texts are less evident in his preaching except on patriotic days when the text is more of a motto or refrain.

In his preaching Schleiermacher did not read a manuscript but spoke extemporaneously after considerable meditation. He used only a small sheet with headlines. He often wrote this during a Saturday afternoon fellowship when it was assumed that he would simply round off what was previously meditated upon. It was known that on such occasions he would absent himself for a time and write his notes in a quiet corner.

The dialogical character of Schleiermacher's mind found expression especially on the professorial rostrum. He did not read lectures, but spoke to his hearers extemporaneously after careful preparation. His prodigious memory enabled him to present even detailed facts without the aid of a manuscript. Many ideas came to him for the first time in his lectures and in contacts with his audiences. Only then did he commit them to paper, thus making the impulse of the hour literarily fruitful.

It is astonishing that he complained to friends about his lack of knowledge of theological literature. He could even write that they would be horrified if they knew how great it was.[36] On his own admission his distaste for theological reading was due to the fact that the theological sciences are mostly pursued by those who have no feeling for religion. Today we might perhaps say that what he missed in most theologians was existential involvement, their own elemental relation to the reality with which they deal in their reflections. It seems that here external dialogue, e.g., with poetry or philosophy, offered more creative stimulation than tarrying in his own theological métier. The uniting of church and state, he thought, might have contributed to this established distancing of theologians.

In his dealings with students, of which the later physician Adolf

36. Dilthey, pp. 751-52.

Müller gives an enthusiastic account,[37] Schleiermacher's sociable and dialogical nature made a particularly great impression. Müller was greatly enamored of him, and only his respect kept him at a distance. Every Friday Schleiermacher gathered some students to whom he was especially close for tea. They could stay as long as they wanted, for he retired to bed only around 2 A.M. His young guests were delighted at the lively way in which their teacher opened himself to them and entered into conversation with each of them. He never tried to remain aloof like a "star." He was equally accessible to all people, whether the heads of his fellowship, his students, or his candidates for confirmation. What he wrote down in concentrated form was thus the fruit of what came to him in lively discussion. In all this we see his gift for friendship, for which, as for love, his spirit always had a vacant place. He wanted to embrace with love every single being, from uninhibited youth in whom freedom is stirring to the ripest maturity. He greeted each distinctive being with love, seeking its relation to humanity, not its external rank in the world. He had love for a person as he found this relation and understood the person. Only as much as the person understood him could he show that person.[38] Communication and friendship shaped his life so deeply that he found in them the relation of life and death. Death is the ending of all human relationship. The life of friendship is a beautiful sequence of harmonies, and when a friend leaves the world the basic note of fellowship fades. Work in that person ceases and part of life is lost. By dying every loving creature dies, and those who lose many friends finally die at their hands, being shut off from working in those who were their life, so that, being pressed in upon themselves, their spirits consume themselves.[39] This is how he puts it in the highly Romantic language of the *Soliloquies*.

In this way Schleiermacher gives expression to his humanity.

II. SCHLEIERMACHER'S MAIN THEOLOGICAL WORKS

To prevent this chapter from expanding into a book, I must leave out a great deal. I am concerned only with Schleiermacher's *theological* intentions as they are presented in the *Speeches* and *The Christian Faith*. The richness of these works makes only a brief survey possible. I must

37. Dilthey, pp. 758-59.
38. *Soliloquies*, II, pp. 45-46.
39. Ibid., IV, pp. 87-88.

thus confine myself to the leading chapters. Of his wide-ranging writings on philosophy, hermeneutics, and biblical exposition I could give only a vague impression in the biographical sketch above. I will try to bring in one or another—more by way of association—in the theological analysis. I cannot ignore them completely, for Schleiermacher's theology receives its essential impulse from outside theology and can hardly be thought of apart from the correlation with everything human and consequently with the primarily *non*religious dimensions of humanity. The new thing that comes into theological history with him is that he breaks out of the ghetto of orthodoxy and pietism, of the inner ecclesiastical and theological sphere as a whole, and scans universal horizons. As he sees it, even moral teaching and philosophical metaphysics belong within the walls of the ghetto which he is crossing.

But things are more complicated than that. The strongly shaped system, with its fine architecture and beautiful symmetry, and in which his many-faceted thought tries to find appropriate room for itself, can also in another way become a prison which cannot hold his intellectual life as a whole. Schleiermacher's Christ is always more than his theology and stands out at every corner. Hence we cannot understand the greatest nineteenth-century systematician apart from his sermons, in which he speaks freely, directly, and unreservedly, i.e., without regard for his system. The pulpit and the rostrum are the two crucial points in the ellipse of his spirit. Along these lines we shall try to uncover the safety valves which allow the surplus pressure of the system to escape and which enable him to say elsewhere what he leaves unsaid in the system itself.

A. *SPEECHES ON RELIGION*

1. Survey

The date of publication should be noted. The work came out on the threshold of the new century in 1799. To be exact, the manuscript was ready on the morning of April 15 at half past nine. The previous night, as he wrote to Henriette Herz, he was full of the *Speeches* and lay for hours without sleep. What kept him awake was not the heat of working, for the work went slowly and quietly, but a mixture of paternal joy and fear of death. For the first time he had a lively sense that it would be a pity if he were to die that night.[40] A few days before he remarked to the

40. *Briefe*, I, 147.

same correspondent that his Christianity, which he had not yet come to in the *Speeches*, would seem very original to his friend Sack, but was really very old.[41]

In the word *original* Schleiermacher denotes the problem of the book. For in his usage it means having an original view of things. The opposite—a "copy"—is the traditional view taken from the views of others. Being derivative is precisely what he wants to avoid. Hence he resorts, not to dogmatic tradition, but to individually experienced feeling and his own contemplation, the living source of religion in himself. Yet he can also describe that which becomes clear to him on this march to Christianity as something very old. What he means is that even the doctrines of the Christian tradition have arisen as a kind of rationalization of religious feeling which is experienced directly, as an objectification of trust and love and fear. Only later, when these have become doctrines, is the soul of creative feeling expelled from them, so that they become verbal corpses. For static concepts last longer than the glowing, fiery life which flows into them to create formulas. Hence, thinks Schleiermacher, as I lead on to a new view of religion and religious productivity, and make a new theological beginning, paradoxically I also lead back to the original sources of all religious writers and church theologians. We must seek religion where it is still enthusiasm, glowing lava and not cooled off rock.

Only when this is clear can we understand the extraordinary fervor of the *Speeches* and the way they embrace both past and future. Schleiermacher realizes that in this respect he is at a turning point of the times as well as the centuries. He is not mistaken in thinking that he is inaugurating a new epoch in theological thinking, a beginning which he himself will surpass in his later work. For the first time we emphatically find here what Semler is the first to intimate, namely, that all theological communications have recipients, and that this helps to determine their form and content. The recipients are contemporaries such as Schleiermacher saw especially in his Romantic friends.[42]

Being contemporary involves stress on what is peculiar to the time, such as we see in the sense of being at a turning point of the times and the sense of contrast between past and future.

This is even plainer in the later *Soliloquies*, in which Schleier-

---

41. *Briefe*, I, 145.
42. These friends did in fact listen, e.g., Novalis and Tieck, and after some initial reserve Schelling. Goethe and Schiller had less time for this glowing Romantic enthusiasm. Only later did Schiller make some approach to Schleiermacher (letter to Zelter, July 16, 1804).

macher refers emphatically to the present intellectual situation, and to the thinking of the present generation, to which he feels that he is a stranger, the prophetic citizen of a later world.[43] I suspect (but am not quite sure) that this is the first instance of reflection on "our time" and its significance for proclamation. The theologian and systematician as well as the preacher is bound to his time. He can speak only in correlation with questions of his own day and in solidarity with his contemporaries.

This means implicitly that theology is a historical phenomenon. Its form, intention, and address are in constant flux. Theology and preaching have a history. No forms of teaching are valid once and for all. We can count on no perennial theology. Although the term *modern* occurs sporadically in the 17th century,[44] only with Schleiermacher does the modernity of theology become a program.

I will now sketch the structure of the *Speeches*, then analyze more closely its central message in the first two *Speeches*. What I want to show in these texts is the first stage in the development of what will come to maturity in *The Christian Faith*.

Structure

The first *Speech*, called an "apology," begins with a theme that is vital to Schleiermacher, that of the recipients. He is addressing the "cultured," and especially skeptics for whom the phenomenon of Christianity, whether orthodox or rationalistic, blocks access to religion, putting them off. He approaches the cultured in this *Speech* with a surprising maneuver which runs contrary to all that they expect from a religious tract. The general opinion thus far has been that culture leaves the mythical childhood stage of the age of religion behind, and that no notice must be taken of the defensive reactions of out-of-date champions of religion, i.e., church leaders and pastors. Schleiermacher, however, speaks in the name of culture. The cultured must be truly cultured. The theologian Schleiermacher does not demand of his readers that in order to make contact with religion they should discard their presuppositions and renounce secular wisdom. He tells them instead to be true to themselves, to maintain their identity as critical intellectuals. He will meet them on their own ground and let them see that he himself is one of them and yet can still confess that he is religious.

The second *Speech* deals with the material nature of religion in

43. *Soliloquies*, III and IV, pp. 49-88.
44. Cf. *EF,* I, 30ff.

order to make it plain that religion is not a foreign body which has to be accepted but that without suspecting it the cultured have constantly been dealing with it in their own sphere. Since we shall be looking at this *Speech* more closely, I will be content here simply to indicate its purpose.

The next *Speech* deals with religious education. Here Schleiermacher first asks the basic question whether religion can in fact be taught, communicated, or handed down. If his thesis is correct that religion can derive only from an original experience, the acceptance of religious theses from others is highly debatable. In secularized psychological categories, which emphasize experience, Schleiermacher is here raising the same problem as occurs today in homiletical and catechetical textbooks: If the Holy Spirit decides the when and where, if faith cannot be manufactured but is given, can the aim of Christian education be to make Christians, or, in Schleiermacher's terms, to teach religion? In brief, his own solution is that if we impart what is most proper to us and hence give ourselves, a spark flies, and it ignites in others a flame that is fed by the materials already present in them as religious subjects. There is thus a kind of Socratic releasing of what is most proper to them. It is impossible to detach religion from this personal character which is kindled by the personal. It is impossible to spread it by suggesting that it corresponds to suprapersonal and universally valid norms.

By such norms Schleiermacher means the rules of understanding and utility. The rules of understanding claim comprehensibility. One can only be intolerant toward those who reject them. They shut themselves out of the society of rational people. But rules of this kind are alien to religion. Hence they cannot serve to make it teachable or to give it the quality of comprehensibility. The rules of utility, or pragmatic recommendations, cannot do justice to religion either. On the contrary, they ascribe to religion the dubious role of being a mere means to nonreligious ends.

Schleiermacher himself sees three legitimate ways to religion which we shall meet again in the discussion of religious speech and which may, then, be simply listed here: self-contemplation (anthropology), contemplation of the cosmos (cosmology), and artistic sense (symbolics). In all three we are related to the universe and thus exposed to religious experience.

The fourth *Speech* deals with the social aspect of religion, or church and ministry. It thus presents an ecclesiology corresponding to the view of religion. The church is defined as a fellowship of religious people grounded on the need to share. When the heart is full, the mouth speaks. The heart is full of religion. Religion, then, involves communication. The church comes into being as the institutional form of this urge for fellowship.

In this church of religious people the bond, then, does not consist of a dogma or confession on the basis of which one is a member of the body of Christ. It does not consist of a word of revelation, a kerygma, which is the basis of the church, which creates hearers for itself, and in the name of which the members of the church assemble. It consists of subjective religiosity. The religious "sense" is the common factor. But the intensity and endowment in this field of experience are unequal, as are also the ability and the need to present the contents of experience and objectify them in words.

Yet the inequalities are secondary. They are not antitheses which must be decided in the name of truth, of an objective fact from which there can be no deviation. In the field of subjective religiosity there can be no confessional stance or uniformity of this kind. This religiosity comprises the widest variations and modifications. Hence the church of religious people has to be tolerant. Its thrust toward fellowship, its need to share, inclines it daily toward organization, toward acceptance of the regenerate, the instruction of children, and the forming of social institutions. It becomes a popular church with a vital center of outreach.

Passionately, and even with some intolerance, Schleiermacher turns against state patronage (as he later does in practice in the liturgical conflict). The worst foe or enemy is always that which comes from outside, whether in the form of a dogmatic authority or in that of institutional direction, such as happens in a state church. Religion always grows from within outward, not vice versa. All that can come from outside is stimulation which produces inner growth and helps to trigger it.

The final *Speech* deals with religions, religious history, and the place of Christianity in it. It is particularly interesting because it carries an apology for positive religions and for the special position of Christianity. According to Schleiermacher's view of religion, which we have to study more closely, this is by no means self-evident. One might be inclined to suspect that he is content with religiosity in general and does not think it unconditionally necessary to belong to a specific religion and therefore to a historical concretion of the religious. Since he comes up here against the special instance of the Christian religion, we must spend a little longer on this issue in spite of the brevity of our sketch.

Religion has to individualize itself and divide into many positive religions because no one can have religion in totality, we being finite and religion infinite. The unavoidable individualizing of religion, however, does not halt with the positive religions. For when we settle in one of these, we again specialize and give it a personal form. We might use Goethe's formula here, namely, that the religious mystery declares itself in an infinite series of finite forms, including religious forms. Innumerable forms of religion are thus possible.

This division into positive religions can lead to perversion. Schleiermacher thinks that the reaction of the cultured to this will be sensible; they will resist it. They fear—and he himself shares this fear—that such forms of religion will force their adherents to fix on one form, to be kept within unnatural limits, and to become the victims of absolutism (and hence also of intolerance). They would be entangled in a system of abstract concepts and theories. When this happens—and here is the perversion—the infinite is made finite and all that remains of religion are the dead cinders of the outgushings of the inner fire that is contained in all religion.

Nevertheless, Schleiermacher warns his hearers and readers that we do not do justice to the positive religions if we see in them only a drift in this direction. In principle the individualizing positive religions are simply fragmentary particles of the one total religion. A specific religion arises only when one view of the universe is made the central point of all religion and everything is referred to it. Thus within what is finite and individual the sense of the infinite and total is developed in this individualized religion. For this reason one may view it as a fragment of the one complete religion which does not force us into a dreadful fixation on this single piece. For the individual religions are only microcosms in which the macrocosm of religion is reflected. Thus we have the whole in the part. What is individual and finite has symbolical significance. To grasp that is to be protected against the perversion of making the specific absolute or the finite infinite.

This is how Schleiermacher opens his apology for positive religions. They are a sign that religion seeks to develop itself on all sides in as many ways as possible, and that only by way of these forms of development do we have access to it. To settle in a specific religion is to have a secure dwelling and citizenship in the religious world.[45] In our individual religion one view has to be dominant or else it is worthless. To struggle against this positive and arbitrary element is to struggle against everything definite and real. The only alternative is the natural religion so much lauded by the cultured.

But for Schleiermacher the generality of this natural religion

45. In this connection Schleiermacher repeatedly uses the words *dwelling* and *to dwell*.

makes it weak and unreal. The lack of personal development and individualization manifests itself in the fact that its adherents seek in vain a wealth of strongly marked features. He himself has never found such. If by religious freedom we simply understand—as those who confess natural religion obviously do—a freedom from all need to be or see or feel anything specific, then we ourselves are nothing specific, and there is nothing original, as we might put it today. Religion, then, plays a very feeble role in the minds of such lemurs.

Using the indefiniteness of natural religion, which is neither positive nor historically individual, Schleiermacher paints an excellent and very precise portrait of these rationalists. He makes it plain that this secret religion of the cultured is not at all the climax of religious history but denotes only decadence and degeneration. It is as if natural religion has no real pulse or blood vessels or circulation or temperature or assimilative power or character of its own. It is everywhere mixed up with morality and natural sentimentality. In conjunction with these it moves sluggishly and rarely. Only in part is it distinct from them. Its adherents, then, fish in muddy waters. Decrying everything specific as dead letter, they give themselves to what is indefinite. What is to be found in the hazy sphere between stiff systematicians (who deal only with the empty formulas) and shallow indifferentists (who shun everything definite or historical) no longer shows any trace of the spirit of a religion.

The apology for positive religions cannot mean the unconditional acceptance of the one we prefer. Schleiermacher brings this out in his presentation and criticism of Judaism. Here we see his reservations about the OT.

In Judaism[46] the idea of the universum shines through only in a very limited way. It is reduced to the concept of universal direct retribution, to a reaction of the infinite against everything finite. Implied is the sacredness of the tradition in which the fulfilments of retribution are recorded. The limited viewpoint that characterizes Judaism grants only a short span to this religion as a religion. It died when its sacred books were finished, for Jehovah's dialogue with his people was then seen to be ended. Certain political elements maintained a sickly existence for a time. But this was simply the distasteful phenomenon of a mechanical movement from which life and spirit had long since departed.

With no little tension we anticipate Schleiermacher's effort to work Christianity into his idea of individualized religions. Is it simply one of these religions and perhaps interchangeable in consequence? Or

46. He means by this what we today would call the whole complex of the religious history of Israel and the Jews.

is it marked by high privileges and perhaps absoluteness? Formally, Schleiermacher's solution reminds us of that which we shall encounter later in the religious philosophy of Hegel. I venture to state it as follows. In Christianity the idea of religion has found its most adequate form. We see here the congruence of idea and form. Schleiermacher begins the section in an almost hymnic way.

The central theme of religion is present in Christianity because it is governed by two poles, namely, our alienation from the final reality that Schleiermacher calls the universum, and the overcoming of this state. Perversion and redemption, enmity and mediation, are the two inseparably related sides of the Christian view. Since Christianity sees the universum best in religion and its history, resorting, as we would say nowadays, to a salvation history, it develops religion itself as material for religion, and thus achieves a higher potency in the individualizing of religion. By "higher potency" Schleiermacher has in view what is specific and unique in Christianity, what I have called the congruence of idea and form, something that is found elsewhere in weaker potency.

The full presence of religion in Christianity expresses itself even more clearly in the aim of Christianity, i.e., an infinite holiness. By this Schleiermacher does not mean an ideal of perfection—this would mix religion with the alien matter of morality—but a sense of never wholly leaving our alienation from religion, a constant striving. Never content with what is achieved, Christianity even in its purest views and most sacred feelings still seeks traces of the irreligious, of the trend toward the finite which is opposed to the universum. He thus finds the true and wholly valid state of humanity in the relation to religion, and it seems that Luther's thesis that we are always righteous and sinners at the same time is present here in very different terms. Essential safeguards are built into Christianity against rigidity and stagnation. It is subject to constant self-criticism and self-purifying, to constant sifting. For Christians, then, the dominant note of all their religious feelings is a holy sadness. In this regard, he admits, there are many distortions and perversions which he has no wish to excuse. Over against them we must cling to the idea of Christianity.

Naturally, we must discuss what significance Christ has for this idea. We will see later, especially in *Christmas Eve,* and then in *The Christian Faith,* that Christology is a difficult morsel in his system which he works hard to swallow. The difficulty relates to the fact that Christ is a historical figure, an objective or "brute" fact, which cannot be reduced to an idea. It is important, then, to see how his wrestling with the problem begins in the *Speeches.*

The beginning is relatively harmless because the historical background of Christianity is still obscured. Christ appears in the fifth *Speech* as a mere idea, i.e., the idea of the mediator. He thus fits smoothly into the schema of alienation and redemption.

The opening thesis is that everything finite needs the mediation of something higher so as not to move further away from the universum and be scattered in emptiness and nothingness. If Christ has this mediatorial function, he himself cannot possibly need mediation, and hence he cannot be finite. To discharge his function, he has to belong to both the spheres that must be reconciled. He must have both a divine and a human nature.

What Schleiermacher is saying here in allusion to the Chalcedonian term *nature* undergoes a reinterpretation which has prototypical significance for his later Christology. He appeals to Matt. 11:27, that no one knows the Father but the Son. The word *know* leads him by association to the point that the special feature in Christ is his consciousness. Here the word occurs which will be the key both to his later Christology and to his theology in general. "This *consciousness* of the uniqueness of his religiosity, or the originality of his view, and of its power to impart itself and to promote religion, was also the *consciousness* of his office as mediator and of his divinity." The ontological term *nature* now becomes *consciousness*. Already intimated, then, is another later theme, namely, that it is the power of Christ's God-consciousness that accords him fulfilment, that makes him a model for humanity and its fragmentary state, that also lifts him above humanity and assigns him divine predicates.

Another feature of the later works also occurs here for the first time. As he will do for the rest of his life, Schleiermacher wrestles with the question whether Christ is the last and definitive revelation of God, whether he can ever be surpassed.[47] As we read toward the end of the fifth *Speech,* Christ never claimed to be the only object of the application of his idea, or to be the only mediator. He never pretended that the views and feelings that he could impart encompassed all religion. How could he? The possibilities of God-consciousness are always a matter of "more" or "less," and in principle allow for emulation. This implies a relativizing of Christ which does not exclude expectation of another and a higher.

But it is as if Schleiermacher cannot quite say this, as if he is

47. As we shall see, his answer is wrapped in some obscurity. Starting theologically with the consciousness, he has to consider in principle the possibility of surpassing by an even higher consciousness. In the sermons, however, he expresses his definite conviction that Christ is final and no other is to be expected; cf. the Advent sermon on Matt. 21:9 (1843 ed., II, 5ff.).

afraid that his approach in the *Speeches* will prevent him from confessing what is obviously still his conviction at this time, namely, that Christ is final and definitive, and that we need expect no other.

In the fifth *Speech* he makes a strenuous effort to escape from the christological obscurity into which he seems to be led at this point. (It is here that his later, incessant wrestling is intimated.)

How can Christianity finally perish? he asks. (And it will have to perish if its founder is only a transitory and not a final figure in history!) But the very phenomena in the history of Christianity which seem to be signs of exhaustion, rigidity, and perversion, and hence to intimate its destruction, show that neither the gates of hell nor any earthly power can prevail against it. For the living spirit that dwells within it may sleep long and often, and in a state of rigidity withdraw into the dead husk of the letter, but it always reawakens when a change in the spiritual world is favorable, and puts its sap in motion; and it will often do so still.

That which is eternal in every positive religion, and that which is superior in Christianity, finds adequate expression and grants resurrection from every upset. Christianity, as we have seen, provides for critical reflection which keeps its final goal in view.

Yet Schleiermacher has to consider the possibility that at least the historical forms of religions, including Christianity, are subject to decay, will find a place in the repository of history as the monuments of an earlier time, and are thus irreversible. Is not a recognition of transitoriness contained in Christianity itself inasmuch as it is more historical, and more humble in its glory, than all other religions? But what does such a recognition finally mean? Does it not mean that Christ himself shares this transitoriness as the normative factor in the personal form of Christianity?

Again the christological problem is the real point, for in it the two elements coincide: the divine, eternal reality that is above time, and the historical, time-bound form. The two dimensions meet in the mediator.

How can Schleiermacher avoid this dead end into which his thinking seems to crowd him? Is there any escape? Does he not have to revoke the divine nature of Christ, which he has accepted, if he agrees that his human nature, as a member of history, is transitory?

I have stated the conflict in which he finds himself more clearly than he himself does. I have made explicit what is only implicit in the text of the fifth *Speech*. I thought I should do this because I find the same conflict in his later christological struggle. When we look at this we find all these conflicting thoughts at issue.

Schleiermacher tries to free himself from the fetters in which he has caught himself by two considerations. (We witness here a true drama of thought.) First, he does not speak of the end of Christ himself, which would cause us to look for another, but of the end of his mediatorial function. The time will come—he himself intimated it by referring to John 4:21, 23—when no mediator will be needed, but the Father will be all in all. Second, the problem of time arises again. If in the foreseeable future the mediatorial function will come to an end, we shall again confront the possibility of a surpassing of Christianity, and with it the possibility that the higher form of religion will find a new representative whom we then have to await. This would again challenge Schleiermacher's christological understanding.

At this extreme limit where the problems of history and eternity, of positive religion and religion as such, come to a climax, Schleiermacher seeks an eschatological escape. The time when Christ's mediatorial function ceases will never come. It lies—he fears!—outside all time, on the far side of earthly history. Thus the problem of a surpassing of Christ does not arise. Rather frivolously, but in a way that illumines the situation, one might say that in God's kingdom we neither woo nor are wooed—hence there is no mediation.

So long as time endures, there will always be Christians and the Christian mediator will be active. Does this mean that the Christian religion, being superior to all others, will be solely dominant in humanity as the only form of religion? Will it, as the absolute religion, drive out all others? Schleiermacher definitely wants to avoid this conclusion. In this regard the arguments he does not use are almost more important than those he does. He does not say—as he easily might have done—that Christ's mediatorship does not arise for other religious areas or that other religions have their own mediators. Such questions, which again raise and lie athwart the christological problem (John 14:6), are not considered. Schleiermacher simply uses the argument that Christianity (not Christ himself), in view of its corruptibility and its melancholy history, does not think it has the competence to drive out other religions. Paradoxically, this sense of its own relativity is for Schleiermacher the best proof of its eternity. In the name of this paradox he can champion the thesis that innumerable forms of religion are possible.

We have now received a first impression of how complicated the web is in which Schleiermacher weaves together the Platonic idea of religion, with its earthly, historical gradations, and the monopoly of Christianity (if one may put it thus), with its historical relativity.

2. Axis: The Understanding of Religion in the First and Second Speeches

Before the hero takes the stage in Schiller's *Wallenstein*, we are told a great deal about him indirectly, so that we look forward to his appearance with tense expectation. The same applies to religion, the chief character in the *Speeches*. In the preliminary survey we follow its many-hued reflection in several variations, and we then turn to it directly. It opens its role in the apology (First Speech). The point here is to see before whom it is playing and to whom it applies: the spectators and hearers.

The First Speech. Four aspects are presented. First, we have the address and the kindling of a readiness to listen. Second, we have a confession of solidarity with those who are addressed. This vouches for the sincerity of the speaker. Third, we have an appeal to existential interest by exposition of the human relation to religion. Finally, distorted ideas in the religious sphere are dispelled.

Regarding the first point, the apology opens with a closer look at those who are addressed, namely, the cultured among the despisers of religion, the secularized. It takes up a concern that orthodoxy never even considers. No longer must the critical world of culture feel left out. Displaying his recognition of the situation of intellectuals, Schleiermacher says that he realizes that they no more honor the deity in sacred stillness than they visit the deserted temples, that in their tasteful dwellings there are no longer any household gods but the sayings of the wise and the songs of poets.

The filling of the present life with meaning, and its refinement, have absorbed transcendence. Culture has made the cultus superfluous. The educated have made their own universum, as Schleiermacher says later. They are too exalted to think of that which created them. They have succeeded in making this life so full and varied that they no longer need eternity. In modern terms, they have a secular religion. The transitory itself has become a symbol. The incorruptible, as the sphere of supernatural transcendence, the hereafter, is a fraud of poets and parsons. (This is how Nietzsche put it later; Schleiermacher uses loftier terms, but it amounts to the same thing.)

In regard to these statements we must note that Schleiermacher does not make them disapprovingly. He does not speak of the curse of secularization, of this-worldliness, of the confusion of Creator and creature. His estimate is positive. The emphasis in life and religion has swung from transcendence to immanence. Schleiermacher's message here is in tune with the panentheistic thrust of Goethe's *Prooemion*, in which God moves the world inwardly, activating himself in nature and nature in himself, not merely impinging upon it from without. In fact, there is evidence here of the panentheistic influence of an intellectual tradition characterized by the names of Bruno, Shaftesbury, and Spinoza.[48]

This panentheism, in which God is brought into the world and is its vitalizing principle, is the classical position in the secret religion of the cultured whom Schleiermacher is addressing. He sees a specific mode of this-worldliness at work in them and not the self-resting finitude of Tillich's critique of secularism.[49] On this view of things the world is a closed system of natural forces and functions which humanity tries to direct without regard for any basic meaning. The finitude that Schleiermacher has in mind, however, rests in something sacred, no matter whether it be called God, the universum, or the ground of meaning. Or, better, this sacred thing rests in it. This world, then, is not autarchous. The eternal is what makes it this world, and it adopts it as such. Strictly, then, it is no longer finite. It takes on the numinous significance of the universum.

Panentheism in this sense is before Schleiermacher his whole life long. The first important emergence of an author usually produces labels that will always be with him. As the secret religion of contemporary intellectuals dominates the *Speeches,* so Schleiermacher will later strive passionately to overcome it (in spite of some remaining traces). He turns vehemently against all those who, as he thought in the Introduction to *The Christian Faith,* accepted a pantheistic or a general philosophical approach.[50]

The "cultured" whom Schleiermacher names as his audience think of themselves as mature and autonomous people, and the author promises to respect their dignity and not to try to force orthodox dogmas upon them. In Socratic fashion he will try to trigger certain religious processes which they have for a long time unwittingly carried within them. He can call them to himself only if they are capable of rising above the common state, taking the difficult way in the inwardness of human nature, and finding there the basis of thought and action.

Regarding the second point, i.e., confession of solidarity, Schleiermacher seeks to win a hearing, not by addressing the cultured authoritatively from outside, but by assuring them that he is one of them

48. Cf. Dilthey, pp. 180-81.
49. This term occurs constantly in Tillich; cf. first *Die religiöse Lage der Gegenwart* (1926), e.g., p. 104.
50. Cf. the *Sendschreiben an Lücke,* which will be discussed later.

and will argue on their own ground. He will have nothing to do with the superstitious and barbaric complaints whereby attempts are made to reerect the breached walls of a Judean Zion and its Gothic pillars. As one human being to others he will simply speak about the sacred mysteries of humanity. He will do so with no ulterior motive. He will speak only out of the inner and irresistible necessity of his nature. They may rest assured that here is one human being speaking to others, all bound together by their common humanity. The author has broken with those traditions which like hardened walls block all access to religion. There is no need to fear any ruts. Readers may confidently entrust themselves to him.

Regarding the third point, the appeal to the existential interest of his readers leads Schleiermacher to point out that all people have a religious relation, i.e., a relation to the universum. If this can be shown, then fear of the supernatural strangeness of the bearers of revelation vanishes. Such bearers are simply an enhancement or final culmination of that which is in all of us. We thus find in them something familiar or analogous. We all have religious talents; prophets and divine messengers have religious genius. We are all religious people; they are the most religious.

How, then, does Schleiermacher elucidate this common humanity and the related existential relevance of religion? He analyzes the human relation to the universum and tries to show that in the natural human being[51] it is one-sided and broken, but its fragmentary character is overcome in prophets and divine messengers, the most religious of people.

Life involves attraction and repulsion.[52] Attraction involves a force that tries to draw everything around it to itself, and as far as possible to penetrate its inner being. It seeks enjoyment. The opposite force is the longing to extend the inner self, to permeate everything with it, to impart it to everything. This force is an active one. It creates the world and culture and brings freedom and relationship, power and law, right and decorum.

Neither force can fully represent the idea of humanity. We can achieve self-fulfilment, or self-identity, only at the point of indifference between these poles where an almost perfect balance unites the two. This basic law of cosmic harmony finds perfect form in certain very religious people, the prophets (among whom Christ is here numbered).

51. Schleiermacher does not himself use this phrase.
52. We are reminded of the first verse of the *Orphische Urworte* and Goethe's commentary on it.

In every age the deity sends those in whom both forces are fruitfully united, equips them with wonderful gifts, and makes them interpreters of its will and works and mediators of that which otherwise would be eternally cut off. On the one side such people make use of surrounding things, on the other they are filled with an impulse to permeate spiritually, to leave the impress of their spirit on the world, and thus to act as heroes, lawgivers, inventors, masters of nature, and good daemons.

In this regard Schleiermacher tries to effect a synthesis of religious and secular genius. Both types are intimately related to the cosmos, having brought the two fundamental forces into balance.

It is important that along these lines religion is set alongside other human capacities. This should gain the attention of the cultured, who have hitherto thought that religion has to do with the supernatural and has no contact with their ordinary humanity. In fact religion is in some sense the most natural thing in the world. Even God's emissaries do not belong to some other world. They do not strike us as strange. They simply represent in fulness and balance that which we are fragmentarily and one-sidedly.

Thus the most religious people are not just mediators between God and us, but mediators also between limited individuals and humanity. They are advocates of the human. At an unexpected place we here run into an intimation of Schleiermacher's later Christology. In Christ we find the same characteristics as in these forerunners (as one might call them). Being human, in the sense of *The Christian Faith*, is the same as being like God, or, in the author's later vocabulary, having a consciousness of God,[53] such as Christ had in prototypical perfection.

Being human is adequately represented by the humanity to which the great mediators lead us. The term *humanity* is so common in Schleiermacher, especially in the *Soliloquies*, that we must devote some moments to it.

In most cases it might be explained as follows. In each individual we find the universal forces of attraction and repulsion in different degrees. Hence we can have only a broken image of the universum. By the law of statistics,[54] however, humanity as a whole, as the sum of an infinite number of individuals, contains the two forces in equal amounts. In the form of a balance, then, humanity enjoys that which in individual examples is present only in imbalance. All humanity,

53. Feeling and contemplation of the universum are more important categories in the *Speeches*.
54. At least this is how one might put it today.

then, is the representative of true and perfect man;[55] hence its high dignity.

The most religious people and their secular counterparts (heroes, lawgivers, etc.), being exceptions who have achieved the balance that is proper only to the whole, represent this total humanity. They are this humanity in microcosmic form. They are its image and likeness.

Only now can we see why Schleiermacher grants them mediatorial rank. They mirror God and his creative purpose, and they are also prototypes of humanity, which they represent. In other words, when the idea of the divine (or the universum) is fully reflected, the idea of the human is also achieved.

At the point of indifference of the two forces, at this most religious point, if one might use the phrase, the final mysteries of the universum are declared. Here is the source of every insight and prophecy, of every holy work of art and inspired speech. Religious revelation does not come through contingent communications from God by way of supernatural acts. How could the moderns whom the author is addressing find any meaning in such a *Deus dixit*? How could they receive anything from it? Revelations take place wherever humanity is seen as a reflection, wherever it is in harmony with the universum, wherever the polar forces in the universum strike a balance. When this happens, as it does in the genius or the mediator, we do not find dogmas that we reject as foreign bodies, but our own humanity speaks to us in its full perfection, and our own humanity is addressed and awakened by it. There are thus communicated holy thoughts and feelings, but in a light play in which different rays of light are now united and then break apart again. The slightest word is understood. We do not have the thundering voice of prophetic herald cries. With a light whispering something is stirred within us which awaits this movement.

When Schleiermacher reaches this central point in his mystery religion, his speech flames with eschatological fervor. The day will surely come when revelation is our common legacy, for even in individuals the polar forces are coming more and more into balance. The biblical pictures of the eschaton are interpreted in terms of this idea of harmony. Thus on the basis of Jer. 31:33-34 and Ezek. 11:19-20 it is said that the time will come when no one will need a teacher, for all will be taught by God. When the sacred fire burns everywhere, there is no need of fiery prayers to bring down fire from heaven; the quiet stillness of holy virgins will maintain it. We must seek out the heavenly sparks which are present when a holy soul is touched by the universum.

55. Cf. the similar view of Kant.

None of the great religious leaders, from ancient prophets to modern mystics, has ever, when moved in this elemental fashion, conceived of the idea of attempting the huge labor of setting up theological systems and thus replacing the divine spark with cold metal. When Schleiermacher himself later attempted such a task in the greatest systematic theology of the century, it was with a question mark on the margin. As mentioned, this mark is to be found in the sermons, in which the witness tries to speak about experiences that he cannot put into the system.

Regarding the fourth point, in his apologetic venture Schleiermacher tries also to rid the minds of the cultured of false and distorted ideas of religion. He has particularly in mind dogmatic and systematic hardenings of that which is fluid fire in its original state.

At the end of the first *Speech* he attacks the pragmatic falsification of religion. We find this abuse when people think that religion is needed to maintain law and order in the world, to come to the aid of shortsighted human vision and limited human power with the thought of an all-seeing eye and infinite force.[56] Undoubtedly, no service is done to religion when it is degraded into a mere instrument of government and subjected to ends outside itself. Since the second *Speech* continues in similar vein, we may let this one reference suffice.

The Second Speech. This address, which echoes some of the themes of the apology, has a negative and a positive part. The negative part is in the main a continuation of the clearing away of common misconceptions of religion. The author's main concern here is to distinguish religion from metaphysics and morality. Since moralism seems to be the chief misunderstanding, still deep-seated in the minds of people today (e.g., in their use of the term *sin*), and since we carry this post-Kantian mortgage in so much of our preaching, it is on this aspect that we shall dwell. The positive part deals with the essence of religion and defines it as the contemplation and sense of the universum.

---

56. In his *Lehre vom Staat* (WW, 1834ff., Part 3, vol. 8), which we cannot discuss here, Schleiermacher deals with law and order, the state and society, authority and freedom, and democracy too, in the light of his theologically developed view of humanity. He thinks that the positivistic and authoritarian *Deus dixit* of orthodoxy is reflected in a similar political structure, i.e., absolutism. Corresponding to absolutism is a strict separation between the supernatural and the natural which lets God intervene arbitrarily in history. But he opposes an extreme liberalism as well as absolutism. Authority has to be based on the will of the whole or it becomes aristocratic caprice. Extreme liberalism, in which the state dissolves in society, also has theological associations. An individualistic view of the church corresponds to it. Christ is no longer the creator of a higher common consciousness but a model for individual conduct which in promoting interests impinges on those of others. Cf. the searching study by Y. Spiegel, *Theologie der bürgerlichen Gesellschaft. Sozialphilosophie und Glaubenslehre bei Schleiermacher* (1968), esp. pp. 199-200.

I will first discuss the differentiation of religion, the clearing of the ground conceptually. At this point Schleiermacher shows himself to be a forerunner of what since Kierkegaard would be called an existential thinker.

His starting point is the statement that religion shares a common theme with metaphysics and morality, namely, the universum and our relation to it. In terms of modern ontology one might say that all three deal with the being in which we exist. In the second *Speech* there are only three possible ways of relating to the universum. We may *think* the totality of being, in which case we engage in metaphysics; we may *act* in it, in which case our relation is moral; and we may *feel* it in a religious relationship.

The difference is not that the three spheres have different objects, for the object is the same. The difference lies in the relation to the object. (We have here an intimation of the approach to Kierkegaard's existential thinker, for whom everything depends on the relation to the object.) Instead of relations we might also speak of different angles from which the universum is viewed. The important thing is that the object itself changes for me as I come under the influence of the different relations.

An example that is closer to home might help. I can have very different views of historical figures according to my relation to them. Thus I might be a contemporary who is for or against them, an impartial historian, or one who sees them from the standpoint of a certain philosophy or ideology. Historical figures and their roles change as I see history as, e.g., a race or class struggle, or as I interpret it idealistically or materialistically.

Only when the three modes of viewing are rightly integrated and work together does there arise the true subjectivity which properly reflects the universum and can achieve an adequate partnership with it. Here again we have a complementarity which needs various colors if we are to reach a true reflection.

In other words, we properly encounter the universum, the totality of being, only when we encounter it with the totality of our humanity and not just with one sector of our mind or activity. When we formulate Schleiermacher's postulate in this way, we see plainly how much his concept of humanity contributes to his view. We also see here things that are essential in his hermeneutics. I have in mind the appropriateness of subjectivity to the object with which it has to do in knowledge, will, or feeling. Here again we come across the problem of relationship.

For Schleiermacher a blind and uncritical knowledge of an object is impossible. If we attempt it, we miss the object itself. We unwittingly produce our own object and regard it as the real object, in this case the universum. Thus Schleiermacher charges idealism with destroying the universum that it seeks to fashion. He perhaps has Hegel in view with his idea of the self-development of the world spirit which our finite spirit sees in the cards and perhaps puts there. Or he may have Fichte in mind, whose I posits what is not I, and hence the universum. At any rate, the creator of an idealistic system demotes the universum to a mere allegory, the empty shadow of our own limitation.

If we want to know the universum, we cannot speculate uncritically and at large. We must have achieved an impression of it prior to reflection. We have to know it in direct experience, as religious people, before we engage in reflection. This is what Schleiermacher attempts in the second *Speech*. Only at this stage of development can he show what subjective attitude is appropriate to the universum.

The truth can be had only within a subjectivity which is already determined by the matter of knowledge, i.e., by the object. Here too, then, there must be a being in the truth (John 18:37), a determination by it, if the truth is to shine forth. There is an analogy between object and subjectivity and in it the object plays the dominant role.[57] The universum speaks and reveals itself to us. The supposed object is in truth the acting subject in the partnership between us and the universum. It discloses itself, therefore, only to a specific and open subjectivity. To that extent it plays the dominant part. The universum demands an appropriate attitude. It can be viewed only as the viewer is influenced by what is viewed (in this case the universum) and is determined by it.

Understandably Schleiermacher, like Kierkegaard after him, develops his theses in opposition to Hegel. Again like Kierkegaard, he regards Hegel's approach as wrong, although without naming him.

Kierkegaard's objection to Hegel is that he rejects the existential thinker who participates inwardly. He sees the world phenomenon only from without as a self-development of the spirit. He sees it only from the standpoint of the spectator who need make no decision.

Schleiermacher's objection is not that Hegel puts God, the absolute spirit, within the universe, not outside it, and sees him at work in various stages of self-evolution. He could hardly object to this, for he thinks along the same lines himself. No, his objection is the different one that Hegel does not begin with the numinous force of the universum, into which humanity is integrated as a tiny particle, but constructs the universum out of his own finite spirit. He dares to do this because this finite spirit thinks it is identical with the absolute spirit, the formative principle of the universum. These ideas are at the back of Schleier-

---

57. In his hermeneutics Schleiermacher deals with this analogy in connection with the divinatory principle.

macher's objection. In them the universum is not taken seriously. We ourselves in all our limitations are its masters. We make it the empty shadow of our own limitations.

This gives us already Schleiermacher's decisive objection to the confusion of religion and metaphysics. Metaphysics has a distant, rationalizing attitude to the universum. Metaphysicians do not see themselves humbly as parts of it. They give their limited minds the hybrid role of grasping it conceptually and thus mastering it. In seeming to construct it, they destroy it.

More narrowly Schleiermacher has in view two different types of metaphysics: that of Kant as well as that of Hegel (the references are plain enough even though he mentions no names). Hegel is meant when he speaks of metaphysicians who classify the universum, who deduce the necessity of the real, who spin out of their own minds the reality of the world and its laws. Kant's transcendental philosophy is meant when he refers to a metaphysics that begins with our finite nature, with the limited sphere of our own epistemological capacity, and seeks to determine from our own power and receptivity what the universum can be for us and how we have to view it. In such cases we cease to approach the all-powerful universum without preconceptions. Metaphysically corrupted,[58] we claim that the structural conditions of our own epistemology (the categories and forms of perception) decide how and to what extent we can see the universum and it can manifest itself to us.

Morality, like metaphysics, also renounces direct receptivity and has a different relation to the universum from religion. The arguments in favor of this distinction develop the same basic thought. Moralists, unlike religious people, no longer live and move in the universum. They distance themselves from it. They misuse it, at least when claiming religion as a guarantee, by seeking to derive duties from it and thus making religion into a code of laws.

The misunderstanding of religion is that morality begins with the sense of freedom and wants to subject everything to it, whereas religion breathes where freedom has become nature again; it sees us beyond the play of our special powers and personality, i.e., where wittingly or unwittingly we have to be what we are. Schleiermacher's *homo religiosus* is like Goethe's daimon, which sees itself as a microcosm of the universum.[59] Being part of the universum, will and duty are

---

58. Kant, of course, would not call his philosophy a metaphysics, but opposes his transcendentalism to (dogmatic) metaphysics.

59. Cf. the strophe *Ananke*, which equates law and will; we will only because we should.

inseparably identical. But morality divides them again. What is a unity in religion falls apart in morality. The final reason why this happens is that moralists set us apart from the universum, no longer view us as part of it, do not accept us as something sacred from the hand of religion.

Naturally, there has to be morality or ethics. Schleiermacher willingly accepts this.[60] Morality is part of the many-colored picture which is needed if there is to be an expression of the fulness of being and of our relation to it.

Morality has a malign influence if it does not supplement the religious aspect of the universum but replaces it or intermingles with religion. It also has a malign influence if it becomes our only mode of relating to the universum, for it then becomes the magna carta of an antithesis between us and it. For Schleiermacher, then, everything depends upon defining the original contours of religion and not letting it be confused with other spheres of the spirit. He thus pursues passionately what will later be called the religious a priori (e.g., by Troeltsch) so as to ensure for religion autonomous and independent rank in the human consciousness.

These distinctions prepare the ground for a development of the content of religion, i.e., of the religion in which we achieve our own identity because we achieve a sense of our integration into the universum. For Schleiermacher openness to religion means a sense and taste for the infinite. He defines the content of religion as contemplation of the universum and feeling for it. These terms call for analysis.

What is contemplation? We have seen already that the disclosure of the universum is not the same as the activation of our own perception as though we were penetrating the universum with our own thinking, feeling, and willing. The activity, if one may put it thus, is on the side of the universum. It discloses itself. Perception is due to the influence of what is perceived on those who perceive it.

60. Cf. the *Soliloquies*, where the unity of freedom and necessity is reflected on the ethical level. But on this level their equation is not achieved in the same way as it is as a primal experience on the religious plane. Ethically, freedom claims clear primacy (I, pp. 18-19). The necessity that confronts it is not Kant's causality and hence an alien ineluctability. It derives from the infinite totality of spirits. This sets a limit for the finite and individual because of the freedom of other finite individuals. Freedom comes up against freedom itself, i.e., that of others. This type of necessity is not a pure antithesis to freedom but simply a reflection of a world that I fashion in holy fellowship with the totality. I with my own freedom am a member of the infinite totality of spirits and a co-creator with it. Thus freedom itself posits the sphere of necessity and restricts itself. Everywhere holy freedom is first (loc. cit.). Only in the name of this primacy can we speak of the unity of freedom and necessity in the ethical (as distinct from the religious) sphere.

Two contemporary examples might help to illustrate this. Thus R. M. Rilke, looking at the torso of an ancient Apollo, says that from being a mere observer he, too, is perceived, and hence he has to change his life. Again, Heidegger thinks of truth as the self-disclosure of being.[61] Being makes itself known to being. Things light up for us. This does not take place from within ourselves but through that which confronts our thinking, i.e., being. Our thinking responds to the claim of being. Thinking is originally the echo of the grace of being.

What is it that discloses itself? Schleiermacher again differentiates the experienced universum from a conceptual system in which one thing follows from another. A system of perceptions is an abortion of thought. In it our perceptions are a chaos in which the unifying factor can be supplied only by our intellect. This apparent weakness is significant from a religious standpoint.

One thing cannot be deduced from another in the universum because each thing is true and necessary in itself and every point is a world. We do not comprehend the individual things on which everything depends if we put them in a higher nexus, but only if we view them as a microcosmic reflection of the whole, so that unconditional emphasis falls on them precisely as individual things. Goethe, too, finds in each tiniest part of the world a symbol. The monadology of Leibniz gives this view classical expression. The monads are qualitatively separate. They have no "windows" through which to communicate with others. Again there is no systematic nexus. They agree in virtue of a preestablished harmony, not in virtue of an intellectually deducible dependence. In all this there echoes the original mythological view that the individual processes of nature (e.g., the rhythm of the seasons or the events of birth and death) are similitudes of something universal.

As religion consists essentially of symbolical contemplation, it can actualize itself only in an original act of contemplation. This contemplation cannot be taught or shared. It can take place only existentially. As Schleiermacher attempts in this speech, we can bring people to the point where their own contemplation is triggered. We can maieutically kindle the slumbering disposition for it. But we cannot impart religion. Religion is more than information or reflection about its nature. These are only imports. We simply take them over. They are never more than cultural experiences. Those who are taught in this way still stand just as helplessly before the closed gates as does the student of philosophy in *Faust*.

Strictly, then, the second *Speech* does not offer a treatise on

---

61. Heidegger, *Was ist Metaphysik?*, "Nachwort," p. 43 (cf. *Being and Time*).

religion. It takes the form of an exercise by which the author tries to get his readers to engage in religion for themselves. This reminds us in many ways of Lessing, the coach of the Enlightenment, who in his own fashion makes it clear that we are not to believe on authority, or to be represented by others, but to act on our own·and to invest our own humanity in the religious act.

Schleiermacher despises what is merely talked about and not experienced. At this point he vents his wrath on the cultured. They have not generated the perceptions for which they have the formulas. Their feelings are mere copies, like strange faces or caricatures.

Because everything individual has its own symbolical autonomy, the field of contemplation is infinite. According to the standpoint we choose in the bodily world, we shall not merely see the same objects in a different order but find new objects in new areas. Contemplation is infinite and the process of contemplation unending because there are infinite angles from which to view the universum. This is a new indication that religion can never be changed into logos or philosophy, for these restrict the infinity of angles by the fixing of finite references. Fundamentally, religion cannot be transposed into any other idiom, especially not into morality, for the moral attitude is most at odds with the religious attitude. Religion is rapture, ecstasy. Hence moral impulses cannot be released by powerful and shattering religious feelings. By their very nature these feelings weaken our ability to act and invite us to quiet and devout enjoyment. Religion can only accompany our human acts like sacred music. We are to do things *with* religion, not *because of* it.

Schleiermacher makes it plain that religion leads neither to reflection nor action when he points out that as we are perceived by the universum we are blinded and are thus put in a position that is the very opposite of objective seeing and assessing. Even if we escape from this blinding, the impression of being overpowered is still with us in all our further seeing. If the eternal world acts on the organs of the spirit as the sun does on the eyes when it blinds us, then everything else disappears at this moment, and for a long time after all the objects that we see are stamped with this image and surrounded by this glory. Thus religion accompanies all further thought and action. There takes place what Rudolf Otto has described as "divination."

As distinct from contemplation, what is feeling? We best proceed by looking at the first stage of the development of religious experience, and I will try to aid the understanding of the reader with various illustrations and associations.

Schleiermacher speaks in this connection about the first mysterious moment that arises in sensory perception before contemplation and feeling divide, when sense and object flow together and become one, prior to their return to their original places. This first process is on the border of consciousness and long before all reflection.

I will use a common experience by way of illustration. I am in a gathering in which I find a member of the audience more interesting than the address. I look at this person from behind or from the side without realizing why. This is Schleiermacher's sensory perception. It is not conscious. I do not intend to hypnotize the other. I am not aware of looking at the person. Yet I and the other are not apart. The person is present in my soul. But suddenly there takes place what usually does take place in such cases. As if reached by a second transmitter, the other looks round. At this moment distance sets in. I suddenly become aware that my gaze has been fixed on another, and on whom. The picture of the other is present to my soul. The other has affected me, and there takes place what Schleiermacher calls contemplation. As Schleiermacher says in this regard, feeling works its way up from within and spreads abroad like the redness of shame or desire on the cheek.

In that first moment something takes place in me. It does not just work on me; it takes place in me. This is feeling. Separate at a second stage, contemplation and feeling are together for a mysterious moment. If we may venture a definition, contemplation is that which works on me and joins me to the universum. In contrast, feeling is what is worked in me. For a first moment they are together. This is a mystical moment. It is "the supreme blossoming of religion. If I could create it for you, I would be a God." It is the climax of religion simply because in it I merge with the universum and that is fully present which later exercises are designed to conjure up. A famous passage in the second *Speech* offers a vision of this supreme moment. There is something astoundingly similar in Goethe's *Werther*,[62] as a comparison will show.

Thus Schleiermacher speaks of lying on the bosom of the infinite world, of being at this moment its soul, of feeling its forces and infinite life as his own, of its being his body as he permeates its muscles and members as his own, of contemplation arising like a separate figure before him, of its mirroring itself in his open soul like the image of the beloved in the eyes of a young man, and of feeling then arising from within. Werther experiences a similar moment as one of extreme and almost intolerable happiness which fills him to the point where his art cannot bear it. The misty valley is before him, the sun rises on the edge of the dark forest, he lies by the brook on the grass, he feels in his heart

---

62. Cotta ed., vol. V, 11, 135. Cf. also Hölderlin's *Hyperion*, SW, III, 9.

the presence of the Almighty who has made us all in his image, he feels the breath of the All-loving One, heaven rests in his soul like the figure of the beloved, and he then thinks: If only he could express this, if only he could put on paper what is so full and warm within him, so that it might be the mirror of his soul as his soul is the mirror of the infinite God. But to do this he has to break again the unity with the universum. The supreme moment has to pass, contemplation and feeling have to separate. Werther could not draw a single line at this time, and yet he had never been a greater painter than in such moments.

Hölderlin, too, refers to self-forgetful union with the eternal world which is broken by the slightest disturbance and gives way to alien reflection. Union with all that lives means that the human spirit lays aside the scepter, and thoughts give place to the image of the world that is eternally one. Hölderlin often stands on this high place, but then a moment of reflection casts him down. The world that is eternally one vanishes, nature closes its arms, and he stands before it like a stranger and does not understand it. Man is a God when he dreams and a beggar when he thinks. When inspiration goes he is like an unsatisfactory son whom his father has put out and whose gaze is fixed on the poor coins that pity gives him by the wayside.[63]

If we grasp, not this truth, but this moment[64] aright, we see religion set in a zone which is immune from any rational or historical attack. In saying this I come to the point of Schleiermacher's project and indeed of his whole theology, although his means of reaching it might later change. The *Speeches* are a crucial work not least because they reveal this point for the first time, and perhaps most clearly and forcefully.

One may perhaps sum it up in a single sentence by saying that Schleiermacher wants to put religion in a secure zone. (This is why he ascribes to it its own a priori.) He does this not only for the sake of his cultured readers who had the Enlightenment questioning of religion, of positive Christianity, at their back, but also for his own sake.

Like few of his contemporaries he saw how religion was being and would be brought under attack by science and history. He had an inkling of the relativism that was to come.[65] If we then call him an apologist, as the dialectical theology especially did, then let us not think of him merely as a protagonist and propagandist to those outside (as

---

63. *Hyperion*, SW (1957), III, 9.
64. We recall the significance of the "moment" or "instant" for Kierkegaard and others after him.
65. We shall come to this when discussing the *Sendschreiben an Lücke*.

the link with his cultured readers might lead us to do) but as one who is also arguing with his own doubts and wrestling for intellectual honesty. Biblically speaking, he is trying to give to every one a reason for the hope that is in him (1 Pet. 3:15). The debate is between the spiritual and the natural man within. The aim of this debate is that the whole person should be the subject of faith and that there should be no cleavage of consciousness. Only with this reservation can I allow Schleiermacher to be called an apologist. In this regard Barth as well as Brunner seems to have a blind spot. Neither, then, can do justice to Schleiermacher.

3. Results: The Theological Intentions of Schleiermacher

Schleiermacher is trying to secure religion against two main attacks, the rational and the historical.

As regards the rational attack, Schleiermacher begins by warning us against basing religion on the experience of nature, its majesty and regularity. What he means by contemplation of the universum and feeling for it is something very different from natural religion or natural theology. Here we have at most only the outer court of the sanctuary of religion. The sense of the invisible that we achieve along these lines is philosophical rather than religious. Why? we might ask with surprise on a first reading. Overpowering experiences of nature do not mean religion because they do not make us members of the universum but immediately plunge our spirits into inner debate and stimulate reaction to the universum.

For one thing, that which is at first incomprehensible and numinous raises the question of the first cause and force, and at once this sets us at the distance of (philosophical) reflection. Again, we react to the powers of nature, not by accepting them as blind superpowers, but by trying to protect ourselves against them. Jupiter's terrors no longer frighten us now that Vulcan has made us a shield against them. For the wounds inflicted by Mars, Aesculapius has shown us means of healing. The gods that seem to be behind the forces of nature, and that cause them to affect us religiously, contradict themselves and are in conflict, so that Promethean man can set them against one another and emerge as victor from their common wars.

The true religious person realizes how dubious is the impression that is made by the quantitative infinitude of space—Kant's starry heaven—or of power. Not only does it provoke a rational, nonreligious reaction; the main point is that from a religious standpoint the most limited body is just as infinite as all the worlds. The eternal that indwells the world as spirit is just as perfect and manifest in what is least as in what is greatest. The *tremendum* in nature—its size and power—is not a religious *tremendum*. For the ruder children of earth it might have had preparatory significance for religion, but the cultured and enlightened for whom Schleiermacher writes have long since passed the naive stage of still slumbering reason.

We see here an advance indication of the later feeling of absolute dependence in *The Christian Faith*. Relative dependence, against which we try to protect ourselves, has no religious quality. Only that on which we are absolutely dependent (including our ability to react) deserves to be called divine. Only the certainty with which this form of dependence penetrates our subjectivity is a religious feeling. Schleiermacher does not go this far in the *Speeches*. We have here only a negative preamble to what he will say in *The Christian Faith*. His aim is to prevent the misunderstanding that even the most impressive relative dependence in the natural sphere can awaken religious feelings.

Since religion teaches us to see in the smallest thing a microcosm of the whole, and since it thus involves an infinitude of aspects of the universum, humanity as a whole is the true subject of religion. Individual examples, as one might say today, are complementary. Only together do they constitute the subjectivity that is commensurate with the fulness of the universum. The force of individuality for Schleiermacher is that each is a compendium of humanity. The one personality embraces human nature as a whole. Total humanity, representative of human nature, is the I made manifold, clearly delineated, and eternalized in every change.

As regards the historical attack, a short methodological discussion is necessary if we are to understand it. What are usually called Christian dogmas are not a sum of timeless doctrines. Dogmas are abstractions from facts of history, or, more precisely, of the salvation history that the Bible recounts. The historical question thus arises in two ways: first, as dogmas must validate themselves before the forum of holy scripture and its statements, and second as the Bible itself is questioned regarding the reliability of its factual statements.

When the latter question is raised, historical criteria involve a basic problem, for salvation events do not fit them. We have already pointed out (in relation to Troeltsch) that these criteria embrace causality, analogy, and immanence. But these criteria do not hold when a transcendent event intervenes in our history (we need think only of the Easter stories). In this situation two reactions are possible. On the one hand, the historical criteria may declare themselves to be inappropriate to such objects. They then call themselves in question. But obviously only historians who believe in the objects can accept this. On the other hand, it may be stated in the name of the criteria that the objects of faith are historically unreal, and we then have the results that we noted in dealing with Reimarus.

Since Schleiermacher has chosen the cultured of the world as his partners in dialogue, he has the second reaction in view. He thus seeks a sheltered zone that will be secure from history and its criteria.

I cannot adduce specific statements in the *Speeches* in which he expressly says this. At this point I have to see the earlier Schleiermacher in terms of the later, i.e., in terms of his concern, expressed to Lücke, that secular disciplines, especially history and natural science, are increasingly pressuring Christian faith, and that for this reason we should find in good time arguments that will create an unassailable basis for the Christian religion. If we follow through this basic line in his thinking, we shall come across hints of it already in the *Speeches*. Schleiermacher undoubtedly has in view the historical problems of the cultured of his day when he exerts himself to give Christian dogmas a meaning which will enable them to withstand historical doubts and objections, and indeed not to be affected by them. I had to make this prior observation to justify my understanding.

A few examples must suffice in illustration of this attempt to find protection against history.

For the reasons mentioned, miracle stories are particularly delicate face to face with historical criteria. They seem to belong to a primitive stage of humanity and they especially irritate the cultured and enlightened. What is a miracle as Schleiermacher sees it?

A miracle is simply the religious name for an event. Even the most natural and everyday event can be called a miracle if the religious view of it is the dominant one. Here we see clearly the sheltered zone that Schleiermacher seeks.

A miracle is not for him a transcendent intervention that breaks into the closed sphere of our finitude. Such an intervention might be contested as a historical fact. Instead, Schleiermacher puts miracle in the subjective sphere. It is simply an aspect, a standpoint from which I see natural events. It is the symbolical view of things which finds a representation of the universum even in what is smallest. But if miracle is just a way of looking at things, seeing them from an eternal standpoint, then lurking historical criticism is thwarted, for it has no object. This way of understanding miracles is typical of the way that all Christian concepts are understood in the *Speeches*.

Revelation, for example, is a new and original view of the universum, an original receptivity to an individual experience of the universum, not one which is alien or simply mediated through others. Revelation is equivalent to inspiration. It is the religious name for freedom, for it leads to a direct and spontaneous expression of religious feeling which imparts itself, so that the view of the universum is transmitted to others.

This form of free and direct receptivity is strictly differentiated from what is commonly called faith. Perhaps it is an opportunistic accommodation to the cultured, for whom the word *faith* had been spoiled by the Enlightenment, that Schleiermacher refrains from correcting their time-bound misunderstanding of faith by reference to Paul or the Reformation, and instead strengthens his readers in their dubious prejudices. He accepts the fact that the popular faith to which he refers simply accepts what another has done and thinks and feels what another has felt and thought. The intended reaction of the reader is that religion has nothing to do with faith, and that we may thus dispense with faith.

But Schleiermacher goes further. He asks what the holy scriptures contain apart from what others have thought and felt. They are the hardened forms of what was once glowing lava. For those who are directly gripped by the universum, however, the lava is again flowing fire, so that they no longer need the scriptures, or at the most are stimulated by them, and may perhaps produce holy scriptures of their own.

Every holy scripture is simply a mausoleum of religion, a monument that a great spirit was present but is there no longer, for if he still lived and worked, how would he attach such great value to the dead letter? It is not those who believe a holy scripture that have religion, but those who need none, or might make their own.

At this point we undoubtedly see a crisis of the *word* in the theology of the young Schleiermacher. The word ceases to be the true medium of revelation, of God's self-declaration. We ourselves are not centrally understood as hearers and recipients of this word. Speaking to his cultured students, the new Socrates simply seeks to release religious powers that slumber within them. He is not trying to lead them to listen to something outside but to discover something inside. For the Socratic of religion the word—we see here the shadow of Feuerbach—is no more than a verbal projection, the discarded shell of a released religious force, a relic, the snow of yesteryear.

If earlier we pointed to certain parallels between Schleiermacher and Kierkegaard, this Socratic approach makes the distinction between them apparent. Kierkegaard can say that there is something Socratic about him,[66] and yet Socrates, that noble rogue of paganism,[67] is for him

---

66. See *The Journals of Kierkegaard*, ed. A. Dru (New York, repr. 1959), p. 143.

67. Cf. W. Rehm, *Kiergegaard und der Verführer* (1949), pp. 447ff.

the climax of secular humanity, and he thus stands in contrast to Christ, whose concern is with God and his transcendent thoughts of salvation and gifts of grace which we can never produce for ourselves but which have to be received. In the maieutics of Socrates the aim is to bring to birth what is already there. Learners are themselves the truth and may thus set aside the teacher and stand on their own feet. Thus the goal of Socrates as a teacher is to make himself superfluous.[68] The teacher is simply the occasion of a process in which we discover what is proper to us. According to Plato's Socrates this is actualized only by recollection (anamnesis), for it is hidden deep within our humanity.[69] For Kierkegaard the truly Christian element, what he calls religiosity, the thing that differs from what we find in Socrates, is that we are built up by something outside the individual. Individuals find edification, not by finding an inner relationship with God, but by relating themselves to something outside.[70]

Apart from a certain use of the term *existential* by Schleiermacher, the two are thus linked more by the antithesis between them. This antithesis consists finally of the fact that Schleiermacher, unlike Kierkegaard, has no radical understanding of sin. For Kierkegaard existence has gained power over us. We are thus unable to transport ourselves "back into the eternal by way of recollection."[71] Sin, especially in its form as original sin, tells us that subjectivity is untruth.

Hence only separated and estranged humanity can be released maieutically. Schleiermacher's view can find no place for this phenomenon of ontic alienation, for personal categories are needed to describe emancipation from God.

If we are to look in the *Speeches* for a term corresponding to Kierkegaard's view of sin, we should have to select *misunderstanding*. The cultured despisers of religion are in truth religious people reposing in the universum; the only thing is that they do not know it. Schleiermacher wants to release this knowledge maieutically. He can thus move and stay on the level that Kierkegaard calls Socratic and pagan.

The self-disclosure of the universum to its parts, i.e., to those parts that have consciousness, does not take the form of a dialogue between the self-revealing God and us the recipients. In the biblical and Christian sphere we are essentially those who are addressed by the word, called by name, and made capable of receiving the word. The word comes from outside. In Schleiermacher, however, we listen to ourselves

68. Kierkegaard, *Philosophical Fragments* (1946), pp. 17ff., 50ff.
69. Kierkegaard, *Concluding Unscientific Postscript* (1941), pp. 216ff.
70. Ibid., pp. 497-98.
71. Ibid., p. 186.

and find that our own inner being is a microcosmic reflection of the universum.

We thus have emancipation from everything that takes the form of word. The word is not the foundation stone of the event of creation on which our human existence rests. It is simply the relic of purely secondary processes which take place elsewhere in others as their reactions to basic religious experiences. Even if the word is still viewed as God's word, this makes no difference to its relativity, for it is always an open question whether God is here a cipher for the universum or the fetishist deification of a specific being.[72]

In the discussion of the idea of God we thus have a critical climax to Schleiermacher's Socratic approach. "In religion the idea of God is not so highly placed as you suppose," we read toward the end of the second *Speech*. We already suspect why Schleiermacher is playing down this idea. For him the deity can be one way of viewing things religiously, for the idea of God fits the view of the universum. It can come to expression as monotheism, polytheism, or fetishism. Hence it is hard to see why a religion without God should not be better than one with God. Someone who views the universum as the one and all, even without the idea of God, might have more religion than the best instructed polytheist, for a plurality of gods reveals a way of viewing things that does not see the universum as a comprehensive unity but as an indefinite mass of heterogeneous elements and forces. Schleiermacher points to many different ways in which different pictures of God result from different viewpoints, and he asks us not to regard it as blasphemy that belief in God depends on the direction of fantasy, which is the highest and most original thing in us, all else being only reflection on it.[73]

The idea of God is thus a function of contemplation and imagination. These keep their religious character even without this cipher and in other expressions. Here we see the extreme opposite of the God of the Bible, who has such primacy over us that he projects us to himself and for the first time makes us religious people.[74] In the

---

72. In Hölderlin, who had not a little in common with the young Schleiermacher, the gods are emanations of Father Aether, whose cosmic fulness is too powerful to be borne undivided. Aether here means much the same as Schleiermacher's universum.

73. Cf. Goethe's relating of monotheism, polytheism, and pantheism, which he regards as complementary.

74. We find only a remnant of this view in Schleiermacher when he points out that humanity is not his all, that his religion strives toward the universum of which humanity is only an infinitely small part. He thus magnifies an idea of God in which God is qualitatively different from humanity, a totally distinct individual. But

Speeches we find (or do not find) the God of the present state of our subjectivity. God has secondary rank, as in Kant, in whom he is a postulate of practical reason or a cipher for the unconditional nature of moral commands.

We again see here how Feuerbach's theory of projection seems to be very close. It is restrained by one barrier that is pushed aside by Feuerbach. For Schleiermacher the universum is still the generative power of being. Religious people, who produce the image of God, are grounded in it. In this image they cause the universum to be mirrored (unless they renounce such mirroring). For Feuerbach, however, humanity is definitively the true and final reality. All else—the universum as well as ideas of God—is no more than projection. Max Stirner can only provide this theory with a final grotesque refinement.

The cultured can breathe again when they hear Schleiermacher say that everything in religion is enclosed in their subjectivity. They feel freed from all ties except that to the universum, which varies at will. It may easily be forgotten that Schleiermacher's main thrust is originally against special ties, against orthodoxy. He summons us away from heteronomous infiltration to self-achievement. Subjectivity can become a sphere of nonobligation, and almost indifference. All debates about truth threaten to be relativized as mere conflicts in the sphere of the word. Subjectivity becomes a city of refuge in which we are spared the hardness of that which meets us outside. Religion takes place in isolation from all action, thought, or decision. Subjectivity is a place where the calm of contemplation is everything.

In all the theological themes heard thus far, one sees how Schleiermacher can take them up into this religion of subjective experience even though they undergo a profound change of sense in the process. The situation alters, however, when he begins to discuss eschatological themes like immortality. Here the flight into subjectivity reaches its most critical point, at which it has to take a kind of oath of dogmatic revelation.

It is noteworthy that Schleiermacher speaks of immortality. He uses it as a surrogate for resurrection, which is completely displaced and does not occur at all in this context. Yet even the word *immortality,* which is more Greek than Christian,[75] and which has to do duty for eschatology, is an alien body that the Schleiermacher of the *Speeches* cannot assimilate. For it involves an interest in individual survival. But this

---

this does not alter the basic idea that even when he is understood thus God is simply a function of contemplation.

75. Cf. *EF,* III, 386ff.

interest is against the basic aim of religion, namely, that so far as possible we should become one with the universum and merge into it. *Hen kai pan* has no place for individuality as an antithetical construct. Schleiermacher seems not to be afraid of what I find to be a tasteless wresting of the saying of Jesus in Matt. 10:39 (those who lose their lives for his sake will save them, and those who save them will lose them) when he puts it on the lips of the universum and sees in it a demand to avoid a paltry concern for personal eternity. Instead he summons his readers to try to give up their lives for love of the universum, to seek to destroy their individuality and to live in the one and all. Immortality in religion can mean only becoming one with the infinite in the midst of finitude, becoming eternal in an instant.

Here is the sharpest contrast to what had previously been understood by Christian eschatology. There are two theological reasons for the change.

First, we see here in a particularly striking way what it means that impersonal union with the universum replaces personal encounter with God. In personal encounter I am called by name, addressed as a person, received into eternal fellowship, and given a permanent or immortal standing in it.[76] Personal fellowship maintains the person. The name is a Hebrew synonym for the person. When a name is named it can no longer disappear from God's history with us. Hence the saying of Jesus cannot mean (as Schleiermacher thinks) the individual elimination of believers: quite the contrary. Yet Schleiermacher has to take it this way. The impersonal universum, as in any monism, can allow room for personal individuality only as an improper mode of being that has to be overcome.

Second, the flight into subjectivity leaves an eschatological gap[77] because theological statements are possible only about things that one can feel, perceive, and experience. In the eschaton, however, we are no longer the subjects of feeling, perceiving, and experiencing, so that there can be no statements in this dimension, and ultimately the only possible word is negation, a reference to the disappearance of subjectivity and individuality. Here, at least theologically, the dead end is plain for a course that seeks to escape the heteronomy of orthodox doctrines and to lead contemporaries to a point which permits a personal and

76. Cf. Luther's commentary on Genesis (WA, 53, 481, 32, LW, 5, 76): Where God speaks, those with whom he speaks are immortal. The person of the God who speaks and the Word of God show that we are creatures with whom God wills to speak eternally and immortally. Cf. *EF,* III, 386ff.; *Living with Death* (Grand Rapids, 1983), pp. 130ff.

77. Brunner is right at this point in his work *Die Mystik und das Wort.*

committed confession in which all one's humanity participates. What a mutation! Yet is it really a mutation? The protest (against orthodoxy and philosophical metaphysics) and the attempt to enter the sphere of those addressed can push the cause that is represented in a direction that is not foreseen. It might be that the author himself is then no longer true to himself. We shall see that in fact the total Schleiermacher is not speaking here. His authorship is complete only when he escapes the twofold influence of the *Speeches* and becomes himself. This real Schleiermacher will meet us in *The Christian Faith* and in his sermons.

4. Epilogue: The Soliloquies

As already mentioned, the *Soliloquies (Monologen)*, which came out soon after 1800, are the ethical counterpart of the religious *Speeches*. They are much less significant and influential. Because of their stylized rhetoric, rhythmical at times, they are hard to read today. Their relation to the *Speeches* is like that of *Die christliche Sitte* (1843, ed. L. Jonas) to *The Christian Faith*. In both cases the ethics is secondary and derivative.

Although Schleiermacher, as we have seen, sharply differentiates religion from morality, the fact remains that religious people have to act in the world. Thus the question arises about what implications religion has for our orientation and action in the world even though no casuistical imperatives can be inferred from it. Religion and ethics seem finally to be linked only at the level of motives, not of programs of action. They meet only in the basic sphere of anthropology where our self-understanding as religious people is at issue.

Schleiermacher begins with the signs of deficient anthropology which he notes among the cultured of his day and which he sees to be grounded in a lack of religion. The religious emptiness and superficiality against which he inveighs in the *Speeches* work themselves out in a life-style. Instead of moving on to freedom, people are enslaved to the spirit of the age, to natural egoism and individualism. Hence Schleiermacher summons them to turn to the depths of their own humanity where finite temporal being is rooted in the eternal and we realize that we are members of humanity. This is the "moral virtuosity" wherein we find humanity in ourselves and thus discover that individuals represent it microcosmically. In this way a bad emancipation, a plunge into individualism, can be avoided, and true freedom can be won.

This return to the basis of existence is what religion also seeks, so that here is the link between religion and ethics. The conclusion of the work shows in hymnic style what a happy fulfilment of life—beyond all the gloom of sullen ascetic duty—this return to our origins brings with it. Eternal youth and joy gush forth from a sense of inner freedom and its work. The author has grasped this and will never let it go. He can laugh as the light of the eyes fades and silver hairs rise up among the gold. Nothing that can happen troubles him. The pulse of his inner life remains strong even to death.[78]

The striking thing in this work is the unbroken way in which one may find these original sources in both religion and ethics. There is no need of turning, of *metanoia*, of a break with the past, of repentance. One finds no sign that we are at odds with ourselves, that in every ethical imperative, whether it be the Decalogue or the categorical imperative of Kant, one may see a protest against the self. The reason why there is no break is that nothing is said here about sin or the fall. Here is a gap in Christian knowledge that Schleiermacher can never quite fill even later. His doctrine of sin will always be fragmentary. Was he afraid to present it to religion's cultured despisers, to obscure the bright light of their enlightenment with this cloud?

B. *THE CHRISTIAN FAITH*

1. Basic Theology (Introduction)

A presentation of Schleiermacher's theology may be grouped around the problem of the word. We have already seen some signs of this significance of the word. In the *Speeches* it is a secondary factor. In some sense it is a disruptive verbalizing of religious experience. It is disruptive along the lines of Schiller's saying that when the soul speaks, alas, it speaks no more.

The situation is different in *The Christian Faith*. This is focused on Christ. But Christ is a historical phenomenon that comes to us through the medium of the word. Hence the rank of the word has to change. Christology is a goad that forces the author to take up into his view of the Christian religion something that comes upon us from outside.

The thing that links the works is that subjectivity, whether as contemplation and feeling or as self-consciousness, remains the central theme. This is possible even along with the primacy of the word, for the word does not simply go forth but also comes to us, so that the situation of those whom it addresses is also a theme. This is all the more true in *The Christian Faith* inasmuch as it is not written for critical intellectuals,

78. *Soliloquies*, pp. 102-3.

who might force the author to leave out opportunistically things that he dare not say to them, but for people as such, as conscious beings. The aim, then, is to harmonize that which comes from outside, represented by Christology, with the conditions of the human consciousness. We shall have to see whether this harmonization is accomplished without concessions either on the one side or the other.

We shall first ask why the work bears the title *The Christian Faith* (or *Die Glaubenslehre*)[79] rather than *Dogmatics*. The title shows that the object of research is not a systematically demonstrable nexus of Christian doctrines relating the primitive state and the eschaton, or to sin and redemption. The author is definitely not looking at things from the standpoint of the creed with its trinitarian grouping of the objects of Christian faith. There can be neither a systematic nor a historical linking of the facts of salvation. Once again Schleiermacher is describing subjectivity, this time believing subjectivity, the Christian consciousness. In this regard he adopts a position that is essentially different from that of the *Speeches*. This is clear at once when we consider how far faith can be made the subject of teaching *(Glaubenslehre)*.[80] Faith might be regarded as a psychological process whose essence is seen in the "how." In this regard it is a theme in religious psychology.[81] This looks at the emotions at work in faith, e.g., the feelings of being seized, of dependence, of the need for security, of guilt, etc. Yet even this approach cannot stop at isolated psychological subjectivity. For psychology cannot avoid the fact (or ought not to do so) that these are processes in human subjectivity, and psychologists betray at once what their understanding of humanity is. If they see in people only bundles of nerves or the agents of mechanistic processes, as some materialistic psychologists do,[82] then they can see in the emotions of faith only expressions of the psyche (cf., e.g., Freud). If, however, they see in people beings that are referred to an outside reality and that transcend themselves, then they will see in the psychological processes a reflection of the relation that takes people up into itself from without.

That religious processes in the psyche are in fact a reflection of

---

79. Strictly the title is *Der christliche Glaube* . . .

80. The use of *Glaubenslehre* has become fairly common during the last two centuries; cf. the works of A. Schweizer, I. A. Dorner, D. F. Strauss, A. Philippi, E. Troeltsch, H. Stephan, etc. Cf. *EF,* I, 14ff.

81. Cf. W. H. Clark, *The Psychology of Religion* (New York, 1958); W. Hellpach, *Grundriss der Religion* (1951); R. Otto, *The Idea of the Holy* (1958); E. Spranger, *Die Magie der Seele,* 2nd ed. (1949); W. Trillhaas, *Grundzüge der Religion* (1946); G. Wobbermin, *Die Methoden der religiös-psychologischen Arbeit* (1921).

82. Cf. my *Being Human—Becoming Human* (1984), pp. 413ff.

that which affects me from without is the main thesis of the two greatest psychologists of religion, Schleiermacher and Rudolf Otto.

In Schleiermacher we are referred to the universum. This claims us and manifests itself to us. It is also characteristic of Otto that, although he studies the subjective processes in religious people, he does not see these as psychological projections but describes them as impressions. For he analyzes the holy as a power that seizes us; he does not analyze holy people as an anthropological type. Naturally, the feelings of awe and fascination that Otto describes as basic religious experiences have a subjective dimension. But they are simply a reflection of the *numen*, which is as such, trans-subjectively, a *numen tremendum et fascinosum*. Thus consideration of the subjective side, including that of faith, has its limits.

The question naturally arises, however, whether we should not describe faith differently from the very outset, namely, in terms of its object.[83] The central significance that Schleiermacher accords to Christology in *The Christian Faith* shows that he has the object in view. Why, then, does he write a doctrine of faith instead of a dogmatics, a presentation of the object?

From all that we have said thus far, it is easy to see the answer. He views the doctrines from the standpoint of their appropriation. Their appropriation is the act of faith, the moment of acceptance, the transition from outside to inside.

We see some similarity here to one aspect of the Reformation. Thus Melanchthon says that to know Christ is to know his benefits. This means that we cannot do Christology by studying Christ in himself, e.g., the "how" of the two natures. We have to speak of his history with us, of his work on (and then in) us. The "faith alone" of the Reformation, however, shows that the stress is on the question of how I can be drawn into the saving reality of Christ, how I can let myself be appropriated by Christ. For a modern doubter like Schleiermacher, the accent has shifted to the opposite question, namely, how Christ can be brought into the apparatus of my consciousness, how I can appropriate him under its conditions, and thus utter my confession of him in such a way that it is my own confession.

What Schleiermacher is trying to do in *The Christian Faith* is to show how we can take up the historical fact of Christ into our consciousness and what must happen in this consciousness to make this possible.

His argument is that those who will not put this question run

---

83. I have already shown how resolutely Luther does this when he makes the subject of faith and the subjectivity of the experience completely secondary to the object, describing the subject as merely a mathematical point.

the risk of simply repeating the faith of others and going along with the Christian tradition without really coming to faith and being the true subjects of their own faith. Orthodoxy is the issue, not merely in the sense that what is believed is correct, but also in the sense that my act of faith is correct, that I perform the act myself.

This being Schleiermacher's intention, he presses hard on the theological conscience of all of us. He attacks us with the question whether and how far as Christians we have perhaps done no more than accept the collective suggestion of the Christian tradition, whether our confession might not simply be a mechanical cliché, whether we are not substituting alien sentiments and cultural experiences for original encounters. For all our material criticism we must not miss the abiding validity of this challenge. Many great theologies do more through their questions than their answers. That of Schleiermacher is one of them. But this also brings us to a point from which to survey *The Christian Faith*.

Our first thesis is that two factors are at work in it. The first is a historical fact, which may be summed up as the fact of Christ. The second is the system of categories with which this fact is accepted, understood, actualized, and existentially appropriated. Schleiermacher begins with these categories in the Introduction (§§ 1-31). We shall later see what misunderstandings this approach caused and with what arguments he defended it.[84]

By beginning with the pious Christian self-consciousness, Schleiermacher is not trying to establish a theology of consciousness but simply doing preparatory work with a view to taking the historical person of Christ into the consciousness. He does not want to make the consciousness a *norm* whereby to decide whether biblical statements are binding. He is simply considering how these facts may come into the consciousness. He understands the consciousness as the *place*, not the norm, of appropriation. (Whether he is successful in keeping these two things apart is another question which we shall have to consider.)

That the consciousness is for him the place of Christianity and its appropriation may be seen from the way in which he localizes Christianity in religious history as a monotheistic form of faith belonging to the teleological orientation of piety, but distinguished from other religions of the same group by the fact that everything is related to the redemption accomplished by Jesus of Nazareth (§ 11). The teleological orientation of piety means that the presentation of the moral task forms the basic type of pious states of mind.

---

84. Tillich's principle of correlation is similar in some respects; cf. the concluding essay on Tillich below.

In thus assigning Christianity its place in religious history, Schleiermacher constructs a typology of religion. Christianity is a form of monotheism related to a founding personality. But this is not the decisive point. The real question is that of the religious rank of the founder. Does he really belong to the category of a founder, or is he more than Moses or Muhammad? The typology is accepted formally but it does not contain any essential statements.

One might best make the following twofold statement. First, as Christianity seeks to become my conviction or way of faith, it has to pass into my consciousness. Second, insofar as it occurs in history and is tied to the historical figure of a redeemer, it has to fit into the analogies of religious history. Both the consciousness and religious history thus have the significance of a place and not a norm, at least in intention. We have to be clear about this, for if not we shall make the mistake of thinking that we are simply presented with a new edition of the *Speeches*, but with a more strongly Christian coloring.

The important thing is to note how certain definitions confirm the formal character of the allocation of place. First, we need to see what Schleiermacher would have us understand by consciousness or self-consciousness. In itself the piety that constitutes the basis of all ecclesial fellowships is neither knowledge nor action but a determination of feeling or of the immediate self-consciousness (§ 3). The delimitation from knowledge and action takes up the arguments with which a similar delimitation from metaphysics and morality is made in the *Speeches*. The appeal to feeling also reminds us of similar statements in the *Speeches*. But in this regard a step is taken beyond the *Speeches*. The substitution of self-consciousness for feeling removes the imprecision of the latter term. It does so by excluding unconscious states. These are, so to speak, unreal. One might think of swoons or dreams in which something is felt but it bears no relation to concrete existence.

The word *consciousness* is made more precise by the addition of the adjective *immediate*. A mediated consciousness would be characterized by concrete objects, by orientation within the objectifiable world. But here we have a state of consciousness that lies beneath the subject-object correlation. In clarification one might think of Kierkegaard's usual distinction between anxiety and fear. Fear arises from dangers which the consciousness can pinpoint objectively. Anxiety is a nonobjective sense of threat which cannot be pinpointed.

The decisive point, however, is the material content of this immediate self-consciousness. Schleiermacher provides this in a crucial section of the Introduction (§ 4) which we must go into in more detail.

The key concept is that of the feeling of absolute dependence.

To elucidate this term, Schleiermacher offers a more penetrating analysis of the word *self-consciousness*. This begins with the question: What is the self of which we are conscious?

This self is on the one side a constant entity that remains identical with itself. In clarification one might say that there is an identity between what we were as children and what we are as adults and old people. This identity is what Goethe calls entelechy.

On the other side, however, the same self is a variable entity, for along with its constancy it has a "changing determination." It cannot produce this itself, for otherwise we could not distinguish between the constant and the variable elements. Yet we can make the distinction even in regard to Goethe's entelechy. For both *tyche* and *eros* affect the entelechy, i.e., the constant I that lives its own life and fulfils itself according to its own laws. Even if this impact cannot finally change or twist the entelechic I but is in fact shaped by it, there is still a variable element which cannot be said to be present when the entelechy develops only solipsistically. Mere development (§ 4.2) or explication displays only the constancy of what develops. But we do not just develop; we also have a history. We are exposed to fate and encounter others. In spite of its identity, then, the self is a changing determination.

For this reason, says Schleiermacher, the self-consciousness contains two elements. It posits itself and it is also non-self-posited. It is, and in some way it has also become (§ 4.1). As I find the latter element in my self-consciousness, I address something other than the self, i.e., that from which it has its determination and without which the self-consciousness would not be what it is.

When I view the I with reference to what it is in itself, in its identical core, I have its self-activity before my eyes. But when I see it in its being with others and with reference to its changing determination, I think of its receptivity.

In connection with these definitions Schleiermacher develops two other concepts which are significant for all that is to follow, namely, the concepts of freedom and dependence. (I am presenting all this in more detail, not only because of its material importance, but also in order to give readers some idea of the precise arguments which even stylistically distinguish this presentation very radically from that of the *Speeches*.)

The feeling of dependence is produced by what is common to all the determinations of the self-consciousness which overwhelmingly express the impact upon receptivity from somewhere outside. We continually react to things, heat and cold, friendliness and rejection. In so doing, we show that an impact is made on us. In contrast, the feeling of freedom has to do with all the determinations of the self-consciousness which affect our own predominantly positive activity.

The important thing is that concretely both feelings are only partial and conditioned, or, as Schleiermacher would say, inauthentic. Our self-consciousness, as the consciousness of our being in the world, expresses itself only as a series of shared feelings of freedom and dependence. In fact, our own free activity is always broken. We know that it is limited by the freedom of others. Similarly, dependence is never alone either in the social or in the astronomical sphere. Even the cosmic bodies that affect us always trigger at least a small measure of resistance in us.

As the fourth and main section tells us, however, we do find in ourselves a basic feeling in which we are *absolutely* dependent, i.e., dependent without sharing or condition. This feeling is the common factor in all the different expressions of piety. It is also that which distinguishes piety, as a religious phenomenon, from all other feelings.

In fact, this feeling is unique and isolated among the feelings, for other feelings know only a *conditional* sense of dependence admixed with a sense of freedom. Hence the question of the origin and reference of this feeling can never be answered by pointing to an immanent object or to the totality of temporal being. Over against these there is only a conditional dependence and we have at least a minimal capacity for resistance or freedom. The concept of *absolute* dependence implies a sense that we ourselves, along with all our capacity for freedom, are dependent. We have not freely attained to freedom. We find ourselves in it. We are endowed with it. As free people, we are thus finally dependent.

Hence the feeling of absolute dependence points to something that transcends the totality of being in space and time, finding no equivalent in this being. This something we call God, who is distinct from all other being.

Note closely how Schleiermacher opens the question of God here. He expressly does not do this by saying that the feeling of dependence is conditioned by some prior knowledge of God (§ 4.4). In this preamble he emphatically does not want to begin with the doctrines of a positive religion and hence with a *Deus dixit*. He explains this in the letters to Lücke. He is afraid that the secular world, especially natural science and history, will pose radical questions to the Christian religion which it will not be able to withstand, for a confessional Nevertheless and an empty apologetics will not be an adequate defense. Hence he wants to find an impregnable rock for religion in the sphere of the general and secular consciousness—a rock to which he can appeal at any time. Thus the basic intention is the same as in the *Speeches*. The only difference is that the level of reflection is incomparably higher. A subtle chain of argument replaces Romantic enthusiasm.

This is why Schleiermacher introduces the word *God* only as a corresponding term—one might almost say a cipher—for the feeling of absolute dependence that is deeply rooted in the consciousness. God is simply the name for an existential reference, with no material content. One might speak here of the author's interest in a religious a priori which will provide theology with an epistemological basis equal to that of other sciences.

An example taken from decades of theological examining might help here. When I ask what is the basic religious feeling in *The Christian Faith,* and the student answers: The feeling of absolute dependence on God, we have a clear failure. The student has badly missed the point by presupposing a prior knowledge of God, which Schleiermacher expressly contests.

The concept "God" is the most direct reflection of the feeling of absolute dependence, its interpretation, as it were. It first denotes that which is codeterminative in this feeling, and to which we attribute our existence. This means that all the remaining content of the idea must be developed out of this prior and basic content (§ 4.4).

What does this mean? It means that no theological statement about God is possible which describes his being as such. Such statements can be made only in connection with the feeling of absolute dependence and can be elucidated only in their anthropological reference. This is particularly clear in Schleiermacher's description of the divine attributes: the eternity of God (§ 52), his constancy (§ 52, Postscript), his omnipresence (§ 53), his unsearchability (§ 53, Postscript), his omnipotence (§ 54), his independence (§ 54, Postscript), his omniscience (§ 55), and his other qualities (§ 56).[85]

The correlation of God and our self-consciousness means that we cannot describe isolated attributes but only this reference. The angle from which we can formulate doctrines is thus plain. We have to begin with living human states, not the ideas of divine qualities and modes of action (§ 30). In no case can the qualities that we ascribe to God denote anything specific in God but only something specific in the way that we relate the feeling of absolute dependence to him (§ 50). Every attempt to deduce such qualities from the divine nature itself is speculative, for it presupposes that we know this nature (§ 50.3). Having no support in our self-consciousness, it cannot be accepted by it.

---

85. Cf. G. Ebeling, "Schleiermachers Lehre von den göttlichen Eigenschaften," *Wort und Glaube,* II (1969), 305ff.

Schleiermacher's treatment of God's eternity might serve as an example of the way that he deals with the divine attributes (§ 52). If, as in the second section, we view eternity only as infinitely extended time, then we do not do justice to the fact that the sense of absolute dependence points to an understanding of God according to which he does not occur as an object in the immanent structure of time and space. For on this view of eternity only the final points in temporal duration are denied, and God is made subject to the temporal schema and is thus set among immanent objects. Hence we can make about God only such statements as remove for God not only the limits of time but time itself, taking him radically out of temporality.[86]

I shall close this consideration of the feeling of absolute dependence with a final thought in which the knotty problem of *The Christian Faith* is particularly plain.

If it is true that this feeling can never relate to immanent objects and values, then God has to be viewed as radically nonobjective. In modern terms, and along the lines of Bultmann, one might say that we cannot have God in a myth if by this we mean an attempt to grasp him in a history which we can pinpoint objectively. To relate the idea of God to a perceptible object, except by way of arbitrary symbolism, is always a corruption, whether it be transitory, as in a theophany, or constitutive, as when God is seen as a perceptible individual being (§ 4, Conclusion).

Here we see all the problems that Christology, which is grounded in history and proposed for the consciousness from outside, necessarily poses for a theology that is developed out of the consciousness.

In such a theology the relating of the idea of God to specific historical phenomena is possible only if such phenomena are regarded as symbolical. Dionysus and Apollo, if we might use them as examples, symbolize different dimensions of existence.[87] In Homer's *Iliad* Hera and Aphrodite symbolize *eros* and the sanctity of marriage, which is contested by Helen. And Christ? He finally symbolizes humanity, for which he has prototypical rank. Insofar as this symbolizing yields to the direct presence of the *numen*, there is "corruption." God is integrated into what is present, or degraded as a fetish. In any case, we have an inappropriate anthropocentricity.

This leads us to the decisive question that we have to put to Schleiermacher. If the religious self-consciousness defines God as nonobjective in principle, can Schleiermacher really prevent a contesting of the

---

86. It is surprising that although Schleiermacher constantly refers to Augustine in such contexts, he does not adduce Book 11 of the *Confessions*.

87. W. F. Otto, *Die Götter Griechenlands*, 2nd ed. (1934).

real intervention of God in history, a real incarnation? Can he avoid the final upshot of Zwingli's theology, i.e., no "is" but only a "signifies"? We might think of the tradition of Abelard, in which God is a transpolar principle of indifference and cannot wrestle historically with evil, so that the passion of Jesus is simply a dramatic or symbolical demonstration which displays God's openness to sinners, overarching both good and evil. How can Schleiermacher avoid the conclusion that the only binding religious statement is not the event of salvation itself but interpreted history, i.e., history seen in the light of its significance or symbolical character?

If we really have to say that he cannot avoid such conclusions, we can do so only with the sense that we are witnessing a definite tragedy of thought. For the approach by way of the self-consciousness was meant to protect theology (against philosophy, science, and politics). But was not this an all too human protection and hence finally an (involuntary) surrender and a ferment of dissolution? Do not theological thoughts surreptitiously take over and lead us where we do not want to go? Theology has to interpret and understand. It thus needs hermeneutical tools, which Schleiermacher's sense of absolute dependence is meant to be. But cannot the means revolt and set itself up as a norm? Might not thinking become guilty of a fault when it is intending to combat another fault—in this case the rigidity of orthodoxy?

Schleiermacher himself seems at times to have some inkling of this when he confesses that "one age bears the guilt of others and can seldom undo it except by fresh guilt."[88] In this regard it is important that in his sermons he often adopts a position outside his systematics and proclaims directly things that his systematic construction does not allow him to say.

2. Sin and Christology

The Understanding of Sin

When we try to speak about sin along Reformation lines, we must state it as a cardinal principle that sin is a transgression against God, an evasion of God that comes to expression in self-assertion and above all in lovelessness.[89]

This means three things. (1) Sin is a real happening between

---

88. *Briefe* (1858), II, 343.
89. See G. Bader's brilliant analysis in "Sünde und Bewusstsein der Sünde. Zu Schleiermachers Lehre von der Sünde," *ZThK* 1 (1982) 60ff. Cf. the elder brother of the parable, Luke 15:25ff.

two persons. It has the removal of peace as a historical result. (2) To know what sin is we have to know who the God is against whom we sin (Ps. 51:4). Negatively, this means that a sense of sin cannot derive from self-analysis. Sin is a relational concept, but self-analysis can bring only moral evil to light. (3) Sin, then, is just as much an object of faith as is he against whom we sin. And as I do not control the knowledge of God but may suppress it (Rom. 1:18ff.), so it is possible to know nothing of sin or to suppress its knowledge. Sin is linked to darkness or blinding, so that I do not see myself. (With tongue in cheek one might say that it is linked to stupidity. It is mercifully hidden from oneself.)

We can count on the fingers of one hand the instances in which we find these three constitutive elements of the understanding of sin in Schleiermacher. Since the concept of God is in him secondary to the consciousness, sin cannot be understood as a history with God that transcends the self; it has to be developed out of the consciousness. This means that a sin that is not tied to the sense of sin is unthinkable. Sin is the consciousness of sin. It can be spoken of only when the sense of it is present (§ 68.2).

In the sense of sin we see that sin is a positive resistance of the flesh to the spirit (§ 66), or, more precisely, to that spirit in which the sense of dependence, and hence the consciousness of God, is manifested (§ 66.1). The sensory consciousness which forms in the flesh as the adversary of the spirit is not permeated at every moment by the God-consciousness (§ 66.1). Even if we may assume that the God-consciousness wholly determines one moment of life, we have only to see that the sensory elements are strengthened from without to realize that the God-consciousness is at once set aside.

We see here something that occurs in every theology based on the consciousness, e.g., in Pietism, which had a marked influence on Schleiermacher, who in many respects remained a Pietist of a "higher order." The role assigned to the consciousness brings us up against the fact that it has only a limited capacity, so that when one thing is dominant in it, it cannot absorb others. In Pietism this may be seen grotesquely in Zinzendorf, and partially in Spener, with regard to the sexual libido. The capacity of the consciousness does not allow love of the Lord to exist side by side with sexual desire in our emotional potential. Hence for the Savior's sake the libido has to be excluded from sexual intercourse and new children of God have to be conceived without desire. The starting point in the pious consciousness necessitates a strict control of what is received into the heart because of its limited capacity.[90] Believers must seek to exercise *apathia* even in marriage.

90. Cf. F. Tanner, *Die Ehe im Pietismus* (Zurich, 1952), e.g., pp. 123ff., 182.

As regards the rise of the sense of sin, Schleiermacher thinks that it results from an unequal development of discernment and willpower (§ 68). From what remains of our original perfection we see how superior are states which unite with the God-consciousness without restricting it. Thus the self-consciousness is stimulated, but the corresponding mobilization of the will lags behind. The influence of the God-consciousness on contents of the consciousness that are carnally determined is out of step with the expanding God-consciousness itself. There is no synchronization. A knowledge of our inadequacy—or sin—finds a home in the gaps.

This sketch of Schleiermacher's view of sin makes it plain how far from the NT he is at this point. We have only to think of the very Platonic form of his concepts of flesh and spirit, which bear little relation to the NT terms *sarx* and *pneuma*.[91] We see here remnants of his monism. The result is that sin can be thought of only as negation, as that which hinders the God-consciousness, not as an active rejection. We can suspect already what this will mean for Christology. Alienated humanity and sinless perfection can easily be reconciled, so that there is no point in wrestling with the doctrine of the two natures and its paradoxes. The secret of Christ's person does not lie in the miracle whereby the Savior assumes the schema of fallen humanity, stands by us between God and Satan, and overcomes the antithesis. No, Christ is only quantitatively an exception. He is the end point of a line on which we find various examples of the relation between flesh and spirit.

Since Schleiermacher tries to integrate almost all areas of traditional teaching into his thinking, we may be interested to find out how he defines original sin, i.e., sin in its suprapersonal character, sin as it goes beyond the limits of the individual consciousness. He moves over at this point from psychological to sociological categories. He finds a supra-individual kingdom of sin (as Ritschl would later call it), a common nexus of influences into which individuals are caught up. Hence he has to reckon with collective guilt, especially as in virtue of this nexus individuals are representatives of the race and help to form the nexus. This reinterpretation of original sin found a following in the 19th century.

Christology

We have already come across the decisive problem in Schleiermacher's Christology. Beginning with the self-consciousness, and making this the grid in which he places all his theological statements, is he not forced to do systematic violence to the figure of Christ, which occurs in history

91. Cf. *EF,* III, 21ff., 44ff.

and is not (like the idea of God) posited in the self-consciousness? Will not this figure be an alien guest that breaks through the system unless it is artificially manipulated, assimilated, and reconstructed?

Schleiermacher tackles the problem quite early, and first in the work *Christmas Eve* (1806). The dialogue form, perhaps taken from Plato, enables him to present and contrast various positions represented by the four characters.[92]

The first, Leonhardt, is the youngest in the party assembled for Christmas, and he opens the discussion. We learn indirectly that he is a critical rationalist, but he has little positive to offer. He finds in the birth of the child a symbol that forms the heart of the feast and he defines the Christian tradition more in terms of its intellectual values than of biblical teaching. He grants that traditional Christianity has a powerful presence but stresses that the ongoing Christian consciousness has long since detached itself from the historical figure of Christ, so that Christ's birth and his real presence in history have little connection with Christianity. Yet he does not want to miss the Christmas feast with its symbolical references to birth, night, and light, and he thus raises his glass to it.

The second character, Ernst, argues vehemently for Christ's historicity and its direct significance today. If we commemorate someone, we must know who this is. Yet it is a matter of the idea of redemption as well as historical remembrance. Redemption is the only principle of joy. The idea of it has entered life with the historical figure of Christ. Redemption means restoration to our original nature in which the present antitheses between appearance and reality, or time and eternity, do not exist, and new harmony is reached.

If Ernst tries to present the human nature of the Redeemer and to see in him an extreme possibility of human nature, the restoration of its original undivided form, the third speaker, Eduard, tries to deepen this thought by relating it to the Johannine Prologue. He interprets the incarnation of the Word as the emergence of a divine principle in human nature. In order that this principle, the final basis of human nature, should be seen through every estrangement, it had to be exemplified in one man, in a person who needed no new birth but was born originally of God. In Christ we see the terrestrial spirit originally fashioning itself as self-consciousness in the individual.

The final speaker, Joseph, does not want to add to what has been said. But he deplores the dialectical reflection which has burdened the joy of Christmas and is sorry for the women present, in whose feelings

92. Cf. Schleiermacher, *Kleine Schriften und Predigten*, ed. H. Gerdes (1980), pp. 223ff.

this joy finds more vital reflection. The ineffable object generates in him, too, an ineffable joy which he expresses all the same with Romantic eloquence and which inspires him to sing Christmas carols.

In all four addresses there is one element which we find again in Schleiermacher's mature Christology. It is as if all the voices in his breast come together at this point. But Ernst and Eduard are closest to his main concern. In them we have a hint of how he will harmonize the self-consciousness with the historicity of Christ. The figure of Christ is the bearer of an idea which finds adequate realization in it, so that we have here a congruence of idea and figure. This is the idea of non-alienated humanity, and to us who are depraved specimens of humanity this idea is both close and distant.

Schleiermacher's doctrine of Christ's person (§§ 92-105) begins with the conviction that the Redeemer does indeed come as a historical figure but that he is not to be deduced from this figure, having brought something basically new into history. The new aeon that dawns with him is really new, as is the new creation that he effects. If not, we could not grasp the uniqueness of what Christianity understands by redemption. We should have only a historical program of redemption such as other religions, e.g., Judaism, might also undertake.

If Christ is squeezed wholly within history, he has to be thought of solely in terms of history. In this case Christianity is simply a continuation of Judaism. It is merely a new development of Judaism and Jesus is only a more or less original and revolutionary amender of Jewish law (§ 93.2).

If Schleiermacher thus clings to the nonderivability of Christ, to his transcending of history, we find here an expression of his interest in the supernatural nature of Christ, in that which the older doctrine of the two natures was also stating in its own way, although for reasons that we need not go into here Schleiermacher speaks of Christ as only relatively supernatural (§ 94.3).

But how can even this fit into his schema of thought? He tries to achieve integration with the help of the idea of a model, i.e., by seeing in Christ the original model of humanity.

If in Christ this model has become historical and actual with a view to inaugurating a new common life (the new aeon), Christ had to come into the old aeon of sinfulness but not from it. He cannot be deduced from it. He is a miraculous phenomenon within it. He is in history, but as a special case he does not derive from it. He can be explained only out of the common source of spiritual life by a creative divine act[93] in which the

---

93. On this view the virgin birth is not an obligatory tenet of faith; cf. § 17.2.

concept of humanity as the subject of God-consciousness comes to absolutely supreme fulfilment (§ 93.3). Negatively, this means that as a historical figure Christ is outside history. He is not subject to prior influences that spread sin and disrupt the inner consciousness of God. He can be understood only as an original act of human nature, i.e., as one who is not affected by sin (§ 94.3). Only in this way can we see that in him we have a saturation of nature with God-consciousness and that he is thus a perfect representation of the original image of humanity.

As a first finding we may make three points. First, the fact that Christ is a model (and not just a moral example) means that he cannot be derived from the history of the old aeon, which is affected by sin. Second, this model fulfils the idea of humanity as the most perfect subject of God-consciousness. Christ is saturated with God-consciousness. There is no room in him for any opposition to it. He is man before the fall. Third, this model comes into history uniquely and exclusively in him.

The exceptional position of Christ seems to be threatened, however, by the thought in the teaching on sin that the conflict between flesh and spirit, and the temporal development of this conflict, are part of the essence of humanity. If Christ is called the perfect bearer of God-consciousness, is he not exposed to this all too human development and the related division, and is not his status as a model challenged thereby? Does the Redeemer himself have to be redeemed if he is to achieve this saturation with God-consciousness?

Schleiermacher, however, thinks that the possibility of sinless development (beyond the division) is not incompatible with human nature. Sin is a perversion of this nature, and is not essential to it (§ 94.1). In this sense he describes the growth of the personality of Jesus from early childhood to the maturity of adulthood as a steady transition from a state of purest innocence to one of purely spiritual force (§ 92.4), beyond all the revolts of the flesh which might threaten a spirit that is saturated with the consciousness of God.

This enables Schleiermacher to offer a striking variation of the two-nature teaching which removes its dialectical and paradoxical elements. Quoting various Protestant confessional writings (§ 96), he says that in Jesus Christ the divine and human natures were conjoined in one person. But how does he view this conjunction seeing he cannot possibly adopt the old ontological concept of "nature"? He thinks divinity and humanity are united in Christ by the God-consciousness. The Redeemer is like all others in virtue of the identity of his human nature but distinct from all others in virtue of the steady force of his God-consciousness, which was a true being of God in him (§ 94). In place of the ontic being of God in Christ we here find his spiritual presence as consciousness *(Bewusst-"sein")* in Christ.

Although this view differs radically from the ontology of the two-nature teaching and does not involve the intratrinitarian speculations which that entails,[94] Schleiermacher does justice to faith's concern in the doctrine by seeing in Christ's human nature a brotherly solidarity with us and by finding in the supreme force of his God-consciousness his divinity and hence his power to redeem.

In the latter emphasis he shows how far Christ is from solidarity with the people of this aeon and how different he is in virtue of his essential sinlessness and absolute perfection (§ 98). The new thing in this reinterpretation of the two-nature doctrine, and the thing which makes it radically different, is the lack of an infinite qualitative distinction between deity and humanity. The distinction is reduced to a quantitative one. In the form of a graph they are end points on one and the same line of humanity. The extent to which a person achieves what humanity ought to be differs according to the degree of God-consciousness in that person. Christ achieves the fullest degree; he is saturated with God-consciousness. Thus the divine element in Christ is precisely that he is a perfect man. With the help of the God-consciousness the infinite qualitative distinction between deity and humanity can become a quantitative one. Being divine can be understood as a supreme stage of being human. Hence the difficulties in the older Christology, which manifest themselves in paradoxes as they attempt a synthesis of qualitatively different elements, are all avoided.[95] Perhaps it is not too bold to see once again at this point some traces of the religion of the *Speeches*. Here again the human is a kind of microcosm in which the divinity of the universum is present, although only in the one true man, who is for this reason divine.

3. The Sermons (the Problem of Eschatological Statements)

When discussing the *Speeches*, I pointed out that a theology based on the religious consciousness, no matter whether this consciousness be defined as contemplation and feeling or as the sense of absolute dependence, runs into particular problems when it has to make eschatological statements. Schleiermacher himself says that the things that can be said

94. By no means accidentally, then, Schleiermacher supports the Trinity only with lame arguments and only at the end of the work gives it the treatment he could not avoid (§§ 170ff.). Cf. also his essay "Über den Gegensatz zwischen den sabellianischen und den athanasianischen Vorstellung von der Trinität" (1822), WW, I, vol. II, esp. p. 564.

95. Cf. earlier in this century the similar Christology of E. Hirsch, e.g., in *Jesus Christus, der Herr,* 2nd ed. (1929).

in this area are not doctrines to which we can ascribe the same rank as those previously presented (§ 159). He does not want to talk of doctrines in the sphere of eschatology, for the content of eschatological statements is beyond our capacity to grasp and hence cannot be a description of our real self-consciousness (§ 157.2). This is in fact the real reason why he can have no true eschatology. As the subjects of self-consciousness and God-consciousness, we cannot pronounce on states of which we are no longer subjects (§ 158.1).

We shall thus refrain from discussing Schleiermacher's detailed theses on, e.g., the last judgment (§ 161) or the return of Christ (§ 160). Only one place is interesting in relation to what we have to say about the sermons. When it is a matter of the survival of the personality (§ 158) he becomes ambivalent. The dominant thing in his system, the self-consciousness, is not a geometrical place to which we can ascribe survival. The reign of the God-consciousness is perfectly attained with the renunciation of the survival of personality (§ 158.1). Yet in his doctrine of Christ's return he speaks about the abiding union of the divine essence and human nature. This nature cannot be so tied to a specific body that it is involved in the destruction of this body. Everything concerning it has to be thought of in connection with the union and seen as an act of this union (§ 160.2). This means that personal immortality, the same as that of Christ, has to be ascribed to human nature (§ 158.2).

This immortality is inferred not from the self-consciousness, but from Christology, or, more precisely, from the modified form of the two-nature teaching. But this argument for survival is illogical as well as indirect. If the God-consciousness does not imply the assurance of survival, but can get along without it, the same applies to the God-consciousness of Christ, whose force constitutes his divine nature.

Here, then, is the place in Schleiermacher's eschatology where a thesis occurs (that of immortality) which is like an erratic block in his system and defies every attempt to integrate it into that system. It seems that here we suddenly hear the voice of the preacher overpowering for a moment that of the systematician. For the preacher has other sources for his statements; he does not have to draw his water from the canals of the system.

In the present context, we need to say of Schleiermacher's eschatology only that the omission or reinterpretation of traditional statements is predetermined by the system, which has its basis in the self-consciousness.

For this reason the sermons serve as an essential corrective in this area. In the pulpit he often (although not always) breaks the fetters of the system and engages in daring proclamation of which he has certainty in faith. As a Christian he is broader and more open to the Christian tradition than he is as a theologian. I will give a couple of examples in which eschatological convictions come to expression that we never find in *The Christian Faith*.

First, when preaching at the funeral of his son Nathanael,[96] he movingly expresses his grief at the death of this much-loved boy and rejects the customary but unconvincing words of comfort that are usually spoken by the graves of children. Human consolations, e.g., that the child is spared a great deal, are no help. For those accustomed to sharp and serious thought, such things leave a thousand questions unanswered. Yet he then goes on to speak of that which grants him true comfort, and in so doing he strikes a note and opens up perspectives that are different and broader than anything his system might have adopted or offered. His whole comfort and hope are in the modest but very rich scriptural saying that it does not yet appear what we shall be, but when he appears we shall see him as he is, and also in the powerful prayer of the Lord, that he wills that where he is, there also should be those whom the Father has given him. Supported by this strong faith and sustained by childlike resignation, he thus says from the heart: The Lord gave him, the name of the Lord be praised that he gave him to me, that even if only for a short time he gave this child a bright and happy life warmed by the loving breath of his grace.

The second example is from an Advent sermon on Matt. 21:9 (prior to 1826).[97] This sermon, which proclaims Christ's uniqueness and absoluteness, goes much beyond what *The Christian Faith* allows us to say. For the force of the God-consciousness that constitutes Christ's uniqueness does not rule out in principle the possibility that another might come in whom is found the same saturation and who might have another task in another age. Possibilities are thus implied (although not developed) which are said to be open in the *Speeches* and which allow of even greater advances. In this Advent sermon, however, which appeals to scripture and not to the self- or God-consciousness, testimony is given to the definitiveness of Christ. When we say to Christ, "Blessed is he who comes in the name of the Lord," we do so not only with a sense that none of those who have come before him in the name of the Lord can be compared to him, but also with the sense that he is the last to have come in the name of the Lord. Now that Christ has appeared and is present, we should not expect any other. None will ever come who will touch human hearts with the same inspiring force and make them ready

96. *Predigten*, IV (1844), 880ff.
97. *Predigten*, II (1843), 5ff.

once again for the reception of eternal life. For those who believe in him have already passed from death to life. None will ever come who will bring us a more perfect word of God, for the voice has sounded once and for all that preaches the gospel to the poor and causes the dead to come forth out of the tombs. We can expect no new revelation from above, for the work of divine grace and mercy is done and all God's promises are Yes and Amen in him; those who see him see the Father. In him alone we can bring salvation to others. We must point to him alone. All those whom in future generations the Lord will select for his service will come in the name of Jesus of Nazareth, with us bend the knee before him, and with us confess that salvation has gone out and always will go out from him alone. Those who will not receive the saving teaching of heaven from him will wait in vain for another.

This certainty of the definitiveness of Christ, which transcends the schema of *The Christian Faith,* is attested also by the words of the dying Schleiermacher at his last communion as they are reported by his wife.[98] After the words of institution he said: "I cling to these words of scripture; they are the basis of my faith." He himself pronounced the benediction, and he then added: "In this love and fellowship we are and remain one." A few minutes later he died (Feb. 12, 1834).

E. SCHLEIERMACHER'S SELF-INTERPRETATION IN HIS LETTERS TO F. LÜCKE

In the reactions of contemporaries to *The Christian Faith* Schleiermacher was affected most by the repeated charge of pantheism, which appeals to the more general religious philosophy of the Introduction. He protested resolutely against the inference, made even by his friend K. I. Nitzsch, that he was trying to absorb specific Christian knowledge into general religious knowledge.[99] In fact, in his development of the general religious self-consciousness, he himself had had in view the God-consciousness developed in the Christian church (Lücke, 28-29). He had not borrowed from elsewhere, whether from philosophy (28, 31, 38) or from pre-Christian doctrines of God such as those found in the OT (29, 42-43).

Why did he engage in this broad preamble to his true presentation of the faith? Why did he put his presentation in the form and indefinite sphere of this perilous Introduction (32-33)? Why did he not

98. *Briefe,* II, 510ff.
99. Lücke, p. 28; the references that follow are to the same work.

begin with the material statements of dogmatics, especially as he thought it possible to take this course, and in preliminary deliberations spoke of the warmer coloring that it would give his statements? He admits expressly that for a long time he lovingly considered keeping to this order (33-34).[100]

It is a scholarly consideration that provides the decisive reason for the debated beginning with the general self-consciousness and the attempt to locate the Christian God-consciousness in it (54). Or, rather, it is the corresponding concern. For if we simply begin with positive scriptural statements (e.g., about miracles) and a plain *Deus dixit*, in our statements of faith we shall not be able to distinguish between what is vital and what is less essential, and we shall thus dig in behind "outer works" (e.g., uncritically accepted biblical accounts of miracles). But in so doing we shall blockade ourselves against scholarship. This blockade, this starving ourselves of scholarship, will become a mortal danger to those who simply maintain their Christian confession thetically but do not consider its relationship to what is said by science and history or discuss the question where this Christian confession is to be located in the landscape of the human spirit. This lack of reflection has fatal results.

For science will then see in theology only a sum of inaccessible and abstruse theses, it will feel repelled by it, and it will be forced to unfurl the banner of unbelief, so that Schleiermacher agonizingly raises the question whether history finally has to mean an equation of Christianity with barbarism and of science with unbelief (37).

Thus his firm conviction, and his aim in presenting the Christian faith as he does, is that every dogma that really represents an element in our self-consciousness (and is not a free statement hanging in the air) can and should be interpreted in such a way that it does not entangle us with science (40). Only the exposition of the connection between faith and consciousness, only the affinity of faith to the human spirit, can see to it that science does not have to declare war on us. Nor,

---

100. His disciple A. D. C. Twesten (1789-1876) later attempted this order in his unfinished lectures on the *Dogmatics of the Evangelical Lutheran Church*, 2 vols. (1826-1837), hoping thereby to make it plain that dogmatics is closely tied to the church. He begins with the given matter of the church's teaching and tries to overcome the limits of the subjectivity from which in his view Schleiermacher's statements about the contents of the faith, especially in the doctrine of God, obviously suffer. Yet unwittingly the definition of religion in terms of feeling plays a role in him too, although in Christianity the experience of regeneration controls this subjective side. Since Christ himself says that regeneration is a condition of participation in his kingdom, and is also a work of the Holy Spirit, we have here more direct access to the contents of faith than by the general feeling of absolute dependence.

in taking this course, do we do any injury to the miracle of miracles, the manifestation of the Redeemer (40).

We can hardly avoid seeing that an essential step beyond the *Speeches* is taken here. In the *Speeches* religion as contemplation and feeling was to accompany other aspects of life, but it was sharply distinguished from other intellectual regions, especially metaphysics, morality, and science. It was set in a special religious province with its own territorial sovereignty. In *The Christian Faith*, however, it is no longer provincial. The whole concern is to show its connection with other dimensions of the spirit. In the *Letters to Lücke* Schleiermacher fears that a kind of schizophrenia, a cleavage of consciousness, might gain the mastery over us. We have to undergo a sharp switch when as historians or scientists (or technicians) we enter the religious sector, which is blockaded off from all others. What is feared might be discerned in some types of fundamentalism, in which critical and mentally alert engineers uncritically cling to an extreme doctrine of verbal inspiration and hold the two spheres completely apart.

The Christian faith is not to be deduced from the general self-consciousness, as the charge goes against Schleiermacher. He simply wants to give the Christian faith a general and formal location (55) so as to spare it the danger of losing contact with the human spirit and thus pushing this spirit back into paganism.

Whether he can really stop at a formal relation between self-consciousness and faith is another question. We have seen how surreptitiously, and against his real intention, the relation can take on normative rank and become a principle in the selection of doctrines. To what extent this occurs may be seen from the sermons, in which he seems to be free from the pressure of his own formulas and can give free rein to the spontaneity of his personal assurance of faith.

Is it not a law of all systematics, we might finally ask, and not just the fate of Schleiermacher, that he becomes the captive of his own beginnings? A theology is justified only by that to which it is oriented. Its method of mastering this conceptually remains under the spell of the fall. Here is the element that needs forgiveness—the *peccatum in re*—in every theology.

CHAPTER 8

The Influence of Schleiermacher

I. IN LUTHERANISM: J. C. K. VON HOFMANN

In the deliberations that follow we shall be guided by the question of how far it is possible, if it is possible, to keep to Schleiermacher's starting point in the self-consciousness when theological thought is essentially controlled by the Lutheran tradition and also, as in Hofmann, by a stress on salvation history (with the accent on the "history"). Is it possible, and if so how far, to relate a definite orientation to an outside factor, to the facts of the biblical event of revelation, with this subjective approach? Interest in this possibility is heightened if I mention that already in Hofmann, who is influenced by Schleiermacher, "fact" is a basic concept, and the term is like the alien metal of a meteor on Schleiermacherian soil.

To clarify a first relation between the two theologians, which will later be considerably differentiated, I might compare their intentions.[1]

First, Hofmann bases his concept of knowledge, at least in the academic and theological field, not on methodological considerations, but on the possibility of systematization. A system is characterized for him by the fact that the material may be brought under an independent, controlling thought and can thus be presented in such a way as to form a single and closed conception. In Schleiermacher's theology the feeling of absolute dependence had this function. We shall see later what Hofmann puts in its place. At any rate there is undeniable similarity in the intention to establish a system.

Second, for both of them theological knowledge is possible, not as extraneous materials—the teachings mediated by the Bible or the church—are ordered or deduced from some first principle,[2] but only

---

1. See *Enzyklopädie*, pp. 18-21.
2. *Schriftbeweis*, I, 11.

as these materials are related to a state of the inner I (self-consciousness, feeling, or experience) and thus, as one might say today, "internalized," i.e., appropriated. In neither of them, then, can theological science be described without taking the role of subjectivity into account. For this alone is the place where there can be assurance of the truths of faith, assimilated truths. It is thus clear that both theologians fall within our designated theme of doubt and appropriation. How differently they define subjectivity we shall see later. For the moment we simply maintain that subjectivity is something that they have in common.

A. BIOGRAPHY

Johann Christian Konrad von Hofmann (1810-1877) was the most influential of the great thinkers of Erlangen. His connected expositions of the NT are still used today. He was strongly influenced by his home life, which came under the impact of Swabian Pietism and Bengel, and also by Christian Krafft, the very powerful preacher of the Reformed church in Erlangen. His thinking was thus steered in the direction of the theology of scripture and experience. As a student at Berlin he listened especially to Ranke and had some thought of becoming a historian. Only after his student days, and more by way of literature, did Schleiermacher make an impact. Hegel, however, repelled him; his philosophy of history robbed Hofmann of all taste for philosophy.[3] He found in it an apparently nonhistorical attempt to do something against which Ranke's empiricism had immunized him, namely, to deduce the plethora of historical phenomena from a supreme principle.

Nevertheless, Hofmann's systematic theology obviously bears remarkable formal and structural analogies to Hegel, so that again and again there has been reference to his Hegelianism. There are indeed formal similarities, above all in the fact that both start with a total view of history. What for Ranke is the goal in the form of universal history is for both, if for different reasons, the starting point of thought. For Hegel the point of all history is the necessity, the "reason," with which the world spirit develops and manifests itself historically. For Hofmann the point is the illumination by the pneuma that enables us to see the whole panorama of salvation history, and of world history within it.

Hence we have here one of those special but by no means rare cases in which a repudiated philosophy formally penetrates a theological system. This observation should protect us against overvaluing formal

3. See P. Wapler, *Das Leben J. von Hofmanns* (1914), p. 25.

features.[4] It is an open question whether this lack of harmony is the cause or the result of the rejection of Hegel.

Along with his theological labors Hofmann held many honorary posts in missions at home and abroad. He was a member of the Bavarian General Synod. He also took a lively interest in politics for some years and championed the progressive party that worked for German unification. Many-sided as his activities were, his teaching work was central along with his theological writing. He was the theological head of the Erlangen faculty in a period of great fruitfulness.

Bibliography. His main works were *Weissagung und Erfüllung,* 2 vols. (1841-1844, cited as *Weissagung*); *Der Schriftbeweis,* 2 vols. (1857-1860); *Enzyklopädie der Theologie* (1879, cited as *Enzyklopädie*); *Biblische Hermeneutik* (1880, cited as *Hermeneutik*); *Die heilige Schrift des NT zusammenhängend untersucht,* 11 vols. (1862-1886); *Theologische Ethik* (1878, cited as *Ethik*); *Interpreting the Bible* (Minneapolis, 1959, repr. 1972). Works about Hofmann include A. Hauck, in *RE,* 3rd ed., 8, 234ff.; M. Kähler, *Geschichte der protestantische Dogmatik im 19. Jahrhundert* (1962), pp. 212ff.; K. G. Steck, *Die Idee der Heilsgeschichte,* Theologische Studien 56 (Zollikon, 1959); J. Wach, *Das Verstehen,* vol. II (1929); P. Wapler, *Das Leben J. von Hofmanns* (1914); E. W. Wendebourg, "Die heilsgeschichtliche Theologie Hofmanns in ihrem Verhältnis zur romantischen Weltanschauung," *ZThK* 1 (1955) 64ff.

B. BASIC THEOLOGICAL INTENTION

The closeness of Hofmann to Schleiermacher is immediately apparent when we consider the theological method that Hofmann uses in order to reach assurance of salvation and in order to present it. The fact that we have to discuss this shows that he was not a Lutheran in the conventionally orthodox sense, or he would have been content simply to recapitulate and systematize scripture and the confession. He is a theologian of the age after the Enlightenment and Schleiermacher to the extent that he does not primarily ask what we have by way of objective facts and truths of salvation but how these may be known and appropriated and how one may be sure of them. After the Enlighten-

---

4. Cf. F. Gogarten's polemical work against K. Barth, *Gericht oder Skepsis* (1937), in which he accuses Barth of Hegelian identity speculation that distorts his firm theological intention. Cf. my "Die Krisis der Theologie," in *Theologie der Anfechtung* (1949), pp. 59ff.

ment, one might say epigrammatically, questions of method, not substance, become the key questions in theology.

How does Hofmann handle the methodological problem? He proposes two different ways in which theological knowledge—the knowledge of appropriation—might be achieved. The first is the systematic way, and it tells us how and where doctrine may be known for certain. The second involves a historical journey, and it tries to ascertain the facts regarding the biblical and ecclesiastical event of salvation of which we have assurance. The order of inquiry—systematic questions first, then historical questions—is typical, for it puts first the problem of certainty, of my relation to the facts of salvation, and only then makes the facts themselves its theme.

Hofmann, then, begins with what he regards as certain and indisputable, with a fact that has axiomatic rank. What does he mean by this? Nothing is closer to him, nor forms a more certain starting point, than that he is a Christian. This is closer to him than that he is a human.[5] In this present fact he has to seek Christianity, for this is the personal fellowship with God and humanity that is mediated in Jesus Christ.[6] If theologians begin with the fact that they are Christians this does not mean that they begin with their individual subjectivity (as in the case of Schleiermacher's feeling of absolute dependence). For it is only in the community that we experience the personal fellowship with God and humanity that defines being a Christian. Being a Christian is thus bound up from the very first with personal union (with God) in the community of God through Christ.[7]

Theological reflection, then, is not an individualistic undertaking. It takes place within the community. Membership in the community, in virtue of which we may have the certainty of fellowship with God and hence of personal salvation, is for its part grounded in the fact of baptism, and therefore once again in a fact, not in a purely inner assurance through the testimony of the Holy Spirit. The witness of the Spirit simply confirms this fact, giving it its comforting Yes.[8] If one might draw a line from the I-certainty of Descartes to Hofmann, one might say (somewhat boldly): "I am baptized, and therefore I think theologically." This does at least express the fact that in Hofmann Christian certainty arises out of the fact of present Christianity, namely, out of my being a Christian in the community as this is guaranteed by baptism.

5. *Ethik*, p. 16.
6. *Schriftbeweis*, I, 8.
7. Ibid.
8. *Weissagung*, I, 51.

The other great representative of Erlangen theology, F. H. R. von Frank, criticized and modified Hofmann's approach[9] in his two-volume *System der christlichen Gewissheit* (1870-1873). Yet he adopted and developed the same basic approach in regard to certainty. At issue, he thought, is the organic self-development of certainty from the seed (of regeneration) in which the whole organism is already contained and preformed, although without denying influences on the seed from outside or asserting its development simply in terms of itself. The point is that all the life that comes into relation to it from outside becomes its own life, assimilates itself to it, and is taken up and developed by it as its own, as it brings with it the nature of the organism (I, 119). One may see here how the idea of the organism makes the Christian I the decisive point in the question of certainty.

Hofmann, then, begins with an analysis of the Christian. He does not begin with a past event narrated in the Bible but with the fact of present Christianity. Theology is free knowledge (in God) only when that which makes a Christian a Christian, i.e., an independent relation to God, in scientific self-knowledge and self-expression makes the theologian a theologian, only when I as a Christian am the most proper material for my knowledge as a theologian.[10] What makes me a Christian, as the reference to baptism shows, is regeneration.[11] If, then, I perceive and analyze as a reality that which I have experienced as regeneration, I come up against the salvation history that is at work in me and that I see reflected microcosmically in the reality of my personal salvation.

Only in the light of the complete certainty of a reality that I experience as present can I inquire into the totality of a salvation history into which I am integrated as, so to speak, its provisionally ultimate point. The eternal as the presupposition of the historical is the first thing to which the historical present leads. The system begins with this present.[12] Here we see the drift of the inquiry.

We have to remember that for Hofmann the eternal is not to be regarded abstractly as Platonic timelessness or supratemporality. It meets us as the historical fulfilment of an eternal relation, as the center of the history of this fulfilment.[13] This means that Christ as the center of history, as the one who is present eschatologically, as the one who is not bound to time, represents the eternal. If, then, I begin with the

9. Cf. *Geschichte und Kritik der neueren Theologie*, 2nd ed. (1895), pp. 255ff.
10. *Schriftbeweis*, I, 10.
11. Ibid., p. 23.
12. Ibid., p. 13.
13. Ibid.

now of my being a Christian, this means that I begin with the Christ who is active in the present and doing his saving work now. But knowledge of this Christ is based on the Jesus of Nazareth to whom the Bible bears witness. Hence, beginning with the present Christ, I have to ask about the historical Jesus. This is why Hofmann refuses to find the basis of Christianity, i.e., of the present reality of Christ, in the history of Christ and the apostles, i.e., in past history. Christianity rests primarily on the present Christ, who then has himself, the historical Christ, as his presupposition, who points us back to this historical presupposition of his presence.[14] We do not begin with the presupposition, but with its present consequences, when we initiate our theological reflection.

This is why Hofmann in his *Schriftbeweis* adopts the strange method of devoting a few pages to an analysis of his personal Christianity, especially his experience of regeneration, and then devotes over fifteen hundred pages to an unfolding of the implications of this experience, namely, the event of salvation to which the Bible bears witness.

C. THE RELATION BETWEEN PRESENT AND PAST IN SALVATION HISTORY

The result is a very complicated correlation between the present experience and the past history of salvation. The present experience of my being a Christian by regeneration provides me, in Kantian terms, with the forms of apprehension and the categories whereby to understand the biblical history of salvation. This history, as a complex of facts outside any subjectivity, then confirms the validity of my experience.

Note here the anxiety of Hofmann lest his certainty be challenged as one-sided either in the sense of being a purely subjective experience and hence becoming a nebulous feeling of dependence, as in Schleiermacher, or in the sense of being content with questionable historical assertions which can never display the totality of the plan of salvation.[15] This is why Hofmann begins with the subjective experience of being a Christian but then sees to it that this subjectivity is not mere inwardness by relating theological work to facts that are independent of the theologian's scholarly work and are thus transsubjective. He finds such facts in the directly certain reality of the regeneration of the

14. *Enzyklopädie*, p. 28.
15. As Hofmann sees it, this is the weakness of Ranke and the reason why he has to take a different path from his great teacher. Cf. Wendebourg, *ZThK* 1 (1955) 66ff.

Christian, and in the history and existence of the church and holy scripture.[16]

Thus Hofmann's deliberations move on two intersecting lines, first that of an analysis of the Christian I, second that of history. The point of intersection is the geometrical place of certainty. In other words, the starting point of theological thinking is the experience of the present event of salvation. The historical inquiry is then a kind of commentary on this experience which also confirms it. Present and past, subjective experience and transsubjective fact, permeate one another dialectically. The certainty of our salvation does not rest on the Spirit's witness to our sonship but on the fact of our baptism to which the Spirit gives his comforting Yes. Similarly the certainty of the community does not rest on the witness of its living fellowship with Christ but on scripture, which the Spirit confesses in every assault. If we are asked what it is that assures us that this inner agreement with the content of the Word flows from the Holy Spirit, we answer that two or three witnesses confirm the truth. The agreement between our need of salvation and the narrated facts of salvation on the one side, and between these and the empowering Yes that we receive in ourselves on the other, grants a certainty that cannot be given by any proof.[17]

Hence systematic reflection, dealing with both present Christianity, i.e., the experience of the Christian I, and the historical high points of salvation history, involves a relation of mutual penetration and confirmation. The question is whether the results of historical research are in harmony with those reached on a systematic path.[18] Only with the establishment of such harmony does the moment of certainty come.

There has been much criticism, and occasionally merriment, that Hofmann is engaging in a conjuring trick when from the top hat of the experience of personal regeneration he produces a whole brood of historical rabbits. Obviously, he must have manipulated all this in advance. His proof from scripture thus suffers from the fact that it is an extended proof from experience, and his proof from experience that it is already a proof from scripture. Twice, then, he is begging the question.[19]

I must admit that I do not wholly understand this objection, for

16. *Schriftbeweis*, p. 23.
17. See *Weissagung*, I, 51. Frank, too, speaks of the agreement between need and reception as a confirmation that in regeneration we do not have an outside authority but something that is made our own and is thus certain (*System der christlichen Gewissheit*, pp. 108ff., 114).
18. *Enzyklopädie*, p. 26.
19. Barth, *Protestant Theology in the Nineteenth Century*, p. 614.

on closer inspection what looks like a begging of the question is none other than the well-known hermeneutical circle. I have to have a preunderstanding of the text that I am to understand, and I then find this in it, yet not in such a way that I simply find it confirmed, but in such a way that the text surpasses and corrects it. (It is thus unfortunate to speak of a hermeneutical "principle," which leaves the impression of something we can never get beyond.) That which Hofmann calls the experience of being a Christian (i.e., regeneration) constitutes the preunderstanding of the biblical text, or of the text of salvation history. It rests on first and relatively naive encounters with it, especially by way of the proclamation of the community in which Christians find themselves. The contact with the text that comes to light in the preunderstanding effects a relationship of analogy and coordination with it which makes possible, as we saw earlier, a divinatory understanding. Christians who engage in theological reflection then lay claim to this.

If we view things in this light, the quantitative mismatch between the short systematic discussion and the long historical section loses its grotesque character. The systematic preamble is simply establishing the analogy between Christian existence and the salvation history that determines it. It is thus bringing to light the categories of understanding. It is also locating the gap in the hedge through which one can see an extensive landscape.

What disturbs me about the relation that Hofmann sets up is something very different. A justifiable material concern arises when Hofmann finds all salvation history implied in the Christian experience of the individual theologian. This seems to be the thing that worries critics when they consider the extreme implications. It would have been different if Hofmann had made Christianity as the total community, or, better, the church, the subject of spiritual experience, and thus arrived at the formulation that theology (not the individual theologian) makes Christianity's experience of faith the theme of its discipline.

D. DECISIVE QUESTIONS

The following questions thus arise which will partly take up again what has been said and partly lead on to a second train of thought: (1) Why does Hofmann choose, like Schleiermacher, to begin with the subject? (2) What goals does he hope to achieve with this method? (3) What is the result, especially as concerns the understanding of salvation history.

1. Why Does He Choose This Theological Path and Not Another?

We might give the summary answer that other paths do not lead to certainty. On the one hand, Hofmann does not think that certainty can be attained with the help of philosophy, although his reasons for this differ from those of Schleiermacher in his rejection of metaphysics as a basis for religion. The repellent features in Hegelian speculation might perhaps stand psychologically behind Hofmann's argument that philosophically established truths cannot be binding for Christians and hence leave them in uncertainty. Why, on the other hand, certainty cannot be achieved on the basis of historical research we have already seen. Historians can give certainty only outside their own situation.[20] Furthermore the historical facts of biblical salvation history can be known only indirectly by way of the church. Thus the danger might arise (cf. the *Enzyklopädie*) that I uncritically adopt the church's confession in which I have a concentrated form of them. In the Roman sense this would hand me over to a church hierarchy, or to mediation by a hierarchy, and I could have no direct certainty.

This is why Hofmann begins his appropriation of the facts of salvation at the point where there is direct certainty already at the start, i.e., with the experience of regeneration and the factual sign of baptism.

2. What Goals Does He Hope to Achieve with This Method?

He first wants to achieve a relation to history which nowadays we should call existential. Starting with the experience of regeneration, with the Christian I, and then inquiring into salvation history on this basis, he asks about what is significant, about the history that is relevant to him. Significance means not only valid truth such as we find in philosophy but the truth of historical facts which accomplish something and make me an effect. The inquiry shows that biblical facts have different degrees of significance. Some are closer and some more distant. The perspective varies.

The first and nearest way in which theology can be certain about its content begins with the very common factor of the personal experience of salvation which makes a Christian a Christian. It leads from the immediately certain fact that forms the content of this to the presuppositions of this fact which must themselves be facts. As a student of

20. We have here a thought that Martin Kähler develops later in *The So-called Historical Jesus and the Historic, Biblical Christ* (Philadelphia, 1964), namely, that history can give only a relative certainty, and that an unconditional truth such as we have in faith cannot be based on a relative thing of this nature.

history sees behind the circumstances of an age the prior facts that have brought them about, and as a student of science finds causes from effects, so the theologian finds the whole of sacred history in its essential results, and can learn its beginning and progress from its provisional conclusion. Does not God's relation to us in Christ, of which we have certainty by personal experience, have all this as a presupposition, and is it not the result of all that which constitutes the essential content of salvation history?[21]

From the high points of Christian experience and history Hofmann also seeks to prove that these are congruent, mutually confirming one another and thus offering a supreme degree of certainty, as we have seen. Kähler rightly points out that R. Rothe, who is quoted in the *Enzyklopädie*, uses a formally similar method. What the theologian speculatively sketches (Hofmann would call such speculation systematizing) has to be compared with the reality (Hofmann would call this salvation history). If the two do not agree, the speculation must be corrected.[22]

3. What Is the Result for the Concept of Salvation History?

Hofmann gives the answer in his other great work, *Weissagung und Erfüllung*. As we have seen, he bases the certainty of salvation on the linkage of various facts. Regeneration as personally experienced salvation causes us to ask about its presuppositions, which must themselves be facts. History as a succession of facts is thus prophecy. Each stage in its development points beyond itself until it finally embraces me, the Christian, in its operation and makes me a fulfilment of its prophecies.

Prophecy here is not just a spoken word of prophecy. History itself is prophecy. The prophets simply express historical facts in their sayings. If they make promises, they are simply commenting on what is already present and given as promise in the events of salvation. Thus J. M. Robinson says that biblical salvation history is the speech event in which the history of Israel expresses itself so as to become historical.[23] Similarly, Heidegger finds in elucidatory history not merely a history of thinking about the problem of being but a kind of self-disclosure of being by way of history. Salvation history, then, does not lie in the

21. Cf. Hauck, *RE*, 8, 239. That the term *salvation history* as it is used here played so significant and controversial a role later is due to contemporary Lutheranism; cf. not only Hofmann but also A. Vilmar, *Die Theologie der Tatsachen wider die Theologie der Rhetorik* (1856). On Vilmar cf. W. Hoff, *A. Vilmar* (1912-1913).

22. *Geschichte der protestantischen Dogmatik*, p. 216.

23. See J. M. Robinson, *EvTh* (1962) 137.

prophetic interpretation of history but in the history that demands this interpretation.

It is astonishing how fully Hofmann's statement that history itself has prophetic significance is taken up by O. Cullmann, especially in his work *Salvation in History* (1967), where he says that in biblical salvation history we have a kind of chain of saving knowledge and presentation in which a new event and revelation are joined to prior revelation and set it in a new light.[24] Cullmann distinguishes three things. The first is the bare event which the prophet must witness and which nonbelievers may also experience although they see no revelation in it. This statement lies close to Hofmann's concern to begin with the experience of the believing I, for only thus do we have access to the bare events. The second thing is the revelation of a divine plan which discloses itself to the prophet in and with the event and into which he inserts himself in faith. The third is the establishment of a connection with prior revelations, and their new interpretation.[25]

If, then, history itself is for Hofmann prophetic history into whose fulfilment he knows that he is integrated as one who is regenerate, this presupposes a total understanding of the historical nexus from its beginning at creation to the final and eternal relationship between God and humanity. I can see the rank of the individual event, whether as prophecy or fulfilment, only as I can see the relation of an individual fact to the end result.[26] Hofmann thus assumes that as a Christian he has access to the whole course of history, to universal history, and that he has this access at the beginning and not at the end of his studies, as in Ranke.[27]

With what right and on what grounds does Hofmann claim this access to the whole historical process? One might answer summarily that the experience of regeneration is a kind of microcosmic concentration of all salvation history, a "recognition" or anamnesis of it in the present.[28] This experience points me to Christ as the center of history and from this center to its advance prophetic manifestation,[29] and also, after this provisional conclusion, to the final fulfilment. Thus the whole of history

24. Cullmann, *Salvation in History* (1967), p. 90.

25. Ibid., p. 91.

26. Hofmann, *Weissagung*, I, 32.

27. Ranke and the whole historical school begin with detailed empirical research and only by way of this try to find the great connections which finally offer universal historical perspectives. Characteristically, Ranke says that each epoch is immediate to God. Hofmann takes the opposite path; cf. Wendebourg, *ZThK* 1 (1955) 71ff.

28. *Schriftbeweis*, I, 8.

29. Ibid., p. 13; see *Weissagung*, I, 40; *Hermeneutik*, pp. 36ff.

is a prophecy of Christ. It reaches its provisional fulfilment in him, and he himself is a prophecy of the consummation.

This is disclosed to us in the witness of the Holy Spirit. What is this witness but a revelation of God which declares the end of all history in a provisional conclusion?[30] Thus Christ as the center of history is a constant factor which is at work in all of it, which determines its course, and which thus enables us to see its whole course in every phase.

In distinction from Ranke, Hofmann does not think that this total view of history results from adding together the individual aspects. It is not a finding of research. It is given when the experience of regeneration leads us to inquire into salvation history. This experience enables us to understand history, i.e., to see how individual facts relate to the whole nexus and how they are to be integrated into it.

Hofmann owes to his teacher Ranke a delight in historical detail and research, but he takes a radically different path in his method of research and his view of understandability—a path which has some formal similarity to that of Hegel, with whom he had a love-hate relationship. For Hegel history is the self-actualization of the absolute Spirit. It is thus determined by reason, and this offers Hegel a total view of history. Those who view the world rationally, the world also views rationally. There is a reciprocal determination.[31] For Hegel, too, this total view is possible because he sees himself at the end of this historical self-development and he thinks of his own philosophy as the result of all prior philosophies, which are contained in it.[32] In the light of this final summation he can understand all the things that are summed up in it.

Despite the formal similarities, we should not overlook the material difference between Hegel and Hofmann. In Hegel it is the speculative identity-philosophy that puts him in the position above history in which he can see the whole historical panorama. In Hofmann, however, it is the eschatological gift of the pneuma that grants this possibility, for the witness of the Holy Spirit is already at work in regeneration, and on this basis the Spirit enables him to see the course of history as an expression of the living and present God in the world, and especially in humanity, as a work of the Spirit on the soul.[33] Hofmann certainly sees world history in the light of its end, which is declared already in its provisional conclusion (Christ). But unlike Hegel he is not himself at the end; he is still in the attitude of one who waits.

30. See *Weissagung*, I, 33.
31. Hegel, *Die Vernunft in der Geschichte*, p. 7.
32. Cf. Wendebourg, *ZThK* 1 (1955) 79.
33. *Weissagung*, I, 16.

The total world panorama with which Hofmann begins in this way embraces not only biblical salvation history in the narrower sense but God's universal world government, and hence pre-Christian and non-Christian spheres as well. Even in these spheres one may see foreshadowings of true salvation history, and the schema of prophecy and fulfilment is already in force, although pagans do not know it. For if all things, great and small, serve to unite the world under Christ its Head, then there is nothing in world history which something divine does not indwell, nothing which is necessarily alien to prophecy.[34]

Christ is the eternal God, and therefore he is present in advance presentations, in prophetic forms, long before his incarnation. Without realizing it pagans felt him in creation, but without differentiating him. Cadmilus and Dionysos and Adonis name him and bewail him too soon, long before he died on the cross. Pagans also know of God's Son much too soon, long before Jesus is exalted as the Son of God and made Lord over all.[35] In Roman history, too, Hofmann finds the foreshadowing of future events in earlier ones, so that again we have a kind of prophecy and fulfilment. Every triumph through the streets of Rome was a prophecy of Caesar Augustus . . . , God in a human, Jupiter in a Roman citizen. By giving its victors these honors Rome announced that in the future it would rule the world through the divinely honored Imperator. The meaning of the triumph is not fulfilled in the repeated processions, nor that of the Passover in the annual Passover feasts. The true content of both is future. The prophecy contained in them is yet to be confirmed.[36]

Whether it be the Roman triumph, the Passover, pagan cults, or biblical ceremonies, the eternal Christ embraces all history before and after him. He is prototypically prefigured in it all. And he himself is a prefiguring of the final end of history which is already present in him as its provisional conclusion.

In this view of the history of Israel and the world I see some similarity to J. G. Hamann, although I cannot prove any direct influence. I have in mind Hamann's question whether we can know the past without understanding the present.[37] I also think of the way in which he goes beyond the history of revelation to Israel and sees something at work in other nations which reminds us of prophecy in Israel and is the analogue to similar obscure presentiments.[38] At any rate, the history of

34. Ibid., p. 7.
35. Ibid., p. 39.
36. Ibid., pp. 15-16.
37. Hamann, "Kleeblatt hellenistischer Briefe," Letter 2, *Schriften*, ed. K. Widmaier (1921), p. 366; ET in R.G. Smith, *J. G. Hamann* (1960), p. 187.
38. "Golgatha und Scheblimini," in *Schriften*, p. 286.

revelation to Israel (as Hofmann might also say), along with Hebrew poetry, is a kind of basic model of all the true history of our divine race and its destiny of glory.[39] Thus the field of world history always resembles the large field that is full of bones which are very dry, and there is no breath in them until the prophet prophesies to the wind and speaks God's word to it (i.e., to the Spirit of prophetic power).[40]

The analogies to prophecy in world history can be disclosed, then, only by the divine word. Nature and history are the two great commentaries on the divine word, and this word is the only key to unlock knowledge in either.[41] The books of nature and history are simply ciphers, hidden signs, which need the key that opens up holy scripture and is the purpose of its inspiration.[42]

D. CONCLUDING CRITICAL APPRAISAL

Bultmann puts to Hofmann the rhetorical question what theological relevance his union of systematics and history can have. He then adds at once the objection that it obviously cannot prove the validity of Christ, since Christ has to be known as the goal of history before the significance of Israel's history can be seen in the light of Christ.[43] But this is to assume that Hofmann wants to bring a proof, which is most unjust, since only "understanding" is at issue. Here again, then, it is sublimely suggested that Hofmann is guilty of begging the question. We have refuted this criticism already and made it clear that what we have here is simply a hermeneutical circle.

More serious is the objection of Kähler[44] that Hofmann is deceived when he thinks he can move on from the fact of my inner life, i.e., my experience of regeneration, to the long history of Israel, messianic expectation, and much else. But the question has to be put to Kähler whether this is what Hofmann does, whether he does really spin the latter out of the former, to put it rather maliciously. Is it not his true aim to show that only those who are caught up into the saving event can understand salvation history because only they are set in the relation of an analogy that makes such understanding possible? Is not Hofmann working out the categories which enable us to see and understand an

---

39. To Herder, Aug. 6, 1784 (*Schriften*, p. 356).
40. "Kleeblatt," 2, 365-66; ET p. 187.
41. "Brocken," p. 179 (ET p. 166); E. H. Gildemeister, *Leben und Werke*, I, 138.
42. "Brocken," p. 188; ET p. 172.
43. Bultmann, *Glauben und Verstehen*, II (1952), 170.
44. Kähler, *The So-called Historical Jesus*, p. 221.

object, the object of salvation history? Has it not always been an essential feature of the Christian tradition to relate theology to a specific state of existence and thus to differentiate it from a neutral and noninvolved religious knowledge?[45] At the decisive point did Hofmann really have anything else in view apart from this rooting of theological work in Christian existence, apart from the fact that only eyes that look at the sun can see the sun, as Goethe put it? This seems to be the point of what he is doing, and it is hard to fault it theologically.[46]

The main problem, in my view, is to be found in the way that he carries out his purpose. Undoubtedly, schemata from the philosophy of history, with a Hegelian coloring, form a dubious scaffolding. The formal use of the schema of prophecy and fulfilment leads often to violent historical constructions. Ideas of progress and evolutionary structures play a role that is alien to the biblical understanding of history. Later generations, which are under the spell of other philosophies and the spirit of another age, can easily see how Hofmann is under the spell of the philosophy and common ideas of his own time. Yet what does all this amount to? Do we really have here more than marginal criticisms of the execution which do not touch the core of what he intends to say? Is not a doxology still a song of praise—to the comprehensive Lord of history who has taken me up into his own history—even though we may sometimes catch atonal elements or false notes along with the biblical melodies? Is not the dominant theme in this historical construction, namely, the correlation between the regenerate I and the presuppositions of this regeneration in salvation history, is not this the decisive indication of what Hofmann regards as theologically relevant? It is an indication that regenerate Christians are themselves taken up into that salvation history and that in virtue of the eschatological quality of the pneuma they are certain of its end and of God's final triumph. This experience of the I is very different from a mere apologetic mask in which the modern biblicist is justifying himself before the spirit of the age.[47]

45. Only if we study religion and such related themes as religious psychology and sociology can we take a different view.

46. The only possible objection is that Hofmann overloads the individual experience of salvation. It would be better to substitute the church's I for the individual I.

47. Cf. Barth, *Protestant Theology*, p. 612.

II. IN THE REFORMED WORLD: ALEXANDER SCHWEIZER

A. BIOGRAPHY

A. Schweizer, who came from a family of Zurich pastors, lived from 1808 to 1888. After his theological examination a patron who recognized his gifts provided him with a scholarship which enabled him to visit German universities. He spent his time mostly in Berlin, where he was especially attracted to Schleiermacher, with whom he had a close relationship. He undertook the editing of Schleiermacher's ethical lectures in 1835 under the title *Entwurf eines Systems der Sittenlehre*. He shared with Hofmann a dislike for Hegel but also the unmistakable influence of Hegel's thought on various parts of his system.

Bibliography. Schweizer's first main work was his *Glaubenslehre der evangelischen reformierten Kirche, dargestellt und aus den Quellen belegt*, 2 vols. (1844-1847, cited as *Glaubenslehre*). Although as a systematician he broke away from tradition and attempted a theological approach essentially shaped by his great teacher, he believed that one should not lose sight of the link with older Reformed dogmatics, especially as the strong influence of Lutheranism irritated him, and over against it he wished to set the theological profile of Calvinism. This emotion-laden purpose is present in and through the wide-ranging and detailed scholarship.

The second work is in the history of dogma, *Die protestantischen Zentraldogmen in ihrer Entwicklung innerhalb der reformierten Kirche (vom 16. bis 18. Jahrhundert)*, 2 vols. (1854-1856). Here we see for the first time that he regards a strict form of predestination as the dominant central dogma of his church. For the rest he establishes historically what he had presented systematically in the *Glaubenslehre*. His anti-Lutheran feeling may be seen in the way in which he attacks especially Melanchthon's weakening of election. He takes issue particularly with the Formula of Concord, above all with its thesis that grace alone is the predestinating ground of salvation but that those who are lost owe it to themselves.[48]

His chief systematic work is *Die christliche Glaubenslehre nach protestantischen Grundsätzen*, 2 vols. (1863-1869); this is the main work that we must briefly discuss in the present context.

---

48. Cf. "Solemn Declaration," XI, 7-8, 41-42 (Tappert, pp. 616ff.).

B. SCHLEIERMACHERIAN APPROACH

In several ways Schweizer shows himself to be a disciple of Schleiermacher. First, we have this intention, which is too easily classified and dismissed as "apologetic." Like Schleiermacher, he does not want to stay with earlier dogmatics, which he describes with some acerbity, nor simply to continue tradition. What the fathers regarded as the truth of faith is not without more ado *our* truth. The constellations of understanding have changed. We have to seek new approaches to truth if we are to bear credible witness to the faith and reach the level of the theological reflection. At the very beginning of the *Glaubenslehre* he writes the revealing words that the fathers once confessed their own faith, and now we try to believe their confessions; to teach a truly credible faith has become an urgent need.

Second, Schweizer, like his teacher, begins with the self-consciousness and aims to develop all Reformed teaching on this basis, at least to the extent that traditional dogmas are feasible, i.e., may be taken up into the modern self-consciousness. Along these lines a few dogmas are left out which were previously fundamental, e.g., those of the Trinity, Christ's deity, satisfaction, substitution, and the inspiration of scripture. Unlike Hofmann, he is not thinking of a self-consciousness that is determined by the experience of regeneration and therefore of a specifically Christian fact of salvation. He has in view a basic and universal theistic feeling—that of absolute dependence on God. His addition "on God," or "on the Infinite or Absolute,"[49] is a typical variation on Schleiermacher's phrase, to which we shall return. In contrast to Hofmann, however, he thinks in terms of a universally religious self-consciousness rather than a Christian one. In this he is closer to Schleiermacher. Some other points support this impression.

(1) Schweizer, too, subsumes Christianity under the master concept of religion in the first part of his *Glaubenslehre*, and he regards all other religions, e.g., the natural religions of the heathen and the legal religion of Israel, as lower pre-stages of the Christian religion, to which they necessarily lead "sooner or later" in the historical process. Schweizer constructs a rather strained division of religious history into epochs of natural religion, legal religion, and redemptive religion. It is characteristic of the force of his system that he postulates an original natural religion even though he himself can say that nowhere is there any historical proof of it.[50]

49. Cf. *Glaubenslehre der evangelischen reformierten Kirche*, I, 135.
50. Ibid., p. 257.

(2) When Schweizer deals with the self-consciousness of the present community, its consciousness of faith, he finds here a mixture of Christian doctrines with the time-bound elements of scientific convictions, cultural legacies, and philosophical opinions. This mixture is unavoidable if Christian dogma is not merely to be a legally understood creed to be believed but is to be appropriated by vital people in their own age. The approach by way of the self-consciousness sees to it that there is no division between faith and modern knowledge such as Schleiermacher fears will overtake a merely ongoing orthodoxy in his *Letters to Lücke*.

(3) The approach by way of the self-consciousness has another implication. It involves a selection of traditional truths. The living religious self-consciousness represents the present stage of the development of the Christian faith and it is thus allergic to demands that are tied to earlier stages and that are thus time-bound and meaningless for the present consciousness. In this way "positive" elements in the tradition of Christian truth are ruled out. (We have already mentioned some of them.) Since everything that is conditioned by a specific time or place is to be eliminated, Schweizer presses finally toward an idea of perfected religion that is detached from history and that only in this way can be universal, i.e., the religion of all humanity. It is hardly surprising, then, that this theory, based on the self-consciousness, has implications that are close to the religious schema of the rationalists. There are times when we seem to hear the voice of Lessing in his *Education of the Human Race*. He, too, developed the history of Christian truth in terms of the rational self-consciousness, and for him the goal was a free-floating idea of truth detached from all historical conditioning.

(4) On this basis Schweizer attempts a synthesis, greatly reduced by his process of selection, between the present self-consciousness and the Reformed dogmatic tradition. Fundamentally his intention is the same as we find in Schleiermacher. If I am right, however, the difference is that in him we do not have the exegetical and homiletical correctives which kept Schleiermacher from being led astray by his passion for systematizing.

C. PREDESTINATION AND ABSOLUTE DEPENDENCE

The crux of Schweizer's synthesis is his concern to interpret the feeling of absolute dependence as a kind of preliminary of what he calls the chief and central dogma of Calvinism, the doctrine of predestination.[51]

51. We have seen that unlike his mentor, Schweizer indicates the source of dependence in God or the Infinite. In Schleiermacher we simply have an undefined

The feature of this doctrine is the thesis of God's omnicausality. This is the basis of the Reformed confession, and for the self-consciousness it means a sense of the total dependence of all being and events, and for the objective consciousness a view of things in which all that is and all that occurs are a self-revelation of the Absolute, which as the ground (i.e., cause) of all being determines and permeates all things.[52]

That the doctrine of predestination in this radical form which makes God the cause of all things does in fact dominate Reformed teaching has rightly been contested. It was so even in Schweizer's day.[53] Peter Barth has pointed out that predestination is only mistakenly called the central doctrine in Calvin's theology, since in the 1536 *Institutes* it comes within the doctrine of the church and is not an isolated dogma (Select Works, I, 86ff.).[54] Although Karl Barth has fundamentally modified Calvin's doctrine in a christological direction, we may see in him some dependence on the later Calvinistic doctrine of the decrees which is in part analogous to what we find in Schweizer.[55]

If in the later Reformed doctrine of the decrees all that happens is foreordained from the foundation of the world, there can never be anything unconditionally new. Even the Christ event is not a new thing. It is not an unforeseeable act of God and turning point of the aeons that breaks the necessity of a predetermined historical process. It is simply an explication of what is already laid down. The abstractness of this system of causes takes all the contingency out of history. This may be seen in Schweizer, although in this context we can only illustrate it in terms of his doctrine of sin and his Christology.

For him the fall is not due to the fact that God enters into free partnership with us and runs the risk of abandoning his complete determination of all things. The fall is for him a transitional point and link in a necessary process foreseen in supralapsarian fashion. (It has to be according to this view of predestination.) Within this process the good needs the polar antithesis of the bad. The bad is not guiltily brought into being by a misuse of human freedom. We are not responsible for it. It has to be. This is an implication of all monistic systems (which work with a monocausal doctrine of predestination). And it is not without

---

feeling whose basis is only later sought in transcendence on the ground that the feeling of dependence is only a partial or conditional one in the empirical world.

52. *Glaubenslehre der evangelischen reformierten Kirche*, I, 135.

53. Cf. J. H. A. Ebrard, *Christliche Dogmatik* (1851).

54. Peter Barth, "Die Erwählungslehre in Calvins Institutio von 1536," in *Theologische Aufsätze K. Barth zum 50. Geburtstag* (1936), pp. 432ff.

55. See *CD*, II/2; cf. G. Gloege, *Heilsgeschehen und Welt*, Theologische Traktate 1 (1965), 77ff. Cf. also *ThE*, I, 203ff.; II, 2, 706ff.; ET I, 110ff.; II, 576ff.

some piquancy that in this regard, like his Lutheran counterpart Hofmann in another respect, Schweizer is following in the steps of the Hegel whom both abhorred. What is for Hegel a necessary moment in the self-development of the Spirit is for Schweizer a necessary result of total predestination. Evil is a mere transition in a predetermined process.[56]

This necessity applies also to the rise of the religion of redemption and hence to all christological statements. In Hegelian terms, the religion of redemption is the dialectical antithesis of the legal religion that precedes it (and that we need not go into here). Yet we do not have here an intervention of God, whose wonderful counsel brings about the turn that is hymned in the carol which speaks of a lost world and of Christ being born. Because redemption is a mere phase in a necessary process which finally brings about the self-actualization of the idea of religion, the event of redemption is not tied to, or effected by, the historical incarnation of Christ or the event of Jesus of Nazareth. Instead, the evolution of the primal decree of predestination, which fixed already the phases of natural and legal religion, continues in the necessary rise of the religion of redemption. That this should take place is grounded necessarily in the nature of things (i.e., in God's omnicausality).[57]

We again have Hegelian thinking, which A. E. Biedermann puts most consistently on the theological plane, when for Schweizer the principle of redemption is no longer identical with the historical person of Jesus but is already present potentially and is simply given historical expression, not brought to birth, by Christ.[58] Christ actualizes "the divine-human idea . . . in himself to the same full extent as he fully bears religion in himself."[59] Christ is the realized idea, the form, which with the greatest religious adequacy expresses the idea of redemption. As Schleiermacher would say, he is the model for all Christians as they strive in fragmentary fashion to achieve the same adequacy.

Thus Schweizer's theology ends in ideas and principles which abandon all God's saving acts for timeless validities. Is not God himself just an idea of predestination, the first and determinative cause of all things?

56. *Glaubenslehre*, I, 273.

57. Ibid., p. 324.

58. Thus Biedermann, too, can say that the Christian principle (of redemption) first entered human history in the religious personality of Jesus but is contained eternally in the being of God and man as their true religious relationship. This is in opposition to the form of church teaching which personifies the principle (*Christliche Dogmatik* [1868], p. 583).

59. Schweizer, *Glaubenslehre*, II, 105.

D. THEOLOGICAL DEAD END

It seems as though Schleiermacher's theology reaches a certain state of exhaustion in Schweizer. We see in him the end of the possibilities that this approach contained. The mediating theology implied by this line of thinking has reached a climax and become one-sided again. It is mediating and yet it is not mediating.

Schweizer first presents it indeed as a mediating theology. Like his teacher, he tries to synthesize opposing trends and positions and hence to keep both. On the one side we have the approach by way of the subjective self-consciousness of the modern Christian, and on the other the church's traditional teaching whose religious content is to be retained in the consciousness in spite of all the criticism of elements bound to time and place. Representatively, the feeling of absolute dependence is interpreted as a kind of reflection of radically understood predestination. Schweizer also mediates between rationalism and Romanticism, between rational faith in the Enlightenment sense and "feeling." In this regard he strives to overcome a polarity that Schleiermacher definitely retains. We thus find in him a vacillation which, when it becomes an end in itself (as it never is in Schleiermacher), is insipid in spite of all the skill in presentation and systematic construction.[60] We seem to have an inkling in advance how the "golden mean" will go toward which he always steers us. The same mediating trend means that he must always react allergically to theological extremes and radicalisms. Thus he played a vital role in the blocking of the call of D. F. Strauss to the theological faculty at Zurich.

Yet Schweizer was not a mediator but in his later years followed the narrow track of a rationalistically tinged religion of ideas and principles. He himself might have viewed this, too, as mediation. Opposing opinions often seem to be muted when we free them from their time-bound limitations and find in them a suprahistorical idea. A theology of history which distills ideas leads to easier systematizing than things that are historically conditioned. But then the system of ideas easily becomes a Procrustean bed in which living traditions are compressed and limbs that will not fit are lopped off.

Readers can only follow such a process with disquiet. For one thing, it equates what is regarded as the idea and criterion of Christian truth with the individuality of the theological author, or at least with his generation and the spirit of the age. Thus Schweizer's dominating

---

60. Barth has something similar in view when he says—perhaps rather mischievously—that Schweizer puts us to sleep (*Protestant Theology*, pp. 575-76).

interest in relevance hardly produces a reliable kerygma to which we can cling. For another, every truth may be deduced in advance from this given or presumed idea, and there is thus no longer any true mediation, only an act of ever new self-confirmation along the line of presupposed ideas.

From this angle Hofmann is a much richer thinker. Taught by Ranke, he had an openness to historical detail which, along with his extended exegetical work, prevented him from falling victim to the formalism of systematic construction and the dissolution of the historical element in ideas and principles.

Thus Schweizer's theology leads into a dead end. He himself had no disciples to continue the tradition of Schleiermacher in spite of his developed art as a systematician. After him, indeed, theology seems to be tired of systems. Historical questions come to the fore.

Yet Schweizer's theology did not go out of circulation (in our own generation there are similarities in Bultmann) because it was opposed and defeated. It went out of circulation because people became tired of the monotony of its questions and answers. These became hackneyed. We should note how significant this factor is in the history of theology and how many theologians have died of it. I recall a conversation in which it was suggested that the influential school of Ritschl did not perish because it was defeated in argument but because Ritschl's disciples died off and no one was any longer interested in theses of this type.

This is a very human aspect of theological history.

CHAPTER 9

Interlude: The New Humanism or Human Liberation

I. THE TERMS *HUMANITY* AND *HUMANISM*

One point has always been with us in our portraits of the Enlightenment and Schleiermacher, namely, that the persistent and overarching theme of doubt and appropriation makes humanity itself—adult humanity—the true theological theme. This may mean that as rational beings we can appropriate only that which accords with rational criteria. We refuse to make the surrender which is necessary if we deliver ourselves up to an alien authority that is beyond our own control, even and precisely if this authority comes with the claim to be divine revelation or to proclaim divine commands. We want religion to confirm and foster our dignity as rational creatures. Religion is acceptable, if at all, only as a service to humanity.

Yet as in Schleiermacher humanity may also be an independent theme of theology as our religious subjectivity or pious self-consciousness is regarded as the primary factor in human existence, and revelation, and even God himself, can thus be discussed only as they come within the compass of this subjectivity.

The move to this new self-consciousness in which we are autonomous bearers of certainty cannot be reversed. Our deliberations have shown, however, that it need not mean our self-elevation as surrogate gods. The way is still radically open to transcendence, or it ought to be open to it, even if only under certain conditions. As nineteenth-century developments make plain, there is also, of course, the possibility that along these lines humanity may finally make itself the end of all being. This need not happen in the Promethean fashion of Nietzsche or the

255

comparatively smaller form of Feuerbach. It may happen in a more restrained way as follows. When humanity sees itself as the end of all being, it finds meaning and destiny only in its own optimal self-fulfilment and the bringing of its own entelechy to its fullest development.

This position we call the new humanism. I will not choose Herder as an example, as is often done. Herder does indeed coin the term *humanity* (at least in the sense in which the educated world now uses it). Yet if many of the features of classical humanism may be found in him, he is not its purest type (if one may be permitted to use such a summary concept). In virtue of his theological life as General Superintendent at Weimar and as a preacher of the gospel, he leaves open a reference to the transcendent by his very calling. At the same time one can see how this element seems to be under the constant threat of being absorbed and assimilated by the human factor which is striving for liberation.

In this regard it is valuable if rather depressing to see how all this comes to expression in his confirmation courses for the ducal children at Weimar. Herder prepared for them a special catechism with many questions and answers. The little princes and princesses had to recite these as a public profession of faith. Thus in a catechism for Caroline Louise, Princess of Saxe-Weimar and Eisenach, the religion of Jesus is depicted as a means to bring human nature, which is identical with the divine element in us, to its full development.[1] We are not to be oriented to our eternal salvation but salvation is to be of help to us in becoming human. The religion of Jesus is not true because Jesus worked miracles—although neither here nor elsewhere does Herder contest this—but its supreme humanity is its one true proof.[2] If one asks whether baptism does violence to children[3] (by working heteronomously against the ideal of self-development), the answer is that it brings them into a community of people in which they are promised a good education, i.e., one which for the new humanists can only serve their self-development.

Although there is here a plain tendency to absorb the transcendent in humanity, Herder still retains a certain openness to it. Where the Bible is set up, it maintains its history with us in spite of every heresy and secularism. Where the figure of Christ is present to the consciousness, even if it be understood only as an example of noble human dispositions, it continually breaks out of the walls of its ideological prison and rises from the conceptual grave of humanism and other restrictive systems.

1. 1806 ed., Part 4, pp. 255ff., 262.
2. Ibid., pp. 265, 281.
3. Ibid., p. 283.

Hence Herder is *not* the classical representative of a new humanism that is oriented to pure immanence. He no doubt turns aside from orthodox dogmatism. Yet he has doubts about the opposite extreme as well, i.e., deistic or neological immanentism. He takes in some sense a middle way, or, as one might also say, a way of compromise.

The person whom one might really describe as a model of the new humanism is Wilhelm von Humboldt.[4] I will not attempt a full portrait of this many-faceted and highly differentiated personality but focus only on one aspect which seems especially to represent the point of the new humanistic view of humanity. His letters provide us with fruitful material for this purpose.

But first we must try to establish clear definitions of humanism and humanity. This is necessary because the terms imply a very definite anthropology. But is it really so definite? Perhaps the terms are too many-faceted and ambivalent to allow us to fix their meaning precisely. Although there may be a common denominator in the different uses, what we mean by humanism in our humanistic school undoubtedly differs from what Erasmus meant by it. And this again differs from the new humanism of Humboldt, and especially from the aims of the Humanistic Union in the late 20th century.

Humanity denotes a moral attitude that is oriented to values which can claim recognition by all who respect the dignity of the human. These values might be described by such terms as human obligations, rights, love, and worth. All such values are aimed polemically against anything that would divert us from our destiny or reduce us to animals, especially egoism, the instinct of self-preservation, eudaemonism, everything purely instinctual, and finally, according to the Marxist version of humanism, that we are made the mere plaything of historical processes such as the class conflict, and hence "alienated." With the idea of humanity the demand is made that we must resist the pull of the natural or of processes. Related to this is the fact that it is often easier to show what is *in*human than what is human.[5]

Since the norm of what is more than nature is not only the basic but also the most common definition of the human, we have in it a measure of the human that transcends all peculiarities and breaks through the barriers of race, people, religion, status, and class. But there can be differences in the way that we define this element. (1) It might

---

4. For convenience I will quote him where possible (but not always) from H. Weinstock's selection, Fischer Bücherei (1957, cited as Fischer).

5. This is blatantly true of the anthropological statements of Herbert Marcuse; cf. my *Kulturkritik der studentischen Rebellion* (1969), pp. 44ff.

be defined cosmopolitically, as in Stoicism. (2) It might be understood as something historical, as in Lessing, who perceives a development that is at first very limited and restricted (Israel) but gradually expands and finally, in the eschatological stage of history, will give rise to the pure, universal humanity of a society of rational beings with no distinctions (not wholly dissimilar to the classless society of Karl Marx). (3) It might finally occur only in individuations in the wealth of an infinite fulness of forms and modifications, as in Herder. Here it is pointed out that creation means that everything is made after its kind. The task, then, is to recognize the common, connecting element, humanity, in the rich fulness of forms. The divine aspect of the race is the formation of humanity. All the great and the good, lawgivers, inventors, philosophers, poets, and artists, all noble people in their different roles, in the education of children, the fulfilment of duties, by example, work, institution, and teaching, have a part in this. Humanity is the treasure and profit that is sought in every human endeavor, the art of our race. To fashion it is a work that must be unceasingly pushed forward, or else, higher and lower classes alike, we shall sink back into raw bestiality.[6] In spite of the wealth of differentiation, Herder thinks that the various forms of humanity share a common theme. By appealing to what is common and suppressing what divides, humanity seeks to achieve a universal ideal which has its presuppositions in all of us. A common layer is thought to underlie the stratum of differentiation.

Thus far one might say (with a grain of salt) that the Christian view could be subsumed under this very general concept. Such an attempt does, of course, raise difficulties if we stress the positive side, namely, the values already enumerated. These cannot be simply equated with the Christian view of humanity. For this view does not involve a mere general love of others. Christian *agape* has a specific point without which it is unrecognizable, e.g., when it is understood as a moral "work." *Agape* entails two things that differentiate it from a general idea of humanity.

First, it is grounded in a movement of love that begins in God. I know that God loves me for no reason in the sense that I am unworthy of this love, and I know that I ought to show the same love to my neighbors even when they do not arouse any such love, even when they are unworthy of it, or are indeed my debtors (cf. the parable of Jesus in Matt. 18:23ff.).

Second, this love is possible only when it is not aroused by the immanent value or dignity of others—adequate though this may be—but when it relates to what Luther calls their alien dignity. He means by this their infinite value on the basis of the fact that God has entered into

6. Herder, *Werke* (Suphan), 17, 138.

a history with them, that they are under the patronage of eternal goodness, that they are "bought with a price" (1 Cor. 6:20; 7:23). What Harnack calls the "infinite value of the human soul" does not consist in the fact that neighbors have for me a specific interest or functional value. It consists in something outside me, in a relationship, not a quality.

For all the differences between Christian *agape* and the ideal of humanity there are certain formal similarities. (These make it possible for representatives of the two to work together, e.g., in social service.) Thus in both the general and the Christian forms of humanity there is a turning aside from self-alienation, whether in its general form as crass egoism or brutality or in its specific form as the way of the prodigal into the far country, the forsaking of the father, the attempt to be as God. It is an axiom of Christian anthropology that those who lose God lose themselves. Since a relationship with God is not at our disposal but may be had only by grace, liberation from self-alienation is not achieved by human resolve or initiative but only by a gracious visitation.

One might speak of "Christian humanity," but in so doing one has to realize that the similarities to general humanity are only formal and essentially negative. They do exist in this sense. It is important to state this, for it sets Christians in contact with natural humanity. It shows that we are dealing with humanity. Yet the implied presupposition is always that God is dealing with humanity. We thus have in view the humanity of God.

As we have seen, the ideas of humanity that occur in the history of thought—notwithstanding their variety—all have the same goal of total self-fulfilment. But what path leads to this goal?

Humanism attempts to answer this question of the means to a fulfilment of humanity. The relation between the terms *humanity* and *humanism* is this: Humanity is the goal, and humanism is teaching about the way to achieve it. Classical humanism points to the way of life indicated by Greco-Roman antiquity. Humanism is as it were the anthropological scaffolding which the humanitarian intention fashions as the form of reflection with whose help it may be fulfilled. Behind it stands the conviction that a perfect humanity is not an abstractly constructed ideal but that it took form in antiquity, especially among the Greeks. Hence the study of classical antiquity developed as the best means of achieving humanity.

When we look at the pertinent terms *humanity, humanism, classicism,* and *culture,* we are not surprised to find that they are Latin terms. The surprising thing, however, is that it was and is chiefly the Greek world which represents humanity in classical antiquity.

In fact, it has been pointed out that there are no Greek equivalents for either *humanity* or *humanism*. The word *philanthropia* does not embody the essence of what is meant by the human but only a friendly approach to others (being nice to them). The absence of such general concepts as humanity is due to the fact that although the Greeks did think in terms of human fulfilment, they found it among themselves, or at least among those who spoke Greek and were permeated by Greek culture. (This applies even to the ethics of Aristotle.) What sounds like a general imperative: "Become what you are by learning," is not thought to apply to those outside the sphere of Greek culture. When Greek culture pushed beyond the national frontiers, the Greeks did not think that this made it a universal culture. They thought instead that those who were not Greeks became Greeks, that they adopted the Greek ideal of *paideia,* and that they were thus integrated into the circle of Greek culture.

It was the Romans who in some sense internationalized the concept of the human and regarded it as something applying to all people. They thus burst through the national limitations of the Greek understanding of *paideia.* They discovered the fact that culture can be transported. Their empire possibly served as a foundation on which they could build a general understanding of the human. This did not mean that Roman poetry and art broke loose from their Greek origins. It meant for the most part that the forms and content taken over from the Greeks were, so to speak, generalized and oriented to what is universally human. The Romans made Greek *paideia* into "education."

Thus humanism has its roots in both Greek and Roman antiquity. Obviously, then, the forms and content of the classical tradition can be known only by way of these two classical languages.

We may sum up our elucidation of the terms by saying that humanity is the epitome of the human and the related human openness, and that humanism is the path to a fulfilment of humanity with the help of the great paradigms that the art, literature, and philosophy of Greek and Roman antiquity set before us.

Humanism takes many forms in the course of history. We cannot go into these and must refrain from discussing the fascinating tension between, say, Petrarch and Blumenberg.[7] Instead, we shall turn to the

---

7. H. Blumenberg, *Die Legitimität der Neuzeit* (1966). One of his theses on secularism (in opposition to Gogarten) is that the only alternative to the nominalistic maximal God which many find too oppressive is an antigodly self-deification, a humanistic atheism and anthropotheism. Cf. C. Gestrich, *Neuzeitliches Denken und die Spaltung der Dialektischen Theologie* (1977), pp. 130ff.; W. Pannenberg, "Christianity as the Legitimacy of the Modern Age," in *The Idea of God and Human Freedom* (1973), pp. 178-91.

form of humanism that develops in German classicism, the so-called new humanism, and we shall try to expound its basic thoughts with the help of the representative figure of Wilhelm von Humboldt.

Even though I leave it to readers to consider the implications, I would point out that many problems in the recent turbulent struggle for university reform become more understandable when we see in them an antithetical reaction to Humboldt's new humanism. Apart from purely technical and organizational questions, the call for reform finally touches the fact that the work of the university is based on Humboldt's ideal and is obviously set in conflict with industry and mass society. Thus the question necessarily arises whether the ideal of individual self-fulfilment does justice to the new situation.

II. A MODEL OF THE NEW HUMANISM: WILHELM VON HUMBOLDT

Bibliography. H. Weinstock, ed., Selection in the Fischer Bücherei (quoted as Fischer); Anna von Sydow, ed., *Wilhelm und Caroline von Humboldt in ihren Briefen*, 17 vols. (1906ff.); A. Leitzmann, *W. von Humboldts Briefe an eine Freundin* (Charlotte Diede) (1909); R. Haym, *W. von Humboldts Lebensbild und Charakteristik* (1856): T. Litt, *Das Bildungsideal der deutschen Klassik und die moderne Arbeitswelt* (1955); E. Spranger, *W. von Humboldt und die Humanitätsidee* (1909); idem, *W. von Humboldt und die Reform des Bildungswesens* (1910); H. Weinstock, *Die Tragödie des Humanismus* (1953).

In what follows I shall not attempt to paint a general portrait of Humboldt but simply to sketch some of the main features of his anthropology that are relevant to our study.

In his life as well as his teaching Humboldt is a perfect type of his new humanism and its implications. For him we are all ends in ourselves, or (to prevent misunderstanding) our individualities or entelechies are ends in themselves. In self-enjoyment personalities find the supreme happiness of the children of earth. The echo of Goethe here is deceptive, unless one restricts it to the one passage in Goethe.[8] Elsewhere we find in Goethe very different emphases from that on self-enjoyment, self-analysis, and contemplation of one's navel. The personality, as he sees it, may be known and actualized only in outward

8. Cf. *West-östlicher Divan;* Artemis, III, 353, where fulfilment comes by way of love, but not self-giving love.

action. We know ourselves, not by contemplation, but by action. If we try to do our duty, we shall know what is in us. We shall know how to come to ourselves.

If, however, as in Humboldt, our own entelechies are the direct goal of self-actualization, this aim can be achieved only by fully exploiting our individualities, only by developing all the seeds contained in them, only by traversing the full horizon of our being. Only thus shall we find our identity. Hence we must develop to the full all our intellectual, moral, and aesthetic abilities. Virtue is the balance of spiritual capacities, as Humboldt can write to Caroline, adopting the Platonic view of *dikaiosyne*. The real goal is not a happy life but the fulfilment of one's destiny and the exploiting of all things human (letter from Rome, March 24, 1804).

In view here is not just the development of utilitarian functions but the formation of humanity. This kind of formation can result only when each aptitude of the personality is given its due. The most human people are those of Greek *dikaiosyne* who actualize this "to each its own" in their inner and outer being.

Some quotations from the letters to his wife Caroline (née von Dacheröden) will perhaps clarify this.[9] (We may laud the periods when communication could not take place merely by phone but had to be by writing.) Humboldt, like Schleiermacher, writes mostly to important women (including his wife) who stimulate him, their receptivity serving to stir up creatively the male heroes of the spirit. He makes no claim to special advantages, to talents, knowledge, or learning, but he does claim the advantage of being human, of being a developed person. His aim is not to use certain functions for some purpose or other, but to develop himself. The true goal is the supreme and most proportionate formation of one's total powers. The formation of individuality is the final goal of the cosmos.

If we recall that in virtue of our humanity we may supposedly lift ourselves above egoism and lower animal drives, we may say—this is almost a theological criticism—that a kind of nobler or sublimated egoism comes to expression in Humboldt's desire for self-fulfilment, in his programmatic curving in upon the self. When life is understood in this way, it is not oriented to service. It is not there for others. It does not receive itself or achieve its own existence in this way as a by-product (Luke 12:31). The very opposite is the case. Humboldt, the new humanist, is there for himself, for the final goal of his own individuality, and he lives by the hope that the world itself will then be a by-product.

9. So far as possible I will follow the Fischer edition, pp. 8ff.

The sum of his wisdom, in which the relation between the I and the outside world, being and function, self-development and service, comes to expression, might be formulated as follows.

While he might hold himself ready for public service, his private life follows its own inclinations or destiny. He has not been made to found or establish anything. His inner personal determination has the goal of learning and experiencing more deeply and richly than others what humanity is and of bringing this inner unity and independence to bear on various forms of activity. When he thinks about the fulfilment of his personal destiny, this does not exclude his being outwardly useful in various ways.[10] When he lives for the self, for his own entelechy, other things may follow as by-products. Paradoxically, this means that those who are egoistic in the higher sense may act very altruistically. When duties claim him, or he acts on behalf of his family, he writes that he does not feel unhappy, even though what is most proper to him would not speak thus, or not wholly or completely so.[11] He is not as he would be by his own will or desire, but as he is willing to be for them. He does what he does freely and with inward joy, but much that is infinitely unique in him remains unsatisfied and is not even touched at all.

Communication, then, does not release what is proper to the personal self. This has to come out directly. It can at most express itself in the dearest love. Only in a general civil sense is it true that those who lovingly make others happy make themselves happy too. This does not apply to higher entelechies, which cannot give themselves to others, because something essential remains silent and undeveloped if they do. This essential part of the self has to be willed directly and can come to development only in a kind of self-cultivation. When we will the self in this way, others benefit by it.

This is the sublime egoism that is a reversal of Christian *agape*. The Gospels leave us in no doubt that to the degree that we are there for others—God and neighbor—we are also there for ourselves and find our own identity. The prodigal who goes into the far country and tries to live for himself, to develop himself without hindrance by free living abroad, loses himself and falls victim to self-alienation. Those who want to win their lives, who make their lives ends in themselves, will lose both them and themselves (Matt. 10:39; 16:25; John 12:25). The son finds himself again only when he finds the father again (Luke 15:24).

Theologically, the deliberate cultivation of the self belongs to the theology of glory in which we are finally the losers. It is opposed to

10. Ibid., pp. 153-54 (to Caroline, June 28, 1810).
11. Ibid., pp. 161-62 (to Johanna Motherby, March 7, 1810).

the theology of the cross in which we spend ourselves in service for others and in so doing gain all things. We may recall the story in which Peter says that he has left everything so as to follow Jesus. He received the answer that no one who has left house or brothers or sisters or mother or father or children or land for the sake of Jesus and the gospel will not receive a hundredfold in this time houses and brothers and sisters and mothers and children and lands, with persecutions, and in the age to come eternal life (Mark 10:19ff.). Our true destiny and our transfigured individuality—as we may surely say also—are thus achieved in self-giving. The grain of wheat has to fall into the ground and die to itself if it is to come up again and fulfil its destiny (John 12:24).

In this light we can see why Humboldt, rejecting this view of things, can call himself a "true pagan" and say that historical Christianity was always alien to him, that he was never religious, and that he had no liking at all for the imposing ideas of traditional religion. He was well aware of the abyss that separated him from the Christian understanding of *agape*.

It is important that we should set Humboldt's theses on self-fulfilment against this background of the Gospels. Only then do we see clearly that the direct cultivation of one's own entelechy as an end in itself is a higher egoism. This self-fulfilment is not a by-product of service, or, in Goethe's terms, action or activity. It is a direct cultivation of the ego. In debate with Humboldt we have to be clear in principle that there are things that we can desire directly and things that we can desire only indirectly. Houses, brothers, sisters, and fields (to use the examples mentioned) may be higher goods but they are not to be desired as ends in themselves; they can only be added. In the Gospels and Paul even good works are not to be desired directly. They can come only with the status of the new and transformed creature.[12]

Many statements show that Humboldt's desire for *direct* self-actualization rests on an egocentricity that is not just sublimated but drastically enhanced. Thus he tells K. G. von Brinkmann that even if he died in old age he would never leave behind a work that would keep the remembrance of him intact.[13] For he never does anything for the sake of the work which is direct and outside him, but for the sake of the energy which is indirect and inside him. He has no searing passion to shape culture. The only thing that finally grips and interests him is the

---

12. Cf. in philosophy Kant's view of happiness as the supreme good. I cannot desire it directly, for this would mean eudaemonism and an anti-ethical attitude. It can only accrue eschatologically when I do not aim at it directly.

13. Fischer, p. 170 (Sep. 3, 1792).

active I which develops itself culturally, so that the work is a means of self-development. Again, he can say that he lives infinitely in his own mind.[14] For he has now set about living only to himself, impertinent as others might find this. He is convinced that all the world's unhappiness and trouble is due to the fact that people have less concern for themselves than for others. If only they would all set about living to themselves! He lives in and for himself and every day accepts the loneliness that Gentz calls dreadful.[15]

It is typical of his position that the only thing he can say to Matthias Claudius (the absolute opposite of a narcissistic humanist committed to self-development, the model of a person who accepts the self with gratitude from the hands of the Creator) is that he amounts to nothing at all. So Schiller tells us—and agrees—in a letter to Goethe dated Oct. 23, 1796. One may doubt, of course, whether someone like Goethe, who had a good relation with Jung-Stilling, would go along with this snobbish judgment.

In the letter to Johanna Motherby already quoted, Humboldt can also say, of course, that this focus on the self needs the friendship of others in order that it may find outward expression. Obviously, this kind of self-communication is part of self-actualization. The self seeks to flow out in words and in this way to find its way to itself.

What opportunity for love does this afford? The love that it makes possible cannot be real self-giving, for the self has to be the goal. In fact, the love that Humboldt has in view does not make the other the object of self-giving. It does not treat the other as an "other" at all. It treats the other instrumentally. It makes the other an assimilated part of the self.

Women with their supposed lack of independence are admirably suited for this. We read with astonishment that a wife should merge completely into her husband and find her autonomy only in his will and thoughts and demands, and her feelings only in subjection to him, whereas the husband should remain completely free and independent regarding her as a part of himself that is ordained for him and to live in him.[16] One wonders how Humboldt would have fared in an age of women's liberation!

In Humboldt the new humanism seems to push on to a point where fixation on self-fulfilment breaks down the last wall that might protect us against self-deification, namely, the recognition of others who

14. Again to Brinkmann, Oct. 23, 1792.
15. To Brinkmann, Dec. 27, 1792.
16. To Johanna Motherby, Apr. 24, 1813.

share the same human dignity and hence cannot be a mere means to an end, even the end of one's own self-fulfilment. For him women are merely the soil in which the masculine self can grow and achieve its destiny. Max Stirner's *Einziger und sein Eigentum* is not far away. It might seem to be cynicism, but in a macabre way it is meant seriously, when Humboldt adds that wives, although apparently abased, should be honored by the men whom they serve as divine, obviously not merely because they help them fulfil their destiny, but also because in so doing they fulfil their own.

Could one say more plainly that this love is only sham love? It is lordship over others. It degrades them as one's own creatures. They are a mere echo of oneself. They serve only one's own activity and pleasure. This is why Humboldt chooses women, or a certain type of women, to write to, i.e., weak women, probably like Johanna Motherby, of whom he boasts that she never had any need to be known. Such women do no more than reply cleverly and serve masculine self-reflection. Men, perhaps, are less adapted to do this, although we find satellite types among them too.

This love which makes others part of oneself is certainly not the opposite of egoism. It lacks all the marks of *agape*. It is unfair, for it denies to others, even though they be enraptured women, even the most elemental claim to individuality and selfhood that is confessionally claimed for oneself. Personality is for Humboldt the supreme good of the children of earth so long as it is one's own. The personalities of others are burdensome; they interrupt the cultivation of one's own higher self.

Undoubtedly, Goethe's humanism is much more humane and differentiated in this regard. Faust, of course, uses Gretchen to fulfil his own entelechy. She is for him merely a transitional point on the way, just as he storms through the faculties in the search for himself and for the bond that inwardly holds the world together. Nevertheless, he learns that Gretchen is a living self that cannot be just a means even to the highest ends. He learns from her fate what guilt is. Goethe avoids the flirting of the new humanism with the absolute selfhood of one's own person. Faust's I is referred to sharing and caring love "from above."

Humboldt's belief in the unconditional selfhood of the person leads him finally to the postulate of immortality. Thus he notes in his later years (March 1832) that the spirit that has had the force to break free from the whole and think for itself remains forever and does not cease to be independent.[17] He does not summarily ascribe immortality to the soul. Immortality has to be earned; all do not achieve it. There

17. Cf. Fischer, p. 223.

may also be a return to general "natural" life in which a personality that has not awakened, or has hardly awakened, is extinguished again. There is a spiritual individuality to which all do not attain, and this distinctive state is unique and imperishable. That which cannot shape itself thus will return to general natural life.[18] When we depart from the earth we leave behind all that does not belong exclusively to the soul and that is not independent of an earthly relationship.[19] This Platonic statement echoes the idea that immortality is bound up with the condition that what belongs to the soul or the entelechy has to be developed and freed from all connection with earth.

Although Humboldt has an almost exclusive interest in his self-development and self-enjoyment, we should remember that he still held public office and in high positions of state left his impress on the developing German university. How do we harmonize this creative outward activity with his introverted goal of self-actualization?

We have already hinted at the answer to this question in quoting a letter to von Brinkmann in which Humboldt says that he never does anything for the sake of the work but for the sake of the energy that is indirect and within him. In the same letter he says that his whole striving is to accept as it is the objects that life offers, and to hold on to them until he has transformed them into his inner self. Among these objects he counts the tasks of shaping culture and the university. These things are not important as creative ends outside the I but because they help to develop the I as it modifies itself according to the nature of the object. Thus the claim for service that reaches him from outside (e.g., to develop the university) stirs up and awakens in him some slumbering potential. Without this stimulus the ability would be in a state of incubation and would not become virulent. Strictly, it is not dedication to a public task that stimulates Humboldt but the thought that this task can be internalized and help to develop the self in a way that could not previously be foreseen. Before accepting a public office one has thus to ask what opportunities it might afford for the mobilizing of potential energies in oneself.

To sum up, we might say that I do not gain the self by being there for others (as Christian *agape* implies) but that as I gain the self I am there for others and they gain something also.

The critical undertone throughout this sketch of Humboldt should not prevent us from saying that this anthropology of the new humanism, dubious though it was, was very effective so far as culture

18. In 1830 to Caroline von Wolzogen.
19. In 1833 to Charlotte Diede.

and the university were concerned, and that the ideal of all-around personal development has remained influential even to the present day, at least as a point of discussion. Even the hypertrophy of such introverted cultivation of the self can take on positive significance as an antitoxin when it is proposed as an alternative to pragmatic educational programs. Such programs set the goal of preparing students for vocations instead of making them cultured persons. They thus have functions in view instead of the *subjects* of these functions. The technical functional aims undoubtedly carry with them the risk of crippling the people, of making them mere *homunculi* with only partial functions. We see this in the specialists who have been characterized as specialized idiots. Typical in this regard is the prevailing expression: "From my angle I see things thus. . . ." Society today threatens to become an accumulation of special interests and of people with special interests, and hence to lose the totality, and with it the question of total meaning. Instead of a standpoint from which to seek the whole, we use artificial standpoints that can see no more than limited sections of what is present. Of a similar cast are the functionaries who have lost sight of the broader context and are thus uncritical and helpless when faced with indoctrination, so that they are wax in the hands of ideological dictators.

Over against such dangerous constriction Humboldt can in fact mount a counteroffensive by championing a concern for the totality of the person. He does this in a one-sided way that is often pathological. He thus arouses opposition to the dronelike self-enjoyment of the flattered personality. Nevertheless, as a corrective to the pragmatism that is taking over today, his idea that the university is a place for the development of the whole person unquestionably has historical importance.[20]

III. RESULTS: THE NEW HUMANISM IN THE WORLD OF MODERN TECHNOLOGY

In spite of the corrective, the epoch of technology and industrialism has obviously plunged the ideal of the new humanism into a crisis. The way in which T. Litt has explored and uncovered this crisis in his *Das*

20. For its importance in the founding of Berlin University cf. Humboldt's *Antrag auf Errichtung der Universität Berlin* (July 24, 1809), addressed to Friedrich Wilhelm III, and the cabinet order of Aug. 16, 1809, in W. Weischedel, ed., *Idee und Wirklichkeit einer Universität*, Dokument zur Geschichte der Friedrich-Wilhelms-Universität zu Berlin, 1 (1966), 210ff.

Bildungsideal der deutschen Klassik und die moderne Arbeitswelt has theological significance as well.

Litt thinks that the modern crisis, with the possibility of National Socialism as a background, lies in something for which the anthropology of the new humanism paved the way. More precisely, it arises out of the discrepancy between the world of work, which seeks to fashion everything afresh, and a cultural ideal that arose in the age of Winckelmann, Goethe, and Humboldt. What is this discrepancy?

It arises because the autonomy of many industrial processes detaches itself from the human subjects and becomes increasingly independent of personal attitudes and motives, i.e., of the cultural state. The unity of what happens, e.g., in an industrial process, needs to be present only in theory. It is present only in the total program. Those who stand on the practical side do not need to perceive this unity in order to fulfil their functions. Indeed, they cannot do so. They simply have to carry out the orders of the controller or theoretician. According to Marx this is the basic evil of the division of work. In an industrial society it results in a reduction of activity and the loss of meaning.[21] Dependents have only a partial function in the process and do not perceive its total structure.

Some systems of ideological government make a virtue out of this lack of perception. They make it a means of achieving lordship. Only the esoteric clique of leaders understands the total processes and their goals. The rest are blind executives. They thus have the responsibility only of carrying out decisions, not making them. (In the trials at the end of World War II this produced the defense that the accused were simply carrying out orders without knowing the general plans or their goals.)

We undoubtedly gain the impression of a discrepancy here between the ideal of self-development in the new humanism and this reduction of the human to a partial function. Yet this is not the real problem. The real problem may be seen only when we recognize that

21. A utopian twist in Marx's vision of a communistically structured industrial society, which seems grotesquely unreal today, is remarkably parallel to the new humanist idea of harmoniously self-developing humanity. As a counterpoint to the rending of humanity by the division of labor, there occasionally hovers before Marx a communist life-style which makes it possible, in opposition to that division, freely to choose one thing today and another tomorrow, to hunt in the morning, fish in the afternoon, and keep cows in the evening, without being a huntsman, fisherman, or cowherd, or critic, as the fancy may take one ("Deutsche Ideologie," in Karl Marx, *Die Frühschriften*, ed. S. Landshut (1953), p. 361; cf. R. Friedenthal, *Karl Marx, Sein Leben und seine Zeit* (1981), pp. 205ff.

the new humanism has actively (if unintentionally) contributed to the rise of this new form of reduced humanity—or nonhumanity. Paradoxical though this may sound, the indications listed by Litt are unequivocal.

(1) If our only destiny as human beings is to develop our humanity, this means that all outside values and processes are devalued and even despised in the name of inner cultivation. But this dehumanizes and anthropocentrically perverts all that life and history pose in the way of demands, values, and experiences. Reality is simply nourishment whereby one may transform the world into one's own possession. Unless our work in the world has the rank of an independent, creative task, it simply serves to refine us until we become a harmonious work of art in human totality.

(2) This has two further consequences. First, we become unreal ghosts bearing no relation to what does in fact govern the world outside. Dreaming that we are subjects and ends in ourselves, we overlook and suppress the degree to which we are also the objects of outside factors,[22] determined, e.g., by the social situation or economic and other structural forces. If we do notice this, we resist this "fixation"[23] and adopt an attitude of protest in assertion of our own existence. Although the term *existence* belongs to a different plane of reflection from that of Humboldt's cultural ideal, a common factor is that in both we find the same self-assertion of the I, which confronts all outward factors from outside in an attitude of alienation and hostility, so that under another sign we have the same cultivation of self as in the new humanism.

Second, the self that is occupied with itself lets the processes of the hostile world outside run on without control or direction. It takes no responsibility, either theoretical or practical, for these processes. It despises them. It seeks to escape them by moving outside them, whether in the form of Humboldt's solitude or the existential variation. The question of the autonomous forces of the economic process, or social development, is not a theme for philosophy. Only the question of how the self can escape fixation by processes, how I can break through and transcend my role as a mere functionary, as one who is thus "fixated," has the dignity of being such a theme. Thus the sphere of historical process is no longer our responsibility. It is treated as a purely outside sphere.[24] It is uncontrolled and abandoned to its own autonomy.

22. For a survey of this aspect and its theological significance see the Indexes to *ThE* under "Autonomy."

23. Cf. J.-P. Sartre, M. Horkheimer, and T. W. Adorno.

24. Cf. Albert Camus, for whom the world is incomprehensible, absurd, and chaotic. We now live in a world without illusions. We feel alien in it. Cf. the

Hence the world of work, of conflicts, of competition, and of the strife of pressures and interests, is relegated to a zone of anonymous obscurity and left to itself. All this forms a dark foil to the light of humanistically or existentially understood selfhood. In this sense O. F. Bollnow can say of Heidegger's understanding of existence that before the unconditional radiance of our own existence the rest of the world fades into a meaningless background.[25]

The new humanism's lack of interest in the world (except as it serves self-actualization) makes the world inhuman. It can mean social disaster for a whole class when this class is left to itself as humanistically uninteresting. This class vegetates. It is condemned simply to discharge mechanistic functions. For it the summons to make the self a harmonious work of human art can only be a macabre farce.

Thus this form of humanity produces an inhuman world. It also provokes the Marxist reaction. In his early works Marx seeks to wrench us out of humanistic and solipsistic isolation and to see us in the context of basic material events. Although he shares with Feuerbach the thesis that religion is an illusion, he attacks him—and although Feuerbach is a left-wing Hegelian, not a new humanist, the charge would fit Humboldt too—on the ground that he isolates us solipsistically. Feuerbach does not see that the religious disposition itself is a social product and that the abstract individual he analyzes has a specific social form.[26] There then follows the summons to change the world which philosophers have simply interpreted in their different ways.[27] Only this attack on social structures, not their abandonment, can restore alienated humanity. If we want to speak of a Marxist humanism—and we may rightly do so in the case of the young Marx—the initial aim is to make the world more human so as to enable people to be their true selves. But this carries with it an (unspoken) summons to the new humanism to cease promoting the self-fulfilment of an elite at the cost of the rest. It should recognize instead the motive impulses and forces of the suprapersonal sphere of history and on the basis of this knowledge intervene in this sphere and bring it under control. On the Marxist theory, as on Hegel's, freedom is insight into historical necessity.[28] The

---

understanding of the world in the book *Chance and Necessity* (1970) by the molecular biologist Jacques Monod, a friend of Camus.

25. O. F. Bollnow, "Existenzphilosophie," in N. Hartmann, ed., *Systematische Philosophie* (1942), p. 356.

26. Cf. Karl Marx, *Die Frühschriften*, ed. S. Landshut (1953), p. 341, Thesis 7 on Feuerbach; ET *Early Writings* (New York, 1975), p. 423.

27. Ibid., Thesis 11.

28. See F. Engels, *Anti-Dühring* (1948), p. 138.

new humanists, then, are not free for all their proclamation of humanity and freedom. Cradled in illusions about human self-fulfilment, they do not see to what extent nonhuman forces share in the formation of humanity and make it their object.[29]

Thus the new humanism has led the humanity influenced by it into a fateful curving in on the self. It has separated the person from the historical structures, and thereby generated a destructive individualism whose consequences are almost the exact opposite of what it intended. The concept of curving in on the self suggests the implicit theological criticism that runs throughout this chapter. We have here a focus on the creature that does not see its creatureliness and hence posits it absolutely. The cult of humanity thus becomes the self-enjoyment of personality. This represents an abstract individual: abstract both in its isolation from concrete existence in the world and also in its isolation from the Thou insofar as communication and love do not seek an independent other but only the other in its function as a midwife helping to give birth to the personal entelechy. Hence this kind of new humanism, as we find it in Humboldt, attacks the very basis of creaturely being. This is the theological background of the criticism outlined here.

29. For a startling example cf. W. Leonhard, *Child of the Revolution* (1959), p. 385.

CHAPTER 10

Immanuel Kant

Bibliography. Kant's *Werke* are quoted from the editions of the *Philoso-phische Bibliothek* (PhB) and W. Weischedel in the Suhrkamp-Verlag (cited as Weischedel). Interpretations: K. Barth, *Protestant Theology in the Nineteenth Century* (1973), pp. 266-312; A. Schlatter, *Die philoso-phische Arbeit seit Descartes* . . . , 4th ed. (1959), p. 107; C. Gestrich, *Neuzeitliches Denken und die Spaltung der Dialektischen Theologie* (1977). Cf. also *ThE*, I, and *EF*, I.

Personality and Work: E. Cassirer, *Kants Leben und Lehre* (1921); H. S. Chamberlain, *Immanuel Kant. Die Persönlichkeit als Einführung in das Werk*, 2nd ed. (1909); K. Fischer, *Immanuel Kant und seine Lehre*, 2 vols. (1898-1899); A. Gulyga, *Immanuel Kant* (1981); K. Vorländer, *Imman-uel Kants Leben* (1911). For the lively accounts of three of his students and assistants cf. L. E. Borowski, R. B. Jachmann, and A. C. Wasian-ski, *Immanuel Kant, sein Leben in Darstellungen von Zeitgenossen* (Berlin, 1912, quoted as *Zeitgenossen*).

I. BIOGRAPHY

Kant was born (1724), lived, and died (1804) in Königsberg, and seldom left it. He never traveled out of East Prussia. Fifteen years after gradua-tion, and after refusing a professorship of poetry (!), he became profes-sor of logic and metaphysics, and taught until ill-health forced him to retire in 1796.

The data of his uneventful life suggest that in distinction from Schleiermacher no very penetrating analysis of his personality is neces-sary to understand his works. To be sure, he was set in a specific

273

intellectual context and this background is significant for his thinking. But his character and personal life are integrated into his work and seem to merge into it. At any rate, they do not seem to transcend it in any way, again in distinction from Schleiermacher, in whose case the man and the Christian do not find exhaustive expression in the theological system. In Kant there is no path from the personality to the work. The path runs the opposite way. His personality and life-style and friendships and social life are of primary interest only because they reflect all the convictions and principles set forth in his work. In this sense the contemporary depictions of his faithful followers are especially important.[1] They are uncommonly enthralling and amusing, and they evoke a profound response.

Kant's teaching—this seems almost inconceivable in a large modern university—took place chiefly in his own house. His closest fellow-workers or assistants were very much interwoven in his private life. Their work was not restricted to the academic sphere. They took care of him when he was ill and old and frail. They performed the most menial services out of untiring love for their honored master. During his younger years Kant appears in these reports as a charming host who engages in light conversation, elegantly dressed and liking a good table.

Essentially, however, we find in his life-style a reflection of his teaching and convictions. This may be seen especially in the fact that his daily conduct was regulated by fixed and rigorously kept rules and maxims. He rose early, and his servant had to light his lamp for the purpose notwithstanding his sleepy protests. He took a midday walk by which his neighbors set their clocks. He would drink only wine and water because beer was so full of nourishment as to be more of a food than a drink. If in the choice of a wife one were to have an eye to material factors as well as the qualities of a good housewife and mother, it would be better to look for money because (in an age of little inflation) this would last longer than any beauty or charm, would make for more solid happiness, and would tie the bond of marriage tighter, since well-being fills a man with loving gratitude to his wife. Yet Kant was susceptible to female beauty and grace. Even after his seventieth year, he always seated the particularly charming Miss A. at table on the side of his one good eye.

Even in the provision he makes against all the possible mischances of life, especially ill-health, his suggestions have something categorical about them and remind us of unconditional ethical rules.

1. See *Zeitgenossen*, esp. the last contribution by A. C. Wasianski.

Thus he has a theory about keeping out bugs and also about the structure of a complicated belt to prevent varicose veins; he constructed one for himself. His assistants had always to be ready to see to it that his routine was not disturbed. The *Metaphysik der Sitten* and especially the *Anthropologie* are full of rules of this kind.

The way in which Kant saw the world throws light on his doctrine of the categories, as a short story told by R. B. Jachmann shows.[2] In a gathering in which a born Londoner was present, Kant described Westminster Bridge so exactly (its length, breadth, height, proportions, etc.) that the Englishman asked him how long he had lived in London and whether his subject was architecture. (This is only one of many examples.) In such cases Kant did not describe the impression that the bridge had made on him but was interested in the "principles" of its construction. H. S. Chamberlain discusses the difference between Kant's eye and that of Goethe in this regard.[3]

At the end of his life Kant went into a mental decline. He could no longer understand his own work or even everyday terms, so that he used abstract analogies for what he meant. He could understand abtractions to the very end, and in the greatest weakness could recite analogies even when he did not recognize his closest friends.

II. KANT'S PLACE IN THE EPISTEMOLOGICAL SITUATION

We recall the theme of our inquiry up to this point.[4] The subject of modern theological history in its dialogue with contemporary issues focuses on the two terms *doubt* and *appropriation*. Doubt arises when one begins to question what has hitherto been regarded as self-evident. One must question everything when one begins to find in oneself criteria of what is true and false that can no longer be ignored. These criteria rest on the claim of the newly discovered self-consciousness to adulthood, and in particular they derive from reason.

Doubt, then, implies a conflict between two authorities that claim a monopoly of truth. On the one hand is the authority of tradi-

2. Ibid., p. 136.
3. Chamberlain, *Goethe*, pp. 38ff.
4. Since I believe that a study of Kant is basic for budding theologians (as well as for philosophers in other faculties), I beg the indulgence of instructed readers if in the first part of this chapter I carefully and rather didactically take beginners by the hand and am not afraid to be very rudimentary. Initiates may skip §§ I and II and begin with the critical discussion in § III.

tional revelation founded on the Bible. On the other hand is that of emancipated humanity represented especially by reason.[5]

The problem of appropriation then contains the question whether and how far the Christian claim to truth can be harmonized with the new criterion of truth, and whether, under what conditions, and with what exclusions, it is still acceptable. What is the position of Kant within this process of doubt and appropriation?

He gives a revolutionary turn to the questions triggered especially by the Enlightenment. Whereas previously the great inquiry had been conducted in the name of an authority of reason that was regarded as self-evident, Kant made reason *itself* a question and the object of criticism—self-criticism.

When Kant uses the word *criticism* he does not mean that reason as an organ of knowledge is criticizing something, e.g., the alleged knowledge of others. He means that this organ is criticizing itself. This gives rise to the paradox that reason is at one and the same time both the subject and the object of criticism, that it is both judge and accused in the one person. What is questioned is not some previous knowledge but the act of knowledge itself. This is what leads to a Copernican revolution in Kant. His goal is to bring reason to understanding. In doing this he completes the Enlightenment but also shakes it to its foundations by discovering the limits of a reason that had hitherto operated and argued and criticized blindly and without restriction.

According to Kant's definition, enlightenment is emergence from self-inflicted immaturity, i.e., the inability to use one's understanding without guidance by another.[6] But what is this understanding that I have to use? Perhaps it is not simply the bashfulness of the understanding that it thinks it needs the guidance of others. Perhaps it is its pride, its lordly ignoring of its incompetence, that *makes* it dependent on the guidance of others. The first need, then, is to show the understanding the limits of its competence, to bring it to itself.

Kant wants to be the one who will help the understanding come to itself and hence become adult. It is important to see that this is where his thinking starts. He puts our epistemological competence under the microscope. He has every reason to do so in the light of the history of

5. I say "especially" because in Schleiermacher and his school the self-consciousness of religious humanity rather than reason forms the critical court.

6. See "Was ist Aufklärung?" in Weischedel, XI, 53; ET "What Is Enlightenment?" in *The Critique of Practical Reason and Other Writings in Moral Philosophy*, tr. and ed. L. W. Beck (Chicago, 1949), p. 286. We have already discussed the ethical continuation (the guilt of immaturity).

philosophy. I will try to clarify these beginnings of Kant's thought with some illustrations.

Like an unruly horse, reason has a tendency to run wild without considering how much breath it has or how far it can go. It thus explores areas that are outside all our experience. It constructs metaphysical systems, doctrines of God and immortality, atheistic philosophies, worldviews, and theosophies. In all its pushing into the basis and meaning of being, it obviously never puts the self-critical question whether it is not getting beyond itself with this excessive speculation, whether its structure does not tie it down within specific boundaries of knowledge. It simply rides off into its metaphysical hunting grounds.

At this point the resemblance to the wild horse ceases. For the horse soon runs out of breath and has to stop or suffer a heart attack. But when reason wanders off into the Milky Way and speculates on ultimate substance (Spinoza), or preestablished harmony (Leibniz), or the preexistence of ideas (Plato), it never runs out of breath but unceasingly establishes its heaven-storming systems. In so doing it uses exact logic and its conclusions are impeccable. Not for nothing does Spinoza speak of his geometrical method. He borrows it from mathematics, the most precise of all the sciences.

The great metaphysicians are not dabblers. We can find no holes in their arguments. The exactness of their conclusions is just as great when they speculate about God and immortality, the finitude and infinity of the world, and what lies beyond all heavens.

But if this is so, where does reason stop, where might it be mistaken about itself? The answer is simple. A crisis arises when we compare the different philosophical systems. They are without inner contradictions and yet they contradict one another. From the pre-Socratics to our own time we find materialism and idealism, positivism and metaphysics. They can all appeal to reason and to the logic of their conclusions.

When we see the contradictions we have to ask how they arise. This question provides a material starting point for Kant's critique of reason. The result of his analysis may be summarized as follows.

Reason makes no error in its heaven-storming speculations, One cannot point to any mistake or gap in the geometrical system of Spinoza. The error does not lie within the system. It is to be found in the fact that reason starts with premises and strives after goals that are beyond its competence, or, more precisely, that lie outside the objectifiable sphere of experience and are thus metaphysical. When reason enters this zone its conclusions are uncontrollable even though logical steps might be formally irrefutable. In this region reason is adrift.

Another illustration might help beginners. If we enter the stratosphere without the proper oxygen apparatus, our biological constitution is not suited to it, our thoughts become confused, we fantasize, we hear organ music, we see rainbows and bright-colored circles, and we think all these things are real whereas in fact they are simply the projections of our wandering imagination. Something similar, Kant thinks, happens to thinkers who leave the oxygen-soaked sphere of human experience and roam about in the transcendent intellectual stratosphere. They become helpless wanderers in the field of dream and fantasy.

Everything depends, then, on the delimiting of the sphere of epistemological competence. As we must determine how far our biological equipment permits us to travel, so we must determine how far our mental equipment enables us to travel in the field of knowledge. Only when the radius is fixed and we stay within it can we know for sure that we are operating in a certain sphere of cognitive competence. Anything else involves arrogance and results in blindness. But what is this radius of knowledge?

I think it important that beginners should grasp as clearly as possible the starting point of Kant's epistemological deliberations, and I will therefore let Kant himself describe it for us.

In the Preface to the first edition of the *Critique of Pure Reason*, Kant says that reason begins with principles that are unavoidable in the course of experience, and that experience shows to be adequate. As examples of such principles one might point to $2 \times 2 = 4$, or to the rules of experience deposited in proverbs. Reason functions smoothly in the sphere of normal experience, in which knowledge is subject to constant self-control and demonstration. But on this basis it then ventures higher (as its nature demands) to "more remote conditions."[7]

What Kant means by these "more remote conditions" I might try to clarify by another illustration. Reason might ask what were the conditions for the outbreak of World War II. It could answer that one of them was the Versailles Treaty with its momentous consequences. But then another—and perhaps the main one—is a fatal figure like Hitler. But these conditions do not arise out of the void; they have other causes. Thus reason has to push its inquiry further back, and the further back it goes the more hazy everything becomes. Yet reason is still staying within the limits of possible experience, and it can establish and illustrate its statements.

Finally, however, in its retrospective inquiry it comes upon the

7. For this and the following see Weischedel, III, 11.

fact that wickedness, anxiety, and sacred egoism are in the world, that these give rise to repression, self-assertion, and the drive for power and prestige, and the result is all that which like a demonic impulse pushes history on as far back as we can trace it.

We might carry the illustration further. When reason has reached the remoter conditions, it takes the final step to the remotest conditions, and its penultimate question is how evil has come into the world. Division comes here, for reason gives opposing answers. Thus Hobbes says that we have in principle a wolfish nature, but Rousseau says that the first to claim property and fence it off poisoned what was originally our good human nature. Reason cannot decide between these antithetical answers. We venture at this point anthropological axioms which are not objectifiable. We confront uncontrollable positions or metaphysical hypotheses.

But then, to round off the illustration, the ultimate question arises: Whence comes evil? Does it come from God as a first cause that is in itself a dualistic principle? Or does it come from a diametrically opposed power, a demonic principle, as Marcion thought? This final question, which touches on the very structure of being, certainly cannot be settled within the sphere of our experience.

When Kant thinks of this kind of regress, he is under the impression that by nature reason obviously does not contain any restraining mechanisms that might cause it not to engage in this infinite regress. He notes that when it presses back to prior conditions its work can never end because the questions never stop. Why they do not stop we can easily show.

Researchers and philosophers may *resolve* not to ask, and may thus refrain or stop themselves from doing so. Yet every answer raises new questions which confront them whether they like it or not. The need to ask is outside our control. Reason thus finds itself compelled to resort to principles which surpass all possible experience and seem to be so secure that our common reason assents to them. (We recall the questions of the origin of evil, the finitude or infinity of the world, God, etc.). In the process it plunges into obscurity and contradictions from which it may indeed conclude that somewhere there must be hidden errors, but it cannot track these down because the principles it uses, being beyond the limits of experience, do not recognize the test of experience. Metaphysics is thus the battleground of endless debates.

Here we come upon the antinomies,[8] e.g., the opposing theses

8. Kant deals with the antinomies in Book 2 of the "Transcendental Dialectic" in his *Critique of Pure Reason*.

that the world has a beginning in time and has spatial limits, or that it has no such limits and is infinite (the first antinomy). These antinomies show that reason is outside the field of its competence and is thus confused. This observation sets the task of fixing the limits of experience. How do we find these?

Naturally, only by asking what may be experienced. To answer this question I must ask what reason can do, and I can answer this question only by putting the structure of reason under the microscope. I may again refer to the example of the alpinist or space traveler. On the basis of the biology of the human organism I may discover to what height one can safely ascend without aids. To do this it is not necessary to go to the limit experimentally. It is enough to investigate the necessity of oxygen to our human constitution. This will give the required height. Along similar lines Kant examines the constitution of reason.

He finds that knowledge is restricted to the sphere of objective experience. Experience here is the combination of two processes: a simple acquiring of knowledge from impressions, and a cognitive penetration of what impressions afford. We thus have a union of sensory perception and a determinative element of rationality, the function of understanding. Only as these two activities come together is there a sphere of transparent and controllable knowledge. What we experience, e.g., a book or desk, does not tell us about things in themselves. All that we encounter in the objective area is preformed by our ability to perceive and know.

In everyday life we can establish the influence of our organs of knowledge by various examples. To the uninstructed a chemical laboratory is a chaos of retorts, pipes, tubes, and unintelligible labels, but the trained chemist finds in all these things an orderly cosmos of meaningful contrivances. A deer finds in a highway that crosses its territory only a kind of clearing. It cannot grasp what a road is, and thus (when inexperienced) it runs into danger in crossing it.

This means that our ability to perceive and understand affects the images that experience sets before us. The biologist Jakob von Uexküll in his book *Niegeschaute Welten* (1957) tells us in lively autobiographical form, and with no direct reference to Kant, how differently we see the world according to our constitution. Konrad Lorenz, in his brilliant work *Behind the Mirror* (1977), raises the problem how our perceiving apparatus affects our view of things. He both supplements and criticizes Kant. He supplements him by showing how the perceiving apparatus arises genetically from our correspondence to the world around us. He criticizes him for not seeing the ontic analogy between knower and known, and with his concept of the thing in itself removing reality from that analogy.[9]

The affecting of the images of experience by the subject of knowledge may be seen in the fact that all the things that we experience are in time and space. Time and space are not something outside. When could I ever see either the one or the other?[10] They are forms of perception that we bring to outside things and with whose help we fashion it. They are thus contributed by the subject.

Again, the contents of experience occur in the sphere of causality, of categories of understanding. We cannot think of anything that is not caused, that is not an effect of something preceding it. Hence we have always to look for causes. To have to do so, to experience things from this standpoint, is part of the structure of our understanding, of our destiny as thinkers. We ourselves are this destiny, for it is our mental constitution that causes us to see and experience thus. We always bring ourselves with our epistemologically conditioned nature. We play a part when we know.

This is why we are not a blank slate that simply receives impressions (cf. British empiricists like Locke). The slate has a hand in what is written on it. Once again an illustration will help. Certain stupid people are supposed to have tried to capture the sunlight in a sack. But unfortunately a sack is not a suitable container for the purpose. A film, however, whether color or black and white, is different. It has an active layer that is receptive to light. It can thus take an impression and plays a part in the production of a photograph.

Since our knowledge is grounded in the principle of causality, we can see why it has a tendency to press back in an infinite regress. It finally has to ask what came first. Hence mythical cosmogonies arise, or theogonies, or the problem of aseity.[11]

In this crossing of the boundaries of experience with ultimate questions, in this transcendental impulse, we have the stretching of a category that belongs constitutively to the functioning of the understanding. The understanding betrays itself here into difficulties and entanglements that denote its structure.

Kant's decisive inference from all this is that we can never know things in themselves but only our encounter with things. Our knowledge operates within the subject-object schema. The two constitute one

---

9. Lorenz, *Behind the Mirror* (1977), pp. 8-9, 14-15.
10. Augustine already touches on this problem in Book 11 of his *Confessions*.
11. Aseity is independent being in and of oneself (*a se*) such as is ascribed to God.

another. We are subjects inasmuch as we are affected by something outside, Kant's thing in itself. This sets our apparatus of perception and understanding in motion. It triggers our radar. The work of the categories commences.[12] The objects that meet us in this way are always fashioned already and thus bear traces of the fashioning subject. Hence our statements and judgments, whether they be in mathematics or physics, or simple statements like "this tree is green," do not tell us anything about real being, but only about the way things seem to us, the way they appear within the subject-object relation.

Radar, for example, does not show me things themselves (ships, hills) but only things as they are worked over and electronically transformed. It projects the objects on a two-dimensional screen. It makes them smaller. It does not present them as we see them but according to the solidity of their substance. Rain, hail, wood, and stones all give rise to special effects. To be able to use radar we have to know how the gadget works. The peculiarity of the instrument decides how the images occur. What appears on the screen is thus a combination of what is really there and the working of the instrument. In anthropomorphic terms, the instrument as a subject is affected by outside impressions, puts them in its own categories, and then produces them in a form determined by the categories.

In the same way I myself am always present with my own apparatus when I receive outside impressions. That which I experience, and about which I make statements, is the thing as it appears to me or as I bring it to light. The subject of experience always plays a role.

In Kant's view I never reach the essence of things because I never perceive the things themselves but only my relation to them. Everything is relative to me. I do not pierce the veil of being. To try to do so is to engage in dreaming and roving metaphysics. I only see myself looking at the veil. I do not look out from the center of the world to the horizon. I always see both myself and the horizon at one and the same time.

We need to state the matter another way and say that the image I have changes according to the standpoint of the beholder. This minor alteration gives us the starting point of modern microphysics, which has explored afresh the relation between onlooker and object. In microphysics a change of stance changes the way of looking at particles, so that we cannot speak about physical processes apart from the subject; we cannot speak about the constellations of particles in themselves. Hence in quantum theory we are not dealing with particles in them-

12. For an ontological development of this aspect see Eugen Herrigel, *Urstoff und Urform* (1926); idem, *Die metaphysische Form* (1929).

selves but with our knowledge of them. A sign of this relation between the observer and the field of observation is that we might see the same things from different angles. Werner Heisenberg put this philosophically when he said that now for the first time in the course of history we confront only ourselves on the earth. The I whom Kant discovered in the subject-object relation is now increasingly to the fore in the sphere of microphysics.[13]

Yet we can also go back thousands of years to Greek antiquity and find an artistic foreshadowing of Kantian epistemology in the discovery of perspective. Ancient Egyptian art did not know perspective and tried to depict objects as they are in themselves, e.g., a warrior, a fish, or a bird. The discoverers of perspective (Apollodorus of Athens and Agatharchos of Samos) brought to light the relation between observer and object.[14]

We may thus have things only as they are in relation to us. This is the feature that Kant has in common with the discovery of perspective and quantum theory. But this means that the self—as Kierkegaard says in *Sickness unto Death*—is no longer the Cartesian ego, a point that is finally isolated. The self is itself a relation, whether to God who has posited it, to others, or to the outside world in general.[15] If I were to define a human being I should have to speak about a relation. This is an existential variation on Kant's epistemological theory. Here we have the radically new position in epistemology that may rightly be called a "Copernican revolution."

III. THE RELATION BETWEEN THINKING AND BEING

The following discussion might bring to light the basic significance of Kant's findings.

The fundamental problem of philosophy has always been the relation between thinking and being. I have to put the epistemological process on the one side or the other.

I might begin with being. Like the ancient Greek atomists Leucippus and Democritus I might ask what are the smallest and most

13. Cf. W. Heisenberg, "Das Naturbild der heutigen Physik," in *Die Künste im technischen Zeitalter* (1954), pp. 45ff., esp. pp. 60, 62; idem, *Physik und Philosophie* (1959), pp. 61ff.; idem, "Quantenmechanik und Kantische Philosophie," in *Der Teil und das Ganze* (1969), pp. 163ff.
14. On perspective cf. *ThE*, III, §§ 3261ff.
15. Cf. my *Being Human—Becoming Human*, pp. 134ff.

elementary particles of being. Or like Plato I might think about the nature of being and ask how it discloses itself to the knower (aletheia). Or like Spinoza I might inquire into substance, or like Hegel into spirit, or like the materialists into matter, as that which is at work in all being.

Asking along these lines implies a certain presupposed relation between thinking and being. The thinker is part of the being that is investigated, part of the "one" that divides in the polarity of subject and object. Thus in Hegel the absolute spirit that is at work in being thinks itself in the finite spirit of humanity. Materialists, too, see the thinking I, not as standing over against cosmic matter, but as part of it. Thinking and knowing are for them functions of the substance of the brain which is part of matter. Knower and known are one. There is merely a difference of function within identical being. This is the situation when we begin on the side of the object, of being.

A second possibility is that of beginning with the I, as Descartes does and later Fichte. In this case I try to deduce from the thinker the totality of the being that is present in the act of thought. To put it briefly, one might say that according to the standpoint of the epistemological process one either locates the I in being or being in the I. Either way we have a monism under one sign or another. Prior to Kant every conceivable change was rung on these alternatives during the course of philosophical history. Thinking on the matter had as it were exhausted itself. (This is true only with reservations, since we find conceptions of this kind after Kant as well.)

Kant, however, separates thinking and being and establishes a solid dualism. The thinking subject and objectifiable being confront one another. Neither may be deduced from the other. The relation is not causal; it is that of subject and object.[16] Nevertheless, the two are tied together. When I say "world," this means that I am talking about "my" world, for there is for me no world outside my own experience, or at any rate no such world exists for me. Similarly, when I say "I," I do not refer to a self-enclosed monad (Leibniz), but to an I that finds reflection in the world. The starry heaven and the I as the bearer of the moral law are in correlation with one another.[17]

---

16. Cf. A. Schopenhauer's doctoral dissertation, *Über die vierfache Wurzel des Satzes vom zureichenden Grunde*, *Sämtliche Werke*, ed. J. Frauenstädt, vol. I (1877).

17. Cf. the *Critique of Practical Reason*, PhB 186, Great Books 44, p. 360. Kant calls the relation between the manifoldness of objects and the unity of the consciousness "transcendental apperception" (*Critique of Pure Reason*, Weischedel, III, 167-68).

IV. FIRST SURVEY OF THE THEOLOGICAL INFLUENCE OF KANT'S EPISTEMOLOGY

In the first instance the concept of faith seems to be clarified by Kant's critical undertaking. Confessional orthodoxy had regarded faith chiefly as the acceptance of traditional biblical stories and sayings as true (the principle of *fides quae creditur*). The saving contents of the Bible are put on the same level as its cosmological statements. The creation story is taken to be a scientific cosmogony. Verbal inspiration necessarily results in a leveling down of all biblical statements.[18] Accounts of God's transcendent interventions (cf. a miracle like that of Josh. 10:12-13) are regarded as immanent processes of which one can give objective historical accounts even though no causes can be found for them within the range of our experience. The empirical and the transcendent merge epistemologically.

Is it surprising that questions arose about the validity of all this? At any rate, dogma seemed to be more and more forced on people. They had to accept it without asking why. In so doing they had to reject scientific theories (such as that of evolution) and the work of historical criticism.

But now, in Kant, transcendence is taken out of the zone of knowledge. No proof of God is possible along the lines of the Pythagorean theorem. No universal judgments may be made about basic Christian truths, since they all involve the transcendence that is outside the zone of knowledge. One cannot prove the deity of Christ or miracles. God does not exist (cf. M. Mezger's use of a phrase of Emil Brunner's) in the same way as Lake Constance or the Himalayas or other objects of this type.

Is not faith hereby assigned to its lawful and appropriate sphere? Do we not have here an enlightening and liberating separation of the dimensions of being? The this-worldly sphere of experience is allotted to reason. It contains the legitimate objects of rational knowledge. Everything transcendent (or religious) is the content of faith. Is this not plausible? Does it not establish a clear relation between faith and thought?

In fact, many theologians—from Schleiermacher to our own

---

18. For a more recent example cf. T. Flügge, the OT teacher at the Free University of Hamburg, who in his book *Affenmensch, Weltall, Bibel* (1958) says that Adam was created in 4134 B.C. and tries to prove the astronomical possibility of Josh. 10:12-13 and Isa. 38:8 (pp. 6, 20, 64). Cf. also H. Echternach, *Es stehet geschrieben* (1937), who calls Luther's translation a binding and verbally inerrant Bible for the church and theology (p. 9). In criticism cf. Gerhard Ebeling, "The Significance of the Critical Historical Method for Church and Theology in Protestantism," in *Word and Faith* (Philadelphia, 1963), pp. 17-61; and my own discussion of verbal inspiration in *EF*, III, 191ff.

times—have thought so. Using Kant's approach Schleiermacher and Troeltsch conclude that if God (or, in Rudolf Otto's term, the numinous) does not belong to the sphere of objective knowledge, then we must seek the contents of religion with the help of other forms of certainty, e.g., in feeling or inner experience. For this reason we cannot prove them by argument. Do we not see and recognize Kant's Copernican revolution behind all this?

(1) Already in Luther we find foreshadowings of what Kant means by the subject-object relation that determines our experience. Not a few theologians have traced a historical line from Luther to Schleiermacher by way of Kant.[19] But this line is not by a long way so straight and consistent as its champions obviously think. At most one might discern certain associations—no more!—which it will be worth our while to consider.

The basis of these associations is a certain transcendentalism in Luther. Characteristically, Luther does not ask about God in himself but about God for me, Immanuel, the God who stands in some relation to my subjectivity. God in himself is for Luther the hidden God, e.g., the Lord of predestination (Deus absconditus). To this God I have no access. Hence I must flee to the revealed God who discloses himself to me in Christ (Deus revelatus).

The Large Catechism brings this out when the first question in exposition of the first commandment is what it means to have God or what God is.[20] The two questions are one and the same. And the answer is that God is one in whom one can find all good and refuge in every need. Thus to have a God is to trust and believe in him from the heart. Only the trust of the heart makes both God and false god. If faith and trust are right, God is right. Faith and God belong together. That on which our heart hangs and relies is our God. The exposition of Ps. 51 is to the same effect when it says that the proper theme of theology is sinful man and the justifying God who is the Savior of sinners.[21] Any inquiry or discussion outside this is in error.

The two references both point in the same direction. That faith and God belong together expresses the truth that I cannot speak about God apart from the fact that he has won me to faith. The proper object of theology, then, is not God in himself but God's relation to me or

---

19. Cf. G. Wobbermin, e.g., in "Die Frage nach Gott in Luthers Gr. Katechism," in Festgabe für J. Kaftan (1920), pp. 418-35; idem, "Luther, Kant, Schleiermacher und die Aufgabe der heutigen Theologie," ZThK (1924) 104-20. Cf. also the typical title of his Festschrift: Luther, Kant, Schleiermacher (1939). One might also refer to T. Siegfried, Das protestantische Prinzip in Kirche und Welt (1939).

20. LBK, p. 560; Tappert, pp. 365ff.

21. WA, 40, II, 328; LW, 12, 303ff.

relevance for me. Hence Luther makes the sinner and the gracious God the common theme of theology. Theologically, I am always dealing with a relation. As I cannot speak about God in himself, so I cannot speak about human beings in themselves. They, too, are involved in a relation.

Luther's insistence on a relation between God and us necessarily raises a decisive question of principle which at once sets Luther at a radical distance from Kant and calls in question the directness of the line that links them. This question is as follows: have we approximated God in himself to ourselves? Have we set him in a relation of which we ourselves are the fixed point? In other words, has God become a mere predicate of anthropology, a mere function of faith, an object that is constituted by it, an object that we simply think in addition to our believing?[22] Or, conversely, has God accommodated himself to us, has he accepted solidarity with us in the incarnation, has he condescended to us in love?

Only the second approach can appeal to the Bible. There God accommodates himself to us, accepts our questions, and speaks our language. In every age he wants to be proclaimed afresh and relevantly in the language of the time. He does not want to be a timeless God in himself who is not in relation to us. Melanchthon expressed this truth in his famous statement that to know Christ is to know his benefits, what he does for us.

(2) Kant's thesis of the subject-object relation in our experience is much more cogently stated in Schleiermacher, although even here the decisive question of principle has to be put, as we have shown. In Schleiermacher God is seen expressly and exclusively in his relation to the self-consciousness, to the feeling of absolute dependence. All the fundamental Christian statements about creation, sin, and redemption may be expressed as states of this self-consciousness and may thus be formulated as anthropological statements.

(3) In Bultmann's existential interpretation, too, the connection of theological statements with the subject of experience plays an essential role. Like Kant, although without referring to him, Bultmann strictly rejects as mythological any entry of God into the empirical world, the immanent world of experience. The point of comparison that establishes his affinity to Kant is that in the biblical texts he is not interested in the historical "in themselves" of the records but in their "significance." The significant thing is the relation of the texts to existential problems, e.g., care, anxiety, guilt, and the sense of finitude.

22. Thielicke here uses the dubious concept of *Glaübigkeit* with its suggestion of "credulity." In a footnote he explains that he thinks it legitimate in the context.—TRANS.

These themes are not triggered by the texts, by revelation; they are already present. Their formulation is taken from philosophy, especially Heidegger's earlier ontology. The resultant interpretation of the Bible that is oriented in this way to our existential state is thus described as "existential." It is possible only within the horizon of the subject of experience. We have here a special nonobjective form of experience, that of faith. Within these limits Bultmann is very much in the tradition of Kant and Schleiermacher.

V. THEOLOGICAL INTERPRETATION OF THE CRITICAL WORKS

A. PRELIMINARY NOTE

From all that has been said it is clear that Kant's work cannot produce any metaphysical ontology in the sense of showing what inner bond holds the world together. Such a bond cannot be the object of our experience. One cannot display it concretely. One cannot say: Here it is, be convinced, and repeat my experiment (as one does in physics). Lying outside my objectifiable experience, this bond cannot be the theme of a strict philosophy that limits itself to what can be said objectively. This is true even though the philosopher be personally convinced of the existence of the bond.

How does Kant fare, then, when on the one hand he does not want to deny that in our thinking we are striving after the totality or nexus of being, and on the other hand he does not think that we can objectify this nexus and hence should not give ourselves to metaphysical speculations?

He finds help by assigning the individual dimensions of being to different organs of reception. When I develop the mind's potential in every direction, I make all the dimensions of reality its theme insofar as this is possible. In other words, Kant makes the totality of being the theme of philosophy according to the different functions of my power of judgment. Here, too, he remains faithful to his Copernican revolution by positing a relation to the knowing, acting, and feeling (i.e., aesthetically receptive) subject.[23]

Thus the understanding, as the theoretical organ that contains a priori the principles that constitute our experience, relates to the

23. Here and in what follows cf. the *Critique of Judgment*, esp. the Introduction, § 9.

sphere of what may be experienced objectively. Judgment (e.g., the power of aesthetic judgment) relates to teleologically determined structures (e.g., works of art), and it regulates the judgments of taste. Such judgments are not the result of pragmatic considerations or tendentious appeals (e.g., in placards) but of universal and purely disinterested pleasure.[24] Since individual idiosyncrasies and special interests are ruled out, this alone can claim general subjective validity.[25] Finally, practical reason determines action in the sense that ignoring individual desire and fancy it gives us maxims that are valid for all and can be made the principle of universal legislation.

In sum, seeing that Kant is convinced that all the reality that we can experience is related to our consciousness and its structure, he need only analyze the detailed dimensions of the consciousness and he will have at the same time an analysis of the reality accessible to us, of the being that we may experience.

In writing the three *Critiques,* then, he has written a kind of biography of the world from the noetic standpoint. In the *Critique of Pure Reason* he determines what being is knowable. In the *Critique of Judgment* he shows what is accessible to us in our feelings, the teleological order of the world and of works of art, purified from everything contingent, the world as an orderly structure. In the *Critique of Practical Reason* he relates the source of moral duty to the sum of ends, the final end that constitutes the order of things.[26] As Fichte would later put it, he sees the world as material for the doing of our duty.[27] Thus Kant deals with the totality of the world and keeps its dimensions in view but always very strictly within the subject-object relation.

I will now examine the main critical works, but only from the standpoint of Kant's theological relevance and influence.

B. *CRITIQUE OF PURE REASON*

Mathematics is the field in which one may see most pregnantly the function of pure or theoretical reason. Mathematicians can largely ignore the epistemological source of observation that merely records. To establish the Pythagorean theorem we do not need to keep on

24. *Critique of Judgment,* § 2.
25. Ibid., § 8.
26. *Critique of Practical Reason,* Part I, Book I, chap. 3.
27. In connection with the last two *Critiques* cf. my *Das Verhältnis zwischen dem Ethischen und dem Ästhetischen* (1932).

measuring a triangle. We can calculate the relations of the sides once and for all. Thus the form of knowledge and statement used in mathematics consists of synthetic judgments a priori. What does that mean?

Again I will simplify for those who are less instructed. Kant distinguishes between analytic and synthetic judgments, and within the synthetic between those that are a priori and those that are a posteriori.

A statement is analytic when the predicate is contained in the subject, as in the statement that a circle is round or a = a. Such judgments involve identity and are logically tautologous.

In synthetic judgments, however, the predicate is not contained in the subject. A new epistemological statement adds it. We thus have an extended judgment. When I say that the sun rose yesterday morning, rising is not part of the concept of the sun. We have here a judgment in which the sun is related to a planet, i.e., our earth. The statement says more than what is contained in the concept "sun." Extended synthetic statements may be either a posteriori or a priori. The former are subsequent to experience and the latter prior to it. The former follow on experience, the latter are its basis; they precede it and make it possible.

The statement that the sun rises every morning is an example. This may be either an a posteriori or an a priori synthetic statement. It is a posteriori when I look out every morning and prove by my own experience that the sun rises every morning without exception. It is a priori when I take a different course and arrive at the statement with the help of mathematical calculation of the course of the planets. In this case the mathematical conclusion does not rest on my experience but is its basis. It shows why I do in fact experience the sunrise every morning, and have to do so.

That which relates to the possibility of the a priori grounding of objective experience by pure concepts and principles, Kant calls the transcendental condition of rational knowledge. That knowledge is transcendental which sees how a priori elements that are independent of our experience still relate to objects of experience and receive confirmation from it.[28]

A priori for Kant is thus an epistemological rather than a psychological feature. It does not denote that which precedes experience in time but that which transcends it materially, i.e., a validity of rational principles that is not based on experience but forms its basis and makes it possible.

Synthetic judgments a priori are universally valid. The basis of their validity for Kant is that their content derives from reason itself.

28. We must not, then, confuse the terms *transcendent* and *transcendental*.

Since all of us have reason, judgments deriving from rational principles are interrelated. No one can evade them. With judgments a posteriori (from experience) the situation is different. One experience may contradict another. Some may say that humanity is good whereas the pessimism of others denounces it as bad. This is according to our constitution or our experiences of others. In the case of an a priori statement like the Pythagorean theorem, however, the derivation from rational principles that are independent of experience results in objective and universal validity. There can be no differences of perspective, no different experiences, no party positions.

I must point out again—if not, everything is wrong—that this derivation from rational principles is not blindly or arbitrarily possible. Thus no such principles will help me to make judgments on God (proofs of God), immortality, or the infinitude of the world. If I attempt this—and Kant does so experimentally—I reach the above-mentioned antinomies which are an indication of lawless reason (*nous anomos*). Although rational judgments do not derive from experience but precede it, they can relate only to the objective sphere which is the basic content of experience. For this reason they can be the foundation of experience.

But if reason normally stays within the assigned subject-object relation, it does not grasp things in themselves, their *hypokeimenon*, but only their appearance, things as they are preformed by our modes of perception and categories, things as they are made perceptible and rational. Reason relates only to objective being. It cannot make judgments about being itself. It makes judgments only about things that it fashions itself. To put it theologically, all our knowledge is anthropomorphic.

After this brief survey of the basic ideas of Kant's critique of reason, we may pause for a moment and consider its implications.[29] The natural sciences took little notice of Kant's Copernican revolution because the epistemological consideration whether the objects of experience are things in themselves or things as they appear was a matter of indifference to them. Only microphysics—as I have shown from Heisenberg—saw the significance of the subject-object relation, if from another angle. For it, Kant was of interest in a wholly new way. In general, however, science treats as nature that which Kant calls appearance.

Historians, too, are unaffected by Kant's epistemological theory. Some basic discussions occur in history which are partly influenced by Kant's approach. I think especially of hermeneutics, and above all of

29. Cf. Schlatter, *Die philosophische Arbeit*, 4th ed. (1959), pp. 122-23.

Dilthey's argument that we can understand in historical phenomena only that which is already contained in living perception, i.e., in the intellectual disposition of the subject, as a kind of bridgehead. But this has little relevance to practical historical research. For the hermeneutical reservation still accepts as historical reality, and not as mere appearance, the things which may be perceived historically and proved from the sources. Concretely, historians do not relativize things and events because of the reservation. They do not make them mere appearance. They simply say that they themselves might not have any affinity to some of them.[30] These events do not fit into my horizon, my subject-object relation—but they are still events. Not all of them are accessible to me because the capacity of my mental constitution is limited. Yet what I know is a real thing that encounters me. I have to do with real people like myself and destinies like my own.

We constantly have the impression that in history only a thin film is accessible to us and broader and deeper dimensions are cognitively concealed from us. Plato's ideas are an example. Every student can answer questions about them. But what do they really know about them? Plato reached his *theoria* only on a high plane of meditation. But who of us has reached this plane today when we speak about his ideas? How, then, can we really know them? Who of us has reached the point where we have the categories and forms of perception for a possible *theoria*? Since we have not reached Plato's point of perception, in Neo-Kantianism the Platonic ideas can be twisted into abstract general concepts. This is what I mean when I speak about only a thin film of history being accessible.

In religion the application of Kantian principles has been quite different. For Kant, religious and theological statements belong to the sphere of dogmatic metaphysics. In this sense they transcend experience. In them reason can roam at will and antinomies result. In this area only postulates[31] lie within the competence of philosophy. We cannot achieve anything more than hints or indications.

Certainly it is due to Kant's influence that religion occupies in the general consciousness today a completely different place from the one it occupied in previous epochs. For Luther, and up to the end of the Middle Ages and the Enlightenment, the question of truth was a criterion. The disputation between Luther and Eck offers an example.[32]

---

30. Thus the book of Revelation seemed remote in the 19th century but took on new relevance in the Third Reich and World War II.

31. *Heischesätze* is Jung-Stilling's word for "postulates."

32. At Leipzig, June 27 to July 7, 1519.

Both stood there with open Bible and tried to show that biblical truth was on their side. The post-Kantian consciousness, which is no longer self-evidently committed to this truth, can hardly think that a normative court like truth applies in a sphere where the organ of truth, i.e., reason, has no competence.

The theological objections of average people (if one might give them rhetorical form) are as follows: How do we know the things found on the first and last pages of the Bible (the creation stories and eschatological statements)? Do not the insoluble contradictions of religions, confessions, and theological schools show that we are here moving in regions which are not open to objective experience (and hence to synthetic judgments a priori)? Do we not have in this region judgments which are unverifiable in principle? How can the question of truth have the rank of a criterion in religion when the organ of truth, i.e., reason, is out of place in this sphere?

Religion is not allowed any interest in the question of truth. The argument runs as follows: How can you claim a concern for truth when you deny the competence of reason (e.g., in proving God) and appeal for faith? We willingly believe what we want to believe, but not what is true. This homespun wisdom is revealing. It leads on to the further thought that we have a vested interest in what we want to believe. Thus behind religious statements, which raise a nonverifiable claim to truth that transcends reason, there does not lie a real concern for truth but a vested interest. Along these lines Feuerbach finds in religion a projection of our hopes and fears. Marxism calls it the opium of the people which seeks to offer the consolation of a better world for present misery and in so doing prevents people from bettering their own lot by revolution. Certain persons have an interest in this ideological result and make the priests their helpers. The mistrust expressed here always finds something else behind ostensible motives. It seeks to press below the surface and unmask the latent interest.

Such theses are not directly triggered by Kant. They are conceivable without him. Yet we should not link the ideological problem in Marxism, and the associated atheistic phenomena, merely with left-wing Hegelianism. Although this has hardly ever been done, we should link it *also* with Kant.[33]

33. For the pragmatism which presupposes the thesis of immanent empiricism, cf. esp. Anglo-American philosophy, e.g., John Dewey, *Ethics* (1908), and William James, *Pragmatism* (repr. 1965). Even in the later 19th and early 20th century, European philosophy took a similar turn (Nietzsche, Henri Bergson, Georges Simmel, E. Mach, H. Vaihinger).

C. CRITIQUE OF PRACTICAL REASON

We should note that Kant's ethics ascribes no less a role to the subject than does his epistemological analysis. In the philosophy of practical reason, too, ethical objects are in a sense phenomena that the moral subject itself brings into being. This is so clearly put that one may plainly discern an essential similarity between the two great *Critiques*. I will briefly show what is at issue.[34]

We may first recall some of the general features of pre-Kantian ethics, although excluding Reformation ethics. We make this exclusion because in Luther, as in Paul, the formal antithesis to Kant is not so pointed as in the moral theology of Scholasticism. In Luther moral objects, or the objects of the concrete obedience of faith, are linked with the believing subject. The Pauline statement that whatever is not of faith is sin (Rom. 14:23) occurs in many forms.[35] Naturally, the opposite is also true, that what is done in faith cannot be sin. The 1520 theses on whether works contribute to grace express this very pointedly: Even adultery, if committed in faith, is not sin. If we pray to God in unbelief, we commit an act of idolatry (Theses 11-12).[36] The work does not make the person but the person the work.[37] Acts, then, are totally qualified by the subject or person. We find something similar in the Gospels, e.g., when Jesus says that what comes from the inner heart, not what is outside, makes us unclean (Mark 7:14-23).

It is hardly surprising, then, that in virtue of this linking of moral worth with the subject, Protestant theology has often supposed it had found an ally in Kant. Wilhelm Herrmann, who taught both Barth and Bultmann, even thought that he should (and could!) erect a Christian superstructure on a Kantian basis in order to achieve a Reformed theological ethics.

But how about the understanding of ethics in the Middle Ages and the Enlightenment? We find here fixed moral values based on natural law in Scholasticism[38] and on human rights in the Enlightenment. Thinkers could say unequivocally what is good and express their knowledge in lists of virtues. "Virtue" might sound subjective to our ears, but note that here moral value is an objective entity and is not

34. Cf. in interpretation Heinrich Barth, *Philosophie der praktischen Vernunft* (1927), esp. pp. 335ff.

35. Especially in works against the Antinomians; cf. *ThE*, I, §§ 599ff.; ET I, 130ff.

36. WA, 7, 231-32.

37. WA, 39, I, 283, 9.

38. Cf. *ThE*, I, §§ 610-719; ET I, 383ff.

constituted by the virtuous disposition of the subject. A person is virtuous who does this or that, who seeks this or that virtue, who achieves, e.g., righteousness, love, or other values.[39] One might venture to say (in Kant's terms) that these are ethical virtues in themselves, although they are no more to be seen directly than Kant's "thing-in-itself." For an ethical process to result these values have first to be worked out and adopted by the subjects. They have to go through their system of categories. The resultant ethical product is the disposition.

How is that? Kant says that only that can be ethical which I do for an ethical motive. The disposition, the subjective ethical "habit," is what qualifies the works.

But what are these ethical motives? We best begin with a negative answer. They are present only when I do not act in self-interest or when I do not act to gratify or satisfy impulse. Kant calls egotistic or self-interested motivation "eudaemonism." In contrast to the doing of duty, it is action out of inclination. With the sharpness of a detective he searches out all motives which might suggest eudaemonism.

Thus it is present when I am motivated by objects, when I am directed from outside. What objects? (The illustrations are my own, but they keep strictly to the line of Kantian theory.)

First, we might think of objects that incite ambition, the desire for power, or the sexual libido. Acts motivated by such objects definitely fall below the ethical level. Every ethical act is constitutively linked to responsible decision. But here there is no decision; impulse takes over. I act like an animal within the causality of the libido.

Nevertheless, I may not be driven merely by impulse but may act according to the above-mentioned moral values. But this does not have to mean that I escape the nexus of causality and impulse. Even when I have ethical values in view, deep down I may be driven by two questionable impulses.

Thus I may be driven by moral inclination, e.g., a certain natural goodness which impels me to active love of others, but "impels" me, so that I am in fact driven by impulse. A sublime egoism is thus at work here.

Schiller spoke ironically about Kant's mistrust of the ethical quality of inclination when he said that it would rob friendship of its ethical rank: "I like my friends but I do so out of inclination. It vexes me that I am not virtuous." For all his admiration for Kant,[40] his work

39. For a more modern ethics of this type cf. Max Scheler, *Der Formalismus in der Ethik und die materiale Wertethik* (1927). On this cf. my *Das Verhältnis zwischen dem Ethischen und dem Ästhetischen* (1932), pp. 46-65, and *ThE*, I, §§ 1932ff.

40. Cf. Schiller's last letter to Kant, June 13, 1794, PhB, vol. 103, 47.

Anmut und Wurde is implicitly a polemic against him. For Schiller the "beautiful soul" in which duty and inclination come together is the real ethical pinnacle. Virtue, then, is an inclination to duty.[41] Only when virtue is natural to us is moral thinking achieved, for so long as the moral mind uses force, natural impulse will have to oppose force to it. Bravery might be mentioned as an example of what Kant himself has in mind, for it might be suspect as an ethical virtue because it derives from the desire for medals and hence from ambition.[42]

The second doubtful possibility is that I might act against inclination but not ethically because I do it, e.g., out of fear of punishment or fear of divine judgment. Thus the instinct of self-preservation is the motive and this is again a kind of egoism. Kant would say that once again I am driven by natural causality instead of becoming a free ethical subject. Theologians call this kind of motivation "servile fear."

In other words, I cannot find any true ethical values outside the ego. For I may seek to practice such values as love of neighbor or obedience to God with the help of motives that rob them of their ethical quality. I may found an orphanage, but only so as to name it after me and thus appease my desire for prestige.

As in Kant's theoretical philosophy, I am thus referred to the final points of orientation of reason itself, this time in the principles of the practical logos.

A new form of a priori arises here in the ethical sphere. The objects that motivate are no longer sought outside in the world of experience. They are no longer based on experience. Experience means direction from outside and hence contingency, for it means that we can all follow our feelings and keep to our favorite values, so that action depends on our constitution or caprice or the situation. Action that is motivated in this way can never have an unconditional character. It is conditioned and contingent. In contrast, the rational principles of the practical logos mean inner direction, or what Kant calls "autonomy." They are thus protected against contingency and bear the mark of universal validity. Kant calls ethical imperatives of this unconditional kind "apodictic."

The opposite are conditional acts that depend on certain outside conditions. They are based exclusively on materially based rules of wisdom and shaped by the decisions of practical judgment. Thus the strategic and tactical plans of a general staff rest on discussion of what to do in such and such cases. They are a function of conditions. Such

41. Ibid., p. 130.
42. Thus, as cynics observe, medals are not always earned.

conditional actions are a massive contradiction of the ethical a priori, for the conditions under which I act are always shaped by experience, by concrete historical situations, and by similar contingent factors. The resultant decisions, then, can never have the rank of universal validity.

In contrast, the sphere of ethical norms demands maxims and principles of action that apply always and everywhere no matter what the concrete conditions may be. Only applying these protects us against opportunism, tactical compromises, and the like. These alone make apodictic unconditionality possible.

Max Weber in his famous address "Politics as a Vocation," given during the revolutionary winter of 1919, discussed the structure of conditional and unconditional action.[43] He distinguished between an ethics of disposition, which is close to Kant's postulate of unconditionality and which he ascribes to the saints, and an ethics of responsibility, which, as in politicians, must take possible consequences into account, and is thus tied to conditions. The essential question that results is how I may have an ethical motivation or even discern it.

First, I arrive at it by accepting the categorical imperative that is mediated to me by the practical logos of my conscience. I recognize this by the fact that, unlike impulses, it is universally valid. Because it is universally valid, it can only be *formal*. Things that are material, e.g., casuistical applications, are imparted to me by the outside world, by experience, so that what is experienced, and what is felt to be desirable or demanded, differs with each individual. Since the result can only be judgments or rules of practical wisdom, the imperatives found in this sphere lack any universal validity. The formulation of the categorical imperative is thus as follows: Act in such a way that the maxims of your will may at any time be valid as the principle of universal legislation.[44] This formulation has all the features that we have noted thus far.

The universal validity that may be seen in it derives from a principle of reason that is at work in universal legislation. It thus applies to everybody. A principle of this kind can respect human dignity, which for Kant means that the humanity in each of us is sacred. This means again that we can use everything at our disposal as means to our ends apart from human beings themselves, for these, being rational creatures, are ends in themselves. They are subjects of the moral law, which is holy, in virtue of the autonomy of their freedom.[45] The fact that they are ends in themselves, and cannot be exploited as mere instruments,

43. Weber, *Essays in Sociology* (1946), pp. 77ff.; cf. *ThE*, II/2, 3601ff.
44. See *Critique of Practical Reason*, § 7 (PhB, 36), Great Books 44, p. 302.
45. PhB, 102, ET p. 328.

is a universal principle which is worthy to shape laws that are universally valid.

Again, the formal character of the ethical demand may be seen in the categorical imperative. It does not offer a material program that I must fulfil. It simply fashions maxims, which are for Kant subjective principles or opinions of the individual will.[46] At issue, then, are unconditional principles of the disposition that ought to motivate us. Thus one might think of the fact that we are ends in ourselves as one such principle. One might cite the statement of Jesus that the sabbath was made for us (not vice versa). In Kantian terms, institutions like the sabbath ought to serve us as means; we ourselves should never have purely instrumental significance for institutions.

Maxims of this kind are independent of historical factors or situations. Only when I have grasped these unconditional maxims do I turn to the world of experience and look for objects on which to work out the maxims. To apply Kant's thinking to a modern problem, I might ask how the fact that we are ends in ourselves impinges on the question of abortion. Is the fetus part of the organism of the mother, so that along the lines of the popular slogan that her body is her own she can abort it or keep it as she wills? Or does the fetus stand under the taboo of independent humanity with the rank of an end in itself?

This is how Kant conceives of ethical motivation. The situation in experience cannot be material for primary motivation but only material for the actualizing of my maxims and my original ethical decision. But then the concrete form of actualization is subject to judgments by which I interpret the material (situations, objects, etc.), which are thus conditioned, and which may turn out to be quite different in a given case.

One might say that the ethical motivation is the same in all who respect the categorical imperative because it derives from rational principles and is thus universally valid and unconditional. But the concrete implications of the motivation may differ, for in the transition from maxims to concrete cases I have to interpret reality. In this interpretation my standpoint and criteria will allow for individual deviations and make them conditional, e.g., on such things as my social position, my class, my capitalist or socialist premises, etc. The pluralism of opinions and decisions that arises in this second act of the ethical process does not, however, affect the universal validity of the ethical motivation. This remains in spite of the variety of inferences drawn from it.

46. Ibid., pp. 297, 317.

Formally, then, Kant faces much the same problem as does theological ethics. One sees this when church synods try to take up a common position in face of everyday problems, e.g., abortion, nuclear weapons, etc. The synod might agree on the theological principles (in formal analogy to Kant's universally valid maxims), but different assessments of the situation will lead to completely different attitudes. We thus have the same combination of unconditional principles (of faith) and conditional implications, consent in motivation and pluralism of inferences.

We return to the question of how we recognize ethical motivation. Our first reply was that we do so as in our conscience we accept the categorical imperative with its formal, nonmaterial validity.

The second answer is that we are sure of ethical motivation when we are aware of freedom. But how does this come about? Not by reason finding a break in causality within the sphere of experience. This is impossible, for causality is one of the categories of theoretical reason and hence reason finds it in its sphere of objects. It would be untrue to itself were it to try to find a break in causality.[47] No, I experience my freedom from practical reason as my conscience, along with the demand that I "should," assures me that I "can."[48] Freedom and unconditional practical law point to each other.[49]

Outwardly, the moral subject cannot have any claim to freedom; all is law. But even in extreme cases, such as kleptomaniacs, those who seem to be determined are for Kant free and responsible, and must be addressed as such. Even if it were possible for us to see so deeply into a person's mode of thinking that we could know the slightest impulses and even if we knew all the external influences affecting that person, so that we could count on the future with the same certainty as with an eclipse of the moon or the sun, we should still maintain that that person is free.[50] To try to uphold freedom unconditionally in spite of the epistemological difficulty that we cannot objectify freedom with the help of theoretical reason, Kant resorts to a speculative construction. Causality, he argues, occurs only in the world of phenomena where the

---

47. Theoretical reason does know something about freedom, not in the objective sphere, but nonobjectively as the possibility of absolute spontaneity, and hence as an analytical principle in the epistemological process. To find the truth it has necessarily to presuppose something unconditional in every series of conditions; see *Critique of Practical Reason* on the deduction of principles, PhB, p. 57, ET pp. 307ff., and cf. Weischedel, I, 31-32.

48. *Critique of Practical Reason*, PhB, 35, 182; ET p. 328.

49. Ibid., p. 34, ET p. 302.

50. Ibid., p. 115, ET p. 333.

categories of reason are in play. The thing in itself, which is outside experience, i.e., which is not made an object of experience by the forms of perception and the categories, is not under causal determination. From this Kant concludes that the moral subject, insofar as it experiences freedom, has the role of a thing in itself.[51]

The "ought" that practical reason declares and the "can" of which the moral subject is assured give the moral subject autonomy. It is required not to subject itself to any purpose which is not possible by a law that might derive from the will of the subject itself.[52]

The theological question that is to be put to Kant at this point might be phrased as follows: Where is God's place in this system? He certainly cannot be the original author of the law, the starting point of the ethical system. For if the moral imperative goes back to his command, the autonomy which is the crux of the system seems to be eroded. For Kant God's law can only be a *heteros nomos*, or can it? (We shall come back to the tension between heteronomy and theonomy at the end of the chapter.) In any case, since the system cannot be based on God, the concept of God can come in for Kant only at the end as a kind of appendix. It cannot be located among the synthetic judgments but can arise only in a continuation of deliberations aimed at an analysis of the moral subject. For Kant this means that it has the character of a postulate, a construction that is designed to help us out of deep existential frustration caused for Kant by the idea of the practical logos. What is this frustration?

According to Kant, as we have seen, I am an ethical person only on the negative condition that I do not act eudaemonistically, that seeking happiness is not part of my ethical motivation. But the difficulty is that happiness as human self-fulfilment is one of the elements of humanity. Kant saw this when he defined it as the state of a rational being for which everything in life goes as it wishes and wills. It thus rests on the agreement of nature with its whole purpose and with the essential basis of the determination of its will.[53] The combination of a fulfilment of both duty and inclination is for Kant the supreme good. Happiness as the congruence of nature and goal means for Kant no less than that a human being fulfils its destiny or, in modern terms, finds its identity. All of us have an image of what we should be and we know no peace until we achieve it. Happiness involves an integration of existence and destiny.

51. Ibid., p. 111, ET p. 331.
52. Ibid., p. 102, ET p. 328.
53. Ibid., p. 143, ET p. 345.

The flaw is, however, that seeking happiness cannot be an ethical motive because, being eudaemonistic, it corrupts the purity of the unconditional and categorical imperative. A paradoxical situation results. The supreme good which is a synthesis of duty and inclination cannot be willed directly and yet it is the individual's destiny.

In this difficulty Kant resorts to the postulate of God. To put it very pointedly, he needs a deus ex machina who will combine that which ethical motivation keeps apart. Rather oddly, Kant thinks that in this regard he has hit on the Christian principle of morality, for this, too, espouses the autonomy of pure practical reason, not the theological heteronomy of a *Deus dixit*, not making the knowledge of God and his will the basis of its laws, but only the attainment of the supreme good on the condition of following these laws, and finding the true impulse to do so, not in the desired results, but solely in the idea of duty in whose faithful observance the worthiness of the attainment alone consists.[54]

Hence the question of God does not come at the beginning of ethics—Kant means Christian ethics!—but only in a concluding reflection, i.e., when the unconditionality of ethical action raises the question of happiness or self-fulfilment, which seems to be ruled out as a constitutive element of human existence.[55]

Although Kant may think that he has hit on the basic intention of Christian ethics with his solution, one has to note that according to this approach Christianity—at least in some respects—comes under the suspicion of eudaemonism. At any rate, it does so when God is put at the beginning as the author of the law. (And who would try to argue that this is merely a theological exception?) When this is done, does not obedience to the law tend to have the goal of making oneself pleasing to God, or to induce a servile fear which makes the fear of punishment a pseudo-ethical motive?

The theologian Luther put this question self-critically, and in working through it he engaged in an experiment of thought, i.e., the idea of resignation to hell. Even if in spite of my justifying faith God were to damn me to hell, I should not let go of him. To do so would show that my faith is merely the device of a selfish desire for salvation with whose help I hope to attain it like those who find their basis in legal righteousness. In truth, then, I am not in faith seeking conformity to God. Faith is simply, in Kantian terms, the means to an end, to the selfish, eudaemonistic end of securing God's good pleasure in me. What faith really means for me, whether it is selfish calculation or unselfish self-

54. Ibid., p. 148, ET p. 348.
55. Toward the end of the *Critique;* cf. Weischedel, IV, 693.

surrender, is shown by this condemnation to hell. If I still praise God in hell, I show that in faith my concern is not with self but with God and his right to dispose of me as he will. In this case, God cannot leave me in hell but has to draw me to himself. For with this praise even out of hell I have attained to the conformity that he wants from me. I am justified before him even in the deepest depths.[56]

One may see, then, that even though, as in Luther, God as the Lord of the first commandment[57] stands at the beginning of theological thinking, this does not entail the de-ethicizing of ethics or its corruption into a kind of eudaemonism. Kant failed to grasp the gracious promise of the gospel and therefore the background of the Pauline and Reformation "by faith alone." Hence he could not understand the proper relation of the law to the gospel.

J. H. Pestalozzi (1746-1827), in a letter to Lavater, has a remarkable parallel to Luther's discussion of resignation. It goes back to his meeting with the mystic Johann Mesmer vom Thal. "For fourteen years," he said, "I have struggled to possess God and to achieve perfection, and I have not succeeded. But even in hell, if I were to die now—and because I do not have the righteousness which I seek I should be damned—I would love God and long for him and know that he would love me in hell and save me and give me his righteousness."[58] The French theologian F. Fénelon (1651-1715) also says of unselfish love that it means that we must be able to love God even though we know that God will damn us.[59]

D. EXCURSUS: HEINE'S IRONICAL CRITICISM OF KANT

Heine attacked the late introduction of God and his reduction to the rank of a mere postulate. His criticism is so broad that he treats Kant as the initiator of the idea of the death of God long before Nietzsche.[60] Kant is responsible for the disturbing news of God's death. Kant has emptied heaven, he has put its whole garrison to the sword, the Lord of the world swims in his blood, there is no more mercy or fatherly goodness, the immortality of the soul is at its last gasp.[61] One might ask, of course,

56. WA, 46, 389ff.; LW, 25, 380-81.

57. *EF*, II, 200, 209; P. Althaus, "Gottes Gottheit als Sinn der Rechtfertigungslehre Luthers," in *Theologische Aufsätze*, II (1935), 1-30.

58. F. Delekat, *J. H. Pestalozzi* (1926), p. 64.

59. See ibid., p. 36.

60. Heine, *Religion and Philosophy in Germany* (1959); cf. *EF*, I, 232ff.

61. Heine, *Religion and Philosophy*, p. 119.

whether Heine did not notice that Kant did not intend any denial of God but found in the theological incompetence of reason the possibility of securing a safe sphere for faith. He did see this, but he says that when he finds someone debating the existence of God a peculiar anxiety arises within him, a sinister sense of oppression such as he once experienced in London at New Bedlam (an asylum), when, surrounded by mad people, he lost sight of his guide. Doubt of God is doubt of life itself; it is death.[62]

The fact that for Kant God is not a basic experience or axiom, that he is brought in later on the margin, that he is reduced to a mere postulate, that he is a squatter on the edge of the universe, an emigrant to the hereafter who leaves hardly a trace in the cosmic nexus—all this arouses a kind of ontological terror in Heine.

Without experiencing the same fear, Schopenhauer in a letter dated August 21, 1852, takes Kant in the same way.[63] He has done a fine job of evicting God in spite of his bulletproof definition with the help of a disguised cosmological proof. Thus Kant's God is a corpse. The writer finds no pleasure in the stink of a cadaver.

Heine goes so far as to throw doubt on Kant's integrity in making this postulate and to accuse him of putting God out in the first *Critique* and then smuggling him back in through a side door in his ethics for pragmatic and sentimental reasons. According to Heine Kant sees that his old and faithful servant Lampe has been robbed of his last support by the declaration of the death of God. His face is swept by anxiety and tears. So Kant has pity on him, for he is a good man and not just a great philosopher. Half in kindness and half in irony he says that Lampe must have a God or else he cannot be happy. Practical reason says so, and hence it will guarantee the existence of God. He thus resurrects the corpse of deism which pure reason had slain.[64]

Kant is for Heine the final point in a theological line on which God increasingly loses substance until Kant gives the decisive blow to aged Jehovah.[65] But before this happens, God has to roam the world. First he becomes increasingly spiritual as a mere synonym for reason or the cosmic soul, and then as no more than a postulate. This figure which is now peripheral and has no influence in the cosmic nexus whimpers tenderly like an indulgent father, a friend of all, a well-wisher, a philanthropist. Nothing can help him. As in Wolfgang Borchert's *Draussen vor*

---

62. Ibid., p. 115.
63. The letter is to J. Frauenstädt; cf. O. Lindner, *A. Schopenhauer* (1863), p. 553.
64. Heine, *Religion and Philosophy*, p. 119.
65. At the end of Book 2.

der Tür he is like a foolish old man who can no longer do anything for us but only weep the tears of helpless senility. Do you hear the bell ringing? Kneel, they are bringing the sacraments to a dying God.

In the final evaluation of Kant's theological statements we shall have to ask whether God really means no more for Kant than what practical reason has to say about him. Might it not be—this is the crucial question—that Kant left the theological contents of the faith untouched, that he thought other forms of certainty were possible than those provided by theoretical and practical reason,[66] and that he was dealing only with the problem of what may be said within the confines of his critical transcendentalism? Might it not also be—to use a rather more mundane example—that he was rather like a scientist who confesses that in his special field (e.g., biology) he finds only faint signs from which he can learn hardly anything about God, which might be taken in other ways,[67] but which in any case do not show us *who* has passed this way. If we assume that this scientist is a Christian, then his faith as such is not based on these traces. It has hardly anything to do with them. It is based instead on experience in a qualitatively different dimension.

The question that arises in relation to Heine's criticism of Kant's ethical concept of God is more complicated, however, than this more popular example might suggest. To deepen it we must ask whether liberated reason, which relies only on itself, which does not "receive," and which does not see itself any longer in the light of a basic relation to God, really has to imply the rejection that Heine fears. What shape will the theological criticism of reason take—a criticism which there can and must be?[68] We shall return to this question when we contrast theonomous and autonomous ethics.

Samuel Collenbusch, the physician and leader of Wuppertal Pietism (1724-1802), is a true antithesis to Heine, but at one point he takes Kant's view of God in much the same way, for in a respectful letter to Königsberg he suggests that this postulated God no longer seems to be one on whom one may set one's hope and in whom one may rejoice at the resurrection of the dead.[69] He is sorry that Kant has nothing good

66. E.g., Schleiermacher's "feeling" or Troeltsch's "experience."

67. Cf. the different interpretations of Teilhard de Chardin and Jacques Monod.

68. Cf. *ThE*, II, §§ 1321ff., and esp. the searching book by S. Scharrer, *Theologische Kritik der Vernunft* (1977).

69. Barmen-Gemarke, Jan. 23, 1795, in H. Cremer, *Aus dem Nachlass eines Gottesgelehrten* (1902). Collenbusch was influenced by the theodicy of Leibniz and the Swabian theosophist Oetinger. J. H. Jung-Stilling constantly mentions him in his *Lebensgeschichte* (1976 ed.).

to hope for from God either in this world or the next. He himself hopes for many good things from God.

E. PHILOSOPHY OF RELIGION: *RELIGION WITHIN THE LIMITS OF REASON ALONE*

What Kant offers in this work is a philosophical view of religion dealing with what since Blaise Pascal has usually been called the God of the philosophers. Pascal used the phrase on his *Mémorial,* which was found after his death in the lining of his coat and dated November 23, 1654. The decisive statement runs: "The God of Abraham, the God of Isaac, and the God of Jacob—not of the philosophers and scholars."[70]

In his philosophical view of religion Kant does not deal primarily with the contents of Christian revelation, although some of these occur, e.g., the nature of God, the Son of God, justification, sin, the exposition of scripture, etc. His decisive aim, rather, is to find within his epistemological theory that which reason may say about religion, and to ask constantly to what extent the contents of Christian revelation may or may not be harmonized with immanent rational knowledge.

The key to his understanding of *Religion Within the Limits of Reason Alone* lies once again in his belief that religions have ethical roots. Subjectively considered, religion is the knowledge of all our duties as divine commands.[71] This is a most pregnant expression of his thesis that God is not a normative court at the beginning of all ethical reflection. First we have certainty regarding our duties. This certainty derives from the principles of the practical logos. Putting it sharply, one might say that religion is a means to the end of clarifying the unconditionality of moral obligation by giving these duties a divine author. The "as" in the definition almost reminds us of Vaihinger's "as if," as though we had here a hypothetical assumption. It "almost" does so, for although for Kant there is no proof of God's existence, all serious and credible moral striving for the good finds the idea of God unavoidable.[72] Hence the

70. Cf. Pascal, *Die kleinen Schriften,* ed. W. Rüttenauer, Sammlung Dieterich, vol. 16, 126-27. Among modern philosophies of religion one might mention in this regard Karl Jaspers, *Philosophical Faith and Revelation* (1967) (important for his comparison of Galileo and Bruno; cf. *EF,* II, 307ff.); W. Weischedel, *Der Gott der Philosophen,* 2 vols. (1971-1972); H. Gollwitzer and W. Weischedel, *Denken und Glauben. Ein Streitgespräch* (1965); cf. also D. Rössler, *Die Vernunft der Religion* (1976).

71. Kant, *Die Religion innerhalb der Grenzen der Blossen Vernunft,* PhB, p. 179 (ET *Religion Within the Limits of Reason Alone* [1960], p. 142).

72. Ibid.

author of the law is not for Kant a fiction that is invented for pragmatic reasons, as he is for Vaihinger, but an idea which the ethical consciousness cannot avoid, and which must be respected as a given factor no matter how it be evaluated ontologically.

Naturally, this religion of reason must be differentiated radically from that of revelation. But are the two incompatible? For Kant the mark of revealed religion is that I have to know in advance that there is a kind of divine command, and to recognize it as my duty. In rational or natural religion, however, the opposite is true. I have to know in advance that there is a kind of duty before I can take it to be a divine command.[73]

Kant, however, does not see any total antithesis here, for even revealed religion must regard certain principles as natural. Thus the term *revelation* can be related by reason to religion only because the concept of religion, being derived from obligation to the will of a moral lawgiver, is itself a rational concept.[74] Thus the religion of revelation is an addition to that of reason, a kind of superstructure. Obviously, this means that the substructure of rational religion has normative significance and thus serves as a criterion for what reason may accept in the superstructure of revelation. Philosophical ethics does not just carry the train of her mistress revealed theology but also lights her way. Is she, then, really the maid?

I may refer in this connection to Kant's work *Der Streit der philosophischen Fakultät mit der theologischen*.[75] Kant is ready to accept the proud claim of the theological faculty that the philosophical faculty is its maid so long as it does not chase or silence it.[76] But his statement has an obvious ironical undertone, for he says that it is an open question whether the maid carries the torch in advance or the train behind. Who, then, is the mistress and who the maid?

An example will show how the function of rational religion as a criterion works out in practice. We might choose the understanding of the Christian doctrine of original sin. Can original sin—Kant speaks of radical evil or an inclination toward evil in human nature—be harmonized with Kant's ethical conceptions? How can one think that the ethical subject, the autonomous self that gives itself its own laws and is its own judge, is also evil (in the sense of Gen. 6:5)? The idea of autonomy is built on ethical self-confidence. Individuals are aware of representing

73. Ibid., p. 180 (ET p. 143).
74. Ibid., p. 182 (ET p. 144).
75. Weischedel, XI, 279ff.
76. Ibid., pp. 290-91.

humanity.[77] They are bearers of the practical logos. They have the rank of ends in themselves. Hence the ethical I knows no court that may question or judge it. It merely *adds on* the idea of God as the author of the law. God as such is simply a symbol of the unconditionality of ethical commands. The I is itself the final authority.

A second consideration seems to make it almost impossible that the thought of original sin might be integrated into Kant's ethical system. Kant made it an axiom that we *can* because we *ought*. Hearing the practical logos carries with it a sense of freedom. But the doctrine of original sin involves a sense of the bondage of the will, of the truth expressed in Rom. 7:15ff.: "I ought, but I cannot."[78] In fact, Kant constructed his ethics with no reference to original sin. How then on his presuppositions can he build a bridge to the Christian doctrine of sin? How can he harmonize the religion of reason with that of revelation?

There seems to be so little possibility of building a bridge that certain pessimistic statements in Kant's anthropology sound to the reader of the *Critique of Practical Reason* like a foreign body. Thus in the section on egoism Kant can say that from the day we begin to speak through the I and advance the self, egoism strides on irresistibly.[79] Again, in the chapter on the nature of the species, Kant says that only the species, not the individual, fulfils the purpose of nature and achieves its destiny, namely, that of developing good out of evil by its own activity.[80]

Kant also points out that nowhere—in spite of the fervor of his anatomical teaching—does he say that we are good. If he did, it would be hard to propose a doctrine of radical evil. No, we are not at first either good or bad. We are made for good.

To say that we are created good can mean only that we are created for good. Our original disposition is good. We ourselves are not yet good. Only as we either do or do not take up into our maxims the impulses that this disposition contains do we become either good or bad.[81] The fact that we have good inclinations can mean only that we have a chance to be good, a potential for good, not that we are in fact good.

Thus it seems that the idea of radical evil is possible. Presuppos-

---

77. Individuals are unholy enough, but humanity must be holy to them in their persons (*Kritik der praktischen Vernunft*, PhB, p. 102; ET *Critique of Practical Reason*, p. 328).

78. On Rom. 7 cf. *EF,* II, 234ff.

79. Weischedel, XII, 408.

80. Ibid., p. 684.; cf. *ThE,* I, §§ 1610-14.

81. *Religion innerhalb,* PhB, p. 47 (ET p. 40).

ing a particular interpretation, Kant will even accept the statement that we are evil, or, borrowing from the doctrine of original sin, that we are evil by nature.[82] But what does he take this to be saying?

In Kant's sense the fact that we are evil can mean only that although we know the moral law we take up occasional deviations from it into our maxims. We are thus halfheartedly ready for the good; we allow ourselves the freedom to make exceptions. The fact that we are evil by nature means that this halfheartedness is not just an individual matter but a liability of the whole species. It is human not to subscribe totally to the categorical imperative. To sin is human. Thus Kant seems to have been impressed by the statement of an English member of parliament that every man has his price for which he will sell himself.[83] He adds that if there is really no virtue for which a degree of temptation might not be found which will overthrow it, then what the apostle says might well be universally true, namely, that we are all sinners, that there is none that does good (according to the spirit of the law), no, not one (Rom. 3:23).

Yet Kant constructs safeguards against possible misunderstandings. That we are evil by nature must never be taken to mean that this characteristic is an inference from the concept of the species. This would be to subject us to the (causally determined) law of necessity. But then there could be no guilt and we would have no responsibility. Kant introduces instead the idea of subjective necessity. This can be presupposed in all of us, even the best. It a natural inclination to evil. Since this is self-caused, we may call it a radical and innate evil in human nature (though still one brought upon ourselves).[84]

In conclusion, one must also point to something that Kant does not say directly but that is relevant to his interpretation. The fact that we are moral subjects rests for him on a supreme certainty. It follows from a fact that is known a priori, namely, that the practical logos speaks in my conscience. But the fact that we are evil rests only on a secondary certainty. It rests on the observation, a posteriori, from experience, that in the battle between duty and inclination, between will and impulse,

---

82. Ibid., pp. 32-33 (ET p. 27).

83. Ibid., p. 40 (ET p. 34).

84. Ibid., p. 33. For the rest Kant thinks the idea of the transmission of sin is an inappropriate one. Not without irony he traces the understanding of this idea through the medical, legal, and theological faculties. What disturbs him about it is obviously that it makes me the object of the guilt of others instead of the subject of my own guilt (pp. 42-43, ET p. 28). The same objection is made today. Thus Ernst Jünger comments: "Original sin? This means transferring the guilt from the one who botches the matter to the one who is botched" (Siebzig verweht, II [1981], 430).

we have a tendency to loosen the bond of duty and sometimes at least to follow impulse.

For Kant, then, sin does not have the primal certainty that it clearly has for me before God (when in principle it includes much more than the concept of moral evil). Theologically, the fact that I am a sinner becomes a direct certainty face to face with God's holiness, and it separates me from God ("'Depart from me, for I am a sinful man, O Lord.' For he was astonished . . . ," Luke 5:8-9). Sin in the Christian, not the moral, sense becomes an object of *faith* when we have faith in *God*. The concrete experience of being a sinner has the significance merely of adding confirmatory indications, although even these are not restricted to moral evil in Kant's sense.

This way of experiencing evil cannot have a place in Kant's system because he introduces the concept of God only later as a postulate and has already constructed all the decisive principles of his anthropology *without* it. He can thus refer to sin only as an *inferred* certainty which is included in the system later. But sin then has to be moral evil, and a change into another genre follows. So far as I can see, Kant only once relates sin to faith, and even here he means faith only in a transferred sense as belief in the moral law after the manner of reflection as distinct from mere attachment to the letter.[85] Here, then, to use Kant's own metaphor, philosophy is not the maid that follows, holding the train of her mistress, but the maid that goes ahead, lighting her way.

VI. GENERAL INFLUENCE OF KANT'S PHILOSOPHY

In the next chapter we shall be studying the influence of Kant on certain representative figures (e.g., A. Ritschl and W. Herrmann). At the end of this chapter, however, I want to formulate the decisive questions that Kant puts to theology and theology to Kant.

First, in the *Critique of Pure Reason,* as we have seen, Kant can point out that he has had to suspend knowledge or restrict its scope so as to make a place for faith.[86] As a maid he has rendered theology a service by establishing the philosophical basis for the possibility of faith. He has made it impossible for philosophers to pursue dogmatic metaphysics and thus to enter into competition with religion. In his sense we might say, then, that he has done two things for theology and Christianity.

85. Ibid., p. 31 (ET p. 26).
86. Weischedel, III, 33.

(1) He has made a place for faith by excluding knowledge—the synthethic judgments of theoretical reason—from the sphere of transcendence. Hence knowledge can no longer compete with faith.

(2) He has made it impossible that an atheistic metaphysics should disturb the certainties of faith with the weapons of thought. For, as we can prove nothing in the transcendent sphere, so we can refute nothing. As every theology has great need of purified concepts of eternity, omnipotence, omnipresence, or everything outside the world, it is absolutely obligatory for it to apply itself to transcendental apperception, i.e., to the function of theoretical reason, which is limited to the sphere of experience.[87] Only such an undertaking can provide a sure judgment on where its sphere of competence begins.

In fact, many theologians, even some who follow it unwittingly, have gratefully found support in Kant's philosophy. What are freethinkers and monists and materialists and metaphysicians really after? In the narthex of faith, in critical discussion of the competence of reason, it has long since been apparent that in our domain nothing can be either proved or refuted.

But the question arises whether Kant's thought can be used in such simplistic apologetic maneuvers. Is it really no more than a support for theology at this point?

Only those can think so who regard the objects of faith merely as transcendent entities. But the incarnation is an unmistakable sign that everywhere Christian theology has to do with this world, with God's gracious turning to our concrete life. Even when the Gospels speak about transcendent regions like heaven and hell, they do not offer a topography of the hereafter but show how these regions are significant for life here and now. The parable of the rich man and Lazarus is a classical example.[88] It does not deal with the situation in the next world but with the destiny of the five brothers in this world.

Precisely in his concern to take philosophy out of transcendence and make it a preserve for theology, Kant had a fateful influence by helping to promote the idea that there is a clear distinction between this world and the next. With some exceptions this idea is less at home among theologians than among many political ideologists. Thus many managers feel they may rightly regard the fashioning of this world as their exclusive privilege, making the next world the ghetto of the church and its proclamation. But those who read Kant more closely will find it hard to base this conclusion on the original

---

87. *Critique of Pure Reason*, 2, 3, 7 (Weischedel, p. 563).
88. Luke 16:19-31; cf. my exposition in *Das Bilderbuch Gottes* (1982).

texts. For he himself does not make so unequivocal or thorough a distinction.

That there is at least some imprecision in Kant is clear at least in the area of practical reason. For example, does he really assign the Ten Commandments, which are in the Bible the content of revelation, only to the next world? Do they have the meaning only of a radical and authoritative *Deus dixit?* If so, Kant could leave them uncritically to the theologians. He could say that there was nothing for him to investigate here as a philosopher, for they were starting with a presupposition that he could neither prove nor disprove, namely, that God is the author of the commandments. This is something that one has to believe. One can only believe it. He may freely abandon this sphere to them.

In fact, however, Kant does *not* say this. Instead, he views the categorical imperative as the criterion for the question whether God's commands (or ostensible commands?) are in harmony with autonomy, whether they thus have the rank, as possible maxims of my will, of being able to become the principle of a universal law. In spite of the *Deus dixit* preamble their imperative content always applies to the present world of concrete action. Philosophy is not a maid or a mercenary providing protection. It is a censor before which one must come to the extent that certain imperatives have an affinity to my this-worldly autonomy. Since the religions of revelation and reason cannot conflict, as we have seen, and the religion of reason has primacy for Kant, it is just possible theoretically that the *Deus dixit* preamble might be contested by the criteria of practical reason.

This question whether one can stand before Kant as the advocate of autonomy and censor of honesty was probably more important for theological Kantians than any joy at his supposed helpfulness. (This is certainly true of Wilhelm Herrmann.) Here at any rate Kant's fateful distinction between this world and the next is by no means clear.

Third, in his role as censor Kant's philosophical religion can leave theologians surprisingly free to make statements that transcend reason—at least in passing. The idea of the supreme good which is inseparably bound up with a pure moral disposition can even lead Kant to the abyss of a mystery, i.e., that of the question of God's role in this. We ourselves cannot achieve the combining of fulfilment of duty and happiness, which is the supreme good. We are thus forced to believe in the cooperation or arrangement of a moral world ruler.[89] But one cannot deny that it is then an open question whether beyond everything

89. *Religion innerhalb*, PhB, p. 161 (ET p. 130).

that we might do, in the mysteries of supreme wisdom, there might not be something that only God can do to make us acceptable people.[90]

Spurred on by the idea of the supreme good, Kant thus arrives at a theological concept of grace, i.e., cooperating grace, to use the theological term. But he has hardly said this before he makes two qualifications.

For one thing, he adds at once that one cannot more seriously misuse this view, which goes back to revelation and sacred history, and even make of it a dangerous religious illusion, than by regarding this faith in God's work, and confession of it, as a means of making ourselves pleasing to God. For in this case fear would be an underlying motive, and we should thus slip back into an opportunism that devalues everything ethical.[91]

Kant even more decisively and radically avoids plunging into a theological discussion of grace on the basis of another consideration, namely, that while we may, he thinks, accept the general presupposition that grace will do what nature cannot do in us, nevertheless we cannot make any further use of this idea.

Why not? First, because we know nothing at all about supernatural aid. We are here on a slippery slope, not on ground secured by reason. Second—and this is where the main accent falls—this is much too lofty an idea, so that we are well advised to keep at a respectful distance from it, as from a sanctuary. But the numinous awe that Kant pleads here is not the main reason for his reserve. He states his main reason in the same sentence. If we count too much on the assistance of supernatural grace, we may fall victim to the illusion that we can do miracles or perceive miracles in us, and this would make us unfit for any use of reason.[92] Hardly, then, has Kant reached the transcendent sphere of the problem of grace, and been forced to do so, before he turns away from it, because the loftiness of the idea might disrupt sober dealings with autonomy and with the duty mediated by it. Finally, then, religion is a reflection in a mirror from which we must turn aside as quickly as possible so as to find our nearest duty. Here, and here alone, may one catch the heartbeat of Kant.

Fourth, by developing the concept of God only in terms of practical reason, and by furnishing religion only with ethical categories, Kant contributes essentially to a moral understanding of Christianity. Even in the popular consciousness today, at any rate on the secularized

90. Ibid., p. 199 (ET pp. 158-59).
91. Ibid., p. 200 (ET p. 159).
92. Ibid., p. 224 (ET pp. 179ff.).

margin of national churches, Christianity is still something which in mythical form expresses that which with the direct certainty of our practical reason—the conscience—we know already as good and evil. (Not a few parents, bringing their children to worship or to instruction for confirmation, give as their reason their belief that the children ought to know about good and evil.) Later the mythical husk can be stripped off. When we reach maturity we know autonomously that which as children we can learn only by theonomous illustrations, namely, that the alpha and omega of life is to learn to do right and to harm no one. The religious element is simply an interim form of this principle. The concept of God, in Kant's sense, helps the immature to gain an impression of the unconditionality of their duties. For God is absolute (even a child can see this), and therefore the duties that he lays upon us are also absolute.

Fifth, in conclusion we must engage the weightiest question that Kant's philosophy formulates for all of us. For Kant contests the possibility of an ethics that is theonomous in the strict sense, at any rate for the adult consciousness. Theonomy is for him heteronomy.

Every theologian must face this question. So must all philosophical thinkers who try to integrate Christianity into their systems and to find a secure place for it. If we cannot answer this question we have not dealt with the basic problem of theology. From the time of Kant this question has haunted the history of theology, and not that alone, but also the general consciousness. To arm ourselves for the encounter, we shall now test and investigate systematically the problem of theonomy and autonomy to see if we have really to choose between them.

VII. SYSTEMATIC CONSIDERATION OF THE RELATION BETWEEN THEONOMY AND AUTONOMY

In view of all that we have said, is not the idea of theological ethics a self-contradiction? In post-Kantian thought, it seems, there can be ethics only if it has as its theme decisions that are taken within an autonomous moral consciousness. An authority that orders us from outside, the kind of authority that the supposed commands of God lay claim to, heteronomizes the moral consciousness. Theonomy thus appears to be a kind of heteronomy. It seems, then, that theology cannot in principle set up an ethical discipline within its own sphere, or even find a place for it. If it claims that it can, it is trying to reverse the wheel of time and making a frantic effort to conserve a medieval and pre-Kantian consciousness.

Now in the face of this objection we have to admit at once that we cannot reverse the question that has been abroad since the Enlightenment, and especially Kant, namely, how the *nomos* of God relates to our autonomy, how the command of God can be brought into harmony with our conscience. In the Middle Ages, and even in Luther, the conscience rests on the authority of the church or of God's Word. It is thus a filled out conscience with a norm. There is no need for reflection on it. But humanity today faces the fact that the conscience still proves its existence and functions even when it is released from all authorities and emptied of all content. The movement toward human autonomy has in some sense come to a head in our day. In every important issue we have learned to rely on ourselves without resorting to the working hypothesis of God. Everything seems to go on just as well without God as it did before.[93]

There can be no reversing or invalidating of this experience that I have within me a conscience, or, more generally, a functioning moral criterion which is and remains active even in an autarchous world. Kant's demand that I must be responsible even for obedience to God's commands, that I cannot just accept them heteronomously as commands, is an irreversible demand.

If we cannot deny this irreversibility, i.e., if we can no longer go back on autonomy once it is brought to light, but if we also cannot strip Christian ethics of its axiomatic theonomy, it seems that we have to try to bring into a synthesis two things that are irreconcilable in principle. It seems as though we were having to try to conceive of wooden iron or a square circle. Is not the very idea of theonomous autonomy paradoxical?

To deal with this elementary objection we would do well to examine the concept of autonomy more closely, putting the main stress not so much on *nomos* (law) as on the meaning of *autos* (self).

What does this "self" mean? For Kant this self is the solitary person that participates in the intelligible world by reception of the practical logos. As moral persons, then, we are fundamentally autarchous. To look outside the self for reasons for what we do in the world destroys the moral structure of the ego. The moral self is the isolated self that listens to itself and shuts itself off from what is without. The way outside comes, as we have seen, only at the second stage of the moral process, namely, when the self that is ready to act seeks outside objects in which it can work out the disposition that is formed in the inner I.

We may illustrate this by love of neighbor. For Kant, the impression made on me by my neighbor does not, as we have also seen, provoke

93. Dietrich Bonhoeffer, *Letters and Papers from Prison* (1973), pp. 325ff.

my readiness to help or my love, i.e., my disposition. The very opposite is the case. There first forms in me a noneudaemonistic readiness to help. I have tested its ethical character by the criterion whether it can be given the status of a principle of universal legislation. Only then do I look for a neighbor on whom I can practice it. This is why we say that for Kant the self is the isolated and autarchous moral ego. A prior anthropological decision underlies the concept of autonomy.

This leads us to an important consideration. In the encounter of autonomy and theonomy the decisive question is not so much what we mean by *nomos* or what is the source of *nomos*. The main emphasis falls on the question of our prior anthropological decision, namely, what we understand by *autos*.

Christian theology has a different view of this *autos* from that of Kant. In Christian thought the self is to be understood only in relation to God. It is the I that is created by God, that has fallen away from him, and that is visited and called to redemption by him. We can make no theological statement about God that does not imply this relation.

If we still try to make such statements, we find ourselves in the inscrutable and inaccessible sphere of a God in himself, a *Deus absconditus*. The only possible object of real knowledge of God is Immanuel, the God who discloses himself in a history with me. To know God is to know his history with us, to know God "for me"—if we might adapt the well-known saying of Melanchthon.

But the reverse is also true, namely, that we can make no theological statement about the human self that does not imply its relation to God. If we still try to make such statements we find only physical or psychological functions with their appropriate organs, or we go on to engage in metaphysical hypotheses and speculations. In any case we miss the point of human existence if we detach the self from the relation to God.

Connected to this is the fact that we can only *believe* in the human self, for the God who determines its being is also an object of faith. The infinite worth of the self and its inviolability cannot be established empirically. To empiricism history offers only the fact that the self can be exploited in various brutal or more refined ways. On this view I might come to agree with Nietzsche that we are no more than vermin on the earth's crust. Naturally, we might arrive at more enthusiastic diagnoses. But we cannot reach the heart of the self.

If we take it seriously that we can define the self only in relation to God, then the self of autonomy takes on a specific quality. We find the self only as we come to God. Apart from this we miss it.

The parable of the prodigal son makes this plain (Luke

15:11ff.). The prodigal's way into the far country is an attempt at self-understanding without the father (or God). But the prodigal is not, as he thought, a self-resting entelechy. His self is his existence as a child. This existence does not become free by detachment from sonship, for the alternative to sonship is servanthood. It becomes free when it leads to adult sonship (cf. Gal. 4:1-7). Freedom is assured when the saying that "all things are yours" is linked with the further saying that "you are Christ's" (1 Cor. 3:21, 23).

It is thus plain that on this level theonomy and autonomy cannot be antitheses, for God is not for us a *heteros nomos*. To be with God is to be with the self; not to be with God is to miss the self.

But a distinction is needed. There is the possibility that God might be for us a *heteros nomos*. Attention is drawn to this situation by the doctrine of the law within which Luther said that when I meet God only in the law I am forced to react to him with opposition, with servile obedience, or even with hate. I am not on the side of the divine law. I am its adversary, at least with one stratum of the self (Rom. 7:22-23). Inasmuch, then, as the law alone denotes my relation to God, it is for me a *heteros nomos*. On the human side its counterpart is the servant in every conceivable form, either the servant who renders unwilling and anxious service, or the saboteur, or the servant who runs away, suppressing the image of the fearsome God and replacing it with wishful images, either mythical or mental.

We might say, then, that if we start with the natural self God is in fact heteronomous. Thus the objection with which we started is right even if in a different sense from that intended. Redemption, however, means that I not merely learn afresh to understand myself but above all that I *receive* a new self, that my old man perishes and I become a new creature.[94]

A suitable autonomy necessarily corresponds to this new creature. For as I am called to existence in the truth, I *will* it. I will to be what I am. God's summons, then, is not that of a stranger against whom I must defend myself in my autonomy. Instead, God calls me as a Father in whom I find my autonomy as his child. What I previously thought of as autonomy I now see to be a very sublime form of self-alienation—a way of escaping final questioning.[95]

In this light it is evident why Paul calls *love* the fulfilling of the law (Rom. 13:10). To love God is to will what God wills, to be one with his will.

---

94. In the NT this new creature, and therefore the possibility of love, are the work of the Holy Spirit; cf. *EF,* III, 4ff.

95. Cf. *ThE,* I, §§ 1613ff.

This will has reached me as the will that loves me, that discloses to me the father/child relationship. The demand to love God the Lord with all one's heart and soul and mind is no longer an alien law. It does not have the typical mark of such a law, namely, that of provoking opposition and dividing the I. For those to whom God has shown himself to be the one who loves, this demand means the release of a new spontaneity of the whole I. The I is fully present in the response of love. Its will—because love is reciprocal—is involved in this spontaneity. Those who really love, even at the human level, do not choose love as one of several possibilities from which they select this possibility and reject the others. Love comes without being chosen, and the will is involved in it.

Real love (in distinction from eros) is thus free of conflicts. It needs no resolve or decision. I do not have to win over the opposition to it in an inner parliament.

One might interject here the thought that in a sick and purely physical sexuality the tormenting thing is that the self is not really present, that only the bodily libido is released, that the heart and mind are not engaged, and that consequently they are not satisfied. Thus sexuality without love is robbed of its fulfilment, for a self-liberating sexuality can never be total.[96] Thus there have hardly ever been so many sexual problems as there are today under the sign of liberation movements and endless television programs on the arts of love.

True love engages the *whole* person. It does not come about through a conflict of choices. It invests itself totally and undividedly. In it the will does not contend against opposition (as in Kant's view of duty). It wills that which love urges. It is an element in love, or, better, its agent.[97]

Thus Jesus can use a remarkable expression when he says that love of neighbor is "like" love of God (Matt. 22:30). This has to mean that in respect of love God and neighbor are not different realities. God makes my neighbors what they are for me, for he has bought them with a price and drawn them into the same history of his love as myself.

Thus the act of love is indivisible. It can be divided neither in respect of its *object* (God and neighbor, cf. Jas. 2:14ff.; 1 John 4:19-21) nor in respect of its *fulfilment,* as though only one half of the self were in the act and the other half outside. This twofold indivisibility is conceivable only if God wins love from me, and by calling me to fellowship sets up a new self, a new creature.

96. Cf. *ThE,* III, 520ff.
97. There is here a purely formal analogy to Schiller's concept of the beautiful soul.

When this happens, I cannot say in the strict sense that I have become another person. I have to confess that I have found my way to myself, to my *true* self, and that in God's eyes I have become congruent with my "design." By becoming theonomous (not one who resists under the law but one who conforms to God under the gospel), I thus attain to autonomy in the *real* sense.

There thus dissolves the originally assumed contradiction between the ethical idea of autonomy and the idea of theological heteronomy. Our earlier thesis still stands, namely, that we cannot go back on the newly discovered autonomy of the moral consciousness. We cannot say that servile obedience to the divine commands is an ethical attitude of the self. Indeed, we might go further and say with Kant that for the sake of the dignity of the moral person the claim of supposed commands, even though they maintain their honorable origin on Sinai, can be accepted only if the commands first come before the censor of the ethical consciousness and receive its approval, only if the ethical consciousness clearly sees in them an objectification of the imperative that sounds forth in itself. The one basic distinction from Kant is that for Christians the ethical consciousness at issue is that of a *new* I, the I of the adult child. On this different level the formal structural marks of autonomy are exactly the same. Indeed, the discovery of these marks by Kant, and the various attempts to establish them since Kant, e.g., in existential philosophy, can be very helpful to theologians. For they serve to clarify on the philosophical side the difference between servile obedience and childlike love (*oboedientia servilis* and *dilectio filialis*).

VIII. APPENDIX: KANT'S VIEW OF SOCIETY: THE RELATION BETWEEN MORALITY AND LAW

After the above survey of Kant's ethics it might seem that he never gets beyond the individual aspect. The categorical imperative certainly speaks about the principle of universal legislation and thus goes beyond the individual sphere. But the way from the individual to the universal is left to individual judgment. Individual reason decides whether one's maxims satisfy the principle of universal legislation and how the maxims are to be realized in concrete action in such a way as to harmonize with what is universal. Our present concern, which leads to objections to this ethical conception, is with the observed fact that we obviously cannot begin in this way with ourselves and our own conscience as though we were the first subject. We find ourselves in a nexus with what has gone before. We are thrust into this. We belong to a specific time and a specific social situation. This helps to determine and shape us. One part of this is that a common mind surrounds us. Certain ideas of values, a certain life-style, and a kind of collective consciousness tell us how we are to think about this or that, and what we have to do or not do.

Do not these suprapersonal suggestions imply a limitation of my autonomy, or, more accurately, of my achievable autonomy? Even more sharply, are my maxims really mine? Or do I merely imagine so when in reality I am simply a representative and spokesman for the common mind, so that being free, an *autos,* is a task rather than a gift? Here is a critical question that has to be put to Kant. It raises problems that occupy us today. In putting it, therefore, we are true to our plan of entering into dialogue with thinkers of the past.

Kant is not silent or helpless in the face of this question. He gave much thought to our relation to given social factors. His main concern in this regard is with law, i.e., public legislation. He sharply distinguishes this area from that of individual morality, although not totally separating them.

The most important sources are to be found in his *Metaphysik der Sitten* and *Über den Gemeinspruch: Das mag in der Theorie richtig sein, taugt aber nicht für die Praxis.*[98] Although I do not explicitly go into it in what follows, I would draw the reader's attention to some formal analogies between Kant's view of the distinction between morality and law and Luther's doctrine of the two kingdoms.

The problem for Kant is as follows. As the bearers of personality and freedom, we are ends in ourselves. Hence there neither can nor should be any social structure that robs us of the privilege of being our own masters and makes us like domestic cattle that are used for service at their owner's will and without their consent.[99] But is the moral consciousness enough to prevent our degradation to the status of domestic cattle. Kant doubts it. Why?

Well, we have to consider that we have in our minds the idea of rights. The categorical imperative is present to us and hence a sense that in accordance with the principle of universal legislation we have integrated our freedom into a society of law. But against this stands a great "but," for because of our hardness of heart it might be that we are unable

---

98. *Metaphysik der Sitten,* PhB, 42, pp. 33-48, 261-337; *Über den Gemeinspruch: Das mag in der Theorie richtig sein, taugt aber nicht für die Praxis,* Weischedel, XI, pp. 125-72. I quote mostly from the latter work and for this purpose use the reprint in F. Jonas, *Geschichte der Soziologie* (1968), I, 212ff. (quoted as *Gemeinspruch*).

99. *Gemeinspruch,* p. 215.

and unwilling to develop and act accordingly.[100] At this point Kant intentionally echoes a term that Jesus uses (*sklerokardia,* Matt. 19:8) when he justifies the Mosaic law of divorce. Divorce was not in the plan of creation (it was not *ap' arches,* Matt. 19:8b), but God allows it because of our situation after the fall, because of our hardness of heart.[101]

Kant undoubtedly has in view certain anthropological conclusions from experience to which we referred in our analysis of radical evil. Because of the unreliability of depraved humanity it is natural that a superior power operating according to the rules of prudence can and should keep order. But is nothing but power a match for human disorder? Kant calls the resort to power a leap of desperation, a *salto mortale.*[102]

If, however, laws and the sanctions of a society of law are unavoidable because of our moral weakness, the question arises at once whether this does not mean tyranny and heteronomy, whether it is not anti-personal and anti-ethical. Kant's answer to this self-critical question serves not only as a basic defense of the threatened autonomy but also as an evaluation from historical experience of the result of the state's use of force.

He sees both a negative and a positive implication. The negative one is that when the state reacts against hardhearted and morally unstable citizens merely with force undirected by law, it makes everything worse. It does not check the citizens but provokes a similar counterreaction. They, too, resort to force and thus make the moral constitution unsure. The positive implication is that when practical reason finds in laws nothing that corresponds to its own normative functions, all the influences on human choice are unable to fetter the freedom of choice. When the right speaks out clearly in laws, i.e., when they are not just force but are in harmony with the human sense of right, then in spite of radical evil human nature is not so corrupted that it will not hear the voice of right with respect. In this similarity between law and morality, order obtains.

There has to be, then, a certain agreement, ruled by the moral sense, between rulers and the ruled. One might say that Kant, although he never used the term, found the nature of authority in this consent.[103]

Yet here a question must be put to Kant which he in his historical

---

100. Ibid., p. 218.

101. Cf. *ThE,* III, §§ 2140-42; ET III, 101ff.

102. *Gemeinspruch,* p. 218.

103. Cf. *Religion innerhalb,* Weischedel, VIII, 753, 827; cf. *ThE,* II/2, §§ 1154ff.; ET II, 8ff.

situation could not perceive with the brutality and radicality with which we know it today. I have in view the perversion whereby an illusory consent can be obtained by psychological tricks, e.g., by an ideological changing of the consciousness (through propaganda or brainwashing). In this way the formation of moral maxims can be taken out of the hands of individuals and a *heteros nomos* can be given the appearance of autonomy.[104] In this regard we have to think of every form of manipulating the subconscious. Its inhumanity lies in the fact that it attacks the center of personal decision and renders the use of material and ethical criteria impossible.[105]

Kant allows that the individual conscience with its categorical imperative is not enough to enable us to live together in society. Because of our hardness of heart there is need of a higher order equipped with sanctions. This order imposes laws which are similar to individual morality but differ from it inasmuch as they are compulsory. Kant's problem is to show how this suprapersonal order (in the form of the state) can serve the final goal of free personality, how law and morality can achieve a certain consensus and yet in such a way that law has morality as its goal and the state is there for individuals, not the reverse. This is how it has to be if the fact that we are ends in ourselves is to be respected, and with it the core of Kantian ethics.

Kant's solution is this. He finds in the resolve to come together in society a contract. This contract differs from all others. In the usual sense contracts are agreements for specific purposes (purchases, rents, etc.). But coming together in society, forming adult individuals into a common entity, is itself a purpose. This purpose, which is in itself "duty," the supreme and final condition of every external duty, is the human right in the form of compulsory laws which define what is ours and protect it against all others.[106] What is inviolably ours is undoubtedly the primary human right. To be our own masters is the right to free personality. (In modern terms, there is no collective in which the individual is merged.)

The problem of harmonizing law and morality finds its solution in the paradox that freedom is guaranteed by force so long as force has a moral basis. The only task of force is to prevent individual freedoms from colliding and destroying one another. It must see to it that the limits of individual freedom are discovered and respected. At root the only problem is that of the implications of the fact that those who are

104. *ThE*, II/2, §§ 154ff.; ET II, 43.
105. Cf. Vance Packard, *The Hidden Persuaders* (1957).
106. *Gemeinspruch*, p. 212.

called to freedom do not live alone or develop unopposed in the world. They are structurally interwoven with other individuals who have the same claim to freedom. They have to communicate with them. They are called to "socialize"—to use a modern term.

To establish a way of living together in society Kant advances three principles: (1) The freedom of each member of society as a human being; (2) the equality of each member as a subject; and (3) the independence of each member as a citizen.[107] In this connection we must be content simply to discuss the first of these, the principle of freedom, since this impinges directly on the problem of law and morality. The other principles have a particularly historical interest.

If freedom is to be safeguarded by compulsory laws, then in addition to agreement with moral law and especially human rights, a decisive requirement is that the compulsion should be purely formal, that it should in a sense have no content. An example of a purely formal demand is when individual freedom must be restricted so as to fit in with the freedom of all.[108] It is essential in this regard that the legal compulsion should have an external character. It cannot impose inner demands, demands on the disposition, for these are in the province of the practical logos of the individual conscience.

Here again there is some resemblance to Luther's doctrine of the two kingdoms in which the state, representing the secular kingdom, has merely the task of regulating society but may not subject those entrusted to it to any "message," to any material norm of conscience (as takes place in ideological systems of government).[109] Since the regulation is external, the power of the state is kept to a minimum (as distinct from the maximum influence exerted by totalitarian states). Negatively, this means that the compulsory law of the state must not have any empirical goal.[110] By this Kant means that it must not have any material content, e.g., that of steering its citizens into a program of happiness of its own devising, and of forcing the corresponding "message" on them.

We naturally think in this regard of Kant's definition of happiness in his philosophy of religion. Happiness is congruence with our destiny. It is part of the supreme good which cannot be directly achieved by us here and now. It cannot be arranged, not even as the provisional and this-worldly happiness of well-being which we must certainly

107. Ibid., p. 213.

108. Ibid., pp. 212-13.

109. Cf. my essay "Absolutheitsanspruch und Toleranz," in *Religionsfreiheit*, ed. H. Helbling (1977), pp. 27ff.

110. *Gemeinspruch*, p. 212.

pursue. For no others can force me to be happy in *their* way (as they conceive of human well-being). We must all seek happiness in the way that seems good to us so long as we do not not violate the freedom of others. Being in a well-arranged and protected order may well promote a feeling of happy satisfaction with the existing state and make it seem to be a state of national well-being, but this general state can only be the basis on which we must all have the right to fashion our own specific happiness. A government which orders happiness and thinks that it alone knows what it is and what is fitting for its subjects forces the latter into immature passivity and is thus the greatest conceivable despotism. In Kant's sense the ideological totalitarian states of the modern period, and the theocratic ones of earlier times, come under this verdict of despotism, because they will not let public order be simply a basis on which we may all be our own masters in the sense of ethical autonomy, and may all decide on the specific forms of our own self-fulfilment (in a free choice of happiness). They make happiness the object of a total manipulation which even takes in the conscience and every personal sphere.

We may conclude that Kant does not just think individualistically. He reckons with the given factor of a social structure that embraces individuals. When he defines the relation between the two fields, that of individual self-determination and that of suprapersonal order, that of morality and that of law, his decisive thesis is that the ordering of social life must never be an end in itself. "The sabbath [symbolizing institutions] was made for man, not man for the sabbath" (Mark 2:27). This primacy of individuals and their ethically related freedom must be the starting point of every Christian doctrine of the state and society. We have constantly had reason to show why some naive theological ideas must be resisted which portray Kant as representing Christian ethics in general. Here, however, is one of the points in Kant's thinking where his torch can light the way of a theological ethics.

CHAPTER 11

Theological Kantians

I. ALBRECHT RITSCHL

A. PORTRAIT OF THE MAN AND THE THEOLOGIAN: HIS PLACE IN THE HISTORY OF THEOLOGY

After Schleiermacher, Ritschl was undoubtedly the most influential theologian of the 19th century. Materially, this influence may be seen in the fact that, following Kant and Lotze, he pioneered moralism in Protestant theology and its sphere. His broad and enduring impact led to the formation of a definite school which dominated theology for several decades. As we speak of "Barthians" in this century, so they spoke of "Ritschlians" in the last. The leading Ritschlian, Wilhelm Herrmann, taught both Barth and Bultmann. We can understand the two dominant schools of our own century only against the background of Ritschlian thought and in reaction to this background.

Some theological writers who have been influential in the first decades of the 20th century were also shaped by Ritschl's school. I need mention only the greatest of them, Adolf von Harnack, whose works and cultural activity extended well beyond the fields of the church and theology. His student Martin Rade (1857-1940) helped to echo Ritschl's theology for a long period (1888-1949) through his significant journal *Die Christliche Welt*, which was always open to dialogue. Modern readers of Karl Holl's justly famous essays on Luther will come across Ritschl's moralizing tendencies in his interpretation of Luther's doctrine of justification. God's judgment acquits us now because God already sees in us those whom one day he will have made ontically righteous.[1]

---

1. Cf. Holl, *Gesammelte Aufsätze zur Kirchengeschichte*, I, 2nd ed. (1923), 111ff.; III (1928), 525ff.

Hence it is not just because of a concern for theological history that we look at Ritschl, but because by his own influence, and even more so by that of his great disciples, he is so closely related to the theological situation today. As soon as his name is mentioned at all in the present generation, he suffers from the reputation of being unimaginably dry, flat, superficial, moralistically monotonous, and dogmatically simplistic. Karl Barth made no small contribution to this disparagement. Although Barth can be very amiable to theologians who are long since dead, and can even at times draw a very loving portrait, one finds nothing of this in his presentation of Ritschl. He deals with him briefly and churlishly at the end of his history as though it were a distasteful duty. This is not merely due to the fact that his lectures were under the pressure of time at the end of the semester. His scorn comes out vividly in a circular to friends dated 3.26.1922, when the mildness of age had not yet put a brake on his hostility: "To be a proper professor of theology one must be a sturdy, tough, insensitive lump who notices absolutely nothing, much like the blessed Ritschl. . . . I reread some chapters in his biography in the afternoon, shuddering as I did so. Or will I perhaps in time become such a blockhead? Either one day explode or become quite certainly a blockhead?"[2]

How is it possible, I might ask, that such a supposedly cold theologian of the relatively mild 19th century, who suffered from kerygmatic anemia, should produce and stimulate such a militant and pugnacious theological fellowship as the Ritschlian school? Liberal theology and the cultural Protestantism of the turn of the century, which go back very largely to Ritschl, were in their own way imposing phenomena worthy to be attacked as the main enemy by the dialectical theologians. A soft and impotent theology consisting only of skin and bone does not usually achieve such honor. The more I have studied Ritschl's theology the more it is clear to me that he found a word for his age, and that his theology is thrilling when it is heard in dialogue with the historical moment. In his doctrine of the moral person one may see a first attempt to wrestle with the mechanistic pull of the machine age and the depersonalizing trend of widespread philosophical evolutionism. It would be foolish to find in this testimony an appeal that we should apply this theological conception to our own time. A theology is ultimately responsible only to its own age.

Albrecht Ritschl was born in Berlin in 1822, the son of the later General Superintendent and Bishop of Pomerania, Karl Ritschl. He spent his student years in Bonn, Halle, and Heidelberg. He began his

---

2. K. Barth and E. Thurneysen, *Revolutionary Theology in the Making: Barth-Thurneysen Correspondence, 1914-1925* (Richmond, 1964), pp. 92-93.

academic work in Bonn. His main years as a professor were spent at Göttingen. The life-style of a professor at that time was very different from what it is today. If I am right, Ritschl only twice gave addresses outside his classroom or synods.

Ritschl's life flowed fairly evenly, mostly at his desk, where he wrote his large tomes. Yet he did not have so peaceful a time as Kant. He had to fight many theological and ecclesiastical battles. Like Lessing, he had his Pastor Goeze in the form of champions of orthodox or positive theology, who attacked him in many tractates and polemical writings, as well as at clergy conferences and synods. He was also a member of the Prussian Council and Consistory in Hanover, and notwithstanding many complaints, he was pleased that as a professor he thus had a hand in the church's activity and government. Twice he was Prorector of the University of Göttingen. He thus developed some social polish and gave a highly regarded address on the occasion of the 150th anniversary of the university. This address shows that he could be politically as well as ecclesiastically contentious, for in it he tries to prove how wrong ultramontanist historical critics are when they bring against the Reformation the objection that it is the mother of all later revolution and disintegration. His own thesis is that ultramontanist and conservative forces have a common root with liberalism and social democracy in the medieval outlook with its totalitarian tendencies (as we should put it today). The Reformation replaced this outlook, especially on his own understanding of the Reformation, which he obviously has in view, although he does not state it. He thus rejects the charge that the Reformation is responsible for every false development in recent times, and hoists the papists with their own petard.

From the force of this address we may see that Ritschl knew how to speak in public, commanding attention and stirring up feeling. He did not engage in emotional rhetoric but maintained the calm of academic argument. Yet he knew which nerve ends to touch. A theology which had political relevance could count on the response of its contemporaries. Thus he admitted to his disciple H. Scholz that if he did not want to be totally colorless he had to speak politically.[3] He was certainly not spineless or bloodless, as the dialectical theologians thought.

Ritschl always thought in terms of fronts. He was thus essentially political even in his theology. A first front was the rising mass society of the industrial age, which he perceived perhaps more clearly than any other theologian,[4] and against which he tried to strengthen the

3. August 22, 1887, in O. Ritschl, *A. Ritschls Leben,* 2 vols. (1892-1896), II, 495.
4. Except for Alexander von Oettingen, Harnack's other teacher. We may

threatened human personality with Christian means. Ritschl sensed the coming climate of collectivism even though he never to my knowledge used this term.

Two other fronts were Pietism and Roman Catholicism. He found Pietism alien because of its narrowness and otherworldliness. Roman Catholicism he viewed as medieval, and he disliked its ontological frame of thought. To him this was outmoded. He felt himself to be modern and post-Kantian. We can imagine with what delight he reacted to a Roman Catholic like von Döllinger, who displayed the kind of sublime confessional self-irony that one often finds in liberal Roman Catholic clergy. Döllinger supplied water for the mills with which Ritschl crushed the Middle Ages and every dogmatism. I cannot resist telling a little story which illustrates Döllinger's irony, and when taken up by Ritschl gives evidence of a sense of humor that is often contested.[5] The story goes that in a nunnery in Bologna whose abbess was the sister of Benedict XIV, the pope was celebrating high mass, and when the nuns kept on repeating *genitum non factum*, the pope found it too much, and turning to the altar, he interrupted the singing with the words: *Sive genitum, sive factum, pax vobiscum.* As Ritschl had a taste for this kind of amusing anecdote, so he liked social jollity. Thus he often invited the young people to dances in his house, and was amused by the taste for dancing shown by the son of a Pietist, who could satisfy at Ritschl's home a desire that he could not satisfy at that of his parents.[6] Ritschl also found pleasure in telling about the mistakes made by the lazy, the dull, and the scamps and rascallions at examinations.[7]

I have mentioned these rather more engaging features of Ritschl in order to counteract certain prejudices. Having discharged this task, I must now say a few things about his theological development, which was not without influence on his later system.

In his youth Ritschl was chiefly interested in history. He felt the impact of the school of the Hegelian F. C. Baur, and himself became a Hegelian. But he soon noted the strongly constructive element in Hegel's dialectical view of history. It seemed to him that history had here

---

see that Oettingen had an eye for social change in his work *Die Moralstatistik in ihrer Bedeutung für die Sozialethik,* 3rd ed. (1882); cf. H. Krimmer, *Empirie und Normativität. Die Moralstatistik A. von Oettingen,* diss. Hamburg (1973). Naturally, one might also mention Ritschl's younger contemporary A. Stoecker, for he took note of the development of the fourth estate. But his encounter with the new situation is on a different plane from that of Ritschl and von Oettingen.

5. Cf. the letter to Harnack on Aug. 29, 1881, in O. Ritschl, *Leben,* II, 375.
6. Ibid., II, 368.
7. Ibid., p. 449.

been planned in advance by thought. Naturally, this could happen only at the expense of hard, contingent facts which defy systematization. In his first great historical work, *Die Entstehung der altkatholischen Kirche* (2nd ed. 1857), a history of the early church, he definitely broke the spell of Hegel under which he had hitherto stood. In opposition to Hegel's intellectualism—his exclusive orientation to the abstract idea—he put the will, and the personality shaped by it, at the center of his thinking. A transition thus took place from Hegel to Kant, and this explains the ethicizing trend of his theology.

The influence of Kant throws light on two other aspects of his theological position. His recovery from the trauma of Hegel brought with it vehement opposition to any infusion of metaphysics into theology. In this respect he felt that Kant was a philosophical ally. The opposition brought with it an orientation to historical facts, especially in the field of the Bible. What gave him such an influence on his contemporaries, and lent to his theology the appearance of a word of liberation, was this. The theologians of his day were tired of philosophy. The Neo-Kantians and Neo-Hegelians had exhausted them. M. Kähler, who was himself no Ritschlian, movingly describes the situation.[8] The so-called positive theologians, oriented to the saving facts of the Bible, were deeply shaken by the rise of historico-critical research and either spent their strength in not very credible apologetical defensive skirmishing, or tried to suppress the new threat by "circling the wagons." Ritschl, however, seemed to open up a new approach to the biblical data, and especially to the central events of justification and reconciliation, an approach which critically tested their validity from the new historical standpoint, but which tried to get to the data themselves by way of the criticism, and which thus passed through the flame of critical research instead of turning aside from it in horror. Many theologically alert contemporaries heard a new note here. Ritschl formed a school.

Furthermore, Ritschl's Kantianism, along with his spiritual disposition, explains his aversion to Pietism. The dominant ethical accent of his theology makes the spiritual domination of the world, its permeation by the Christian spirit, the motto of his thought. Pietism seems to him to be a degenerate form of Christianity by reason of its hostility to culture and its esoteric conventicle-form. Similar reasons caused J. H. Wichern, who was very Pietistic in his piety, to struggle against Pietism because it had forgotten its mission to the world. August Tholuck,[9] the leading Pietist

8. M. Kähler, *Geschichte der protestantischen Dogmatik*, p. 246.
9. His most famous book, and a good example of Pietist theology, has the title *Die Lehre von der Sünde und vom Versöhner/oder die wahre Weihe des Zweiflers* (1823).

at Halle, had had a large following, but his students left him in droves, accepted the confessional theology, and forswore Pietism. Finally, for many semesters he left his empty lecture room and returned home.

At the same time Ritschl in his dry and factual style avoided any echo of Pietistic emotion or devout subjectivism. It was against his nature and against contemporary taste to find a place for these. He did not like "testimonies." Paul Gerhardt's chorale "O sacred head, now wounded," which is based on a Latin hymn, he rejected as alien and medieval. But this does not prevent him saying a verse from Gerhardt to himself on his deathbed. Time and again, especially in the case of Schleiermacher, we have noted elements in the personal religious life which cannot be reduced to theological reflection, but in which the Christian is more than the theologian. Here is perhaps one such element in Ritschl.

B. THE SYSTEM: AN ELLIPTICAL THEOLOGY

Bibliography. Primary Works: *Die christliche Lehre von der Rechtfertigung und der Versöhnung*, 3 vols. (1870ff., cited as *Rechtf.*), ET of vol. III: *The Christian Doctrine of Reconciliation and Justification* (repr. 1966); *Unterricht in der christlichen Religion*, 3rd ed. (1886), which was planned as a high-school primer but for reasons that are obvious today did not fill the bill, serving instead as a compendium for theological students; *Geschichte des Pietismus*, 3 vols. (1880ff.); *Theologie und Metaphysik*, 2nd ed. (1887); *Fides implicita* (published posthumously, 1890).
Secondary Works: G. Ecke, *Die theologische Schule A. Ritschl und die Kirche der Gegenwart* (1897); H. R. Frank, *Zur Theologie A. Ritschls*, 3rd ed. (1891); G. Hök, *Die elliptische Theologie A. Ritschls* (1942); M. Kähler, *Geschichte der protestantischen Theologie im 19.Jahrhunderte* (1962 ed.); F. Kattenbusch, *Von Schleiermacher zu Ritschl* (1892); O. Ritschl, *A. Ritschls Leben*, 2 vols. (1892-1896, cited as *Leben*); H. O. Wölber, *Dogma und Ethos* (1950); P. Wrzecionko, *Die philosophischen Wurzeln der Theologie A. Ritschls* (1964), with special reference here to Kant and Lotze; M. Kähler, *Dogmatische Zeitfragen*, II (1898), esp. pp. 1-38.

Goethe once said that what even the great want to say can be stated in very few words. His point is that each of us has one thesis which is simply expressed in many different forms. I will begin by trying to say what this thesis of Ritschl is.

It amounts to this. Human personhood can be safeguarded and protected against the pull of depersonalizing materialism only if, following the Reformation, we make the unconditionality of the conscience our basis, make personhood possible by union with Christ, support it by membership in the community, and in this way develop impulses so as finally to achieve a human order controlled by the laws of virtue.[10]

This attempt to formulate Ritschl's basic thesis makes it apparent at once that he is treading a line that runs, or seems to run, between Luther and Kant. The strictness with which Kant maintained the obligatoriness of the law and the clarity with which he displayed its moral character on the basis of freedom show that he did not merely transcend the principles of the Enlightenment but also renewed the moral outlook of the Reformation.[11] This does not mean, however, that Ritschl adopted a purely receptive and uncritical attitude toward Kant. He bemoans the fact that Kant found a pointless struggle between the impress of the religious ideas of Christianity and the claim of morality to unconditional autonomy, even though this does not spring from any lack of faith on his part, but from the overhasty dogmatizing of the critical principles of his moral teaching.[12] Ritschl is indicating here that he means to overcome this unresolved tension in Kant's thought by means of theological reflection.

The very terms used here (e.g., "moral outlook of the Reformation") show how far Ritschl's modern thinking really is from the Reformation. But this should not prevent us from fixing on the point of departure where Luther and Kant seem to intersect. On this view Luther is characterized by the fact that he refused to let conscience be represented by the institutional authority of the church. On the basis of his principle of faith alone he saw us in our immediacy to God and therefore conferred adulthood on us. In Ritschl's view, then, he already freed us for autonomy, at least to the extent of removing from us the heteronomy of ecclesiastical authority.

Along these lines Ritschl's school comes to see in both Luther and Kant the champions of the modern age and to see in itself the theological representative of the modern spirit that also takes up the Christian tradition. This is certainly not to be regarded as a tactically meant assimilation to contemporaries. Ritschl seriously adopts the post-Reformation and post-Kantian plane on which he lives and thinks, and he seeks to reunite it with a critically *purified* Christian tradition.

We can understand the unheard-of effects of Ritschl's thinking in the 19th century only if we catch the underlying ardent and even

10. In this regard cf. A. Stoecker, and in Holland A. Kuyper (cf. *ThE*, II, 2, §§ 4234ff.; ET II, 598ff.) for similar tendencies.

11. *Rechtf.*, I, 431.

12. Ibid., p. 459.

triumphant mood. The aim is to build a completely new style of Christian chapel on the landscape of a totally changed modern world. The purpose is not to restore. It is not to go back to what our predecessors believed. New elements of the faith are to be brought to light which can be integrated into the grid of changed values and which will suit the critical sobriety threatened by materialism. Freethinkers and liberals and monists and salon intellectuals may be shocked that to a large extent there is agreement with them in attacking the dark Middle Ages, the ossifications of dogmatic history, and the metaphysical superstition of the church. Ritschl himself shares with Schleiermacher the fervent desire to be modern, to be contemporary, and therefore to open up access to the Christian tradition for his own age.

We shall first look at the theological effect of Ritschl's concern to stress the autonomous and self-responsible individual. Two points call for notice.

First, Ritschl maintains that religion assists our moral nature by helping us to achieve inner independence of the two dimensions of nature and society, and not to be absorbed by either. All religion is an interpretation of the struggle known to some extent by us all in the sense that the superior spiritual forces (or force) that are in or over it maintain or protect for the personal spirit its claims or independence against the obstacles of nature or of the natural operations of human society.[13] Thus the knowledge of God is demonstrable as religious knowledge only when God is thought of in connection with the fact that he guarantees for believers the position in the world which overcomes the obstacles it poses, so that they can no longer be reabsorbed by it.[14]

This means that the concept of God is given a radically different place from that given it by metaphysics—including Scholastic metaphysics—with its proofs of God. For this, God is simply a synonym for the religiously neutral concept of world unity, so that personality (that of God as well as ours) is brought within this unity instead of differentiated from it.[15] That which as world threatens my independence may be either nature or society. Ritschl obviously thinks that both of them, along with natural causality, might swallow us up. He presumably has in mind what we today would call their "autonomy."

Second, our moral independence is seen from the further standpoint that we cannot be derived genetically from the world nexus.

13. Ibid., III, 17; ET *Christian Doctrine of Justification and Reconciliation,* p. 17.
14. *Rechtf.,* III, 198.
15. Ibid., p. 17.

Christianity has no place when the sphere of our spiritual life and social action is not set over against a general explanation of the world but thought of in terms of the general grounds on which the world is explained. To include ethics within the concept of the cosmos is the mark of a pagan outlook. The moral privilege of the human person thus depends on its participation in the kingdom of God, which cannot be derived from a genetic explanation of the world. It consists of the dominion over the world that is given thereby.[16]

What Ritschl calls a pagan outlook (i.e., deriving humanity from a genetic explanation of the world), we nowadays, since Bultmann, usually call a mark of the mythical. On this level F. Gogarten opposes to mythical thinking the Christian understanding of our historicity, historicity being precisely what Ritschl means when he speaks about the antithesis between the moral person and the world. The mythical world is, for Gogarten, the world as it and the forces that sustain it are honored as divine, and as we derive our existence from it, and make it secure by piously adjusting to its order. In calling us children and heirs (Gal. 4:1-7), Paul takes us out of this mythical integration into the world and calls us to independent historical existence.[17]

A new problem thus arises in Ritschl. If we overlook this, as Barth and the dialectical theologians do, we cannot do justice to him. What is this new element?

The struggle with modern secularism had essentially taken place thus far on the field of history. We need only recall the problem of certainty in Lessing, and especially his complaint that the accidental truths of history in the biblical tradition can never achieve the same degree of certainty as the necessary truths of reason. In Ritschl, however, the main point is the threat to personal existence, the threat that comes from nature and society.

Nature played some part in the Enlightenment, but almost solely from the standpoint that as a world of things, which can be investigated and which makes strictly logical statements possible, it stands opposed to the airiness of all supranatural speculation. Ritschl, however, raises a very different problem concerning nature. He reflects upon it inasmuch as attempts are made to deduce humanity from it, to conceive of humanity in terms of nature's genesis. We have to consider what creative impulses toward debate with the current anthropology deriving from Darwin are involved in this approach of Ritschl's. Without (to my knowledge) making these inferences, one

16. Ibid., pp. 24-25.
17. F. Gogarten, "Theologie und Geschichte," *ZThK* 3 (1953) 348-49.

might say that his denial of a genetic derivation for us puts at his disposal the decisive argument in this debate. He implicitly rejected the pitifully dilettante attempts to evade the threat of Darwin by opposing the evolutionary theory itself and rejoicing at every gap in the transition from animals to us.[18]

With Ritschl's rejection of a genetic derivation for us, we find a similar rejection of derivation from the social situation or our reduction to purely social beings. Such a derivation would mean for Ritschl the misunderstanding of society as nature and natural effects. We must again consider the implications of this rejection. Here is the most serious argument against a Marxist anthropology even though Ritschl himself does not look in this particular direction. In the Göttingen of his day this was not a real problem! We must also bear in mind that here is a prophylactic thought—it might be used against some modern theories of the environment—which the church soon forgot to its hurt, and the ignoring of which meant that there was hardly any theological wrestling with the then materialistically aligned social democracy. At least potentially Ritschl opened the door to such discussion and indicated the direction in which it might go.

The basic outline of Ritschl's system is simple, perhaps too simple. He does not depict it, in Reformation fashion, as a circle whose center is justification but as an ellipse with two main points, justification and reconciliation (or divine sonship) on the one side, and the kingdom of God on the other. He was convinced that divine sonship, or freedom from and above the world, must be a leading theme in dogmatics, as must also the idea of the kingdom of God. These were the main goals of Christianity in the context of practical religion and morality. But unfortunately neither traditional dogmatics nor the Reformation confessions had linked them. The idea of the kingdom of God, which he added to the Protestant tradition, did not suffice alone, for all that it expresses is that Christianity is morality. The fact that it is also religion can be maintained only by the other idea (divine sonship). This is the essence of what Ritschl had to offer, and he is concerned that people should hear it and take it to heart.[19]

We now turn to the two points of the ellipse.

18. W. Elert gives vivid and ironical examples of this futile apologetic in a book which is now unfortunately forgotten, *Der Kampf um das Christentum* . . . (1921), pp. 231ff. Although he deals with Ritschl, I found in him no reference to the way that Ritschl went beyond this apologetic.

19. Cf. the letter to his friend L. Diestel dated 3.20.1873; *Leben*, p. 148.

1. The Kingdom of God

The kingdom is not for Ritschl eschatologically transcendent. It is moral. This may be seen from the fact that he takes over the similar concept in Kant and as it were Christianizes it. He does not borrow uncritically from Kant. He objects that the way in which Kant gives to religion the quality of a mere appendix or postulate within practical reason is defective from the very outset.[20] He himself has a very different view of the role of religion when he links it with ethics. Yet he starts with Kant's idea of the kingdom of God and quotes Kant's formulation that the kingdom is a uniting of humanity by the laws of virtue.[21] He Christianizes this definition in two ways.

First, he concentrates the laws of virtue, plural in Kant, into the one law of love. Jesus himself understood by the kingdom the organization of humanity by action whose motive is love.[22]

Second, he correspondingly views Christianity as a center or reservoir of power which sends powerful impulses of this law of virtue into society. He thus arrives at the definition that Christianity is the monotheistic, complete, spiritual, and moral religion which on the basis of the saving life of its Founder, the foundation of the kingdom of God, consists of the freedom of divine sonship, includes the impulse to act in love, is oriented to the moral organization of humanity, and establishes happiness as the basis of fellowship with God and the kingdom of God.[23]

We see here that Ritschl, like Kant, very closely relates religion and ethics, but, unlike Kant, he takes away from religion its secondary character as a kind of appendix and puts it in first place. For his definition begins with the divine sonship that is established by Christ and that brings all else with it. The impulse to act in love follows upon divine sonship, and this in turn is oriented to the moral organization of humanity. Happiness or beatitude is achieved with the coming together of the initiatory beginning (fellowship with God and divine sonship) and the resultant end, the kingdom of God. It seems to me that Ritschl has in view a new kind of Christian version of Kant's supreme good.

Nevertheless, we cannot avoid the question whether Ritschl is really putting the spiritual (or religious) event of divine sonship in first place. Might it not be that he understands the initiation in divine sonship in such a way that the organization of humanity, the kingdom of God, is the true goal or final end of a development for which divine sonship

20. *Rechtf.*, I, 445.
21. Ibid., I, 444; III, 11.
22. Ibid., III, 12.
23. Ibid., pp. 13-14.

is only the necessary beginning? Is the moral conclusion the true goal and religion merely the means or sine qua non for reaching it? If so, what is the real point of putting religion first? Is it *really* a sign of its primacy and hence of a reversal of Kant? We shall keep this question in mind in our further deliberations.

Another question—and a more obviously rhetorical one—arises at this point. Does Ritschl's concept of the kingdom really have anything at all to do with the eschatology of the NT? Does Ritschl's kingdom transcend history? Is it a *coming* kingdom? Does it break in upon us from above? Or is it the climax of history—a climax which God's saving work initiates but which we bring about with the freedom that this work gives us? Is there not something here that is very like what we find in secularism, e.g., in Marxist eschatology with its classless society, in which the historical future is a substitute for transcendence? If so, Ritschl's theology is open to the suspicion that it is on the same secular level and does not transcend this level. And then we do not merely have accommodation to the questions of the age but the open assimilation of Christian theology to the form of the world (cf. Rom. 12:2), and with it a surrender of one of the basic elements of NT eschatology.

If in Ritschl the *eschaton* does not transcend history but is regarded as its immanent goal, we may assume that Ritschl has hardly any understanding of the *proton* which corresponds symmetrically to the *eschaton*. In his scheme of thought there is no place for the relation between creation and the fall. His idea of moral personality forces him to throw out the concept of original sin, because the traditional doctrine is untrue to his own theological point, namely, our dominion over the world, our nonderivability from its nexus. He criticizes Augustine for deriving inherited sin from the natural link between children and their sinful parents.[24] This integration into a natural nexus is precisely that which gives an extreme shock to Ritschl's Kantian spirit (as it had shocked Kant, as we saw). For this reason Augustine can supposedly find in his teaching only an argument for human *weakness*, not for human *guilt*.[25]

Ritschl realizes very well that evil is not restricted to the self-responsible act of the individual but has also its suprapersonal side. He wants to find for this side, which is at least found in the doctrine of original sin, a place in his own system. But how?

He interprets this suprapersonal aspect of evil and sin with the help of a concept which corresponds exactly to the kingdom of God on

24. Ibid., p. 316.
25. Ibid.

the negative side. He speaks about a kingdom of sin.[26] The kingdom of sin is a substitute for the theory of original sin which clearly validates all that the concept of original sin rightly intended, though it fatefully perverted it by mixing in alien elements.[27] What it rightly intended is the suprapersonal dimension of evil.

Obviously borrowing from Kant, Ritschl finds this suprapersonal element in a *social* phenomenon to which we are subject. He begins with Kant's idea of an evil "inclination," which we best understand if we use the Scholastic term *habit* (Latin *habitus*). This inclination is imputed to the moral person as its own act. The rooting of the person in the social nexus means that the evil present in individuals accumulates by reciprocal stimulation, and as a result sin acquires the effect of a law which it does not have in and of itself.[28] It does not have this because this inclination, which becomes collective and surrounds us like the atmosphere, does not have its basis in the divine government of the world or our human disposition for freedom. Hence this suprapersonal evil in the kingdom of evil has neither an originally theological nor an originally ethical basis. It arises, as we would say today, through a sociological law from outside, through the immeasurable interaction of sinful deeds which unites all of us.[29] There thus comes a reciprocal rise or crescendo of evil. But whether we think of the individual sin that is most clearly seen in responsible decision or of the collective social infection that is the sum of human decisions and hence is still our responsibility, in every form sin is the opposite of the good and it runs contrary to the recognizable moral goal of the world.[30]

We can hardly avoid seeing in this understanding of original sin a revolutionary modification of the content of the doctrine, although Ritschl is trying to establish this content and to free it from dregs that distort its meaning. In the Christian tradition original sin is not traced back to the sociological law of accumulation as in Ritschl's kingdom of sin. It means that God's rejection is never addressed to us as the first rebels. The rebellion has already taken place; the fall is behind us. The history of the fall has been going on a long time when we come on the scene. Ritschl fears—and because of this fear he has a blind spot—that this view of sin thinks that we derive from a genetic natural nexus, a corrupt nexus, so that *guilt* is changed into *fate*, we are thus relieved of

26. Ibid., pp. 304ff., 326ff.
27. Ibid., p. 320.
28. Ibid., p. 325.
29. Ibid., p. 357.
30. Ibid., p. 353.

responsibility for it, and original sin can no longer be imputed to us. His main objection to the traditional view is that when we understand the suprapersonal side in this way it takes away personal responsibility.

In answer we might turn to Luther's arguments in *The Bondage of the Will* in which he tries to show that even a will that is in bondage (and not just a will that sees itself as free and autonomous) has to accept responsibility for its rebellion. Luther distinguishes between *coercion* and *necessity*. If I am forced into sin by outside coercion, e.g., by the natural causality of birth, then this sin cannot be imputed to me. I am merely the effect of the process of transmission and am not responsible. But for Luther there is also an inner necessity of my human nature to which I have to say "I" and in face of which I cannot speak of an "It" that comes upon me from without.[31] I myself, then, am the subject of this necessity, and I will and do as I am.[32]

Nevertheless, even if the doctrine of the kingdom of sin cannot be a legitimate form of the doctrine of original sin, Ritschl's reference to the possibility of a social accumulation of evil does have its point. We find an impressive example in Georges Bernanos's observation in *The Diary of a Country Priest* that "the seed of evil as well as good drifts everywhere. . . . Our hidden failings poison the air that others breathe, and a fault whose core one poor person unsuspectingly bears within will never ripen into fruit without having this destructive influence."[33]

In the sociological reinterpretation of the doctrine of original sin we find a tendency that may be seen elsewhere in Ritschl. He tries to plant all theological concepts in the soil of anthropology. Hence Kant's concept of God (on the margin of ethics) has unintentionally left its mark on him. The doctrine of the wrath of God is an example.

In Christian tradition God's wrath is his reaction to sin. Ritschl cannot think that there are emotional elements in God which are outside the human sphere. He regards God as the epitome of love, the good God. As in Abelard, this love of God is a suprapolar principle of indifference which embraces contradiction.[34] Thus the idea of a wrathful God has no value for Christians; it is a theologoumenon with neither home nor form.[35]

31. Clemen, III, 125, 23ff. (*Bondage of the Will*; cf. *ThE*, I, § 1438; ET I, 62).
32. WA, 18, 709. The terms *coactio* and *necessitas* occur sometimes in the Roman Catholic doctrine of merit; see Denzinger, 2003.
33. George Bernanos, *The Diary of a Country Priest* (New York, repr. 1989), p. 195.
34. On Ritschl and Abelard cf. *Rechtf.*, III, 345. Ritschl also approves of post-Schleiermacherian theologians who espouse an Abelardian type of theology, e.g., A. Schweizer; cf. *Rechtf.*, I, 554, 559. See Kähler, *Dogmatische Zeitfragen*, II, 32, 35.
35. *Rechtf.*, II, 154.

Yet once again Ritschl does not simply eliminate the traditional theologoumenon. He tries to keep one aspect of its meaning by planting it in the soil of anthropology. The wrath of God is a mythicizing expression, projected on God, for our sense of distance from God, for the horror of that distance which sin has triggered in us.[36] God does not hide from us or reject us. Metaphorically, it is rather that in our earthly atmosphere the effects of sin bring clouds over the sun and hide it. When we have fallen into sin we can no longer see the sun of the divine love. We are filled with mistrust. We think that God has wrathfully hidden himself from us. In truth, it is we ourselves who have hidden ourselves from him.

After these remarks on the negative factor of sin, we must now ask about the overcoming of sin, i.e., about justification and reconciliation. This brings us to the second point of the ellipse.

2. Divine Sonship (Justification and Reconciliation)

Although, following Kant, Ritschl continues to anthropologize theology, he does more than continue Kant's work with theological means. In his introduction to volume III of *Justification and Reconciliation,* without expressly mentioning Kant, he shows how he goes beyond his master in two ways.

First, he differs from Kant by putting the Christian community rather than the moral I of the individual at the center.[37] He does this because he wants his theology to be christocentric and because it is by the community that I experience its possession of forgiveness by Christ's work, and therefore Christ himself. I learn about Christ through proclamation, and therefore through the community. "Authentic and complete knowledge of Jesus' religious significance . . . depends, then, on one's reckoning oneself part of the community which He founded, and this precisely in so far as it believes itself to have received the forgiveness of sins as His peculiar gift."

Second, Christ is radically other than a purely ethical entity, than a mere author of new legislation or promoter of the ideal of humanity. He is more than an example that we are to imitate. He prevents imitation by *confronting* his disciples as the author of forgiveness, not as a model. We must first appropriate the forgiveness that he offers if we are to undertake to imitate his religion and his moral achievement.

Although ethical tendencies may be seen here, these are some

36. Ibid., II, 21, 148ff.
37. For this and the following quotation, see ibid., III, 1ff.; ET p. 2.

new notes compared to Kant. We catch in them a remote echo of the Lutheran doctrine of law and gospel.

In sum, we might say that God may be known only in Christ and that we learn about Christ only when we are addressed within the community of the forgiveness that he won. "If we can know God aright only when we know him through Christ, we can also know him only when we put ourselves in the community of believers." In such contexts there may even be some central Reformation statements about forgiveness which go much beyond the moral understanding that is present elsewhere in Ritschl. Sin, he can say, "can be appreciated only in virtue of the forgiveness of sins which is Christ's special gift."[38]

What does Ritschl mean by forgiveness? In Luther's sense forgiveness might be described only as a change in God. The God of the gospel overcomes the author of the law, so that there is in him the Nevertheless of a turning to fallen humanity. God for Luther is not just the dear Lord whose attitude to us is one of timeless benevolence. Forgiveness is rather an act of God, or, put somewhat anthropomorphically, God's overcoming of himself, the victory of his grace over his holiness.

This transcendent history in God is something that Ritschl cannot discuss because it contradicts his reduction of theology to the dimension of human existence. In forgiveness there is no change in God but a change in us (cf. Abelard again). God's turning to us, forgivingly, sees to it that the mistrust disappears from our hearts which as an emotion of guilt naturally separates the offender from the offended. Thus God reopens the broken fellowship and stands by the saving goal which he has in view "for higher reasons."[39]

The anthropologizing of theology may be seen here in the fact that it is not God who suffers from the breach of fellowship with us; the exclusive concern is the healing of the sense of guilt in us. Forgiveness means that we are given the chance of returning from mistrust and hostility against God to a fellowship of trust and peace.[40]

We come up against a peculiar tension in Ritschl's thinking, however, which prevents complete anthropologizing and leaves his theology open. (Critics who overlook this openness are guilty of unfair simplification.) For although Ritschl can conceive of no history with God, no resolve or emotion on his part, although (like Abelard) he puts all history on the human level, nevertheless he still thinks in terms of an

38. *Rechtf.*, III, 7.
39. Ibid., p. 60.
40. Ibid., p. 495.

act of God to the extent that it is God who sets aside our mistrust. It is also an act of God, a creative act of his will, when he justifies us and sets us in fellowship with himself.[41] The judgment expressed in justification is creative because God does not receive people who are already ontically righteous[42] and declare them to be righteous; he receives and justifies sinners. The judgment is not analytical (one of identity) but synthetic (one of extension).[43] At this point Kant's terminology penetrates deep into the heart of Ritschl's doctrine of justification.

This creative side of justification shows and implies that Ritschl repudiates the understanding of God as an *idea* and instead speaks of God under the sign of personal will. God is an active God in Ritschl's thought. This is why we do not find in him an immanent or closed system. His system is open even if the opening is only an emergency exit and it is hard to say where it leads, whether to the regeneration of a transcendent view of God and an overcoming of the anthropologizing, or to Feuerbach, who can see in an active and personal God only the projected alter ego of an active and personal human being.

The anthropologizing thrust is clearer in the second concept that is a theme in Ritschl's Christian doctrine, namely, reconciliation. This has a greater range and distinctness than justification or forgiveness. Justification is simply God's declaration that he is kind and gracious to sinners. It gives them the chance to respond. In contrast, the term *reconciliation* means that those who are pardoned and respond set aside their passivity, orient themselves to God, enter into his purpose, and in this way reciprocate God's action.[44]

The anthropologizing element that we sense here is that we ourselves let ourselves be reconciled to God by abandoning our mistrust and reservations. Obviously, it has always been one aspect of the event of reconciliation that there is this reaction or response on the human level. In Paul's view, however, this is significantly only the second act in a process in which God lets himself be reconciled and his wrath turns into favor (2 Cor. 5:18-19). Here reconciliation is a miracle that none can postulate. It is an act of God in which the gospel breaks through the schema of law. For this turn in our history with God, as we have seen, Ritschl can find no theological place. In him God does not overcome himself in love (so that forgiveness costs him something, we are bought with a price, he spends himself for us). For Ritschl God is the personified

41. Ibid., pp. 20, 22, esp. pp. 103, 112.
42. He accuses the Pietists and Thomists of holding this view of God.
43. Ibid., pp. 76, 102.
44. Ibid., pp. 74-75.

state of a suprapolar principle of love. The only act is that he declares himself to be the dear Lord and thus accomplishes, not an ontic change in himself but a noetic change in us. For Paul the imperative "Be reconciled to God" is a consequence of God's new turning. For Ritschl, however, it is the totality of reconciliation. We do not have an actual turning of God but a permanent state of God's turning to us which we can know and to which our trust can actively respond. We ourselves restore divine-human symmetry by believing.

Naturally, this affects Ritschl's Christology. Christ cannot be an aeonic change or act of God in actualization of love. He can be only the one who reveals a constant love, who draws our attention to it, who teaches us about it.[45] Yet Ritschl sees in him something qualitatively different from what the Enlightenment meant when it called him a teacher and lawgiver. Teachers make themselves superfluous when their students appropriate for themselves what they are trying to contribute. For Ritschl, however, Christ is the abiding center of the Christian religion and differs fundamentally from other founders like Zoroaster or Moses.[46]

What is the lasting and definitive element? Why is Christ more for his followers than the temporary occasion of their religion and legislator for their conduct?[47] The simple answer is that Jesus undoubtedly experiences, and attests to his disciples, a new relationship with God.[48] One might say, then, that Christ is the perfect Revealer of God because like none other he stands in an immediate, face-to-face relation to God.

This side of Christ's significance relates to the point of the ellipse that is called divine sonship. Christ in his immediacy tells us that God is our Father and that we are his children. In so doing he changes us from mistrustful children troubled by a bad conscience into reconciled and trusting children. This is his function as Revealer.

Again—and this brings us to the other point of the ellipse— Christ is a model of spiritual lordship over the world, so that this can then be experienced by the members of his community.[49] In both his immediacy to God and his lordship over the world Christ is an example and model for his community.

The two qualities of Christ as perfect Revealer and open model of lordship over the world come together for Ritschl in the predicate of

45. Ibid., pp. 358ff.
46. Ibid.
47. Ibid., p. 359.
48. Ibid.
49. Ibid., p. 360.

deity. A supreme, definitive, and uniquely privileged relationship with God may be seen at the two points of the ellipse.[50]

Obviously, Ritschl has great difficulty in bringing the passion of Christ and the event at Golgotha into this schema. That he should reject Anselm's interpretation follows from his closeness to Abelard. There can be for him no question of sacrifice or self-giving on the part of the Crucified to bridge the abyss between God and us, for there is no abyss on God's side, there is only an apparent abyss on ours, due to our mistrust, and we simply need to be cured of our illusion by experiencing through the Revealer the inalterable kindness of God. Hence Christ does not *do* anything by his passion (there is nothing to do). In good Abelardian fashion, he simply *demonstrates* something.

What does he demonstrate? For one thing he displays a constant love which is not deceived by the fact that those he wills to save reject it. This love shows itself to be such by surviving all possible resistance, never being a mere echo, and remaining the same through every form of repudiation.[51] Again, Christ's readiness to suffer, and his patient bearing of death, prove in spite of all opposition that he is faithful to his calling in the service of the moral dominion of God and the actualizing of the kingdom of God.[52]

Like his figure as a whole, Christ's suffering is thus an example and a pointer. In his being, teaching, and conduct, he is the model and prototype of a relationship with God which should constantly compel his people to imitate him.[53]

C. CONCLUDING EVALUATION

We thus leave Ritschl with an impression of ambivalence. On the one hand he points to the future and is "modern" in his own hour. In face of the developing industrial age and the corresponding mass society, in face of the economic and social autonomies whose profile was becoming increasingly sharper, he represented the independence and apartness of the moral person. As a thematic task of theology, the way that the Christian religion strengthens this personhood—dubious though it may be—shows that theology has to take up a position vis-à-vis the problems that are raised by the new global constellation.

50. Ibid., p. 361.
51. Ibid., p. 420.
52. Ibid., pp. 447, 420.
53. Ibid., p. 360.

Nevertheless, Ritschl's system is a grandiose attempt to integrate revelation into a given thought-schema, i.e., Kant's anthropology, and we have seen that this involves wrenchings, reinterpretations, and reductions. Notwithstanding the stress on the significance of the person, can we really speak of a personal God in Ritschl?[54] Has not God become simply a timeless idea of love? If God's own aim—to be love—is identical with his concern that humanity should be an end in itself, does not this mean that God himself is no more than the means to an end, namely, that humanity should be an end in itself?[55] Does not this make religion merely a way of bolstering morality? Could not Ritschl define the kingdom of God (organizing humanity by action in love) without mentioning God (although secondarily God does take on a certain importance as a paradigm of love)?

Nevertheless! The above question marks do not denote purely rhetorical questions. The questions are real ones, open ones.

If Christ were merely an instrument to aid morality, then he ought to make himself superfluous when his Socratic aid has released personhood and achieved lordship over the world. But Ritschl repudiates any ascribing to Christ of no more than interim significance. He does so decisively. There is for him no time when Christ will be relegated to the past and we may look for another. Christ is for him definitive and once-for-all. At most we can only ask whether his theological constructions are adequate to establish this "once-for-all." But how are we finally to evaluate a theology, by its goal and intention or by the means of thought with whose help it tries to find its way there? Do we not have to say finally of theology, as a work that is made up of many acts of human thought, that it is justified only by its orientation? (It is to Christ that we look.)[56]

Thus Christ might have been more for Ritschl than his thought-schema on its own permits. (I have already pointed out that he read to himself a verse from Gerhardt's hymn on his deathbed.) As in the case of other theologians we should not forget that there are extra elements which show that the Christianity transcends the theology. We see this in Ritschl not merely in lack of congruity between the reflective Christology and the nonreflective faith but above all in the role that the community plays in his thinking. Because he thinks as a theologian within the communion of saints, he lives in communication with its Christianity

---

54. Ritschl does in fact lay great stress on the personality of God; see *Rechtf.*, III, § 30.

55. Cf. Kähler, *Geschichte der protestantischen Dogmatik*, p. 259.

56. Cf. the hymn: "O sacred head, now wounded."

and tradition, not as a monad, so that his theology stands always under correction by it. A theologian of this type is always a hearing person who in principle is open to revision. This is true of Ritschl because he questions all the philosophical presuppositions of his thought, and is able to remold them, by seeing that truth may be known only when those who know *are* in the truth, and therefore when the union of Christians with Christ—and not just a general humanitarianism—is the presupposition of all theological thinking.

A theology lives by this extra element. This is what makes it vital, always pointing beyond itself and ready to receive impulses which press it forward. This extra element is always handed down. By it even the authors of dubious theologies (and what theology is *not* dubious?) remain in the communion of saints as fathers of faith and as partners in dialogue with those who come after them.

In other words, this is how it is that there is no purely past theology which has nothing more to say to later generations. Whatever deserves the name of theology has never been taken over by the spirits of its own age but always lives by the Lord who for his part has led the spirits captive (Col. 2:15) and is immediate to every age. Theology is bound to this Lord by that which does not fit into any schema, by the extra element which may perhaps seem to be inconsistent from the standpoint of the immanence of the system. Often the inconsistent element may be the genuinely kerygmatic element (like the definitiveness of Christ in Ritschl, which hardly has an adequate basis in reflection). Will not Christ continually rise up again out of the conceptual tombs of systems instead of sharing their corruptibility?

II. WILHELM HERRMANN

Bibliography. Primary Works: *Die Religion im Verhältnis zum Welterkennen und zur Sittlichkeit* (1879); *Der Verkehr des Christen mit Gott* (1886, cited as *Verkehr*), ET *Communion with God* (1906); *Ethik* (1901); *Gesammelte Aufsätze,* ed. F. W. Schmidt (1923, cited as *Aufsätze*); *Dogmatik,* ed. M. Rade (1925), ET *Systematic Theology* (1927).
Secondary Works: H. B. Asseburg, *Das Gebet in der neueren anthropologischen orientierten Theologie,* Diss. Hamburg (1921), esp. pp. 85ff.; K. Barth, "The Principles of Dogmatics according to Wilhelm Herrmann," in *Theology and Church* (New York, 1962), pp. 238-71; M. Beintker, *Die Gottesfrage in der Theologie W. Herrmanns* (1976); cf. pp. 120ff. on Herrmann as the teacher of Barth and Bultmann;

R. Bultmann, "Zur Frage der Christologie," *Faith and Understanding* (1969), pp. 116ff., esp. pp. 132ff. P. Fischer-Appelt, *Metaphysik im Horizont der Theologie W. Herrmanns*. Forschungen zur Geschichte und Lehre des Protestantismus, 10, XXXII (1965), 215ff.; idem, "Zum Verständnis des Glaubens in der liberalischen und dialektischen Theologie," in *Freispruch und Freiheit*, ed. H. G. Geyer (1973), pp. 68ff.; E. Fuchs, *Hermeneutik* (1954), pp. 27ff.; F. Gogarten, "Theologie und Geschichte," *ZThK* (1953) 339ff.; H. Grass, *Ostergeschehen und Osterberichte* (1956), pp. 268ff.; G. Koch, *Die Auferstehung Jesu Christi* (1959), pp. 90ff.; T. Mahlmann, *Das Axiom des Erlebnisses bei Wilhelm Herrmann*, Diss. Münster (1962); H. J. Rothert, *Gewissheit und Vergewisserung* (1963).

A. BIOGRAPHY

Herrmann was born in 1846 and died in 1922. He was first influenced by Halle Pietism, then belonged to the Ritschl school. His ethics were essentially shaped by Kant. More decidedly than Ritschl he was often at odds with historico-critical biblical research. Especially in Christology he sought a new possibility of unconditional certainty. From 1879 he was a professor at Marburg. Here he gathered a large and influential body of disciples, who were impressed by his penetrating thought, his passionate search for certainty, and his warmhearted piety. Barth and Bultmann were the most outstanding of his critical but always grateful students.[57]

B. THE STARTING POINT: THE DISTINCTION BETWEEN GROUND OF FAITH AND THOUGHTS OF FAITH

As the red thread that runs through the history of modern theology, I have mentioned the double theme of inquiry into the hitherto self-evidently accepted contents of tradition on the basis of the newly discovered autonomy of the religious and moral subject, and the question whether and how far such contents can be adopted afresh within the new criteria. We find the same persistent questions in W. Herrmann.

His vital question is how we may find certainty of faith now that our new understanding of the world and the self has blocked various

57. Cf. Barth, "Klärung und Wirkung," in *Zur Vorgeschichte der KD und zum Kirchenkampf*, ed. W. Feurich (1966), pp. 240ff.

routes to such certainty, so that we cannot simply accept traditional Christian statements.

What are the obstacles?

(1) As a post-Kantian theologian, Herrmann realizes that the metaphysics of a religious outlook that goes beyond the horizon of our experience can offer no support. It moves on a different level. Herrmann is not just opposed, like Kant, to the insubstantiality of any such metaphysics. He has another objection to its unsuitability.[58] Religious reality cannot be reached on the plane of the objective discovery of reality which points to a union of being and event that is free of all contradiction. Inquiry that seeks such objectification leaves no place for the involvement of the will. But it is the will that religious reality claims by setting final goals for it. The apparent problems of a religious outlook that are contained in objectifying thought about the cosmic nexus, namely, that God does not seem to have a place in this nexus, do not really touch the nerve of this outlook. This outlook is dealing with the will and the nonobjectifiable person. At this point we catch the voice of Ritschl.

(2) A further challenge to the Christian view of truth arises out of the dignity of the moral person as Kant expounded it. Enlightenment humanism had already seen that this dignity is mortally threatened if faith violates the unity in the spiritual life of the Christian,[59] if the situation is reached (cf. Lessing's dictum) that a person is a pagan in the head and a believer in the heart. In modern terms, this means no less than the forfeiture of personal identity and is thus an attack on the person. If we ask about the unity of the world and the implicated unity of the person in such a way as to seek this unity in an objectively demonstrable relation, the religious outlook cannot be included. For what it has in view cannot be grasped objectively. It thus leads to that fateful split of consciousness.

The position is different when we seek the source of unity in the subjective sphere, in the life of a concrete person as this is shaped by the contemplation of a supreme good. Being finds unity in this final goal. Only this schema offers the presupposition on which the question of cosmic unity makes sense. Since for the concrete person the final end lies in the absolute and unconditional moral ideal which displays its universal validity to all of us, and since the Christian revelation stands in an inner relation to this ideal, there is no more place for the dreaded split between the Christian religion and the understanding of the world.[60]

(3) For Herrmann the worst threat to Christian certainty comes

58. *Die Metaphysik in der Theologie* (1876), p. 8.
59. *Die Religion im Verhältnis . . .* , p. 246.
60. Ibid., p. 246.

from history. In history, i.e., in the Bible and the church's tradition, we find the event of salvation on which the Christian faith rests. But how can conditional historical certainty be the basis of the unconditional certainty of faith? How can the absolute rest on relative foundations? Herrmann is threatened by the same attack as Lessing. It is posed by the fact that the truths of history are contingent. He, too, sees the broad and ugly ditch between what was and what is.

Modern critical research makes the problem worse for Herrmann. This research engages in constant subtraction (Kähler). Christ as the central figure of faith becomes a historical Jesus that we find hard to grasp. Where, then, can we find a secure zone in which there is a firm faith that no historical questioning can erode? This question links Herrmann, who was in the middle of the erosion, to Schleiermacher, who foresaw it.[61]

Yet it was not just the threatened erosion of the facts of salvation history that troubled the great Marburg scholar. Tradition posed an equally strong threat to the foundations of faith's certainty. In tradition we have the burden of centuries of reflection. Does faith mean believing all the thoughts of faith? But how are we to distinguish between the ground of faith and the thoughts of faith? Where does the message of the resurrection belong? Is it a ground of faith, as Paul presents it in 1 Cor. 15? Or should we put it with the thoughts of faith as the supremacy of Jesus over death leaves its impress on reflection and finds mythological expression? (We see at this point the influence of the inquiries of Herrmann on Bultmann.)[62]

The basic direction in which Herrmann seeks relief from these problems of certainty may be considered from three angles.

First, and negatively, historical research can offer no possibility of finding in Christ the basis of faith and therefore certainty of faith. If the person of Jesus is so certain for Christians that we see in it the basis of our faith and the revelation of God present to us, this conviction does not rest on a historical judgment.[63]

Second, that which forms the constant basis of a Christian's religious experience is not a sum of thoughts of faith but the man Jesus. It is thus a concrete figure which we encounter as something indisputably real in the same historical sphere as that to which we ourselves belong.[64]

Third, the decisive question is this: If the man Jesus is the

61. Cf. the Second Letter to Lücke.
62. Cf. my essay "The Restatement of New Testament Theology," in *Kerygma and Myth*, ed. W. Bartsch (New York, 1951), pp. 138ff.
63. Herrmann, *Communion with God*, p. 60.
64. Ibid., pp. 49ff.

ground of my faith, if this man is found in the history that embraces both him and me, but if the means of certainty available to history— namely, historical research—cannot serve as the ground of faith, what access to him can I have? It is here that Herrmann introduces a category of experience that we should now call "existential" and that consists of the impression made by the whole life of this person on our experience.

He does, of course, think that we begin with tradition. We take note of the historical facts. Yet the ultimate reality cannot be reached by a purely historical investigation. It is reached only when we are aware of the enrichment of our own inner life by contact with the living Jesus.[65] At this point, to use Lessing's metaphor, an electric spark leaps over to me which enhances my inner life and makes me certain of what I experience. This is obviously the same sort of experience as we find in R. M. Rilke when he looks at the torso of Apollo: "There is no place that does not see thee; Thou must change thy life."[66]

What place is it that sees me thus within Christology and changes my life? What is this reality that cannot be put in purely historical terms but which touches me in my personhood and convinces me of its reality?

To see what it all finally amounts to we must pierce through secondary traditions such as the apostolic reports and teachings, the thoughts that were suggested to their faith, and all that does not seem to be incontestable fact.[67] Again, Herrmann might say with Lessing that accounts of miracles that others experienced are not miracles that we ourselves experience. For Herrmann everything comes back to personal experience and therewith to direct certainty.

Only after setting aside everything that is derived and of second rank can that which no doubt can remove be clear to me in all its power and significance. This is the picture of the inner life of Jesus. Here, paradoxically, we may speak of the historical Christ, although historical research does not find him but only the person who is seeking eternal life in history.[68] The paradox—I use the term in Herrmann's sense— lies in the fact that this picture of the inner life of Jesus, which cannot be historicized, convinces those that seek after God that in it there is something historically real even though it runs contrary to all previous experience and is miraculous in the strict sense of the word.[69] Only the

---

65. Ibid., p. 61.
66. Rilke, *Werke* (1980), II, 313.
67. Herrmann, *Aufsätze*, pp. 320-21.
68. Ibid., p. 321.
69. Ibid., pp. 318-19.

personal can kindle the personal. Hence faith, which is the supreme phenomenon of personal life, is generated only by the spiritual power of persons. Witnesses reach us with their witness. But they point us away from themselves to the ultimate ground of faith, the personal life of Jesus. To be cast down by his power is the basis and goal of all that we may count as life or the development of faith.[70]

What Herrmann thus calls the inner life of Jesus has anthropological and theological implications: anthropological inasmuch as in the God whose work is nowhere so apparent in us as in the power of the person of Jesus over us, the moral thoughts that stir within us take on personal life, Christ being the representative and fulfiller of final moral norms, or, as one might say, the incarnation of the practical logos;[71] and theological in the sense that in the loving turning of Jesus to us, in which the forgiveness represented by him is plain to us, God himself meets us in his human manifestation, draws us to himself, and enters into communion with us in him.[72]

We block access to what Herrmann calls the inner life of Jesus if we are afraid of the psychological-sounding formula. Obviously, for theologians of our generation, for whom the so-called historical Jesus is largely unknowable and a very problematical figure beset by questions, the inner life of this figure is wrapped in obscurity. The controversies regarding the messianic self-consciousness of Jesus are enough to make this plain.[73] But Herrmann uses the phrase ontologically, not psychologically. He understands it to imply the identity of Jesus with his task or cause. He has in mind his unconditional loyalty to his calling, his fellowship with the Father, and his being there for us, which symbolizes God's own address to us.

Schleiermacher, too, did not mean psychologically what he in his own way said about the inner life of Jesus (without using the phrase). When he said that Jesus was filled with a constant force of God-consciousness, he meant this more ontologically as the one being of God in him. For Herrmann, then, the inner life of Jesus is a cipher for his unbroken fellowship with God.

This central concept of the inner life of Jesus brings us close to Christ and analogically makes him understandable. For in him the moral thoughts that stir within us take on personal life. Yet the concept

---

70. Ibid., p. 325.
71. *Verkehr*, p. 85.
72. Ibid., pp. 117-18.
73. Cf. Bultmann, *Theologie des Neuen Testament* (1953), § 4, with bibliography.

also puts us at a distance from him, for the identity of person and task is on a scale beyond us. It is precisely this combination that gives him power over us, making us unconditionally certain of him and changing our lives. This is why Herrmann makes the concept of the inner life of Jesus the keyword in his Christology. I will give a few examples.

(1) In his manifestation we see God himself, who discloses himself to us and draws us to himself. In what he does in us there arises the idea of a person which can be adequately expressed only in the confession of his deity.[74] Instead of "idea" we might use "thought of faith," i.e., the necessary thought of Christ's divine rank. In the word *deity* there is expressed the result of an encounter with his person.

This sequence, i.e., encounter and then the predication of deity, is the point of what Herrmann imparted to his contemporaries as a liberating word. For in the light of this order it is evident how meaningless is a theological and homiletical dogmatism which burdens needy people with the sine qua non that if they want to be redeemed by Christ they must believe in his deity. Instead, we must tell them that if they want to be redeemed by Christ they must learn from the fact of his person that God is in communion with them, and then they will of themselves, as it were, speak about his deity.[75]

As already in Ritschl, the concept is taken out of the two-nature schema, or an ontology of nature, and made an ethical predicate. According to Kant the cleft between divine and human will, between being and obligation, is "human"—in the sense of "not divine." In Christ, however, we have an identity of being and obligation, of person and destiny. We thus have deity. Deity does not express an infinite qualitative distinction from us but a fulfilment of humanity, the *pleroma* of the human, the fulness of human destiny. The deity of Christ symbolizes, not humanity in contradiction, but, as in Schleiermacher, unique and true humanity.

At the same time it is plain that Herrmann is adopting ancient trends in the history of dogma. He is not on the side of Alexandrian Christology (e.g., that of Cyril), which along the lines of the two natures assumes a unity of substance between God and humanity (*henosis physike, kat' ousian*). He is following the Antioch line of Theodoret, who assumes a unity of the divine and the human in terms of ethical disposition and conduct (*henosis schetike*).

(2) The way in which Herrmann approaches Easter faith is also true to his starting point with the inner life of Jesus. As he cannot regard

74. *Verkehr,* pp. 117-18.
75. Ibid., p. 103.

belief in Christ's deity as a sine qua non for our being drawn into communion with God, so he cannot recognize belief in the fact of the resurrection as a condition of the same kind. The two statements regarding Christ's deity and his resurrection on the third day force themselves upon me when I have already passed into the temple, i.e., when I encounter the inner life of Jesus. The trust in his person and cause which develops in consequence contains the thought of a power over things which necessarily sees to it that Jesus, having perished in the world, gains the victory over the world.[76]

The Easter stories in the NT cannot for this reason be a basis for my faith, quite apart from our inability to reconstruct what really happened from these stories.[77] Even for the disciples themselves the appearances of the risen Lord are not the basis of their faith. Already in their intercourse with Jesus, i.e., their experience of his inner life, they have had imparted to them the certainty that he is their Redeemer. The appearances are a kind of divine support which confirms the saving significance of his death. Hence they would have to say that even without the appearances they would have received the certainty that the death of Jesus was not his failure or a refutation of his obedience but had the point of a fulfilment. The decisive thing about him, the power that overcomes death, becomes clear for them with the encounter with his person. The extra appearances are simply confirmatory. God gave them the function of strengthening the threatened faith of the disciples after the crucifixion. Their relative significance shows us who come later that that which historically is attested only indirectly cannot be a basis for faith. The sole ground of faith is our own direct experience of the person of Jesus and his inner life. For us, too, it is here that there resides the certainty that death cannot hold him.

Herrmann's interest in statements of this kind is always the same. He takes the truths of faith down from the leveling plane of timeless dogmatic rank, integrates them into the vital historical encounters of believers, and as regards their significance relates them to the role that they play in such encounters. The main distinction that results is between the ground of faith and the thoughts of faith. Real, original faith has a direct relation to its basis. It thus starts out with experience of the person of Christ. This is, as it were, the primal Christian experience. If faith were to begin with reflection on the ground of faith, with the thoughts of faith (the deity of Christ, the appearances on the third day, the virgin birth, etc.), then we should not have to do with the primal

76. Ibid., p. 80.
77. *Dogmatik*, p. 18.

experience but at most with shared experiences. Hence Herrmann can attack the Pietist practice of imaginary intercourse with the exalted Lord.[78] Here the primary encounter with the historical person of Jesus tends to be replaced by one's own ideas and imaginings. Yet Herrmann did not contest the presence of the exalted Lord, for faith has experienced his power over death.[79] The confession of the presence of the exalted Lord, however, can develop only in faith and must constantly refer back to the beginning of faith, to experience of the historical Jesus. Only in him does God turn to us understandably and comprehensibly, so that only he and not the exalted Christ takes the rank of Revealer.[80]

The point of Herrmann's dogmatic concern is obvious. He wants to stress the original inwardness of the truths of faith, to break away from dead and impersonally accepted traditions, and to penetrate to the real core of Christian truth. One might formulate his question thus: How can the person of Jesus as the incarnation of revealed truth be direct in spite of its historical distance? Or, conversely, how can I be "immediate" to the person of Jesus?

As Herrmann seeks in this way to make Christian truth present, we note a movement of theological thought that meets us repeatedly in different variations. Always by way of doubt there is a renewed appropriation of Christian truth. Doubt arises because we suspect that this Christian truth can no longer correspond to the presuppositions of modern thought, and especially not to the claims to autonomy that are raised by the ethically and religiously adult subject. The overcoming of this problem and the opening up of new possibilities of appropriation for faith come about in such a way that within the categories of our apparatus of intellectual reception a place can be found where Christian truth can be accepted and appropriated by us, whether this place be in the sphere of reason (Kant) or in that of experience (Schleiermacher, Ritschl, and Herrmann).

This distinctive and constantly repeated development means that what seems to be a new affinity to Christian truth—its acceptance into our intellectual system—will at the same time bring about a distortion, restriction, and alteration of the truth of faith. Herrmann is an example.

Christ can be the object of a statement of faith for me only insofar as he is drawn into a relation to me which is experienced in the conscience

---

78. *Verkehr,* 1st ed., p. 200.
79. Ibid., 7th ed., pp. 233-34.
80. Herrmann, *Die Gewissheit des Glaubens und die Freiheit der Theologie* (1887), p. 46.

and can be presented in moral categories. The fact that Christ transcends this relation, that he is more than my faith in him, that his person is more than his work, even than the work of faith in me, that God is greater than our heart, than our experience of him (1 John 3:20)—all this remains outside the competence of our receptive categories.

These categories, and with them the anthropological presuppositions which prove to be open to the reception of Christian truth, and which I try to put at the disposal of this truth, surreptitiously take on normative rank. Even though the initial motive is to let them be a mere means to understand this truth, there quickly comes about a revolt of the means. On the basis of the anthropological presuppositions I can say in advance what a competent christological statement can be, i.e., simply that in which Christ proves to be an incarnation of the norms that I know already through conscience. This given system of norms within which alone I can experience Christ and his inner life becomes, then, a Procrustean bed which makes manipulations and changes necessary to fit him in.

The constriction and reduction of christological statements to which I allude may be seen in every theological conception that begins by defining the conditions of acceptance and assimilation. We need only think of Bultmann, in whom Herrmann's approach is obvious. I recall the statement already mentioned, namely, that the understanding of accounts of events as God's action presupposes a preunderstanding of what God's action can be.[81] This does not allow for that fact that God's action might leap across the bastions of my preunderstanding and my conditions of reception, that God might transcend them. Instead, these conditions are given normative rank and hence a power of manipulation. They are indeed palm branches and clothes that are spread out on the path of the king as he enters Jerusalem. They ought to help to prepare his way and render him service. But they might also fix his way. And will the way then lead to Jerusalem?

This is the development of thought that is particularly striking in Herrmann. Yet there is no place for Pharisaism on the part of those who know from later experience what will be the results of this development—an anthropologizing of theology. For what theology is not subject in some way to a similar fate? (The champions of such a theology may cast the first stone.)

Theology is a work that needs forgiveness. There is no immaculate conception of theology. All that can be achieved outside the admission of the need for forgiveness is simply that theology sees itself

81. Bultmann, *Glauben und Verstehen*, II (1952), 231.

as one moment, a brief interim, in the discovery of Christian truth, and that as such it is ready to be outdated. The feet of those who will carry it off are already at the door. And did not the theologian Wilhelm Herrmann, who commands such respect and is so full of character, realize that only too well? His relativizing of the thoughts of faith seems to be witness to such an awareness. But did he and could he also realize that much of what he called the ground of faith reaches into the zone of the thoughts of faith and is sicklied o'er with the pale cast of thought? I merely ask.[82]

C. MARTIN KÄHLER'S CHRISTOLOGY IN CONTRAST TO HERRMANN'S

The great biblical theologian Martin Kähler undoubtedly comes from a very different theological root from Herrmann. They stand alongside one another like two tall firs. But when the winds of time shake them, their tops occasionally incline toward one another and momentarily touch. In view of the theological fury found elsewhere we may note with envy how these two great contemporaries come together and then withdraw again, but always with politely expressed material and personal respect. They were gentlemen of the old school, if one will.

For all their differences they shared a concern to achieve a direct relation to the person of Jesus, to overcome the gap of time between him and us, and not to let history be a wall of separation. At issue in both is the possibility of personal experience in which we may be mastered by Christ as he comes to us.[83]

It sounds almost like a saying of Herrmann when Kähler states that we cannot make our faith in Jesus dependent on the future results of historical research nor on the debate about a biography of Jesus. What counts is a tradition which has in itself the power to convince us by its divine authenticity. The datum has to be directly accessible.[84] What gives this immediacy of conviction, even regarding the Bible, is our experience and the perceived vitalizing and enriching.[85]

For Kähler, too, the Gospels are not meant to give us a history of the founding of the church or biographical materials for a life of Jesus.

---

82. On the development at issue here cf. *EF*, I, esp. chaps. 1–4.
83. Cf. Herrmann, *Aufsätze*, p. 310. For Herrmann's treatment of Kähler cf. pp. 310-21. Our quotations from Kähler are mostly taken from his *Der sogenannte historische Jesus und der geschichtliche, biblische Christus*, 2nd ed. (1928); partial ET *The So-called Historical Jesus and the Historic, Biblical Christ* (Philadelphia, 1964).
84. *Der sogenannte historische Jesus*, p. 19.
85. *Die Wissenschaft der christlichen Lehre* (1966), p. 49.

They are testimonies of faith to Jesus the Christ. Herrmann agrees.[86] That there are such testimonies is not for Kähler a matter of touching up by community theology, or of later and secondary addition; it is a matter of the work of Christ's own person. The mature—the historically mature—personality is not a private individual *behind* his work but one who lives *in* his work.[87] What is this penetrating work that Jesus has left behind him? According to the Bible and church history, it is none other than the faith of the disciples.[88] The NT texts, then, are testimonies to this awakened faith, records of the preaching that founds the church.[89] Hence the historical Christ, the real Christ, is the *preached* Christ.[90] This insight frees faith from dependence on the shifting picture of the so-called historical Jesus, which is subject to the subtractions of historico-critical research and therefore, as a conditioned picture, subject to academic fads, can never form a basis for the *unconditional* certainty of faith.[91]

Although Herrmann welcomes some of Kähler's insights (e.g., his demand for immediacy to the person of Jesus, his reference to personal experience, and his stress on the kerygmatic point of the Gospel records), he expresses reservations when he finds that many of his own most important themes are *not* present. He concedes that a Christ that is found behind the NT tradition, the so-called historical Jesus, cannot be a basis for faith. Yet he argues that the Christ that the tradition itself portrays (Kähler's historical, biblical Christ) cannot serve as such a basis either.[92] Why not?

He accuses Kähler of not differentiating sharply enough between the *ground* of faith and its *content*.[93] The NT message undoubtedly arises out of experience of the risen and exalted Lord. Hence it is not just a record but a testimony of faith. But the full content of Christian

---

86. *Aufsätze*, p. 311.

87. *Der sogenannte historische Jesus*, p. 63, ET p. 63.

88. Ibid.

89. Ibid., p. 22.

90. Ibid., p. 66, ET p. 66.

91. Modern investigations of the historical Jesus have had the same experiences but have a different point. They no longer try to give faith a historical basis but want to be a corrective to a purely kerygmatic theology which, as in Bultmann, treats the theology of the primitive community as the final point of inquiry and thus threatens to be riveted to a mythologoumenon. Cf. E. Käsemann, *Exegetische Versuche und Besinnungen*, 3rd ed. (1964), I, 187ff.; II, 31ff.; cf. *Essays on New Testament Themes* (1964), pp. 15ff.; G. Ebeling, "The Question of the Historical Jesus and the Problem of Christology," in *Word and Faith* (1963), pp. 288-304.

92. Herrmann, *Aufsätze*, p. 315.

93. Ibid., p. 311.

faith grew gradually and hence it cannot be a basis for those who are only just beginning to believe. Furthermore, the error threatens to intrude that we can find help by sacrificing our judgment and submitting to the assurances of believers who have already experienced that growth.[94]

Herrmann thus expresses the same fear as A. Schweizer, that by simply accepting the NT testimonies of faith we shall be believing the faith of others and not achieving the immediacy to the figure of Jesus that Kähler desires. For this reason the Christ that faith sees in its fulness, the risen and exalted Christ, cannot be the final resting place and ground of faith. Christ in the radiance of his glory, as the redeemed learn to see him, cannot render us this service. This is the *content* of faith but not its final *basis*. If we let go of that which gives our personal conviction its sure support and independence, we are not protected against the essence of Roman Catholicism, against being referred to the mediations of others, of the church, and hence not attaining to the immediacy of our own experience. A faith that can be handed over to this apparatus (the Roman church) will not come about so easily if it inquires into its final ground.[95]

Here is the nerve of Herrmann's concern, for which, he thinks, Kähler has no feeling. Everything focuses for Herrmann on two questions: First, what certainty is so overpowering that it makes a non-Christian into a disciple? And second, how can this certainty cling to the ground of faith that it finds through all the vacillations of our inner life,[96] not just in moments of exaltation but also in the deepest exhaustion of the soul?[97]

Herrmann begins with doubt and testing and asks what remains in this ultimate sifting. All else that faith experiences in its history with Christ, with the risen and exalted Lord in the radiance of his glory, all that the church's history of faith has discovered in the fulness of reflection, he certainly does not deny, but agrees with Kähler in acknowledging it. But at a pinch all this can be jettisoned and the union with the person of Christ need not fade. For all this (to put it pointedly and with some exaggeration) is theological comfort that the reflection of faith constructs for itself. One can live without it. It consists of advanced outposts but is not the inner line on which everything depends for Herrmann. Hermann's concern is with the steel core of Christian

---

94. Ibid., p. 312.
95. Ibid., p. 313.
96. Ibid., p. 315.
97. Ibid., p. 316.

certainty. To find that he can experimentally strip off all the husks—the thoughts of faith, to use the term again.

At this point, however, Herrmann thinks that Kähler parts company, and hence his objection that Kähler does not distinguish between the content of faith and its ground. To put it figuratively, Kähler blinds those who are seeking faith and longing for redemption with a 1000-watt lamp; he surprises them with the overpowering brightness of the historical Christ, with the developed fulness of the church's Christology. But this cannot help seekers. He himself simply lights a little candle which will illuminate the tiny corner of what is essential, the corner where the person of Jesus is credible. How can Jesus be credible to us? Only as we are taught to look to that which gives a sure support and independence to our personal conviction.[98] But this is his union with the Father, his rooting in the ultimate normative court, the personified union in him of being and obligation. In short, we find in him, in fulness, that which lives in all of us at least as an object of search.

We thus come back to the starting point, to the point where the similarity between what we find in the person of Jesus and what lives in us as moral beings causes a spark to leap across and generates immediacy and even subjugation.

The difference between Herrmann and Kähler is not just that Herrmann has a pastoral concern for beginners and doubters whereas Kähler's life and thought center on the explication of faith—this is only conditionally true. The decisive difference is that Herrmann bases certainty on the similarity between our anthropological presuppositions and that which meets us in the person of Jesus, whereas Kähler finds the ground of certainty in the gift of the Spirit whereby Christ overcomes our closedness and makes himself present to us. The choice is made in the sphere of pneumatology.[99] The problem is that of Cartesian and non-Cartesian theology. Herrmann belongs to the Cartesian side, i.e., to that of an anthropologically controlled theology.[100]

D. HERRMANN'S ETHICAL VIEWS

Since, as we have seen, the dogmatics had already a basic ethical frame and thus had an anthropological tendency, only a few references are

98. Ibid., p. 313.

99. Cf. *Dogmatische Zeitfragen,* I (1898), 137ff. For Kähler's pastoral concern cf. pp. 110ff.

100. Cf. *EF,* I, Part 1.

needed to present Herrmann's ethics itself. It is clear that in Herrmann the understanding of the moral person and its independence rests on Kant's concept of autonomy. Appealing expressly to Kant, he defines moral conduct as the perfection of the will. By this he means independence of the environment and its influence and heteronomy, i.e., self-determination. A mark of this independence is that the will is constant, that the will as it is determined by the practical logos achieves a fixed direction that nothing outside can modify. We undoubtedly have our inner independence solely in the fact that we can present to ourselves that of which we can say that we always will it. All views of the moral finally come together in the thought that inner concentration in a disposition that we can and must think of as the unchangeable form of our will is moral or good.[101]

For Herrmann, then, a theological ethics rests primarily on the universally valid phenomenon and the agreed independence of moral knowledge. He can thus cite Kant as an authority for his analysis of the ethical.

Only because there are morally grounded persons can there be a human society. Such a society lives on the basis of trust. But there can be trust only on two conditions.

The first is when we know that people do not act out of eudaemonism, i.e., within shifting constellations of interest, but in obedience to an unconditional will. They are then accountable. We know the inner flight plan which they have to follow. We trust their inner independence. But our trust is then based on something which by its very nature is not provable. We cannot objectify the ground of trust because we cannot objectify the moral person as such. How, then, can we venture to trust? We can do so only on the second condition. This must be met if there is to be trust.

This second condition is that I can trust others only if I know that I am required to take up myself the attitude that inspires trust. Only those who are honest enough to demand of themselves that which they regard as trustworthy in others have the courage to trust. Those who have no such inner stability cannot trust it in others.[102] Hence a society based on trust, as distinct from a collective or a fellowship of interests, can be present only with the mutual relations of morally independent people. This basic thought runs through all the later sketches of cultural and political ethics.[103] Only a common commitment to ultimate norms binds us to one another.

101. *Ethik*, 2nd ed., §§ 6, 14-15.
102. Ibid., § 10, esp. §§ 27-28.
103. Ibid., §§ 26, 27.

But how does this ethical approach that is adopted from Kant work out theologically? Can it take on theological relevance when it is self-contained, has its sole basis in the universal human conscience, and leaves no place for a *Deus dixit,* e.g., in the form of a command, in its development? For Herrmann faith can be relevant only in those who are already morally complete, as it were. What, then, can it add to the existing autonomy? What is it that needs to be rounded out by Christianity?

Herrmann gives his ethical section the title "The Christian Faith as the Power to Do Good" (§ 21). The definition of what is good is offered by an independent ethical court which is not theologically governed. But faith gives us the power to do the good that this court independently determines. What is meant by this?

At this point Herrmann incidentally, lightly, and superficially touches on some of the deep themes that we find in Paul's wrestling with the law. If the ethical comes to us as an imperative: "Thou shalt," it is true that the law cannot make us righteous (Rom. 8:3; Gal. 3:11) or lead us to a fulfilment of our divinely ordained destiny. It is not as though Herrmann relates himself expressly to these Pauline insights. Yet one can hardly avoid the impression that they are in the background when he says that left to our moral knowledge alone we cannot attain our goal.[104] Suddenly this does not sound at all Kantian.

Why, when referred to the moral imperative and left to our moral knowledge alone, are we betrayed and sold out? Why are we unable by means of the purely ethical law to do justice to ourselves and to our allotted dominion over the world? What is this moral imperative on which our will breaks?

Now the Kantian categorical imperative can mediate to me my inner autonomy and help me to the dignity of moral subjectivity freed from externally directed and impulsively eudaemonistic motivation. This is for Herrmann the basic presupposition of moral existence (and in this regard he takes his decisive points from Kant). Yet the task of personhood amounts to more than this. For so long as this personhood merely constitutes itself and maintains its autonomy, it merely looks out for itself and is stuck in what we should now call individualistic self-fulfilment. But our destiny is to be free in our wills from the compulsion merely to look out for ourselves.[105] Our destiny is to be free to live for others. So long as we are referred only to our moral knowledge, we never get beyond the unresolved tension be-

104. *Ethik,* §§ 21, 113.
105. Not in a material sense but in terms of moral self-fulfilment, as in Kant; see ibid., § 113.

tween ethical self-actualization and self-denial,[106] i.e., unselfish self-giving to others. Herrmann at least suggests here the possibility that self-fulfilment alone might be a finally sublimated egoism.

How does this tension arise and why can we not attain our true goal (at least when left to our moral knowledge alone)? The answer for Herrmann lies in our unmastered relation to the world. Here we come up against a moral barrier that lies between us and our destined goal. We are hemmed in morally by our being in the world. We cling to the world because it nourishes us and we are afraid of it, because it destroys us. When we are bound by the desire for things and by fear of their power, we are closed to others. We are then too much concerned about ourselves to be able to live for others.[107]

At this point Herrmann's ethics seems to entail no less than a final questioning of the Kantian beginning which forms the basis of his doctrine of the moral consciousness and its autonomy. For where do we find in Kant this restriction by a moral barrier with which the world blocks our way to ethical self-fulfilment? (Even what Kant says about radical evil bears no relation to such a barrier.) Herrmann, then, is not convinced that the moral subject is really independent of the world or superior to it. Left to our moral knowledge alone, we are enslaved to desire and anxiety, to hope and fear. This enslavement triggers an anxiety that forms an insuperable barrier on the way to the true ethical goal, namely, to self-denying giving to others.

This analysis of our being in the world and its moral liabilities enables Herrmann to see the significance of Christian faith for ethics. Faith can help us to achieve what we cannot do by moral knowledge alone. It can give us power to overcome the barrier, the restrictive tension between moral self-fulfilment and loving self-denial. Faith enables us to achieve this fulfilment of the moral task in two ways.

First, it makes the thought of the omnipotent God true for us. If it is God who works in the world, we can lose ourselves neither in delight in the world nor in sorrow and care.[108] Even the unlimited uncertainty of our existence, even the death that confronts us, need no longer be repressed by us. They all become a sign of the mysterious depth which the almighty God has given our existence. The experience that contact with the morally perfect Spirit does not cause us to sink in a sense of our impotence but raises us up inwardly; this miracle of grace changes the world for us.[109] In this changed world the barrier is taken

106. Ibid.
107. Ibid., § 111.
108. Ibid., §§ 111-12.
109. Ibid., § 112.

away which through desire and anxiety causes us to circle egocentrically about ourselves and blocks any readiness to give ourselves to others.

Second, God does not merely work in the world but in Jesus comes to us in a personal life as one who loves. This is the second factor that frees us from ourselves and makes self-giving possible. Significant here is what Herrmann said about the inner life of Jesus, namely, that it is a being for others, and that by it our own personal lives are kindled for personal self-giving. Once the moral power of Jesus touches us, his sacrifice for those who are lost without his faithfulness, the manifestation of his personal life as a proof of the love of almighty God, we become so rich that we can take an interest in others and live for fellowship. In the moment of religious exaltation we feel free for what we understand in its moral necessity.[110]

This, then, is the point. Left to the moral consciousness alone, we know the necessity of the unconditioned, of the good. But we lack the freedom to do it or even to want to do it. Herrmann has abandoned Kant's postulate of freedom, which is related to the assurance of the practical logos that "we can because we should." He takes empowering for freedom from other sources, from the miracle of grace that changes the world for us and gives us the power to overcome concern for the self.[111]

Without adopting the traditional vocabulary, Herrmann harks back to the Reformation distinction between indicative and imperative. The imperative of the commands has its basis in an indicative positing which we do not control but which God's turning to us imparts, and in so doing makes it possible for us to will and to do. When we think of Herrmann's Christology, we see that his understanding of this divine turning is still tied formally to the Kantian schema. Yet we see that the reference to the indicative message of salvation bursts through this schema at every point. We have certainly not understood Herrmann if we do not see the purely instrumental rank of the schema. Yet we are not unaware that instrumental means—even in theology—are constantly in revolt, so that the phenomenon arises which we call a necessary development of thought.[112]

---

110. Ibid., § 115.
111. Ibid., § 112.
112. On the problem of the indicative and imperative cf. *ThE*, I, §§ 315ff.; ET I, 74ff.

CHAPTER 12

G. W. F. Hegel

Bibliography. Primary Works: *Werke*, 18 vols. (1832-1845); Suhrkamp ed. in 20 vols. (1970-1971) (cited as Suhrkamp); *Die Vernunft in der Geschichte*, ed. G. Lasson (PhB 171a); *Encyclopädie der Philosophischen Wissenschaften* (PhB 33, cited as *Encyclopädie*). Selected texts, ed. F. Heer, in the Fischer-Bücherei (1955, cited as Heer); E. Hirsch, ed., *Die Umformung des christlichen Denkens in der Neuzeit* (1938), pp. 260-302.

Secondary Works: Apart from Kuno Fischer, *Geschichte der neueren Philosophie* (1901), and W. Dilthey, *Gesammelte Schriften*, IV (1959), 5-258, see the theological interpretations in K. Barth, *Protestant Theology in the Nineteenth Century* (1973), pp. 384-421; P. Cornehl, *Die Zukunft der Versöhnung* . . . (1971): W. Elert, *Der Kampf um das Christentum* (1921), §§ 3-5; C. Freyd, *Gott als die universale Wahrheit von Mensch und Welt* . . . , diss. Hamburg (1982); W. Krötke, *Sünde und Nichtiges bei Karl Barth* (East Berlin, 1972), esp. pp. 33ff.; A. Schlatter, *Die philosophische Arbeit seit Descartes. Ihr ethischer und religiöser Ertrag*, 4th ed. (1959); H. P. Schmidt, *Verheissung und Schrecken der Freiheit* . . . (1964); H. Thielicke, *ThE*, I, 203ff.; *EF*, I, 259ff.; III, 338ff.; *Living with Death* (Grand Rapids, 1983), pp. 86ff.

I. BIOGRAPHY

Hegel lived from 1770 to 1831, when he died of cholera in Berlin. As a boy he studied philosophy and theology at Tübingen. Here his friendship with Hölderlin and Schelling influenced him more than his studies. Schlatter, who suffered not a little from the school at Tübingen and the people there, remarks rather bitingly that it no doubt resulted both in his constructive skill in dialectics and in mastering life, and also in his philosophical self-awareness, which has it that philosophy is the end which the world spirit has thus far reached as the sum of 2,500 years of very serious work.[1] Those who know the institution that educated Hegel, writes Schlatter,[2] will often have tiny, even very tiny, examples before them of what alien constructionism and highly developed self-awareness the students (and their fellow student Hegel) experienced, and of what may also be seen in Hegelians who were also educated there like D. F. Strauss and F. C. Baur; like Hegel they have no knowledge at all of the world and an inability to perceive reality, but in childlike and childish fashion they blunder dreaming through the world with a self-awareness that knows no caution, break, or limit, but takes delight in the achievements of its own thought and boldly sets for itself the highest goals.[3]

Since Hegel is often put on a pedestal it is perhaps admissible to bring up these rather spiteful references to his early years, especially as this caricature fits in with the portrait of Hegel that is constantly found among his opponents, e.g., Kierkegaard.

Hegel began to teach in Jena in 1801 and gave lectures that covered all the philosophical disciplines and later mathematics as well. His *Phenomenology of Spirit* (also called *Phenomenology of Mind*) was written at this time. In Jena he also saw Napoleon, whom he admired as a figure of world history. As he wrote to his friend Friedrich Neithammer, he saw the emperor, that world soul, ride through the city. It was a wonderful experience to see such an individual, here focused on a single point, riding on a horse, but reaching across the world and ruling it. The world spirit on a horse![4] Financial difficulties forced Hegel to leave Jena and to take a temporary post as an editor in Bamberg until he received a call to become rector of a high school in Nuremberg in 1808. Although he did not feel well here, being beset by problems[5] and hoping vainly for a professorship at Erlangen, he wrote his *Science of Logic* in two parts in 1812 and 1816.

He finally received a call to Heidelberg in 1816. During the short two-year interim there his comprehensive *Encyclopädie der Philosophischen Wissenschaften* was written.

1. Schlatter, *Glockners Jubiläumsausgabe,* vol. 19, 685.
2. Ibid., p. 173.
3. Cf. the semi-ironical student song which refers to Uhland, Hegel, Schelling, and Hauff as the rule that strikes no one as strange.
4. Cf. the correspondence with J. Hoffmeister, PhB, vols. 235-37.
5. The school has not even a "toilet . . . the story is too shameful and terrible."

In 1818 his painful course reached its academic crown with a call to the first philosophical chair in Germany at Berlin as Fichte's successor. In a famous inaugural address on October 22, 1818,[6] Hegel lauded the Prussian state that he had previously criticized. It had now accepted him. It was the place where hitherto silenced scholarship might now speak again, and the free realm of thought might flourish anew. Hegel referred to the despair of reason that was now behind us and that had been largely caused by the banality and insipidity of what was called enlightenment. He appealed to the spirit of youth, the courage of truth, and faith in the power of the spirit as among the first presuppositions of philosophical study.

Because of his recognition of the Prussian state Hegel is often called the Prussian state philosopher and accused of political opportunism, especially as Prussia at this time was not really a refuge for the freedom that he extolled. In a later letter (December 1830) to the lawyer Karl Göschel, who inclined to his philosophy, Hegel shows that the accusation is a misleading simplification. He draws attention to the dangers to freedom when it becomes doctrinaire and gives rise to new forms of intolerance. The Prussian state is a bulwark against this type of freedom.

Yet understandably Hegel's philosophy is open to the charge of opportunism, not because of Hegel's character, but on material grounds. If its premises demand that the rational structure of history be shown at all costs, this naturally leads to a justification of what is there, especially when the results seem to confirm it.

Not surprisingly, Hitler's rhetorical address to the Reichstag on January 30, 1939 (after the incorporation of Austria), was viewed as a kind of popularized Hegelian philosophy. What was the "providence" that seemed to confirm the success of Hitler's acts but a popular shadow of Hegel's world spirit? In this regard Eduard Spranger could say on March 1, 1939, that divested of its pious framework Hegel's philosophy is nothing but a naked theory of progress and success.[7]

When his works brought renown to the Berlin chair, majors, colonels, and councillors attended his classes, much to his delight. More important was the fact that many people who later achieved eminence attended, and his impact was seen even when they later opposed or modified his system. Among them we may mention S. Kierkegaard, D. F. Strauss, the Russian revolutionary M. Bakunin, and the great American historian, politician, and diplomat G. Bancroft. Karl Marx

6. Cf. Heer, pp. 65ff.
7. Klaus Scholder, *Die Mittwochsgesselschaft* (1982), p. 32.

was at the university only six years after Hegel's death, and he listened eagerly to his disciple Eduard Gans and studied Hegel intensively while at Berlin.[8]

Whether positively or negatively, the range and significance of Hegel's intellectual and political influence is indescribable, especially through the left-wing Hegelians and chiefly the Marxists. He is without parallel among philosophers in this respect. Even the dialectical theologians do not escape his impact. On the left wing one might mention Feuerbach, Bruno Baur, and Max Stirner. Politically, we find such names as Marx, Engels, Lassalle, and later Lenin. Even revisionists like Roger Garaudy and cultural critics such as Adorno, Horkheimer, Marcuse, and Habermas are just as influenced in their approach by their debate with Hegel as Ernst Bloch is. One might continue the list in the spheres of philosophy, theology, and history, and it extends even to our own time.

Unavoidably, even this short biographical sketch leaves a strong impression of Hegel's significance and effect. We might close, therefore, with the satirical note of a student, Karl Grün, who heard him with mixed feelings, like Ludwig Feuerbach, whose correspondence he later edited.[9] Grün noted that the stiff skeleton of Hegel's thought lacked flesh and blood but was correct down to the smallest detail. Apodictically convinced, it convinced others, creating the world as Jehovah created it on the first day, explaining everything, positing necessarily, dialectically making every antinomy into a nomy, forcing all things under law, applying to everything in heaven and on earth and under the earth, conceptually reconciling humanity with himself and the world, and leading him finally to the absolute spirit to which infinity joyously overflows out of the cup of the whole world of being.[10]

II. FOUNDATIONS OF THE SYSTEM

Hegel's system is often called a philosophy of self-confident reason. Finally, every system, i.e., every effort to present all reality in an orderly context, from a specific angle, and with the help of constitutive prin-

---

8. R. Friedenthal, *Karl Marx* (1981), pp. 79, 82, 87.

9. L. Grün, ed., *L. Feuerbach in seinem Briefwechsel und Nachlass* (1874). The above reference is from vol. I, 15.

10. Schopenhauer gives way almost to paroxysms of hate when he calls Hegel a shallow charlatan who with unparalleled insolence combines absurdity and nonsense. Cf. R. Spaemann and R. Löw, *Die Frage Wozu? Geschichte und Wiederentdeckung des teleologischen Denkens* (1981), p. 188.

ciples, is based in some way on confidence in the agreement of thought and being, of noetic and ontic reason. As Stoicism saw, a system presupposes that reality may be conceptualized and that there is in it something rational akin to our own mind. As we saw earlier, this comes out very naively in the rational religion of the Enlightenment. This religion finds the possibility of knowledge in the fact that God (deistically viewed) has made the world and ordered it for the best (as the optimism of Leibniz showed). God has established our world rationally and ordered it morally. In the end righteousness will always triumph, lies will not last, the sun will bring things to light. God has also made the reason with which we grasp the world. Thus thought and being, subject and object, both go back to the same Creator. No wonder, then, that reason finds itself confirmed in the world, that it finds reality satisfactory and akin, since it goes back to the same source.

Antiquity and the Middle Ages could even give being the quality of truth. This quality is the presupposition of its knowability. Being is true because the Creator has envisioned it. Thought and creation are alike to him. Being is thought being. The absolute spirit, the Creator Spirit, stands behind it. It conforms to thought; it is shot through by logos. Hence our thinking is a thinking of God's determinative thoughts after him. We are capable of this because our reason is a particle of the ontic structure of thought.

Thus for Anselm truth is not just a matter of logical judgment. It is part of the being to which the judgment relates. A thing can be true when it accords with the plan of creation, when its nature and destiny are congruent. In such a case it has the quality of *rectitudo*. Hence the truth immanent in being can be progressive (unlike that of logical judgment). There may be more or less truth according to the degree of congruence. Quartz is more true than silica and crystal than quartz by reason of greater *rectitudo*.[11]

Whereas for the Middle Ages being as God's work shares eternal truth and human work is contingent and perishable, Giambattista Vico (1668-1744) initiates a radical change which brings us into the modern era.[12] In place of Anselm's certainty of being which derives from faith in God, we find in Vico a monstrous ocean of doubt with only a tiny corner of earth on which to plant our feet.[13] Where is this little patch of certainty? Vico's answer is that real knowledge is always the knowledge of causes, and therefore we can have truth and certain knowledge only

11. R. Allers, *Anselm von Canterbury. Leben, Lehre, Werke* (1936), pp. 88ff.
12. K. Löwith, *Meaning in History* (Chicago, 1949), pp. 115ff.
13. Cf. Vico, *New Science*, § 40; cf. Löwith, *Meaning in History*, p. 119.

of what we ourselves have caused and made. But we did not make the cosmos. Its final causes are thus impenetratably hidden from us. There is no certainty there. Certainty arises only in areas which were previously thought to be contingent, i.e., in human acts, in history. We are to turn to what we have done. Facts or facticity[14] will now take on significance as the sphere of the certainty that was previously found in being. Here is the break beyond which modern historicism begins.

A distinction arises here which we might briefly summarize as the distinction between a theological and an anthropological age. In the theological age, exemplified in Anselm, only the Creator Spirit knows the work of which he is the creative cause. But he gives his creatures the possibility of thinking his work after him, by letting them participate in his own thoughts and opening up their spirit to his. The anthropocentric age initiated by Vico detaches itself from the nexus of being, thinking it can find certainty only where we ourselves act as causes and can thus understand what we have made.

This distinction helps us to get a first impression of the extent to which Hegel tries to grasp the totality of being and to weave it into his system. What seems to be an antithesis is here forced into a synthesis because there can be no antithesis between the world spirit—Anselm's Creator Spirit—and the emancipated human spirit. We ourselves are simply one aspect of the absolute spirit, or, better, of its evolution. We are thus finally identical with it. There is, then, no exclusive distinction between a theological and an anthropological age, between a sacral and a secularized age. The two are simply stages and phases in the same self-development. First we have the phase of the absolute spirit in itself. This is the age of immediacy and transparency. Then we have the age of the finite spirit as this frees itself and the world spirit takes on an alien form. Finally, the antithesis is removed by a return to synthesis.

What is new here as compared to Kant?

For Kant the systematic approach by way of the all-embracing monon of the absolute spirit involves a metaphysics whose basis lies beyond all possibility of knowledge. Kant fixes the limit of what may be known by defining our relation to being through the subject-object correlation. He then establishes what can be a theme of objective knowledge on the basis of the subject's epistemological structures. Even though there might be no identity of the finite and the absolute spirit— to claim that there is would be metaphysics!—and even though there is no identity between subject and object, there is still for Kant a link between thought and being. We are to think of this, however, as analogy

14. Along with mathematics, which we need not discuss here.

rather than identity. The objects of experience are spirit of our spirit because they are stamped by our forms of perception and our categories.

Even the world beyond our experience, the realm of the thing in itself, stands in this primal relation to us, and we may see a glimmer of reason in it. For even if our world of experience is shaped categorically by our reason, it is not created by our reason. It is an objective sphere because the thing in itself affects our receptive organs. In relation to experience, then, reason, for all its contribution of the categories, is receptive rather than creative. The many phenomena that we perceive and know are expressions of an ontic background that is itself necessarily varied and that affects us in many different ways. Reason has not invented the variety. (Reason is not rich in Kant but is fairly uniform in its functioning.) The variety derives from that which affects us. It is the richness of a being that we do not know directly, as it is in itself, but only as it meets us within our own noesis, by which it thus seems to be shaped.[15]

In Kant, then, there is a certainty of reason. Being can be assimilated by reason because it is itself rational. Here we have one of many possible confirmations of our thesis that every philosophical system rests on the self-confidence of reason. A system can be erected only because the author is certain that reality may be grasped in rational concepts, that reason is not alone at a lost position but can count on finding something similar to itself in reality.

In contrast, existentialism is an enemy of systems because it has lost confidence in reason and fundamentally reflects only on our human self-understanding and self-development as we are cast into an alien world that is threatened by finitude and futility. Existential philosophy does not even want to produce a system. It treats any such intention with scorn and contempt. (We need think only of Kierkegaard's attacks on Hegel.) It is not that its proponents lack the power of systematizing. It is rather that they have lost the indispensable prerequisite of systematizing, namely, the confidence that thought and being are in a pre-established harmony and are analogous to one another.

O. F. Bollnow illustrates this lost confidence in being from Heidegger, who restricts the world to the mode of what is there, to the sphere of the technically useful, to the deficient world of naked and meaningless reality. In him we find no spheres of meaningful reality, whether we think of the organic life of animals and plants or the realm of human culture. Similarly, Karl Jaspers orients the world to a concern for external things. The whole world becomes a meaningless back-

15. Cf. Eugen Herrigel, *Urstoff und Urform* (1926).

ground when confronted by the unconditional radiance of one's own existence.[16]

When a system is present, one may assume as a premise what we earlier called the divinatory principle of hermeneutics, namely, that understanding rests on the agreement (analogy) between the one who understands and what is to be understood. When hermeneutics relates to the understanding of texts, this is easy to say and grasp. For the person who is to be understood (Plato or Bruno or Leibniz) is a rational being like ourselves. But philosophical systematizing goes much further as regards its hermeneutical premises. It is confident that the world itself bears the same relation to us as the literary texts of a rational being, that it is spirit of our spirit.

Hegel presses these premises to the full. As noted, he speaks not merely of the analogy but of the identity between knower and known. The world process is a process of thought. Human life is a process of thought, no more than this, but this even in what we declare to be nature and reality.[17] All processes—and in Hegel especially history, for he is less successful in expounding the thesis in relation to nature—are materialized thought processes of the world spirit. In simplified form one might say that all that is and happens consists of thoughts of God that have taken form as reality.

Thus far one might think that we have here a variation on Enlightenment deism with its belief in a rational Creator and the rational world that he has made. The new thing, however, is the role that Hegel allots to the rational human spirit. For the Enlightenment and Kant the knowing spirit stands over against the known world. There is a subject-object relation. This relation arises—cf. Kant—as reason encounters itself, knowing reality as it is impressed by its own forms and categories of perception. But there is still encounter. In Hegel, however, identity holds sway. What does this mean?

Hegel sees in the finite human spirit a transitional point in the self-development of the world spirit. Primarily, of course, the finite human spirit is just an entity like any other form of reality, e.g., a tree or a rock. But one decisive feature marks off humans from all other beings, namely, consciousness or self-awareness.[18] But what is this consciousness, and what does it know?

We do best to give a negative answer first. Of itself and on its

16. See O. F. Bollnow, "Existenzphilosophie," in *Systematische Philosophie*, ed. N. Hartmann (1943), pp. 313-430; cf. p. 356.

17. Schlatter, *Die philosophische Arbeit seit Descartes*, p. 175.

18. Cf. Heidegger, *Being and Time* (New York, 1962), §§ 31ff.

own initiative this finite consciousness cannot see in reality the self-development of the spirit as though it stood over against this reality. What we have here is the world spirit knowing itself. To this end it simply uses the finite consciousness as its instrument, as a means of self-consciousness. It thus fashions for this finite consciousness the physiological presupposition of the brain. On the one hand, one might say (with some reserve) that when I reflect, the world spirit reflects in me. On the other hand, it simply *manifests* itself in stones and flowers and natural phenomena. In such things it discloses itself with different degrees of clarity. (One might think again of the crescendo of silica, quartz, and crystal in Anselm.) In me, however, as the finite spirit the world spirit awakens to consciousness of itself.

Hence if I write a philosophy of history as Hegel does, it is not a biography of the world written from the distance of encounter but an autobiography of the world spirit as this looks at itself through my consciousness.

The unheard-of and earth-shaking effects of this (initially) simple figure of speech will be hard to understand if we do not bring to light the feeling for existence that slumbers in it. Our starting point was the extraordinary confidence of the thinker in himself and his thought. Naturally, if I am simply the medium through which the world spirit thinks, I can think with extreme self-confidence. My self-confidence is similar to the apodictic assurance of the prophet who does not rest on his own shifting knowledge of the truth but who speaks in the name of God and is simply the mouthpiece for his word. The point of comparison between the prophet and the Hegelian philosopher is the instrumental rank of human utterance. The finite consciousness is taken into service. Another speaks through it.

The self-confidence underlying this conception is so radical that Hegel could seriously express the conviction that the history of philosophy was closed and summed up in him. He could reduce all that had previously been said to the formula that we have in it the history of the world spirit thinking about itself and pressing on to ever greater clarity. The previous stages in the history of philosophy and theology are for Hegel stages in the history of the spirit's consciousness. In the first stages the spirit is tied to the instrumentality of sensory images or mythologoumena, but it then rises up from these to the immediacy of concepts.[19]

An obvious conclusion is that Hegel's philosophy is not just a new system but that all previous philosophies from the Pre-Socratics to Kant are elements in it, are taken up into it, and are seen to be stages

19. *Encyclopädie*, §§ 20-21, 486.

in the self-consciousness of the spirit. Unconsciously, they have all helped the self-consciousness of the spirit to reflection. They have been precursors like John the Baptist. Hegel himself is the Christ of knowledge. He has come as a kind of philosophical Savior. The first stages of knowledge have the same relation to him as in the Apologists (Justin Martyr) the kernels of truth in ancient philosophy (the *logoi spermatikoi*) have to the Christian revelation of the (cosmic) Logos. He, Hegel, sees the secret meaning behind these processes of thought. He perceives that they are forms in the morphology of the spirit. Hence he does not overcome what has gone before. He transcends it in the twofold sense of both removing it and also adopting it.

If we were to try to put Hegel's self-confidence in a single formula we might say that for him there is a final identity between thought and what is thought, between knowledge and what is known. We can illustrate this with the help of three questions.

First, what is it that is thought? It is the world in the plenitude of its forms in space and time. But this is not just thought by me as a random rational individual. We have here forms and realizations of the thoughts of the world spirit.

Second, who does the thinking? The world spirit is the subject of thought whose thinking is objectified in the forms of the intellectual world.

Third, how does the world spirit think? It thinks, or reflects about itself, by means of the forms that emanate from it. One of these forms has the gift of consciousness. It bears the charism through which the world spirit can think about itself. I, the finite spirit, am this form.

Hence the self-confidence of the thinker rests on the fact that another thinks through me. I simply reproduce the music that the world spirit makes. If one will, one might say that my own will is excluded. (Astonishingly, or not so astonishingly, Hegel lays little stress on the will.) It is no accident that for Hegel necessity lies in the self-development of the spirit, and freedom is understood not as the claiming of the will but as insight into this necessity.[20] In Marxism this is the basis of the essential antithesis to the individualistic view of freedom in the Western tradition.[21]

Three results follow. (1) Thought in Hegel's sense has the same degree of unconditionality as prophetic certainty. The world spirit is the guarantee that I will not miss the reality that it has produced. (2) I achieve a total view of being. I see in it God himself. The spirit is in all things, whether merely manifested in certain forms or self-reflected in

20. *Vernunft in der Geschichte,* p. 40.
21. Engels, *Anti-Dühring* (Berlin, 1948), p. 138.

a rational being. From the spirit I myself, being spirit, have access to all reality. All reality is rational. This is an axiom in Hegel's system. I myself simply reflect this cosmic reason. Hence all reality is accessible to me. (3) I am thus immediate to all reality. There can be no question of a "thing in itself" that is distant from me and that I can know only from its reflection within my own range of experience (as in Kant). To put it rather sentimentally, I am at the very heart of things. I see the mystery of the world face to face. For I myself bear the features of the power that is at work in every cosmic form as spirit.

Although Marx stands Hegel's doctrine of the spirit on its head, he retains some of the same self-confidence. The vehemence and force of the Marxist conception rest on the fact that the revolutionary proletariat are (or ought to be) convinced that their will is oriented to what history wills. Their freedom to change the world is identical with the necessity with which the dialectical process of history proceeds. This idea of the cosmic law and of the harmony with it that gives the revolutionary will its assurance is a final remnant of Hegel's doctrine of the world spirit—even if in inverted form.

All this raises for us a decisive question. It might seem as though, when the world is seen in this way, it will reflect the spirit that forms it in a static and petrified way, as a kind of monument. But I perceive that the world is in movement. Natural processes unfold in it. Above all, it has a history. It is full of dramatic events. How does it come about that there is this movement in it? The answer to this question is by no means obvious in the light of what has been said thus far.

The question where and how movement may be found in the system is a pressing one because Hegel's world allows for no will or motive power that might produce dynamic elements. The spirit is not a willing, personal being, but a thinking being. The principles of the occurrence in which it unfolds itself are the principles that are immanent in reason. The forms of thought that Hegel ranges under the concept of categories[22] are the structures of occurrence itself. The question of how there can be any occurrence is thus an urgent one. If the world spirit is only a thinking spirit, and if we are only a medium whereby it may think through our finite spirit, where are we to find the dynamism or the motive power of events?

The question is the more intense when we consider that thought is properly a contemplative act, that in the vivid Marxist terminology coined from Hegel we can only interpret world occurrence, but not change it by active intervention (although for Marx the proletariat has

22. *Encyclopädie*, §§ 20, 43ff.

revolutionary force because it is not just a fellowship of interpretation but also of resolve). Will not Hegel's thought lead, then, to static nonhistoricity? Yet his philosophy of history, of active processes, has been his most influential work. How are we to explain this?

To this problem of movement, of historical dynamic, Hegel has an astonishing solution which itself makes history in its influence on Marxism. He begins by arguing that thought is not just contemplative, as it is not just receptive or interpretative. It is itself a dynamic event. Hence no active or dynamic thing like the will needs to be added to it. It is itself active. The processes that are permeated by the spirit have a share in its dynamic.

But where are we to find this element of movement in thought? We find it in the fact that concepts change into their opposites and involve movement in the threefold act of thesis, antithesis, and synthesis. This process opens up an unforeseeable future, for the threefold act is constantly repeated. The synthesis becomes the intiatory thesis of a new sequence.

At first the dialectical principle characterizes only the logical movement of thought. But since events are spiritual, it then characterizes real processes too. For instance, in historical processes we speak of the swing of the pendulum. Collectivist tendencies trigger the reaction of a new individualism and vice versa. The resultant synthesis produces a fresh negation. The Marxist doctrine of revolution adopts this dialectical principle. One is tempted to find traces of it in the history of the universities from the late sixties. But we can leave this to the imagination of the reader.

Hegel's greatest difficulty is that of applying the dialectical principle to nature and its laws and mutations. He certainly tried to interpret the natural process as a process of thought.[23] But we are left with the impression—we cannot pursue it here—that the effort fails, and indeed that this failure brings the whole system into question.

In history, however, the dialectical principle may be seen more clearly, not only as we find factual examples of the threefold act, but especially because history is the sphere of human existence, of beings that are exemplary bearers of the finite consciousness in which the absolute spirit knows itself and hence manifests itself most directly.

We see this in Hegel's doctrine of the individual. This opens with reflections on historical individuals.[24] The approach is not accidental, for prominent figures like Alexander the Great, whom Hegel takes as a

---

23. Ibid., §§ 245ff.
24. *Die Vernunft in der Geschichte*, pp. 74ff.

representative, reflect a relation of the finite spirit to the absolute spirit which is the ideal case, present only fragmentarily in normal individuals.

An essential feature of historical individuals is that they are filled with great passions. Passion is their ego's energy. It is an almost animal impulse whereby they devote their energy to a cause and thus win power, extend their ego, and further their plans of aggrandisement. That they have passions and are ready to satisfy them is the condition of their achieving something worthy. Hence they cannot be immoral.[25] Moral objections come from schoolmasters and psychologists who see only the desire to achieve fame and conquest and think they are superior to the great because they themselves do not have such passions. They thus focus supremely on the peculiarities of great historical figures as private persons, and along the lines of petty psychology interpret the great and transcendent factor of their passions in the light of the banal and everyday.[26]

It is true, Hegel concedes, that historical individuals seek to satisfy themselves and not the well-meant aims of others.[27] They give free rein to their passions. But without their knowing it the satisfaction of their passions is used instrumentally by the world spirit. This spirit incorporates them into its overarching plans. They come within its design. One might call it the *cunning of reason* to make passions work on its behalf. World reason remains aloof from antithesis and conflict. It keeps itself intact and untouched in the background while those that do its work suffer loss, hurt, and destruction.[28]

Historical individuals do not derive happiness from this destiny of theirs. They are favored by fortune to be leaders in purposes which form stages in the progress of the universal spirit. But apart from this "substance" of their being they are also "subjects" or individuals with wills of their own. The related split between their own desires and the purposes whose unsuspecting instruments they are does not make for their happiness.[29] (In this regard Hegel seems to have in view the same concept of happiness as that of Kant.)

A further recollection of Kant seems to cause Hegel to ask in this context whether the cunning of reason does not degrade individuals as a mere means of the world spirit and thus contradict their personal rank as ends in themselves. Hegel tries to avoid this conclusion by

25. Ibid., pp. 79-80.
26. Ibid., pp. 80-81.
27. Ibid., p. 82.
28. Ibid., p. 81.
29. Ibid., p. 78.

arguing that there is a side in individuals which is not at all subordinate (instrumental) but eternal and divine. By this participation in the eternal and divine, individuals have a part in the ends of reason and are thus ends in themselves. Since the eternal and divine is not apart from them, they fulfil themselves and their own purposes by serving the purposes of the world spirit. They are not just means because as the agents of morality and religion they are referred to their final purpose and may consciously relate to it.[30]

In this context it is no accident that the question arises whether individuals can be guilty. The possibility of guilt expresses that which constitutes personal dignity as distinct from animal innocence.[31] Guilt arises for Hegel when individuals isolate themselves from the universal, seek wealth, external fame, etc., and reject the summons to good, moral, and just purposes which seek to be executed and secured among and in them.[32] For Hegel evil in the Christian sense is neither a wilful and conscious contradiction of God nor a disruption of personal fellowship. It is an indolent and venial pursuit of one's own purposes. At this point the question may be put—we shall have to explore it later—whether we do not have to regard this stage of emancipation as simply a transition in the dialectical process and therefore as a necessary stage. This teleological understanding of evil will imply a sharper distinction from the unconditional and radical concept of sin in the biblical sense.

As a result of the theologically relevant discussions of personal individuality in Hegel, we may state that there is no real place for individuality in his system. Individuals in their particularity are continually erased and cancelled so as to be absorbed in the universal and supraindividual in whose service they stand. (Not last or least it might have been this feature that led Kierkegaard to put the "individual" in the center in his violent contradiction of Hegel.)

In discussing Marxist anthropology we shall later note how the restriction of individuality in favor of the universal worked itself out in Marx and provided an argument for his collectivist tendencies. The concern of Marx is with the development of "social organs" which reduce our individuality and make us organs of the socially universal.[33] Human liberation can be achieved only when individuals merge into the species.[34]

30. Ibid., pp. 84-85.

31. Ibid., p. 85.

32. Ibid., p. 86.

33. K. Marx, "Nationalökonomie und Philosophie," in *Die Frühschriften*, ed. S. Landshut (1953), pp. 237, 241.

34. "Zur Judenfrage," in ibid., p. 199; ET "On the Jewish Question," in *Early Writings* (New York, 1975), p. 234.

For Hegel such supraindividual structures as the state and law are more akin to the absolute spirit than individuals. Individuals are no more than means and transitional points in the self-fulfilment of this spirit, but such structures are its true "material" and the site of its actualization in the form of the objective spirit.[35] At any rate, individuals have for Hegel something quite different from the alien dignity that is assigned to them in Luther's theology and that gives them the accent of unconditionality.

III. PHILOSOPHY OF RELIGION

We shall now take up the question of the implications of the system for an understanding of religion and ultimately of Christianity.[36] I must refrain from conducting a guided tour in every corner of this multi-faceted work after the manner of a Baedeker. We must ignore the history and typology of the religions as they are unfolded with the help of Hegelian dialectic and limit ourselves to points that are theologically relevant. As Hegel's philosophy is a summarizing, elucidating, and transcending of the whole prior history of philosophy, so contemporary Christianity is regarded as the summarizing, elucidating, and transcending of the whole prior history of religion. We shall take a brief look at the religious process that leads to this end.

A. RELIGION IN GENERAL

The issue in religion, too, is the coming to consciousness of the absolute spirit, which achieves knowledge of itself in the religious subject. Religion is the relation of the spirit to the absolute spirit. Only thus is the knowing spirit also the known. Religion, then, is the self-consciousness of the absolute spirit.[37] In finite knowledge the absolute spirit knows itself, and the finite spirit knows its knowledge to be that of the absolute spirit.[38] There thus follows a statement which brings to light the mystical side: "Without the world God is not God."[39] But why does the absolute spirit need the world?

---

35. Hegel, *Die Vernunft in der Geschichte*, pp. 89ff.
36. Cf. esp. *Vorlesungen über die Philosophie der Religion*, in *Werke*, XI-XII (1832); ET *Lectures on the Philosophy of Religion* (1984-85).
37. *Werke*, XI, 128.
38. Ibid., p. 122.
39. Ibid.

The answer is given in two steps. First, God is undeveloped and formless without cosmic space, without the world. Alone, he would be pure *eidos* in Aristotle's sense. He would be mere concept or infinitude, the abyss of nothingness into which all being sinks.[40] To God's being there thus belongs his reality, which Hegel can think of only in terms of self-development. A spirit that does not exist in real forms, that is without objectification, that is limited to pure transcendence, is merely potential and not kinetic energy, if one might use a physical analogy. When still at this stage, the world spirit is no real God. At most it is only God-expectant, a possibility awaiting actualization.

Second, the spirit without the world is not God because it cannot achieve consciousness of itself without the finite spirit; it cannot be really there in Heidegger's sense.[41] A God without self-consciousness, and hence without the attribute of omniscience, is obviously not God. As Angelus Silesius might say, God cannot live for an instant without me.

We have seen that Hegel's identity speculation finally leads to the same point as the mystical doctrine of God in me and me in God, or as Eckhart's doctrine of the ground or spark of the soul. We are surely not guilty of any theological exaggeration if we say with Kierkegaard that here the self-confidence of thought turns into hubris.[42] For in such speculation God is not the Lord who in the form of creation out of nothing makes a world distinct from himself, and who in the silence of primeval time is still the triune God.[43] Instead, this God is tied to the existence of the world and humanity. "You shall be as God"; indeed, we are not merely "as" God; we are no less than those who make God possible as one of his modifications.

B. POSITIVE RELIGION AND THE ABSOLUTENESS OF CHRISTIANITY

One might easily imagine how Hegel evaluates the historical religions. They are simply forms of religion in general and are arranged hierarchically.[44] Mounting up from primitive forms of natural religion by various stages (the OT and Greek and Roman religion) to a religion of spiritual individuality, they display an increasing clarification in the

40. Cf. *EF,* I, 260.
41. Cf. *Encyclopädie,* §§ 416-17, 566; *EF,* I, 263.
42. I refer only to Hegel and am not placing mystical piety under the same verdict.
43. Cf. *ThE,* I, §§ 712-62, 1330-53; ET I, 79-80.
44. Cf. the Table of Contents of the *Lectures on Religion.*

self-consciousness of the absolute spirit until this self-consciousness achieves complete adequacy in the absolute religion of Christianity.

What do we normally mean—this preliminary question is useful—by the absoluteness of Christianity?[45] We mean the exclusiveness of its truth. In the history of theology this meaning comes to expression in the thesis that Christianity is the most perfect religion or the epitome of all religion. Thus for Harnack the uniqueness of the gospel is that it is not a positive religion like others, that there is nothing particularistic about it. This does not mean that it is not part of the history of religion. On the contrary, it can only mean that it is religion itself.[46] In the gospel the historical phenomenon is congruent with the very idea of religion. Rudolf Kittel expresses the same thought more vividly (and more crassly) in his hymn of praise to the OT when he finds in it the blossoming of all ancient religion and the instrument with which the master can bring in absolute religion. When we consider with what purity and majesty the idea of God finds expression in Israel, the idea of God as moral will; when we consider how the idea of personality develops out of this; when finally we come under the influence of the powerful moral and social universalism whereby humanity itself becomes a great union of moral and religious personalities, or a kingdom of God, then we have to allow that the OT is so close to religion as such that we can do no other than maintain its truth and abiding worth for all its weaknesses in detail.[47]

In Hegel, whose echo we catch in Harnack and Kittel, absoluteness does not denote a supreme quantitative enhancement. It points to the transition from quantity to quality, to the point where an entity—a historical religion—becomes fully congruent with the concept of it. Whereas the natural religions display the self-consciousness of God only in cloudy or muffled form, with an admixture of such alien elements as superstition and fetishism, this self-consciousness has become direct and fully adequate in Christianity. Here the finite spirit has become a clear mirror for the absolute spirit.

Two elements mark this concept of absoluteness. First, it is the final stage in a purifying development, in the self-development of world reason. The concept of religion comes into its own here. The gospel does not stand over against religion, as dialectical theologians like to say.

---

45. Cf. *EF*, III, 345ff.

46. Harnack, *Das Wesen des Christentums* (1900, repr. 1950), p. 38; *What Is Christianity?* (New York, 1901).

47. R. Kittel, "Die Zukunft der alttestamentlichen Wissenschaft," *ZAW* (1921) 84ff., esp. 96-98.

It is the end point in a series. It belongs to the genus of religion, as Hegel would put it. Second, Christianity is a form of knowledge in which the absolute spirit comes to knowledge of itself through the medium of the finite spirit, which it uses in philosophy too, and in every form of thought. Hence the Christian religion (and with it the subjective act of faith) is part of the nexus of knowledge.

This implies, first, that Christianity is a phenomenon of the human consciousness and comes within the context of culture. When revelation is understood thus, when as a stage in the self-development of the spirit it is spirit of our (finite) spirit, then there can be no contradicting it. We cannot decide against it. It cannot be a scandal. Lucifer is not interesting as a fallen angel, as Satan, whose fall is the antithesis of the ascension. He is interesting because in him the angels see one of themselves. Even a fallen state is a stage in the self-development of the spirit. It is supreme alienation, the movement of antithesis in the dialectic of the logical process. Lucifer is still an angel in the negative mode of the phase of alienation. There can thus be no contradiction, no No, for spirit cannot decide against spirit. The inclusion of Christianity and religion in the human consciousness makes it easy for the left-wing Hegelians, and especially Marx, to interpret everything religious as the time-bound product of the socially tied consciousness, as a functional superstructure.

A second implication of the thesis that Christianity belongs to the general nexus of knowledge is that it ceases to be a "historical" religion in the strict sense. By its historicity we mean that it tells me of the mighty acts of God, evoking my astonishment, and giving me contingent news that I cannot tell myself. The news of the forgiveness of sins is the news of a divine visitation that cannot be postulated, of a breaking of the regular nexus of sin and guilt. The appearance of Christ is a shining of light in the darkness that cannot be a construct of thought. It is the miracle of the change of aeons. It is not the self-development of God in the process of history, but an intervention in this process.

Such contingent impartations as are associated with miracles can have no place in Hegel because they contradict the necessity of the process of thought and occurrence. For Hegel events are a necessary and logically conceivable self-unfolding of the spirit. This means that the true content of Christian faith is to be vindicated by philosophy, not by history. Hence in studying religion we do not go historically to works, beginning on the outside; we go to the concept. To begin with what is positive, i.e., with history known by narration, is the necessary way in education. Childishly naive piety accepts the truth as authority, as the impartation of a *Deus dixit;* it is quite satisfied with this. In such faith the true content is present but the form of thought is missing. Philosophy deals with the form, though the content remains the same. In this way naive faith is freed from an authoritarian tie to history and becomes reflective knowledge to the extent that we proceed scientifically. Along these lines it is the aim of Hegel's lectures to reconcile reason and religion.[48]

In sum, we may say: (1) That philosophy—to adopt Kant's comparison—becomes the mistress of theology because it alone provides the criteria by which to present the truth content of the Christian religion, detaching it from the authority of purely historical impartations and making it an evident element in the proclamations of the spirit. This is possible only because the same applies both to revelations that come in history and to what may be said of history in general, namely, that they are the work of reason and that philosophy alone can adequately interpret them. Philosophy has a papal monopoly in exposition. (2) Christian truth, then, is plainly dehistoricized. The point of all Christian doctrines is proclaimed in history (as a self-evolution of the spirit), though at its core it is not tied to history but is timeless and always present. The thrust is the same as in every theology of consciousness and not just Hegel's.

These conclusions may be illustrated from any one of the various Christian dogmas. I will sketch Hegel's understanding of reconciliation, the Trinity, and sin.

1. Reconciliation

Since all contradictions can be only antitheses in a dialectical process, and hence elements within the identity of the spirit, they are never radical or unconditional contradictions but are always interim and conditional. Hence there is no need of a reconciliation which demands the intervention of a third party or at least a deliberate Nevertheless which reconciles the two parties in the antithesis. What brings reconciliation is simply a process of knowledge. The two parties in antithesis come to know one another, to see that their opposing positions are simply stages in the same process or elements of one and the same spirit. There is thus no act of reconciliation. There is only the recognition of an already existing state of reconcili..ion. Within the *complexio oppositorum* it is perceived that there is a monon which overarches the polarity and holds the two sides together. The concept of unconditional and radical antitheses is a prephilosophical figment that is naturally present

48. Hegel, *Werke*, XII, 266ff.

at a naive stage when the event of salvation is depicted historically and the true meaning of history is not yet seen.

Thus in the definition of absolute religion as the religion of truth and freedom the third thesis is to the effect that the first stage of reconciliation posits a contradiction between God and a world that is by nature alienated, and that reconciliation is the negation of this cleavage as the two recognize one another and come to know their real nature.

In other words, an active reconciliation is out of the question because of the unity and identity of the spirit that transcends all antitheses. What is historical takes place only on the plane of the self-unfolding of this identity. Antitheses are thus transcended. What we really have are historical stages in the development of the consciousness. We are dealing with a noetic event by which antitheses come to know one another, i.e., to know that they are reconciled.

This, then, is the synthesis of things that seem to be opposed and alien. This synthesis is not a creative act. It is always present and timelessly in force. Only its noetic perception has the form of a historical process. The Pythagorean theorem is always valid, but Pythagoras, who discovered it, was a historical phenomenon who found it in the historical process of thought. What seems to be the event of reconciliation in the Bible is thus, in Abelard's sense, no more than the dramatic demonstration of something that is timelessly valid. Similarly, the union of the divine and human natures in Christ does not rest on the actual miracle of incarnation (John 1:1) any more than our reunion with God is due to an act of redemption by Christ. What happens is simply that in christological symbols we have a manifestation of the timeless state of reconciliation between God and us—a manifestation that the antithesis is no more than dialectical. The unity of the divine and human natures has to be objectively revealed to us. This took place with the incarnation of God. The possibility of reconciliation lies in the perception of the existing unity between the divine and human natures. We can know that we are adopted into God inasmuch as God is not alien to us.[49]

It would be almost an anticlimax to stress how different is the NT view of reconciliation as the miracle of the act of God's love which we can never postulate (cf. John 3:16; 2 Cor. 5:19; Eph. 2:16). Under cover of the same terminology there has been a radical departure from the meaning of the biblical concept of reconciliation.

49. Ibid., p. 235.

2. The Trinity

In Christian theology the doctrine of the Trinity safeguards the historic-ity of revelation. It expresses in a formula the fact that the saving event has its context in the one God who as Creator and Redeemer reveals himself to be both present and future. According to the Apostles' Creed with its trinitarian structure, the triunity can be defined only by the historical events of creation, incarnation, and the outpouring of the Spirit at Pentecost.[50]

One may suspect that it was the number 3 in the doctrine which gave Hegel the idea that we have here a confirmation of the threefold structure of his dialectic. (1) God the Father is thought, i.e., the eternal content which remains the same in its manifestation. (2) God the Son signifies the distinction of the eternal nature from its manifestation in the finite spirit even in nature. (3) God the Holy Spirit is the synthesis as the eternal return of the alienated world and its reconciliation with the eternal nature. The Trinity, too, is taken out of contingent history and put in the necessity of the dialectical process of thought. A theolog-ical confession which interprets God's history with the world is under-stood philosophically and transposed into a formula—a true change of genre—which expresses that dialectical necessity and thus becomes a philosophical formula. Hegel is not denying that the biblical accounts relate to historical events. His point is that these events are emanations of the reason that holds sway in history. As such they are illustrations (or primers) for a textbook that contains the philosophy of the spirit.

At root all antitheses are resolved in this system which is based on the dialectic of thought and the self-development of the spirit. Whatever is in motion is so in a monistic sense only as a process of knowledge within a static system and its identity. (Stylistically the kinship to the thought of Origen is thus unmistakable.)

One may judge what serious consequences this conception has for the monistic reinterpretation of Christianity—a reinterpretation that is the more sinister inasmuch as a facade of Christian terminology remains intact (sin, reconciliation, trinity, divine humanity of Christ, etc.) while behind it a substantial change of content takes place. We do not have here a protest against Christianity but the most dangerous transformation of Christianity in the modern era, the transformation of faith into thought, of the historical into the permanently valid, and of

50. Cf. *EF,* II, 129-83, for my contention that the doctrine of the Trinity is an expression of the contingent work of salvation that God has done. On Hegel's doctrine of the Trinity cf. K. Fischer, *Geschichte der neueren Philosophie,* 8, 996ff.

theology into philosophy. Hegel's philosophy is like an apparently harmless Trojan horse. It bears a Christian emblem. But from inside it, once it is within the walls of the church's Troy (dragged in by theological Hegelians), there spring Feuerbach, Strauss, Marx, and all the rest. These attack the Christian front in a partisan warfare which Hegel initiated under the cover of Christian concepts. It is understandable that the left-wing Hegelians, and later Feuerbach and Marx, should find in Hegel the methodological principles of a criticism of religion which would lead inevitably to atheism.[51]

Hegel resolves all the dualisms of Christian theology (God and the world, holiness and sin, law and gospel, etc.) in an all-embracing monon which makes dialectical antitheses into controlling syntheses. In a general survey we may tabulate as follows the theologically significant examples of such resolution.

C. DIALECTICAL RESOLUTION OF ANTITHESES

1. The Gospel and the Religions

These are all integrated into the development of the self-knowing spirit. Christianity is subsumed as a species under the master concept of religion. Religion itself, one might say, is subordinated to the chief concept of the absolute spirit that comes to adequate reflection in philosophy. In this regard Hegel distinguishes himself from a synthetic theologian like Schleiermacher, who assigned to religion an independent province of its own and prepared the way for the later doctrine (cf. Troeltsch and Nygren) of a special religious a priori. At least doctrinally, Schleiermacher gave Christianity a special place within the religions, not in virtue of a speculative unity of form and content, and therefore not in terms of a Hegelian absoluteness, but on the basis of a historical reference to the person of Christ.

A tension between the gospel and the religions such as is, on any understanding, the basis of mission, can no longer be normative in Hegel's system. The only possibility is a dialogue between them with the goal that each will see itself in the other and thus merge into the peaceful monologue of the world spirit. Those who once vigorously espoused the thesis of the absoluteness of Christianity can easily and quickly accept the tame postulate of a mere dialogue (as has happened among many missiologists today, and as is symptomatic of a fatal loss of salt). Hardly

51. R. Garaudy, *Dieu est Mort. Étude sur Hegel* (Paris, 1962), pp. 428-29.

anyone notices that there may be heard here the distant thunder of the Hegelian herd.

2. God and Humanity

This antithesis yields to a final identity as the absolute spirit recognizes itself in the finite spirit and the finite spirit sees itself to be a vessel and transitional stage of the absolute spirit.

3. The Accidental Truths of History and the Necessary Truths of Reason

The antitheses between these truths troubled Lessing and was a sustaining motif in his theological deliberations. But it now falls away, for reason and history are reconciled. Lessing with his historical problem is undoubtedly much closer to the event of the gospel than Hegel, and there can be no doubt on which side Pastor Goeze of Hamburg would have been had he had to choose. The synthesis which Hegel puts in place of Lessing's cleavage is quickly adopted by the left-wing Hegelians. Thus Strauss makes it the occasion for his skeptical thesis that we are not to take history as history but as allegory or myth.[52] A historical process which is changed into dialectical necessity involves the dissolution of history and consequently of a revelation that comes to expression in history.

4. The Polarity of Good and Evil

This, too, is finally dissolved. The result is a destruction of the biblical view of sin as unconditional contradiction of God.[53] In paradise prior to the fall human beings have the innocence of animals. Their consciousness is "natural." But this state has to be transcended once the consciousness of the spirit intervenes. They cannot be accountable so long as they exist in unconscious and childlike innocence.

Hegel thinks it a defect in the metaphorical conception of paradise that union with the good is depicted as an existent state, for

---

52. Cf. C. Hartlich and W. Sachs, *Der Ursprung des Mythosbegriffs in der modernen Bibelwissenschaft* (1952). The authors show that when Strauss raises the suspicion of myth this implies a critical departure from his master (pp. 121ff.).

53. This presentation draws on sections of the *Vorlesungen über die Philosophie der Geschichte* which are printed in Brünstadt's edition (pp. 41ff.) but not in PhB. Cf. also *Religionsphilosophie*, Jubilee ed., 16, 73ff.

here there can be no true good. Such goodness is achieved only when we leave our original natural state, as we have to do in order to become conscious. Becoming conscious means entering the polarity of good and evil. The fall, then, is the eternal myth of humanity whereby we become human.

The fall is necessary, and evil is simply a transition in the dialectical process. The journey to the far country—to use the illustration of the parable of the prodigal—is a necessary dialectical detour on the way home. We arrive at the synthesis by way of the antithesis.

André Gide has similarly depicted the far country as a productive transition. In his story the returning son sends the youngest brother, who does not figure in the parable, into the far country in order that he may achieve maturity there. One may also think of Schiller's understanding of the fall as the happiest day in world history.

Here again it is plain why Golgotha is not needed as an act of deliverance to overcome the unconditional contradiction of God by sin. Golgotha can be no more than the demonstration of a reconciliation that is posited in the dialectical process itself. To use our illustration again, when the prodigal returns to his father, he does not now say: "Father, I have sinned against heaven and before thee; I am no more worthy to be called thy son" (Luke 15:21). He no longer receives inconceivable acceptance from his father in spite of every expectation or dialectical postulate. No, as perceived by Hegel, the prodigal says on his return: "I have now discovered my identity and I come before thee as the one thou dost desire. In the far country I have become the one I was designed to be." And in the father we no longer have a miracle of acceptance. The father simply draws the conclusion from what the productive change in the far country has accomplished.

Evil on this view is not the sin of the Bible. Indeed, staying in a state of nature is evil for Hegel. It is staying in the father's house, in paradise. The older brother who never leaves home is the representative of evil. (He is, of course, a negative figure in the parable of Jesus, yet not because he stays at home, but because he does not share the father's joy at the prodigal's return and finds merit in his staying at home.) If we are to fulfil our destiny, we must spend a productive period in the far country. We must go out freely and voluntarily. But this means that we must enter into the teleology of evil which will lead us to the telos of a return. Hegel's interpretation of the story of the fall carries a critical undertone when he comes to speak about the prohibition of eating the tree of the knowledge of good and evil, i.e., of entering into the polarity and its teleology.

Alexander Solzhenitsyn alludes at times to the fact that it is the teleological reinterpretation of evil that makes it evil. Thus in face of the evil figures in Shakespeare, Dickens, and Schiller, he asks whether these are people who consciously do evil, whether they are wicked people. But he denies this. To do evil we must first think that evil is good or lawful.[54] Thus ideology depicts evil as something that serves the good. By way of certain practices in Maxist Stalinism, do we perhaps have here an echo of the dialectical mitigating of evil initiated by Hegel? Nicholas Berdyaev, too, wrestles with the monistic dissolution of evil in his book *The Power and Reality of Evil.*

If evil is no longer seen as an unconditional antithesis of good which cannot be harmonized with it teleologically, then the possibility of decision is removed. For no matter what I do, no matter how I act within the polarity of good and evil, I always fit in with the teleological process and help to achieve the happy ending of synthesis.

T. W. Adorno in his essay "Kritik" has pointed out that Hegel's view leads to the elimination of criticism as well as decision.[55] Those who trust their finite and fallible reason are scorned. One need not be a sociologist to detect behind the mockery of reason and of attempts at world betterment the soothing preaching that seeks to pacify subjects. Subjects are seen as people who in their stupidity do not like the decisions made by their rulers and cannot see that finally everything is for the best, that the world spirit in the rulers, in its form as an objective spirit, will finally prove to be superior to the individual understanding. Adorno wants to fix here on the point in Hegel's philosophy at which he establishes the unconditional authority of the state over its subjects. Along the lines of laissez-faire, subjects can uncritically fit in with the movements of the world spirit and trust its superior manifestations, e.g., in rulers.

The transcending of all antitheses in a teleological process raised against Hegel the diametrically opposed objections of Kierkegaard and Marx. In each case the opposition was so basic and radical that it contributed essentially to the rise of the objectors' own views. Hegel's philosophy could not produce an ethics, Kierkegaard argued, because its stance was that of a spectator. It does not really let me exist *in* history. I am an onlooker outside it. I see the whole panorama from the standpoint of the world spirit. We have already shown the implications of this. Hegel cannot take history seriously, including salvation history, because he dissolves all historical facts in logical processes. This applies to himself as one who acts in history, for he sees himself to be

54. Solzhenitsyn, *Gulag Archipelago* (New York, 1974).
55. *Die Zeit* 26 (1969) 22.

unable to make any decisions and must bow to the law of laissez-faire, which results in a subject-mentality. We need only think of God coming among us in human clothing, not in the sense of real incarnation. Even he cannot act or decide. He sees the end from the beginning. He sees that after all the adventurous dialectical movement everything will have to come under his sway. He is thus denied the possibility of bold and authentic and responsible decision. Is not Hegel, too, in this position when he introduces the world spirit?

To history and historical action there obviously belongs a finite consciousness which does not mount above its finitude by attributing to itself an identity with the absolute spirit. When we act we are "blind" in Goethe's sense. We have to be so. If we were not, there would be no dialogue or debate; we would be caught up in the monologue of the world spirit.

Insight into this difficulty in Hegel also stands behind the thesis of Marx that we have not to *interpret* history but to *change* it. Marx noted the lack of any place for decision in Hegel. In the Marxist view of freedom as insight into necessity, we find a remnant of Hegel's dialectic of history. Yet in the absence of the presupposition of the identity of the finite and the absolute spirit, or of speculation about the spirit in general, this insight itself becomes an act which necessarily pushes us out of the state of extreme social alienation into the certainty that when the proletariat revolt they will have the will of history on their side, so that the insight inspires their own active will. We still see the philosophy of Hegel in the wings, but it has been displaced, and on the stage we now see active people who have set aside speculative dreaming and found ideological stimulation in the agreement of their own will for change with the thrust of history.

This, then, is Hegel's position in or *above* history. He hears the whisper of the world spirit. It says to him: "You are like the spirit that you grasp, not me." But he grasps this spirit, for he is part of it. Because of this, history stops. It is at rest in a very different way from what Hegel had in mind when he expressed the conviction that the whole history of philosophy was summed up in him and had reached its end. The finite spirit, we have said, can act only when it is blinded, when it is only finite, when it knows no escape from its finitude. (The overcoming of finitude in the Christian doctrine of the resurrection is another matter.) Hence history stops at the very moment when the finite spirit transcends itself in Hegel's sense. Concepts alone glide noiselessly on, but we humans have ceased to grasp ourselves precisely because we *think* we have done so. We are confronted by the self-judgment of hubris.

IV. CONCLUDING QUESTIONS

We have briefly sketched the vast complex of Hegel's thought and tried to grasp its architectural scheme. I will close this attempt by trying to formulate some questions that have to remain open in Hegel and that press for answers in the next decades and up to our own time. The very fact that we find such open questions means that we support the thesis that Hegel is not a conclusion, as he thought he was, but that by summing up all previous thought he constitutes a synthesis which as a thesis has to produce new antitheses and thus initiates a new dialectical game. History goes on, and it is given a push by the questions that remain open in Hegel.

What questions? I will take up two which, I believe, have representative significance. The one is theological, the other more generally intellectual.

A. THE THEOLOGICAL QUESTION

When Hegel finally abolishes history as history because its regularly determined course leaves no room for the contingent element (which explains the insignificance of individuals), the resultant theology finds difficulty and disruption in the figure of Jesus Christ. In a plain attack on Hegel, Kierkegaard formulates the difficulty as follows. The offense—the philosophical offense—in the figure of Christ is that in him an individual and not suprapersonal humanity is God,[56] even though the individual lies on the far periphery in the self-development of the spirit. Faced with this offense, we must choose between two christological alternatives.

We might base our theological thinking on the fundamental historical fact of Jesus Christ. In this case our basic attitude in the history that he triggered and that is at work in us will be one of *decision* rather than *insight*. How can we gain access to the figure of Christ by way of insight when this figure cannot be subsumed under a master concept or type and there is thus no objective access to it? As Kierkegaard sees it, the objective uncertainty in which we are set releases an "infinite passion of inwardness" which there can never be in Hegel's insight-philosophy.[57] This philosophy of noncommitment is thus the true enemy for Kierkegaard.

56. Kierkegaard, *Training in Christianity*, pp. 26ff.
57. Kierkegaard, *Concluding Unscientific Postscript*, p. 188.

The other possibility is to start as Hegel does with the axiom that history is the self-unfolding of the spirit. In this case I have to reinterpret the figure of Jesus Christ so as to fit it into this schema. Above all, I have to depersonalize and deindividualize it. Agreeing with this result of Hegelian Christology, and using it to destroy the traditional picture, D. F. Strauss reduces it to a famous formula when he says that the idea does not realize itself by putting all its richness in a single example and begrudge it to all the rest, expressing itself perfectly in this one and imperfectly in all others.[58] The idea unfolds itself in an infinite series of finite forms which complement one another in mutual alternation. On this view the historical person of Christ yields to his symbolical significance, which represents something suprapersonal and closer to the spirit. There is no doubt that this suprapersonal element is understood in terms of the thought of humanity that is familiar to us from Kant and Schleiermacher. No place remains for the offense of thought of which Kierkegaard spoke, namely, that God appeared in an individual.

B. THE GENERAL INTELLECTUAL QUESTION

For Hegel, as we have seen, everything real is rational. The correlation of reality and reason is viewed, as it were, from the side of reason. He describes it as the self-development of the spirit.

The question, however, is whether one cannot view the correlation from the other side. Might one not say that in the sphere of reality, of the material, observation points to dialectical laws according to which the processes of evolution take place? In the course of evolution matter then produces an element which achieves consciousness with the rise of the human brain.[59] This consciousness then forms ideas which plainly mirror material circumstances and are to be understood as reflections (ideologies) in this sense.

In this case everything in Hegel is reversed. The sign is changed. Hegelianism becomes materialism. The dialectic of history is materialistic. In short, what happens is what we find among the left-wing Hegelians.

Hegel is defenseless against this development. Instead, he ini-

58. Strauss, *The Life of Jesus* (1892), § 151, pp. 779-81.
59. This kind of materialism, which goes rather beyond what is usually called the materialist view of history, is championed in the Marxist sphere by F. Engels in *Dialektik der Natur. Notizen und Fragmente*, p. 554.

tiates it, and hence in many respects finds confirmation in it. There are two main reasons why this is so.

First, this reversal is the antithesis to the thesis of Hegel's philosophy. What happens in left-wing Hegelianism is both a very paradoxical refutation of his system and at the same time a confirmation of his dialectical schema. Although there is liberation from Hegel, and his philosophy is stood on its head, he is still the secret father in the background.

Second, Hegel is defenseless against this development because there is no room for decision in his thinking. From Hegel's standpoint, it is not for us to say whether the correlation is to be viewed from the side of spirit or that of matter. The antitheses must come to know one another and see their common basis in identity. That they do so is the real reason why, even after the left-wing reversal, Hegel is still seen to be the genealogical ancestor.

CHAPTER 13

Theologians Influenced by Hegel

I. A. E. BIEDERMANN

Bibliography. Primary Works: *Die freie Theologie oder Philosophie und das Christentum in Streit und Frieden* (1844); *Unsere junghegelsche Weltanschauung oder der sogenannte neueste Pantheismus* (1849); *Christliche Dogmatik* (1869; 2nd ed. in 2 vols. 1884-1885).
Secondary Works: W. Elert, *Der Kampf um das Christentum* (1921), pp. 113ff.; H. R. von Frank, *Geschichte und Kritik der neueren Theologie* (1895), pp. 181ff.; O. Pfleiderer, *Die Entwicklung der Protestantischen Theologie in Deutschland seit Kant und Grossbritannien seit 1825* (1891), pp. 139ff.; R. Stähelin, in *RE*, 3rd ed., pp. 203ff.

A. BIOGRAPHY

Aloys Emanuel Biedermann was born in 1819 by Lake Zurich. He studied in Basel, where on his own confession the reading of D. F. Strauss made a stronger impression than any of his own teachers. Only much later, when *Der alte und der neue Glaube* came out in 1872, did he painfully draw away from this "ominous book." He next studied in Berlin, where he was much influenced by Hegel's philosophy. In 1843 he became a pastor in Basel-land, and here he wrote his first work, *Die freie Theologie . . .* (1844), which expresses a Hegelianism that brings him close to Feuerbach when he says that in the idea of God the human consciousness objectifies what is for it its universal, eternal, absolute, and authentic nature.[1] The book had a

1. Cf. Biedermann, *Die freie Theologie*, p. 83 (quoted by Stähelin, *RE*, p. 204).

strong impact in Switzerland (both for and against), and according to Stähelin led to the relaxation of obligatory confessional standards. Biedermann now wrote his main work, the *Christliche Dogmatik* (1869). Along with his church work he devoted his last years to a revision of the dogmatics. This does not represent any change of theological position but engages in discussion with friends and debate with opponents. He died at the beginning of 1885.

B. THE QUESTION OF THE TRUTH OF DOGMA

Among the theological disciples of Hegel one might hesitate whom to choose in illustration of the way in which Hegel's philosophy of the spirit affected professional theology. We are confronted by many figures in whom the reception of Hegel's identity dialectic takes very different forms. In this context I need mention only the most prominent: K. Daub (1765-1836), P. K. Marheineke (1780-1846), O. Pfleiderer (1839-1908), and of course, that gifted historian F. C. Baur (1792-1860).[2] I select Biedermann for my sketch because one may see in him how a theologian who is rooted in the church's fellowship, and who seeks a church that is free and yet in no sense emancipated from tradition, handles the impact of Hegel's philosophy.

Yet it is not just a matter of Hegel himself, although Biedermann in the preface to his dogmatics confesses, not without some irony, that his opponents are not entirely wrong to mock him as the Swiss campfollower of an aberration that has long since been outmoded in the metropolis and in other official centers of German scholarship. In fact, he owes a great deal of the nourishment for his philosophical thinking to the philosophy of Hegel. But the strongest influence of Hegel was indirect by way of a Hegelian. In particular it was D. F. Strauss who forced Biedermann to put Christian doctrine on a new and greatly reduced basis. This reduction, Biedermann thought, is due especially to Strauss's convincing criticism of the personal character of God, of an individualistic doctrine of immortality, and of the absolutizing of an individual like Jesus. Such things cannot be brought into harmony with the final identity of the finite and absolute spirit.

The inferences that Biedermann drew from these negations, and the positive goals that he saw for his theological work, we learn from

---

2. On Marheineke see Barth, *Protestant Theology*, pp. 491ff.; on Baur see W. Dilthey, *Gesammelte Schriften*, IV (1959), 403-32; Barth, *Protestant Theology*, pp. 499ff.; Hirsch, *Geschichte der neueren evangelische Theologie*, V (1949), 518ff.

the *Christliche Dogmatik,* his one great work, which is marked by the crispness and pregnancy of its language, by its perspicacity and historical erudition, and not least by a bold and uncompromising consistency, while always preserving a judicious character and never lapsing into fanaticism.[3]

While recognizing the criticisms of Strauss, in distinction from Strauss Biedermann is always seeking the truth content of Christian dogmas. To distil this out, he uses scholarship, for this brings to light the contradictory and time-bound ideas in church dogmas and enables us to get at the "concept." The religious content of dogmas is their truth as thus reduced to the concept. Biedermann's final aim is positive. He wants to contribute a stone in the building up of a free Protestant Christian church.[4]

In trying to find this truth content Biedermann comes up against the basic problem that affects every theological system of the period under discussion, namely, doubt as to the concrete content of the Christian tradition (especially the admixture of intellectual content and mere depiction), and also the problem of how there can be new appropriation, how the objective data can be harmonized with the subjective receptive capacity. Only when such harmony is attained can the church, and the believers united in it, be free in Biedermann's sense.

The involved question of the objective truth content of dogma and the possibility of subjective agreement Biedermann answers by demanding an identification of divine and human authority.[5] In the obviously Hegelian terminology this means that the finite spirit must understand itself in its identity with the absolute spirit. At the same time the way in which Biedermann describes the finite spirit as the believing subject and stresses the role of the individual in the appropriation of absolute truth—reminding us of Kierkegaard—makes it plain that there has been a shift of emphasis as compared to Hegel. At the center we now find the free individual in a church which only thus can be free.

In the life of the human spirit religion is the most general thing and yet also the most individual, the most binding and yet also the most liberating. In content it relates to that which stands universally above us all. In form, however, it is the relation of the most inward I to the universal, a direct matter of the individual heart and conscience. Hence the ethical fashioning of the objective religious fellowship (the church) is the supreme but also the most difficult social problem of humanity.

3. Unless indicated, my quotations are from the 1st ed. (1869).
4. *Christliche Dogmatik,* § 82.
5. Ibid., § 79 (pp. 107-8), § 82 (p. 109).

For here it is in a special way a question of uniting two basic elements, the universal factor that forms the organism of fellowship and the personal life of the individual. The ideal is the strongest and most express freedom sustained by the strongest and most conscious fellowship. Only thus can one dissolve all the human authority that might force the faith of the individual and achieve an identification of divine and human authority which will safeguard individual freedom and hence make a free church possible.[6]

To find the truth content and hence to open up the possibility of new appropriation is thus to reach the point where the identity of the finite and absolute spirit is evident and where divine and human authority are not separate. In spite of this Hegelian schema it is plain that the emphatic role of the individual and of matters of the heart and conscience is not taken from this schema but derives from the gospel and is thus a disruptive element in the Hegelian dialectic.

Biedermann's dogmatics is worked out in accordance with his goal of developing a truth content that can be appropriated—only thus can the individual conscience remain free—and reducing what is meant in depictions to concept.

After an introduction on theological principles (the nature of religion, religion and science, and the principle of Christian dogmatics), a comprehensive historical section deals empirically and statistically with the biblically attested facts and sayings of the old and new covenants. Thus we have a carefully differentiated Synoptic, Pauline, and Johannine Christology. Dogmatic themes (Christology, theology, anthropology, and soteriology) are then interwoven as the discussion continues in the form of a history of dogma.

The core of the dogmatics, which the empirical account merely serves in the form of a collection of materials (although it consists of 496 pages and 561 sections), is the critical and speculative part. Here we have the real scientific dogmatics, i.e., a full criticism of the form of church dogma according to no other standard than that of autonomous thought.[7] What Biedermann means by the form of dogma is the psychological form of depiction which as the abstractly sensory presentation of an intellectual idea contains within itself a rational contradiction. To be able to appropriate a dogma honestly—which is Biedermann's goal—depictions have to be made transparent to the idea which is the core of dogma. When this is found, the contradictions disappear.[8]

6. Ibid., § 82 (p. 109).
7. Ibid., § 563 (p. 497).
8. Ibid., § 564 (pp. 497-98).

We must be content to give just a few examples in illustration of the speculative method of Biedermann as it is indicated by the architectonic structure of his work. I will choose for this purpose two typical issues which are important in Hegel too, namely, the personality of God and the fall. These examples will enable us to conjecture how Biedermann handles other dogmas as well (e.g., Christology).

C. THE QUESTION OF GOD'S PERSONALITY

Already in discussing the biblical material Biedermann points out how offensive it is if we form our opinion of God's personality after the analogy of the human ego. For this ego subsists in a sensory ego that is distinct from it as spirit. The same is definitely not true of the God of the Bible. Even when the idea of personality is cautiously applied to God, we are in the half-light between a purely spiritual conception and one that is suprasensory-sensory.[9] The speculative section has to deal with this.

In doing so, it finds that the concept of personality does not go with that of spirit (as it applies to God) but only with that of finite spirit, and therefore in strict thought we are to deny it to God.[10] Personality and finite spirit are overlapping concepts. But an analogous application of the concept of person to God is not possible, for as finite spirit the concrete personal subject is not pure spirit (as God is) but as an indivisible unity it is conjoined with nonspiritual, sensory, natural presuppositions. Thus the analogous attributing of the concept of personality to God lands us in hopeless contradictions, for at every point we have to adopt it again even though it is not absolutely applicable. For this reason the attempt to transfer Hegel's distinction between the finite and the absolute spirit to a distinction between finite and absolute personality rests on an illusion.[11]

Personality is inadequate as a term for God, for it is incompatible with the one term which is adequate, namely, absolute spirit. Personality is simply an adequate term in which to picture the theistic concept of God as all the essential elements in the idea of God are summed up in the concept of the absolute spirit. But for this reason the personality of God is in science the shibboleth of a theism of pure depiction which cannot mount up scientifically from depiction to pure thought.[12]

9. Ibid., § 170 (pp. 171-72).
10. Ibid., § 716, 7 (p. 645).
11. Ibid., § 716, 6 (pp. 643-44).
12. Ibid., p. 646.

The Hegelian background is plain in the speculative thinking through of dogmatic opinions, in the mounting up to pure thought. Nevertheless, hardly has this been stated speculatively, hardly has God been exalted for scientific thought into a pure, depersonalized spirit, than thinking that is related to the consciousness of the Christian community cuts across the speculative schema and forms a disruptive element within it. For even if man is personality as finite spirit, and God as absolute spirit is not, we suddenly have the astonishing qualification that the interaction of religion is always personal, and this not merely in subjective depiction but in objective truth, for between the infinite and the finite spirit this interaction must always take place within the life of the finite spirit and wholly in the form of this spirit.[13]

This is indeed an astounding statement. Biedermann has accused others of constantly having to readopt an application of the category of the personal in relation to God,[14] and now he does the same himself. He does it abruptly and emphatically at the end. How is this?

The forsaking of Hegel in the midst of a plea for Hegel comes when Biedermann considers the concrete situation of the community, i.e., when it hears God's word and prays, when it enters into interaction with the absolute spirit. This concrete dialogue between God and us or us and God cannot be subsumed into the eternal monologue of the spirit with itself which Hegel overhears. Here the finite spirit represented by the community suddenly takes on a different value. It is no longer a mere transition in the self-unfolding of the absolute spirit. It becomes a partner in dialogue. Against his prior premises, Biedermann argues that this is not just a subjective depiction but objective truth, that it is the substance of truth in all that may be said for the postulate of a personal God.[15] What we have found to be the case so often may be seen here once again. The Christian in Biedermann transcends his schema of theological thought.

D. THE QUESTION OF SIN

The Hegelian background may naturally be seen in the understanding of sin and evil. A short reference may suffice.

Within the biblical and historical material there is a careful debate with supralapsarian theories and the Calvinist doctrine of an

13. Ibid., § 717 (p. 647).
14. Cf. ibid., p. 644.
15. Cf. ibid., p. 647.

absolute decree of predestination.[16] Biedermann's decisive concern comes out here. He does not want sin to merge into a suprapersonal process, whether this be a determination arbitrarily posited by God or a teleological evolution that embraces the two poles of good and evil. He wants to maintain its character as imputable guilt for which we are personally responsible. This concern obviously brings him into tension with Hegel's understanding of evil as a mere transition in the self-development of the spirit.

Even when Biedermann does adopt the idea of transition—how can he suddenly not be a Hegelian at this classical point in Hegelianism!—he gives it an essential nuance which derives from his traditionally shaped theological thinking and not from Hegel. As he puts it, in the process of the development of spirit, with absolute necessity we have to go through the alternative of sin and obedience, and hence the inner temptation to sin, but not sin itself.[17] The absolute necessity of the transition relates only to the experience of the division with our determination as spirit.[18] This is the disposition of our existence and no more. What we make of it for good or evil belongs to the moment of self-determination. What takes place before this is not yet sin.[19] We see at this point a theologian who knows about guilt, forgiveness, and justification, and who obviously realizes that the act of justification would be superfluous if sin lost its specific weight as the mere transition in a process.

It is natural to suppose that here again the personal Christianity of Biedermann breaks through the Hegelian schema from within. His own faith, rooted in the community and tradition, is like a partisan that has infiltrated the Hegelian schema and that operates within its theoretical territory. It is hard to integrate the whole of Biedermann's Christianity into his system. There are all kinds of loose ends. His Christology makes this apparent. But instead of following this up in his dogmatics, I will turn to a letter which is impressive in its directness. He wrote it the year before his death (Nov. 18, 1884) to an Erlangen colleague of a very different theological orientation, H. R. von Frank.[20] In it he said that subjectively and objectively God's love is the supreme fact for believers. It is so for him in the full sense, no matter how abstractly he expresses its nature. Hence this is how it is with him regarding the real religious

16. Cf. ibid., pp. 423, 601, 608, etc.
17. Ibid., § 772 (p. 672).
18. Ibid., p. 673.
19. Ibid., p. 672.
20. H. R. von Frank, *Geschichte und Kritik der neueren Theologie* (1895), pp. 187-88.

fact of eternal life,[21] in the light of which he can quietly and deliberately view the transfer to an afterlife as the mere projection of an inner reality, as he has to do according to his epistemological presuppositions— without harming in any way the content of true religious faith.

In the same letter he touches on the relation of his personal faith to the theoretical conception of his Christology. The inner life of Jesus is for him the pinnacle of humanity whose incommensurable greatness in contrast to the religious life of all others is highlighted for him by the historical fact in such a way that it generates in him the kind of faith that the NT authentically presents to us as apostolic—a faith which is pro- duced by the evangelical portrait of him. He thinks so highly of the inner life of Jesus because only in the light of it can he grasp historically, rationally, and commensurably the mythological depiction of him from the resurrection visions onward. The force with which his personal faith resists encirclement by the theological system and enables him to escape imprisonment by it could hardly find clearer manifestation.

The transforming of a mere picture into an abstract idea enclosed by it is neither halted nor denied as a necessary process of thought that we have to undertake. Yet there is another process that essentially transcends in significance this process of thought, at any rate when we think of its relevance to the spiritual ego. This higher process is for Biedermann the objective process in which he traces back mytho- logical christological depictions to their origin in the inner life of the person of Jesus. This in its greatness is what produced and fashioned the depictions. They are not a projection of the imagination of the community. They result from the person of Jesus coming to expres- sion—as one might perhaps say—in this imagination. The person of Jesus reproduces itself by means of this imagination. The imagination is not itself productive.

Two things seem to me to be significant in this regard. First, the goal of faith (in distinction from a theoretical, systematic conception) is not the abstracted, depersonalized idea which is for the Hegelian Biedermann the truth content of dogmas. The goal is a person in history which in contrast to the depictions to which it gives rise obviously cannot be transformed into an abstracted content of ideas, a mere concept.

Second, the true problem of faith for the Christian in Bieder- mann is not finally the changing of time-bound depictions into the truth content of dogmas (as idea) so as to give them a commensurably adequate character. No, once the Christian has grasped the incommen-

---

21. In the *Dogmatik* he contests individual existence after death with very Hegelian arguments; cf. §§ 962ff.

surable greatness of the inner life of Jesus, he can understand the mythological forms of expressing this inner life. This inner life and not a dialectical or rational principle is now the hermeneutical key to an understanding of the christological statements of the NT. Only in this light, as he said in his letter, could Biedermann grasp historically, rationally, and commensurably the mythological depictions.

In keeping with this is the fact that on his deathbed he read the hymns of Paul Gerhardt. C. J. Riggenbach, who tells us about his last hours, says at the end that his heart plainly broke through his system.[22] Conclusions of this kind, which are common in the present book, are not meant to enrich difficult theological reflection with the spice of edification. Instead, I am convinced that serious dialogue with past thinkers is possible only if we keep in view the elements that transcend their systems. Only then can we speak with them within the communion of saints that embraces us all. Apart from this they become mere objects of historiography.[23]

II. KARL BARTH

A. FREEDOM AND NECESSITY IN BARTH'S UNDERSTANDING OF GOD

Essentially more important than the Hegelians of the 19th century are the ongoing shock waves of the Hegelian earthquake in the 20th. They may be seen especially in the great Karl Barth, although one has to overcome some scruples in putting him among those who were influenced by Hegel and presenting him as a Hegelian. In fact, this label is wholly inadequate, not because it is unimportant to establish the theological relevance of his structure of thought as it was in fact influenced by Hegel, but because Barth was a theologian grounded in biblical exegesis and thus had a corrective by which to bring himself to order, guarding against enslavement to systems and being prepared for happy inconsistencies (which are, of course, more apparent to his readers than to himself).[24]

22. See von Frank, *Geschichte und Kritik*, p. 189.

23. Formally, this is not just a theological concern, as may be seen from the fact that when a historian of philosophy like W. Windelband wants to enter into dialogue with past philosophers he needs a common basis with them and finds it in "European humanity," which has put its view of the world and its assessment of life in scholarly concepts; see his *Lehrbuch der Geschichte der Philosophie*, 12th ed. (1928), § 2. In this way he steers clear of mere historiography.

24. Cf. his evasion of universalism, which I discuss in *ThE*, I, 208; ET I, 100ff.

I will ignore the purely formal Hegelianism that one finds in Barth. This appears in the fact that his theology can be called dialectical or in its tendency to paradox ("impossible possibility"). Here we have obvious traces of Hegelian dialectic. Theologians who either like or dislike Hegel are often ready to use paradox because of a certain similarity in thought-structure. For all his material opposition to Hegel, Barth stands close to him in his style of thought and expression. As he himself admits, "I myself have a certain weakness for Hegel and am always fond of doing a bit of 'Hegeling.'"[25] As regards the chapter on Hegel in his theological history, many of Barth's theological colleagues from the 19th century might envy this great philosophical step-brother the many tokens of respect, love, and hope that are paid to him. How is it that there are so many similarities in thought-structure when the relationship is materially such a broken one?[26]

In reply I will look at the matter from various angles. First, many of the principles of Barth's doctrine of God trigger associations with Hegel's concept of the absolute spirit. Thus in regard to the freedom of God according to which he first wills to be himself, Barth tells us that God is not dependent on anything that is not himself or outside himself, that he is not determined by anything outside himself, that he is not subject to any necessity other than himself.[27] The statement that he is not subject to any necessity other than himself is meant as an argument for God's freedom and independence. Yet his freedom is subject to the need to be himself.[28] Being himself in his freedom enables him to determine himself as the gracious God and the author of the covenant even prior to the foundation of the world. For all the difference from Hegel's view of necessity, what the covenant of grace implies is astonishingly close to Hegel's idea of self-development. Significant in this regard are the questions why there has to be a creation and why it has to be disrupted and denied by sin, death, and the devil. Ignoring differentiations, we may say that in each case the answer is that these things have to be in accordance with God's free will.[29] Reflections of this kind sound as though the principle of grace which God resolves on from the outset unfolds itself with necessity both in relation to that which is

25. E. Busch, *Karl Barth* (Philadelphia, 1976), p. 387.

26. The same question might be put to younger theologians who are influenced by Barth and Hegel, e.g., Pannenberg; cf. *EF*, III, 3, 337ff. On the general problem of Barth's Hegelianism, cf. C. Gestrich, *Neuzeitliches Denken und die Spaltung der dialektischen Theologie* (1977), pp. 236ff.

27. *CD*, II/1, 560.

28. Ibid., p. 561.

29. Ibid.

similar to it and close to it, like creation, and to that which is alien, like sin, death, and nonbeing. The only nuance—which is meant to be theologically significant but which seems to me to be very tiny—is that the necessity of self-development is not deduced (as in Hegel) from the nature of the spirit but from the nature of God as God has freely resolved upon this, namely, to be the gracious God. Under this new sign of a free resolve, however, the event of salvation develops with necessity. Even the story of Christ loses its historical contingency and becomes the mere executing of the original resolve.

Barth plainly struggles against making the process automatic. This may be seen especially in his distinction between God's efficacious will (i.e., his positive creative will) and his permissive will. But even when God permits the disruption of his creation by sin, this does not rule out the fact that his will as Lord, if not as Creator, eternally accepts into his foreordination, and therefore into his will, the fall of the creature and the whole kingdom of evil. Do we not have here a purely dialectical distinction, and can the argument really resist the pull toward the view that the negative as well as the positive history with God is grounded equally in the pretemporal self-determination of God as the gracious God (the only difference being that we have here his will as Lord and not as Creator)? Does not the occurrence of negative factors in creation, of its alienation, of sin, form in Hegel's sense an antithesis that God needs in order to demonstrate his victorious goodness? Thus Barth says that when we ask why God permits these negative factors, we can only answer that in them we really see his true and supreme goodness to his creation, that its obedience and salvation will not just be nature, a necessary process, but deliverance from the edge of an abyss. Hence the abyss has to be part of the landscape.[30]

The divine movement made in the covenant of grace has its basis in the fact that God posits himself as the triune God, i.e., as the one who is in relation to himself. Only because he is a God in intratrinitarian relation to himself can he be in relation outward in the movement of salvation history. Here is a speculation that is very close to Hegel. As Barth sees it, grace in the form in which we know it can have and be divine reality only because it has and is divine reality in this un-fathomable form in God himself. Only on the basis of its prior form in which it is not yet a special movement, not yet condescension, not yet the overcoming of an antithesis, but the pure liking, grace, and favor that binds the Father to the Son and the Son to the Father through the Holy Spirit—only on this basis can it become what it is in the form in

30. Ibid., p. 595.

which we know it, namely, movement, condescension, and overcoming. And on this basis it does become this insofar as it has and is divine reality in the form in which we know it.[31]

In this way the event of salvation itself—the Christ event as well as my own incorporation in the event of redemption—is dehistoricized in the same way as in Hegel. It becomes merely an unfolding and executing of what God has foreordained before all time. It is not a new thing—there is no NT—but simply the actualizing of a divine *habitus* (if one might put it thus) that God has chosen for himself in the freedom of his original resolve.[32]

Second, this brings us to the doctrine of the decrees, which is part of the Reformed tradition and which in Barth helps to form a bridge to the philosophy of Hegel.[33] Reconciliation in Jesus Christ— Barth has the decrees in mind—is the first great act of God's faithfulness to himself and therefore to us also—his faithfulness in the execution of the counsel and plan that he had from the very first and that he willed to bring to its goal in all circumstances.[34] H. U. von Balthasar rightly puts the rhetorical question whether this merging of *proton* and *eschaton*, which in this identity become the true agent in the whole intervening process, is not finally spirit of the spirit of Hegel.[35]

In the original decrees—or decree, as Barth would say—creation, fall, reconciliation, and redemption are all foreseen, so that they acquire the character of a necessary unfolding of the original decree. This again confirms the fact that there can be nothing that is historically and contingently new. Reconciliation is not God's reaction to human sin. The abyss of sinful rebellion—to take up Barth's metaphor—is foreseen in the decree of reconciliation itself.

Nevertheless, there *is* something new in Barth. This new thing represents a nuance that breaks through the net of formal similarity to Hegel. In Hegel the finite spirit knows itself in its identity with the abso-

31. Ibid., p. 358. Freyd, *Gott als die universale Wahrheit von Mensch und Welt* (diss., Hamburg, 1982), pp. 122ff., uses the doctrine of the Trinity to show how close Barth is to Hegel, the only difference being in nuances.

32. On Barth's doctrine of the Trinity cf. Pannenberg, "Die Subjectivität Gottes und die Trinitätslehre. Ein Beitrag zur Beziehung zwischen Barth und der Philosophie Hegels," *KuD* 23 (1977) 25.

33. On the historical background of the doctrine cf. *ThE*, II/2, §§ 4039-67. Cf. also O. Ritschl, *Dogmengeschichte des Protestantismus*, III (1926), 291ff.; F. Flückiger, "Vorsehung und Erwählung in der reformierten und der Luther. Theologie," in *Antwort. Festschrift für K. Barth* (1956), pp. 509ff.

34. *CD*, IV/1, 47.

35. H. U. von Balthasar, *Karl Barth. Darstellung und Deutung seiner Theologie* (1951), p. 218.

lute spirit, and it can thus mount up of itself into the self-development of the spirit. Barth rejects as "natural theology" this view of the original decree and its historical emanation. For the fact that the covenant of grace is the first thing that may be known and said about God and us in our relationship to one another is something that we may perceive only as it makes itself known, only as it is fulfilled—which is what took place in Jesus Christ—only as it is really and truly fulfilled.[36] Hence the Christ event is not a new thing as a historical event. As such it is simply the execution of the original self-positing of God as the gracious God. This event, however, discloses a new thing to us that we cannot tell ourselves or establish speculatively (as in Hegel). This new thing is knowledge of the primal decree. Hence the new thing in the NT is noetic, not ontic. What Barth understands by revelation here is noetic disclosure, information, demonstration. Abelard greets us from afar in Barth.[37]

On the path from the OT to the NT there is no historical progress. One might be inclined to use in this regard a metaphor that Barth uses in ethics when speaking about the Christian community and the civil community, i.e., that of two concentric circles. Insight into the decree of reconciliation is found within the whole compass of revelation. The OT is the outer circle, but there is an increasing concentration on the center, on the true point, until the process reaches a provisional end in Christ. The metaphor of concentric circles shows vividly that there is no historical progression of events but a progression of disclosure, of God's (noetic) self-revelation.[38]

Third, the significance of the event of salvation (and perdition) as an execution of the primal decree takes on sharp contours, as one would expect, in Barth's doctrine of predestination. I must be content here to refer to my express presentation of this in the *Theological Ethics*.[39]

Fourth, we have already pointed out that evil, or sin, is en-

---

36. *CD*, IV/1, 45.

37. This helps to explain why in some extreme followers of Barth we find a nontemporal identification of OT and NT salvation history, Christ being present equally in both OT and NT and the latter simply being a noetic explication of the former. Cf. W. Vischer, *Das Christuszeugnis des Alten Testaments*, 2 vols. (1934-1942); ET of vol. I = *The Witness of the Old Testament to Christ* (London, 1949); H. Hellbardt, "Abrahams Lüge," *Theologische Existenz heute* 42; idem, "Die Auslegung des Alten Testaments als theologische Disziplin," *ThBl* 16 (1937) 129-43. Cf. *ThE*, I, §§ 571ff.

38. On Barth's "nonhistoricity" cf. Freyd, *Gott als die universale Wahrheit*, pp. 125-26.

39. *ThE*, I, 205ff.; ET I, 98ff.

visaged in God's primal decree (according to his will as Lord, not Creator). The result is that by the law of monistic thinking Barth is betrayed into a suspicious closeness to Hegel's understanding of evil as a mere transition.

He comes closest of all when he interprets sin in terms of his idea of predestination.[40] Unlike traditional Calvinists, he does not relate reprobation to a certain contingent element in humanity, and therefore to a mass from which God chooses. God rejects himself by means of the incarnation of the Son. He takes rejection to himself. In the strict sense, then, election and rejection are no longer a drama between God and us but an intratrinitarian event, a drama in God (which formally reminds us once again of the spirit-monon in Hegel). In Jesus Christ God elects and rejects himself.[41] As he thus ascribes our reprobation to himself and speaks a pretemporal Yes to us, it becomes impossible for us to understand evil, revolt, our human self-assertion, as an element of tension in our history with God. This history—to put it strongly—threatens to become a panentheistic movement which again has the character of a monologue of God.

In fact, in a remarkable development of the thought of Augustine, Barth depicts evil only negatively. It is only the possibility of the existence of the impossible, the reality of the existence of the unreal; it can have only the power of impotence.[42] Evil, then, is nothingness, which like chaos prior to creation has no power of its own, but can occur in a theological statement about creation only as a possibility which God contemptuously passes over, which he rejects, and which obviously belongs to the past.[43] Evil is not something authentic. It exists only in a negative mode. It is that which God does not will. It lives only by the fact that God does not will it. It does live by this, for what God does not will as well as what he wills is powerful, and hence cannot be without some real correspondence. What really corresponds to the divine non-willing is nothingness.[44]

Barth, then, ascribes a real dimension to evil.[45] Yet having no ontic autonomy, it cannot be understood in terms of itself. It appears only, as it were, as the reflection of a reality. It is present only as God

40. Cf. the careful essays by G. Gloege, "Heilsgeschehen und Welt," *Theologische Traktate*, I (1965), pp. 77ff., 133ff.; H. U. von Balthasar, *Karl Barth*, pp. 142ff.; W. Krotke, *Sünde und Nichtiges bei K. Barth* (1971). Cf. *ThE*, I, 207ff.
41. *CD*, II/2, 1ff.
42. Ibid., p. 170.
43. *CD*, III/1, 108.
44. *CD*, III/3, 352.
45. Ibid.

passes it over and does not will it. Only by the very tortuous and artificial thought that even God's nonwilling is powerful, is nothingness not just nothing but a negative mode of being. And just as evil has a real dimension, and is distinguished from nothing, only in its negative relation to the divine nonwilling, so it has its sham existence, not by itself, but only falsely by human error.[46] In relation to Jesus Christ, however, one cannot say in any sense that evil has objective existence, that it subsists at all except for our eyes that are as yet closed, that it is something really to be feared, that it is a factor that really counts, that it still has a future, that it still presents a danger and can bring about our ruin.[47]

B. THREATENED EVACUATION OF THE HISTORICAL

The loss of a history with God in favor of a pretemporal perfect tense finds expression not only in the setting aside of the event-character of the incarnation but in this context especially in the disappearance of eschatological expectation. For it is now possible to speak only in the perfect tense. The world is no longer the victim of evil. The Christian no longer has to respect evil now that it is a thing of the past, a wasp without a sting. We must not think of nothingness as though real liberation and redemption from it were still a future matter, an event that has still to come.[48] We no longer await anything, for everything has already happened. Nothing can be consummated, for we already participate in the consummation.

Over against this G. Gloege has assembled rich materials from the NT (the Synoptists, Paul, and John) to show how much the community is constantly under assault, is warned against the powers of seduction, and in its provisional and contested faith awaits a consummation in which alone the definitive conquest of evil will come and provisional faith will yield to definitive sight.[49] The community waits in an ongoing history. It is still in an imperfect tense. It is assaulted by the reality of evil. Its knowledge is not the conviction that evil has become nothingness and that it thus lives in the perfect tense of victory; it is the certainty that it has the promise, that evil will not gain the mastery over it, that it will defeat temptation.[50]

46. Ibid., p. 350.
47. Ibid., p. 363.
48. Ibid., p. 364.
49. Gloege, *Theologische Traktate*, I (1965), 247ff.
50. On the end of history with the "perfect" cf. also Regin Prenter, "Glauben und Erkennen bei Karl Barth," *KuD* (1956) 176ff., esp. 190-91.

The implied loss of history threatens to result in a cyclical movement of the salvation event. This is a symbol of the nonhistorical in contrast to the line, the progressive span of time. This cyclical character means that Barth is forced toward universalism. For this is an appropriate expression for God's universal and pretemporal Yes to humanity.

C. APPROXIMATION TO UNIVERSALISM

In fact, Barth does constantly border on this doctrine. He tells us that we are forbidden to make of the open number of the elect in Jesus Christ the closed number of the classical doctrine of predestination, in distinction from whom all the rest are reprobate.[51] This thesis is directed against a double outcome of history and moves toward a universal monon of salvation. Yet Barth tries to avoid the logic of the statement by saying that we must not make the open number of the elect in Jesus Christ into the totality of all people. This is impossible because in Jesus Christ we are dealing with the personal, living, and therefore free will of the God who stands over against the world and everyone in it. The NT never says that the world as such is elect, nor can we say it without doing violence; we can say only that the election of Jesus Christ has taken place for the world, i.e., in order that through him that event might take place in it and to it.[52]

This argument is a remarkable one, for it evades a systematically necessary deduction by arguing positively that the NT does not make this deduction. It seems to me that Barth ought to have asked why the NT does not actually have this doctrine, and whether the other eschatological deductions that the NT does make do not rest on different premises from those that we find in Barth's theology, especially that of the preexistent God-man. A theological thesis can be judged by its implications—and perhaps even more by those that are suppressed with the help of the deus ex machina that they are not biblical.

Barth's other argument against the logic of universalism is no more systematic than the scriptural one. It consists of a reference to the dubious theological company (Origen, Schleiermacher) in which we set ourselves if we espouse such a doctrine. We have to say that both arguments are secondary and heteronomous. It is not clear how Barth could escape the Hegelian doctrine of universalism if he followed the

51. *CD*, II/2, 422.
52. Ibid.

drift of his own thoughts. Nonetheless, it is understandable why he should do all he can to avoid this conclusion even if his avoidance is more one of will than of reason. For the universalist thesis would be an open confession of the nonhistorical cycle. It would be an admission that salvation history does not consist of divine events and turns and resolves but that it simply brings noetically significant demonstrations of primal facts and is an intratrinitarian circle. In fact, it is this in Barth. But he could hardly admit this directly.

What takes place for Barth, then, is not an ontic event in the strict sense but only a demonstrative event, a process of indication and cognition. At this point we have a remarkable parallel to Bultmann's understanding of salvation history, in which it is not the case that something happens, but self-consciousness comes.[53]

D. THE BASIC QUESTION OF THEOLOGICAL THOUGHT IN BARTH

Our conclusion is that certain similarities to Hegel in the structure of Barth's thinking have not been without autonomous influence on his theological conception. The differences from Hegel amount to no more than mere nuances and shifts of emphasis. Yet we should not overlook the fact that Barth does maintain one important distinction which shows that his intention is different from Hegel's. For Barth God is not a principle which unfolds and finds and realizes itself as the absolute spirit in a dialectically necessary process. At the beginning of God's covenant of grace we find the freedom of the divine counsel. The covenant of grace as the original decree is the free act of the faithfulness of God.[54]

Barth is concerned to oppose the concept of freedom to Hegel's understanding of necessity.[55] In some places, too, Barth tries to put brakes on the dialectical thrust of his starting point, e.g., in his discussion of the personality of God, in which he can accuse the Hegelians Biedermann and D. F. Strauss of either eliminating the concept of personality or presenting it as an inadequate and inferior concept, so that God is for them a mere idea.[56]

---

53. Cf. my essay "Erwägungen zu Bultmanns Hermeneutik," *ThLZ* (1955) 705ff.

54. Cf. the thesis to § 57 in *CD*, IV/1, 3.

55. On this understanding of freedom see *CD*, II/1, § 28, "The Being of God as the One Who Loves in Freedom," pp. 257, 297ff. On Barth's concern to oppose the concept of freedom to Hegel's understanding of necessity see ibid., pp. 311ff.; IV/1, 197ff.

56. See *CD*, I/1, 136ff., 358.

Nevertheless, we still have to ask Barth whether this reference to God's freedom is enough to break the fetters of Hegelian dialectic. Can it really help sufficiently in this regard when the freedom of God that is proclaimed in this way serves God's willing and determining of himself as the gracious God,[57] and yet what he wills then unrolls as the unfolding of the primal decree, and in the process—in analogy to Hegel's dialectic—embraces both positive and negative factors, and leaves no place for historical contingency?[58]

Yet this critical question to Barth cannot be our last word. Instead, we here come up against a basic theological question which is provoked by the controversy with Hegel.

No theological utterance can use special concepts that are adequate to its special theme. It always borrows concepts from speech in general, and especially—at the higher level of reflection—from the vocabulary of philosophy. We have already dealt with the fact that in the process there is often (and perhaps always) a revolt of the linguistic means. By using such concepts, theology allows the partisans of alien ideologies to slip into its temple. We thus arrive at the thesis that theology is not justified in what it says concretely, for this will always be a mixture of its own truth and alien elements; it is justified by that to which it looks. Theology takes a servant form which is no less than a human following of the incarnation of Christ. The incarnate Word, being found as a man (whether in conduct or concept), is both revelation and concealment at one and the same time. The concealment of Christ's incarnation, the hiddenness of his kingship, is that it can be interchanged with something else, e.g., the figure of Christ with that of a teacher of the Torah, or the events of the years 1 to 30 with no more than a section of religious history.

What we see here on the level of history is repeated in the sphere of proclamation and on the level of theological terminology. The spoken and written word, the confessions of the church, and the concepts of dogmatics can be confused with words that the world utters. The prophet on the right hand, the prophet on the left, and the worldling in the middle all belong together when seen from outside. They wear the same clothing when seen from outside. The concealment of God's revelation in Jesus Christ and the church's theology is that of interchangeability, whether historical or conceptual.

The mystery of revelation is that only the servant recognizes the

---

57. *CD*, II/1, 561.

58. It is not by accident that in such contexts Barth can speak of our being in a circular course in which there is no break (*CD*, II/1, 37).

king, not the onlooker on the outside. The king's voice is heard only by those who are of the truth (John 18:37), and who thus see that all the history taken into his service (salvation history), and all the concepts taken into his service (theology and doctrine), look away to him, and that this looking away to him justifies them even though they are perhaps clothed in a dubious philosopher's cloak and not in the appropriate wedding garment. It would, of course, be fatal to make a virtue out of this necessity of theology—its bondage to the secular wisdom of philosophy. It would be fatal to identify it with the servant form of its Lord. The servants must constantly remember and tell themselves that their inadequate, interchangeable terms must again and again repent and hate themselves and slay themselves. This repentance will keep them from making their poverty and indebtedness and sinfulness an occasion for boasting or for the naive cleverness of sinning boldly.

It is only with such a reference that I can close this section on Barth. Barth is more and other than a Hegelian when we consider where he is looking. This does not mean that we should not take into account the revolt of the philosophical means that he takes from Hegel. It also means, however, that we should not overlook his own struggle against this revolt. And it means above all that we theologians are all in the same plight. We have a fatal tendency, however, to see it only in others, to miss the blind spot in ourselves. But sharp-eyed diagnosticians will already spot it.

Because F. Gogarten sees in his earlier friend and later opponent Barth only a representative of (Hegelian) identity speculation in theological garb, I have brought arguments along the above lines against this interpretation. I have in mind Gogarten's once famous and now almost forgotten book *Gericht oder Skepsis. Eine Streitschrift gegen Karl Barth* (1937). This is a classical instance of the way in which even the sharp-eyed reflections of a theologian can overlook the phenomenon that I have called "interchangeability."[59]

III. RICHARD ROTHE: THE SPECULATIVE OUTSIDER

Bibliography. Primary Works: *Die Anfänge der christlicher Kirche und ihrer Verfassung* (1837); *Theologische Ethik,* 1st ed., 3 vols. (1845ff.), 2nd ed.,

---

59. My essay against Gogarten bears the title "Die Krise der Theologie. Zur Auseinandersetzung zwischen Barth und Gogarten über 'Gericht und Skepsis,'" in *Theologie der Anfechtung* (1949).

5 vols. (1869ff.); Preface to C. A. Auberlen, *Über die Philosophie Oetingers*, 2nd ed. (1859); *Zur Dogmatik* (1863, 1869); *Stille Stunden* (posthumously published aphorisms).

Secondary Works: Barth, *Protestant Theology in the Nineteenth Century*, pp. 597-606; A. Hausrath, *R. Rothe und seine Freunde*, 2 vols. (1902-1906); T. Heckel, *Exegese und Metaphysik bei R. Rothe* (1928); E. Hirsch, *Geschichte der neueren evangelischen Theologie*, V, 166ff., 365ff.; E. Jundt, *Auflösung der Kirche im totalen Staat? R. Rothes Gegenwartsbedeutung* (1940); cf. on this A. Deutelmoser, *Luther, Staat und Glaube* (1937); M. Kähler, *Geschichte der protestantischen Dogmatik*, pp. 103ff.; F. Nippold, *R. Rothe. Ein christliches Lebensbild*, 2 vols. (1873-1874); E. Schott, "R. Rothes These vom Aufgehn der Kirche im Staat," *Theologia viatorum* (1959) 257ff.

A. BIOGRAPHY

Rothe was born in 1799 and died in 1867. His intellectual development was in many stages which find reflection in the tensions of his theosophical system. A mild rationalism characterized his home. He then encountered Romanticism in Novalis. At Heidelberg Hegel and Daub began to have their lasting influence. Pietism in the impressive figure of his mentor Tholuck had an impact on him in seminary at Wittenberg. From 1824 to 1828 he was a pastor in Rome, and this period broadened his outlook, especially, although not exclusively, in relation to the treasures of culture. It freed his Pietism from the conventicle narrowness which in Wittenberg had given the taint of sin to all openness to the world, even dancing and recreation.

Thus "purified," Rothe accepted a call to direct the Wittenberg seminary in 1828, and he there composed his important work *Die Anfänge* (1837), which in spite of its historical character foreshadows his later doctrine of the merging of the church in the state. He was called to a professorship at Heidelberg in 1837. Here he also directed the newly founded seminary for practical theology, and his main work, the *Theologische Ethik*, was published. This contains his whole speculative system (on its dogmatic and philosophical sides). After a five-year interval in Bonn, he returned to Heidelberg as Professor of Church History, Exegesis, Systematic Theology, and Practical Theology. He gathered around him a host of students whom he greatly inspired. He must have been a fascinating teacher with considerable intellectual gifts. One fruit of this period was his *Dogmatik*, which significantly augments his main work on ethics. In his last years, especially after the death of his mentally sick wife, whose illness had cast a shadow over his life for a long period, he suddenly plunged actively into the ecclesiastical politics of Baden. He was greatly mourned when he died in 1867.

After tracing Hegel's influence up to our own time in Barth, we now turn back a century and take a look at the Hegelian outsider, Richard Rothe.

It is not easy to characterize in a few strokes a bundle of contradictions like Rothe. Even placing him in the history of theology is difficult, for he was a maverick to whom no rubric convincingly applies. The fact that he has been put among the mediating theologians is significant, for in him we have a mixture of such heterogeneous elements as Hegelianism, Pietism, theosophical speculation, and secularism—to mention only a few. Yet to call him a mediating theologian is superficial. The title as little applies to him as does that of a "militarist" to Carl von Clausewitz. (Clausewitz was this, but he was also more than this.) His best place is among theologians who were influenced by Hegel, for his speculative and deductive system not only reminds us of Hegel but over long stretches of reflection is in fact stimulated by him.[60] Nevertheless, this characterization leaves many loose ends. Hardly have we found one trend in Rothe than we must add a "but." Rothe was a Pietist who lived in close contact with his Savior, but he did not have the narrowness of Pietism. He was a Hegelian, but he was also a supranaturalist. He was a supranaturalist, but he was also one who in his *Ethik* cast theological light on astronomy and physics. He was a theosophist, but he was also open to the cultural and social movements of the modern world. He called this "being pious in the open air."

It is no wonder that in his own age Rothe attracted very different people with his uniting of such different things as pious inwardness and abstract speculation. In this regard we might call him the Karl Heim of the 19th century (whom he resembled in both stature and appearance). Yet he appealed also to someone so different from Heim as Ernst Troeltsch, who admired in him one of the few spiritualists who sought and achieved contact with the rapidly changing cultural, social, and technical landscape of the modern world. Walther Köhler even called him Troeltsch's favorite old man.[61]

---

60. Hegel's influence was not only direct but also by way of Rothe's teacher at Heidelberg, Karl Daub, who was a follower of Hegel.

61. W. Köhler, *Ernst Troeltsch* (1941), p. 202. Rothe left many traces in the works of Troeltsch; see esp. his memorial address in 1899 and also *Gesammelte Schriften*, I, 3rd ed. (1923), 935ff.; IV (1925), 498-99, etc.

B. SECULARIZATION AS THE ABSORBING OF
THE CHURCH INTO THE STATE

Along with his attractive uniting of Pietism and openness to the world, its was especially Rothe's understanding of what we now call secularization that was not only noted by his contemporaries but that also raised a problem that still engages us in controversy. Rothe's ideas on the subject recur in various forms no matter whether he himself is recalled or we simply find similar thoughts. (I will return to this later.)

We shall first have a look at this most strongly influential idea of Rothe's and then consider the speculative framework in which it is found.

The thought of secularization first announces itself in Rothe's early work on the beginnings of the Christian church. According to the sayings of Christ the Christian religion is to find consummation as God's kingdom on earth. The church, summoned to serve religious ends, is a first form of this, but it necessarily presses on to a more comprehensive actualization of the Christian spirit in which the moral task imposed in and with religion can be discharged. The institutional form in which the actualization of the Christian spirit, or the kingdom of God on earth, is achieved, is for Rothe the state. The state is the perfect sensory form of the spirit. It is the realization of all moral life. As the church presses toward this perfect form of its mission, it makes itself superfluous and is absorbed into the Christianized state. The perfected state completely excludes the church.[62] Even the cultus—in the form of culture—is taken over by the state. Thus the church has only interim significance, although it is still important in the present age. The thoughts expressed in the first part of this inquiry are integrated into investigations which deal especially with the rise of the church.

The fact that Rothe finds in the state the religiously vitalized organization of moral reason and can thus regard it as an actualization of God's kingdom on earth—an actualization which integrates the church into it and thus makes it superfluous as a separate entity—this fact shows clear traces of Hegel's view of the state. For in Hegel the state is the self-conscious moral substance which has knowing subjectivity as its content and its absolute goal, willing the rational for itself.[63] Insofar as the state is aware of its destiny as mediated by the spirit, and does justice to it, the final goal has supremacy over the individual. In the power of the state as we thus understand it, and as it understands itself,

---

62. Rothe, *Gesammelte Schriften*, IV, 81.
63. *Encyclopädie*, § 535.

religion and philosophy are identical, and one may thus infer that religion and the church have no special status independent of the state. Only in the principle of the spirit that knows its own nature is absolute power present, so that the state, religion, and the principles of philosophy merge into one and reconciliation is effected between reality and the spirit, between the state, the religious conscience, and philosophical knowledge. The morality of the state and its religious spirituality are mutual guarantees.[64]

This transition of churchly religion into the perfected state as its new and final bearer is systematically developed in the *Ethik*. To be sure, the story of redemption which proceeds from Christ its center begins with the founding of the church. This is at first an alien body and counterforce over against the world, which is morally out of joint. The church is the beginning of the power of spiritual life that is brought into the world by Christ. But it is not the final goal. For the spiritual and moral vitalizing of the world that it effects makes it superfluous once the christianizing effect outstrips the churchly cause. When the end is achieved it dismisses the means, which has now discharged its function. Nevertheless, the church is significant as that which gives the first push to this development, and we ourselves still live in the initiatory phase, so that we still need the church. Although the Christian fellowship as the provisional, churchly form of the kingdom of God on earth cannot begin as the state, but only as the church, nevertheless the necessary result of its own life-development is the gradual replacement of its form as the church by its (political) form as the state.[65]

The evolutionary Hegelian concept of progressive permeation by the spirit in the institutional form of the state is provided at once, however, with the usual "but." "But" the perfecting of the kingdom of redemption does not come with an immanent development; it belongs to the invisible and suprasensory world. Certainly, it is not conceivable without the spiritualizing and Christianizing that begin in the historical process.[66] Yet as the agents of this development we ourselves are incapable of reaching the goal and setting up God's kingdom on earth. To achieve this there is needed—if one may put it thus—a supranaturally redemptive intervention such as is promised in the Lord's *parousia*, in the perceptible reappearance of the Lord in his glory.[67]

The disruptive episode of sin explains why the speculative

64. Ibid., § 552.
65. *Ethik*, § 578 (p. 181).
66. Ibid., § 583 (p. 187).
67. Ibid., § 586 (p. 189).

Hegelian development does not coincide with its empirical course and a final appeal has to be made to the *parousia*. We shall see, of course, that Rothe's view of sin itself bears Hegelian features. Yet the decisive thing is that Rothe sees in it a power that prevents the moral development of the natural human race from following its normal course.[68] At the beginning of Vol. 3 of the *Ethik* Rothe can specifically note the discrepancy between the theoretical and the actual course of the development: The normal course of the moral process is not the actual course; the latter is decidedly abnormal.

We already see here how impossible it is to place or categorize Rothe. In his idea of secularization immanentist Hegelian notions coincide with the NT message of supranatural redemption and its transcendent basis. The particular impact that this conception of Rothe's, and the thesis of the church's merging into a Christianized world, made upon his contemporaries, and their further development of it, take various forms.

First, comfort might be found (astonishingly) in the thought that the forsaking of the church by the masses, and especially by intellectuals, which is everywhere to be seen and which fills the devout with anxiety, no longer needs to be understood negatively as a falling away, since secularization may now be viewed as an effect of Christianity itself. Christianity exists not merely as a conscious Christianity practiced in worship but also wherever its cultural diffusion has made it our second nature.[69] Finally, then, Christ's own work pushes on to the Christianizing of culture by way of unchurching, and we may thus see the triumphant march of Christ.

But was not this an illusion? Rothe had called sin a blocking mechanism in the development, and might not sin lead to real apostasy instead of the Christianizing of the world? Might not the state, instead of becoming the bearer of the objectified Christian spirit, develop into the ideologized, atheistic, totalitarian state?[70]

Gogarten, whose concept of secularization is similar to Rothe's, shares with him (although on a different basis) the conviction that secularization is a child of Christianity. But he does not identify the resultant product with Christianity in secular form. Historical experiences that Rothe could not have to the same degree perhaps helped to

---

68. Ibid., § 480 (p. 41).

69. This reminds us formally of the thesis of Marx that our social being can become our second nature; see *Frühschriften*, ed. S. Landshut (1953), pp. 199, 237, 241.

70. Cf. the works of Deutelmoser and Jundt.

bring it about that Gogarten distinguishes from legitimate secularization a secularism that represents a self-resting secularity that has radically broken free from God.[71]

Second, Rothe is in another respect the pioneer of theological ideas which are still under discussion. In the remoter zones of Christian influence, where there is no direct and conscious contact with Christian truths (as in the church), but these are present only as our second nature, there necessarily arises a phenomenon that Rothe calls "unconscious Christianity." In recent decades this idea, introduced as Rahner's "anonymous" (or not yet actualized) Christianity, has played an important role, especially in the theology of mission, and not just in Roman Catholic circles.[72] The concept undoubtedly raises the problem that no clear-cut decision can be made any longer between Christianity and non-Christian religions (or a purely secular this-worldliness). The two dimensions are viewed synthetically and are either related in a way similar to the nature-grace construct of Thomism or along the lines of haziness and clarity, of the *logos spermatikos* and the total truth of the Logos, as in the early Apologists. This leads to a tendency to approximate the Christian message to pre-Christian and post-Christian positions, since the Christian message brings only a mutation within the homogeneous corpus of truth.[73]

I am probably not mistaken if I conjecture that the idea of unconscious Christianity helped to influence Rothe because of his association with the founding fathers of the German Protestant Union and the initiation of religious liberalism. His own expressed aim in all this was to help those who are alienated from the church to return to it. The newly formed Union (1863) would help by bringing the church closer to them and reconciling it with these children whom it knows no better than it is known by them.[74]

We cannot fail to see the seeking missionary love that speaks here nor the zeal to reclaim the alienated. Yet it is an open question

71. Cf. Gogarten, *Verhängnis und Hoffnung der Neuzeit* (1953) and the review by W. Joest in *KuD* 3 (1953) 339ff., esp. p. 349.

72. Cf. K. Rahner, *Theological Investigations*, VI (1969), 390ff. Criticism, which applies to Rothe too, may be found in B. Stoekle, *Mysterium salutis*, II (1967), 1057ff.; J. Ratzinger, *Das neue Volk Gottes* (1969), pp. 339ff. For a striking application to mission cf. Raimundo Panikkar, who believes that the confession of good believers in any religion is really oriented to the one, holy, catholic, and apostolic religion (*Religionen und die Religion* [1965], p. 168). The problem is at least implicitly addressed in the *Ad gentes*, § 61 of Vatican II.

73. Cf. *EF,* III, 365-69.

74. H. Hohlwein, *RGG,* V, 3rd ed., p. 645.

theologically whether the idea of secularized and unconscious Christianity does not lead to an assimilating of the mentality of those who are sought, to a surrender of Christian distinctives in the attempt to meet the alienated, to a dropping of everything in Christian truth that might disturb them and be a block to them. The almost total doctrinal freedom that Protestantism proclaimed, the abandoning of dogmas and confessions, raises the suspicion that Rothe viewed this way of assimilation and unrestricted tolerance as a possible one. What would supposedly protect him against the charge of opportunism and the willing surrender of all that his piety holds dear is his idea of secularization. Within the resultant relation of church and state this form of encounter had to appear to be theologically valid.

The influence of his idea of a movement from the church to the world may be seen in others as well as in Gogarten. We might better and more cautiously speak of conceptual similarities, since there can hardly be any question of direct influence. We search the theological literature in vain for associations or the quoting of his name. But for all the differences we find some closeness in a work like *The Christian Church and the Old Testament* by the Dutch Calvinist A. A. van Ruler.[75]

Van Ruler does not think that the theocratic ordinances of the OT were limited to Israel; they were directed to the whole world. In salvation history he finds not only a narrowing down from the nations to the people of Israel, from the people to the remnant, and from the remnant to an individual. He also finds an expansion "from the Messiah to the Spirit, from the Spirit to the conscience, from the conscience to the state, from the state to the cosmos."[76] Similarly, although Christ is at the heart of these movements,[77] he is not to be regarded as the goal of OT salvation history. He is simply an episode, an intervening means to accomplish the divine rule on earth which is sought.[78] Hence the goal of creation is not grace, the covenant, or (religious) salvation. In this salvation God's concern is with created reality, that it may subsist before him as a totality, a universe.[79]

Thus Christ is a mere interim with a transitory function like

---

75. Originally published as *Die christliche Kirche und das Alte Testament* (Munich, 1955); ET Grand Rapids, 1971. Gerhard von Rad told me that nearly every semester he urged his students to wrestle with van Ruler because (like Rothe) he did not fit into any of our normal types and was thus inspiring and challenging. I have invited him to my own seminars for the same reason. Cf. *ThE*, II/2, 744ff.

76. Van Ruler, *Christian Church*, p. 69.

77. Cf. O. Cullmann, *Christ and Time* (1964), pp. 94ff.

78. Van Ruler, *Religie en Politiek* (1945), p. 172.

79. See Van Ruler, *Christian Church*, p. 68.

Rothe's church.[80] The state has a function which—although without Hegelian influence—reminds us of Rothe. It is in a representative sense the order of a world whose sanctification is the aim of salvation history and which God has in view already in the decree of creation. The state is an earthly, or, better, a messianic form of divine sonship.

Van Ruler certainly does not have Rothe's idea of secularization. His concern is the sanctification of the earth, which he takes from the OT, and which he owes essentially to Jewish exegesis of the OT, especially that of Martin Buber. Yet the similarity to many of the thoughts of Rothe should not be overlooked. This is another reason why we should not just discuss present-day theology but draw the ideas of those who have gone before us, which are mostly disregarded, into the debate.

C. THE METAPHYSICAL BACKGROUND

Rothe's doctrine of the subsuming of the church in the state is part of a comprehensive speculative system which has links not only with Hegel but also—although with no express reference—with Descartes. We recall how Descartes deduced both the existence of God and that of the world in all its dimensions from the concept of God as an entity than which no greater can be thought. Similarly, Rothe speculatively deduces the existence of the world, its history, and salvation history from the primal entity of God as the absolute spirit.

In this respect we may note two basic differences from the identity philosophy of Hegel.

First, Hegel never thought of proving from concrete reality his inferences from the self-development of the spirit. He presupposed that harmony between them would be self-evident. Rothe, however, specifically decided to set up reality as a control. In § 4 of the *Ethik* he argued that a speculatively established system must prove itself by not being in contradiction with empirical reality but elucidating it. He unconditionally accepted the need to control speculation by experience.[81] When he perceived an actual divergence between the empirical course of the process and what speculation would prognosticate to be the normal course, he was led back (as we have seen) to the abnormality of the interlude of sin.

Second, Rothe does not begin, like Hegel, with the self-development of the absolute spirit. He begins, like Schleiermacher

80. "Christ is an emergency measure," ibid., p. 69.
81. *Ethik*, p. 20.

(whom he does not greatly care for), with subjectivity, with what Schleiermacher calls the feeling of absolute dependence. Yet Schleiermacher does not provide a model which he follows without reservation. Here again we have a "but." He does not have in view a feeling of absolute dependence in the sense of something universally existential (cf. § 4 of Schleiermacher's *Christian Faith*). To base speculation on a general I-consciousness belongs for him to the sphere of philosophy. Rothe's concern is with theosophy, which begins with the already posited God-consciousness of pious Christians.[82] In its basic state this consciousness is experience and religious feeling. To the extent that it is vitally strong, it moves out of the purely emotional zone into that of reflection, first to religious thinking in the narrower sense, then to more comprehensively speculative theology, which penetrates the whole of being and sees it to be grounded in God.[83]

To this consciousness God is the absolute. His life is the absolute process of life and self-generation.[84] Since God as the absolute spirit furnishes himself with self-consciousness and free self-activity—and with both in the absolute sense—he directly determines himself as I or personality.[85]

As God thus posits himself as I, dialectical logic demands that he differentiate himself—in Fichte's sense—from all that is non-I, but also that he himself posit it. If God determines himself as absolute essence and thereby achieves the thought of himself, then with an unbreakable logical necessity he directly and simultaneously thinks the thought of the other, of his opposite, of a being that is not everything that he himself is.[86]

After the manner of Hegel, then, God's self-development leads to creation. This initiates a process of increasing spiritualizing, beginning with a radical antithesis to God in matter, and finally leading by several intervening creaturely stages, which we need not discuss here, to human personality, which is also furnished with self-consciousness and self-activity. The moral development of humanity proceeds with constant spiritualizing as God increasingly indwells it and purifies its creaturely being into divine likeness.[87]

In this stage of the process there is a decisive turn similar to that which occurs when the church is absorbed into the state. As God creates in us a personal counterpart, he hands the world over to us so that we

82. Ibid., pp. 34, 52.
83. Ibid., § 6.
84. Ibid., § 28, p. 104.
85. Ibid., § 31.
86. Ibid., § 40, p. 154.
87. Ibid., § 117.

may control nature and make it ours. From this point on, the process is no longer dependent exclusively on God's creative initiative. It is now the responsibility of human personality, being in some sense delegated to it. At this point natural creation becomes moral creation, or history.[88] This is the sphere in which humanity develops its own initiative as God's vice-gerent. As the church merges into the state, the representative of secular action, so religion is not so much dissolved in morality but becomes particularly virulent on its moral side. (We again come up against the "but" at this point.)

If we were to read Rothe's *Ethik* only thus far, we might be inclined to see in him a precursor of the death-of-God theology which the American God-is-dead fellows (and a German woman among them!) made so fashionable, seeing in it the theological goal of secularization, in the 1960s and 1970s.[89] On this view the primary school of religion has had its day. Those who have come of age must let the theistic God go his way and take up his task for themselves. What this actor God (Christ) did—play God under conditions of impotence—is open to us. We can play God for one another.[90]

At this turning point there begins the abnormality of the historical process as it has now come under human control—an abnormality that no longer corresponds to the speculatively deduced course of the process. The first to be awakened to personality fall victim to dependence on their material nature, which binds them and hampers them in their moral task.[91] This is the great "but" of the fall, of an anti-godly enslavement from the outset, from which we cannot break free by reason of the polarity of good and evil that comes with self-determination. Rothe, then, finds himself forced to abandon the natural process that corresponds to the self-unfolding of God as absolute spirit and to postulate a supernatural corrective intervention by God that reminds us of a deus ex machina.

In place of our weak human action comes God's redeeming action in which he creatively introduces into our old natural humanity a new beginner of the human race, a second Adam.[92] This one can

88. Ibid., § 82, p. 393.
89. Cf. esp. T. J. Altizer, W. Hamilton, and P. van Buren. On the history of the idea cf. *EF*, I, 232ff.
90. D. Sölle, *Stellvertretung* (1965), p. 192.
91. *Ethik*, § 480.
92. I am sure that this new positing by God does not wholly fit the idea of the deus ex machina. It is foreseen, although it does not come within the a priori deduction of the absolute spirit, in which nothing supernatural of this kind can be foreseen.

transform the old natural humanity from matter to spirit.[93] Christ, the second Adam, does this by making it his religious task to develop his own fellowship with God into complete union, and also by making it his moral task to unite himself with humanity in a bond of absolute fellowship, and to do so out of love.[94] From this point onward the fellowship of redemption is the determinative principle of development.[95]

The zigzag line of progress that Rothe sets up with this supernatural intervention, and that he substitutes for Hegel's dialectic, continues as the initiative in progress seems to fall back on regenerate humanity once the redemptive correction has been made.

The religious fellowship of the church, which is founded by Christ and which is the preliminary form of the kingdom of God, spreads abroad the Christian spirit in the world, so that the form of the church can merge into the political form of the state. Nevertheless, as we have seen already, God's kingdom cannot be consummated by us alone. The consummation belongs to the invisible, suprasensory world and will come only with the perceptible reappearance of the Redeemer in his glory.

Thus the whole human process oscillates between logical developments and transcendent interventions, between the normal, the abnormal, and the correction, until the absolute spirit that is there at the beginning, and that resolves on self-unfolding, comes to itself again. In distinction from Hegel, this coming back to itself does not take place within an all-embracing monon but in such a way that in the form of the *parousia* there is at the end a final act of redemption that transcends the monon.

Insofar as Rothe follows a monistic line, moving within deduction from the one original principle of the absolute spirit, the autonomy of such a system sees to its similarity to other monistic philosophies. Thus there is a striking resemblance to a thinker of our own century, the Jesuit paleontologist Teilhard de Chardin,[96] for whom the world process, which embraces both nature and history, leads from God (point Alpha) to God (the final point, Omega), and does so in such a way that from the point of inorganic nature a spiritual element is infused into the bearers of the process and becomes increasingly stronger until total spiritualizing is achieved. In this process inorganic nature at the first

93. *Ethik,* § 519, p. 119.
94. Ibid., § 541.
95. Ibid., § 565.
96. Cf. my critical chapter on de Chardin in *Being Human—Becoming Human* (1984), pp. 449ff.

stage corresponds to Rothe's matter. The second stage is vitalization, which brings the self-propagation of organisms. The third stage is that of differentiation and leads on to primates. This development is like a multistage rocket with humanity at the tip. The comparison shows the teleological nature of this spirit-directed evolution. The fourth stage is that of cerebration. It crosses the frontier from the biosphere to the noosphere. Self-consciousness comes, and with it the awareness of evolution. In us evolution achieves consciousness of itself. There is thus a break here that resembles the break in creation that comes for Rothe with conscious and responsible human personality. Like Rothe, de Chardin says that after this break evolution no longer develops on its own. Humanity shares responsibility for its further course. It can want it and promote it. The fifth and final stage is the culmination when matter becomes completely transparent to the power that illumines and spiritualizes it. At this point Omega, evolution ends and leads on to mystical union with God. Here all things come together, find their explanation, feel secure, and come into possession of themselves.

Within the monistic structure of such thinking, whether in Rothe or de Chardin, sin is a stage that has to be gone through; it is a transition in Hegel's sense.[97] For Rothe sin is theoretically necessary. It comes within the general teleology. Yet it is a difficulty, for it disrupts the speculatively calculated course of the world-process and makes the development abnormal (as we have seen). This is not so in Hegel.

At this point Rothe's Christian knowledge—his knowledge of sin—breaks the speculative smoothness of the process and gives rise to one of his many inconsistencies.

D. CONCLUDING EVALUATION

In Rothe we find the common themes of the age under discussion: wrestling with doubt of traditional Christian truth and a concern for new appropriation. One sees this especially from his biography. His encounter with the world of culture and politics, which takes place first in Rome, shows him how esoteric is the conventicle Pietism of his beginnings. The this-worldliness of the secularized masses, and especially of the cultured despisers of the Christian religion, cannot be reached by the insider thinking, the pious language, or the world-renouncing life-style of the little flock of Pietism. The missionary zeal which Rothe's love of the Savior nurtured led him to question his

97. On de Chardin's view of sin, see ibid., pp. 471ff.

Christian past. Could it really be the goal of God's saving history to save a little flock of devout people while the rest were committed to perdition? The disproportion between the sacred remnant and the gigantic host of the rest was too great not to cast doubt on God's government of the world. Rothe could save his faith, and appropriate it the more seriously, only if he could find some theological point in the disproportion. He thought he found it when he saw that God's way of salvation leads by way of the church to a secularizing of the Christian message, that the church is only the starting point for a spiritualizing and Christianizing in the cosmic sense. In this case secularization could be understood as a work of his Savior and it would no longer give rise to the dreadful thought that the world had slipped out of his hand.

Rothe's cooperation in founding the Protestant Union was a sign that he wanted to affirm secularization and see in it a sign of hope. He sought to borrow from the treasures of Hegelian dialectic the conceptual means whereby to understand the secularizing of Christianity and a divine plan that embraces the whole cosmos. He had a concern that the secularizing of Christianity would not be able to bring about a permeation of the state and the world with the Christian spirit, that empirical observation would seem to indicate a movement to naked this-worldliness that leaves no place for God at all. This concern never left him. The thought of the disruptive factor of sin helped him when he had to face this speculative dysteleology. But he knew as a Christian that the divine plan of salvation provided for victory over it. And he could make strenuous efforts to interpret it as a divinely foreseen transitional stage and in this way to stay close to Hegel's system. Behind the speculative system we plainly see the Christian Rothe with his love of the Savior, his love of humanity, his struggles, and his winning through to new hope and its conceptual basis.

For this reason one cannot say that Rothe's system is a closed and strictly executed one. We find in it many breaks, inconsistencies, and transcendent interventions. His thinking is not what it pretends to be when he says that it develops out of itself and is thus self-thinking in the strictest sense.[98]

Much as the disruptive elements permeate his system and disturb the architecture of his thought-structure, spoiling its beauty with alien elements, one is still forced to ask whether it is not precisely these inconsistencies that validate Rothe as a Christian theologian even as they break the system. In fact, he did not do what he was trying to do. He did not spin the world and the salvation event out of the mere idea of

98. *Ethik*, § 2.

that which is unconditionally perfect. He knew them already from his experience of the world and of faith. His prior knowledge takes precedence over his abstract speculations. Fundamentally, his conception of God, the world, and history, which he worked out with the help of Hegel (and also Schelling and Fichte), does not have the function of generating Christian knowledge. It simply brings order to it and gives it the compactness of a well-constructed system of thought.

Thus things are perhaps the opposite of what they seem to be in Rothe. The essential thing is not the Hegelian framework within which he forces the theological doctrines of God, creation, the fall, and redemption. The essential thing is the prior Christian content. It is the Christian life behind the thinking. This essential thing is then adorned with idealistic dialectic in an attempt to commend it to the educated who have forsaken the church and to offer a coherent intellectual account of Christian teachings.

This may seem to be straightforward enough, but in Rothe, of course, it is not. The "but" that occurs so often is again disruptive. For the prior Christian knowledge, as we have seen, shatters the speculative inferences and again and again brings the Christian witness to the fore. It relativizes the intellectual constructions and makes of them no more than marginal notes. Nevertheless, the intellectual means constantly revolt and conceal the Christian contents. (We need think only of the understanding of sin, which is saturated with Hegelianism.)

Rothe, then, is marked by the problem that afflicts all theology, as we have had occasion to see earlier. His theology is justified, not by what it says intellectually, but by that at which it looks.

Naturally, this does not offer immediate amnesty to theological ambiguity. In the sphere of human criticism we have to consider how far a theology lets itself be mastered by its intellectual means, especially the philosophies to which it lays claim. In this regard, while we respect Rothe as a devout Christian and a man of pure humanity, we are frequently forced to shake our heads, and not, we hope, pharisaically.

CHAPTER 14

Left-Wing Hegelians

I. DAVID FRIEDRICH STRAUSS

Bibliography. Primary Works: *Gesammelte Schriften*, ed. E. Zeller (1876-1878); *Das Leben Jesu*, 1st ed. (1835), 2nd ed. (1837); ET (of the 4th German ed.) *The Life of Jesus Critically Examined* (Philadelphia, repr. 1974); *Streitschriften zur Verteidigung meiner Schrift über das Leben Jesu und zur Charakteristik der gegenwärtigen Theologie* (1837); *Die christliche Glaubenslehre* . . . (1840); *Das Leben Jesu für das deutsche Volk bearbeitet* (1864); *Der alte und der neue Glaube* (1872). Biographies of U. von Hutten (1858) and Voltaire (1872); *Literarische Denkwürdigkeiten* in *Gesammelte Schriften*, I, 1-80; *Ausgewählte Briefe*, ed. E. Zeller (1895).
Secondary Works: G. Backhaus, *Kerygma und Mythos bei D. F. Strauss und R. Bultmann* (1956); K. Barth, *Protestant Theology in the Nineteenth Century*, pp. 541-68; C. Hartlich and W. Sachs, *Der Ursprung des Mythosbegriffs in der modernen Bibelwissenschaft* (1952), pp. 121ff.;[1] E. Hirsch, *Geschichte der neueren evangelischen Theologie*, V, 492ff.; Gottfried Müller, *Identität und Immanenz* . . . (1968); F. Nietzsche, "D. F. Strauss, der Bekenner und der Schriftsteller," in *Unzeitgemässe Betrachtungen* (1873; we will cite the repr. in WW, II, 25ff. [1922]); A. Schweitzer, *The Quest of the Historical Jesus* (New York, repr. 1968); J. Wach, *Das Verstehen*, II (1929), 271ff.; T. Ziegler, *D. F. Strauss*, 2 vols. (1908); idem, *RE*, 3rd ed., 19, 76ff.

---

1. A prize work on a theme set by the present author.

A. BIOGRAPHY

Strauss was born in Ludwigsburg in 1808. He studied theology at Blaubeuren and Tübingen. At both the strongest impact was made by F. C. Baur, whose teaching on myth greatly influenced him. Strauss was the first of five candidates at Tübingen to finish with a top grade, which is very seldom given (only once during the nine years I taught in Tübingen). After taking a doctorate Strauss rounded off his studies at Berlin, where he especially wanted to hear Hegel. But Hegel died of cholera at this time, so that he had little personal impact. Strauss associated with his disciples and read his works instead. This made him a Hegelian for a time; Schleiermacher remained alien to him.

After Berlin he returned to Tübingen and taught philosophical courses as an inspired and inspiring Hegelian. But then came the first of many crises in his life. The professors of philosophy envied him his large following and he had to withdraw. In his involuntary freedom he wrote his first work on the life of Jesus, which had on contemporary theology, and indeed on a wider sphere, the shattering effect of an earthquake, and which took on fateful significance for his later life, since he had in fact disqualified himself for any ecclesiastical or academic service. The Württemberg church put him in a girls' school in Ludwigsburg, but he did not stay there long, particularly as the storm about his book forced him into increased literary work in its defense.

While he worked on successive editions of the book, the prospect of a professorship at Zurich opened up. This caused him, not opportunistically but for the sake of the office for which he had studied, to soften or at least to question his theses on the life of Jesus. He was called to the professorship, but the cantonal authorities withdrew the call under pressure of a popular protest stirred up by the pastors. One cannot dismiss the conjecture that this new blow, which Strauss felt to be unjust and theologically constrictive, left him with a permanent resentment against the official theologies of the time. It is, of course, impossible to measure the extent to which this resentment contributed to the fury of his destructive polemics.

He was now an independent author, and as such he published the lectures that he had planned for Zurich under the title *Die christliche Glaubenslehre* (2 vols., 1840-1841). This is a scholarly work which bears witness to systematic virtuosity in its structure. He uses the history of dogma as an instrument of criticism: "The true criticism of dogma is its history."[2] By way of theses and their rationalistic dissolution, this leads

2. *Die christliche Glaubenslehre*, p. 71.

finally to what is full of significance from the standpoint of philosophical knowledge. But here, as we shall see, the Hegelian synthesis of faith and knowledge, or depiction and concept, breaks down, and the two come into antithesis. Various Christian doctrines, e.g., eschatology, can no longer be integrated into any form of knowledge.

After this work Strauss kept silence for two decades. During this period he entered into an unhappy marriage with the opera singer Agnes Schebest, who had no feeling for his theological work and could obviously neither cook nor keep house, so that a sense of abandonment came into his private life as well. The marriage soon ended in separation, but the pain of it lasted for some time.

As a deputy from Ludwigsburg in the Landtag Strauss tried to engage in politics. Politically, he was far from being a revolutionary. He shunned anything that had to do with the people or the masses, and therefore the Social Democrats too. The trauma of the mass campaign against him at Zurich had (perhaps) left its mark. Nietzsche spitefully notes his later patriotic enthusiasm in the war of 1870.[3] He traces it back to his fear of the people, the Social Democrats, that Strauss expresses admiration for Bismarck and Moltke, and he quotes his hope that those who champion the masses and revolution might be able at least to see up to the knees of such exalted figures.[4]

Another great theological work finally came out in 1864. This was a new *Leben Jesu für das deutsche Volk bearbeitet* (Life of Jesus Revised for the German People). The title was a misnomer, for the book was too scholarly to be able to reach the general populace. Nor did it have anything like the impact of the first *Leben Jesu*. In spite of the new methodological approach, it advanced in principle no new theses. Here again the aim is to evaporate mythically all the supranatural features (especially eschatological) that have clustered around the person of Jesus. Whereas in the first book he did not think he could present the supposed historical core of the story of Jesus as a unity, he now starts with this core.[5] Yet the result is essentially a failure, for of few great men of history are we as inadequately informed as Jesus.[6] What we have are fictional records.[7] Thus the biographical material is a tissue of conjectures, though these show one thing plainly enough, namely, that the possible contours of his life bear little resemblance to the Christ of the church.[8]

3. Nietzsche, WW, II, 49-50.
4. Ibid., p. 74 (quoting from *Der alte und der neue Glaube*, p. 280).
5. *Das Leben Jesu* (1864), p. 161.
6. Ibid., p. 621.
7. Ibid., p. 157.
8. Ibid., pp. 5-6.

Readers soon get the impression that Strauss uses the meager biographical materials for his own poetic stylizations, which in some sense replace the mythical exaggerations. He projects a liberal picture of Christ as a "beautiful soul" in which humanity comes to consciousness of itself.[9] Among those who advance the human ideal Jesus is in the front rank. He adds features that were not there before him, or had not as yet been developed.[10] Strauss is not wholly clear in this regard. For while this picture of Jesus is being formed, he can say in the same breath that we must distinguish the historical Christ from the ideal Christ. By the ideal he means the original of humanity as it is present to human reason. The development of the religion of Christ into a religion of humanity is the ineluctable outcome of recent spiritual development. Jesus—the historical Jesus—is the essential motive power behind this. It is perhaps due to the weakness of the outline given by the sources that the goal of the development of the ideal of humanity colors the biographical investigation and then leaves it blank again the very next moment. Strauss is clear that what we know historically about Jesus cannot have the stamp of definitiveness on the way to that ideal. If someone were to arise in whom the religious genius of the new age takes flesh as that of the age of Jesus did in him, then such a one would not need to borrow from Jesus but would carry on his work independently.

The last work of Strauss, *Der alte und der neue Glaube* (1872), was written in a pamphleteering style which enabled it to reach a wider public than the *Leben Jesu*. We shall speak about this work later. It had the honor of catching the—scornful—attention of Nietzsche, whose work reached Strauss just before his death. He died in 1874 and did not receive a church burial. A young friend who gave a eulogy was harassed by the Swabian "quiet in the land." Even the grave of Strauss was thus a focus of controversy.

B. INTELLECTUAL PHYSIOGNOMY

A system like Hegel's identity philosophy was sooner or later bound to raise the question whether his all-embracing world spirit can really comprehend as a monon the totality of heterogeneous elements. As we have asked already in the chapter on Hegel, did not this synthesis lead to inertia, to an affirmation of the status quo? (just as Hegel thought that the history of philosophy had reached its end with himself). Could no

9. Ibid., p. XVIII.
10. Ibid., pp. 625ff.

new factors arise in history to force a revision or at least a modification of the synthesis?

We shall see that for Strauss it was the rise of historico-critical research, and the influence of F. C. Baur as its representative, that brought to light a new element that could not be integrated easily into the Hegelian schema. The unavoidable result was that the Hegelian school split into a right-wing group on the one side and a left-wing group on the other. (There were other reasons for this about which we shall speak later.) The right-wing group insisted on Hegel's synthesis, and in the words of Strauss lost touch with the intellectual movement of the age. The left-wing group came increasingly to the conviction that the peace made by Hegel between philosophy and Christianity was defective in principle.[11] This false peace meant in theology that respected dogmatics were like sausage-meat in which orthodox doctrine was the meat, Schleiermacher's theology the fat, and Hegel's philosophy the spice.[12] For this reason Strauss counts himself on the left wing, which seeks to separate the things that are artificially united and to take account of the realities involved.[13]

Disgusted by the compromises that he found everywhere in the theological sphere, Strauss makes his own theology a kind of acid that separates things. Over against every synthetic both-and he is a zealous supporter of either-or. By constitution as well as circumstance he is a polemicist and destroyer. His thrust is mainly negative, and when at the end he sketches something positive in his last work, it is so weak and unconvincing that Nietzsche heaps scorn on him as a cultural Philistine. The point of his work is always attack.

The reasons for this are complex. Aggression is not just for the sake of aggression. He is moved by a passion for the truth, which he sees to be everywhere deformed, painted over, and destroyed. To get at the truth he has to hew away on the right hand and the left. His zealous Swabian temperament might also have plunged him into controversy. One also suspects that behind his destructive passions lay a very human resentment, the traumas due to the envy, stubbornness, and pettiness of his opponents. If he had been given a position and respect and spared his enforced martyrdom, then his biobrapher A. Hausrath thinks that his theological path would have been less

11. *Glaubenslehre*, p. 4.
12. Ibid., p. 70.
13. For similar reasons we find right-left splits in other schools, e.g., that of Heidegger, in which Sartre represents the left wing, or even that of Dietrich Bonhoeffer; cf. Hanfried Müller, *Von der Kirche zur Welt* (1961).

swayed by negation.[14] When he hoped to become a professor at Zurich, we find indications of this other possibility.[15]

Often he seems to feel that he is between two stools because this position alone seems to validate his commitment to the truth, which will flirt neither with the right nor the left. He obviously kept his distance from the positive theology that accepts the supernatural and smooths over biblical problems. But the Liberals and the Protestant Union are too halfhearted for him. They do not plainly renounce the older faith. They are content with patching and botching, and thus run into even greater absurdities.

Strauss unconditionally sought his own way, part extrovert and part introvert. His motives and approaches were always those of reaction, and they were heavily fraught with emotion. Yet the complete line of his thinking is direct. He maintains his identity and fulfils himself. Things that affect him from outside maieutically serve his own self-development.

His biographies support this view, especially those on Hutten and Voltaire. In these he largely detaches the entelechies of his subjects from their historical setting. He does not merge them into a general picture of their time but is exclusively interested in the laws of their inner development. In spite of the climate in which he constantly moved, Strauss was essentially a "loner." He was unable and unwilling to attach himself to any group or integrate himself into it. Even his great influence never led to the formation of a school.

He was certainly not driven by a conscious urge for self-fulfilment. Indeed, he tended to forget himself. This is why he could be helpless when he consciously asked about himself and where he was going. Not by accident we have from the years of his silence the verses in which he says that he is undoubtedly in a strange land, that he does not know where his home is, that he does not know whether it is a dream that he has two fine children, that he is not sure whether his relation to his wife is one of love or hate, that he does not know whether he is an unbeliever, as people say, or devout, and that while he does not fear death, he is not sure whether he has not long since been dead.[16] A half-light rests over his whole life. The directness of the development of his entelechy goes hand in hand with a helplessly questioning disorientation, piety with unbelief, revolutionary protestation with bourgeois conservatism (to a degree that Nietzsche could describe as Philistine).

14. A. Hausrath, *D. F. Strauss und die Theologie seiner Zeit*, 2 vols. (1976ff.).

15. Cf. the Preface to *Zwei friedliche Blätter* (1838), in which he does not withdraw but (incidentally) questions his early doubts as to the authenticity of John's Gospel.

16. WW, 12, 64.

This half-light lies over his theology, especially his Christology. He could never break free from the figure of Christ even though he regarded it as historically almost unknowable. He was frightened and repelled by its mythical enhancement, and yet he pointed always to its suprapersonal meaning. Either-or might be the maxim of his life, and yet the history of Jesus in the Gospels reduced him to helplessness. On the one hand it awakened in him the feeling that Jesus is a paradigm of humanity, but on the other hand the sources could not give firm contours to this feeling. Hence he could not decide whether to advance or retreat. Finally, toward the end of his life, he replaced the mythical stylization of the figure of Jesus by the community with his own poetic exaggeration in which Christ is a "beautiful soul" in Schiller's sense, a personification of perfect goodness, the most human of all human beings. His thinking never ceased to circle around the meager historical fragment. He never thought of setting aside that which it seemed he could never grasp, and resorting instead to metaphysical conceptions of his own based on his own view of life.

Interpreters of Strauss have time and again called him a historian with no systematic force. (Even Barth is hardly an exception.) I find it moving and almost tragic that the pitilessness of his critical probing not only evaporated the mythical element in the church's Christology but reduced the remaining historical remnant almost to nothing, and yet that this last poor fragment so fascinated him that he could never break free from it and become simply a philosopher. With one small finger he still clasps the horns of the altar.

C. MYTH AND HISTORY: THE BROKEN RELATIONSHIP WITH HEGEL IN THE FIRST *LIFE OF JESUS*

Strauss was a committed Hegelian when teaching at Tübingen.[17] Yet an important break came when the suspension of his philosophical lectures led him back to true theological work. In this he did not proceed in a pure Hegelian, i.e., speculative, manner. Under the influence of F. C. Baur he took up historico-critical investigation and therefore the question of historical fact.[18] Along the lines laid down by his master, his

17. Along with the 1835 *Life of Jesus* cf. the essay "Das Verhältnis der Hegelschen Philosophie zur theologischen Kritik," in *Streitschriften* (1837), Heft 3. I owe this reference to Hartlich and Sachs, *Der Ursprung des Mythosbegriffs in der modernen Bibelwissenschaft.*

18. Baur in *Kirchengeschichte des 19. Jahrhunderts* (1862), p. 359 (cf. Hartlich and Sachs, *Ursprung*, p. 124) can point out that the critical spirit in the work of Strauss

purpose in all this was always to reduce the historical depictions that he discovered to "concept."[19]

But here the Hegelian notion of reason in history and its necessary course left him in the lurch. This notion might work when historically demonstrable connections were present. In such cases the philosophical interpreter could indeed try to see the dialectical triad in them and in this way to detect the logic of the world spirit that is immanent in history. But this construction falls to the ground when the actual course of history is obscure, as it was for Strauss when he came to the life of Jesus. He could possibly interpret an established historical process along Hegelian lines, but he could not reconstruct along these lines a process that could not be established. He could not deduce a historical process from the idea of rational necessity. He could not "prophetically" replace absent historical verifiability by what I might call a retrospective philosophical prophecy.

For these theses, which he stated in Heft 3 of the *Streitschriften*, Strauss found a model in the christological statements of the Gospels. The principle of an absence of presuppositions, respect for which Strauss in his book on Jesus demanded of all historical interpreters of the Gospels, had to lead to radical criticism of the information they gave, and made everything nebulous when it was asked what really happened in the years A.D. 1-30.

Among the criteria of the verifiability of historical events Strauss reckoned principles which would later recur in Troeltsch. These principles are related to the axiom that nature and history form a nexus of cause and effect. Causality, succession, psychological law, and analogy determine events, and these are all recognizable.[20] This axiom is the presupposition for doing justice to the principle of an absence of presuppositions. When we respect this axiom, however, the biblical stories, in which the nexus is broken at many points by the intervention of divine causality, cannot possibly be regarded as history.[21] But what is left if these transcendent interventions are rejected?

The historical vacuum which opens up here cannot be filled up speculatively. Hegel does indeed state speculatively that the idea of divine-human unity in Christ is the point of Christianity and is the basis of its absoluteness. But we cannot infer from this idea that this synthesis

---

does not come from Hegel. Hegel and his followers never developed this kind of historico-critical element. It represents a new beginning in Strauss.

19. *Streitschriften*, Heft 3, 57.
20. *Das Leben Jesu*, pp. 100ff.
21. Ibid., p. 81.

took shape in the one individual Jesus and thus found representation in history. In Heft 3 of the *Streitschriften* Strauss gives an impressive example to show how impossible is this transition from the general idea to the special case. Thus the idea of beauty or virtue has to have reality, but can I deduce from this that some specific person has to be beautiful or virtuous?[22] It might be essential to ideas—cf. our discussion of historical personages—to manifest themselves in individuals, and even to make some individuals the bearers of their absolute content. This holds good as a general statement. But it is not essential to ideas that one specific individual alone should be a full actualization of them.[23]

Thus Hegel's idea of divine-human unity is a good one, and Strauss pays homage to it, but it has no bearing on the question whether this idea is actualized in the individual Jesus. This question can be decided only by a historico-critical analysis of the accounts. But the attempt at such an analysis does not help. For the elements in the Gospels which bring Jesus into conformity with the idea of divine-human unity occur in the gaps in the historical net, i.e., where what we have is not history, but supposed transcendent interventions replace causally effected immanence.

Strauss concludes, then, that Hegel's philosophy cannot decide whether that which the Gospels report really happened. When the question of truth is related to that of fact, when it is not answered by an assertion of what is generally valid, then the question of truth is left open in Hegel.[24] Thus the approach by way of a historico-critical analysis of the life of Jesus leaves Strauss with the feeling that at an essential point in his search for truth Hegel has nothing to offer.

The inductive and empirical inquiry of Strauss—one might call it his left-wing Hegelian motif—brings to light a gap in the Hegelian system. It thus establishes a new relation to reality and truth and throws doubt on the system to an extent that Strauss can hardly overlook in his own historical hour. Nevertheless, he attempted, as we shall see, to work out a new approach to the system in spite of the difficulty.

The critical investigation of the life of Jesus brings Strauss up against a problem that never arose for Hegel,[25] namely, that of distinguishing what is empirical from what is supernaturally embellished, or history from myth. This is first done with the help of a negative principle of

---

22. *Streitschriften*, Heft 3, 69; cf. Hartlich and Sachs, *Ursprung*, p. 127.
23. *Streitschriften*, p. 125.
24. Ibid., p. 68.
25. It does not do so because for Hegel history and myth are both depiction that has to be reduced to concept; cf. Hartlich and Sachs, *Ursprung*, p. 131.

We see our limitation, imperfection, and alienation. We thus posit God as our opposite. God is infinite, we are finite; God is perfect, we are imperfect.

It is natural to relate the anthropological reversal of the Christian religion very emphatically to the incarnation, to God become man, and hence to view the concept of God as a human entity as the core of the idea of incarnation. The incarnation is nothing other than the actual sensory manifestation of the human nature of God. The reversal reaches a climax for Feuerbach—in chap. 5—when he says that the humanity of God denoted by the figure of Christ is the hypostatizing of what we in our humanity know and experience as love. The point is as follows.

1 John 4:8 tells us that God is love. The essence of love is here defined by that of God. This love is thus distinguished from our natural human love. For Feuerbach, however, God personifies our love. The idea of God is a hypostatizing of our love. Hence, as H.-J. Kraus rightly observes, what we should now read is that love is God.[59] If the idea of God is subsumed under that of (human) love, then in chap. 5 Feuerbach has come back to what in different ways is always his basic thesis. The projection of this love in the form of God must be abandoned in favor of the projecting entity. As God has given up himself in love (this is meant ironically, since God is a fiction!), so in love we should give up God. We should practice the self-giving that comes to illustration in the incarnation only indirectly, i.e., as a liberated virtue.

Thus ethics in Feuerbach is no longer vitalized by religion, as it is in Kant. In this regard Feuerbach brings up a problem that is still relevant in modern discussions. The famous statement of Hugo Grotius that natural law, i.e., natural ethics with its norms, would still be valid even if there were no God, has for Feuerbach the sense that ethical values are secure only when they are detached from their theonomous basis, i.e., only when we realize that there is no God. The distinction may be appreciated when we see[60] that what Grotius has in mind is that in natural law God has linked himself so closely to his own order that the latter will be valid even if we assume—as we may not—that there is no God. Grotius is not postulating atheism but is making the point that what God has given is so good that it would maintain its order even without him, and that it is so inalterable that even God himself cannot alter it.[61]

59. Kraus, *Theologische Religionskritik* (1982), p. 161.

60. This is important because Bonhoeffer misunderstands Grotius when he quotes him in *Letters and Papers from Prison*.

61. On Grotius see E. Wolf, *Grosse Rechtsdenker* (1939), pp. 199ff., esp. pp. 209-10, 212, 217.

We may formulate our first findings as follows. First, God is a projection that magnifies the I in its hopes and fears and especially in its contradiction between what it is and what it ought to be. In psychological terms, one might speak of a superego posited by ourselves.

Second, in the modest series of references that point us to the heart of Feuerbach's view, we often find the formula that religion is "nothing other than." This formula is a typical mark of the reductionism which in spite of every effort to be positive amounts to no more than subtraction. This style is found especially in materialism, toward which, as we have seen, Feuerbach increasingly veered. Reductionism marks an intellectual situation which refers us to an existent, objectifiable, and to that extent one-dimensional reality. It comes out in the recurrent formula that humanity is "nothing other than." Thus we read that life is nothing other than a process of consumption or oxidation. Again, in an American journal for psychotherapy, we read that values are nothing other than "defense mechanisms and reaction formations." Again, we humans are said to be nothing other than a biochemical mechanism fed by a system that gives energy to computers.[62]

Third, Ernst Bloch understood Feuerbach correctly when in connection with our cleavage, our division into what we are and what we ought to be, our not-yet and our hoped-for destiny, he thought of God as the hypostatized ideal of what humanity has not yet become in its reality, as the utopian entelechy of the soul, just as paradise is pictured as the utopian entelechy of the world of God. What we have, then, is a projection of *homo absconditus* and his world.[63]

This interpretation agrees with Feuerbach's express conviction that his criticism of religion is not at all negative or destructive in his own mind, but that it has a positive goal. He loves humanity and wants to help it. He refers to this goal in Lecture 3 of *The Essence of Religion*. He wants to make lovers of humanity out of lovers of God, students of this world out of candidates for the next, free citizens of earth out of heavenly and earthly courtiers, anthropologists out of theologians. His concern is to serve humanity and its development. But humanity can come to itself only when in freedom it sees itself as an autonomous theme and is not misled by being encoded in religious ciphers.

Increasing polemical opposition, however, has caused Feuerbach to be remembered primarily as a spirit of negation, the advocate of an "anti." He himself thought that the "anti" was simply the reverse side of his positive, philanthropic goal. He never tired of pouring scorn

62. See my *Being Human—Becoming Human,* p. 436.
63. E. Bloch, *Das Prinzip Hoffnung,* III, 1522-23.

and ridicule upon those clever priests who would not throw away the crutches of religion but instead tried to fit them on their fellows. The dogmatician Julius Müller was a typical target for such tirades.[64] He was the epitome of priestcraft. Priests like him are either dishonest hypocrites if they are clever, or stupid if they are sincere. There is nothing more abhorrent than theologians. In them we find ignorance under the guise of revealed wisdom, vulgarity under the guise of culture. Feuerbach is not a Christian for moral reasons. He does not think that in his day one can be a Christian without deceit and self-deception.[65]

C. CRITICAL APPRAISAL: THE END AND NEW BEGINNING OF APOLOGETICS

We might continue at length and show how all Christian dogmas are viewed after the manner of reductionism ("nothing other than") and hence grotesquely banalized. But in relation to his two main works in criticism of religion, this would hardly explain their enormous influence, particularly that of *The Essence of Christianity*. For in spite of his fiery eloquence (in writing) and the fervor which makes joyful discoveries out of bowdlerizing of Christian doctrines, the monotony of his one, endlessly repeated thesis becomes exceedingly tedious.

His success may be explained only from two angles. First, theologians and educated Christians found in his work some secret questions of their own, especially the question whether what they believed might not finally be a human product. They had to take notice of a refrain that was repeated so directly and so frequently. Second, the many secularized people of his day found on every page of his monotonous unmaskings a new confirmation of the fascinating thesis that formed their starting point. Like all fanatics, they never wearied of the repetition. One might add that the very fervor of liberation which inspired the two works was able to induce a new sense of mission, and hence much more than mere gloating.

Nevertheless, it would be unjust to charge Feuerbach alone with the trivializing of Christianity. He did not arrive at his critical theses by accident, and he is certainly not a hybrid Prometheus. He is a victim of

---

64. Julius Müller (1801-1878) was author of *Die christliche Lehre von der Sünde* (1838ff.).

65. That he had a positive, humanitarian goal was for Feuerbach the essential difference between him and the radically negative Max Stirner, whom he did, however, admire.

Hegelian philosophy and its inability to satisfy the sense of reality in developing materialism. He is also a victim, as we have seen, of the Christianity of his age. In his letters he sometimes chastises the Christianity around him no less sharply than his contemporary Kierkegaard. When his brother Eduard asked him to be godfather to his son and begged him to give up his anti-Christian stance, he refused in an ironical letter (Aug. 18, 1842), telling his brother to pander to the spirit of the age, which could regard a contradictory mixture of Christianity and paganism as Christianity, by giving his son the anti-Christian name of Ludwig and the Christian name of Anselm, thus avoiding all embarrassment. His pain at the emptiness and inauthentic contradictoriness of contemporary Christianity is obvious. The emptiness of its empirical manifestation provided the impetus for his examination of the reality that lay behind such a dubious phenomenon. For all the criticism, disillusioned love may be seen in the background.

If we seek an approach to countercriticism of Feuerbach's theory of projection, I want to begin with what might seem to be the shocking statement that in principle his thesis cannot be refuted by argument. Such a refutation, i.e., the proof that revelation is not a human projection, would imply the possibility of a proof of God.

Naturally, we can fasten on points of detail. But what will an apologetic patchwork of this kind accomplish? If we do not focus on the central theme of anthropologizing, we miss the point and leave the main conception intact.

An instructive example of the ineffectiveness of this kind of apologetic may be found in the debate that raged in the 1930s around Alfred Rosenberg's *Myth of the Twentieth Century*. This very widely circulated work aroused a host of apologetic reactions from the church. The most important and comprehensive was written by anonymous scholars and published as an occasional paper by the diocese of Münster under the title *Studien zum Mythus des 20. Jahrhunderts* (1934). In it the authors sought to counter all the exegetical, ecclesiastical, and historical arguments of Rosenberg and to demonstrate his total lack of scholarship. Although widely circulated, this work of debunking was astonishingly ineffectual. The supporters of the myth did not feel touched by it, since the blood and soil ideology of Rosenberg was for them a vital message. Its opponents felt a gloating satisfaction, but there were no renegades or converts. Not incorrectly, the author of the Nazi myth could say in reply that what he had maintained in the myth would stand even if its historical proof could be refuted at every point.[66] Similarly, the theses

66. A. Rosenberg, *An die Dunkelmänner unserer Zeit* (1935), p. 6.

of Feuerbach are unaffected even though his detailed references from the Bible and church history might be contested at every point.

Feuerbach has done us the unwitting service of radically challenging the traditional apologetics with its mixture of speculation and history. He has thus forced theologians to face the problem of how to conduct a relevant dialogue with those who contest Christian truth. He drives them out of subsidiary theaters, where there is only indecisive skirmishing, to the main front. One might say that he compels theology to abandon matters of detailed tactics for strategic considerations.

In the attempt to make this initiative fruitful, our first point is that in principle there can be no defense of Christianity from outside. Looking at it from outside, one can in fact interpret Christianity in a way that relativizes it psychologically or historically. (Thus in many ways Freud is in this regard a disciple of Feuerbach.) No objective arguments can be found for the overpowering of my existence by the kerygma of the gospel, just as Kant can find no way of proving the fact of freedom. On an outside view, Kant says, all things seem to be subject to causal necessity, so that with a knowledge of the psychological factors we may predict human action with the same certainty as astronomers predict an eclipse of the moon. As Kant says, the certainty of freedom is nonobjective. I have it when I encounter the practical logos of my conscience. The kind of existential certainty that faith has cannot be proved from outside. It is nonobjective. So is the certainty of a reality of God that cannot dissolve into the notion of a mere projection. It cannot be demonstrated from outside.

This might seem for a moment to be a capitulation to the argument of Feuerbach. But it is only a negative pointer to the true subject of debate. To show what I have in mind I sometimes use an illustration. Seen from outside, stained-glass windows in churches are gray. They tell us nothing. They might as well be glazed screens. Only when I go inside do they begin to glow and tell their story and proclaim. To put it sharply, I might say that the Christian conviction of the reality of God and Feuerbach's contesting of this reality are on different planes. The absence of a common plane is identical to the absence of convincing arguments within the premise of objectivity. The certainty of the reality of God and the refutation of Feuerbach can arise only through authoritative proclamation in which the reality comes to light and the theory of projection itself becomes a figment. Only then do I go inside, and the windows speak, and my previous course of life is either suddenly or gradually changed.

The decisive critical question to Feuerbach regarding the choice between theology and anthropology, revelation and projection, seems to

me to be very different from the usual countercriticism that one reads in
his theological interpreters, including Karl Barth and H.-J. Kraus. When
I said that one cannot in principle refute him with arguments, one might
even in some circumstances view Kierkegaard's opposition to Hegel as a
refined form of projection if one is bent on so doing. Kierkegaard
protested most sharply against making Christianity an objectification of
our own wishes and ideals. He drastically stressed its character as offense,
the shocking paradox of it. But he offered no theological defense against
the understanding of his thought as intellectual wishful thinking, or of his
point about offense as merely a tactical trick to enable Christianity to
escape the argument of Hegel (and Feuerbach).

I will thus refrain from the apologetic nonsense of countercriticism, or from taking the same course as Barth and regarding Feuerbach
merely as a storm that rightly engulfs certain anthropocentric theologians of the 19th century (although there is, of course, something in it).
I can take Feuerbach seriously only if I take his basic question seriously.
It is in fact a spear that pierces us and wounds us. I will not respond to
it with the pharisaic gesture of self-reassurance as though under my
cassock or robe I wore a mail-shirt off which the spear would bounce
harmlessly. (This criticism does not apply to Barth or Kraus.)

To turn to what I have called the strategic as distinct from the
purely tactical consideration, I propose the following way of entering
into dialogue with Feuerbach.

In taking Feuerbach seriously, I would go so far as temporarily
to take down my theological barricade, apparently go over to the enemy,
and take a stand on the ground of the projection theory. Let it be
supposed that I have to accept it. I have to give up the transcendent
basis of my faith thus far. I must be satisfied with the horizontal plane
of self-actualization and my resolution to love others. Is this all that may
be said at this point? Feuerbach seems to have no more to say. His total
anthropologizing of religion puts an end to the problem of transcendence. He sets a period behind it. But should not the period really be
a colon? Is it not the fact that only here do we come up against the
decisive question?

The main question is this: Why are we forced to engage in this
form of projection, in this division of the self which causes us to use the
symbol "God" for what we ought to be in contrast to what we are? Can
we be content with the trivial explanation that Feuerbach himself gives,
namely, that the idea of God or the gods is no more than the objectification of wishful thinking?

If we dig more deeply into this question of the origin of the need
for projection of this kind, the alternative of theology or anthropology

obviously changes into a decisive question that is quite new. This is the question of the source of the need for projection. Is it to be explained in terms of the horizontal or the vertical dimension of human existence? We are not alone in putting this question; Karl Marx does too. In closing, then, we come back to Feuerbach's initial question.

(1) Marx contends for an immanent source in his Feuerbach Theses at the beginning of the "Deutsche Ideologie."[67] He respects Feuerbach as a materialist who has inverted Hegel,[68] but he objects to his failure to get behind our projecting and to find the true reason for it in our inventing in religion a heavenly alter ego and thus positing the division into a religious world and a secular.

Marx's real answer to the question of the source of the need to project, and his correction of Feuerbach, is that there is no abstract humanity in Feuerbach's sense but only humanity as it is shaped by social circumstances. It is these circumstances that alienate and warp us. Feuerbach establishes the fact that we are torn apart and in self-contradiction. He deduced from this his idea of the heavenly alter ego. But all this is simply a reflection of our estranged relationships. As Marx so often says, it is these that drive us to imagine a consoling substitute hereafter for the misery of present relationships. For him, then, the crucial thing is to change the world and humanity, and not just to interpret it.[69]

Feuerbach merges religion into humanity, Marx says. But humanity is not an abstraction indwelling individuals. In reality it is a nexus of social relationships. Feuerbach does not engage in criticism of this true reality. He does not see that even religious feeling is itself a social product, and that the abstract individuals that he analyzes belong to a specific social form. Mysteries that lead to mysticism find their rational solution in human practice and an understanding of it.[70] For Marx "practice" means our concrete social situation.

Marx, then, poses a question that Feuerbach never puts, namely, that of the reason for religious projection. He answers it by diagnosing social relationships in the sphere of the horizontal or immanent dimension.

(2) But theologians who enter into dialogue with Feuerbach must also put this question of the source of projection, and in so doing they may well come across a new transcendence.

---

67. Written in 1845-46; cf. *Frühschriften*, ed. Landshut, pp. 339ff.; ET of the Feuerbach Theses in Karl Marx, *Early Writings* (New York, 1975), pp. 421-23.
68. Cf. "Nationalökonomie und Philosophie" (1844), in *Frühschriften*, p. 250.
69. Feuerbach Theses, 11.
70. Ibid., 6-8.

Does not everything depend on our point of reference? From a one-sided psychological or sociological angle the contents of religion might indeed seem to be projection. These sciences, or some schools within them, insist on deriving metaphysics from objectifiable conditions. But from the angle of faith things are very different. Anthropological conditions are now a reflection of divine creation. In the former case the fatherhood of God reflects earthly fatherhood, and for those who have sorry experiences in this regard—cf. Tilmann Moser's *Gottesvergiftung*—a frightfully distorted picture of God results. But in the latter case the image of the earthly father reflects the Father in heaven. On the one side we have an anthropomorphic depiction of the world to come—the alter ego of our human world, as Marx put it—and therefore a projection. But on the other side we have a theomorphic shaping of our earthly, human reality.

If I said that we cannot refute Feuerbach in principle or by argument, this does not mean that we should not put a counterquestion to him. Might it not be that the picture of God that supposedly arises by projection has its basis in the affinity of those who project to what is projected? Might it not be that the picture of God that seems to be a mere appearance to empiricists arises in fact as a reflection that God has impressed upon the psyche? How could we arrive at the idea of a heavenly alter ego were it not that we already bear the *imago Dei* within us, that we are created for God, and that there is by creation an affinity between him and us?

To put it even more sharply, if Feuerbach has stood his master Hegel on his head, might it not be a theological task to do the same to Feuerbach? Not, of course, to make of him a reborn Hegel, but to put to the anti-theologian who anthropologizes religion the question whether projection is not a reflection, a reaction to "something" which has already been said, which has established affinity between the divine and the human, and which, in biblical terms, has made us the divine image? Might it not be that God has become man, that his word has become flesh, that he has been found in fashion as a man (Phil. 2:7)—and Feuerbach has conceived of the abstruse idea that his affinity between God and us, that the analogy of this condescension, is a reason to see in God a projected alter ego of ourselves?

From this standpoint does not the rise of the alter ego idea have a very different look? I put this as a question, not wishing to fall into the assertive style that is customary in apologetics. But it may well be taken as a rhetorical question which will lead readers into trains of thought of their own.

I claim that it is at least just as impossible to refute this theological response to Feuerbach as it is to destroy his own theory by argument. I must justify this "at least," however, because it confers a certain argumentative advantage to the theological side, and might thus seem to be somewhat inconsistent with our prior course. (For thus far we have avoided arguments and tried to show that Feuerbach's thesis and the theological antithesis are an open question from that standpoint.) Are we suddenly plunging back again into argument under the imposed form of a question? Are we relapsing into the style of apologetics? I am not prepared to go that far. We have here a choice, and reflection will not force us to go one way or the other. Yet there is one consideration that might upset the plain and self-evident nature of Feuerbach's theory of projection. It stands on a nontheological level.

Peter L. Berger has rightly pointed out that mathematics is a science in which in a sense the mind projects.[71] Without contact with nature a mathematician can construct mathematical universes which come into his head as pure products of his own understanding. This is especially true in astronomical mathematics, which can calculate in advance the position of the planets, and the telescope will later confirm the accuracy of the calculations. How is this possible? The only answer is that nature, or the universe, is itself constructed mathematically, that it is permeated by the logos. Only because there is this analogy between the ontic logos outside and the noetic logos in me can it be true that mathematical projections are not imaginary but reflect an existing logical reality. There is thus an affinity between the logos of thought and the logos of being, as Stoicism stated, regarding it epistemologically as the basis of the possibility of our own comprehension. The mathematically rational relations of the universe have, as it were, a beachhead in my own reason by means of which they can reach me and find reflection in me.

The same question—as a question, not an answer—arises in religion. It is as follows. Might it not be that the possibility of producing the idea of an alter ego rests on the fact that there is an analogy between God and us, an analogy that the Creator himself has established? Might it not be, then, that the idea of an alter ego is not a *production* of my own imagination but a *re-production*?

This question is so basic, and implies such a radical inverting of Feuerbach's view (the inverting of an inversion!) that there is no need for any frantic apologetic attempt to find in the sphere of religion details which cannot possibly be attributed to mere projection. We have now found a level on which to bring against Feuerbach a challenge in principle.

71. Berger, *The Sacred Canopy* (New York, 1967), p. 181.

I am thus in agreement with the essential thinking of Berger when he argues that saying "that religion is a human projection does not logically preclude the possibility that the projected meanings may have an ultimate status independent of man. . . . This would imply that man projects ultimate meanings into reality because that reality is, indeed, ultimately meaningful, and because his own being (the empirical ground of these projections) contains and intends these same ultimate meanings. . . . The most amazing fact about modern science is that these structures have turned out to correspond to something 'out there.' . . . Mathematicians, physical scientists, and philosophers of science are still trying hard to understand just how this is possible."[72] To this one might add at most that long before modern science, others (e.g., the Stoics) were moved to reflect on the relation between thought and being.

The counterquestion or challenge that has to be put to Feuerbach may be clarified by some theological statements which, taken alone, might seem to come close to Feuerbach and to represent an anthropologizing that anticipates him. I am referring for this purpose to a previously quoted saying of Luther, namely, that as we all are in ourselves, so is God to us as an object.[73] One might also add Luther's exposition of the first commandment in his Large Catechism: Only the heart's trust and belief makes God or an idol.[74] These statements seem to suggest that for Luther God is simply a function of our subjective condition, according to which a projection of God or an idol arises. But such a misunderstanding is blocked by the decisive premise of the statements, namely, that we are addressed by God and either open ourselves to him in faith or close ourselves against him. Only then does there arise the subjective condition that Luther has in view, and that entails different views of God in those who open themselves and those who close themselves.

A highly dialectical process and reaction occurs in those who are addressed. But the reality of God as the one who addresses them is always presupposed. We are always in relation to God even if the relation is in a negative mode and the related image of God is projected: an image that corresponds to personal desires, that confirms them, that fits in smoothly with them, and that exerts no pressure. If in both cases the view of God has anthropomorphic features, this is simply because God discloses himself to humans and accommodates himself to their powers

72. Ibid., pp. 180-81.
73. LW, 25, 219 (on Rom. 3:9, Corollary) (WA, LVI, 234).
74. Tappert, p. 367.

of comprehension. It is not because he is a reflection or projection of their subjective state.

As regards the massive anthropomorphisms of the OT (God experiences aversion and loathing, he can be wounded, he can repent, he hates, he also rejoices and is glad), L. Köhler can say that their purpose is not at all to put God on the human level.[75] This is not a humanizing. The point is to make God accessible. The anthropomorphisms avert the mistake that God is an abstract idea or a fixed principle. Because the OT speaks in this way, its God is presented to us as the personal and living God who meets us volitionally and actively, who acts on us, who comes to us. God is the living God.[76]

A careful critical debate with Feuerbach seems to me to be unavoidable because here we have the most radical questioning of Christian truth in intellectual history. Because it is so radical, it is not the most dangerous challenge. More threatening are the theological half-truths which Feuerbach's theory of projection engenders and which continually arise again long after him and up to our own time. Among these half-truths are opportunistic assimilations of Christian truth to the spirit of the age or its integration into given structures, e.g., into Hegelianism or existentialism. Feuerbach has done us the great service of exposing these half-truths by making total untruth out of them. Just because we are all entangled in such processes of thought and alienation, he shows us our own deepest temptations. This is why we have had to spend more time on him even though in fact he has only one basic idea.

D. FEUERBACH AND SUCCESSORS

The impact of Feuerbach has left wide traces in literature, philosophy, psychology, and even theology. Among the great names that bear the impress of his spirit we may mention first Gottfried Keller, who as a student heard his lectures on *The Essence of Religion,* and who in a letter early in 1851 said that Feuerbach was most important for his development because he felt that through him he was enabled to penetrate and grasp human nature more profoundly. He unreservedly accepted Feuerbach's anthropological theory in criticism of religion.[77]

In theology Barth makes a distant and partial coalition with

75. L. Köhler, *Old Testament Theology* (New York, 1957), pp. 22-23.
76. Ibid.
77. Bächthold, *Gottfried Kellers Leben,* II, 168-69.

Feuerbach by finding in religion a last human revolt. In it we are ourselves the creator of God and make him the mere predicate of our own human life and being.[78] For a final breaking of the Feuerbach wave on the theological shore I may refer to the strange death-of-God theology, which now seems to be little more than a theological curiosity.[79]

A large monograph would be needed to give even a sketch of Feuerbach's influence. All that I can do by way of epilogue to the section on Feuerbach is to give some striking and typical examples.

1. Sigmund Freud

For Sigmund Freud, too, religion is a projection, a superstructure of anthropology, especially its deeper psychological dimension.[80] This applies in the question of meaning. Meaning is not for Freud a transcendent and autonomous entity. The search for it reflects a subjective state and is a pathological symptom. Thus in a letter to Marie Bonaparte we find the revealing statement that the moment we ask after the meaning and value of life, we are sick. The idea of God is understood similarly. It may at times have functional significance in the attaining of equilibrium by a balancing of impulses.[81] Under the pressure of danger, depression, and guilt feelings, we may be plunged into the role of helpless children, and then the idea of God aids us by meeting our need for protection.

The idea of a God who loves and forgives alleviates the pressure of guilt complexes. A certain desire for power is pacified when it enjoys certainty that it has the support of an almighty partner. The notion of God can thus relax tormenting tensions of every kind.

God is no more an independent reality than spirit. He has only the rank of a projection which impulses use, just as spirit is an instrument that animal life uses in humans because they lack the automatic self-regulation that animals have by instinct. Life lays too heavy a burden

---

78. Cf. *CD*, I/2, and many other passages in *CD* and *Romans;* cf. *EF,* III, 324ff., 331ff., 345ff. H.-J. Kraus objects to this interpretation of Barth (*Theologische Religionskritik,* pp. 109ff.), but I find it hard to grasp his view that the teaching on other lights in IV/3 presents a different view of religion in terms of Christology. Cf. H. Berkhof and H.-J. Kraus, *K. Barths Lichterlehre,* Theologische Studien, 123 (1978).

79. On this remarkable idea, which occurs first in Jean Paul and Nietzsche, cf. *EF,* I, chaps. 13–15.

80. Cf. the dialogue with Freud in my *Being Human—Becoming Human,* pp. 413ff.

81. Cf. Freud's main works on religion: *Totem and Tabu* (1912) and *The Future of an Illusion* (1927).

on us, says Freud. Hence, to lighten our intolerable lot, we resort to constructions that will help us. These range from primitive intoxication to the sublime narcotic of religion.[82]

Linked to Freud's fixation on the impulsive mechanisms of the psyche is his failure even to consider the question that we put to Feuerbach's theory of projection, and that Viktor Frankl raises against Freud in his writings on logotherapy.[83] Might it not be that Freud is inverting things when he says that God is not the original father-image but that the human father is the original of deity? Where does the reality lie, in the disclosure of the anthropomorphism of the image of God as a projection of the father-model, or in the confession of the theomorphism of the reality that lies behind the creaturely features of the image of the Creator?[84]

2. Ernst Bloch

Ernst Bloch extends Feuerbach's anthropologizing of religion to the social plane.[85] His goal is the end of real misery and the beginning of real happiness, i.e., an end to exploitation, the appeasing of the hunger and thirst for righteousness, the raising up of the heavy-laden, and freedom for the upright to lift up their heads without losing the ground under their feet. Do not the religions give us wrong directions on the way to these goals? An afterlife in which there will be a just distribution of supraterrestrial goods threatens to sanction the unjust distribution of terrestrial goods. With such projections one can easily evade unfulfilled desires for independence, etc., leaving them to God and not working strenuously to achieve them. In this way our God may make us passive.

Bloch's view, then, is that only without faith in a God who intervenes from above can love be concrete and hope alert. Since practical Christianity wants both these things, he develops his thesis that

82. Cf. E. Stadler, "Wahrheit und Verkündigung," in *Festschrift für Michael Schmaus,* I (1967), 285ff.

83. Cf. V. Frankl, *Der unbedingte Mensch* (1949); idem, *The Doctor and the Soul* (1955); idem, *Theorie und Therapie der Neurosen* (1956).

84. As regards critical counterquestions to Freud, cf. A. Görres, "Physik der Triebe—Physik des Geistes," *Gott in der Welt. Festschrift für K. Rahner,* II (1964), 556ff.; *Kennt die Psychologie den Menschen? Fragen zwischen Psychotherapie, Anthropologie und Christentum* (1978). Cf. also the symposium ed. by Heinz Zahrnt, *Jesus und Freud* (1972).

85. Cf. Bloch, *Altheismus in Christentum* (1968), and the passages on Feuerbach in *Das Prinzip Hoffnung* (1959), pp. 288ff., 1515ff. In criticism cf. C. H. Ratschow, *Atheismus in Christentum? Eine Auseinandersetzung mit E. Bloch* (1970).

only an atheist can be a good Christian and only a good Christian can be an atheist. He agrees with Marx, however, in thinking that we must finally break the chain that binds us to transcendence, recognize the mystery of our own being, and believe with Feuerbach that true faith in transcendence is faith in the freedom of subjectivity from the limits of nature, and therefore faith in ourselves. Only when this atheistic deduction is made do the religious symbols of Christianity become a plain text—a text in which, as I have shown, God is the hypostatized ideal of (as yet) unrealized humanity, of the utopian entelechy of the soul. The hidden God has only hidden humanity in mind. The supreme eschatological possibility of this humanity is projected upon an imaginary deity. We must now omit the first part of the saying of Athanasius that God became man in order that man might become God. The transcendent coagulates into our own desires. We thus enjoy an exodus from divine bondage and enter the promised land of autonomy. The Christian orientation to love and hope can be retained even though God is dead.

This reinterpretation of religion changes it but does not abandon it. The sum of unfulfilled wishes and goals comes into focus in the God of the religions. The vacuum left when God is banished is filled by the ultimate utopian goal, by the hope of achieving what is not yet. When wishes are viewed as that which is not yet, they are no longer tied to divine fulfilments—the great fault of religious ages—but to human programs of action and conflict. The world must be changed in keeping with the utopian goal. The religions lacked the initiative to do this because they expected everything from the deity.

Thus Bloch basically reinterprets the religions but does not negate them. For they manifest the ontology of the "not yet" in theistic garb. Thus their identity remains even though an atheistic garb is now substituted for the theistic.

We need hardly put again to Bloch the question that we put to Feuerbach. More important in summing up his following of Feuerbach seems to be an observation of his own in which he puts his own question and laments the loss of transcendence.[86] We live, he says, in a time when the upper world is extinguished and darkness and emptiness are undoubtedly widespread. In the West we have a tolerant pluralistic tedium, and in the East a commanded, ordered, repressed, monolithic tedium. Both show that hormone production is, as it were, out of line. There is a kind of partial eclipse of the sun. Everything is remarkably gray. Birds do not sing, or sing differently. Something is missing.

86. Cf. his address "Materialismus als Enthüllung, published as "Herr und Knecht in der Bibel," in *Wiener Neues Forum* (1967).

Transcendence is weak. Tedium is a lesser forerunner of nihilism: a nihilism of despair that the world is alien to us, that it does not even give us the cold shoulder. For the cold shoulder would be anthropomorphic. No, we have no relations with a cosmos that has no ends. In this sense cosmology is in a poor way; there is no connection at all with soteriology. It seems to be mere superstition to modern science. What Nietzsche prophesied for the 20th century has come to pass: We are moving on to an epoch of nameless misery, *with an underproduction of transcendence*.

We have here a remarkable and strangely contradictory statement. For in Bloch's view the absence of transcendence is the truth. But it is here our destruction. He obviously overlooks the fact that transcendence produces us, not we it, if we are to use this crude economic term. (So Gerhard Nebel in a letter to me.)

We thus catch an echo of the question that we put to Feuerbach. Is this complaint merely a short pessimistic interlude, or is it the moment of truth disclosed in the glade of being?

3. Jean-Paul Sartre

Jean-Paul Sartre has drawn the (as yet) final deduction from Feuerbach's thesis, although, so far as I can see, he has hardly any connection with Feuerbach himself. His concept of existentialism, which differs from the varieties found in Gabriel Marcel, Heidegger, and Jaspers, contains the most radical form of Feuerbach's anthropologizing.[87]

In his work on humanism we find the characteristic statement that according to existentialism, even though no God exists, there is a being in which existence precedes essence, and this being is the human being, or, as Heidegger would say, human reality. What does it mean here that existence precedes essence? It means that a human being first exists, encounters himself, occurs in the world, and only then can become.

We have here an inversion of medieval Scholasticism, or, if one will, its consistent secularization. Following Aristotle, Scholastic thought had essence precede existence. Pure form *(eidos)*, as it is present in God's thoughts, combines with primal matter *(prote hyle)* and produces what is. The divine act of creation, *actus purus*, accomplishes this. Since pure form is the essence of things, and preexists in God's consciousness, it precedes existence, which comes into being only later. Created things, including humanity, have a transcendental origin.

87. Cf. his main work *Being and Nothingness* (1957), and esp. *Existentialism and Humanism* (1948).

The moment God is denied, one can no longer assume the precedence of essence but has to begin with what is ontically present, existence. Knowing itself only as factually present, humanity is a blank slate on which must be written the program of what it wills to be and desires to become under its own rule and on its own initiative. Theology and metaphysics, which view our human destiny as already given and transcendentally determined, are now not merely reduced to anthropology in Feuerbach's sense. The reduction goes further.

Anthropology itself is not a system which has fallen from heaven and in which we are related to what we are and should be, and oriented to values and norms.[88] It, too, is traced back to existing humanity freely deciding what it wills to be and become, and hence rejecting all given norms. We thus have to determine the essence of our being in freedom, in imitation of the divine *actus purus* that has proved to be imaginary.

Thus Sartre occupies toward Scholasticism the same position as Feuerbach does toward religion and Christianity in general. He achieves a full inversion. We create ourselves by determining our essence and setting our goals. This is not just becoming in the sense of Goethe's concept of the entelechy, i.e., the living development of a preshaped form. Nor is it becoming in the sense of Friedrich Rückert's image that lives or is pregiven in all of us and that we have to "be" if we are to be fully at peace.[89] As Sartre's plays show, to become is to wrestle with the world around, not to be degraded to its mere object, to be autonomous over against it, to make it the object of one's own action. For Sartre freedom is the *actus purus* of the self-creator—no less.

Infinite freedom, however, is freedom from responsibility, because no normative entity confronts it to enforce responsibility. Sartre, of course, persistently but unconvincingly seeks to evade this implication of his concept of freedom. We cannot go into the ethical consequences of his view of freedom here. What we can say is that essentially he uses this freedom in such a way as to uphold the independence of existing individuals who are on their own in this way, and he will not recognize the impact of anything that may befall them. He constantly insists that we are self-creators. Thus Orestes in *The Flies* claims independence both of Jupiter and of the past, whether his own, that of the accursed house of Argos, or that of his *polis*. These all seek to fix his destiny. He titanically

88. Cf. the destiny of love and fellowship that Feuerbach discovers in his anthropology.
89. I refer to the verse—whether Rückert wrote it is disputed—in which he says that we all have within us an image of what we ought to be, and so long as we do not live up to it, we are not fully at peace.

bursts through the causal nexus of guilt and retribution that hangs over him. At the end he simply departs through the midst of the Furies (the flies as symbols of the avenging gods), and leaves the order of being and all the things that seek to bind him. Where does he go? He goes to a land in which he is alone. For there is no place where one who lives and thinks like Orestes can live with others. He wants to be a person without a past because what is behind us shapes in part the future that we are making for ourselves and restricts our radius of action. Where, then, does he go? He goes to the land of individuals and their own possessions, the land of Max Stirner.

In his drama *No Exit* Sartre advances his well-known formula that hell is other people (the last scene). Others are my enemies when they wrest from me the self that I am grasping autonomously. They expose me to a sublime form of slavery. They "fix" me, and in so doing they subject me to values which are not my own, which I accept unwillingly, and within which they make me an object. They hold me fast, and take from me my freedom to be myself. I can protect myself against them only by a counterattack in which I make them *my* object[90] and in that way win back my freedom.

I cannot unfold here the complicated dialectic involved in this counterattack in which others have the remarkable double role of both subject and object. In this context it is enough to say that on our own, in freedom, we have no relation to the Thou, that we live in defense and counterattack against the Thou, that we must regard the Thou as one who threatens our own existence.

Thus Sartre has to view any orderly system in which I have to live with others as simply a force of existential destruction against which I must be on guard. The fact that such a system encloses me shows how debilitating it is. Whether its representative values and norms accuse me or excuse me, I am always viewed as an object; I am "fixed." Freedom is identical with solipsism. I do not have freedom; I am it. This is what Orestes says in *The Flies*. He thus sets up a partition between himself and everything around him.

Sartre's later attempt to view the Thou of others as at least partly meaningful because it stimulates one's own existence is forced and inconsistent and secondary. At the heart of his thinking he seeks distance from others and from the web of orders in which one is brought into contact with them.[91]

90. *Being and Nothingness,* esp. pp. 221-302.
91. I wonder if this might be connected with his strange liking for the dropouts, terrorists, and misfits of the sixties and seventies.

The extraordinary confusion in all this, the contradiction between blank slate and responsibility, between self-creation and being thrust into the world, finds succinct expression in the work on humanism. If God does not exist, says Sartre, then no values or commandments confront us to justify our behavior. Neither behind nor before us are there any justifications or excuses in the radiant realm of values. We are alone. This is what is meant when it is said that we are "condemned to be free." We are condemned, for we did not make ourselves, and yet we are free because, thrust into the world, we are responsible for everything that we do. Really only for what we *do*? Not for our nature or essence? It seems to me that Sartre's free radius of action does not reach its full extent here.

Sartre's existentialism carries through from the beginning to the final end. He expresses this in the work on humanism when he says that existentialism is simply a concern to draw the last inferences from a consistent atheistic position. Here we have the orderless world of absolute individuals, and it is noteworthy that Sartre does not feel driven into lively dialogue with Dostoyevski's saying that without God everything is permitted. He does at least perceive from afar the wolfish forces that make the atheistic landscape insecure. Max Stirner sees them more clearly. In Sartre I have always awaited in vain the moment when in place of the lost order he will propose a compact that will allow the Orestes figures to have contact without rubbing one another the wrong way. For when order is expunged, such a compact always arises. The world can never be a mere accumulation of individuals or solipsists.

Sartre, it seems to me, is the provisional end of the dance that begins when Feuerbach proclaims the absence of transcendence.

III. KARL MARX AND MARXISM: QUESTIONS TO THEOLOGY AND THEOLOGICAL COUNTERQUESTIONS WITHIN THE FRAMEWORK OF ANTHROPOLOGY

Bibliography. Fuller details need not be given because the literature is so enormous and many accounts of the life of Marx are available. A more recent and carefully researched biography is that of Richard Friedenthal, *Karl Marx. Sein Leben und seine Zeit* (1981). Among other works cf. W. Bienert, *Über Marx hinaus* . . . (1979); Guilio Girardi, *Marxismus und Christentum* (1968); Helmuth Rolfes, *Der Sinn des Lebens im marxistischen Denken* (1971); Siegfried Scharrer, "Der atheistische Ansatz in der Philosophie von K. Marx," *Glaube und Weltanschauung,*

2 (1978); "Christlicher Glaube und marxistische Religionskritik," *Glaube und Weltanschauung*, 2 (1978); H.-J. Schoeps, *Was ist der Mensch?* (1960), chap. 1; H. F. Steiner, *Marxisten-Leninisten über den Sinn des Lebens* (1970); Leszek Kolakowski, *Die Hauptströmungen des Marxismus*, 3 vols. (1981-1982). For the early works of Marx cf. S. Landshut, ed., *Kröners Taschenausgabe*, vol. 209 (cited as Kröner).

Karl Marx was undoubtedly a great thinker, but it may seem to be paradoxical to include him among theological thinkers. The theological element in him is that of anti-theology. Yet his approach is such as to put questions to theology and to trigger counterquestions. Furthermore, his influence on theological work, not merely in the Socialist sphere, is vast. Without usually noting the impact of the thinking of Marx, under its influence the horizon of meaning of *agape* has basically changed. We no longer equate it solely with Christian love in individual ethics. We see that it has the supraindividual task of altering social structures that harm humanity at large and alienate it. Here tradition left an ethical vacuum which Marx did not fill but which he pointed out. In so doing he necessarily imposed upon theology the task of filling it. More recently the task of filling it has led to the concept of love in structures, which is often misunderstood because it is put to dubious use in the theology of revolution.[92]

Now all the questions of faith find a focus in anthropology, and anthropology is also a key theme in the system of Marx. I will thus take the understanding of humanity as the point of encounter.

A. AUTHENTIC AND INAUTHENTIC HUMANITY

Marxism is primarily a doctrine of social relations. This doctrine is meant to be an intellectual weapon in the fight of the proletariat for liberation. In Marxism this liberation is first economic. At issue is the economic exploitation of workers and their consequent alienation. The basic economic theme might make it seem strange to put the question of Marxist anthropology at all. It might kindle the fear that we are bringing an alien question into the system from outside. Yet the young Marx has a plain and even programmatic doctrine of humanity.

92. Cf. Richard Schaull in H. Krüger, *Appell an die Kirchen der Welt* (1967), pp. 88ff.; on the relation between *agape* and structure cf. my essay "Können sich Strukturen bekehren?" *ZThK* 1 (1969) 98ff.

1. The Place of the Anthropological Question

There are two possible places for anthropology within the Marxist system.

Dialectical materialism says that historical events rest on economic movements and laws, so that history is really economic history. This suggests that humanity is the product of laws, and the word *product* implies that humanity is the result of economic conditions rather than their cause. It cannot be the cause because these conditions follow law, i.e., the law of dialectic, and leave no room for freedom understood as the possibility of intervention. From this standpoint humanity has only a poor subsidiary part to play; it is the result of movements which treat it as an object.

But there is a second and very different way of integrating Marxist anthropology within the system. Thus an expositor of Marxism in the camp of Roman Catholic theology can say that the theme of Marxism as well as Christianity is humanity. What Theodor Steinbüchel means by this is that it is only because of their common theme that the two are polemically interested in one another. If Marxism were only an economic theory, one could hardly think that they would be in such passionate controversy, for Christianity champions no specific economic program and is thus compatible with Marxist economics, as many religious Socialists have noted.

The fact that an anthropological concern stands at the heart of Marxist thought, at any rate in the younger Marx, may be seen at once from express statements. Schoeps rightly states that the younger Marx had much in common with Kierkegaard.[93] Like him, he is concerned about inauthentic, alienated, and authentic humanity, even if his definitions differ. In his criticism of Hegel's philosophy of religion,[94] Marx says that theory can grip the masses once it is ad hominem, and it is ad hominem once it is radical. Being radical means going to the root of things. The root for humanity is humanity itself.

2. Humanity as a Main Theme

If further proof be needed that humanity is the true theme, not just for theory, but for the program of conflict, one may cite the statement that the only practical liberation of Germany is liberation from the standpoint of the theory that declares humanity to be the supreme essence

---

93. H.-J. Schoeps, *Was ist der Mensch?* (1960), p. 33.
94. See Kröner, p. 216.

of humanity.[95] Theoretically, then, the goal of the struggle (again an anthropological thesis) is the resolving of the tension between existence and essence, between objectification (as victim and object) and self-activity, between freedom and necessity, between individual and species. Authentic humanity that is no longer alienated but has come to itself is the solved puzzle of history, and it knows that it is the solution.[96] In this light one has to say that the true theme of Marxist thinking is humanity in its relation to the material conditions of existence, which decide whether it remains chained in alienation or gets the social chance of breaking out to authenticity.

It is important to take into account the concrete starting point of Marxism, namely, the situation of workers in the age of early capitalism. The Marxist ethos is shaped in a passionate revolt against two symptoms of sickness in modern society which are closely related: first, the modern form of slavery, the reduction of a section of humanity to a material mass with the rank of a mere machine, and second, the degradation of humanity as a mere means to an end, this end being the profit of a specific and parasitic class. One thus finds the initial kindling of Marxist movements in the protest against dehumanizing. One might refer, then, to its humanitarian approach.

Justified though we may thus be in finding a due place for anthropology in the Marxist system, we still have to ask how and in what sense humanity plays a part in Marx. The discussion that follows will try to answer this question. It will be a kind of theological investigation of Marx.

3. Economic Humanity

Humanity first figures in Marx as the object of social pity and the resultant social therapy. His question is how to liberate humanity from the alienating and depraving impact of a bungled social structure. Negatively, then, humanity is not the real object of interest. The concern is not the riddle of human existence. It is not human nature, especially in the sense that this transcends economic relations. Humanity is seen only in the context of social and economic conditions. One can change it, and bring it to authenticity, only as one alters this dominating factor. Hence humanity is finally only an exponent or function of this complex of reality.

Marx, then, thinks that he has said all that needs to be said about

95. Ibid., p. 223.
96. Ibid., p. 235.

humanity when he calls it economic humanity. The economic dimension is seen as not merely one—if an essential—dimension of its being; its being is the result of this one particular factor. The part becomes the whole. Theologically stated, Marxist thought has in this formal respect the character of a heresy. The mark of heresies is to make one doctrine the totality and thus to lead to elephantiasis. Marx is a heretic in anthropology when he reduces human existence to a single aspect. We shall thus expect to see, and we shall see, that in spite of his central interest in humanity Marx fails to get at the essence of humanity. His thinking circles around a picture of humanity that is shadowy; one cannot grasp it.

Let us now go to the heart of the matter and investigate this anthropology on its negative side. Marx speaks about dehumanizing and alienation. What does he mean by this? It is to be found in capitalism as he understands it.

4. The Concept of Alienation

One finds the loss of humanity, its reduction to a mere labor force, in the phenomenon of surplus value. Workers do not receive what their work is worth. They receive only the minimum needed for existence. They are thus no more than a dynamic, impersonal labor force. They are not valued as persons who are more than the productivity that nature has invested in them. The theory of surplus value brings to light the pseudo-humanity that lurks in capitalism. Workers are not loved, but they cannot be allowed to starve lest they lose their power to work.

This is found to be completely inhuman because workers here are valued, not as human ends in themselves, but only as the means to an end, i.e., to the achieving of a specific quota of work. Immanuel Kant, as we have seen, regarded it as the heart of immorality not to value people as ends in themselves, but only as the means to an end. The term *labor force* expresses the tendency to treat people as mere objects, for it makes workers a parallel of natural forces like steam and electricity. Since they have to sell their labor, but are also identical with it, this means that they are forced to sell themselves.

The resultant slavery leads to self-alienation. This manifests itself in two forms. Socially and economically, it means deformation inasmuch as people are dominated and controlled by their products. They are not subjects of their products and production; they are their victims and slaves. One section of humanity, the capitalist class, controls the labor of others and uses it as a means to secure its own profits, i.e., as mere human material. Humanity is thus divided into beneficiaries and victims. People are mere objects or functionaries; this is their extreme self-alienation. Classes represent this social or institutional side of self-alienation. The basis of it is the division of labor in virtue of which some have to work for others but do not control the products. Workers, then, are reduced to their function, and a depraved soul corresponds to the degrading function.[97]

Self-alienation may also be seen in religion and ideology. The ruling class fashions ideologies that justify its monopoly, seek to safeguard the class itself, and throw dust in the eyes of the poor so that they will not see their self-alienation or protest against it. As noted, religion is one of these ideologies in the view of Marx. It intensifies and perpetuates self-alienation by giving a substitute comfort so that people do not see their real conditions but hope for a better future in the next world and accept their misery in the present world as supposedly the will of God. They are thus prevented from trying to achieve any real change in their situation, or from effecting it.

Here is the real reason for Marxist atheism. Religion does not deliver us from self-alienation but holds us fast in it.[98] In original Marxism, features are plainly evident which according to the way that Marx understands himself one might call positive humanism. Marx is in fact concerned about humanity and human personality.

B. THE BREAK IN MARXIST ANTHROPOLOGY

Can Marxism keep to its humanitarian approach? This is an urgent question because normally we do not think that it can. The fact that Marxism has set up a state dictatorship shows us that there has been a severe personal loss, that in some forms of its outworking, at least, it does not respect human dignity and freedom as it originally seemed to do, and that in it we run into mechanizing and dehumanizing in another form. (Obviously we in the West need not be proud at this point, for we are in the same boat, even if for other reasons.)

We might argue that the self-understanding of Marxist Leninism is not a consistent development of Marxist ideology but that there has been a profound structural change. Yet even so we cannot evade the critical question; it only becomes the more acute. For it now becomes the very sharp question: How is it that Marxist Leninism has

---

97. Ibid., p. 516.
98. Cf. my study of atheism in *Von der Freiheit, ein Mensch zu sein* (1981), pp. 133ff.

been able to develop out of the original teaching of Marx? How is it that it can still with some justice make an appeal to it? Our central problem, then, is this: How could there be this break within Marxism itself, the break whereby a humanitarian beginning threatens to become so completely inhuman? Do we have an inconsistency here, a derailment, a decline from the ideal? Are we dealing with the very essence of Marxism, or with an aberration from it?

This is a very provocative question. For on the answer to it depends our answer to the question whether Christian theology must reject Marxism or can find correctives in it that show that it may still be open to real humanity, that the link with atheistic anthropology is not unconditionally constitutive for Marxism, that as scientific sociology it may be just as open to Christianity, or remote from it, as natural science. As Christian observers we constantly have to correct ourselves at this point, for to Marxist eyes Christian and bourgeois elements are confusingly mixed in us. At any rate, we must look this possible source of error squarely in the eye.

1. The Idealistic Origin

Perhaps we can advance our answer to the cardinal question by following the second strand that leads us to the rise of Marxism. (The first is the impulse from outside, i.e., conditions in the capitalist order of society.) What we have to expound is the intellectual origin, namely, the way that Marxist thinking derives from Hegelian philosophy. In so doing we must keep especially in view the way in which Marxism, when it argues that it is materialistic, reflects a kind of Oedipus complex vis-à-vis its idealistic origin.

Hegel's basic thought, as we have seen, was that world occurrence is a self-unfolding of the spirit. This spirit does not exist "in itself" over against the world; it exists in the evolution of the world. It moves gradually upward from the stage of unconscious nature to that of awakening consciousness of itself. This consciousness resides in human thought, and this thought has a rich variety of possible developments ranging from that of mere awakening to that of supreme reflection. The last stage comes when we finally raise the whole content of the divine spirit to the level of clear philosophical knowledge.

The essential thing in the controversy between idealism and Marxism is that in Hegel the spirit is not—to put it crudely—"produced" by human thought or even the human brain, as though humanity itself stood at the beginning of every spiritual movement. The opposite is the case. Thinking humanity comes last. First comes the world spirit itself. It knows every stage of its development. It first finds impress in the cosmos of inorganic and organic nature. This shows clear traces of the spirit, for it is a cosmos, a meaningful, spiritual construct with causal and final laws.

Yet the cosmos is only an object of the self-unfolding spirit (at the "being for itself" stage, and hence in self-alienation). It cannot respond with its own consciousness. Only in the human spirit, at a later stage of development, does the absolute spirit become conscious of itself and reflect upon itself. When we humans think, strictly it is not we who think, but the absolute spirit itself that thinks through us. Hence the statement arises to which we have referred already in the chapter on Hegel. The absolute spirit thinks itself in the finite spirit, and the finite spirit knows itself as the absolute spirit.

2. Humanity as the Transitional Point in Spiritual Processes

To achieve an understanding of Marxism, it is important to note that in Hegel's idealistic system humanity itself plays a relatively secondary role. It is only a transitional point in higher spiritual processes, just as later in Marx it is only a transitional point in economic processes. Related to this, as we have also seen, is the fact that Hegel can find no real place for individuals. Human history as the self-actualization of the spirit knows individuals only as inauthentic agents, as points of transition. As mere individuals they rank behind the species, which for its part represents the universal aspect and is thus closer to the idea. One might almost say that the species, being universal, is seeking to bring forth itself as such, and that this process takes place in the sequence of generations, so that individuals must constantly give themselves only the lower rank of transitions, and to that extent sacrifice themselves and wither away.

The incorporation of individuals in the species, so that they act as a race and the race is a supraindividual entity, is thus the first step on the way to the dissolution of individuality, i.e., to death. Hegel expresses the link between love and death when he says that the species continues only through the perishing of individuals, which fulfil their destiny by mating, and then, having no higher destiny, perish.[99] One might almost say that the original disproportion between individuals and the universal is their original sickness and the innate core of death.[100]

In this context Hegel is important in two ways. We now understand more clearly why we had to say earlier that individuals are not the

99. *Encyclopädie*, § 370.
100. Ibid., § 375.

real products of the spirit but mere points of transition that it uses to achieve its true ends and to become conscious of itself. This being so, we can see what is the function of historical personages in Hegel. They do not act on their own initiative, as we spectators might think. They are used instrumentally by the cunning of reason. No matter how vehemently Marxism might react against its idealistic origin, its inheritance is plain, for it, too, ascribes to individuals only a secondary rank in the flow of supraindividual processes.

3. The Break with Hegel

We are now adequately prepared to take a look at the way in which Marxism arose in intellectual history, i.e., at its break with the Hegelian tradition. It has become plain enough that we cannot understand decisive trends in Marxism if we do not consider its idealistic genesis and the influence of idealism even as it is negated. The atheistic and anti-Christian reaction is also understandable only when we realize to what extent Marxism is wrestling with its own origin in this regard.

The young Hegelian school, the so-called left-wing Hegelians, from whose ranks Marx himself springs, feel impelled, as we have seen in the case of Strauss and Feuerbach, to put a provocative question which is present even in Hegel himself, namely, whether the way of defining the relation between the world spirit and the human spirit should not be reversed. Is it really true, this school asks, that there is an absolute spirit that uses human consciousness to become conscious of itself? Is not this an illusion in the sense that the absolute spirit is in fact a projection of the human spirit? In this case the absolute spirit is our alter ego resulting from an optical illusion, namely, from a hidden act of objectification.

This is the decisive reaction against Hegel. Applying the reversal to the concept of God, Feuerbach expresses the reaction when he states that the principle of philosophy does not lie in the substance of Spinoza, the intelligible ego of Kant, the absolute spirit of Hegel, nor any entity abstracted from true reality, but that this principle is the most real of all things, the truly most real thing, namely, humanity itself. Humanity thinks the spirit; the spirit does not think itself in humanity. In this regard individuals are not the most real thing for Feuerbach, but the race or species. The impact of Hegel's negation of individuals may still be seen at this point.

4. The Extreme Opposite

We need not discuss here all the nuances of the Hegelian left. But the extreme left, which typifies the opposition to Hegel, does demand some consideration. The opposition reaches its almost grotesque extreme when Max Stirner says in *Der Einzige und sein Eigentum* (1845) that concrete individuals are the representatives of the one and only final reality. He has in mind people who are freed from every nonsensory reality (and hence from all relationship to metaphysical, logical, ethical, and legal norms), who are thus present, and can enjoy the moment, only as physical beings whose height and weight can be measured. For him there can be only the discontinuous moment. To relate to the future, with the implication of temporal continuity, they would have to presuppose norms and values, and goals at which to aim.

In other words, fullest reality belongs, not to individuals at the intellectual or spiritual level, but to individuals as natural animals quite apart from their intellectual or spiritual existence. The final result has to be that they are reduced to the physical side of their egos. Once they begin to think, they are back in an unreal cloud-cuckoo-land such as we have in philosophy, religion, or ethics.

In this way the individual has to be the only reality. Along with ideal norms, all possibility of communication with others drops away, for this is possible only within relations that have to transcend the individuals concerned and are thus ideal. There cannot even be the idea of a human species, because this implies communication between individuals. Instead of fellowship there is only the coexistence of physical bodies. Here Hegel's doctrine of the absolute spirit has been changed into a nihilistically anarchical and atheistic anthropology which rules out all further development, and even the concept of anthropology itself, for human thought is entering here the realm of the irrational and the illogical, the realm of the silence of reason. The moment reason begins to speak, illusion again overwhelms us.

5. The Reversal to Marxism

We have had to follow the overturning of Hegelian idealism to this extreme at which it becomes the completely materialistic solipsism of Stirner. And we should consider for a moment how comfortless is this world without spirit or morality. In it the funereal silence of nothingness prevails. Lonely individuals are abandoned to the darkness of a lunar landscape. Only when we appreciate this can we see the final and dreadful end of idealism and spot the place in intellectual history where the reversal to Marxist philosophy takes place and seems indeed to be "necessary."

Marx and Engels follow the logic of Stirner exactly. In 1844, writing to Marx, Engels refers to the "noble" Stirner, noble because he has to make an impact if one has the courage to draw from him the final inferences. His egoism, says Engels, is pushed so far, is so mad and yet so self-conscious, that it cannot for a moment remain in all its one-sidedness, but has to turn at once into Communism.[101]

This passage seems to be especially significant because it fixes exactly the point at which Marxism begins. It is also important to see how the law of Hegelian dialectic is at work here. Stirner with his materialistic individualism is the antithesis of Hegel's thesis of the spirit and the dissolution of the individual, as we have seen. The question then arises how the antithesis will develop. There seem to be two possibilities for the construction of a new antithesis according to whether the accent in "materialistic individualism" falls on the "materialistic" or the "individualism."

In the first case there will be an inversion to a new idealism. We need not go into this possibility, although such regenerations of idealism play an acute part in various forms of Socialist revisionism.

In the second case, when the accent falls on "individualism," the antithesis is Communism. Marx claims this possibility. Here again a second feature is important inasmuch as it helps to explain the Hegelian origin of Marxism. In this reversion to Communism the material basis is transcended in the twofold Hegelian sense that it is both negated and overcome and also taken up in a modified form.

This may be seen in two ways: first, in the way in which humanity is set in relation to the material laws of economics that determine its existence, and second, in the way in which the spiritual sector is understood.

C. INSIGHT INTO NECESSITY AS THE BASIS OF HUMAN ACTION

The way in which Marxism views individuals as a function of the historical infrastructure reminds us of their dependence on natural laws. This is particularly plain in the interpretation of revolution as Marx elucidates it with the help of an illustration from the changing of quantity into quality. In the course of quantitative shifts in society, e.g., a quantitative increase of possessions for some and decrease for others,

101. Marx-Engels, *Ausgabe*, III/1, 7.

and an increasing quantitative disproportion between the declining number of those with possessions and the gigantically increasing host of the proletariat with none, the same points of junction necessarily arise as in the transition from quantity to quality. In this case what comes is the point of revolution.

One might think that freedom erupts in revolution, that revolution is a spontaneous and emotional event. Revolutions always seem to mean a break with the law of the drag of the past. People are no longer content to be the mere effect of historical circumstances, e.g., social orders. With free spontaneity they break their chains and declare themselves to be the creators of new circumstances. We still perceive, however, that even as this specific phenomenon of human freedom, revolutions are subject to a way of natural necessity and have the character of physical points of junction. Does this mean that human subjectivity, the whole of the human element, is eliminated? (In this regard revolution serves only as an example.) To press the question, can we discern in this context the typically human situation of responsibility?

1. The Problem of Responsibility

To stay with this concept, the opportunity for responsibility arises when two conditions are met. First, I have to be able to act as a free subject. I thus have to be able to stand by what I do. I cannot be held responsible for what I do in a trance or at gunpoint. Second, responsibility arises when I am able to echo the claim that a higher authority makes upon me, e.g., that of truth. Responsibility means being under an obligation to reply, to make an echo.

Responsibility is not possible in principle, then, when I do not confront an entity to which I must respond and which is thus independent of me. It is not possible in principle when all that I think and do is apart from my personal I and takes place merely in a process that is dialectically conditioned by what is conceived to be my impersonal I. If the concept of freedom still figures in this context (and does any philosophical system reject it?), it can no longer be a mark of free spontaneity but only "insight into historical necessity." We must spend some time on this understanding of freedom.

Wolfgang Leonhard in his famous book *Child of the Revolution* tells us about the remarkable impression that proclamations of freedom made on young functionaries in Bolshevik party schools. For us, he says, freedom was insight into historical necessity.[102] Since we were the only

102. Leonhard, *Child of the Revolution* (1959), p. 385.

ones who on the basis of scientific theories had this insight, we were free, while people in the West, who did not have such theories and were thus ignorant of historical development and helpless in face of it, became the mere football of this development and were not free in spite of their proclamations of freedom.

In other words, the West construes freedom as the ability to do as one wills, unaware of the fact that hidden historical forces direct its supposed freedom and thus make an illusion of it. We must not ignore the seriousness of this challenge. If we make only the confessional reply that this is a betrayal of the free way of life of the West, this is no more than empty rhetoric. It frightens me when I constantly hear the sound of such tinkling cymbals. They signify an uneasy sense of security that is not only out of place but dangerous on the edge of the abyss. The demand at this point is for stringency of thought.

2. The Dominion of Necessity

What does the statement mean that freedom is insight into necessity? Dialectical materialism sponsors the thesis that there is no such thing as an accident in either nature or society. Necessity reigns. Everything that takes place in the sphere of history or human action is ruled by objective laws. These have the stringency of natural laws. Since Communism sees itself as a movement of liberation and wants to change the world and not just to interpret it, it has to face at a very elemental level the problem of freedom. For the wish to change the world logically presupposes the ability to do so.

An answer to the question of the relation between freedom and necessity can be given in this context only in the form of the famous definition of Engels that freedom does not lie in illusory independence of natural laws but in recognition of these laws and the resultant possibility of planning to make them serve specific ends. Freedom, then, is not active intervention in history—how can this be possible?—but collaboration with its laws, planning to make them serve the right goals. Such collaboration naturally presupposes knowledge. This knowledge is knowledge of the laws of movement in the material and economic infrastructure of society.

Above the historical structure of freedom as insight into necessity lies the eschatological freedom of the consummation of history. This second, eschatological form of freedom brings about what Marxism-Leninism calls the leap into the realm of freedom. For with the taking over of the means of production by society, the rule of the product over the producer comes to an end. The necessity of the previous course of history then ceases. It is no longer a kind of controlling force over us. The objective, alien forces that have previously ruled history pass under human control. They concede to us the role of subjects. Only this eschatological phase of history brings the final emancipation of humanity from the animal kingdom, puts it on its own, and gives it the opportunity of achieving unbroken humanity.

Those who know Hegel will easily recognize here the materializing of his doctrine of the spirit. In our development into subjective spirits, says Hegel, we become free and find in all reality a manifestation of the same spirit that comes to consciousness of itself in us as finite spirit. Knowing our identity with that which works in everything objective, we are absolutely free. For freedom is the same as not being determined by anything alien. I am free when I am on my own.[103] In other words, I am free when I will what the world spirit wills and no longer view what it wills as a controlling force. As history is progress in awareness of this identity, it is progress in awareness of freedom.[104] The eschatological sphere of freedom is thus a sphere of perfected humanity in the sense of being on our own.

3. The Dynamic Thrust of History

Following Hegel, Marxists perceive a necessary ascent to freedom in virtue of the fact that they can name the anonymous forces that blind the bourgeoisie and can combine the knowledge of their historical course with their own program of action. No longer, then, do they consume themselves, as the Kantian dualism of freedom and necessity demands, in a conflict with the autonomous necessities of history, with the economic trend, with the laws of mass psychology, and with many other factors in the supraindividual sphere of history. They use the flow of history. They direct its water to their mills. They empower their own dynamic of historical change with the forces of history itself. They thus treat history homeopathically, as it were, as like with like, and not allopathically, in opposition to it.

As distinct from Hegel, we obviously have here an economic consideration. It is a waste of strength to oppose the thrust of history, and it is a conservation of strength to empower one's own will by bringing it into line with that dynamic thrust. The economic factor is not just the theme of Marxist thought. It also controls its method of seizing control of this factor in its thinking, and then actively influencing it.

103. Hegel, *Philosophy of History;* cf. PhB, p. 32.
104. Ibid., p. 40.

We can understand the considerable fascination that this view and this program exert. The attractiveness of the concept rests less on its materialistic basis—this immediately evokes an "if" and a "but"—and more on its insight that freedom here is not just proclaimed as desirable but is exposed to the pressure of reflection. Such reflection brings to light certain controlling forces in history in relation to which freedom can come to itself only when it is not blind and no more than an empty phrase. Those who say "freedom" without being aware of the necessity with which they have to come to terms in some way are at bottom saying nothing at all.

From the Communist standpoint, then, the freedom of the free West does not imply a different desire from the East but rather a different way of thinking. To want freedom as distinct from terror or ideological tyranny points simply to a different view of freedom. Freedom has to have a basis both in logic and in real life. Hence Marxism poses a question of principle that cannot be answered merely by declamation or argument. The problem of meeting this challenge seems to be the great task of thought and decision for adult spirits in the West.

4. The Validity of the Truncation of Humanity

Once again we come up against the reduction of the personal sphere in Marxism, for we are forced to ask whether freedom is not in this way restricted to the mere ability to achieve insight into historical necessity. But what impels us to claim and harness this insight?

As concerns the proletariat, one might perhaps answer that what drives them is their social plight. Seeking to overcome this, they look for tactical possibilities of bringing about their liberation. In so doing, they first establish the course of the historical process, and then work productively with it instead of unsuccessfully opposing it. In this case freedom as insight into necessity is simply the result of economic pressures and not what has always been understood by freedom, namely, the ability to withstand all pressures, to resist laws, and, for example, to achieve a triumph of the freedom of the spirit over the suffering of the body.

If we think not of the proletariat but of people like Marx himself, who are always the ones to expound the theory of history and proclaim their insight into necessity, the above explanation does not fit. For philosophers of Marxism like Marx and Engels are not under the pressure of the fate of the proletariat. Yet they do the work of thinking vicariously for the proletariat. What impels them to claim this freedom? Is it pity for the alienated humanity of the proletariat? If so, then the next question is how this pity arises. What is the worth of these people that makes a life of thinking worthwhile? We find no answer to this question.

If I am right, the true motive force of freedom lies neither in a resort to self-help under economic pressure nor in a concern for the nature and worth of humanity, which remain obscure, and which can be brought to light only if it is stated who these people really are whom there is a readiness to help, e.g., for reasons of love. In the NT love is based on our essential nature. We are beings about whom God is concerned, whom he has bought with a price, and we have to be concerned about those in whom God has such an interest.

5. The Elimination of the Personal Sphere

Thus the personal sphere is eliminated and left obscure. The final thing to be said about us is simply that in our being and consciousness we are determined by the economic infrastructure and hence by the class situation. We are exponents of this situation. Our impulses and decisions are simply a result of the infrastructure. They are reactions to it. They can never be traced back to convictions that have an independent origin in the moral I, in the conscience.

How could such a thing be possible? If there are such decisions and convictions, they are formed in the consciousness. But this merely reflects the economic situation. It is functionally dependent on it. Hence it can produce nothing autonomous. Dominant thoughts are simply the ideal expression of dominant material relations comprehended as thoughts. Relations make a class dominant, and the thoughts are thoughts of its dominion.[105]

One might say, of course, that this diagnosis by Marx has in many ways the significance of a corrective. It shows how wrong is the assumption that philosophy falls from heaven to earth without any presuppositions at all, and how important it is to realize that the social situation does in fact influence the consciousness and its decisions. The primitive thing here, says Schoeps,[106] is simply the belief that the one absolute principle of explaining such complex modes of human action has been found, and that with it one can determine in advance the laws of historical development. It is simplistic to think that our modes of action merely depend, in popular terms, upon the pocketbook. The materialistic principle of explanation does not measure up to the truly

105. Marx, "Deutsche Ideologie," Kröner, pp. 373-74.
106. Schoeps, *Was ist der Mensch?* p. 53.

vast figure of world history. Not even such an ephemeral phenomenon as the Hitler movement in more recent history can be seriously explained in terms of it. Hence the real course of history continually falsifies Marxist interpretations and prognoses even though these, equated with the demands of economic reason, may sound realistic. They fail again and again in times of decision. Why? Because Marxists have a mistaken anthropology, because Marx has too narrow a view of the ontic basis of the human consciousness.

D. DEGRADATION OF HUMAN BEINGS TO MERE FUNCTIONS

In the elimination of personality and the reduction of human beings to mere functions of the infrastructure, we find the basic reason why continually in the world of Communist thought we come up against impersonality in its most varied forms of expression. In this world all thought and action is collective. There is a constant tendency to schematize speech and outlook. The thrust is toward the cliches of propaganda. No place can be left, even as a possibility, for variety or the richness of tension in intellectual structures, for swimming against the tide, for not howling with the pack.

1. Marxist Criticism of Marxism

A sign of how strongly the dangerous possibilities in Marxism have been viewed is evident in the so-called revisionisms, though these amount only to postulates and it is doubtful whether the desired corrections can be effective if Marxism is espoused. We shall mention here only two such revisionist postulates that are especially important in our inquiry. Thus one revisionist, Eduard Bernstein, says that it is inappropriate to study social science as though it were a kind of natural science which sets up various sociological laws as one formulates natural laws, and can then predict future events very accurately with the help of these laws.

Predictions of this kind might not come true, and often have not come true. Thus the proletariat has not become worse off, but with the help of strikes and other social measures (i.e., with the intervention of human initiative, which is not subject to any natural law), there has been a steady improvement of conditions for both the working class and the middle class. In other words, precise prognoses will not work out because they do not take into account the intervention of a purposive rational will. Hence one has to take ethical and ideal values into account and not construe them merely as functional ideologies. Religion, art, and law all affect economic relations just as economics affects the religious and artistic superstructure.

In face of these revisionist proposals from within the Marxist camp, one has to ask in all seriousness how far they reject the true front of Marxism and hence do not correct it but negate it, although this does not mean, of course, the rejection of (some of) its economic insights.

We cannot go into this question. I mention revisionism only so as to show that fear of the impersonalism that obtains in Marxism need not be due to theological prejudices but may be felt within Marxism itself. As early Marxism intervened in favor of humanity over against capitalist society, so revisionism is an intervention in favor of humanity, this time over against Marxism.

An impressive indication of threatening impersonalism may also be found in the atheistic meditation on prayer in an essay by the Marxist philosopher Milan Machovec entitled "Vom Sinn des menschlichen Lebens."[107] Today, he says, we live in self-forgetfulness, being permanently steered and directed from outside. We once made sure of inner dialogue by means of religion. In prayer we did not, as supposed, speak with God, but with the ideal self. Yet we achieved thereby an inner dialogue which enabled us to master life and not to let the inner self be absorbed in outer things. If we eliminate prayer from life without demystifying and liberating the human element contained in it, we lose this inner dialogue, and we fail to objectify and overcome the sense of inner weakness and guilt, i.e., the failure of the empirical I. We thus inevitably suffer a certain inner impoverishment. Sovereign rulers of things who forget the inner self lose the most precious thing in the world, communication with their inner being. In comparison with us moderns, the medieval monks who gave themselves to meditation (i.e., to inner dialogue) were really much more advanced.

Machovec is in a dilemma. He is in solidarity with the Marxist criticism of religion with an unmistakable rationalistic accent. Yet he sees that the Marxist emancipation from theology carries with it a threat to anthropology. The basic role of material things robs humanity of its autonomy and affects its inner freedom. Lacking independent significance, humanity is helpless against the outside world of things. Prayer is commended as an exercise that protects humanity, though it has to be demythicized. Its creative human function must be preserved, but not its original point as a dialogue with God to which the human function is merely incidental.

107. In *Disputation zwischen Christen und Marxisten*, ed. M. Stöhr (1966), pp. 75ff.

Here if anywhere in later Marxism there breaks out powerfully the neglected question of human reality, the hidden question of God.

2. Communist Humanism

This brings us once again to the deep cleft that opens up in Marxism. The notable contradiction between human concern on the one side and the depersonalizing of economic materialism on the other has always been decided, in both theory and practice, in favor of the latter. But has not Marxist-Leninism also promoted the slogan "positive humanism"? Did not Stalin himself—to quote an extreme and prominent figure— use this concept?

A speech by Stalin published by Fritz Lieb is very instructive in interpreting the expression "positive humanism."[108] In an appeal Stalin storms against the fact that there is more concern for a runaway mare than an absentee worker. He says that in the early days of the revolution all the stress had to be on promoting technology. But now we must turn again to those who control it. Technology itself demands this human concern. Note that no categorical imperative or divine command puts the emphasis in humanity; technology does. We must protect capable experts and promote their growth, we must develop people carefully, distribute and organize them correctly in the process of production, and improve their qualifications. This is what is needed if we are to raise up a great army of technically productive cadres.

3. Utility as a Norm

Since this is a common and not an isolated line of argument, we must view it as representative and interpret it accordingly. The new accent on humanity, and the related positive humanism, are not due to the viewing of people as the opposite of the world of the mechanical and instrumental, as those who have personal dignity, whose souls are of infinite value, who are in the divine likeness. The point is that people are needed within the hierarchy of technical means. They have a supreme position in this hierarchy. They direct the machines. They are functionaries in a world of functions. This is their nobility. The issue is not their worth but their usefulness. Here once again the pragmatic aspect is dominant.

The question that has to be put to this form of humanism is as follows. Like the original capitalism that it opposes, does it not make

---

108. *Russland unterwegs* (1945), pp. 262ff.

people a means to an end by measuring their importance by the role they play in the process of production? Frontiers are always instructive places, and here, too, a frontier case makes the "means-to-an-end" position plain. Do we have only material value and a material function? Do we have importance only as we represent economic value? Or even when we are old and weak and of little value, are we still sacred? The latter position alone we believe to be specifically human.

If, however, we are important only as we have material value, our prestige, perhaps expressed in social privileges and rewards, must not be confused with respect for the human person. How little it truly is this one may see clearly from the fact that the result of this line of thinking is the liquidation of useless specimens, e.g., radical nonconformists and dissidents who cannot be integrated.

4. Exclusion of Basic Anthropological Questions

In fact, no inquiry into our true human nature transcends this pragmatic approach. A test will show this. At two points this question seems to be put. The first is when Marx speaks about alienation. Can one speak about alienation without measuring it by the norm of what is meant by humanity in its positive essence?

Strange as it may seem, one can. For we, too, can say fairly accurately what is *not* human. But difficulty arises when we try to say positively what *is* human. Those who know what is bad do not by a long way know what is good. To know what humanity is and what is good, we have to reveal our source of knowledge, e.g., whether people are God's image or functionaries in the economic process. To say what is not human we need not reveal this. For a massive mistreatment of people, as in their cynical exploitation, runs contrary to both views.

But since we usually speak very generally about humanity, the concept is weak and unworthy of credence; it is mere babbling. Mostly we have in view only a symbol for the opposite of what is not human, a negation of the negation. From the mere fact that Marx knows the concept of alienation and therefore of inhumanity, we cannot infer that he knows the positive nature of humanity. One notes the same lack of any positive concept of humanity in Herbert Marcuse.[109]

Does Marx at least know radical evil under the sign, perhaps, of alienation? One has good reason to think that he does not. Leszek Kolakowski is probably right when he points out that the question of radical evil cannot arise here because no radical decisions have to be

109. Cf. my book *Kulturkritik der studentischen Rebellion* (1969), pp. 40ff.

made concerning absolute good and evil; we find only relative values restricted by historical processes.[110] Good and evil can show themselves only in personal and unconditional conviction. Only individuals and their actions are subject to moral judgment. There can be no moral judgment apart from motives, and motives are individual. It thus follows that one cannot make any moral assessment of an anonymous historical process, of its success or failure.[111]

5. Socialism as a Free Act

We have another control available in our test. Marx also has the chance to speak positively about human nature, about authentic humanity, when he shows how we may be freed from our alienation and brought to ourselves. He sets this process under the heading of a leap into freedom. This leap consists of the seizing of the means of production by society and the ending of the rule of the product over the producer. The individual struggle for existence comes to an end. Only thus do we finally leave the animal kingdom and change animal conditions of existence into human conditions. The achievement of true Socialism, which has hitherto been under the control of nature and history, is now our own free act. This is the leap from the sphere of necessity into the sphere of freedom.[112]

Humanity in itself, authentic humanity, is that which is no longer the object of relations but achieves Socialism by its own free act. Yet is this still any more than a negative statement, the negation of a negation? Do we have here any more than the negative assertion that humanity is no longer alienated, without any statement, and without the ideological approach being able to make any statement, what humanity is in a positive sense? How will history continue? Will it continue at all? Obviously there are no longer any hostile forces, whether in society (classes have ceased) or in the human soul, with which humanity has to contend. Is humanity good at last, perfect, without any evil? All this remains obscure. A man like Robert Havemann thinks about it, although along very utopian lines. But to the instincts of leading ideologists the very fact that he introduces the theme seems to be a confirmation that he is an alien body in the system.[113]

---

110. Leszek Kolakowski, *Der Mensch ohne Alternative* (1961).
111. Ibid., pp. 106ff.
112. See *Handbuch des Weltkommunismus* (1958), p. 69.
113. Cf. R. Havemann, *Dialektik ohne Dogma?* (1964), pp. 151ff.

6. A Vague View of Humanity

In Marx we have apparently only one indication of the true nature of humanity.[114] According to him the monstrous power of evil which in the economic disorder of capitalism produces a dehumanized proletariat does not arise of itself but is a work of humanity, which is responsible for it. It is our own doing, says Marx. Our own act becomes an alien power confronting and subjecting us instead of being ruled by us.

Is it accidental that this concept of evil as an anthropological statement is not explained further, that the thought of evil does not occur again except under the sign of alienation? (Or have I simply been unlucky in my search? If so, I would be grateful for help.) In particular, is the idea of radical evil completely suppressed in Marxist eschatology? This simply has a utopian vision of a humanity with no further history— a remarkably unreal, docetic ghost in which we can find no essential features. At this point Marx simply stops portraying humanity, i.e., at the very point where we most expect to see what authentic, nonalienated humanity is like.

Where has the evil gone whose traces Marx can discern in historical humanity? Let us assume that according to Marx the social form of dehumanizing, the exploitation and class structure of society, is the product of evil in humanity; how can it be hoped that humanity will change even if it does remove this product of its sin? To put it dogmatically, will its status change if the act that is responsible for it remains the same? Must we not suppose that the potential energy of evil will come out in new and different kinetic forms even in the classless society, e.g., in individual conflicts, in envy, hatred, and the desire for prestige? The aggressive impulse remains the same.

The picture of eschatologically authentic humanity is hard to grasp because it loses all individual features and becomes the mere substratum of a collective consciousness. Only when individuals have taken back the abstract citizen into themselves and become social creatures in their empirical life and work, says Marx, only when they have seen and organized their own forces as social forces and are no longer separating social power from themselves as political power, can full human emancipation be achieved.[115]

Humanity thus finds fulfilment by ceasing to be individual and by becoming social. Society achieves in this way a full unity of being with

114. See Kröner, II, 5; cf. H. Weinstock, *Die Tragödie des Humanismus* (1960), p. 292.

115. See Kröner, p. 199.

nature. We have here the full naturalizing of humanity and the full humanizing of nature. In other words, humanity works back to its unity with nature and the world. It now wants what nature wants and society wants. All contradictions come to an end, for emancipation terminates everything particular and individual. With Gogarten one might perhaps say that humanity ceases to be historical and becomes mythical again. There is even the development of social organs or collective instincts which express the social will and do not allow humanity in its spontaneity to be any more than the object of a collective, social imperative.[116] The socializing of the means of production gives rise to this social humanity as well.

E. ANTHROPOLOGICAL MISCALCULATION

Is not this humanity an unreal ghost, this being with collective instincts and a collective consciousness? Is there any such thing? Does it not mean that individuals cease to "be" and become only a synonym for the kind of humanity that in the 18th and 19th centuries, even in Feuerbach, is the mere sum of every positive and self-complementing human quality?

This is the great miscalculation. Human nature cannot be eliminated empirically and fulfilled as a mere sum of qualities.[117] But Marx thinks it can. He tries to portray humanity as economic humanity apart from the real course of history. In this way there finally results a docetic shade, because the reality of the human cannot be grasped solely in economic terms. That this does not work out empirically may be seen from the fact that many human phenomena are inexplicable when an attempt is made to explain them solely in terms of economic interests. Can one explain a Luther, a St. Francis, or even a Hitler solely from the standpoint of such interests?

Marxism cannot arrive at a full view of humanity from this angle. For, paradoxically, humanity remains unrecognizable so long as one focuses only on its immanent or functional worth. In a secular sense to believe in human value is simply to believe in human usefulness (in the processes of production or reproduction) and hence to see in people the mere means to an end.

We thus come up against the final mystery of anthropology. Inevitably in every interpretation of human existence another reality shines through the human reality, an alien factor which decisively

116. Ibid., p. 241.
117. This is the theme of my book *Being Human—Becoming Human*.

characterizes humanity. This is because we can describe ourselves only as beings in relation, as beings that stretch out, that are in relation to something, and that transcend themselves.

Either this alien thing that determines us is something material that we serve, e.g., the economic structure in Marxism or biological forces in National Socialism (here we have some form of an immanent essence), or else this alien thing is something unconditional that transcends everything material, i.e., God. In this case we have the alien dignity that is the essential characteristic of the divine likeness. Kierkegaard expresses the difference between these two factors in *Sickness unto Death:*

> The gradations in the consciousness of the self with which we have hitherto been employed are within the definition of the human self, or the self whose measure is man. But this self acquires a new quality or qualification in the fact that it is the self directly in the sight of God. This self is no longer the merely human self but is what I would call, hoping not to be misunderstood, the theological self, the self directly in the sight of God. And what an infinite reality this self acquires by being before God! A herdsman who (if this were possible) is a self only in the sight of cows is a very low self, and so also is a ruler who is a self in the sight of slaves—for in both cases the scale or measure is lacking. The child who hitherto has had only the parents to measure itself by, becomes a self when he is a man by getting the state as a measure. But what an infinite accent falls upon the self by getting God as a measure.[118]

1. Authentic Humanity

The value of the self is decided by its recognition of the entity above or below it with which it is in relation. If this entity is below it, its own rank is decided accordingly. Those who are determined by material things will themselves become immersed in things. Only those who have the alien dignity that a relation to God confers on them can escape the enslaving grasp that seeks to value them materially and that will let them go again once they lose their material usefulness. We see here the protection, the impregnability, and the holy privilege that we enjoy when we are seen to be bearers of that alien dignity. Even in the extreme case when we are no longer of material value we are still the creatures

118. Kierkegaard, *Sickness unto Death,* p. 210.

of God. As the OT puts it, we are the apple of God's eye. God himself undertakes to protect us. To touch us is to touch the Lord himself.

Similarly, it is typical of the NT that it does not refer our human dignity to the supreme achievements of such models of humanity as geniuses and moral heroes, but to little people who are in need of mercy, to the *ptochoi,* to borderline specimens of humanity on the darker side.

Thus the hidden Christ meets us in those who are hungry and homeless and imprisoned and naked and destitute. He makes himself the brother of all of these. If we receive them and visit them and clothe them and feed them, we do it to him. Similarly, Paul can describe as follows the inviolable dignity of the narrow-minded who want to restrict Christian freedom and lay burdens on others: Christ died for them, and therefore we should not offend them (Rom. 14:15; 1 Cor. 8:11). The alien dignity makes them sacrosanct.

We are not referred, then, to ourselves, or to things, or to our usefulness, but to the glory of God that seeks to demonstrate and glorify itself in us. The issue here is our hiddenness in the alien righteousness of Jesus Christ. As we have there infinite value in the eyes of God (for God wills to see us in his Son), so here is our true humanity in the eyes of others. It is the humanity of the Son of God who calls himself our brother. It is hidden as this is, and hence it may be similarly desecrated. Yet it is desecrated and honored in its hidden dignity.

It is not true that we are demeaned by this kind of servanthood, and that the supreme glory of God puts us down as the oriental despot displays his greatness by putting down the slaves around him. The common idea that there is a vast disproportion between the greatness and absoluteness of God on the one side, and the littleness and valueless-ness of those that are related to him on the other, is wrong. The very opposite is the case. The greater the object to which our human existence is related (so long as this "object" is God and not a superior creaturely entity that does at once relativize us and make us small), the more unequivocal and hence the more inviolable our humanity becomes. Those who on the edges of humanity teach us this—those who are either the apple of God's eye or the plaything of human opportunism.

2. The Decisive Insight

We stand by our decisive insight that the view of humanity is always stamped by something alien that is actualized in it. This statement gives us the key to the remarkable and at first sight astonishing fact that in spite of its concern for humanity, Marxism can finally succeed only in treating it as a thing. Having a perverted relation to it, it could not reach it or even catch a proper glimpse of it by reason of the autonomy of this relation. It has never even seen humanity.

Humanity may be stamped by what is under it. In this case the alien material factor distorts humanity and what confronts us is the rigid face of nonhuman nature or the nonhuman because closed mechanism of dialectical puppets. Or humanity may be stamped by what is above it. Then the goal is the glory of God that chooses us as its instrument. Turned toward us, this glory is, in the older language of Christianity, grace.

The great, decisive question is this: By which factor do we see the view of humanity stamped, in what factor do we know that it is upheld or lost? The anthropological question is set before this theological question—and that not merely in the left-wing Hegelians.

Marx himself felt these final conflicts in his understanding of himself and humanity. This is not apparent in his theoretical writings but one may see it in an early poem in which, with what is almost a prophetic glance at his own future, he sees himself as a tragically unsuccessful Prometheus, yet as one who still persists defiantly in his protest. Here the essence that is established from above, the idea of humanity, is at odds with the Promethean view of the self. Lightnings from on high seek to shatter this view. But they can only recoil, and if they shatter his walls he will defiantly build them again. The title of the work is "A Desperate Prayer."[119] It says that if some God has thrust him here in the flood and under the yoke of fate, his worlds are wholly defective, and all that remains is revenge. Marx will avenge himself on the being enthroned above. His strength is a patchwork of weakness and his good is unrewarded, but he will build a throne with a cold and lofty top. Suprahuman horror will be its bulwark and melancholy pain its marshal. If any regard it with sound eyes they will turn back deathly pale and silent, struck by the blind breath of death. The very lightnings from on high will recoil from the iron structure. The Most High may break the walls and halls of Marx, but he will defiantly rebuild them for all eternity.

119. The poem is quoted in Henri de Lubac, *Die Tragödie des Humanismus ohne Gott* (Salzburg, 1950), p. 340.

CHAPTER 15

The Struggle for the Unconditionality of Christian Truth

I. SØREN KIERKEGAARD: EXISTENTIAL UNCONDITIONALITY

Bibliography. Primary Works: E. Hirsch, *Sören Kierkegaard. Gesammelte Werke* (1950ff., cited as Hirsch); H. Gottsched and C. Schrempf, *Gesammelte Werke Kierkegaards* (Jena, 1922ff., cited as Jena); in general the American editions of his works (published by Princeton, translated by Walter Lowrie, et al.) are cited below.

Secondary Works: F. Brandt, *Sören Kierkegaard* (Copenhagen, 1963); H. Diem, *Kierkegaard Auswahl und Einleitung*, Fischer-Bücherei (1956); H. Gerdes, *Sören Kierkegaard*, Sammlung Goschen, vol. 1221 (1966); P. P. Rohde, *Sören Kierkegaard in Selbstzeugnissen und Bilddokumenten*, Rowohlt Taschenbuch (1959).

Monographs: M. Bense, *Hegel und Kierkegaard* (1948); H. Diem, *Die Existenzdialektik von Sören Kierkegaard* (1950); idem, *Sören Kierkegaard Spion im Dienste Gottes* (1957); E. Geismar, *Sören Kierkegaard. Seine Lebensentwicklung und seine Wirksamkeit als Schriftsteller* (1929); E. Hirsch, *Kierkegaard-Studien*, 3 vols. (1920-1921); idem, *Geschichte der neueren evangelischen Theologie*, V (1954), 433-91; S. Holm, *Grundtvig und Kierkegaard. Parallele und Kontraste* (1956); K. Jaspers, *Rechenschaft und Ausblick* (1951), pp. 115ff.; K. Löwith, *Von Hegel zu Nietzsche*, 3rd ed. (1953); W. Lowrie, *Kierkegaard*, 2 vols. (New York, 1938); H. P. Müller, "Welt als 'Wiederholung.' Sören Kierkegaards Novelle als Beitrag zur Hiob-Interpretation," in *Werden und Wirken des AT. Festschrift für Claus Westermann* (1979), pp. 355ff.; A. Paulsen, *Menschsein heute. Analysen und Reden Kierkegaards* (1973); E. Pivcevic, *Ironie als Daseinsform bei Sören Kierkegaard* (1960); W. Rehm, *Kierkegaard als Verführer* (1949); W. Ruttenbeck,

Sören Kierkegaard der christliche Denker und sein Werk (1929); H. P. Schmidt, *Ontologie und Personalismus* . . . , *dargestellt an A. F. C. Vilmar und Sören Kierkegaard,* Hamburg dissertation (1957).

A. BIOGRAPHY

Kierkegaard lived from 1813 to 1855. Except for a short stay in Berlin as a student, he resided in Copenhagen. From 1830 to 1840 he studied theology there, and he concluded his university years with a dissertation on the concept of irony with special reference to Socrates. His melancholy and phlegmatic father, a wealthy merchant, had a vital influence on his inner development. A youthful trauma pursued his father all his life. Once as a poor herdsman, overcome by his wretchedness, he had cursed God. His gloomy piety was passed on to his son, who saw a curse lying on the family. Kierkegaard's struggle to break free from this curse helped to make the question of the grant of a new possibility of being by forgiveness the main theme of his life. The profound melancholy that overshadowed his life, and that had some psychopathic features, was a legacy from his father. In retrospect he once said that in earliest childhood he strained himself under the impact made on him by the melancholy old man, who himself was sinking under the same weight. He was a child crazily and dreadfully disguised as a melancholy old man.[1]

Yet it would be a mistake—although often made—to try to interpret Kierkegaard in psychiatric categories. We see in him that psychological burdens are not just a liability. They also enhance sensitivity to dimensions of life that are closed to more robust natures. This is especially true in the case of a genius like Kierkegaard.

It is no wonder that he viewed himself as an exception and that he failed to integrate himself into the common human or ecclesiastical order. Thus his attempt to go the way of all flesh in marriage failed. His engagement to Regine Ohlsen (1840) was broken off and had an influence on his reflections on the "individual" and his analyses of melancholy.

His first great work, *Either-Or* (1843), brought him renown. It displays the decisive features of his literary output. He likes to use various pseudonyms representing such perspectives as the ethical, the aesthetic, the tragic, and the religious. He himself both is and is not these various writers. He adopts these different positions. The choice of this

1. See Kierkegaard, *The Point of View for My Work as an Author* (New York, 1962), p. 76.

pseudonymous mode of presentation marks him as an "existing thinker." (We shall have a look at this term later.)

The method, which is biographically important, is explained when we ask why he does not write descriptively, critically, or polemically about ethical, aesthetic, or religious people, as, e.g., Eduard Spranger describes these life-styles in their ideal or typical contours.[2] For various reasons Kierkegaard obviously refuses to do this.

First, he does not want to stand aloof from the relevant position. This would presuppose that as an observer he stands above it and faces the reader with the fait accompli of superior critical instruction. As one might say today, he would be making the reader a mere "consumer" of what he has to say. He makes Hegel his archenemy precisely because Hegel looks at all intellectual processes from the superior vantage point of a thinker who thinks he has a full view of the world spirit.

Second, by plunging into the midst of the various views, Kierkegaard takes his readers with him. He gives them the task of identifying themselves with Job, Abraham, Socrates, and many others. This is for them a summons and a challenge. They have to decide whether to accept or reject this identification, whether to exist in truth or untruth. They are thus set under an obligation and can no longer be indifferent spectators. In this sense there is for Kierkegaard no eternally valid truth, only the truth or untruth of one's own being. Not *what* we think is essential, but *how*, the extent to which we are existentially involved, whether we are "existing thinkers." We can be this only as *individuals*.

We thus see why in his lifetime Kierkegaard can never find his way to what is general but always starts back from it. The tendency of the general is to swallow me up, to swamp my individuality, no matter whether it is marriage or some institutional or ecclesiastical connection. Thus Kierkegaard avoids all offices or official tasks as a free author living and writing on his own responsibility. This leads him into violent attacks on the Danish state church and its representatives, who reduce church and state to the same level and swamp them in what is general.

With a similar alarm Kierkegaard foresees revolutionary movements in 1846, even before they occur in 1848,[3] for they advance the tendency to bring everything down to a mass (or crowd) level. This is the issue in his review of the short story "Zwei Zeitalter," in which he refers to the superiority of the category of the generation to that of the

---

2. E. Spranger, *Lebensformen. Geisteswissenschaftliche Psychologie und Ethik der Persönlichkeit*, 7th ed. (1930).

3. He refers to 1848 as the year when the howling was heard that announces chaos; see *Point of View*, pp. 61-62.

individual, and speaks of the disruptive and demoralizing effect of the principle of social cohesion which is being deified in his day. The result is the neglect of the singularity of individuality before God in the responsibility of eternity.[4] In Kierkegaard's sense, an individual exists only before God. Oriented to the social nexus, and merging into it, the individual ceases to be an individual.

Being an individual stamped Kierkegaard's life-style. His inheritance enabled him to live without any job or post. He formed no student attachments. He liked to walk on the promenade at Copenhagen, to visit the theater, and to engage those who met him in Socratic conversation. His striking appearance brought him into the columns of the paper *The Corsair.* The resultant feud led to his reflections on the leveling down of public opinion by the press and the hostility of secularism to the individual.

Kierkegaard died at the early age of 42, worn out by his indescribably intensive activity as a thinker and writer. That he wrote and published his gigantic work in twelve years is almost inconceivable. To the last he was feuding with the official church. At the burial of the highly regarded bishop J. P. Mynster, who had come back from materialistic philosophy—first with the help of Kant—to a biblical Christianity, Professor Martensen extolled him as a witness to the faith. In an incredibly harsh and cynical article Kierkegaard denied that either of them deserved this description.[5] He also applied to N. F. S. Grundtvig, the writer of spiritual hymns and the worthy founder of Danish high schools, such insulting terms as "babbler" and "prophet" and worse. This was hardly appropriate, although in the light of Kierkegaard's decisive and divisive mentality it is understandable when we consider Grundtvig's strange combination of orthodox Lutheranism with a love of Nordic mythology: a freedom for Loke and Thor, for all that the spirit that will not be bound desires.[6]

In this context we cannot pursue even briefly the tremendous influence of Kierkegaard on literature, philosophy (from Gabriel Marcel to J.-P. Sartre), and theology (Barth and Bultmann). Instead, I would refer to the monograph by O. F. Bollnow, which does at least offer some essential insights as regards philosophy and literature.[7]

4. See Hirsch, 17, 90-91.

5. In *The Fatherland,* Dec. 18, 1854, no. 295; see Hirsch, 34, 3ff.

6. See Holm, *Grundtvig und Kierkegaard,* p. 88.

7. Bollnow, *Existenzphilosophie,* 6th ed. (1964); on Bultmann and Heidegger cf. *EF,* I (Index).

B. FROM HEGEL TO KIERKEGAARD

Hegel regarded his system as the synthesis and conclusion of all prior philosophy. But when we continue to think along the lines of his dialectic, as I pointed out in the last chapter, the synthesis of his thought becomes another thesis that provokes an antithesis.

This antithesis, remarkably enough, takes two forms. The first finds the true foundation of being, not in the spirit, but in the material infrastructure. Examples of those who espouse this antithesis are Feuerbach, Stirner, and Marx. The second form finds a representative in Kierkegaard.

Kierkegaard saw in Hegel's gigantic effort to identify thought and being (i.e., to understand the real as the self-development of the absolute spirit, and the finite spirit as the locus of the self-consciousness of the spirit) a vast deceptive maneuver which it was the task of his thinking to unmask in various ways. Hegel's statements about reality imply no reality for Kierkegaard. They are an empty abstraction, and they construct an absurd reality of thought or phantom of the brain. The difficulty in this gigantic effort is that only God himself, as a transcendent entity distinct from finite reality, can be the subject of pure thought. Only this being is at the sovereign distance at which one can see and survey the whole panorama of being below. No finite being can do this, for finite beings belong to immanence and are in the stream of immanent history. According to Kierkegaard, Hegel cannot show—or with the help of a trick can only appear to show—how the finite spirit that is enclosed in history can change into a godlike being that is above history.

Kierkegaard acknowledges the greatness of Hegel. He is well aware of the dangerous possibility of being seduced on to the same speculative path—a real possibility for one of such virtuosity of thought. But he brings one decisive argument against Hegel's philosophy, namely, that Hegel eliminates the "existing thinker." I will explain this term below. At this point I will simply say that Hegel neither can nor will show how as finite spirits and individuals we relate to the truth and have a history in this relation, how, e.g., we decide, how we choose between opposites and alternatives instead of simply recognizing them, riding a dialectical wave, and sanctioning the principle of laissez-faire.

Thus the main theme of Kierkegaard is the problem of the existence of individuals and of the existential relationship of all the resultant reality. His concern is with existential unconditionality. We are not simply finite spirits in Hegel's sense. We have a concrete, multidimensional existence in which intellect, will, emotion, passion, fear, hope, and aesthetic, ethical, and religious subjectivity combine.

C. THE EXISTING AND THE ABSTRACT THINKER

In relation to the necessary distinction it would be an impossible undertaking to give a compendious survey of the highly differentiated dialectic of Kierkegaard's total work, especially as such a survey would have to put us at a distance which could not do justice to Kierkegaard's thinking. In the form of unending reflection, this thought is an appeal to readers to let themselves be brought into the process of reflection, to become existentially involved, to awaken as individuals themselves. Along these lines Kierkegaard tries to prod people. In my presentation, then, I can do justice to him only if I adjust to the style of his thought and am content to try to help my readers to enter into the process, and hence to focus on the decisive points. Here if anywhere the art of portraiture must be that of omission. I am well aware that in adopting this course I am leaving a great deal out. The gaps will perhaps stir some to read Kierkegaard for themselves. For a first encounter with him I might recommend *Training in Christianity*.[8]

The term which brings out Kierkegaard's singularity, and which I thus want to analyze, is that of the "existing thinker." Abstract thinkers, striving for objectivity, ignore the subject of knowledge, disparaging it as an empty and exchangeable husk. In contrast, existing thinkers bring the existence of the thinker into play. "All logical thinking employs the language of abstraction, and is *sub specie aeterni*."[9] Eternity in this sense means outside time and in detachment from history. Things are different with the existing thinker, who includes the thinker's existence in the cognitive act. "It is impossible to conceive existence without movement, and movement cannot be conceived *sub specie aeterni*."[10] Hence abstract thinkers who strive for timeless objectivity have to ignore an existence that is involved in historical movement. This is the one "thing in itself" which cannot be thought, with which thought has nothing to do, because it has turned away from the subject and is oriented to the object. From what is pure thought abstracting? From existence, and hence from that which it should explain but does not even consider.[11]

Further differences may be seen between the abstract and the existing thinker. Abstraction is disinterested, but existence is of supreme interest to those who exist. In pure thought the concern is for relief from

---

8. Kierkegaard, *Training in Christianity* (Princeton, repr. 1972).
9. Kierkegaard, *Concluding Unscientific Postscript* (Princeton, repr. 1974), p. 273.
10. Ibid.
11. Ibid., p. 277.

all doubt, eternal positive truth, and what have you. If Hegelian philosophy is free from all postulates (because it does not follow dotted lines like
Kant, but with its abstract grasp thinks it can present reality in clearly
contoured and connected lines), it achieves this position by way of one mistaken postulate: that of pure thought, which is a phantom or "chimera."[12]

Thus abstract thought is disinterested. Its subject has no part
in what it thinks. The subject is a mere spectator of what results from its
thinking. In contrast, existential thought is highly involved. It has the
passion of *inter-esse*.

Another difference separates theoretical and abstract thinking
from existential thinking. Existence is never complete. It is always
developing. The same applies to thinking that relates to existence. With
being, the related thinking is involved in uncompleted development.
Hence a truth that may be fixed apart from the subject is not true truth.
True truth is not a definitive *result* but a *way*. It consists of a process of
appropriation. Truth is free only when the thinking subject has a *history*
with it.[13] This means that "only then do I truly know the truth when it
becomes a life in me."[14] "For knowing the truth is something which
follows as a matter of course from being the truth, and not conversely;
and precisely for this reason it becomes untruth when knowing the truth
is treated as one and the same thing as being the truth, since the true
relation is the converse of this: to be the truth is one and the same thing
as knowing the truth, and Christ would never have known the truth in
case He had not been the truth; no man knows more of the truth than
what he is of the truth."[15]

It is not that we may finally be the truth (as Christ was). Here
again there is a process of coming into the truth. For existential thinking,
then, there is no complete equation of thought and being—the chimera
of speculative and abstract thinking, and even its supposed possession.
"This conformity is actually realized for God, but it is not realized for
any existing spirit, who is himself existentially in process of becoming.
For an existing spirit *qua* existing spirit, the question of the truth will
again exist."[16]

This is the reason why Kierkegaard opposes systems. By definition systems are rounded off and complete. But there is such a thing
only for God and for those who, like Hegel, usurp his place in hybrid

12. Ibid., p. 275.
13. Kierkegaard, *Training in Christianity*, p. 202.
14. Ibid.
15. Ibid., p. 201.
16. Kierkegaard, *Concluding Unscientific Postscript*, p. 170.

fashion. Only if existing beings could get out of themselves could the truth be for them something complete that they could put in a system. But where is this point? In answer, Kierkegaard finds it only where the existence of the subject has degenerated to a "point" for abstract thinkers. The subject that places itself at this point may thus be changed at will. "The I-am-I" is a mathematical point which does not exist, and in so far there is nothing to prevent everyone from occupying this standpoint."[17]

The upshot is that for those who are existentially involved the truth that discloses itself does not consist of a "what" that may be formulated as a valid result, but of a "how," of the manner of appropriation. The "how" of truth *is* the truth. It is, therefore, untruth to answer a question in a medium (i.e., that of abstract thought) in which the question cannot arise.[18]

D. THE INFINITE PASSION OF INWARDNESS

When Kierkegaard considers how the antagonism between existential and abstract thought works itself out within theological truth, especially in the questions of God, of Christ, and of immortality, he begins with some theses that are important for our orientation.[19]

If we ask objectively about the truth, we reflect about it objectively as an object to which we as knowing subjects relate. We do not reflect about the relation but about the fact that it is the truth, the true, to which we relate. Only when that to which the subject relates is the truth is the subject in the truth.

But when we ask subjectively about the truth, we reflect subjectively on the relation of the individual. If only the how of this relation is in the truth, then the individual is in the truth even if the relation is to untruth.

Kierkegaard illustrates this by the way in which knowledge of God can arise. Abstract thinking that is concerned about objectivity asks about the true God and tries to differentiate him from an imagined God, the idol of paganism. Along this path we engage in an approximation process which seeks to produce God objectively, although this is in all eternity impossible, because God is a subject, and thus exists only for subjectivity in inwardness. For existing thinkers who bring along their

17. Ibid., p. 176.
18. Ibid., pp. 181-82.
19. Ibid., p. 178.

subjectivity, the situation is quite different. They focus their thinking on the relation to this object, and thus take into account themselves and their own existence. Everything depends, then, on their relation in truth being a relation to God. They no longer have God in virtue of an objective consideration, which can only be approximate and can never reach him in all eternity. They have him at that "moment" or "instant," because their relation to him is determined by the infinite passion of inwardness, because they pour their whole selves into the relation to God, and because they are in the truth in relation to him even though their relation is to what is not true, i.e., even though they do not hit upon the true God in it.[20]

It is typical that Kierkegaard uses the concept of the moment or instant in describing the immediacy of the relation to God and the "now" in which it is actualized. The eternal encounters us as something present, in the moment (or instant),[21] as something contemporary. We do not find it in a sequence of time, as though we could find it in some past, e.g., as a historically verifiable event in which God became man, or as though we awaited it as a utopian future. Only a very indirect relation to the eternal would make that possible. No, we have it in the immediate present. Better, the eternal qualifies the present and makes it the moment of direct presence. Otherwise the present disappears in the sequence of times and is rubbed out, as it were, between past and future.

Time is an unending sequence. Life which is in time, and belongs to time alone, has nothing present. "The instant [moment] characterizes the present as having no past and no future, for in this precisely consists the imperfection of the sensuous life. The eternal also characterizes the present as having no past and no future, and this is the perfection of the eternal."[22]

It would be a mistake to think that by the "instant" or "moment" Kierkegaard means only a chronological instant as a particle of time. Strictly, the moment is not for him an atom of time but an atom of eternity. It is a first appearance of eternity in time, its first attempt to arrest time. Kierkegaard can also say that "the instant is that ambiguous moment in which time and eternity touch one another."[23] Only those who are existentially involved experience this moment, for they are passionately interested in their relation to the eternal.

20. Ibid., pp. 178-79.
21. Kierkegaard, *The Concept of Dread*, 2nd ed. (Princeton, repr. 1973), p. 77.
22. Ibid., p. 78.
23. Ibid., p. 80.

Kierkegaard finds another example of the difference between abstract and existential thinking in the way in which we inquire into immortality.[24] Who has the greater certainty, he asks, the one who looks into immortality objectively, who seeks a proof of it, and yet who can achieve only approximate certainty, or the one who turns to it with the passion of subjectivity, as Socrates does? Socrates put the question of immortality objectively, and on this level he could say only: *if* there is an immortality. But on this "if" he risked the whole passion of his inwardness, his whole life. He dared to die. For the sake of this involvement of his existence, his life had to be found acceptable—*if* there is an immortality. Here too, then, the truth lies in the passionately grasped relation to that about which, objectively, we ask with no certainty.

The incarnation is for Kierkegaard the chief example of the difference between objective and existential certainty. For Christ is a phenomenon in history and consequently in time. He is thus open to be misunderstood as a possible object of thought and experience appropriate to time and space. Yet Christ is also the irruption of eternity into time. Objective thinking is not appropriate to this, only passionate existential involvement. How do the two things work together, and in what way are they distinct?

Kierkegaard greatly sharpens the problem by putting it very differently from such famous nineteenth-century theologians as Schleiermacher, Hegel, and Strauss. For all these Christ represented an idea, e.g., that of humanity or that of reconciliation. Ideas are not tied to a temporal moment. On the contrary, they transcend time, and to objective thought they are thus like stars in an eternal firmament. If Christ represents the idea of humanity, for example, time and eternity are, as it were, brought into line. At any rate, a hard collision between them is avoided.

For Kierkegaard, however, the eternal God does not merge into a suprapersonal idea through which he might become the object of our thinking. He becomes "an individual man." This "is the greatest possible, the infinitely qualitative, remove from being God, and therefore the profoundest incognito."[25]

We thus have the task of thinking together irreconcilable things. We face a fact which objective thought, tolerating no contradiction, cannot handle. The irreconcilable can be put only under the sign of the paradox. For objective thinking it thus seems to be absurd.[26] We have

---

24. *Concluding Unscientific Postscript,* pp. 180-81.
25. *Training in Christianity,* p. 127.
26. *Concluding Unscientific Postscript,* pp. 183-84; cf. *Philosophical Fragments,* rev. ed. (Princeton, repr. 1974), pp. 29ff., 39ff.; for a penetrating analysis of the nature of paradox, see H. Vogel, *Christologie* (1949), pp. 164ff.

a paradoxical statement when a concept within the limits of understanding goes hand in hand with one outside these limits. This happens
when, thinking of the incarnation, I have to put together the infinite
God and a finite individual.

In religion the problem of paradox does not arise only in the
meeting of time and eternity. If Kant had known or claimed the
concept,[27] he might well have spoken of the paradox of freedom. This
does not occur in the realm of theoretical reason, but it is asserted in
two ways: first as a condition for the possibility of theoretical thought,
as an analytical principle of pure speculative reason,[28] and second under
the command of the practical logos which also mediates the certainty
that we can if we will. (Cf. the chapter above on Kant.) The understanding cannot conceive of freedom objectively, and to that extent it is
for Kant something paradoxical.

E. THE ETERNAL IN THE FINITE: THE LACK OF DIRECT KNOWABILITY

For God to be "an individual man"[29] involves the paradoxical combining
of eternity with a finite existence in time. Since objective thought
confronts at this point something that transcends its competence, it
cannot make the incarnate Logos one of its objects. The servant form
of God in Christ has the mark of unrecognizability, of an incognito.

What does this unrecognizability mean? It means having the
appearance of something that one is not, e.g., a police officer in plain
clothes. For God to be an individual man involves absolute unrecognizability, and therefore the most profound incognito. For here infinitely
qualitative distance is paradoxically overcome in the identity of a single
person.[30] Strictly, it is not overcome, for the antithesis still means
unrecognizability. But precisely this unrecognizability is a mark of the
God-man. It would blaspheme the miracle of the incarnation to try to
remove it and press on to direct knowability.

This blasphemy occurs when it is assumed that only distance in
time prevents us from knowing him today. If we had been his contemporaries, it is said, his deity would have illumined us. This assumption
results in blasphemous attempts to make him present, as "in the priest-

27. Kant uses the term, so far as I can see, only in an innocuous and
insignificant way in his anthropology; see *Werke*, Weischedel ed., XII, 410.
28. See *Critique of Practical Reason*, p. 307 (PhB, p. 57); and cf. the Preface
to the *Critique of Pure Reason*, 2nd edition.
29. Kierkegaard, *Training in Christianity*, p. 127.
30. Ibid.

prelate's undialectical loquacious climax: Christ was God *to such a degree* that one could at once *perceive* it directly—instead of saying as they ought: He was very God, and therefore *to such a degree* God that He was unrecognizable, so that it was not flesh and blood, but the exact opposite of flesh and blood, which prompted Peter to recognize Him."[31]

Christ's unrecognizability, then, is not for secondary reasons (such as distance in time) that we can overcome. It is constitutive of his divine-human existence, and we blaspheme and desecrate this if we try to make him directly apprehensible. For then we "poetize" him and make him something different,[32] as all those have done—we might add—who have integrated Christ forcefully into their own systems of thought, whether by seeing in him only the difference of a greater force of God-consciousness (Schleiermacher), or by making him the mere representative of some idea of our own, e.g., reconciliation or humanity (Hegel and Strauss).

In Kierkegaard's protest against the assumption—or assertion—of a direct knowability of Christ we have a by no means arbitrary association with the story of the temptation (Matt. 4:1-11) in which Christ rejects the devil's proposal that he should take the easier way of making himself directly recognizable and instead chooses the hard way of hidden servanthood and suffering.[33] Direct knowability would have been achieved if Christ had performed the miracles of making the stones bread or jumping from the temple pinnacle, or if he had validated himself by taking over all countries and kingdoms and thus visibly displayed his divine-human monopoly to the whole world. What would it have meant, however, if Christ had thus exposed himself to objective recognition? Would it have achieved the involvement of existence and not just of some specific interest (e.g., an acceptance with our understanding or senses), and then our return to normal, consoled but not any more enlightened? As it is, Christ, being hidden, claims a very different quality of our *inter-esse* in his servant form. We no longer know him merely as spectators. We have to have a committed relationship with him if he is to reveal himself to us—that of discipleship.

Along the lines of Luther's Heidelberg Disputation we might say that with his negation of any direct recognizability Kierkegaard rejects a theology of glory and espouses a theology of the cross.[34]

31. Ibid., p. 128.
32. Ibid.
33. Kierkegaard discusses this story in his *Edifying Discourses* (Hirsch, 27-29, 92ff.). Cf. Dostoyevski's Grand Inquisitor in *The Brothers Karamazov*.
34. Cf. W. von Loewenich, *Luthers Theologia crucis*, 2nd ed. (1933).

F. THE PROBLEM OF HISTORICAL CERTAINTY

To talk of an eternal historical, i.e., of something eternal in history that must be verified by historical means, is for Kierkegaard a mere playing with words. It leads to the transforming of history into myth, myth being understood here as the putting of something historical in our own circle of ideas and hence as the assimilating of it to our only too human understanding. This inevitably happens because we cannot handle the dialectical contradiction that is posed by the manifestation of God in a single man. What we have here is not just something historical but a phenomenon that can become historical only against its own nature, so that it is an absurdity.[35]

At this point we can see how impossible and even absurd is any attempt to establish the phenomenon of Christ with historical means. We are probably right to assume that it is this incompetence of history that leads Kierkegaard to ignore the historico-critical investigation of scripture that was developing in his day. In this regard he threw out the baby with the bathwater. For even if we accept with Kierkegaard that this approach is christologically deficient, it is surely of material importance to distinguish the sources and to make use of form-critical criteria and other relevant historical data. The question of the historical Jesus is at least posed, and any christological statement has to have, to put it cautiously, at least some basis in the historical Jesus. It has no foundation if it contradicts what is historically established. There can surely be no doubt about that. To eliminate historical data altogether involves the danger of reducing the material definitions of Christology to the mere assertion that in Christ we have the presence of God in an individual. We are right to suspect that this reduction does to a large extent take place in Kierkegaard. He constantly insists on that one point.

At any rate, the alarming contradiction in which history involves us once it comes face to face with the theme of Christ is the result of the fact that with extreme subjective passion, i.e., with a concern for eternal salvation, we are here asking about something that has to have an unconditional character valid both in time and in eternity—for it is thus, with this expectation, is it not, that we ask about Christ. The historical answer to this question can give only a maximal approximation and thus remains conditional and uncertain.[36] But how can the absolute certainty that is demanded here be based on something conditional?

The same problem stands at the heart of M. Kähler's classical

35. Kierkegaard, *Concluding Unscientific Postscript*, p. 512.
36. Ibid., p. 510.

work *The So-called Historical Jesus and the Historic, Biblical Christ*,[37] although here we do not find the same reduction to a mere assertion as in Kierkegaard. As Kähler sees it, if historical evaluation has to deal with the sinlessness of Jesus, his messianic consciousness, his return, his throne in world history or at the right hand of the Father in heaven, then the question remains how this figure who is only just emerging from the mists, how this uncertain remnant of critical subtraction can be the object of faith for all Christians, and especially how it could previously be so in the concealment which, happily, we are just beginning to dispel.[38] Here, too, we have the claim that relative historical certainty cannot be a basis for absolute certainty. Kähler does not quote Kierkegaard (did he know him?), but he, too, uses the divine-human or antihistorical aspects of Christ (sinlessness, messiahship, return, etc.) to show how uncertain is historical exploration.

Kierkegaard offers a human example to illustrate the difference between the certainty that the passionate search for eternal salvation seeks and the limited certainty that historical research can give. Human love demands the unconditional certainty of reciprocal love. But there can be such certainty only in a direct relationship with the beloved, not by hearsay. If a woman in love hears from others that the man she loves, being dead, had really loved her, although he had not assured her of this himself, the witnesses may be very reliable people and the case may be such that a historian or clever advocate would say there is no doubt about it, but the woman herself would soon see the snag, and it would be no compliment to her if she did not, for objectivity is no crown of honor for lovers.[39]

Because Kierkegaard has to say that the appearing of the eternal in time is something absurd that a historian can never encompass, he can regard reliance on historical inquiry as arrogance and even blasphemy. It means trying with the help of history, e.g., with an evaluation of the extraordinary impact of Christ upon history, to arrive at a Therefore: Therefore he was God. Faith, however, grasps him in immediacy, with the infinite passion of inwardness. It thus sees a contradiction here. It is forced to say that to begin with this syllogism is to begin with blasphemy.[40] Kierkegaard, then, waxes merry at the expense of the professor of history who thinks that the brilliant results

---

37. Originally published as *Die sogennante historische Jesus und die geschichtliche, biblische Christus* (1928); partial ET 1964.
38. Ibid., p. 4.
39. Kierkegaard, *Concluding Unscientific Postscript*, p. 511.
40. *Training in Christianity*, p. 32.

that Christ achieves in history offer proof of his divine sonship. For what are these results compared to his return in glory? But this return, in which alone his deity will be manifest, lies outside the realm of historical verifiability. Unlike the results, it is something that one believes—quite apart from the fact that when one examines the results more closely they turn out to be too shabby a kind of glory for faith to speak about them when it has in view the true glory of Christ—the glory which is not brilliant but concealed in humility and swaddled in rags.[41]

In sum, historical certainty runs up against two limits when it confronts the "once-for-all"[42] of Christ, and to ignore these limits is to put blasphemy in the place of faith.

First, it can achieve only uncertain approximation and thus involves the intolerable contradiction of answering the question of eternal salvation with relative and even mistaken information.

Second, historical verifiability presupposes the possibility of understanding and therefore of an analogy between investigator and object. But here we have something totally different, the exception, the special, antihistorical case. It can thus be told us only from outside ourselves. It has to be proclaimed to us.

Kierkegaard constantly alludes to the basic distinction between pre- and post-Christian (i.e., secularized) people on the one side and believers who have been brought into the truth on the other. The former think that the truth is already in them, not brought.[43] Socratic maieutics applies to them. In these we move within the immanence of being and remain in the dialectic of existence. Kierkegaard calls this Religious-ness A: It "can exist in paganism, and in Christianity it can be the religiousness of everyone who is not decisively Christian, whether he be baptized or no." In the second case, Religiousness B, "the edifying is a something outside the individual," and has to be brought as something proclaimed.[44]

G. THE LEAP INTO FAITH

But how can there be any recognition of Christ? In Kierkegaard's sense the question ought to be: How can we leap over historical distance and

41. Ibid., p. 33.
42. On once-for-all, cf. Rom. 6:10; Heb. 7:27; 9:10; 10:10.
43. Kierkegaard, *Philosophical Fragments*, p. 11.
44. *Concluding Unscientific Postscript*, pp. 493ff. (quotations from pp. 495, 498).

win the immediacy of contemporaneity with Christ, the immediacy that faith implies? I need this if it is a matter of "Theme 1" to which the infinite passion of my inwardness is directed, the question of my eternal salvation.

We have already given a first hint of the answer when we said that it was not flesh and blood that enabled Peter to see Christ in his unrecognizability (or incognito) as God in history, but the very opposite, the testimony of the Holy Spirit.[45]

Precisely because Christ discloses himself to us (by the Spirit), he is qualitatively different from a teacher who imparts truth and whose function is to instruct. The false picture of the teacher, which constantly recurs, e.g., in liberal theology, arises at once if we follow the principle of analogy. All education rests on this principle. Whatever the teacher imparts can be received by us only because it is spirit of our spirit and already has a bridgehead in our consciousness. Thus Socrates was the ideal teacher, for he used the maieutic method and awakened and developed that which was already slumbering within us.

Here, however, we have something that does not rest on this presupposition. How can we grasp the truth that God comes in a single person when we are obviously not analogous to this truth? We have no such analogy, says Kierkegaard, not just because we are finite and the infinite that comes here is qualitatively different from us, but also because we are sinners,[46] making the Creator in our own image instead of the reverse (Rom. 1:18ff.), and assimilating the picture of Christ by bringing him into the schema of our own consciousness and mythicizing him in our own light. We exist, then, in untruth, in sinful apostasy, and without any analogy.

This is the decisive reason why in our relation to Christ we get nowhere with Socratic methods. Socrates begins by assuming that the truth does not have to be brought to us but is already in us.[47] As a teacher, then, he has merely the function of releasing what is already there.[48] No such possibility arises, however, if we are sinners whose lack of analogy prevents us from bringing the God who has come in Christ out of his unrecognizability. In sinners who have turned aside from God there is nothing to become virulent after the Socratic manner or to give rise to an Aha experience. The teacher thus faces an impossibility at this point. To proceed he has not merely to reorient the students but to *remake* them

45. *Training in Christianity*, p. 128.
46. *Philosophical Fragments*, pp. 19ff.
47. Ibid., p. 11.
48. Ibid., pp. 17ff.

if they are to begin to learn. But no one can do this; if it is to be done at all, it must be done by God.[49]

What distinguishes God from a mere teacher is that with his offer of the truth God posits the conditions under which the truth discloses itself to me. He *re-creates* me; that is, he transforms my existence, transposing me from the untruth of my being to the truth. If disciples are untruth (and hence we cannot use the Socratic method), but are still people, when they receive the condition and the truth, they do not become people, for they are this already, but they become different people, or, as we might say, new people. This is the divinely effected restoration, the bringing back from the far country of being in untruth (or error) to which, on our side, conversion, regeneration, and faith correspond.[50]

When God re-creates us in this way to being in the truth, when he thus gives to us the conditions under which we may know his truth, can we really call him a teacher? To do so is inappropriate. No, let us call him a Savior or Liberator, for he makes his students free instead of unfree; he makes them free from themselves, releasing those who had imprisoned themselves.[51]

Hence in what we know about God it is a matter of the state of our existence, our being in truth or untruth. Our thinking is merely a function of this state. This is the crucial reason why it can never operate in an objective and purely logical context that is distinct from existence if it is aiming at God (or at his presence in an individual). There are here no timeless relations, for existence is in time, being in constant development.

Thus immediacy to God cannot arise in the static state of a timeless relation, but only momentarily in a leap. The "moment" replaces mediation. Faith as the subjective side of immediacy to God is an event of the moment when the leap takes place. It may be a brief thing in time, "and yet it is decisive, and filled with the Eternal. Such a moment ought to have a distinctive name; let us call it the *Fullness of Time*."[52]

Here once again we come up against the reason why the truth cannot be imprisoned in a system. A system can be only a closed nexus which is detached from developing existence, which consists of media-

---

49. Ibid., p. 18. Kierkegaard uses a Platonic mode of expression when putting a definite article with the word *God;* cf. Niels Thulstrup, "Commentary," in ibid., p. 190.

50. Ibid., p. 22.

51. Ibid., p. 21.

52. Ibid., p. 22.

tion, and within which there is no moment and no leap. It is not as though there were no system at all in which thought and being are bound together. But such a system is present only for God and not for existing spirits in process of becoming.[53] The jab at Hegel is plain enough here.

Since thinking is a function of our existence and its state, it can win through to truth only if existence itself is in truth. As noted already, "knowing the truth is something which follows as a matter of course from being the truth, and not conversely. . . . To be the truth is one and the same thing as knowing the truth. . . . Only then do I truly know the truth when it becomes a life in me."[54]

Here again light is shed on Kierkegaard's resolutely championed thesis that it is "a monstrous error, very nearly the greatest possible error, to impart Christianity by lecturing."[55] In a matter of existence, results and proceeds no longer matter. When Christ transfers his being in truth to us, the way of existence is decisive, not a result that one can formulate. This way, however, is discipleship.[56] Only on this way is the leap possible which leads out of imprisonment in the circle of objectifying thought. This truth takes place as the saving act of deliverance, as the transforming of our existence, as conversion.

H. WHY THE EFFORT OF KIERKEGAARDIAN DIALECTIC?

At this point, having surveyed (or attempted to survey) the complicated dialectical structure of the relation between existence and truth or faith and thought, I take the liberty of asking a very naive question, hoping that it will not remain naive but will perhaps lead us more deeply into Kierkegaard's understanding. The question (I will put it in different ways) is as follows.

Why do we have to have this complicated construction, which is made the more complicated by Kierkegaard's assuming of the ironical masks of his pseudonyms, and therefore not deliberating from a single standpoint but constantly shifting ground? Why is what he has to say so indirect and devious? Even if, like Schleiermacher, he has in mind the cultured among the despisers, who even among them can follow his often broken dialectic, and who, even if they can, will be ready to subject

53. *Concluding Unscientific Postscript*, p. 170.
54. *Training in Christianity*, pp. 201-2.
55. Ibid., p. 202.
56. Ibid., p. 204.

themselves to such exercises? He can indeed, as in the *Edifying Discourses*, speak very simply and in a way that the simplest can understand. Does God really make it as hard as Kierkegaard does to come to faith and to find the point from which to leap?

Again, is not the denial of Christ's direct recognizability, and the resultant resort to paradox, the reason for the whole evil of dialectical complication? Could not God have made himself known more directly and clearly instead of in triply hidden ciphers? The devout in all ages have raised this cry for direct knowability. The prophet sighs: If only God would rend the heavens and come down and make his name known among his enemies, because they can no longer fail to see him (Isa. 64:1). The people ask Christ: "How long will you keep us in suspense? If you are the Christ, tell us plainly" (John 10:24).

A first reply to these questions might take the form of a reference to the fact that in his decided denial of the direct knowability of the divine, Kierkegaard has the Synoptic tradition on his side. (I can only sketch this here.) Christ does not directly claim the messianic title for himself. Mark's Gospel is the book of secret epiphanies.[57] This shows us that Christ's person cannot be subsumed under a given title. He is not apparently known and may not be objectively defined along the lines that such titles suggest. Only in discipleship can disciples come to see who he is, and only then, as the result of an existential encounter, can they accord to him the title of Messiah (Matt. 16:16).

For the same reason Christ chides the desire for signs, the desire for direct knowability through the evidence of miracles, the desire to see instead of believe, the desire for truth without the venture of existence, i.e., without discipleship (Matt. 12:39; 16:4). Even the parables, which didactically come closest to meeting our ability to receive, neither can nor should impart direct knowability. On the contrary, they serve a purpose of concealment so far as those who exist in untruth are concerned (Matt. 13:13).

Thus Kierkegaard has the NT kerygma on his side when he denies the direct knowability of God in a single, finite man and refers to the necessary condition on which alone the truth that is hidden here discloses itself, namely, my transforming from untruth to truth. Only those who are of the truth hear his voice (John 18:37).

Once it is clear that existence and truth hang together in this way, immense tasks are set for my thinking. For only those who are brought back into truth can say in retrospect on what mistaken paths

57. Cf. M. Dibelius, *From Tradition to Gospel* (1935); cf. also W. Wrede, *The Messianic Secret* (repr. 1971). On this whole problem cf. *EF,* II, 290ff.

their thinking—even though it might be inspired by Socrates—previously went astray when it thought that it could reach the truth by way of objective conclusions detached from existence. Those who want to become free for truth must learn to know their imprisonment in a wrong schema of thought. Those who want to attain to the truth that has come to light in Christ can appropriate it only if they perceive how it is with themselves, with their existence. This requires of adult spirits the kind of reflective self-elucidation that Kierkegaard achieves on so high a level.

The second answer to the question of why Kierkegaard's thinking is so complicated takes the form of a reference to what he was opposing, to that to which all his theses are antitheses. This consists of mistaken objective thinking that does not take account of existence. Hegel is a chief representative, although not the only one. Speculatively establishing the mediation of absolute and finite spirit, Hegel thought that he could know Christ directly, but only by an essential falsification, i.e., by his deindividualizing, by his reduction to the mere representative of the idea of reconciliation. In contrast, Kierkegaard views him as the God who comes to manifestation in an individual. He thus bursts open the continuity of Hegelian dialectic. He makes Christ an absurdity for objective reason, an absolute exception that we can speak about only in the form of paradox. This contradicting of Hegel, which either explicitly or implicitly runs through his whole work, might well have contributed to the adoption of a style of thought that is quite different from the abstract dialectic of Hegel.

Yet Kierkegaard does not attribute to Hegel alone the original sin of a direct recognizability of Christ. He finds this sin also in the religious common sense of ordinary culture-Christianity, and especially in institutional Christianity such as he found in the Danish state church. The dominant liberalism of that church produced erroneous syntheses of church and world and faith and reason. By accommodations to the spirit of the age, it sought to avoid the offense of the real Christ, the paradoxical appearance of the eternal in the finite, indeed, in a single individual. It thus came about that Christ was presented as a mere teacher teaching truths that reason could readily absorb.

Against these fateful errors—along with the scorning of the category of the individual as this found expression in leveling down in the dawning age of the masses—Kierkegaard reacted not only with great contempt and mockery (which he did) but also and chiefly with an attempt to show what was the final basis of these collective tendencies. To do this an enormous effort of thought was needed.

The third answer to the question of why Kierkegaard is so

complicated has to take into account the contemporary polemical situation and to convey some sense of the ultimately positive and even creative intention which Kierkegaard had in seeking to overcome his main problem. Finally, as we have seen, this problem was caused by the single fact that an individual is God, that as such he is inaccessible to objective historical knowledge, that there is no direct recognizability. Taken alone, this seems at first to be a purely negative position.

But what might seem to be a dead end for our thinking and seeking was for Kierkegaard a decisive, creative moment. For if I am greatly concerned about a vital question (like that of eternal salvation), but am in objective uncertainty about the answer, my existential passion is stretched to the limit. *"An objective uncertainty held fast in an appropriation-process of the most passionate inwardness is the truth,* the highest truth attainable for an *existing* individual. . . . The above definition of truth is an equivalent expression for faith. Without risk there is no faith. Faith is precisely the contradiction between the infinite passion of the individual's inwardness and the objective uncertainty."[58] That which reason can grasp smoothly, which I can quickly arrive at as a conclusion, does not contain the risk of objective uncertainty without which faith cannot live and there can be no leap, no moment in which is the fulness of time. Hence I do not come to faith without experiencing the shattering of the false objective way of certainty.

Here again, although in a different place, Kierkegaard uses the relation between lovers to illustrate the mobilizing of that extreme passion of inwardness. We have seen that love—even erotic love—was for him a favorite paradigm of the involvement of one's whole existence. This love, too, can be in productive conflict with objective uncertainty. Let us assume that the one who loves assures his beloved of his love with ardent expressions, and his whole being corresponds to these almost to the point of idolatry. He then asks: "Do you believe that I love you?" His beloved answers: "Yes, I believe." But he then hits on the idea of a test to see if she really believes. He abandons all direct communication, makes himself unrecognizable as it were, acts as a deceiver, makes himself an enigma in his conduct. In this changed situation he then asks again whether she believes him in spite of appearances to the contrary. At first he was directly knowable. Love and its verbal expression were in agreement. Everything went smoothly. But now, when the one who loves is hidden under his opposite, the aim is to force the beloved to choose which form she believes to be the true one.[59] She has lost the certainty of objective knowledge. This

58. Kierkegaard, *Concluding Unscientific Postscript,* p. 182.
59. *Training in Christianity,* p. 141.

loss poses a demand for the Nevertheless of faith, the venture of her existence. Here is the point of comparison between this situation and that in which we confront a Christ who is not directly recognizable.

Without trying to improve on Kierkegaard's example, I might point out that a similar maneuver often takes place in the art of love without any need for that kind of theatrical and rather artificial test. It is one of the wiles of an experienced young girl, when being courted, not to accede too easily but to feign indifference. She counts on it that her lover will become more passionate in consequence. By making him objectively uncertain—this is the tactic—she mobilizes his full potential for passion. This is what she wants to prove.

I. THE RELIGIOUS AUTHOR AS "GOD'S SPY" AND HIS UNMASKING

As an author Kierkegaard, too, acts exactly like that lover. He conceals himself. He does not speak directly as a teacher. His style is indirect. The various pseudonyms serve this concealment. Under their mask he is a deceiver, he catches people by guile, he is "a spy in a higher service."[60]

This masquerade does not mean that he wants to deny his identity or to evade responsibility for what he says pseudonymously. No, under all these various names (Johannes Climacus, Victor Eremita, etc.), he himself is speaking. They are stages on his life's way, or at least aesthetic, tragic, erotic, and ethical possibilities within himself. Yet in them he speaks as one who has been brought into truth, as a religious author. Thus the disguise has an ironic tone. He is this, and yet he is not. As he speaks from each angle, not describing from outside but adopting the position, he is making a Socratic appeal to his readers, not with a view to maieutically releasing their own possibilities, but with a view to questioning these, throwing doubt upon them, for even as he ironically adopts an aesthetic or a Socratic position he is a religious author, and he understands these positions better than those who hold them. We do not think our way into being Christians, but out of other things so as to become Christians. The pseudonyms are designed to help people think their way out of being other things. This is the hidden challenge in all of them.[61] On the lips of a rising poet who values his work and allots him a place among those who have suffered for the truth, he puts the words: "Whereas as author he had dialectically a survey of the whole," i.e., all possible existence, which he could survey at strategic

60. *Point of View,* p. 87.
61. Ibid., p. 96.

points only with the help of the pseudonyms, "he understood Christianly that the whole signified his own education in Christianity."[62] Under all the masks that he put on, and in every position that he took up as a spectator, he wanted to be faithful, then, to his identity as a Christian author.[63]

Indeed, the certainty that everything he wrote, even the "tremendously witty" work *Diary of a Seducer*,[64] has a Christian point is the basic theme of his final self-testimonies. In these he confesses that what he is in truth as an author he is as a religious author. His whole activity as an author stands related to Christianity, to becoming a Christian. He used the pseudonyms, or indirect speech, so as to search out the representatives of an erroneous Christianity in their doubtful abodes and to fetch them out. With direct and indirect polemic he reacted against the monstrous illusion of Christendom, i.e., that all those who live in a particular country are Christians.[65] As an example of his Christian identity beneath all the masks Kierkegaard points out that along with the aestheticism of *Either-Or* he wrote the *Two Edifying Discourses* in which one may see the real author concealed behind the pseudonyms.[66] Even *Either-Or* is in the strict sense written in the cloister.[67] Hence it is not as a former aesthete who has now turned from the world that he finally puts off the masks and makes himself known directly as a Christian author. No, he is a person who always, beneath all the masks, has definitely turned aside from the world and its wisdom.[68]

At the end, then, the author takes off the aesthetic garb and ceases to engage in literary saturnalia; the midnight unmasking comes. For finally, at the end of the self-disclosures,[69] the communication of the Christian element must conclude with witness and hence with direct statement. The ultimate form cannot be maieutic. On a Christian understanding truth does not lie in the subject, as Socrates thought. It

62. Ibid., p. 103.

63. We have to take this and the following quotations seriously, so that the view of Jaspers is wrong when he argues that Kierkegaard's Christianity is simply a cipher for a general philosophy of existence. That the Christian element is merely incidental and irrelevant Jaspers claimed even more definitely when he invited me to debate the point in Heidelberg, where we were both teaching at the time (1936-1940).

64. *Point of View*, p. 95.

65. Ibid., p. 22.

66. Ibid., pp. 17ff.

67. Ibid., p. 18.

68. Ibid., p. 98.

69. Cf. W. Rehm, *Kierkegaard als Verführer*, p. 393.

is a revelation that must be proclaimed. The maieutic element can have an important function in Christianity, for most people live with the illusion that they are Christians, and penetrating Socratic inquiry can be useful in piercing through the facade. But finally the maieutic writer must nail his colors to the mast and become a direct witness.

Kierkegaard knows well what the cost is when he drops his pseudonymous masks, abandons all the wiles of the spy of God, and adopts the simplicity of direct witness.[70] He stands there naked and defenseless, and must reckon with the venomous reactions of a disillusioned world. He hears very well the partly spiteful and partly sorrowing reference of a critic who sets the account before him.

> "But what have you done now?" I hear somebody say. "Do you not perceive what you have lost in the eyes of the world by making this explanation and public acknowledgement?" To be sure, I see it very clearly. I have lost thereby what in a Christian sense it is a loss to possess [Phil. 3:8], namely, every worldly form of the interesting. I lose the interesting distinction of proclaiming the seductive craftiness of pleasure, the glad report of life's most subtle enjoyments, and the insolence of derision. I lose the interesting distinction of being an interesting possibility. . . . I lose the interesting distinction of being an enigma, seeing it is impossible to know whether this thorough-going defence of Christianity is not a covert attack most cunningly conceived. This interesting distinction I lose, and for it is substituted, at the farthest remove from the interesting, the *direct communication* that the problem was, and is, how to become a Christian.[71]

Looking back on his studies of what is interesting, he constantly emphasizes that for the sake of the religious background of his aesthetic authorship he needed and sought the help of God.[72] He has the writer already quoted sum up his work along these lines: He served the cause of Christianity. From childhood this was in a remarkable way his life's focus. He did the work of reflection in such a way as to draw Christianity, or becoming a Christian, into it. The purity of his heart was to will only the one thing. Historically he died of a fatal illness, but poetically he died of a longing for eternity, that he might have nothing to do but give thanks to God without interruption.[73]

70. Kierkegaard, *Point of View*, p. 97.
71. Ibid., p. 93.
72. Ibid., pp. 66ff.
73. Ibid., p. 103.

In this sense the most appropriate epitaph might be the pietis-tic (!) verse that the Danish hymn writer H. A. Brorson chose for his own tombstone: "Yet a little while and the fight is won, the conflict ended, and in the hall of roses I shall talk with Jesus without interruption for ever and ever."[74]

J. CRITICAL EVALUATION

Although we cannot go into the rich influence of Kierkegaard in such varied fields as philosophy, literature, and dialectical theology, it seems important to show what his place is in intellectual history and how pivotal this place is.

We have established the fact that a basic tendency of the modern era is that the human subject, whether thinking (Descartes), feeling (Schleiermacher), transcendental (Kant), or believing (Herrmann), acts as the point of reference for every statement. As a rule problems of knowledge and certainty, especially in the area of theology, raise this question of the subject and the conditions on which it can accept religious truth. It is thus especially as rational beings or thinking subjects that we come into view.[75]

The particular significance of Kierkegaard is that by showing the existential reference of every discovery of truth he overcomes this one-sided emphasis on our rational nature. In so doing he has a rich and varied view of existence. Existentially we consist of body, soul, and spirit,[76] so that every aspect is involved. As regards existence, reason is no higher than imagination or feeling, but stands alongside these.[77] If a thinker, who is also an existing person, has lost imagination and feeling, this is just as bad as losing understanding. If instead of achieving an existential contemporaneity of all these aspects we one-sidedly stress the rationally directed academic process, we destroy life.[78] (The concept of contemporaneity that is used here has many implications. Usually it refers to the direct relationship of believers to Christ which transcends

74. See Gerhard Krause, "Ein Sonderfall des sogenannten Ewigkeitsliedes. Zu einem Kapitel dänischer und deutscher Hymnologie," *ZThK* 3 (1979) 360ff.
75. Schleiermacher is to some extent an exception. But in putting his theology on the plane of feeling or immediate self-consciousness, he was guided not least of all by the aim of finding a storm-free zone secure against rational, i.e., historical, philosophical, and scientific, questions. I recall the open letters to Lücke.
76. *Concluding Unscientific Postscript*, p. 307.
77. Ibid., p. 310.
78. Ibid., p. 311.

the gap in time, but here it refers to the simultaneous activity or equal rank of rationality, feeling, and imagination.) The breadth of the existential reference comes to expression in the philosophy that stands under Kierkegaard's influence. Thus in Heidegger (and Bultmann after him) terms like *anxiety* and *concern* are existential things and thus become themes of philosophical reflection. This takes place under the essential impulse of Kierkegaard. Philosophy had never known anything like it before him.

In spite of the enriching of the relation between subject and truth, the limitations of Kierkegaard are plain to see precisely at this point. I will mention just a few of which we have had intimation in what has been said already.

First, Kierkegaard has a very sick constitution burdened with the melancholy derived from his father. He can speak about this very movingly in his confessions. From birth and by education it was his fate not to be a real man. When one is a child and other children play and joke, when one is a youth and other youths love and dance, then as child and youth it is dreadfully painful to be spirit, and the more so if one has the imaginative power to make it seem as though one is the most youthful of all. Kierkegaard knew no immediacy, and hence from the standpoint of genuine humanity he did not live.[79]

If we take seriously his thesis that thinking is a function of real existence, we cannot overlook the pathological burden that this imposed. His constitutionally determined position as an exception could not fail to have an impact on his concept of the individual. Yet it would be a mistake, as I have already pointed out in the biographical sketch, to let our evaluation of Kierkegaard's thought be controlled by a psychiatric diagnosis of this kind (as frequently occurs). The thin walls of this type of sick psyche enhance receptivity to the mysteries and scents of background elements that are hidden from so-called normal people. It may be that Kierkegaard's "individual" is presented in distorted and isolated absoluteness, yet he sees this individual through a magnifying glass that gives him abnormal vision.

Second, by pursuing incessantly the difficulty of knowing Christ historically and objectively, and making nonimmediate knowability the central christological question, Kierkegaard can never develop the full breadth of the gospel, at least in his theoretical works. I have expressed this reductionism as follows. The *content* of Christ's appearance and message retreats behind the *fact* of it, the fact that paradoxically this individual is God. Kierkegaard concentrates on a single point. This may

79. Cf. *Point of View*, pp. 76-77.

be the decisive point but it is not the only one (even though all the others must stand under the sign of it). This focusing on a single point comes to symbolical expression in the temporal concept of the "moment." Kierkegaard touches the soil of historical existence only point by point, as it were. It is perhaps not out of keeping with his style, and certainly no caricature, if we say that he reminds us of a toe dance.

Third, as the one-sidedness derives from the things against which he strives antithetically, the desire for direct knowledge, objectivizing, assimilation to the secular mind, so we must relate his absolutizing of the individual not least or last to the background of collectivist and leveling-down tendencies in the dawning age of the masses. He was essentially right to think that he could find a place for the mass, or the collective as we might say today, only if he began with an infinite, divinely based accent on the individual.[80] Yet it is hard to see how he could move on from this theological view of the individual to a concept that can, for example, establish a theological ethics of politics. It is hard to see what significance he could accord to the institutions, the historical structures (social and economic), in which the individual exists.

The light that falls from eternity on the individual—only an individual can attain to the truth, not "the crowd," which is always in untruth[81]—undoubtedly imparts a truth. "What an infinite reality," Kierkegaard says, "this self acquires by being before God! A herdsman who (if this were possible) is a self only in the sight of cows is a very low self, and so also is a ruler who is a self in the sight of slaves—for in both cases the scale or measure is lacking. The child who hitherto has had only the parents to measure himself by, becomes a self when he is a man by getting the state as a measure. But what an infinite accent falls upon the self by getting God as a measure!"[82] The truth in question is that there can be final self-understanding only before God. A mistaken anthropology necessarily results, therefore, when the I receives its decisive orientation from the animal element below it, or the human element alongside or above it, or the general spirit of the day. Nevertheless, the task of existing involves more than the final orientation to the standard of God. This final orientation has implications for our being with others (and with animals too), and for our position within the orders of the world. Kierkegaard in his toe dance is content with the one point. He focuses solely on individuals in their situation before God. Yet we must be cautious here. This might be a "one-eyed" criticism, since

80. Cf. the biographical sketch and esp. the review of "Zwei Zeitalter."
81. Cf. *Point of View,* p. 112.
82. *Sickness unto Death,* p. 210.

it applies only to Kierkegaard's theoretical reflections on Christianity. His meditations in the many works of edification have a broader horizon. They go into the content of the gospel and unfold it. We have to take these works into account as well.

Fourth, the objective sphere of knowledge, especially natural science and history, is screened off from any relation to the existential perception of truth. Kierkegaard has no organ by which to detect the significance of factual knowledge.[83] He does not even appreciate the historico-critical question of the relation between the biblical record and the actual events. Arguments and objections of this type, which might make people doubters, have no place for him. They contradict the absolute theological premises of his life and thought.[84] The epistemological problem in its totality has a wider reach than finds expression in his thesis that subjectivity is truth. The screening out of other aspects of truth is undoubtedly a result of his making the *content* secondary to the *fact* of existential truth.

Fifth, does not Kierkegaard bracket off the religious dimension from the totality of existence, so that it touches the horizontal dimension only as a tangent does a circle, i.e., at a single point?[85] One need not and should not go so far as Jaspers does when he describes as absolutely ruinous the message of a point-by-point existence and the interpretation of Christianity that this entails,[86] or when he calls Kierkegaard and Nietzsche figures who stir people to come to themselves and then destroy them in the whirlpool of nihilism.[87] For Jaspers they are like birds flying before a disastrous storm. We see in them unrest and haste and confusion but we also note something like circling and staggering and falling.[88] Jaspers obviously has in mind the lack of secularity in Kierkegaard's mode of existence, and hence the impossibility of existing in this way, of being without everything that is human or real in the world.[89]

In fact, it does seem that Kierkegaard takes the relation of radical unconditionality toward God and transfers it negatively to the relation to worldly things (including the institution of the church and Christianity as it is actually lived out to a large extent). There thus arises, it seems, that absence of the human element and that loss of immediate living to which he himself refers in his confessions. In the term used by

83. See von Loewenich, *Luther und der Neuprotestantismus* (1963), p. 180.
84. See Hirsch, *Geschichte der neueren evangelischen Theologie*, V (1949), 490.
85. I am adopting here a figure that Barth likes to use.
86. Jaspers, *Rechenschaft und Ausblick*, p. 126.
87. Ibid., p. 129.
88. Ibid., p. 130.
89. Ibid., p. 128.

Bonhoeffer, he has no relation to the sphere of the penultimate in which there have to be compromises and conditionalities. Similarly, we find in him only a hint of a two-kingdoms doctrine without which there can be no kind of theological ethics (at least for Lutherans!).[90] Kierkegaard has two right hands and no left hand. If one may exaggerate, what he says about redemption applies only to abstract individuals and not to the self insofar as it is involved in political, social, and economic structures, although it cannot remove its individual existence from these structures. When Kierkegaard looks at secular forms of existence (as in his pseudonymous works), they are only play or a masquerade, like the young Kierkegaard imagining himself to be the most youthful of all. Is this play a substitute for what is in fact an absence of secular existence? Why has he not taken the ordinary course of work and marriage? Why does he live the even externally unusual life of an author? We may and must put this question.

One point in the criticism of Jaspers is certainly right, or at least, to put it more cautiously, it does contain an element of truth. If we want to imitate Kierkegaard (which was not his intention) and live this unusual point-by-point existence that isolates the individual on the horizontal plane, then in a reality that is threatened by the loss of meaning we are indeed very close to nihilism. Does there not open up in Kierkegaard's own life a blank of this kind, a vacuum, when as a child he does not play, as a youth he does not flirt and dance, and as a man he shuns the usual structures? Are not whole provinces in this landscape emptied of meaning? Is there not nihilism in this sense?

I am engaging in a daring comparison between a soaring intellectual building and a modest cottage—but with a grain of truth—if I say that there is a zone in which Kierkegaard's existence is in a sense close to Max Stirner. It is quite conceivable that the individual whom infinite reflection reduces to despair will leave the house of Kierkegaard and in the neighboring house become a less complicated if, of course, much more abstract individual.

To be quite open, in conclusion, I do not think that one can live with Kierkegaard alone. It is impossible to slip into his unusual existence and be only his disciple. Can there or should there ever be any Kierkegaardians?

His claim and intellectual rank rest on the fact that he put a warning question mark and exclamation mark on the margin of every theology and anthropology, a red light, as it were, which warns us against any objectification of God or humanity, and especially against

90. Cf. *ThE*, I, §§ 1783ff. and II/2, passim; ET I, 359ff., and vol. II, passim.

any attempt to integrate either or probably both into our own schema of thought. Indeed, Kierkegaard is a corrective not merely on the margin of theology but on the margin of every "ism." These can arise in history and the natural and social sciences when they venture to develop an anthropology out of their objectifying categories, and in so doing take up an absolute position to what is relative, and regard their particular aspect as the whole.

At the same time, as a question mark and exclamation mark, Kierkegaard is not the text on the margin of which the sign stands. At any rate, he is not the text that can shape my life as the *only* word of guidance.

II. ERNST TROELTSCH: UNCONDITIONALITY FROM RELATIVISM

Bibliography. Primary Works: *Gesammelte Schriften*, I-IV (1912ff.); *Die Absolutheit des Christentums und die Religionsgeschichte* (1969, quoted as *Absolutheit*), ET *The Absoluteness of Christianity* (London, 1972); *Ein Apfel vom Baum Kierkegaards* (1921; cf. *Anfänge der dialektischen Theologie* [1963], pp. 134ff.); articles in *RGG*, 1st ed., on Erlösung, Eschatologie, Gesetz, Glaube, Kirche, Naturrecht, Offenbarung, Prädestination, and Protestantismus; posthumously, *Der Historismus und seine Überwindung* (1924); *Glaubenslehre* (1925).
Secondary Works: H. Benckert, *Ernst Troeltsch und das ethische Problem* (1932); idem, "Der Begriff der Entscheidung bei Ernst Troeltsch," *ZThK* 12 (1932) 422ff.; idem, "Ernst Troeltsch," *RGG*, 3rd ed., VI (1962), 1044ff.; W. Bodenstein, *Neige des Historismus. Ernst Troeltschs Entwicklungsgang* (1959); F. Brunstäd, *Über die Absolutheit des Christentums* (1905); H. G. Drescher, *Glaube und Vernunft bei Ernst Troeltsch* (1959); idem, "Entwicklungsgedanke und Glaubensentscheidung . . . ," *ZThK* 1 (1982) 80ff.; F. Gogarten, "Historismus," *ZZ* 8 (1924) 7ff.; W. James in G. Wobbermin, *Die religiöse Erfahrung in ihrer Mannigfaltigkeit*, a German version of *The Varieties of Religious Experience* (1907), 4th ed. (1925); T. Kaftan, *Ernst Troeltsch. Zeitkritische Studie* (1911); W. Köhler, *Ernst Troeltsch* (1941); W. von Loewenich, *Luther und der Neuprotestantismus* (1963), § 17; R. Röhricht, *Zwischen Historismus und Existenzdenken* . . . , Dissertation, Tübingen (1954); H. H. Schrey, "Ernst Troeltsch und sein Werk," *ThR* 12 (1940) 130ff.; P. Tillich, *Ernst Troeltsch* . . . (1924); idem, *Der Historismus und seine Probleme* (1924); H. O. Wölber, *Dogma und Ethos. Christentum und Humanismus von Ritschl bis Troeltsch* (1950).

A. BIOGRAPHY

Troeltsch lived from 1865 to 1923. In his development he was essentially influenced by Neo-Kantianism, theologically by A. Ritschl, philosophically by R. H. Lotze, H. Rickert, and W. Windelband. Schleiermacher's understanding of religion was always for him an object of critical debate. He became Professor of Systematic Theology at Bonn in 1892, and at Heidelberg in 1894. At Heidelberg, in token of his universal interests that transcended the faculties, he also taught in philosophy. In 1914 he accepted a call to teach philosophy in Berlin, and from 1919 also served for three years as an under secretary in the Prussian Ministry of Culture. He felt closely bound to several academic colleagues such as Friedrich Meinecke, Friedrich Naumann, Max Scheler, and Max Weber. His students included Paul Tillich, Friedrich Gogarten, the church historian Walter Köhler, and the authoress Gertrud von Le Fort. The dialectical theology emerged partly in critical dialogue with him, especially in the case of Gogarten.[91]

B. THREE BASIC MOTIFS

At a point when in the name of dialectical theology he was moving away from Troeltsch's view as erroneous, Gogarten confessed that he found Troeltsch's work of the greatest significance, and that no theology could hope to be of any importance unless it entered into fundamental debate with him.[92] The implication is that no one can presume to talk about the unconditional (or revelation) in history without first pursuing to the very limit the possibilities of historical knowledge even in all its mistakes and confusions. Only in this way can we protect ourselves against facile absolutisms and dogmatisms. Only by this journey abroad can we validly come home, turning aside from the path of hopeless relativism. Did not Kierkegaard, one might ask, spare himself the trouble of this detour by the abyss of relativism? With his finding that the way of objective historical knowledge ends in mere conditionalities and approximations, did he not make too confidently and too quickly the leap into paradox? This question suggests itself because Troeltsch was one of the few theologians of his time who not only knew Kierkegaard but studied him and wrestled with him.

---

91. But cf. also the General Index to Barth's *CD* (Index Volume, p. 204). On this relationship cf. C. Gestrich, *Neuzeitliches Denken und die Spaltung der dialektischen Theologie* (1977), pp. 77ff.

92. Gogarten, "Historismus," *ZZ* 8 (1924) 181.

The upshot of his encounter was that he had very serious reservations. Kierkegaard represents an abstract individual detached from his historical context. His Christianity agrees with that of no church or confession or historical form. He champions a very personal and private Christianity in very radical opposition to world, people, state, culture, and church. He disparages all the mediation between God and the world which he regards as the essential interest and work of the church. There thus arises a Christianity of absoluteness, of the either-or. By descent, upbringing, cast of mind, and orientation of life, he belongs to the (mystical and chiliastic) milieu of sectarian religion. He thus fights for a purely individual, abstract, personal, and absolutely radical Christianity. His early death, and his loneliness and oddness, which seem to be connected with his psychopathic disposition, protect him from the need to work out the positive and affirmative side of his religion in some relation to the world.[93] In short, Kierkegaard exists nonhistorically and abstractly. He lives apart from the world's structures. He thus thinks in terms of abstract alternatives, not of mediation.

Similarly unreal and abstract is his view of God. God's nature and eternal creation may well be fully inexplicable and supralogical, but God is not apart from the world. The world is God's world. We thus receive from him the powers of our being in the world. But this gives us the task of so uniting and kneading the existing material of life that its shaping can be an expression of these powers. At every time every living person must fashion the related rule and ideal.[94] God turns *to* the world, not *from* it. He calls us as beings that are involved in history and do not exist as isolated individuals. Our task, then, is that of mediation. Everything else is a capitulation to life.[95] The early church from Paul on sought innumerable arrangements with the world (and maintained its ancient radicalism only in its heartwood as asceticism and monasticism). Luther, too, was permeated with the view that the new man must seek mediation with the world.[96]

Yet for all the distance from Kierkegaard there is a certain affinity with him which one might describe as the existential trait in the thinking of Troeltsch. As he says in the debate with Gogarten, and indirectly with Kierkegaard, he is not inquiring into the nature of Christianity as such, nor into the position that a pastor might take, but only into that by which he himself lives, only into his own position if he

93. See Troeltsch, *Ein Apfel vom Baum Kierkegaards*, pp. 135-37.
94. Ibid., pp. 138-39.
95. *Gesammelte Schriften*, II, 293-94.
96. *Ein Apfel*, p. 136.

has to call that radical theology spiritually impossible for him.[97] In no way, then, does Troeltsch want to speak as a distant spectator of history in Hegel's sense. He does not seek noncommitment; he speaks as one who is involved. The relativism that threatens to overtake history is painful for him, the most painful thing in his life. But only as he accepts it, he thinks, will his search for the unconditional that transcends history be valid.

From this background three motifs emerge which shape his search for Christian truth. The first is concern for the principle of mediation between religion and historical reality. The second is an attempt to find the path from theological or metaphysical dogmatism to existence that is relatively determined and hence exposed to relativism. The third is a passionate concern to escape the grip of relativizing historicism and to find a new way to unconditional truth and values. The goal will always be the same, but the way to it may vary in the different stages of his life.

C. THE HISTORICAL CHARACTER OF HUMAN REALITY (FIRST PHASE)

The linking of the view of God and humanity with reality means for Troeltsch supremely its linking with history. The word *history* has in this context a certain total significance. Troeltsch speaks in the name of the historicism of his day—and the ending "ism" tells us that the conditional nature of all phenomena and norms is taking on an absolute sense. This is in fact the situation in which Troeltsch finds himself and which he adopts. He historicizes all our thinking, including the highest norms. Nothing lies outside this historical conditioning.

Troeltsch is simply giving vivid expression to the intellectual climate in which he did his thinking when as a young man he told the Friends of the Christian World, assembled at Eisenach in 1896, "Gentlemen, everything is tottering"—a statement which Ferdinand Kattenbusch, who represented older and rather shocked participants, rejected as the sympton of a shabby theology.[98]

The statement that everything is tottering implies that the age of a perennial theology, of a solid truth that has been dogmatically fixed for all time, has now gone. It is not as though there is no such truth, as though everything is the mere product of history. But history gives "the" truth changing, polymorphous expressions behind which we have first

97. Ibid., p. 129.
98. See W. Köhler, *Ernst Troeltsch*, p. 1.

to seek it without being able to posit it, or to see it as posited, axiomatically in advance. It is at all events a powerful shock when all eternal truths, whether supernatural truths in the church that have supreme authority, or the eternal truths of reason and the rational constructions of state, law, society, religion, and morality, are sucked into this process of historicizing.[99]

Troeltsch thinks that only a "poor intellectual habit" of rational and superrational dogmatism will invest the term *relative* with all the terrors of what is uncertain and unrooted and aimless.[100] That which is basic to historical knowledge, namely, the art of hypothetical appreciation of alien constructs and their inner and outer presuppositions, has produced unlimited virtuosity in the shifting of our standpoints of judgment as everything is understood and evaluated in terms of itself. For many, therefore, history has become identical with sympathy for everything strange and the renunciation of what is one's own, i.e., with skepticism and academic trifling, with a blasé and unbelieving attitude. This is true at any rate for those of "weak nature," by whom Troeltsch means the victims of a "poor intellectual habit," people who need fixed and solid norms to which to cling.[101]

For Troeltsch the suspicion that he is letting all unconditional norms and standards float away on the stream of history is a misunderstanding that he bewails. At every stage of his life he struggles to establish values that transcend history. But he does not want them cheaply or at any price. The price for him is a costly attempt to find them within and not apart from our present intellectual situation as it is shaped by historicism, and hence to establish them on the given historical foundation. Even though he can advance the formula that "historical" and "relative" are identical,[102] this implies no confession of relativism and no abandonment of the struggle for absoluteness. It simply denotes the renunciation of a false absoluteness that has long since been shown to be untenable.

What does he mean by this false understanding of absoluteness? Alluding to Hegel, he explains the concept of absoluteness in terms of an evolutionary construction of the history of religion in virtue of which all non-Christian religions are understood as relative truths, as early stages of Christianity, which itself represents the absolute, complete form of religion, the being of its very concept.[103]

99. Troeltsch, "Die Krisis des Historismus," *NR* 33 (1922) 573.
100. *The Absoluteness of Christianity*, p. 85.
101. Ibid., p. 87.
102. Ibid., p. 85.
103. Ibid., p. 49.

In this context he has to offer recognition to his older contemporaries F. H. R. von Frank (1827-1894) and L. Ihmels (1858-1933), who champion the supernatural view of absoluteness but who along the lines of modern orthodoxy are concerned not to understand the supernatural factor merely as an authority but to bring it into association with immanent psychological factors as Schleiermacher had tried to do in his own way. Even for modern thought, however, there is something that it cannot absorb. For everywhere in the orthodox tradition everything human is subjective, fallible, sinful, and impotent. There is a need, therefore, for supernatural divine acts which directly and without analogy break into the human reality that is determined by history and transcend the laws that obtain in every other sphere of human life. Here, then, we have a direct causality of God, and hence a delimitation in principle from everything human and historical and from all its purely relative truths and forces.[104] Modern thinking, however, has irrefutably established the continuity of the causal nexus and rendered the dogmatic supernaturalism of the church impossible.[105] Hence the normativity that Troeltsch seeks will have to be different from all exclusively supernatural revelation and different, too, from the absolute fulfilment of the concept of religion.[106]

Nonetheless, we cannot give in to the hope of showing that Christianity is absolute religion with *historical* means, as though this could be demonstrated as a fact in history. Troeltsch is just as shocked at the thought of finding an absolute point in history as D. F. Strauss, whom he cites expressly and who said that the idea does not like to pour out all its riches into one example and favor it above all the others.[107]

The historicism of Troeltsch destroys a final hope of "weak natures," namely, that one might perhaps retain a last element of absoluteness in history by differentiating the kernel from the husk. Such a distinction would have it that we see only the expression of eternal truth which is subject to the limits of temporal history and hence to relativity, but that the kernel enclosed in this husk is something unconditional which may be found in history. As we may see today, this distinction has some affinity to Bultmann's demythologizing. In this the Gnostic redeemer myth and later Jewish apocalyptic are distinguished from the kerygmatic core as its form of expression (or husk).[108] In reply,

104. Ibid., p. 52.
105. Ibid., p. 53.
106. Ibid., p. 57.
107. Ibid., p. 68.
108. Cf. H. Thielicke, "The Restatement of New Testament Mythology," in *Kerygma and Myth*, I, ed. H. W. Bartsch (New York, 1961), pp. 138-74.

Troeltsch contends that the distinction applies only in peripheral details. It cannot be made in anything essential. For in the main, central religious ideas are closely connected with alien ideas of the time that cannot be experienced afresh by us. The result of all nimble attempts at differentiation is that the distinction becomes increasingly difficult and entails a loss of elevating pleasure in the great individual reality of history. Troeltsch finds in such attempts a barbaric lack of musical sensitivity to the melody of history, and even a kind of attack upon it. What is sought, the kernel behind the husk, is not a nonhistorical, eternal, and unchangingly explicated concept, but an individual and vital whole of concrete reality that has developed under these conditions. It is pointless, therefore, to seek a timeless concept behind the mutability of individual phenomena.[109]

D. THE SEARCH FOR THE ABSOLUTE

Troeltsch, then, has tied the knot. The return to a dogmatically decreed or speculatively conceived absoluteness is closed to him, for it can be had only at the price of an abstract universal validity that ignores history. If he stays close to history, he seems to be confronted by a hopeless confusion of values and exposed to the suspicion that historical thinking condemns us to nihilism.[110] Yet this is not the worst of the complications into which he might be maneuvered. How great these are may be seen only when we grasp the following point.

Self-evidently for Troeltsch one can find absolute truth, e.g., Christianity as *the* religious truth, only with the help of historical thinking and not by ignoring it. From the very outset then, as we have seen, there is no hope of finding the manifestation of the absolute at a single point in history or in an individual historical example (Strauss). But another result is even more serious. To follow traces of something unconditional on the basis of history, or even to seek them, one needs a norm of evaluation or a criterion of value. But one cannot derive this from history itself. For on the one side this would mean treating history unhistorically by having an axiomatic value before encountering it and then subjecting the historical phenomena to this. Or, on the other side, I would have to realize that the criterion I import into history is itself

109. Troeltsch, *Absoluteness of Christianity*, pp. 68ff. At this point the similarity to Bultmann ends, for Bultmann does not mean by the kerygmatic core the timeless concept of Hegel.
110. Ibid., pp. 93-94.

historically conditioned, for I too am a member of history, and along with my views I am only one among many of its individual expressions. I thus face the paradoxical situation that the standard of evaluation by which I hope to escape the grip of relativism and to attain to something unconditional is itself only relative and historical. Does it not seem, then, that Troeltsch is leading us out of the older dogmatism, by way of the historical relativizing of values, to extreme relativism?

How can Troeltsch find his way out of this difficulty? How can he be on the track of something unconditional when he is unwilling to leave the plane of historical experience? This is the problem.

We find the first hint of a solution in the observation that the confusion of values in history is not so great and that we are not so helpless or disoriented in face of it. It is surprising to Troeltsch how little history has thus far produced by way of significant content. He also thinks it unlikely that the future will initiate any wild and confusing productivity.[111] Among the few great ideal expressions it seems to him that evaluation is possible. At least, he does not think it ruled out that the great values and contents of intellectual life may be compared, judged by a standard of values, and hence subjected to a common goal (in the sense of something unconditional). Naturally, the standard by which to evaluate the distinctions between such ideal types is not a religious theory deduced from some point a priori, as in Scholasticism.[112]

But how are we to find such a standard a posteriori from history itself? Instead of our importing it and doing violence to history, it must arise in the free conflict of ideas with one another. It thus develops in the encounter with history. As we expose ourselves to this, we acquire criteria. Troeltsch admits, then, that such a standard is a matter of personal conviction, and is in the last resort subjective. But it is not merely subjective. For ultimately it has an objective basis in careful survey, impartial appreciation, and scholarly appraisal. The final decision is, of course, one of very personal conviction, but it is conviction. This means that history convinces me by the evidence of its great phenomena and the values they posit. History itself gives me the standard if I will commit myself unreservedly to it. When I do this, only a few high points confront me. This is the first thing that I learn. Among these I quickly learn to distinguish. For all the subjectivity, then, the standard is not capricious. It rests on objective historical references. For Troeltsch, then, the essence of historical thinking lies in delimiting the

111. Ibid., p. 94.
112. Ibid., pp. 26, 92ff.; for what follows, see p. 95.

sustaining foundations of the values worked out in history, and seeing them in their relations to one another.

In this way Troeltsch arrives at a distinctive concept of universal validity which is radically different from an abstractly and speculatively deduced philosophy like that of Hegel. If by comparison a standard of judgment arises, the comparability and the common relationship of the things compared point to something within them that is common and universally valid. One cannot distil this, however, out of the concrete phenomena in the form of a free-floating idea separate from them. This would again be unhistorical and would put us under the suspicion of previously smuggling in that which we conjure up out of the phenomena as something universally valid. Troeltsch holds on to his historicism by claiming that what is universally valid, expressed in the converging lines of basic movements, and experienced by us as a normative goal or ideal or final aim, is present only in specific individual actualizations, and cannot be detached from these without falling victim to falsification. We find only individual approaches to common goals. This means that the perfect totality that the goals intimate does not itself occur in history but is beyond history and may never be grasped in it except in a conditioned and individually fashioned way. There are thus distinctions in the ways of apprehending the final spiritual goal that hovers before us. There are gradations based on the lesser or greater clarity and strength of the revelation of the higher life. There is also expectation of a final and definitive revelation.

Note the linguistic nuances which weaken the unconditional concept of universal validity and which give it the character of something indefinite that hovers before us. We can only approach it. It hovers in front of us. Being always tied to something individual, it can never be direct. It is always mediated by history, and yet it always remains beyond it. Along this line of thinking Troeltsch finds confirmation in the lines of Goethe that tell us that we may not enter the land of ideas, but may be known on the shore and may cast anchor there so long as we do not think we can conquer the isles.[113] Troeltsch casts anchor in the sea of history, and from this point he surveys afar off in the haze the unattainable isles of fulfilment.

The unconditional or universally valid element of meaning, value, and norm is not for Troeltsch a matter of objective knowledge. Hence he does not feel that he comes under the verdict of Kierkegaard that history leads always to approximation and can never reach the unconditional. Troeltsch knows this—that is why he anchors at a dis-

113. Ibid., p. 106.

tance as long as he is in the ship of knowledge. Yet, seeing the unconditional in that which transcends history, he has the certainty of the unconditional in that which is beyond knowledge, in inkling, feeling, and experience.

This may be seen in religion, in which the issue is certainty of the ultimate. Here he finds the experience of a final, absolute reality. The purely religious experience can be as little fixed, defined, or described as its object, for it is no other than the sense and experience of a final being and a final value that is ascribed to this final being.[114] Because the absolute immutable value which is not temporally conditioned does not lie in history but beyond it, like all that is beyond history it is accessible only to sense and faith. Thus we miss the problem of history if we let it be defined by the false either-or of relativism or absolutism (as Kierkegaard does). In fact, we have a mixture of both, the development of orientations to absolute goals out of the relativities of history.[115] To put the pistol of the either-or to one's breast is the dogmatic method. The historical method is to weigh the both-and—in this case that of the relative and the absolute. The ultimate decision between these experienced values is, of course, a final axiomatic act, but not really in an arbitrary or subjective sense, for its motive is clarified by the weighing and grading of compared values, and hence its criteria develop out of the encounter with history.[116]

E. THE RANK OF CHRISTIANITY IN RELIGIOUS HISTORY

What rank can Troeltsch assign to Christianity when in the manner described he opens himself to an evaluation of the historical religions and tries to win the standards of evaluation from history itself?

He cannot accord it absoluteness in Hegel's sense or regard it as a complete actualization of the concept of religion. This is clear. But what grade of unconditionality can he grant it when he considers the historical individualizations and hence the particular expressions of the unconditional, and when he has, then, to regard Christianity as one such historical expression, and limited thereby? Is not Christianity hopelessly subject to the attack of a religious polymorphism which allows a table of values and thus exposes Christianity as well to relativism?

In the light of his presuppositions, the answer of Troeltsch,

114. See *RGG,* 1st ed., II, col. 624.
115. See *Absoluteness of Christianity,* p. 90.
116. Ibid., p. 31.

which we shall expound first, is an astonishing one. The personalistic redemptive religion of Christianity, which rests on the prophets and Jesus, which has its chief classical witness in the Bible, and which develops an immeasurable richness with its fusion of the ancient and Germanic worlds, is for him the highest and most consistently developed world of religion that we know.[117] The criterion of evaluation that Troeltsch uses here is the personalistic character by which the Christian religion of redemption validates itself. We must not think that the term *personalistic* is open at once to the suspicion of being an abstraction that is imported into history. For in it there comes to expression a question that was of unusual contemporary relevance for Troeltsch. In place of the question of the Reformation, how to find a gracious God, the question now was how to find the soul and love, or how to win a higher personal life from God in our mortally infected humanity.[118] This is *the* question in the life of Troeltsch, and as in the case of his teacher A. Ritschl, it reflects the threatening of personality by mechanistic structures and life in the mass.

Troeltsch thinks that this question, which arises out of history, finds its answer in the Christian religion of redemption, which upholds the privileges of the human person. In this regard the Christian religion takes precedence over others. This comes out most clearly when we see how outside Christianity the forces of religion are bound and hampered by the viewing of God in the being and operation of nature and the idea that humanity is something that merely is, not something that comes to be only in its own self-giving and action. Thus in the nature religions humanity is integrated into the cosmos and there can be no awakening of personality. The same is true in the non-Christian religions of redemption. They assimilate the world and humanity to the substance of God. They thus rule out any encounter of personal partnership.

It is not as though this makes Christianity an isolated phenomenon in religious history. No, it shares certain common features that connect all the higher religions and that come to expression in related basic thoughts and forces and impulses, although outside Christianity these go along with limits that are very hard to cross.

In this connection Troeltsch mentions four thought-groupings in the contemplation of which the higher religious life moves: God, the world, the soul, and the higher supraterrestrial world, the upper world, which arises in relation to the first three. One might say that we have here some of the few great contents that history has produced. And by

---

117. Ibid., p. 117; on what follows see pp. 112ff.
118. *Gesammelte Schriften*, II (1913), 522, 840.

these few great thoughts and their interrelationship one may see clearly that the goals that are sought are most freely and forcefully achieved in Christianity. The criterion in this regard is the higher personal life which is the theme of the Christian view of our relationship with God. Among the great religions Christianity is the strongest and most concentrated revelation of personal religion. It is the only complete break with the limits and conditions of nature religion, and the presentation of the higher world as infinitely valuable personal life conditioning and shaping all else, and this by way of the redemptive linking of souls that are entangled in the world and guilt with the love of God that meets and grasps them.[119]

Christianity, then, is not just the high point but also the point of convergence of all the recognizable lines of development in religion. Naturally, it is still a historical entity, and it thus has all the individual and temporary limitations of historical phenomena. There is no supratemporal "essence of Christianity."[120]

For this reason we cannot prove with strict certainty that it will remain the high point and can never be surpassed.[121] Because absolute truth and the unconditioned are beyond history, the truth is still hidden in many ways, and only the future will bring its unveiling with the judgment of God and the ending of earthly time. Until then we have only a sure faith, and faith for Troeltsch means the epistemologically transcendent form of experience and trust and feeling and testing.

If one cannot prove that Christianity will not be surpassed in some historical future, the devout should not be upset by this. Can they not be certain, asks Troeltsch, that what they have inwardly felt and proved to be true in life can never be untrue to all eternity, and can it upset them, then, if it is a mere belief that so far as we can see we can expect nothing higher than the revelation in Jesus? The devout must be content that they have the deepest and best that there is, beyond which it is pointless to seek anything more, since this does not exist anywhere, and they themselves cannot invent it.[122]

Thus Christianity is the high point of all previous religions and the basis and presupposition of any clear and powerful religion in the future. It is also unlikely to be surpassed so far as we can see.[123]

119. *Absoluteness of Christianity*, p. 112.
120. *Was heisst Wesen des Christentums?* in *Gesammelte Schriften,* II, 387ff.; idem, *Über historische und dogmatische Methode in der Theologie,* II, 129ff. On the origin of the expression "essence of Christianity" cf. Köhler, *Ernst Troeltsch,* pp. 71ff.
121. *Absoluteness of Christianity*, pp. 114-15.
122. Ibid., p. 121.
123. Ibid., p. 131.

Twice when Troeltsch looks at the future from the standpoint of the devout—and he has himself in view—he uses the reservation: "so far as we can see." Can he do anything other or say anything more on the plane of historicism? Can the question that is put to Jesus—whether he is he that should come, or should we look for another? (Matt. 11:3)—find along the lines of Troeltsch the answer that there can be no other? Yes, so far as the horizon of his own European experience is concerned. But are there not other historical perspectives in terms of which we can give no answer—areas of experience that we have to deal with in the problem of mission?[124]

We have still to see how this reference to his own viewpoint takes on new urgency in the later period, especially in his work on historicism. The expansion of his view of religious history calls for corresponding revisions.

F. EXCURSUS: THE CONCEPT OF THE RELIGIOUS A PRIORI, WITH A GLANCE AT KARL HEIM

If the validity of religious experience, along with the absoluteness of Christianity, is rooted in life and feeling, Troeltsch is concerned to give it a place in the context of our intellectual life and to free it from the suspicion that it has a purely irrational basis.[125]

Fundamentally the motivation of Troeltsch is the same as that which we have noted in Schleiermacher. He does not want to make religion a mere appendage of morality, metaphysics, or psychology. He wants to find for it a special autonomy such as Kant ascribes only to theoretical reason, ethics, and aesthetics. At the same time he does not want religion to be left outside the nexus of our consciousness. He presupposes a correlation between the intelligible I and the suprasensory world.

If Troeltsch is not afraid to speak of religious impulse in this regard, it is because he understands by it an inner vitality that precedes all objective awareness (like the feeling of absolute dependence in Schleiermacher) and that rests on an affixing of the soul by something ultimate, the ground that sustains it. One might recall the at any rate

124. Cf. "Mission," *RGG,* 1st ed., II, 1959ff.
125. Cf. Troeltsch, *Arbeiten Psychologie und Erkenntnistheorie in der Religionswissenschaft* (1905); also *Zur Frage des religiösen A priori,* in *Gesammelte Schriften,* II, 754ff. For a critical discussion cf. A. Nygren, *Die Gültigkeit der religiösen Erfahrung* (1922); F. K. Schumann, *Der Gottesgedanke und der Zerfall der Moderne* (1929), pp. 106ff.
126. Scholz, *Religionsphilosophie* (1921), p. 356.

formally similar way in which Kant thinks that the system of categories is affixed by the *Ding an sich*. In religion we are dealing, Troeltsch believes, with a transcendent reality which provokes reactions in our intellectual household. Because these reactions cannot derive from the circle of experience in this world, but are unique occurrences, there applies to them an a priori that is both before and outside all experiences.

The specific religious experience, then, has a sure place in the nexus of consciousness as an independent phenomenon, being shown to be an essential element in our reason when this is taken in the broadest sense.

Although the influence of Kant is apparent here, the impression forces itself upon us that Troeltsch breaks free from Kantian epistemology to the extent that he does not regard the a priori as transcendental in the true sense but psychologizes it, so that it represents an independent psychological-religious potentiality. Heinrich Scholz has devoted a critical investigation to this transformation of the a priori concept to another dimension.[126] We discern in it the impact made on Troeltsch by James's philosophy of religion. This may be seen in the statement that it is as if there were in the human consciousness a sense of the real, a feeling that something is present, an idea of something objectively existent, which is deeper and more universal than any one special feeling that attests to reality according to the view of modern psychology. So far as religious ideas can awaken this sense of reality, in spite of every criticism we have to believe them, even though they may be weak and indefinite almost to the point of being incomprehensible.[127]

When Troeltsch is concerned to establish the validity of experienced religious reality along such lines, polemical intentions also play a part. Thus he attacks his ancient foe, a theology based on the supernatural, which naively and uncritically accepts traditional religion as a given, and never puts the question of the subjective possibility of certainty. Such a theology loses contact with the other dimensions of the spirit and works in the isolation that Schleiermacher already feared in his *Open Letters*. It also arrives at a simplistic absolutizing of Christianity which fails to take note of religious experiences outside the Christian realm. Again, with his idea of the a priori Troeltsch takes issue with certain secular theories which derive religion genetically, especially along psychological or sociological lines. In this regard he has A. Comte, H. Spencer, and L. Feuerbach especially in view.

To come across the name of Karl Heim in this context might

127. Cf. James, *Varieties of Religious Experience*, pp. 26ff.
128. Cf. his main work *Glaubensgewissheit*, 4th ed. (1949); also his early work

surprise readers, because the great Swabian Pietist, Professor of Systematic Theology at Tübingen, was as distant as possible from Ernst Troeltsch in both thinking and personal and spiritual makeup. Nevertheless, there are some points of comparison which bring the two together in this excursus on the religious a priori.

For one thing, the vital theme of Heim's thinking is that of wrestling with the relativistic threat and wide-ranging reflection on the way to the unconditional, to certainty of faith.[128] In this regard he is less worried by the history of religion and more by the relativism deriving from natural science.[129]

Again, in regard to the validity of religious experience, both Troeltsch and Heim have a common philosophical root in Kant's transcendentalism, and especially in the Neo-Kantianism of H. Rickert.[130] Without laying claim to the idea of a religious a priori, Heim takes a similar course to that of Troeltsch in trying to achieve religious certainty with the help of Kant's nonobjective, transcendental ego.

Heim's goal is to overcome rationalism, chiefly that of scientific provenance, for in it he finds the intellectual problem that afflicts the educated of his day in the search for reliable foundations for faith. His method is to vanquish rationalism with its own weapons, i.e., by thinking it through consistently and showing its consequences, which are absurd and with which one cannot live. The meaningless rationalism to which we are led on this level has itself to be relativized. We thus need a bridge which leads from the this-worldly shore of the visible and perceptible world which is open to the scientist to the otherworldly shore of faith which rests on invisible ground.[131] In his many volumes Heim's effort is to find such a bridge and to show that it is of solid enough construction to carry us.[132]

With some similarity to Kierkegaard, but with different emphases, the destructive and critical part of Heim's system opens with an attempt to fix the limits of objective knowledge. Knowledge that is tied

Das Weltbild der Zukunft (1904), and the outline of his whole system in *Leitfaden der Dogmatik*, 2 vols. For a good introduction cf. A. Koberle, *Karl Heim* (1972).

129. See Heim, *Der christliche Gottesglaube und die Naturwissenschaft* (1949); idem, *Die Wandlung im naturwissenschaftlichen Weltbild*, 2nd ed. (1951); idem, *Weltschöpfung und Weltende* (1952).

130. In the introduction to the 4th edition of *Glaubensgewissheit* Heim alludes specifically to Rickert's work *Der Gegenstand der Erkenntnis*, 6th ed. (1928).

131. Heim, *Weltschöpfung*, p. 5.

132. No theologian has ever wrestled so intensively or expressly with natural science as Heim.

133. Heim, *Leitfaden*, pp. 5-6.

to space, time, and causality runs up against infinite causal sequences both forwards and backwards. Looking back at the past, I have to stop at a certain point without being able to explain why the final point was as it was. Looking ahead to the future the situation is the same as I perhaps reach as far as the freezing of the world, and I then have to stop with the admission that I cannot understand where it is all leading, but it simply is so.

The infinite nature of causal processes means that we are always far from any goal and can never grasp the totality of being. The religious question is thus in irreconcilable contradiction with the objective structure of our thought. For this asks about the eternal meaning of my present situation, the why and wherefore, which can be explained only as I have a grasp of the whole which is not available objectively. If the question of meaning—the religious question—is not to be a hopeless one, the forms of thought and contemplation which lead us into the dead end will have to have their basis in a closed totality of conditions which we can neither see nor imagine, since it is indefinite, but the idea of which we have to have if our views and concepts are to have any meaning.[133] The knotty problem which Heim presents is thus as follows. We cannot grasp the whole of reality with objective thought. Yet we cannot dispense with a grasp of the whole, of the totality of all conditions, for we cannot make do without the certainty of meaning. The certainty that cannot be obtained objectively sustains every moment in which something unconditional touches us. This is true when beyond all conditions or considerations of utility we listen to the unconditional demands of our consciences.

What bridge can there be between the categorically defined outward aspect of reality and the inner view of the I with its orientation to the unconditional? Following Kant and Rickert, Heim develops a picture of the world in which a basic fact is the relation between the nonobjectifiable I (as the subject of experience) and the objective sphere of experience.

This view rejects both materialism and speculative idealism. Both these dissolve the basic relation and change it into a causal one. Materialism makes the I a product of the objective world—one among others. Speculative idealism reverses things and makes the objective world a positing of the I after the manner of Fichte. Both views rest on a similar mythological objectifying of the nonobjectifiable,[134] i.e., on an absolutizing of the category of causality and of the objective thinking

134. Ibid., I, 15.

that rests upon it. Since in this sphere there is no possibility of meaning, of grasping the whole of reality, or of the resultant revelation, one may expect the situation to change when a nonobjective reality can be established and taken seriously.

But this fact of the nonobjectifiable I is not taken seriously if I want to view it again from outside. For then I cannot understand my freedom and the unconditional nature of my responsibility, for I am objectified into the causal nexus.[135] Through this objectification there also arises an exclusive relation between the various specimens of the I, as between A and non-A. Thus a specific I can never achieve the certainty that its personal experience is universally valid.

In truth, however, the transcendental I as the nonobjective basis of the empirical world is so close to us that we cannot objectify it; it is always cognitively transcendental. This nonobjective ego lies in a state that is beyond spatial and temporal limits, so that the exclusive relation is overcome that separates one I from another on an objective view. In this state which is above the categories and forms of perception, we thus have the possibility of a grasp of the whole that breaks through the barriers of space and time.[136] A revelation is possible which one receives and all receive in him, a disclosure which comes at one place and unveils the totality of being.[137]

Heim now introduces the concept of God by seeing God within the sphere of nonobjective reality and (in a way that I cannot wholly understand) identifying the nonobjectifiable with God.[138] The negative side of the identification is readily understandable, for we cannot perceive God in the objective world (as Schleiermacher was saying in his own way with his feeling of "absolute" dependence). When this is attempted, we have the blasphemous absolutizing of the finite to which Paul refers in Rom. 1:23. Also understandable is the thought that we can as little see God as we can the nonobjective I, because both are nearer to us than we are to ourselves.[139] Nevertheless, the confusion that we find in Heim between God and the nonobjective I seems to be much closer to the metaphysics of Fichte than Heim himself would care for.

Only after establishing the possibility of a revelation that encompasses the totality can Heim speak about the figure of Jesus, which only by its impress can impart the certainty that Jesus is the bearer of the

135. Kant worked out the implications of this objectifying of the ego in *Critique of Practical Reason*, PhB, pp. 110-11, 115.

136. Heim, *Glaubensgewissheit*, pp. 272-73.

137. Heim, *Leitfaden*, p. 17.

138. Heim, *Glaubensgewissheit*, pp. 245, 273.

139. Ibid., p. 246.

revelation, the heart of human history, and that from him we learn the meaning of the whole. Because Jesus as Revealer himself belongs to the transcendent sphere of the nonobjective, because we cannot know him objectively but only by doing his will and in personal commitment, we are independent of all historical criticism relative to him. We have always to remember that historical science deals with causal connections and hence in principle it is in insoluble tension with that which is certain to us in faith, i.e., nonobjectively.

In this way, then, Heim ties the validity of the idea of God to the affirmation of a specific view of things. This view cannot be enforced, however, for there can be no establishing either the nonobjective I or its basic relation to the objective world. In this decisive question of philosophy we cannot convince one another by logic. But once someone is clear about this transcendental ego which is beyond space and time, and which may thus achieve a grasp of the whole of reality, for that person the basic thesis of criticism has the certainty of an axiom which cannot be proved but which needs no proof because it is self-evident.[140]

It is self-evident—and yet there are those whom one tries in vain to convince concerning it. This philosophical difficulty, which outwardly recalls a vicious circle, constitutes for Heim a theological moment. At this point I confront a final and basic decision which I can no longer make with the help of logical arguments that relate only to the objective sphere. Furthermore, how I decide is not a matter of my own will. Yes and No are not alternatives between which I can choose. Decision has, as it were, been made concerning me when I affirm a view of the world which represents the axiom of the nonobjectifiable ego and which thus makes it possible for me to conceive of revelation. In the moment of choice I already stand in the Yes even though theoretically considered the No is just as possible. I thus hover over the abyss of antithetical possibilities without falling in. This can be so only in virtue of that which is nonobjective. The decision, then, has its basis not in a mark of distinction but solely in the nonobjectifiable itself. If I name this God, I am naming the final decision of God in virtue of which I find myself at this moment in the Yes, i.e., grace, the position which enables me to hover over the abyss without falling in, faith alone.[141]

The question which argument cannot answer, namely, whether I recognize the basic axiom of the nonobjective, transcendental ego, can thus be answered only by a decision, and paradoxically only by one that can be taken only from the position of a Yes that is imparted to me. This

140. Ibid., p. 73.
141. Ibid., pp. 251-52.

means that I decide as decision is made concerning me. This decision concerning me does not depend on my physical or psychological makeup, my environment, or other factors in the objective world, but exclusively on that nonobjective factor which I call God.

To that extent one might say that the final religious decision—like other nineteenth-century conceptions, especially those of Kantian theologians—has a definite similarity to practical reason. A few essential nuances are unmistakable.

First, practical reason does not include only the postulate of the concept of God, as in Kant. It brings acts of decision already into the sphere of knowledge that prepares the way for the concepts of God and revelation. Second, the ethical decisions that practical reason reaches are already enclosed in a theological fact, namely, that decision is made concerning us.[142]

This final perspective, which rests on a decision, and which with the help of the nonobjectivity of the ego opens up an understanding of meaning, a survey of the whole of reality, and hence the possible thought of transcendence (God, revelation, and grace), may certainly be set in analogy to what Troeltsch calls the religious a priori, and to what is for him the condition of being able to locate an understanding of religious truth in the nexus of human consciousness. This analogy—in connection with the attempt to escape the threat of relativism and to find an absolute—is what gave me the bold idea of linking Troeltsch and Heim as an excursus.

It is perhaps related to this connection with a distinct philosophy that Heim's grandiose effort has taken a back seat, or even been forgotten altogether, in ages of other philosophies.[143] Every theology is in debt to its time, as A. Köberle once said. Along these lines one might say that Heim owed it to his time when with the means of philosophical reflection at his disposal he contended for a bridge to transcendence, to certainty of faith.

Only with hesitation do I finally touch on a point which for many—but not all—students seems to lower the honorable status of Heim as compared to Troeltsch.

In Troeltsch we come up against the basis of the conflict between relativism and the absolute which he felt in his own person to the very end and never resolved. I have to ask, however, whether Heim ever felt

---

142. On the significance of ethical decision, cf. ibid., pp. 245, 253ff.

143. Although Troeltsch is partly rooted in the Neo-Kantian philosophy of his time, it is worth considering why he still has greater relevance than Heim. I discuss this question further in what follows.

the same conflict in himself even though he made it the theme of his life's work. A look at his story, in which there do not seem to be any deep crises (although who can finally say?), suggests that his normative concern was not really a deadly struggle with relativism but pastoral compassion for his secularized contemporaries, for the cultured among the despisers whom he saw threatened by intellectual distress in the matter of meaning, and hence by nihilism. If I may put it rather loosely, it seems to me that he was more a deacon of thought who vicariously took this problem upon himself. Perhaps it was less his own need than sympathy with that of others which led him to take upon his shoulders the enterprise of this work of thought. Might this be the reason why we do not find in him the elemental force of intellectual struggle that we detect in Troeltsch? But even if it is, as I suggest, does this "merely" sympathetic love really have to mean the disparagement that is feared? What norm have we by which to decide this?

At this point in the interpretation of Heim we come up against a barrier which we have to respect as one that we cannot cross.

G. THE SHARPENED PROBLEM OF RELATIVISM (SECOND PHASE)

After that excursus we take up again our presentation of Troeltsch. We recall that in his 1902 work on the absoluteness of Christianity he was looking for traces of transcendence in the history of religion, trying to ascribe a special position to Christianity, and granting validity, so far as we can see, to the experience of faith which finds Christ to be final.

The breath of a relativizing reservation which still blows over this concept of absoluteness developed into a storm in the next decade when the ideas occupied him which took shape in his writings on historicism.[144] Already in the preface to the second edition of *The Absoluteness of Christianity* (Dec. 16, 1911) he mentions that the situation in which the work was written was not the same as it is today, and that the problems have become much more acute in the last decade.

What was it that changed for Troeltsch?

In connection with the above quotation we might say that the historical outlook had greatly broadened. Hence many of the previous rankings of values and the previous ideas of absoluteness had become provincial in retrospect. The problem of relativism also has a fresh look.

---

144. Troeltsch, *Der Historismus und seine Probleme*, in *Gesammelte Schriften*, III (cited as *Überwindung*); idem, *Der Historismus und seine Überwindung* (1924; cited as *Historismus*).

The change is stated most baldly in the five addresses on historicism and its overcoming.

A new penetration into the broad field of religious history, and especially an acquaintance with Buddhism and Brahminism, showed Troeltsch that even outside Christianity there is purely human and inward religiosity which in its own way can appeal to inner certainty and commitment. We have to consider that under very different historical, geographical, and social conditions these religious values have taken their own special form suited to the individual localities. Even the findings of science and logic will show strongly individual distinctions, even down to their deepest and most inward basis, under different skies and on different ground. He does not now think, as he did ten years before, that he knows so well what is really universal and absolute in spite of changing relations and possibilities of understanding.[145] Christianity is God's face as it is turned to us Europeans. It is the way in which we in our situation experience and feel God's revelation. It claims us and hence it is redemptive for us. But other human groups in different cultural relations might experience their contact with the divine life in individually very different ways and hence very sincerely experience their own absoluteness.[146]

1. The Involvement of Religion in the Prevailing Culture

Two slogans denote the new outlook of Troeltsch on the relation between Christianity and the higher religions, and in so doing outline for us the new inquiry into absoluteness. These two slogans are "cultural relations" and "individuality."

The historical approach convinced Troeltsch of the deep involvement of the religions, including Christianity, in prevailing cultures. Even the idea of personalism does not have universal validity. It develops in the sphere of Western Christianity and cannot be simply transported to other areas. If we take this involvement in culture seriously, we confront the difficulty that we can compare values only as we do not isolate the religions but compare the total cultural systems of which the religions are an undetachable ingredient.[147] But who dare make such comparisons in view of the complexity of such systems?

The historical approach increasingly nudges Troeltsch away from the theological inquiry which is crucial in his work on absoluteness. It pushes him in the direction of a general cultural investigation. This

145. *Überwindung*, pp. 75-76.
146. Ibid., p. 78.
147. Ibid., p. 79.

weakens the whole idea that Christianity has to be accorded supreme rank as the point of convergence in the history of religion. Such a notion is no longer essential. To put it sharply, we have only our provincial European standards. We may owe their origin to Christianity, but this does not make them less limited. They do not command universal criteria to which we may subject the fulness of cultural and religious individuations. These must be evaluated by their own standards—just as they for their part must consider that these standards apply only in their own sphere.

Relativism thus takes on new force. History does not even achieve approximation, as in Kierkegaard. The eternal inserted into history constantly eludes us, like the artificial hare to which the dogs seem so close that they almost have it, but then it escapes again. The sun of the absolute has hardly begun to shine before a new cloud-bank comes before it like a curtain and obscures it again.

Christianity thus loses its missionary task. It might still have a civilizing role in relation to primitive tribal religions, but this is more a matter of culture than of the Christian ingredient. In relation to the higher religions, however, it cannot engage in missions, for their life-style better meets the specific needs of their cultural sphere than an imported Christianity.[148] At most, what we now today call "dialogue" among the religions might extend our own outlook and help people to find their own religious identity.

The development of individual inclinations works toward the final goal of a syncretistic melting down of that which exists first in the different concretions of religious need. In this ultimate goal we see a metaphysical hypothesis that for Troeltsch lies on the margin of science and cannot be objectified by it, namely, that historical movement will ultimately come to rest in a final unity which in its own movement escapes our grasp, and which is only very inadequately described by such words as unity or totality.[149]

At this point in Troeltsch we come up against the paradoxical fact that in the last resort historicism dissolves the concept of a religious absolute, putting in its way the obstacle of cultural individuations that cannot be overcome, and yet the same historicism obviously calls for a fundamental metaphysical assumption which it cannot itself deduce objectively but without which its subject becomes a disconnected fluctuation of pointless movements.[150] One may debate whether this as-

---

148. Ibid., pp. 78-79.

149. *Historismus*, p. 173.

150. Intimated already in the earlier work *Über historische und dogmatische Methode in der Theologie* (1898), in *Gesammelte Schriften*, II, 728-29.

sumed absolute is imported by Troeltsch into history or arises under the impression that history is not breaking up in chaos but has a final basis of integration. But no matter how the decision goes, there is in any case an absolute that transcends history.

2. The Link between Religion and Individuation

The metaphysical background of history that Troeltsch presupposes comes to expression in the second of the two slogans that mark his view of the history of religion. The concept of individuality has two frames of reference. The first, of Neo-Kantian origin, is purely formal. The second, which derives from his mysticism, is a higher metaphysical one.

(1) The Neo-Kantian tradition within which Troeltsch thinks is what causes him to stress the concept of individuality in his historical work. In this tradition natural science and history differ inasmuch as the former makes supraindividual and universal law its subject, whereas history takes as its theme the specific individual example. Thus Rickert in his work *Die Grenzen der naturwissenschaftslichen Begriffsbildung* (5th ed. 1929) says that methodologically natural science follows a universalizing tendency and history an individualizing tendency. Similarly, W. Windelband distinguishes between the nomothetic method of natural science and the idiographic method of history.[151] On a poultry farm zoologists are interested in egg production and general matters, not in special cases. But when we come to a historical personage like Napoleon, historians are not concerned about what he shares with others (e.g., his military career or physiological matters like diet and digestion, etc.) but in the individual contours. It may be noted in passing that sociological approaches have made a total distinction between the two methods impossible.

Thus Troeltsch cannot treat individual concretions as mere "cases" that he may subsume under a general law. He finds in them the visible representation of innumerable individual processes within a comprehensive whole which we can never see beyond or apart from these cases.[152]

(2) Along with this more neutral concept of individuality is a more metaphysical understanding.[153] In this regard he adopts the Leibnizian idea of the monad. The monad is an "individual totality"— Troeltsch likes this term—which does not exist in isolation but shares a

151. *Präludien*, II, 9th ed. (1924).
152. *Historismus*, p. 120.
153. Ibid., chaps. 2–3.

universal consciousness and thus participates in all reality. The monads are like a series of electric bulbs which are mysteriously connected to the electrical center by an invisible wire, shining out individually but still fed from the center.[154]

The idea of individuality, then, does not embrace merely the facticity of what is specific and unique, as in Rickert and Windelband. It has to do with given individualizations of the ideal, concretions of what ought to be.[155] The ego is not just an individual example. As a human ego it is a personal construct endowed with freedom and responsibility. It must be described not merely in terms of what is but also in terms of what ought to be. It is to be defined in terms of an ideal or norm. If the individual is enmeshed in the general relativity of values, within the relative an absolute is alive and creative.[156] In short, there is a kind of essential and individual identity of finite spirits with the infinite spirit and hence an intuitive participation in its concrete content and active and living unity.[157] In the life and activity of the individual multiplicity of history there comes to expression the activity of the divine life itself. In the relations of history an absolute that transcends history is manifest.[158] For Troeltsch, then, individuality is not restricted to the personal sphere but related to the individual religions, to the religious monads which participate in the absolute, in the general consciousness, but are still the necessary media without which final truth cannot come into view.

Here is the hermeneutical key to an understanding of other religions and cultures. In this regard Troeltsch speaks of understanding what is alien to us.[159] Congeniality and sympathy are not enough. What we need are ontological rather than psychological conditions of understanding, although we still have to have an element of discernment and divination. The ontological condition is that in virtue of our identity with the general consciousness we bear the alien element within ourselves. It participates in the general consciousness in the same way as we do, so that a bond of understanding links us to it.

In the second phase, then, the concept of absoluteness found a decisive place. The question is no longer whether a single historical phenomenon like Christianity can represent the absolute. Christianity, too, can have the significance only of a religious monad which in just

---

154. See Köhler, *Ernst Troeltsch*, p. 367.
155. *Historismus*, pp. 200-201.
156. Ibid., pp. 211-12.
157. Ibid., p. 677.
158. Ibid., pp. 677-78.
159. Ibid., pp. 684ff.

the same way as others participates in the general consciousness. It is simply a finite example in which the infinite is specifically present. The all-embracing absolute lies outside history. It is the condition, however, on which alone finite individualities can meet and understand one another. In this sense, one might say, it is the true religious a priori.

H. CONCLUSION

In sum, we might say that, according to Troeltsch, in the course of development Christianity increasingly becomes no more than the representation of a unity in which the development of the Mediterranean peoples debouches. The totality of the European peoples controlled by Christianity is no more than a small part of the totality of history.[160]

As I see it, the view of this totality becomes increasingly more gloomy. The prognosis of a syncretistic fusion of the religious monads threatens finally to evaporate. The vision of the future that history—or historicism?—can furnish is extremely pessimistic as we have it in the *Glaubenslehre*. We cannot answer the question of final religious and cultural unity. The weariness and exhaustion that can overtake great cultures opposes belief in uniform and mounting progress. So, too, does the rise of new conflicts and difficulties with every new situation. It is hard to envision the final state of humanity as one of uniform earthly perfection; great problems in external life are more likely. The bleakness of this outlook cannot be relieved by faith. There is no possibility of deducing continuous development from this, for the focus is not on an earthly goal but on a broader development beyond this life. Hence we can hardly expect general progress but only new battles on new fronts.[161]

If, however, faith cannot open up positive vistas regarding the course of history and its higher goal, what significance can it have? Faith in a general rather than a specifically Christian sense does at least assure for us at every point in this dubious history the possibility of winning the fight between flesh and spirit with the religious forces at our disposal, and hence of breaking through at every point to eternity. Christian faith is simply a quantitative enhancing of this possibility. In the Christian

160. *Glaubenslehre*, p. 320. These lectures were published posthumously (1925) by Maria Troeltsch on the basis of notes taken by Gertrud von le Fort, although the present references come from the script, not from the freely delivered lectures, and are thus authentic. The lectures were given in Heidelberg.

161. Ibid., pp. 320-21.

certainty of God we have the greatest strength for this breakthrough and can thus ethicize the battle of life as much as is possible for a will that is ready for sacrifice.[162] At any rate, we might add, this is true for the Christian West.

In his final period, as we have seen, Troeltsch presses on to a mystical spiritualizing which obviously brings him closer and closer to Hegel. (We need only recall such terms as *universal consciousness, divine spirit*, etc.) Increasingly, we find him looking away from concrete history to something that transcends it. It seems as if he is turning aside from the present experience of history to history itself. Certainly, he never denies that the way to this mystical reality, which is the final goal as well as the final datum, leads by way of history. The sense and experience of this final reality come from history and not from abstract speculation. Characteristic of his historical thinking, however, is that he now speaks about the horizon or margins of history where a sphere of reality opens up that cannot be grasped by historical study. "On its margins such study moves into a mysterious background of universal life, and without this we could not maintain the independence of its logic and method."[163]

This is a very revealing sentence. The mystical background is not a final result of the encounter with history. It does not lie on the dotted line of a postulate. It is certainly the goal toward which history strives, but it is also the presupposition of the encounter. The logic and method of historical investigation depend on the existence of this all-embracing transcendent factor.

We have already seen how far this is so. Only because the individual monads are related by this metaphysical reality, and stand in final identity with it, can we understand what is alien. But the encounter with history is bound up with this understanding. In its logic and method historical inquiry is a metaphysical undertaking which is sustained, conditioned, and defined at every step by this extrahistorical absolute, and made possible by it as its a priori.

In face of this, one might put what is admittedly an open and daring question. If Troeltsch could have begun again, and done his research on this basis, would he have become another Hegel, an author who starts with the absolute spirit and regards history as its unfolding? Is not this idea of a reincarnation suggested when we read that a final common goal lies in the unknown future and perhaps in a hereafter, and that a common basis resides in the divine spirit which is coming to light and consciousness, which is enclosed in the finite spirit, and from

162. Ibid., p. 321.
163. *Historismus*, p. 87.

whose final unity with this finite spirit all the variety of movement proceeds?[164]

Wherever his way might have led, Troeltsch was at least a pioneer. And the new path opened up or at any rate prepared by him goes far beyond the point where he himself had to break off. Nor can the way to any of the fields in which he worked bypass him.[165]

After him the path has in fact led in a different direction. What followed was dialectical theology. This grew and ripened in antithesis to him. To that degree it did not bypass him. But how about its children? Have they not made a thesis of what was once an antithesis? This could happen, however, only as an antithetical rejection arose against it, so that in theology we do in fact have the new battles on new fronts that Troeltsch expected. The question may be permitted at this point whether his own struggle with historicism and its relativistic consequences is still a live one, or whether one may correctly assume that it has come to an end. Yet there are some problems in the solution of which others cannot represent us, so that in that sense they are never outdated, but are always contemporary in Kierkegaard's sense.

164. Ibid., p. 82.
165. Cf. Paul Tillich on his death (1923) in WW, XII, 175.

Epilogue: Results

THE ANSWER AND CRISIS OF DIALECTICAL THEOLOGY

Historicism reached its end with Troeltsch. History can lead to nothing absolute. The attempt so to harmonize faith's sense of transcendence with history that one is concerned to find traces of transcendence in history was unsuccessful. Whatever was found was provincially limited and subject to individuation. Only too easily it might have been regarded as universal and comprehensive, but a cosmic extension of outlook showed how provincial it was, and made it apparent that even Christianity is subject to the same limitation. Furthermore, religions came to be seen as no more than (modest) parts of much broader cultural circles, and Christianity was banished to the cultural island of the Mediterranean West.

The link between faith in something unconditional and life, or, let us say, history, did not bring the vital rooting of religion, even the Christian religion, that was hoped for, but simply presented with historical means a heterogeneous and polymorphous set of transcendental adumbrations behind which we may not seek.[1] (We should now call it pluralism.)

In face of the historical experience of reality the longing for the unconditional thus found itself consigned to a vacuum which could be filled for Troeltsch only by a leap into spiritualizing, into the far side of history. For those who watch this tragedy of thought this acts as an emergency exit when all other ways to overcome relativism are blocked.

1. Thielicke uses here the fashionable German word "hinterfragen."—
TRANS.

546

After this conclusion, of which the great figure of Troeltsch is a representative, and which is not without its own greatness, a radical new beginning had to come. This new beginning took especially the form of dialectical theology, and in the first instance it came with explosive force in Karl Barth's *Romans*.

To understand the powerful influence of Barth, we must consider that he came not merely at the end of a development, i.e., with the relativistic upshot of historicism and the decay of the cultural Protestantism of liberalism, but that this wider impact started with the breakup of values and institutions at the end of World War I. The elemental impression made by his message at this *kairos* may be compared only with *The Decline of the West* by Oswald Spengler, a work which from another angle touched the nerve of the historical hour.

We have here no less than a prophetic message. It had prophetic rank because it interpreted the historical fate that had overtaken the West in terms of the Word of God, and found in it a judgment on de-Christianized culture and even more so on a de-Christianized Christianity which was forgetting its task. The fact that the interpretation was in terms of God's Word shows already that the standards for the understanding of the *kairos* are not taken from history itself but are found beyond it in a revelation that is directed to history. Thus we do not have here a mere continuation of the theological dialogue in new phrases. How could that be when the dialogue had sunk into a brooding silence (which did not prevent theologians from disguising the silence behind continuing chatter!). No, a new theme was introduced. New questions and criteria were put on the agenda and new discussions with new participants were started.

The vacuum into which this new theology actualized in terms of the Word of God moved was also the vacuum that along with other intellectual and spiritual processes historicism had left behind. This generation saw itself at the end of all human possibilities, including the historical experiment. Barth proclaimed this end.

Nevertheless, proclaiming it in the light of God's Word and in the name of God's possibilities, he was not simply a prophet of woe or even a pessimistic critic of culture. He was the messenger of a new hope. He did not find this hope in history or its regenerative power. No, history, like all other human forces, lay under sentence of death. This corpse defied all attempts to revive it by the creative powers of humanity. The breath which would reawaken the bones on this field of the dead (Ezek. 37) did not blow in history but came from the Spirit of God blowing into the dead world of history as the Spirit of resurrection.

Speaking thus to his age in the name of God's Word, Barth did not at first have a material message in view. He primarily found in God's Word an expression of judgment on the end of all human possibilities. This No understood as a Yes was God's Word for Barth.[2] Within that end, the Yes points to the possibilities of God. Before *Romans* appeared, and during the war, Barth could already say in 1916: "Where faith is, in the midst of the old world of war and money and death, there is born a new spirit out of which grows a new world, the world of the righteousness of God."[3] But we can hear this Yes only when we have first heard the No to all the human arrogance which thinks it can interpret and shape history. "It is because *God* says Yes to us that the No of existence here is so fundamental and unescapable."[4] Hence the new theology carries with it a thorough awakening to the "relativity of all secondary thoughts and things, a readiness for *last* questions and answers, an awaiting and a hastening toward *last* decisions, a listening for the sound of the *last* trump which makes known *the* truth which is beyond the grave."[5]

In the second edition of *Romans*[6] these thoughts find a fiery formulation that often sounds as though a specific rejection of Troeltsch's historicism is in view, as when Barth refers to Jesus as the break between a plane that we know and one that we do not know, or when he speaks of him as the unknown plane that intersects the plane that we know "vertically from above." The eternity that breaks in with the resurrection of Jesus has no connections with time, but as the absolute, transcendent limit of history it strikes it just as indirectly as a tangent touches a circle only at a single point.[7]

In these first stages of dialectical theology the eternal, or, as Troeltsch would say, the absolute and unconditional, is not present *in* time. The resurrection, or, and this is the same thing (!), the return of Christ, is not a historical event. "The moment when the last trump is sounded . . . comes *en atomo,* says Paul, in an indivisible, non-temporal, eternal now. Is it yesterday, tomorrow, today? Is it ever? Is it never? In each case we may answer Yes and No. For, though our times are in God's hands, God's times are not in ours. . . . Resurrection means

2. Cf. Althaus in *ZSTh* (1924) 770.
3. K. Barth, "The Righteousness of God," in *The Word of God and the Word of Man* (Grand Rapids, 1935), pp. 25-26.
4. Barth, "The Problem of Ethics Today," in ibid., p. 169.
5. Barth, "Biblical Questions, Insights, and Vistas," in ibid., p. 83.
6. This is a radical revision of the 1st edition. In particular Barth eliminates what he came to regard as Platonic and Kantian tendencies.
7. *Romans,* pp. 29-30.

the *new world,* the world of a new quality and kind. *Qualiter? totaliter aliter.*"[8]

Along similar lines Barth vividly rejects the idea of a delay in the *parousia* that has allowed the establishment of the church in time and recognition of the world in all its secularity. In *Romans* he is also wildly scornful of those who yield to the temporal expectation of a crude, brutal, theatrical spectacle at the end of the world, and who then, when rightly this does not come, comfortably go back to sleep again. How can anything fail to come when by definition it cannot come anyway?

Christ's resurrection and return do not take place in history. For this reason they can coincide. Both are immediate to each moment of our lives. In a paradoxical way they are thus simultaneous for us, so that to await the *parousia* means simply to take our actual situation seriously as it is and not to sleep.[9]

Barth, then, rejects all attempts to tie revelation to a historical event that we can fix, to understand time as the vessel of eternity, and then if possible (cf. Troeltsch) to look in this time for traces of the eternal and unconditional. In this regard he gives evidence of the influence of that fascinating theological eccentric and friend of Nietzsche, Franz Overbeck.[10] For Overbeck church history is a history of decline. Christianity decays the moment it enters history and makes an arrangement with it, forfeiting the high tension of its original eschatology. Barth agrees. He quotes Overbeck's protest against the historicizing of Christianity. "'Historic Christianity—that is Christianity subjected to time—is an absurdity.' History is precisely the basis on which Christianity can *not* be established; for 'neither Christ himself nor the faith which he found among his disciples has ever had any historical existence at all under the name of Christianity. . . . History is an abyss into which Christianity has been thrown wholly against its will.'"[11]

To express the detachment of the Christian saving event from history, Barth uses in modified form an expression that he took from Overbeck, namely, "primal history." As regards the past, the only possible location for Christianity is not in history, but *before* it as *primal history.* Only nonhistorical concepts, standards, and perspectives can enable us to understand this Christianity which is not Christianity in any

8. Barth, "Biblical Questions, Insights, and Vistas," in *The Word of God and the Word of Man,* pp. 89-91.

9. *Romans,* pp. 500-501.

10. Cf. esp. his *Christentum und Kultur,* ed. C. A. Bernoulli (1919).

11. Barth, "Unsettled Questions for Theology Today," in *Theology and Church* (New York, repr. 1962), p. 61. See also A. Pfeiffer, *F. Overbecks Kritik des Christentums* (1975), esp. pp. 79-97.

historiographical sense, and hence to speak about it and to represent it.[12] Here the implicit antithesis to Troeltsch is given its sharpest edge.

In this context we cannot pursue the different phases of Barth's development that follow this initial thrust. We may simply note that in connection with Christology, and especially the doctrine of the incarnation, his attitude to history changes. We see this in the first form of the later *Church Dogmatics,* in the 1927 Prolegomena to the *Christlichen Dogmatik im Entwurf,* in which he is critical of the idea of suprahistory, and implicitly of his own earlier term *primal history.* In the incarnation God posits himself as flesh, as man in time. He encounter us. This is revelation. Thus and thus far revelation is history—not suprahistory, but history.[13] The concern lest the categories and methods of historiography should again become normative for an understanding of God in the flesh then causes him to state that although history is a predicate of revelation, revelation is not a predicate of history.[14] This means that we learn from revelation what history is, not from history what revelation may be.

The early period of *Romans,* when the infinitely qualitative distinction between time and eternity is to the fore, and when Barth opposed the entry of revelation into history, inevitably involved difficulties for theological ethics.[15] For how can one act with a true basis, program, or goal in a world that bears no analogy to God's will, that is radically apart from it, that lies in the darkness of the divine No lit up "only" by grace? In this worldly night all cats are gray. There can be no distinguishing between good and bad, or more or less good. All that I do is finally corrupt. Can the question of the rightness of my action have any meaning when everything stands under the proviso that all I do even in the best of lives is in vain? The calling into question of the whole complex of our existence and nature, of all our known ways and byways, of all that is serious or frivolous, of all our righteousness and our sins, our beliefs and atheisms and skepticisms, leads in our ethical decisions to a "perhaps and perhaps not."[16]

As regards concrete action in history, this involves only indifference. What other option is there when everything is bad as such?[17] The

12. Barth, *Theology and Church,* p. 61.

13. *Christlichen Dogmatik,* p. 232.

14. Ibid.

15. See Barth, *Romans,* 6th ed. (London, 1933, repr. 1980), p. 10. This throws fresh light on our attempt in chap. 13 above to show Hegelian features in Barth and to argue that his dependence on the doctrine of the decrees later imperils his relation to history (the salvation event).

16. Barth, *Romans,* p. 292.

17. Ibid., pp. 479-80.

existing order, and the institutionalism which in history is formatively and constitutively bound up with it, denote only that we hypocritically clear ourselves.[18] No doubt we criticize concrete defects. But in the last resort this cannot mean that our norm is an improvement of the order or the idea of an ideal order. No, seeing the defects in what is there can only be an occasion for recognizing that what is there is bad as such. If unsettling by God brings us into critical antithesis to life, this is the most positive and fruitful of all possible achievements, Barth can already say in 1919.[19]

We see at this point how the retreat from history, expressed in the formula "vertically from above" and in the comparison with a tangent, is relevant to the working relation to history, i.e., in ethics. Even if casuistic directions are not sought, but only normative points of orientation,[20] we need the decisive premise that there is some analogy (however broken) between God's reality and ours, between God's commands and human norms.[21] If there is here only an infinitely qualitative distinction, an absence of norms results which makes it impossible for theology to say anything about questions of culture, of politics, and even of personal life-style.

Parenthetically, I might offer some biographical illustrations. First, when as students at Bonn in 1931 and 1932 we used to ask our teacher, Karl Barth, for his position on the urgent political problems of the day, he would not take an official stand from the rostrum but would devote private discussions to such issues. This meant that he had nothing to say about the historical present as a theologian. Naturally he had his private views, but these were the "reasonable" views of an alert contemporary. Second, when at Heidelberg (1936-1941) I had many conversations with the friendly neurologist Victor von Weizsäcker, in which we discussed theological neuroses. In this connection he asked how to explain the fact that many (but not all) Barthians could very earnestly proclaim God's judgment from the pulpit but often condone libertinage outside it without feeling any contradiction, but in all good conscience. For myself I could only refer to the ethical indifference which may be noted in the earlier Barth. (The observations of Weizsäcker also related to a period already past.)

It is always a risk to engage in historical interpretation even

---

18. Ibid., p. 478.

19. Barth, "The Christian's Place in Society," in *The Word of God and the Word of Man*, pp. 273ff.

20. This is one of the decisive theses of *ThE*, vol. I.

21. This is not meant in the same sense as the *analogia entis* of Przywara; cf. *ThE*, I, 390.

when it deals with a time that one has lived through. Aware of the risk, I still want to try to work out some of the ecclesiastical consequences of the ethical deficiency.

It sounds almost nonsensical for me to say that the very Barth who would later head the church's resistance to Hitler was responsible in part for the soft flank which enabled Nazi ideology to make its inroads. To be sure, Barth's theology prepared the church to see the threat to its basis of faith, and to ward it off with the battle cry: "The church must remain the church." Yet because of the ethical gap he could not prepare the church to perceive with the same clarity the ideologically controlled foreign policy, cultural policy, and racial policy, and therefore the indirect attack upon the Christian view of life. To that extent Bonhoeffer was right to criticize the Confessing Church for limiting its resistance to an inner church struggle and not taking up its political responsibilities. (We shall see later how under the pressure of such insights Barth later made a theological switch.) Barth's earlier retreat from political ethics, and from ethics in general, left a vacuum into which an anti-Christian politics could move with little opposition so long as it did not affect the direct confession of the church, whether by secularist contradiction or institutional penetration (the "German Christians"). But indirect invasion and infiltration are part of the strategy of totalitarian ideology.

Barth himself would later blame the church's vulnerability to the new paganism on the Lutheran distinctions between law and gospel and the two kingdoms.[22] In this regard he obviously had in mind crude distortions of the distinctions, especially in Neo-Lutheranism.[23] Here he rightly found it damaging that the secular kingdom and its orders were removed from the sphere of theological responsibility and left under the control of the rulers of this world. But he still seemed to have a blind spot and not to see that at the decisive period of its breakthrough dialectical theology had espoused a similar irrelevance of theology to the evaluation of historical situations, although on different grounds. The Confessing Church would hardly have been conceivable had not Barth's theology prepared the way for it. But its initial helplessness in face of cultural and racial infiltration is also hardly conceivable without Barth.

22. Cf. K. Barth, *Die evangelische Kirche in Deutschland nach dem Zusammenbruch des Dritten Reiches* (1946), pp. 26ff.; H. Diem, *K. Barths Kritik am deutschen Luthertum* (1947); H. Schmidt, "Das Kreuz der Wirklichkeit . . . ," *Die mündige Welt,* IV, 79ff.

23. Cf. the dreadful Ansbacher Ratschlag of 1934, which unfortunately even Althaus and Elert signed, or the equally dreadful statements of Bishop Marahrens in 1938 (Diem, *Barths Kritik,* pp. 71-72). For a critical analysis of Luther's teaching cf. *ThE,* I, 359ff.

It is no wonder, then, that dialectical theology broke apart under the pressure of the Third Reich and the sharper questions that it raised.[24] In the present context we can only give a sketch of how this came about.

(1) Emil Brunner noted the ethical vacuum left by Barth, and in a work in 1934 championed the thesis that theology might embrace anthropological insights such as our human endowment with reason and conscience. Apart from this natural light the connection between God's will and our human existence would be inconceivable.[25] Barth replied with an angry rebuff entitled "No!,"[26] in which he argued for the radical ignoring of such insights. As he saw it, we can only pass by natural theology as by an abyss into which we must not look if we are not to fall into it. We can only turn our backs upon it with horror and indignation as the great temptation and source of error, not engaging in it. In a true rejection of natural theology we do not stare at the serpent to be transfixed, hypnotized, and bitten by it; when we see it we beat it with a stick and kill it. A true rejection of natural theology is possible only when there is a final lack of interest in it.[27]

As though the problem would go away if only there were no declaration of interest in it! In fact, the very lack of interest could itself have fateful results. For if the power which impels us toward a natural knowledge of God, and which uses reason and conscience as materials for this purpose, does not become a theme of theological observation and criticism, the danger arises that it will sneak up on us unseen and unthematically, and rob us of the sober criteria by which to unmask it. If appearances do not decieve, Barth himself became a victim in this way. His work *Rechtfertigung und Recht* in 1937, and several pieces during World War II,[28] seem to be very much exposed to the danger of reaching theological verdicts on democracy and totalitarianism not from the theological center but on political grounds, which may be perfectly rational and are sometimes specifically Swiss, but which are all justifiable only on the secular level. At this point natural theology, although it is

---

24. Cf. C. Gestrich, *Neuzeitliches Denken und die Spaltung der dialektischen Theologie* (1977); Klaus Scholder, *Die Kirchen und das Dritte Reich*, I (1977); G. Gloege, "Evangelisches Weltbewusstsein heute," in *Heilsgeschehen und Welt* (1965), pp. 286ff.

25. E. Brunner, "Nature and Grace," in *Natural Theology* (London, 1946), pp. 15ff.

26. K. Barth, "No!" in *Natural Theology* (1946), pp. 67ff. Cf. also E. Brunner, *Man in Revolt* (Philadelphia, 1947), pp. 68ff., 499ff.; idem, *Revelation and Reason* (Philadelphia, 1946), pp. 309ff.; *ThE*, I, 321ff.

27. *Natural Theology*, pp. 75-76.

28. *Eine Schweizer Stimme 1938-1945* (Zurich, 1948).

not a theme and has been dismissed from consideration, celebrates
something of a triumph. Brunner's solution may be open to criticism,[29]
but at least he saw the problem which Barth obstinately refused to see
even as a problem.

(2) Bultmann tried to overcome the nonhistorical element in
Barth's thinking in another way. With the help of Heidegger's ontology
he worked out an anthropological "preunderstanding" which comes
into contact with the kerygma and forms the hermeneutical presupposition for its understanding.[30] In face of this Barth thinks that his
reservations about natural theology and the inclusion of anthropological insights are confirmed. He rightly puts to Bultmann the
question whether the NT message begins with an explanation of the
self-experience of its recipients.[31] Like me, he thinks that the stress on
the anthropological preunderstanding not only forms a bridge for
understanding but surreptitiously becomes a normative criterion for
what a compelling kerygma can be.[32] Here one can understand Barth's
concern to reject natural theology, although the ignoring of the problem
is an excessive expression of that concern and one which involved a
momentous ethical deficiency.

(3) Friedrich Gogarten also tried fill the ethical gap by incor-
porating anthropology in theology. He did this by following E. Grise-
bach—he, too, had someone to vouch for his particular philosophy and
anthropology—interpreting the I-Thou encounter as a created relation
and the orders as institutional forms of the divine law.[33] On this basis
Gogarten arrived at a provisional identification of the law of God and
the nomos of the people, and then it was only a step to acceptance of
the Nazi version of the nomos of the people.[34]

Under the severe ideological pressure of the Third Reich, Barth
inevitably found himself forced into ethical and political positions which
necessitated some change in theological principle. The first requirement
was that he should solve the problem of analogy; without such a solution
he could find no basis for ethical decisions. But how can there be analogy
between eternity and time when their infinite qualitative distinction is

29. Cf. my *Geschichte und Existenz*, 2nd ed. (1964), pp. 104ff.

30. Cf. *EF*, I, passim.

31. K. Barth, "Rudolf Bultmann, Ein Versuch, ihn zu verstehen," *ThSt* 34
(1952) 13, ET in Bartsch, *Kerygma and Myth*, II (1962), 82ff.

32. Cf. *EF*, I, 49ff.

33. F. Gogarten, *Politische Ethik* (1932); cf. my *Geschichte und Existenz*, pp.
120ff.

34. F. Gogarten, *Die Einheit von Evangelium und Volkstum* (1934); cf. also
W. Stapel, *Der christliche Staatsmann. Eine Theologie des Nationalismus* (1932).

maintained? An analogy of being cannot come into consideration, for in it nature and grace are set in a hierarchical structure.[35] Barth thus has resort to the analogy of faith, which is structured in a qualitatively different way. This kind of analogy does not imply an ontic constitution which disposes us to receive God's Word in virtue of natural faculties that may be analyzed as such. Here is an analogy which God actively effects and which thus arises in faith. God creates hearers by opening their ears. He establishes the analogy in faith.

As Barth puts it, we do not have here a "natural capacity in man—it is grace after all that comes to sinners, to incapable men—but as the capacity of the incapable, as a miracle that cannot be interpreted anthropologically, nevertheless as a real capacity which is already actualised in faith, regarding whose existence there is no further room for discussion, whose existence can only be stated, since in becoming an event it already showed itself to be a possibility even before any question about it could arise."[36] In this way Barth believes that if he has not solved the question of contact that Brunner raised, he has overcome it as a question. "Precisely when we describe both the conformity of man to God that takes place in faith and also the point of contact for the Word of God posited in this conformity, not as an inborn or acquired property of man but only as the work of the actual grace of God, our only final word at this point can be that God acts on man in His Word. Because man's work in faith is that on which God's work is done, man can know the Word of God. He knows as he is known by God."[37]

The problem at the back of Brunner's objections, namely, that God in his Word turns to human beings and not to animals or stones, and that our human constitution thus contains a dispositon for the Word, no matter how we describe it, does not of course find a solution in Barth's analogy of faith. Barth again overlooks our natural constitution and our involvement in history. Hence the concept is hardly fitted to establish a new basis for ethics. In this regard it is a kind of emergency bridge which does not seem capable of bearing the weight of decisions in ethics, and especially in political ethics. In fact it is a remarkably open question under what sign Barth adopts his various political positions: a theological sign, a realistic-rational sign, or a specifically Swiss sign.

At any rate, there is a new approach to the problem of analogy. (The *Church Dogmatics* began to come out in 1935.) The established, or as yet to be established, possibility of theologico-political ethics is realized

35. Cf. H. U. von Balthasar, *Karl Barth* (1951), pp. 73ff.
36. *CD*, I/1, 241.
37. Ibid., p. 244.

only when Barth is back in Basel (1935). Here he claims that confession of the first commandment means not only an ecclesiastical decision in the matter of National Socialism but ipso facto a political one as well, i.e., a decision against a state which, being totalitarian, can recognize no task or proclamation or order but its own, no God but itself.[38] With this is bound up a reservation concerning the Confessing Church, for while it has maintained itself ecclesiastically and fought for the purity of its proclamation, it has had nothing to say about the attacks on the Jews, the astonishing treatment of political opponents, the suppression of the truth in the press of the new Germany, and many other things about which the OT prophets would undoubtedly have spoken.[39] Indeed, Barth reproaches himself because when he was in Germany he did not publicly address the political dimension of the Christian task. What had been for the most part his political abstention he now saw to have been a fault.[40]

The true turning to political ethics comes with the work *Rechtfertigung und Recht* (1937).[41] In this work Barth sets aside the two-kingdoms doctrine and tries to work out a theological approach to political questions christologically, i.e., on the basis of justification. Along with divine justification human justice becomes a theme of Christian faith, responsibility, and even confession.[42] On these grounds Barth affirms democracy and the defense of Switzerland.

But in this work, and in the later political works published during and after the war, we may see how inadequate is the solution to the problem of analogy along the lines of an analogy of faith.[43] This analogy carries with it no relation to the structure of the human. Hence it does not open up access to a theological interpretation of human existence in its historicity. To this extent Barth is right when he hesitates and even refuses to speak about a supposed change of mind, and grants only that he has made some political inferences in his later period. In fact the climate of his theology remains unhistorical; we spoke about this when dealing with his relation to Hegel. The introduction of the analogy

---

38. See Barth, "How My Mind Has Changed, I—1928-38"; cf. E. Busch, *Karl Barth*, pp. 272ff.

39. Busch, *Karl Barth*, p. 273.

40. Cf. *Theologische Existenz heute*, N.S. 49 (1956) 91.

41. ThSt 1 (1937). Paul Tillich speaks about the change but thinks the break comes with the work *Die Kirche und die politische Frage heute* (2nd ed. 1938), ET (London, 1939); cf. WW, XII, 324ff.

42. Barth, *Community, State, and Church* (New York, 1960), p. 101.

43. Barth also calls the analogy one of relation when on the basis of Gen. 1:26 he speaks about plurality in the divine essence, *CD*, III/1, 196.

of faith as a basis changes nothing in this respect. It simply leads to difficulties and uncertainties which make it hard for readers to decide whether specific statements in social and political ethics are theologically valid or whether they are simply evaluations which carry special weight because they have behind them the authority of a prominent theologian.

Thus a remarkable cleavage develops in Barth's theological statements. Often (1) we have directly analogous statements which in their directness hardly fall behind what we have in the scholastic doctrine of natural law that is grounded in the analogy of being.[44] But then (2) we find other statements which are simply those of the reason (sobered, of course, by faith) of the Swiss Karl Barth. I will give short examples of both.

(1) Direct forms of analogy that hardly go beyond what the analogy of faith might itself suggest occur both (a) in matters of theological principle and (b) in concrete ethical judgments. (a) In matters of principle we find that Barth deduces the human I-Thou relation, and marriage in particular, directly from the inner divine structure as he expounds it, from plurality in the divine essence. He infers the plurality from God's conversation with himself: "Let us make man in our own image" (Gen. 1:26). God "willed the existence of a being which in all its non-deity and therefore its differentiation can be a real partner; which is capable of action and responsibility in relation to Him; to which His own divine form of life [i.e., plurality] is not alien; which in a creaturely repetition, as a copy and imitation, can be a bearer of this form of life. Man was created as this being. . . . Thus the *tertium comparationis*, the analogy between God and man, is simply the existence of the I and the Thou in confrontation. This is first constitutive for God, and then for man created by God."[45] Is it not obvious that in this characteristic of God's being—that he encloses within himself an I and a Thou—and the being of man—that he is male and female—we have what is in fact a very simple and clear correspondence, and indeed an analogy of relation?[46]

Such texts, which we could easily multiply, force upon us the question of how these forms of correspondence between time and eternity differ from the analogy of being. Am I mistaken if I catch here a very different note from that of a mere analogy of faith? God is now positing more than an analogy that becomes actual in faith. He is positing an ontic correspondence which is always valid. We are dealing

44. Cf. *ThE*, I, 383ff.
45. *CD*, III/1, 184-85.
46. Ibid., p. 196.

with structures of human existence on the horizontal, historical plane. They are not restricted to the circle of believers. In this context, what is the significance of faith, and therefore of the analogy of faith? Does not faith have only the significance that it recognizes the correspondence of God and man, so that it has a noetic significance but not an ontic, as in the analogy of faith?

(b) It is no surprise that this lack of precision in the concept of analogy results in the above-mentioned obscurity in concrete ethical positions. An example of the direct form of analogy, with a christological emphasis, occurs in the work *Christengemeinde und Bürgergemeinde* (1946) (ET *Community, State, and Church* [New York, 1960]). This work views the church, living in the analogy of faith, as an entity that has the task, with its order and conduct, of providing an analogous model for the state, which both can and needs to be like it.[47] The aim is the ascribing of a derived and secondary analogy to the state itself. This analogy finds vivid illustration in the metaphor of two concentric circles with the political entity as the outer circle and the Christian community as the inner circle. Both relate to the christological center. The justice of the state from a Christian standpoint is its existence as a correspondence or analogue to the kingdom of God in which the church believes and which the church proclaims.[48]

The analogy between state and church is carried so far that even detailed state structures are derived from it (christologically). Thus members of the community are united by the one head, Christ. What corresponds to this politically is that civil freedom must always be seen within mutual responsibility.[49] The upshot is that the Christian direction or line in politics always gives evidence of a striking inclination to what we usually call the democratic state.[50] (The "German Christians" might have used an analogy speciously constructed with the help of the one head to argue in exactly the opposite direction for "one people, one country, one leader," if one might be permitted to say this!)

How artificial the analogy is becomes grotesquely clear when we look at some of the details. Thus we read that secret diplomacy contradicts the light that shines in Christ. The day of the Lord has dawned for the community and it lives in this day. The necessary political counterpart is that the community is the resolute opponent of all secret politics or diplomacy. What seeks to be secret is fundamen-

47. *Community, State, and Church,* p. 169.
48. Ibid.
49. Ibid., p. 174.
50. Ibid., p. 181.

tally wrong even in politics. Freedom and responsibility are one and the same thing in the service of the civil community, and hence everything can and must be done before the eyes of all.[51] (I might perhaps be allowed to ask here whether there is not a closer analogy here, not to Christology, but to the—in many ways very happy—situation in a Swiss canton.)[52]

(2) In other instances Barth's political positions are not based on analogies of this kind but are evaluations with no theological support at all, or only apparent support. Confusion is caused here by the rejection of the distinction between the two kingdoms precipitated by the alarming specter of Neo-Lutheranism. For only when such a distinction is made can one make a clear and simple and undisguised secular evaluation and thus escape the suspicion of pursuing a theologically stipulated politics.

Nontheological judgments, which can vary astonishingly in similar situations, occur in advice given in letters. I will give a couple of examples. In a letter to Josef Hromadka, his colleague in Prague, written during the Czech crisis of September 1938, Barth says that humanly speaking the freedom of Europe, and perhaps not only of Europe, stands or falls with the freedom of the Czech people.[53] Is the whole world to fall under the spell of the evil glance of the giant serpent? If the worst comes to the worst, he hopes that "the sons of the ancient Hussites will show a Europe that has become too soft that there are still men even today. Every Czech soldier who fights and suffers will do it for us." Barth can say without reservation that he will do it also for the church of Jesus Christ, which in the dark sphere of Hitler and Mussolini can only fall victim to ridicule or extirpation.[54] This letter, published in Prague on September 24, triggered a propaganda campaign on the part of the Goebbels press which caused great difficulties for the Confessing Church and disconcerted even many of Barth's friends. Thus Franz Hildebrandt, a friend of both Barth and Bonhoeffer, came out in opposition in London. That he evaluated the political situation differently is less important than his failure to understand Barth theologically. Had Barth not taught us to separate political protest and the preaching of the gospel? Had he not taught us that the church must always fight only with spiritual weapons, or, as we might add along the lines of Luther

51. Ibid., p. 174.
52. Cf. *ThE*, II/2, §§ 4068ff., ET II, 576ff.; on analogy in Barth see *CD*, I/2, 144; II/1, 81ff.; III/1, 96; III/2, 220ff.; III/3, 352; IV/1, 149, etc.; cf. also G. Wingren, *Theology in Conflict* (1958), esp. pp. 30, 36.
53. *Eine Schweizer Stimme*, 2nd ed. (1948), pp. 58-59.
54. Ibid.

and his works on war against the Turks, that we are not to engage in crusades in defense of the gospel and the church?[55]

Twelve years later (1950) a German contribution to the military defense of the West evoked passionate discussion. The threat posed by Eastern dictatorship was not unlike that of Nazi dictatorship in 1938. As a result of the violent upset in Prague, the Berlin blockade, and the war in Korea (1950), the cold war had begun. Martin Niemöller and Gustav Heinemann, who were close to Barth, led the campaign against a German contribution. Barth was repeatedly asked to give an opinion. This time, on political not theological grounds, he evaluated the situation very differently. For all his criticisms he thought Stalin's dictatorship was very different from Hitler's. He thus came out against military defense. He thought he could not insist urgently enough that finally and fundamentally the only defense is the positive one of creating just and tolerable social conditions for all strata of the population.[56]

No one contests Barth's right to hold such an opinion. One may admit that historically it is to some extent right. But that is not the point. The real problem is whether a theologian has the right to plead for a decision by the Christian community for which he can adduce rational considerations but no theological arguments. Decisions based on such considerations may come out very differently even when the Christians who take them share the same basic faith, as in the case of members of a synod.

When relative and all too secular decisions of this kind are given theological weight, they threaten surreptitiously to become decisions of faith, articles of the standing or falling church, which then divide the body of Christ.

This actually happened in the next decades when debate about the right method of safeguarding peace and about the peaceful and military use of atomic power and many other things seemed increasingly to shape the church's life far more than faith in the resurrection of Christ. No one can dispute the basic seriousness of these questions. No one can deny that they challenge our responsibility before God and that the church has the task of expressing this responsibility and deepening it spiritually. The only point is that the church cannot make confessional judgments in the sphere of political, economic, and social methods. All that we have are the evaluations of its members according to their

---

55. Cf. Klaus Scholder, "Die Demokratie fragt jetzt um Bewaffnung . . . ," *FAZ* 187 (1981). For a similar letter by Barth to the wife of a Dutch pastor (Oct. 24, 1938), cf. *Eine Schweizer Stimme*, pp. 63ff.

56. Scholder, op. cit.

knowledge, influence, and democratic responsibility. To exalt these into confessional judgments of the church is in the strict sense heresy and a rending of Christ's body.[57]

I am far from blaming Barth himself for this development. Nevertheless, it seems likely that the vacuum of nonhistoricity which besets his theology has contributed to the notable defenselessness of much of the church against this heresy.

What we need is a new basis for theological ethics that will fill the vacuum. (Attempts have, of course, been made in this direction.) Such an ethics will need to think through again the problem of analogy and especially to tackle afresh the doctrine of the two kingdoms. It cannot simply adopt Luther's first effort in a reactionary way and overlook the points at which this is tied to its own age. It must correct the mistakes of Neo-Lutheranism which reached a first climax in F. Naumann and his two gods, and then finally led into a dead end in the case of leading Lutherans during the Third Reich.[58] At root no theological ethics—whether it be that of Calvinism or the moral theology of Roman Catholicism—does not at least implicitly contain the theme of the two-kingdoms doctrine.

CONCLUSION

We have behind us a long and winding way. The last section on dialectical theology hardly forms its conclusion. The reason why I have had to say something about it is obvious. It forms a sharp break between the end of one theological development, symbolized by Troeltsch's hopeless wrestling with an all-relativizing historicism, and a radically new beginning, which on the basis of the infinite qualitative distinction between time and eternity places the revelation of the unconditional on the agenda.

I have tried to show that the radical, analogy-less split between

57. For a crass example of this erroneous theological ethics, which uncritically builds on Barth, cf. the declaration of the Reformierter Bund on the confession of Jesus Christ and the church's responsibility for peace (1982). A unilateral rejection of atomic weapons is here put in confessional style, and an evaluation thus takes on confessional status. Echoes of Barth's Christology may be heard in the statement.

58. Cf. F. Naumann, *Briefe über die Religion* (1903), p. 81; cf. *ThE*, II/2, Index; also the useful collection of materials, "Umdeutung der Zweireichlehre Luthers im 19. Jahrhundert," *Texte zur Kirchen- und Theologiegeschichte*, no. 21 (Gütersloh, 1975).

time and eternity leads to problems in anthropology, especially regarding our historicity and theological ethics, which defy solution on this approach. It was this difficulty that produced the rift in the dialectical school. All its representatives apart from Barth himself sought a new anthropological reference of thought, or the old and well-considered one. This reference found classical formulation in Tillich's principle of correlation.[59] We have here a variation of the familiar problem of analogy, on the relevance of human reality for theological thought.

But this means that the dialectical thinkers and their theological successors have come back to the old lines of inquiry which have occupied the whole period dealt with in this book. Once again we come up against the decisive problems that have been with us since Descartes, the Enlightenment, Schleiermacher's Romanticism, and Idealism. Faith was trying to maintain itself in face of the reawakened reality of humanity, whether the reference was to our rational being, to Kant's intelligible ego, to the finite spirit of Hegel, or to humanity exposed to historical relativity. For those who were investigating faith and its possibility, the reality of the human always gave rise to difficulty. How could people who viewed themselves as rational adults harmonize the Christian faith with their rational norms without yielding to a dogmatism that would essentially divide them? Now that Kant had been on the scene, and shown them the dignity of their autonomy, how could they still be defined theonomously?

Thus the same question has continually come up afresh, although we need not run through all the variations again. The main theme, which is always visible, is that experienced or empirically stressed reality is a problem for faith. The visible challenges the invisible. Sight challenges faith. The temporal challenges the eternal.

Another permanent theme that we catch is that of the question whether and how there can be a fresh appropriation of faith in these crises. Appropriation cannot mean evading the questions that arise or suppressing them and blindly being carried away on the conveyor belt of tradition. It cannot involve any kind of fundamentalism. It can only mean traversing the field of problems that lies before us and seeking the power that is stronger than every assault, that will give us the grace of faith, and that will also show us the credibility of faith. Theological history, as we have seen, is full of victories and defeats in dealing with such matters, and also of sham victories.

For a while the dialectical theology seemed to be opening up a new panorama from which the dualism of assault and appropriation

59. Tillich, *Systematic Theology*, I, 59ff.

had retreated and only the "vertically from above" held the stage. But this was only an interim in the history of theology—not a cessation of breathing but a catching of breath. Then the problem of reality arose again and demonstrated its indelible character. It really seems to be set before us. We have to accept this task. Perhaps the point of our long excursion has been to find this task of theological thinking with the help of those who have preceded us, to see that it is a task for our own time.

Is there, then, nothing new under the sun, even in theology? Has everything already been? Yes, it has already been, and it always will be again as long as this aeon lasts and there is in it both faith and thinking about faith. Yet it will always be again in a new way, and faith will always be a venture. As before, it will involve not a Because but a Nevertheless. It will constantly learn to utter this Nevertheless in face of the reality of the human and therefore in spite of appearances to the contrary. The form of the Nevertheless will vary as (conscious or unconscious) interpretations of the reality change. It can only be a surprise if we are not swept away by the assault of appearances. Along these lines we should have regard to our predecessors in faith, and also in doubt, who in their own ways, hoping or crumbling, have engaged in the same conflict.

"Blessed are those whose course and goal lose themselves in the clouds of those witnesses of whom the world was not worthy" (Johann Georg Hamann).

Appendix: Paul Tillich*

"Paul was ready and concerned to be all things to all men, but with the two exceptions that he would not be a miracle-worker to the Jews or a cultural Christian to the Hellenes" (Martin Kähler, Tillich's teacher).

How can we honor someone whose lot and task it was to encompass intellectually both the university faculties and the traditions of the old world and the new? The entelechy of thought that is at work here in a vital development is determined above all by the fact that it exists in polar fields of force, that it needs tensions both to be constantly created and to be itself creative. As one may see from his career, Tillich stands, then, between different faculties, particularly that of theology and that of philosophy, and in so doing he stands also between different cultures.

Yet the resultant encounters never lead to static syntheses or to an immobile third thing frozen in a Platonic rest above this lively play. The encounters take place in a dynamic movement. They never become fixed events. They are always sharply contoured. They always involve elements in a drama of thought in which the author unceasingly objectifies himself, in which he forms himself and then reforms himself. "The frontier is the most fruitful place for knowledge"—this might perhaps be called the most pregnant orientation of his thinking. The frontier always stands "between." It means encounters, or, as Tillich himself would say, correlations.

---

*This address was given on the occasion of the award of the Hanseatic Goethe prize in the Hamburg Rathaus, 1958. Out of friendship with Tillich I add it to what has already been said, especially as his name often appears in the preceding chapters. Tillich frequently served as a guest lecturer on the Hamburg faculty. On one occasion he taught my classes for a semester while I taught his in Chicago.

Here, then, is the extreme opposite of a type of thinking which continually generates itself parthogenetically, or rather spins itself out of itself. In the case of Tillich the sparks that fire him always come from outside, from confrontation with social reality and art, especially Greek antiquity and expressive modernity, and above all from dialogue with philosophy. Hence his thinking is never isolated. It does not feed on its own thoughts. It is nourished by the eros which links it to existence, to the threat of nonbeing, to anxiety and hope, to the knowledge of being upheld. One might even say that this thinking is ecstatic, not in the psychological sense of irrational flickering—no, this thinking has a steady glow—but in the existential sense that it stands above itself and reaches beneath itself, either way penetrating the deep shafts of existence and striking the mother lode.

Theology, then, does not stand alone in Tillich's thinking. He does not simply transpose a secure faith into the form of reflection. He turns to philosophy as well. This means that he is not just turning a naive faith into a more sophisticated faith. Instead, believing existence is in encounter with thinking existence. The personal union between the two has to be found in a venture. Polarity has to be sustained with intellectual integrity.

The resultant intellectual processes always involve triumphant endurance; they keep watch on the discovered frontiers. This thinking, then, cannot develop autonomously and fall victim to delight in frivolous intellectualism, no matter how temptingly these forbidden fruits must have dangled before the eyes of such a virtuoso of thought. This thinking remains always an ethical act. It is devout thinking, not primarily in what is thought, but in the way it is thought, in the way that the freedom of the committed is lived out and thought out in it.

Tillich finally stands on the frontier between Europe and America. He feels the tension of the hemispheres and makes it creative. He is given a task that is universal even in a geographical sense and becomes one of the leading theologians of the new world. That this occurs is the result of a higher leading which can turn even what is meant for evil into a gracious good. For in 1933—if we may mention this one date at least—he was expelled from Germany as one of the intellectual leaders of religious socialism, and with the help of Reinhold Niebuhr he found a new post at Union Theological Seminary in New York.

Being rudely thrust into a completely new and strange element must have been at first a considerable intellectual shock to a man like Tillich, who had his roots in the traditions of Western Europe, and who was—if I may venture to say it—a thoroughly German thinker, enjoying, not in a conservative or antiquarian sense but with living immediacy, the legacy of mysticism, classicism, and German idealism, so that with the terminology of the German philosophical tradition he must have been an alien, and seemed at first perhaps to be a rather flinty guest to the Americans.

But this master of encounter turned his fear of what was strange, and what threatened to reduce him to silence, into a creative impulse by being ready to accept his lot, transforming his thoughts into another idiom, and in the process achieving a new clarity and simplicity of statement. It is not as though all this were Tillich's own doing. He himself would have been the very last to say that. The gracious visitation which enabled him to achieve this clarification, and which made America a new home for the European exile, was of another kind. And this hour perhaps permits us to say with the angels who bear away the immortal part of Faust: "Love from above has had a part in this."

That love had and has a part is the message which Tillich the man and the Christian not only proclaims but radiates by his very existence. Hence we miss out the decisive feature in the portrait if we present him at this time only as one who thinks and not also as one who loves. He loved when he had to leave his own country and did not feel the resentment of the emigrant. In spite of the terrifying and oppressive mask which covered Germany, he always saw the dear face of his country in its illustrious spirits and above all in his friends. When our land plunged into its deepest misfortune, he did not turn aside but came to our help, and pleaded, excused, and interpreted in love. We shall never forget that in this friend who proved himself in guilt and suffering—*our* guilt and *our* suffering.

It was this love that won the hearts of the young academic generation in America. Behind what might seems at first to be the inflexible shell of inaccessible abstraction, they detected the thinker who not only sought the truth in the sense of what is objectively correct but whose concern was with the truth that can make us free. What he was seeking, then, was themselves, to nourish them with the truth. At the point where truth and love are one and the same, i.e., in Jesus Christ, only they can find the truth who seek people, and only they can seek people who have found being in the truth. Behind the crystallized form of the thinking they thus discerned the pastor, the one who thirsted after young people, as Martin Kähler once said of Tholuck.

If I might illustrate by an anecdote, a student in America once said to me: "When I am bad, I like Hollywood; when I am worse, I like Tillich." This young man realized that here was someone who had found the courage to be and was waiting to bring him to it. Here was someone who knew that being is upheld and who thus knew the secret that against every possible postulate of our own we are graciously affirmed even when we have to negate ourselves.

I almost dare to hope that in saying this I have touched on what is central in Tillich's thinking. At any rate, brevity does not allow me to give a full portrait, to outline the system, but only to reflect my own encounter, and to attempt some interpretation.

In fact, it seems to me that thinking in love is the sustaining motif in the twofold sense that it contains elements of both *eros* and *agape*. The eros aspect (I have in mind Plato's symposium) is that eros is aware of an original unity that has been shattered and that longs to be restored by unification. When we ask about being, and an orientation to meaning within it, the question implies a search for this lost unity. Only because we are separated from being, only because we have this destiny behind us, only because we know this separation of finitude, can we put the question of being at all. He who is infinite does not ask about being, says Tillich, for being infinite, he has the perfect power of being; he is identical with it; he is God. God does not know the question of being. He does not have the eros that asks only out of the depths. Nor do nonhuman creatures know it, for they are not aware of their finitude and vegetate below the eros that would trigger the question.

We humans, however, are so distinct and separate from being that we have to ask about it. This makes us threatened beings. It puts our existence in jeopardy. For when we are raised above being the possibility arises that we may miss it. It is under this threat that Tillich seeks people.

To be sure, he speaks as a systematician, and the hammered-out strictness of the systematic form differs totally from emotional address. But those who look more closely, and have the good fortune to interpret the thinking of Tillich in terms of the man, can never be in any doubt that what he says is aimed at people, and that the goal is to help people in their peril and restore to them the courage to be.

In the last analysis, perhaps, it is the pastor who is using the means of thought. By it he is addressing nihilists. Nihilists can feel the threat of nonbeing so painfully because the preceding experience of being lies behind the realization of nonbeing. The shocking experience of meaninglessness is possible only because there has first been an awareness of meaning and some participation in it. Our very questions derive their vitality from the reality in whose name we ask them.

We cannot, then, escape the fact that being is upheld. Hence the goal of an appeal of thought can only be to assure those who are under threat that they are upheld, to make it clear to them that even their despair is possible only because the power of being has already taken possession of them.

This affirmation, which rings out like a bell above our despair, is not, of course, a matter of surreptitious dialectic. If one might use Hegel by way of contrast, it is not a static point of indifference above the dramatic movement of human hope and despair, human success and failure. It is a grace which must be addressed to us and become an event. Instead of being postulated dialectically as a timeless good, it is a historical happening, a gift, a gracious acceptance.

I can illustrate this comfort of thought—if I might call it thus—only by quoting a sermon. This quotation finds Tillich at a moment when the hidden orientation to people that is implicit in his system in academic form comes to direct expression in proclamation. Grace, he says, with this affirmation in mind, meets us when we are in great trouble and unrest. It meets us when we go through the dark valley of a meaningless and empty life. It meets us when we feel that we have hurt another life—a life which we loved or from which we were estranged. Sometimes at such a moment, he says, a wave of light breaks upon our darkness and it is as if a voice told us that we were still affirmed. Affirmed all the same by that which is greater than thou and whose name thou dost not know. Do not ask the name now, perhaps thou wilt find it later. Aim at nothing, seek nothing, purpose nothing. Simply accept the fact that thou art affirmed.

Do not ask the name—do not as yet ask about him, says Tillich the preacher. Does not this suppression of the vocabulary of the Christian schools in the dogmatic system, and even in the preaching, alienate us at first? Why is there this fear of over-quick answers? Why this "nonreligious interpretation," as Dietrich Bonhoeffer would call it? Why this secular form of Christian proclamation?

Although Tillich, like Kierkegaard, sees a distinction from Socratic maieutics inasmuch as he is not trying to draw some existing knowledge out of people but trying to tell them and promise them something that they cannot tell themselves, we cannot fail to see one Socratic aim. Any direct imparting of the message that rushes ahead of the inner history will necessarily appear to be a dogmatic authority which does not let existence put its own question but crushes the core of the question by over-strong and over-hasty answers. Hence, if I am right, Tillich perceives a great danger in routine proclamation. The assured acceptance of traditional Christianity, and the use of cliches, leaves no room for the believing self but loads only with indigestible alien matter and leads to the declamation of foreign texts instead of a personal confession of their contents.

What is Christian, then, can be achieved only by way of one's own existential question. The task of the preacher and pastor is to teach us to put this question. They must provoke a confrontation with nothingness and meaninglessness. They must bring people to this point. If I am right, in this aspect of thinking pastoral care one may see how Tillich combines Luther's theology with the problems of modern existentialism. When Luther says that temptation makes a theologian, he, too, has in mind a confrontation with the nothingness of despair through which we must all pass if we are not just to have traditional experiences but piece faith into the individual self, not merely speaking about God but in an act of personal appropriation confessing: "*My* Lord and *my* God." And when existentialism speaks about falling victim to anonymity, about the self-alienation of the I through that which throngs upon it from without (whether it be overpowering history in Nietzsche, given *essentia* in Sartre, an imposed system in Kierkegaard, or anonymity in Heidegger), and when it tries to lead back to the self by projecting existence into nothingness, then here, it seems to me, we have the same question of the task of existence.

The nerve of Tillich's system, then, is the idea of correlation. This means that the Christian message can cease to be a doctrinaire authority which causes self-alienation only if as an answer it corresponds to a prior question. This prior question, if one might put it thus, is the call for help of an existence that is threatened by nonbeing. Hence interpretation has to fit all Christian concepts into the form of this prior question. Only then can they be appropriated and lead the self to itself instead of estranging it.

In detail the process of adjustment and interpretation might take the following form. "If the notion of God appears in systematic theology in correlation with the threat of nonbeing. . . , God must be called the infinite power of being which resists the threat of nonbeing. . . . If anxiety is defined as the awareness of being finite, God must be called the infinite ground of courage. . . . If the notion of the Kingdom of God appears in correlation with the riddle of our historical existence, it must be called the meaning, fulfilment, and unity of history."[1]

All the concepts of the Christian tradition occur, but they are all fitted into the schema of question and answer. If in the process they seem at first to be so disguised and altered as not to be recognizable, the point is to bring their true face to light and to show how they apply unconditionally to me. That which is simply accepted and repeated does not apply to me. The direct Christian vocabulary might become a perfunctory merchandising of words that we resist with a secret refusal to be touched by it.

1. Tillich, *Systematic Theology*, 3 vols. (Chicago, repr. 1961), I, 64.

In a conversation with his friend Fedor Stepun he expressed this in a charming way. It has been said of the English, said Stepun, that when they say God they mean cotton. In your case, Tillich, it might be said that when you say cotton you mean God. Why do you not simply say God? Tillich replied that if people no longer understand the word *God* (because they do not see in it an answer to their questions) I will say cotton so long as they understand that I really want to tell them something about God.

Both on the rostrum and in the pulpit, then, Tillich breaks out of the esoterics of sacral speech and prefers secular expressions. His purpose in this nonreligious form of proclamation, however, is not just that of a missionary assimilation to secular people. His concern is not just with the method of telling but with the matter itself.

It is this matter, and the fight for its credibility, for its direct relevance, that has caused this generation, and especially its youth, to listen to his message. For if we are truly brought here to the place of threat, the matter presented does not make faith easier by taking from us the need for a venture of a decision or a leap. Tillich takes up our own prior question and engages in an ontological analysis of existence with a view to the orienting of proclamation, but in no case does he assimilate the message to us and our questions. Our doubt and despair are not removed by discussion. The point is that affirmation or grace is addressed to us and must be grasped by us in a daring leap, i.e., they must be believed by us. The philosopher's toga should not cause us to miss the point that a messenger is speaking to us here. Because he is a messenger, there is no immanent overcoming of doubt. The aim in such overcoming could never be the truth (disclosure) but only the intellectual indication of what is correct. Here the truth is an event. It is the event of affirmation. Hence we have more than a statement that this or that is right. We have a new being by grace.

Perhaps the ontological precision of Tillich's thought is especially calculated to express the matter at issue in an appropriate way and to secure a hearing among the younger generation in particular. For the innermost passion of their search, it seems to me, is not oriented to redemption by way of knowledge or insight but to a redemption that grants a new reality, that carries the future with it, and that means success in the discovery of life. What our generation looks for in Tillich is not something that is thought, however perfect, but actual being by grace—a being which thought proclaims and which sets up signs of reflection that point to a reality which here seeks to express and declare and confer itself.

By its well-considered symmetry and the proportions of its vaulting and pillars, the system may be aesthetically pleasing, like a good piece of architecture. Those who still have a sense of the grace and charm of an able play of thought will delight in the harmonious structure. But those whom a mere love of intellect rules will miss the point of it all, namely, that he who speaks here is the messenger and mediator of a new reality, of a living event. For them the thought will be the mere play of shadows on the inner wall of the Platonic cave; the real aim of this effort of thought, however, is to tear us out of the cave and point us to a reality which transcends all shadows and darkness because it is the power of being itself.

We do Tillich an injustice, then, if we see in his thought only a philosophical ontology which simply works out Christian ideas. This is a misunderstanding, for in the inner chambers of the structure we are told something that we cannot tell ourselves, something that tradition calls revelation. Being is threatened but also upheld by arms from which no despair can break free. We are affirmed even though we stand on the brink of self-destruction. This is not the result of deduction. It is told us by an event. It is a message that is brought to us and that no human being could either think out or write.

The transposition of Christian materials into this schema of an ontology, of a correlation of question and answer, is, of course, a venture of thought. It always carries with it the risk of failure. This is clear to anyone who works in a theological laboratory. The categories with whose help we grasp the thought-content of Christianity, as we must if their unconditional relevance to us is to be plain, are always at the point where their ministry of service may become the dominion of a system. Tillich shares this danger with all those who dare to impart ultimate things to their time, with all those who seize the kingdom of God by force. Few systematicians of such rank keep their charisma in control. Few who make the most of their architectonic creativity do not also have misgivings about such gifts. For theological thinking is also an all too human work which in its fallibility must take comfort in the fact that it is upheld, that it stands under forgiveness, and that the surprises and revisions of the last judgment will not shatter those who do service, who are no Pharisees of thought, who undertake the venture of thought as those who love and not as mere adventurers. The imperative and the consolation that I would link with all of this might be summed up in the saying that we have to venture heresies in order to achieve the truth.

It was part of the background play of the forces of life that we met Paul Tillich in Weimar. If this was not an accidental encounter in the throng of the classical Walpurgis night, but has symbolic power, the point is that Goethe too, according to Tillich, is a figure on the frontier, a figure who sees himself exposed to various forms of transcendence, who knows the menacing onset of magic but also knows that being is upheld, who is aware that love is imparted to us from above. Goethe, then, is one who knows his human form, who as an entelechy puts to himself the question of his telos, who seeks to promote his vital development toward it, and who, according to his *Orphic Sayings,* stands in full, mysterious correspondence with the course of the planets and with the God who moves immanently within the world.

Certainly the frontiers from which the two men look out are different. Yet those on the frontier are a secret order. They have an affinity. They all know and love. Thus today we greet Paul Tillich with respect and joy, *our* Paul Tillich, I am bold to say. To his friends he is like a wanderer between two worlds, and it gives us great pleasure that we in Germany are one of these worlds in whose soil his roots are sunk. We hope that it is not just the categorical imperative that brings him to Hamburg almost every year but a certain yearning for his place of origin. We also realize that when he is with us he has a longing for his students in America. Those who love are themselves much loved. He is thus a wanderer between two forms of longing. This, too, is the fate of those who love. They are awaited. And when they come, the joy obtains that they are there, and that with all their knowledge they do not seek what is most distant but are close to what is closest.

INDEX OF NAMES

INDEX OF SUBJECTS